Whitman Encyclopedia of Mexican Money

Volume I: An Illustrated History of Mexican Coins and Currency

Don and Lois Bailey

Foreword by
Dr. Manuel Galán Medina

Whitman Publishing, LLC
PUBLISHING SINCE 1934
www.whitman.com

Whitman Encyclopedia of Mexican Money
Volume I

Whitman Publishing, LLC
PUBLISHING SINCE 1934
www.whitman.com

3101 Clairmont Road · Suite G · Atlanta GA 30329

Correspondence concerning this book may be directed to the publisher, attn: Encyclopedia of Mexican Money, at the address above.

ISBN: 0794834078
Printed in Mexico

Disclaimer: Expert opinion should be sought in any significant numismatic purchase. This book is presented as a guide only. No warranty or representation of any kind is made concerning the completeness of the information presented. The author, a professional numismatist, regularly buys, sells, and sometimes holds certain of the items discussed in this book.

Caveat: The value estimates given are subject to variation and differences of opinion. Before making decisions to buy or sell, consult the latest information. Past performance of the rare coin market or any coin or series within that market is not necessarily an indication of future performance, as the future is unknown. Such factors as changing demand, popularity, grading interpretations, strength of the overall coin market, and economic conditions will continue to be influences.

For a complete listing of numismatic reference books, supplies, and storage products, visit Whitman Publishing online at www.whitman.com, or scan the QR code on the inside front cover of this book.

CONTENTS

FOREWORD

If you ask yourself for an invention that has been able to survive for thousands of years, competing against other innovations along all these years, certainly money is one them. It has been one of the most important innovations of mankind, touching the lives of the majority of human beings who have lived on this planet.

Notwithstanding the important evolution of technology, it is still difficult to imagine a world without money, either bank notes or coins. Every country has its own. Printed or minted money is still the preferred payment system of all societies; around 70 to 80 percent of all transactions are performed with cash.

In Mexico in particular, the evolution of Mexican coinage is an art that has taken centuries to develop, since the establishment of the Casa de Moneda de México in 1535. Billions of coins have been minted since then, and Mexico has experienced innumerable changes that have been reflected in its coins—showing different minting techniques, the rise of an emperor, the willingness of its people to produce a change. It is evident that every numismatic piece is a kind of document that provides valuable historical data about different cultural aspects of society in the past, because it reflects the ideological context of the epoch.

The *Whitman Encyclopedia of Mexican Money*, by Lois and Don Bailey, is the fruit of their tenacious effort of more than 50 years active involvement in all areas of Mexican numismatics as collectors, dealers, writers, and historical researchers. The work is composed of the rich and intense monetary emissions in Mexico for almost five centuries of history, in four volumes. This is not just another catalog. This is a work well done, more complete and documented; the product of years of study and work, in which the reader will find accurate and actual data about Mexican coinage, its many-sided dimensions, and the reality of the numismatic market.

Additionally, this work is full of rich and interesting historical references, a product of the constant study and intimate proximity of the authors with Mexico, its coinage, its past, and its people; all this working toward the benefit of the book.

As it is known, the Baileys have studied Mexican coinage, along with its history and its culture, for decades. They have collaborated with other distinguished authors, and like few others, they have been distinguished promoters of Mexican numismatics in the United States. Don is a founding member of the United States Mexican Numismatic Association. Mr. Bailey has also received numerous awards and honors during the years for his work with the Banco de México, the Casa de Moneda, the Sociedad Numismática de México, and the Soumaya Museum in Mexico City. One of these honors is the Mexican Order of the Aztec Eagle, awarded by the Mexican government in 2001; it is the highest honor that can be awarded to a non-citizen.

Everyone interested in the history and coinage of Mexico will find these books enjoyable and comprehensive. Every chapter has been designed to provide rich and appropriate background information. The prices of Mexican coins are an important contribution to the market, where accurate, independent price information can help collectors and investors make wise purchasing decisions.

These volumes will be an important reference for libraries and schools and institutions of higher education, wherein collectors as well as numismatists and historians can relate the history of Mexico through a study of its numismatics. This impressive work by Lois and Don Bailey has earned a place in the library of everyone who is interested in Mexican coinage.

Dr. Manuel Galán Medina
Director General of Currency Issue (retired)
Banco de México

HOW TO USE THIS BOOK

Volume 1 is written to be user friendly for the beginning collector as well as interesting to the advanced numismatist. Regular-issue coinage is discussed first, in chronological order by the eras of Mexico's history; the chapters give a summary description of subjects that are expanded upon in volumes 2, 3, and 4. The chapters on regular issues are followed by chapters on tokens, variety and error coins, and pattern coins, then medals, orders, and decorations. Although the numismatic values of collectible Mexican coins are not discussed in this introductory volume, a chapter is provided to help the reader estimate the worth of the precious-metal content of their gold and silver coins, based on a range of spot values. The main text concludes with an overview of the history of paper money in Mexico, from the pre-revolutionary issues to date.

This book contains a unique typeface that attempts to reproduce the devices in the coin legends as closely as possible. For example, the nine-punch appears as **ℵ**, and the mintmarks traditionally depicted in books as **Mo**, **Go**, and **Oa** appear as **M̊**, **G**, and **Ⓐ**, respectively. These characters are general representations of the characters in coin legends and mintmarks. The reader should keep in mind that the positions of dots, annulets, rondules, and so forth, relative to other elements on the coin, can vary. When legends are reproduced in the regular text, they are in a slightly bolder typeface; when they break from one line to the next, hyphens are *not* used unless they appear, verbatim, on the coin.

For many years, U.S. auction catalogs and dealer price lists have sought to accommodate American collectors by using the words "obverse" and "reverse" as would be expected for U.S. coins. Although it is usually noted that U.S. definitions are being used, when those definitions conflict with standard Mexican numismatics, confusion can result. In this book, we apply the terms according to correct Mexican numismatic usage, as defined in *Numismatic History of Mexico* (Alberto Francisco Pradeau, 1938).

Assayers and their initials, when relevant, are listed at the beginning of each section, either by date or in alphabetical order, as is most appropriate for that section. In the year-by-year charts, a slash refers to an overstrike, whether of date, mintmark, assayer, or other element. A hyphen in the assayer or related column means "and": "A-B" means "A and B," and "A-B, C-D" means "A and B, *and* C and D." The term "Unconfirmed" refers to coins that are said to exist or are listed in other catalogs, but have not been verified by the authors or contributors.

"G" numbers are from the classification system developed by Frank W. Grove. "KM" numbers are from the system developed by Chet Krause and Clifford Mishler. "BW" numbers are the Bailey-Whitman classification system, developed for this encyclopedia. Other numbering systems are explained in the chapters in which they are used, and in the glossary.

Subjects addressed briefly in volume 1 will be expanded upon in volumes 2 through 4 as follows, but in catalog format, with expanded historical information, date listings, and technical information such as weights, sizes, mintages, and so on (if available). Numismatic valuations will also be provided.

VOLUME 2: MODERN COINAGE

1. Overview
2. The Coinage Reform of 1905
3. The Coinage Reform of 1992

4. Commemoratives of the 1905 and 1992 Coinage Reforms
5. Mint and Proof Sets
6. Silver Bullion Coinage
7. Gold Medallic Coinage
8. Libertads: Silver, Gold, and Platinum
9. Pre-Columbian Collections

VOLUME 3: EARLY NUMISMATICS

1. Overview
2. Media of Exchange in the Anáhuac Era
3. Carlos and Johanna Coinage
4. Cob Coinage
5. Milled Coinage
6. Coinage of the War of Independence
7. Coinage of Agustín de Iturbide
8. Republic Reales Coinage
9. State and Federal Coppers
10. Coinage of Emperor Maximilian
11. Republic Decimal Coinage

VOLUME 4: THE MEXICAN REVOLUTION

1. Overview
2. Estado de Aguascalientes
3. Estado de Chihuahua
4. Estado de Durango
5. Estado de Guerrero
6. Estado de Jalisco
7. Estado de México
8. Estado de Morelos
9. Estado de Oaxaca
10. Estado de Puebla
11. Estado de Sinaloa
12. Estado de Zacatecas

1

An Overview of Mexican Numismatics

The history of any country can be viewed from a study of its coinage, and Mexico is no exception. The various conflicts in Mexico's history, both political and economic, present a wealth of numismatic subjects for the collector to pursue. A study of these conflicts reveals the entwinement of the histories of Mexico and the United States, including the War with Texas (1836–1845); the Mexican War (1846–1848); the 1914 conflict at Veracrúz; the 1916 invasion of Columbus, New Mexico, by Pancho Villa; and the Mexican Revolution of 1910 to 1920.

Long before the United States and Mexico were heard of, however, before the arrival of Hernán Cortés and the lengthy period of colonial rule in the Americas, the indigenous peoples used other media of exchange. During the period now called the Anáhuac era, discussed in chapter 2, these items included cacao beans, strings of colored shells, *patolquechtli* (small squares of woven cotton material), and gold-filled quills, as well as *tajaderas* (now referred to as "Aztec hoe money") made of copper in T-shapes of various sizes. In later years, tokens were often used as local "necessity" money within Mexico (see chapter 21). In most cases, they filled a need for small coins in the rural areas, and they were used by haciendas and merchants. Some were overstruck on earlier copper state coins.

In 1536 Mexico (then the Viceroyalty of New Spain) issued the first coinage of the Americas. Mexican coins were used in U.S. commerce and were legal tender, by statute, until 1857. Mexican coinage then ceased to be official legal tender in the United States, although it continued to circulate in rural areas. The only Mexican coinage issued under Spanish rule within what would later be part of the United States was the copper 1/2 real known as the "Texas jola," issued in 1818. They were struck in San Fernándo de Bexar (San Antonio, Texas) by José Antonio de la Garza.

The Carlos and Johanna coinage series covers the period from 1536 to 1572. Its coins were issued in silver and copper, with denominations of 1/2, 1, 2, 3, 4, and 8 reales in silver, and 2 and 4 maravedies in copper. (This era is discussed in chapter 3.)

Cob coinage followed the Carlos and Johanna series. These coins were issued from approximately 1580 to 1732, under six different Spanish rulers from Philip II to Luis I. The origin of the word "cob" is debated among numismatists; some say it derives from the Spanish term *cabo de barra*, or "end of the bar"—and the planchets for cob coins were, indeed, cut from the ends of bars of metal, clipped to the required weight, and hand-stamped with die punches. Others say the term comes from the old, English word "cob," which refers, in essence, to a small, rough lump of something (e.g., cob horses are small, thick, sturdy animals, noted for their practicality rather than their beauty).

Many cob coins are, indeed, quite crude, with a good portion of the design missing. "Royal strikes" are an exception to the rule during this era. Struck carefully on perfectly round discs, probably for presentation to the king, royal strikes are very rare. Both gold and silver coins were struck in the cob series. Chapter 4 covers the subject and includes a chart of the Spanish rulers' coats of arms to aid coin identification.

Cob coinage was replaced by milled coinage, so called because it was minted on a screw press rather than hand stamped like the cob coinage. Milled coins were issued from 1732 through 1771 in the Pillar series, and from 1772 through 1821 in the Portrait (or Bust) series, under five Spanish rulers from Philip V to Ferdinand VII. Pillar and Portrait coins were issued in bronze, silver, and gold, and are covered in chapter 5. The milled coinage is historically and numismatically important to U.S. collectors, as some pieces circulated in the United States as legal tender in the nation's early days.

In addition to the colonial coinage discussed to this point, the proclamation medals issued to honor Spanish rulers and the events during their reigns are also highly collectible (see chapter 24). Also widely collected are pattern, experimental, and trial pieces, dating from the 18th century to the modern era (chapter 23).

The War of Independence, 1810 to 1822, brought about the next era of Mexican coinage. Mexico's fight to obtain independence from Spanish rule was led by the heroic Father Miguel Hidalgo y Costilla, with his September 16, 1810, call for liberty: "Viva Mexico! Viva independence! Viva the Virgin of Guadalupe!" Many numismatic oddities—cast coinage, counterstamped and double-counterstamped by both the Royalist and the Insurgent sides of the conflict—were issued during this time. Chapter 6 reviews the coinage of this complex era.

The end of the War of Independence brought Mexico the short-lived empire of Agustín de Iturbide in 1822 and 1823. The first paper money of Mexico (chapter 27) was issued during Iturbide's reign, along with coinage of copper, silver, and gold (chapter 7).

After the abdication of Iturbide, Mexico became a republic; its coinage was issued from 1823 through 1897 in denominations of reales and escudos (as discussed in chapter 8). Within the period of 1824 through 1872, a wide variety of state and federal issues of the real denomination were struck in copper and brass (chapter 9). Those from the state mints were originally authorized by the federal government, but they proliferated to the point that the government finally put a halt on their production. The French intervention of 1863 to 1867, under Emperor Maximilian, interrupted the Republic coinage and resulted in Imperial decimal coinage of copper, silver, and gold (chapter 10). Even so, coinage of the Republic design continued to be struck at some mints during the French occupation.

After the June 1867 execution of Maximilian by Benito Juárez, Republic coinage was officially restored. This was the Republic's first decimal coinage, and it continued until the coinage reform of 1905, with the Liberty Cap pesos continuing into 1909. The Republic decimal series, like the Republic real series, offers bronze, silver, and gold coinages of several types; it is covered in chapter 11.

All of the early coinage of Mexico, from the Anáhuac era through the Republic decimal issues, is presented in greater depth in volume 3.

The 20th century brought the development of a wealth of new coin types and production concepts. Under the coinage reform of 1905, the gold standard was introduced, all the branch mints were closed, and ESTADOS UNIDOS MEXICANOS replaced REPUBLICA MEXICANA on the coinage. After this reform all of the coinage was struck at the Mexico City mint, except for a few occasions when some coins were struck outside the country. They all bear the famous mintmark of Mº. Today's coinage is struck at the modern mint at San Luis Potosí, using the Mº mintmark to denote the Casa de Moneda de México.

The coinage reform of 1992 (chapter 14) introduced the temporary "nuevo peso" denominations, along with the subsequent issues that are in circulation today. Both coinage reforms embraced the idea of commemorative (non-circulating legal tender) coinage, which is made to very high standards and sold to collectors at a premium over their face values. These coins are presented in chapter 15, followed in chapter 16 by Mint and Proof sets, which are packaged and sold by the Banco de México, Mexico's central bank. Silver and gold bullion coinages are covered in chapters 17 and 18, respectively; the Libertad series, in silver, gold, and platinum, in chapter 19; and the extensive coinage of the Pre-Columbian Collections Program in chapter 20. Modern varieties and errors appear in chapter 22. (All of the modern Mexican coinage, 1905 to date, is covered in-depth in volume 2.)

The violent era of the Mexican Revolution of 1910 through 1920 generated a vast variety of coins, tokens, and paper money, all of which is widely collected today. Paper money of the Revolution is covered in chapter 27; the coins are covered in chapter 12 (with previously unlisted issues now in their appropriate locations), and are treated in-depth in their own separate volume, number 4 in this encyclopedia.

The pot of gold at the end of the rainbow of Mexico's fascinating history: copper bucket of gold planchets for 50-peso coins, Apartado Mint, Mexico City, 1980.

2

Media of Exchange in the Anáhuac Era

The explorers of the American continent reported in several publications the results of their investigations into the media of exchange used by the natives. They noted that coinage as it was known to the Europeans at that time did not exist on the new continent.

Dr. J.W. Bastrow, in his article on "el comercio, moneda y cambio de los antiguos pueblos de México," presented at the 11th reunion of the International Congress of Americanists (October 15–20, 1895), had this to say pertaining to money:

> Money, in a broad sense, is some substance representing value, or of accepted value; less bulky and perishable than ordinary merchandise or commodities, used as a medium for the operations of trade, or for the convenient adjustment of balances or differences arising in the business of commerce. In a restricted sense, money is a piece of metal, usually gold or silver, stamped by public authority; it is used as the medium of commerce and known as coin. . . . Money, in its broad sense, was known in Mexico in the pre-Columbian period, it passed current in commerce and was accepted at fixed values.

The Aztec communities had a well-kept accounting of tribal taxes and, for lack of another method, would assign a "vassalage," which is a tax payable in products of a given area in various quantities based on population and wealth.

Lord Kingsborough, in his *Mexican Antiquities*, volume 5, pages 54–89, and volume 9, pages 17–18, lists among the taxes paid: large baskets filled with *cacahuapinol* (flour made of corn and cacao); baskets of *chiampinoli* (which he described as "meal of the Salviæ Chian"); finely woven cotton cloth; round, multicolored feather shields; honey; beans; corn; and implements of war, just to name a few items. Kingsborough named and closed his listing with "something of every thing found in the air, earth or water." There are numerous other published reports on the media of exchange.

Bringing together these items with those discussed in the previous chapter, we have the following list of materials used as media of exchange in Anáhuac (later New Spain and presently Mexico) prior to the establishment of the first mint in the Americas in Mexico City:

- cacao beans, or *cacahoat*
- pieces of cotton fabric, or *patolquechtli*
- stone beads
- Moctezuma's eagles, or *quauhtli*
- quills laden with gold dust or grains, or *canutillos*
- tin planchets
- hoe money, or *tajaderas*

In 1992 the Mexican government issued the first in a coinage series of "The Pre-Columbian Collections," which honored six of the early cultures of Mexico. The six cultures so honored were the Aztec (1992), the Central Veracrúz (1993), the Maya (1994), the Olmec (1996), the Teotihuacán (1997), and the Toltec (1998). These series are covered in Chapter 20

Aztec hoe money *(tajaderas patlachte)*.

Cacao beans *(cacahoat)*.

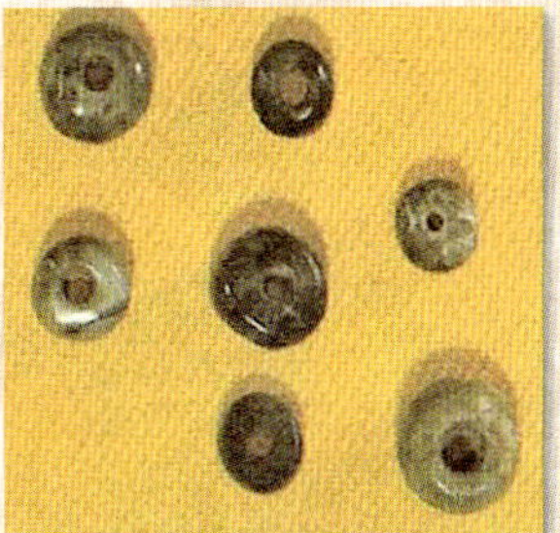

Jade beads *(cuentas)*.

Quills of gold *(canutillos)*.

3

Carlos and Johanna Coinage

The Carlos and Johanna coinage of 1536 through 1557 predated the coins of the United States by more than 250 years. Johanna was the daughter of King Ferdinand II of Aragon, who died in 1516, whereupon Johanna became queen. Charles, the eldest son of Johanna, became co-ruler because "Johanna the Mad" was, as the nickname suggests, deranged. (Her husband was Flemish Philip I, "the Handsome," of Burgundy. When he died, she refused to bury him and carried his coffin wherever she went. At times she opened the coffin so she could have extensive conversations with him.)

The son of Johanna and Philip I, Charles I, ruled Spain as king from 1516 to 1556, most of that time also ruling as Charles V, Holy Roman emperor (1519–1558). He was the grandson of Holy Roman Emperor Maximilian I and Mary of Burgundy. History generally accords him to have been the greatest of the Hapsburg emperors. He inherited the Spanish kingdoms, Spanish America, Naples, Sicily, the Low Countries, and the Austrian lands. In 1556 he abdicated all of his titles and retired to a monastery. His son, Philip II, received Spain, America, Naples, and the Netherlands. His brother became emperor as Ferdinand I.

During the period of the Carlos and Johanna coinage, Antonio de Mendoza served as the viceroy of New Spain up to 1550. Mendoza, the Count of Tendilla, was the first of the Spanish viceroys, and was chosen because Charles I was pleased with his successful diplomatic missions. Mendoza was responsible for bringing the first printing press to New Spain and for establishing the mint, the Casa de Moneda. The issuance of coins began in 1536. Luís de Velasco replaced Mendoza as viceroy through the end of the Late Series coinage.

First striking of coins on the American continent.

The silver issues from the Carlos and Johanna period were 1/4, 1/2, 1, 2, 3, 4, and 8 reales. They were issued in both the Early and Late Series, except for the 3 and 8 reales, which were issued only in the Early Series.

The silver 1/4 real *(cuartilla)* has, within a corded circle, a crowned K on the obverse with the legend KAROLVS . ET. IOA. On the reverse is a crowned I, the mintmark, and the legend HI:SPANIE:ET: IND: (with many varieties within the legend). Reales denominations 1 to 4 have basically the same design, with the Spanish coat of arms on the obverse and a pomegranate below. Several varieties were known to have been issued with the legend **CAROLVS ET JOHANA REGES**, in both roman and gothic letters. The reverse has the Pillars of Hercules, with the motto **PLVS VLTRA** ("further beyond") in various abbreviated presentations. The legend **HISPANIARVM . ET . INDIASRVM.** can be found in different formats with various abbreviations. **KI** replaces the Spanish coat of arms on the 1/2 real.

Carlos and Johanna coinage is referred to by some collectors as the "Pillars of Hercules," and the usage of PLVS VLTRA on the coinage refers to Spain's worldwide dominion at that time. Aloise Heiss, in his *Descripción general de las monedas hispano-cristianas desde la invasión de los árabes*, which was published more than 100 years ago, wrote with respect to the coins of Carlos I and Johanna: "For the first time appears the figure of the columns of Hercules with the modern motto PLVS VLTRA in place of the ancient NON PLVS VLTRA, because Christopher Columbus proved that there were other lands and other worlds beyond the limits placed by Hercules" (volume 1, page 150 of the reprint; translated from Spanish).

Humberto F. Burzio, in his *Diccionario de la Moneda Hispanoamericana*, reports: "Spain in the time of Charles I (V of Germany), adopted in its blazon of arms the columns of Hercules, as symbolism of its world-wide dominion, uniting with it the Latin motto PLUS ULTRA, to signify that, beyond the waters (of Oceanus or the Atlantic) there extended the dominion of its empire" (1958, volume 1, page 81; translated from Spanish).[1]

On November 12, 1545, Viceroy Mendoza decreed that "regardless of what the proportions were previously, the coinage in the Mexico City mint was to be: One-third in pieces of four reales denomination; One-third in two reales pieces; and the remaining third was to be minted in pieces of one real and half real denomination." These denominations are represented on the 1 through 3 reales as dots: one dot for 1 real, two dots for 2 reales, three dots for 3 reales. The denomination on the 4 reales is shown with an arabic numeral **4**. The copper maravedies were decreed by Viceroy Mendoza on June 28, 1542, and were issued in 2 and 4 maravedies. Like the silver Carlos and Johanna coinage, they were issued in both the Early Series and Late Series. The 2 maravedies has a crowned castle on the reverse while the obverse has a crowned **I**, the legend **PLUS ULTRA**, and the mintmark. The 4 maravedies has a castle, a crowned **K**, and the mintmark on the obverse; the reverse has a crowned **I** and a lion and castle. On some 4 maravedies the K looks much like an H.

For both copper and silver coins, those of the Early Series are crudely struck and have the letter K in "Karolvs" (Latin; in Spanish, "Carlos"), while the Late Series uses the letter C in most cases. Early issues use the motto **PLVS** or **PLVSVLT** in a bordered panel, while in the Late Series the panel is missing. Coins of the Early Series have a round-bottomed crown and, in the Late Series, a flat-bottomed crown. In the Early Series 4 reales, the numeral 4 is above the panel, while in the Late Series it is below. The early issues are without waterlines.

Coinage was a measure of the wealth that determined land and family status, and to New Spain was a symbol of stability. The most important purpose of coins was to protect the social status of the hierarchical structure. The coins from this period were hammered by hand, so perfection cannot be expected. Coins are listed herein by Early and Late Series. As their sizes varied, due to the minting process, the weights and sizes described here serve only as guides.

1. Azteca Numismatic Society's *PLUS ULTRA*, volume 5, number 53, 1968, by John Fies.

EARLY SERIES

The first diesinker for the Mexico City mint was Anton de Vides. Assayers for the Early Series (1536–1542), and the denominations issued, were:

1536–1538	Assayer: Francisco del Rincón (initial R) Denominations issued: 1/4, 1/2, 1, 2, 3, 4, and 8 reales
1538–1541	Assayer: Pedro de Espina, or Pedro de la Membrilla (initial P) Denominations issued: 1/4, 1/2, 1, 2, and 4 reales
1540 or 1541	Assayer: Francisco de Loaiza, or Esteban Franco (initial F) Denominations issued: 1/2, 1, 2, and 4 reales
1541–1542	Assayer: Juan Gutiérrez (initial G) Denominations issued: 1/4, 1/2, 1, 2, and 4 reales; 2 and 4 maravedies

Within both the Early and Late Series, there are several varieties in legends and in placement of quatrefoils, mascles, annulets, lozenges, rondules, and other devices.

Special Devices, Early and Late Series

Annulet

Rondule

Quatrefoil

Mascle

Lozenge

Pomegranate

Nine-punch

1/4 real, 0.930554 silver, 0.85 g.

Obverse: Crowned K. Legend CAROLVS . ET. IO... *Reverse:* Crowned I; on both sides of I, gothic M mintmark with rondule above and below M. Legend hI:SPANIE: ET:IND:. *Assayer's mark:* None. *Mintmark:* °𝔪°. *Diameter:* 18 mm. Nesmith 1, BW-3.1, KM-4.

1/2 real, 0.930554 silver, 1.62 g.

Obverse: Crowned KI with gothic M mintmark below. Legend ✠:KAROLVS:ET :IOhANA:RE:. *Reverse:* PLVS and crowned columns, with assayer's mark between columns.Legend:✠:ISPANIE:ET:IRDIARVM. No denomination shown. *Assayer's mark:* R. *Mintmark:* 𝔪. *Diameter:* 20 mm. Nesmith 2, BW-4.1, KM-6.

1 real, 0.930554 silver, 3.40 g.

Obverse: Crowned coat of arms; at each side of shield, a latin M mintmark with annulet above and below. Legend ✠ KAROLVS ✠ ET:IOHA. *Reverse:* PLVS and crowned columns, with assayer's mark between columns. Legend +HISPANIARVM ◊ET ◊INDIAR. No denomination shown. *Assayer's mark:* G. *Mintmark:* °M°. *Diameter:* 25 mm. Nesmith 9, BW-5.1, KM-8.

1 real, 0.930554 silver. 3.40 g.

Obverse: Crowned coat of arms; at each side of arms, a gothic M mintmark with rondule above and below. Legend KAROLVS✠ ET:IOhAN. *Reverse:* PLVSV and crowned columns, with assayer's mark between columns. Legend ✠:hIS:PANIA ✠: ET: INDIARV𝔪. No denomination shown. *Assayer's mark:* R. *Mintmark:* °𝔪°. *Diameter:* 25 mm. Nesmith 3a, BW-5.2a, KM-8.

2 reales, 0.930554 silver, 6.80 g.

Obverse: Crowned coat of arms; at each side of arms, a gothic M mintmark with rondule above and below. Legend :KAROLVS:✠ :ET:IOh·······. *Reverse:* PLVS and crowned columns, with assayer's mark between columns. Legend :✠:hI·SPANIE :✠: ET: INDIARVM. Two rondules above panel between columns indicate denomination. *Assayer's mark:* R. *Mintmark:* °𝔪°. *Diameter:* 27 mm. Nesmith 4, BW-6.1, KM-10.

2 reales, 0.930554 silver, 6.80 g.

Obverse: Crowned coat of arms; at each side of arms, latin M mintmark with annulet above and below. Legend +KAROLV◊ ET◊IOHANA. *Reverse:* PLVS and crowned columns, with assayer's mark between columns. Legend +HISPANIARVM◊ET◊ INDIAR. Two rondules above panel between columns indicate denomination. *Assayer's mark:* G. *Mintmark:* °M°. *Diameter:* 27 mm. Nesmith 10a, BW-6.2, KM-11.

3 reales, 0.930554 silver, 10.30 g. Type 1.

Obverse: Crowned coat of arms; at each side of arms, gothic M mintmark with rondule above and below. Legend KAROLVS ✠:ET: IOhANA:. *Reverse:* PLVSVL in panel spanning crowned columns; assayer's mark between the columns, below panel. Legend :✠:hI·SPANIE:✠:ET:INIARVM. Denomination indicated by three bars above panel and between crowned columns. *Assayer's mark:* R. *Mintmark:* °𝔪°. *Diameter:* 30 mm. Nesmith 5d, BW-7.3, KM-14.

3 reales, 0.930554 silver, 10.30 g. Type 2.

Obverse: Crowned coat of arms; at each side of arms, a gothic M mintmark with rondule above and below. Legend KAR...VS :ET:IOhANA:. *Reverse:* Within dotted circle, PLVS VLT in panel spanning crowned columns with assayer's mark between columns. Legend :◊:hISPANIE ✠ :ET: INDIAVR✠ :m. Denomination indicated by three rondules above panel, between columns. *Assayer's mark:* R. *Mintmark:* °𝔪°. *Diameter:* 31 mm. Nesmith 5c, BW-7, KM-13.

3 reales, 0.93055 silver, 10.30 g. Type 3.

Obverse: Crowned coat of arms; at each side of arms, a latin M mintmark with rondule above and below. Legend +:KAROLVS:ET :IOhANA: DEIGRA:R. *Reverse:* PLVSVLT in panel spanning crowned columns; assayer's mark below panel. Legend :ℵ:hISPANIEℵ :ET:INDIARV ℵ:M. Denomination indicated by three rondules above panel. *Assayer's mark:* R. *Mintmark:* M̊. *Diameter:* 32 mm. Nesmith 5a, BW-7.4, KM-15.

3 reales, 0.930554 silver, 10.30 g. Type 4.

Obverse: Crowned coat of arms; at each side of arms, a gothic M mintmark with rondule above and below. Legend +:KARO LVS:ET•IOhANA•DEIGRA:V. *Reverse:* PLVS VLT in panel spanning crowned columns; assayer's mark between columns, with waterlines below. Legend +:hISPANIE :ET•ℵ INDIARVm•REGES. Denomination indicated by three rondules between columns, above panel. *Assayer's mark:* R. *Mintmark:* m̊. *Diameter:* 31 mm. Nesmith 5, BW-7.1, KM-13.2.

4 reales, 0.930554 silver, 13.60 g.

Obverse: Crowned coat of arms; at each side of arms, a gothic M mintmark with rondule above and below. Legend :KAROLVS:ℵ :ET:IOhANA. *Reverse:* PLVS in panel spanning crowned columns; assayer's mark below panel. Legend :ℵ:hISPANIE:ℵ :ET:INDIARVM:RE. Denomination indicated by numeral 4 above panel. *Assayer's mark:* R. *Mintmark:* m̊. *Diameter:* 34 mm. Nesmith 6, BW-8, KM-15.

4 reales, 0.930554 silver, 12.75 g.

Obverse: Crowned coat of arms; at each side of arms, a gothic M mintmark with rondule above and below. Legend :KAROLVS:ℵ :ET:IohANA. *Reverse:* PLVS in panel spanning crowned columns, with assayer's mark between columns. Legend :ℵ:hIS:PANIE :ℵ:ET:ℵ:INDIAR:V:M. Denomination indicated by numeral 4 above panel. *Assayer's mark:* R below panel. *Mintmark:* m̊. *Diameter:* 34 mm. Nesmith 6d, BW-8.1, KM-16.

8 reales, Carlos and Johanna.

These extremely rare coins were the first crown-sized coins of the New World, and were reportedly minted in 1538. The three known examples came from a salvaged shipwreck. Prior to their discovery in 2000 there had been no known existing examples, and the coins were thought to have been missing or destroyed following Francisco de Sandoval's investigation of the mint (ordered by the Spanish king as a result of fraud charges by Spanish conqueror Hernán Cortés). The coins were made only briefly in 1538, as their size was too difficult to produce.

8 reales, 0.850 silver, 27.18 g.

Obverse: Crowned coat of arms with pomegranate below; at each side of arms, a gothic M mintmark with rondule above and below. Legend :ℵ:KROLVS:ℵ: T:IOhAMA: D:. *Reverse:* PLVS in a rhomboid panel spanning crowned columns, with assayer's mark below. Legend :ℵ:hISPANIE:ℵ:ET:ℵ:INDIARVM:RE. Small Greek cross replaces denomination in field above panel. *Assayer's mark:* R. *Mintmark:* m̊. *Diameter:* 38 mm. Nesmith UL, BW-9, KM-UL.

2 maravedies, copper.

Obverse: Unreadable. *Reverse:* Crowned castle. Legend ISPANIARVM ◊ET◊INDI ARV+. *Mintmark:* None visible. *Diameter:* 25 mm. Nesmith UL, BW-1, KM-UL.

4 maravedies, copper.

Obverse: Crowned K with lion to right and castle to left; below castle, latin M mintmark with annulet on either side. Pomegranate below crowned K, quatrefoil below lion. Legend KAROLVS ◊ET◊IO HANA◊REGES+. *Reverse:* Crowned I, with lion to right and castle to left. Legend +HISPANIARVM◊ET◊ INDIARVM. Denomination indicated by numeral 4 below crowned I, with four annulets at either side of 4. *Mintmark:* ⊙M⊙. *Diameter:* 27 mm. Nesmith plate XII.1, BW-2.1, KM-2.

Early Series

Coins of the Early and Late Series vary widely with respect to assayer marks, mintmarks, and other devices. The examples shown here may differ from the examples described in the text, but the major elements will be the same.

1/2 real. Mintmark °m, assayer's mark °P°. Nesmith 23, BW-4.2, KM-6. 19 mm, 1.70 g.

1 real. Mintmarks are °M° (with M struck over F) at left and °M° at right. Assayer's mark G (on reverse). Nesmith 9, BW-5.1, KM-7. 23 mm.

2 reales. Mintmarks are °m° at left and °m° right. Assayer's mark R (on reverse). Nesmith 4, BW-6.1, KM-10. 27 mm, 6.80 g.

3 reales, Type 2. Mintmarks are °m° at left and °m° right. Assayer's mark R (on reverse). Nesmith 5.b, BW-7, KM-13.1. 31 mm, 10.20 g.

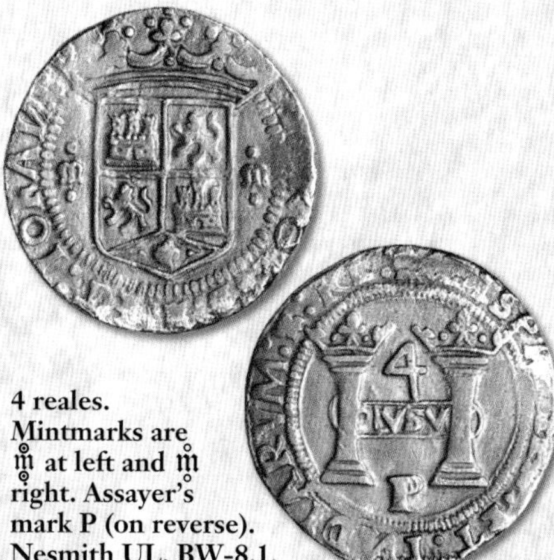

4 reales. Mintmarks are °m° at left and °m° right. Assayer's mark P (on reverse). Nesmith UL, BW-8.1, KM-16. 34 mm, 13.25 g.

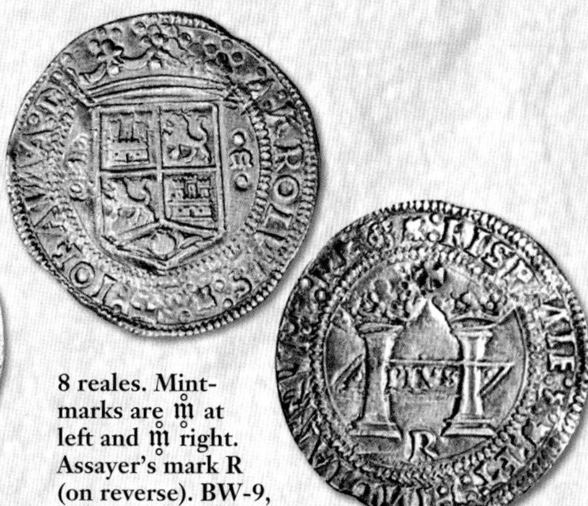

8 reales. Mintmarks are °m° at left and °m° right. Assayer's mark R (on reverse). BW-9, KM-UL. 38 mm, 27.18 g.

Drawing of an early 2 maravedies, reverse only (obverse is blank). Nesmith UL, BW-1, KM-UL.

4 maravedies. Nesmith plate XII #1, KM-2. 27 mm. BW-2.1.

LATE SERIES

The Early and Late Series of maravedies are easy to distinguish, as coins of the Early Series have a round-bottomed crown and the legend KAROLVS, while those in the Late Series have a flat-bottomed crown and the legend CHAROLV.

Assayers for the Late Series, 1542–1557, and denominations issued, were:

1542–1545 Assayer: Juan Gutiérrez (initial G)
Denominations issued: 2 and 4 maravedies; 1/4, 1/2, 1, 2, and 4 reales

1543–1545 Assayer: Alfonso del Rincón (initial R)
Denominations issued: 1, 2, and 4 reales

1543–1546? Assayer: Alonso del Villaseca (initial A; unproven thus far)
Denominations issued: 1/2, 1, 2, and 4 reales

1542–1556 Assayer: questionable, but reported as Luis Rodriguez (initial L)
Denominations issued: 1/2, 1, 2, and 4 reales

Prior to 1554 Assayer: Gómez de Santillán? (initial S)
Denominations issued: 1/4 (unique), 1, 2, and 4 reales

1552–1553 Assayer: questionable, but reported as Luis Rodriguez (initial L)
Denominations issued: 1/2, 1, 2, and 4 reales

1552–1557 Assayer: Bernardo de Oñate (initial O), apparently worked as an apprentice under the assayer "L"
Denominations issued: 1/2, 1, 2, and 4 reales

1/4 real, 0.930554 silver, 0.85 g.

Obverse: Crowned K. Legend CHAROLVS ET IOHAN. *Reverse:* Crowned I with latin M mintmark at left and assayer's mark at right. Legend +HISPANIARVM •ET•IN. *Assayer's mark:* S. *Mintmark:* G. *Diameter:* 18 mm. Nesmith UL, BW-3, KM-5.

1/2 real, 0.93055 silver, 1.70 g.

Obverse: Crowned KI. To left of crowned K, latin M mintmark with annulet above; to right of crowned I, assayer's mark (see note). Annulet between K and I. Legend CAROLVS∘ET∘IOHANNA∘REGS. *Reverse:* Above water, two crowned columns with PLVS on panel. Legend +HISPANIARVM •ET•INDIAR. No denomination shown. *Assayer's mark:* O. *Mintmark:* M̊. *Diameter:* 19 mm. Nesmith 107, BW-4.2, KM-6.5. (*Note:* In the 1/2-real series, the placement of the mintmarks and the assayer's initial can vary among left, middle, right, and below the monogram.)

1 real, 0.93055 silver, 3.40 g.

Obverse: Crowned coat of arms with assayer's initial to left and latin M mintmark to right. Legend +CAROLVS∘ET∘IOHANA ∘REGS. *Reverse:* Crowned columns with PLVSL on panel. Legend +HISPANIARVM ∘ET∘INDIARVM. *Assayer's mark:* A. *Mintmark:* M̊. *Diameter:* 23 mm. Nesmith 104c, BW-5.3, KM-9.

2 reales, 0.93055 silver, 6.80 g.

Obverse: Crowned coat of arms with assayer's initial to right, latin M mintmark to left. Legend CAROLVS∘ET∘IOHANA REGES. *Reverse:* Crowned columns above water. PLV SVL TR on panel with two rondules above SVL. Legend +HISPAN IARVM:ET:INDIARVM:. *Assayer's mark:* A. *Mintmark:* M̊. *Diameter:* 28 mm. Nesmith 109, BW-6.3, KM-12.

4 reales, 0.93055 silver, 13.60 g.

Obverse: Crowned coat of arms. Legend CAROLVS:ET:IOHANAREGS. *Reverse:* Crowned columns. PLV SVL TRA on panel, with 4 below. Legend +HISPAN IARVM:ET:INDIARVM. *Assayer's Mark:* None. *Mintmark:* None. *Diameter:* 34 mm. Nesmith UL, BW-8.3, KM-18.

2 maravedies, copper.

Obverse: Crowned column divides PLVS and VLTR. Latin M mintmark to right of column, pomegranate below. Legend +CHAROLVS◇ET◇IOHANARG. *Reverse:* Crowned castle. Legend +HISPANIARVM :ET:INDIATVM. No marks on reverse field. *Mintmark:* M. *Diameter:* 25 mm. Nesmith 1b, BW-1.2, KM-1.3.

2 maravedies, copper.

Obverse: Crowned column with PLVS to left of column and VLTR to right. Latin M mintmark to left of column and below PLVS. Pomegranate below crowned columns. Legend +CHAROLVS ◇ET◇IO HANARG. *Reverse:* Crowned castle, with M's to left and right of castle. Legend +HISPANIARVM:ET:INDIARVM. *Mintmark:* M. *Diameter:* 25 mm. Nesmith 1a, BW-1.4, KM-UL.

2 maravedies, copper.

Obverse: Crowned column divides PLVS and VLTR. Below column, latin M mintmark with annulet at each side. Legend +HISPANIARVM:ET:INDIARVM. *Reverse:* Crowned castle, with M's to right and left of castle. Legend +HISPANIARVM:ET: INDIARVM. *Mintmark:* ⊙M⊙. *Diameter:* 25 mm. Nesmith 2a, BW-1.3, KM-1.5.

2 maravedies, copper.

Obverse: Crowned column divides PLVS and VLTR. Below column, latin M mintmark with annulet at each side. Legend +HISPANIARVM:ET:INDIARVM. *Reverse:* Crowned castle. Legend +HISPANIARVM: ET:INDIARVM. No marks in reverse field. *Mintmark:* ⊙M⊙. *Diameter:* 25 mm. Nesmith 2b, BW-1.4a, KM-UL.

4 maravedies, copper.

Obverse: Crowned K with pomegranate below and castle to left; to right, a lion with numeral 4 below it. Below castle and to left of crowned K, latin M mintmark. Legend +CHAROLVS:ET:IOHANNA:REGES:. *Reverse:* Crowned I with 4 below, castle and four annulets at left, lion and four annulets at right. Legend . +HISPANIARVM:ET: INDIARVM. *Mintmark:* ⊙M̊⊙. *Diameter:* 28 mm. Nesmith 5, BW-2, KM-3.1.

4 maravedies, copper.

Obverse: Crowned K with pomegranate below, castle to left, and lion to right. Below the lion, latin M mintmark with an annulet above and one to the right. Legend +CHAROLVS:ET:IOHANNA· REGES:. *Reverse:* Crowned I with numeral 4 below lion; castle to left of I, with three annulets below castle; lion at right, below latin M mintmark, which has an annulet to each side. Legend +HISPANIARVM: ET:INDIARVM. *Mintmarks:* M̊⊙ (obverse) and ⊙M⊙ (reverse). *Diameter:* 32 mm. Nesmith 9, BW-2.5, KM-18.

4 maravedies, copper.

Obverse: Crowned K with pomegranate below, castle to left, and lion to right. Below lion, latin M mintmark with an annulet above and to each side. Legend +CHAROLVS:ET:IOHANNA:REGES. *Reverse:* Crowned column with 4 below; at left, castle with three annulets below; at right, lion above latin M mintmark with an annulet to each side. Legend +HIS PANIARVM:ET:INDIARVM·. *Mintmarks:* ⊙M̊⊙ (obverse), ⊙M⊙ (reverse). *Diameter:* 32 mm. Nesmith 9a, BW-2.4, KM-3.3.

4 maravedies, copper.

Obverse: Crowned K with pomegranate below, castle to left, and lion to right. Below the lion, latin M mintmark with annulet above and to each side. Legend +CHAROLVS:ET :IOHANNA:REGES :. *Reverse:* Crowned I with numeral 4 below. Castle to left of I with three annulets below castle. Below lion and to the right of 4, latin M mintmark with annulet above and to either side. Legend +HISPANI ARVM:ET:INDIARVM·. *Mintmark:* ⊙M̊⊙ (obverse), ⊙M̊⊙ (reverse). *Diameter:* 34 mm. Nesmith 10, BW-2.3, KM-3.2.

Late Series

Coins of the Early and Late Series vary widely with respect to assayer marks, mintmarks, and other devices. The examples shown here may differ from the examples described in the text, but the major elements will be the same.

1/4 real. Mintmark ⊙M⊙, assayer's mark S. Nesmith UL, BW-3.2, KM-5. 18 mm, 0.85 g.

1/2 real. Mintmark M̊, assayer's mark O. Nesmith 107, BW-4.2, KM-6.5. 23 mm, 1.70 g.

1 real. Mintmark M̊, assayer's mark A. Nesmith 104c, BW-5.3, KM-9. 24 mm, 3.40 g.

2 reales. Mintmark M, assayer's mark A. Nesmith 104, BW-6.3, KM-12. 29 mm, 6.80 g.

4 reales. No assayer's mark or mintmark. Nesmith UL, BW-8.3, KM-18. 30 mm, 13.60 g.

2 maravedies. Mintmark M̊, Nesmith 16, BW-1.2, KM-1.3. 25 mm.

4 maravedies. Nesmith 7, BW-2.4, KM-3.3. 32 mm.

4

Cob Coinage

There are many theories as to the origin of the term "cob." Some prefer the explanation by Dr. Charles Aby, "from the Irish meaning a lump of anything," while others in the numismatic field believe that the term derives from the Spanish term *cabo de barra* ("the end of the bar").

The planchets were clipped from the end of a bar of refined gold or silver, thus the *cabo de barra.* After the planchets were clipped off the bars, they were weighed to see if they met the standard for the denomination. The planchets were then filed or clipped to bring them to the allowed weight and size, then placed on the lower die. The upper die was placed on top of the planchet and struck with a hammer with enough force to impress the dies' designs on both the obverse and reverse of the coin. Dies were placed in such a manner as to ensure that the mintmark and the assayer's initial appeared on the coin.The mintmark showed where the coin was struck, and the assayer's initial showed who was responsible for the weight and fineness of the coin. A very severe penalty was imposed for undersized and underweight coins. Most of the coinage was slightly under its desired weight, probably within the tolerance of the authorizing decree, but never overweight. Weights and diameters vary in each coin, due to the minting conditions.

Since the coins were prepared without a collar to hold the dies in place and by non-skilled employees who did the best they could with what they had, one will find double and triple strikings, rotated obverses and reverses, and a multitude of different shapes.

Round examples of cob coinage are called "royal strikes," and in most cases these scarce examples have full dates and legends and are almost perfectly round. Some speculate that they were struck to be sent to the king as proof of the workmanship that was taking place in New Spain. The royal strikes are highly collectible but seldom encountered.

Cob coinage was minted in New Spain under several Spanish rulers, as follows. In this text, each ruler's issues are listed separately.

Philip II, 1556–1598

Philip III, 1598–1621

Philip IV, 1621–1665

Charles II, 1665–1700

Philip V (first reign), 1700–1724

Louis I, 1724

Philip V (second reign), 1724–1733

Spanish Coats of Arms

Philip II

Philip II

Philip II

Philip III

Philip III

Philip III

Philip III

Philip III

Reprinted from *Spanish Colonial Coins of North America, Mexico Mint* (A.J.S. McNickle, Sociedad Numismática de México, 1962).

Philip IV

Philip IV

Philip IV

Philip IV

Charles II

Philip V

Philip V

Philip V and Louis I

Charles III and Charles IV, Ferdinand VII

PHILIP II, 1556–1598

The Spanish empire reached its height during the reign of Philip II, son of Holy Roman emperor Charles V and Isabella of Portugal. Philip II became king of Spain in 1556. In 1580 Portugal was united with Spain. Philip II ruled with an iron fist and a diligent eye out for corruption, which was already becoming a problem. His reign became known as the golden age of Spanish art, during which writers and painters created some of Spain's greatest artistic works. His rule also brought the beginning of the end of the empire.

As Spain's power declined, the state's obligations for public services increased. Numerous roads had to be kept up and extended into vast areas that had to be guarded with garrisons for vigilance and keeping order. Cities and towns were established and demanded more public services. Corporations or groups of merchants (artisans, manufacturers, petty traders), the urban poor, and the restless populace had urgent needs, and this expanded throughout the empire. Crowding in the cities created unforeseen problems. Crops failed while speculators cornered the grain market. Numerous riots broke out due to lack of foodstuffs and the means to purchase them. In addition, mine workers who had emerged from slavery—but not from servitude—created other conflicts. The government remained incompetent.

The Real y Pontificia Universidad de México (Royal and Pontifical University of Mexico), founded in 1551, was the first educational establishment in New Spain. Other universities were established, but they were never true universities in the sense of centers of learning to promote the society of New Spain. Instead they were marred with religious dogma, and the king never encouraged new concepts of science.

During this era, Franciscan friars converted Indians through teaching at the missions. The friars brought new skills and technologies throughout New Spain, and in the process, they boosted the economy with the silver coinage of the realm.

1/2 Real

1/2 real, cob, 0.931 silver, 1.69 g.

Obverse: Crowned monogram of Philip II, with mintmark to the left or right, and assayer's initial to the left or right. Legend DEI . GRATIA . HISPANI. *Reverse:* A ball-tipped cross with castle and lion in the quarters. Legend +ET. INDIARVM . REX. *Mintmark:* M̊. BW-11, KM-20.

Date	Assayer	Comment
No date	O	M̊ to left, O to right
No date	F	
No date	F-D̊	F to left, M̊ to right, D̊ below monogram; rare
No date	O	O to left, M̊ to right
No date	O	M̊ to left, O to right

1 Real

1 real, cob, 0.931 silver, 3.38 g.

Obverse: Crowned coat of arms of Philip II, with mintmark to the left or right, and assayer's initial to the left or right. Legend PHILIPVS . II . DEI . GRATIA. *Reverse:* A ball-tipped cross with castle and lion in the quarters. Legend + HISPANIARVM . ET . INDIARVM . *Mintmark:* M̊. BW-12, KM-26.

Date	Assayer	Comment
No date	O	M̊ to left, O to right
No date	O	O to left, M̊ to right
No date	O	Vertical M̊O to left
No date	O	O to left, M̥ to right
No date	F	M̊ to left, F to right
No date	F	M̊F to left
No date	F	M̊ F to right
No date	F	M̊ to left, M̊F/O to right
No date	F-D	F over D to right
No date	F̊	M̊F̊ to left; rare

2 Reales

2 reales, cob, 0.931 silver, 6.77 g.

Obverse: Crowned coat of arms of Philip II, with mintmark to the left or right, and assayer's initial to the left or right. Legend PHILIPPVS : II : DEI : GRATIA. *Reverse:* A ball-tipped cross with castle and lion in the quarters. Legend + HISPANIARVM : ET : INDIARVM : REX. *Mintmark:* M̊. BW-13, KM-31.

Date	Assayer	Comment
No date	O	O to right, M̊ to left
No date	O	O to left, M̊ to right
No date	O	Vertical M̊O to left
No date	O	M̊ with o below right
No date	F	MF to left
No date	F	M̊F to left
No date	F-D	M̊F to left, D to right

4 Reales

4 reales, cob, 0.931 silver, 13.54 g.

Obverse: Crowned coat of arms of Philip II, with mintmark to the left or right, and assayer's initial to the left or right. Legend PHIL IPPVS : II : DEI : GRATIA. *Reverse:* A ball-tipped cross with castle and lion in the quarters. Legend + HISPANIARVM : ET : INDI ARVM : REX. *Mintmark:* M̊. BW-14, KM-36.

Date	Assayer	Comment
No date	O	M̊ to left, O to right
No date	O	O to left, M̊ to right
No date	O	O to left, M̊O to right
No date	O	Vertical M̊O to right
No date	O	Vertical M̊ and O to left
No date	O	M̊O to right, inverted M; rare
No date	O	INDARIVM RX error
No date	O	BHLIPPVS error
No date	O	Phillip III SPAN error
No date	O	INDIARVN error
No date	O	GRATIR error
No date	F	Denom. IIII to right, M̊F to left
No date	F	F and denom. IIII to left, M̊ right
No date	F	Denom. 4 to right, M̊F to left
No date	F	Denom. IIII to left, M̊F to right

Date	Assayer	Comment
No date	F	PHYLIPPUS error
No date	F-D	M̊F to left, D to right
No date	F	Rare

8 Reales

8 reales, cob, 0.931 silver, 27.07 g.

Obverse: Crowned coat of arms of Philip II, with mintmark to the left or right and assayer's initial to the left or right. Legend PHILIPPVS II DEI. *Reverse:* A ball-tipped cross with castle and lion in the quarters. Legend +HISPANIARVM ET INDIARVM REX. *Mintmark:* M̊. BW-15, KM-43.

Date	Assayer	Comment
No date	O	M̊ with extra o below left, 8 to right, DEI GRATIA
No date	O	DEI GRATIA, flat-top 8 right, M̊ with extra o below left
No date	O	O left, M̊ right, DEI GRATIA
No date	F	M̊F left, PHILIPPVS II DEI
No date	F	M̊F left, PHILIPPVS II DEY
No date	F	M̊F, PHILLIPPVS
No date	F	M̊F, PHILIPPVS D
No date	F	M̊F left, denomination VIII vertical
No date	F	M̊F left, words in legends divided by :
No date	F	M̊F left, IISPANIARVM
No date	F	M̊F left, denomination VIII
No date	F-D	M̊F left, 8 dots right
No date	F-D	8F to left, M̊ D right
No date	F	M̊F to left; rare

PHILIP III, 1598–1621

Philip III, the son of Philip II, was a scholar but could never make up his mind. Like so many Spanish rulers, he never challenged the power of the Catholic Church, especially during the Inquisition. Not all was gloomy, however, and Spain still basked in the sunlight of an artistic and intellectual world. Nevertheless, the country was now suffering from serious economic problems that would affect New Spain and the rest of the New World. Due to numerous government restrictions, commerce was never able to expand and thrive.

During this era the raw materials taken from New Spain and the rest of the New World found their way into the hands of the merchants and manufacturers of Western Europe. Some of these materials came back to Spain in the form of finished articles for home consumption or for shipment to the New World. A dependent Spain, itself a colony of the developing countries of Europe, set the stage for the tragedy of Mexican history.

Under Philip III only silver coins in the denominations of 1/2, 1, 2, 4, and 8 reales were struck, with assayer initials of A, D, and F. Dates appeared on these coins for the first time from 1607 to 1620 for the minor reales and from 1607 to 1621 for the 8 reales. Presentation pieces are known for 1607, 1608, 1614, and 1615. (Examples exist under all rulers, but dates are not visible on the planchets due to their crudeness.)

1/2 Real

1/2 real, cob, 0.931 silver, 1.69 g.

Obverse: Crowned monogram of Philip III with mintmark to the left and assayer's initial to the right. Legend **PHILIPPVS . III . DEI . GRATIA.** *Reverse:* A ball-tipped cross with castle and lion in the quarters. Legend **+ HISPANIARVM . ET. INDIARVN REX.** *Mintmark:* $\overset{o}{M}$. BW-11a, KM-20.

Date	Assayer	Comment
No date	F-D	Predates 1607
No date	F	Predates 1607

1/2 real, cob, 0.931 silver, 1.69 g.

Obverse: Crowned monogram of Philip III with mintmark to the left and assayer's initial to the right. Legend **PHILIPPVS . III . DEI . GRATIA.** *Reverse:* A ball-tipped cross with castle and lion in the quarters. Legend **+ HISPANIARVM . ET. INDIARVN REX.** *Mintmark:* $\overset{o}{M}$. BW-11.1, KM-21.

Date	Assayer	Comment
No date	n.v.	Date off flan
1608	A or F	
1609	A	
1610	F	
1614	F	
1620	D	

Note: n.v. = not visible.

1 Real

1 real, cob, 0.931 silver, 3.38 g.

Obverse: Crowned coat of arms of Philip III with mintmark and assayer's initial to the left. Legend **PHILIPPVS . III . DEI . GRATIA.** *Reverse:* A ball-tipped cross with castle and lion in the quarters. Legend **+ HISPANIARVM . ET. INDIARVM.** *Mintmark:* $\overset{o}{M}$. BW-12.2, KM-27.1.

Date	Assayer	Comment
No date	F-D	
No date	F	

1 real, cob, 0.931 silver, 3.38 g.

Obverse: Crowned coat of arms of Philip III with mintmark and assayer's initial to the left. Legend **PHILIPPVS . III . DEI . GRATIA.** *Reverse:* A ball-tipped cross with castle and lion in the quarters. Legend **+ HISPANIARVM . ET . INDIARV.** *Mintmark:* $\overset{o}{M}$. BW-12.1, KM-27.

Date	Assayer	Comment
No date	n.v.	Date off flan
1607	F	1607 over ATIA
1607	F	
1608/7	F	
1608	A	
1608	F	
1609	A	
1610/09	F	
1610	F	
1611/10	F	
1611	F	
1612/1	F	
1612	F	
1613	F	

Note: n.v. = not visible.

Philip III Royal 1 Real

Royal coins were struck with special dies on selected round planchets and may not have the same legend as the regular coinage of the same date and mintmark. The choice examples were probably sent back to Spain for presentation to the king. BW-R12.3, KM-R27.2.

Date	*Assayer*	*Comment*
1608	*A*	*Rare*

2 Reales

2 reales, cob, 0.931 silver, 6.77 g.

Obverse: Crowned coat of arms of Philip III with mintmark and assayer's initial to the left. Legend PHILIPPVS . III . DEI . GRATIA. *Reverse:* A ball-tipped cross with castle and lion in the quarter. Legend + HISPANIARVM . ET . INDIARVM . REX. *Mintmark:* M̊. BW-13.2, KM-32.1.

Date	Assayer	Comment
No date	F-D	Rare
No date	F	Rare

2 reales, cob, 0.931 silver, 6.77 g.

Obverse: Crowned coat of arms of Philip III. Legend PHILIPPVS . III . DEI . G. Mintmark to the left, assayer's initial to the left. *Reverse:* A ball-tipped cross with castle and lion in the quarters. Legend +HISPANIARVM . ET. INDIARVM. REX. *Mintmark:* M̊. BW-13.3, KM-32.2.

Date	Assayer	Comment
No date	n.v.	Date off flan
1607	F	1607 over ATIA
1607	F	
1608	F	
1608	A	
1609	A	
1611	F	
1613	F	
1616	F	
1620	D	
1622	D	Retrograde 2's

Note: n.v. = not visible.

4 Reales

4 reales, cob, 0.931 silver, 13.54 g.

Obverse: Crowned coat of arms of Philip III. Legend PHILIPPVS . III . DEI . GRATIA. Mintmark to the left, assayer's initial to the left. *Reverse:* A ball-tipped cross with castle and lion in the quarters. Legend + HISPANIARVM . ET . INDIARVM . REX. *Mintmark:* M̊. BW-14.2, KM-37.1.

Date	Assayer	Comment
No date	F-D	
No date	F	M̊ left, 4 right
No date	F	F and 4 left, M̊ right

4 reales, cob, 0.931 silver, 13.54 g.

Obverse: Crowned coat of arms of Philip III. Mintmark to the left or right, assayer's initial to the left, and denomination to the left or right. Legend PHILIPPVS . III . DEI . GRATIA. *Reverse:* A ball-tipped cross with castle and lion in the quarters. Legend + HISPANIARVM . ET . INDIARVM . REX . *Mintmark:* M̊. BW-14.1, KM-37.

Date	Assayer	Comment
No date	n.v.	Date off flan
1607	F	1607 over ATIA
1607	F	
1608/7	A or F	
1608	A	
1609/8	A	
1609	A	
1610	F	
1611/0	F	
1611	F	
1612	F	
1613	F	
1614	F	
1617	D	
1618	D	
1620	D	
1621/0/9	D	
1621	D	

Note: n.v. = not visible.

Philip III Royal 4 Reales

Royal coins were struck with special dies on selected round planchets and may not have the same legend as the regular coinage of the same date and mintmark. The choice examples were probably sent to Spain for presentation to the king. BW-R14.2, KM-R37.1.

Date	*Assayer*	*Comment*
No date	*F*	*Rare*

8 Reales

8 reales, cob, 0.931 silver, 27.07 g.

Obverse: Crowned coat of arms of Philip III, with mintmark and assayer's initial to the left. Legend PHILIPPVS . III . DEI . GRATIA.

Reverse: A ball-tipped cross with castle and lion interchanged in the quarters. Legend + HISPANIARVM . ET . INDIARVM . REX. *Mintmark:* M°. BW-15.3, KM-44.2.

Date	Assayer	Comment
No date	F-D	
No date	F	
No date	F	M° and F left, 8 right

8 reales, cob, 0.931 silver, 27.07 g.
Obverse: Crowned coat of arms of Philip III, with mintmark and assayer's initial to the left. Legend PHILIPPVS . III . DEI . G . followed by the date. *Reverse:* A ball-tipped cross with castle and lion interchanged in the quarters. Legend + HISPANIARVM . ET . INDIARVM . REX. *Mintmark:* M°. BW-15.1, KM-44.

Date	Assayer	Comment
No date	n.v.	Date off flan
1607	F	1607 over ATIA
1607	F	
1608	A-F	
1608/7	F	
1608	A	
1608	F	
1609	A	
1610	F	
1611/10	F	
1611	F	
1612/1	F	
1612	F	
1613	F	
1614	F	
1615	F	
1618	D-F	
1618	D	
1620	D	
1621/0	D	
1621	D	

Notes: n.v. = not visible. The 1611 uniface ball-tipped cross REI is a fantasy.

Philip III Royal 8 Reales

Royal coins were struck on round selected planchets with special dies. These may not have the same legend as the regular coinage of the same date and mintmark. The choice examples were probably sent to Spain for presentation to the king. BW-R15.2, KM-R44.1.

Date	Assayer	Comment
ND	F-D	Unique
ND	F	Rare

Obverse legend PHILIPVS . III . DEI . G. followed by date. BW-R15.4, KM-R44.3.

Date	Assayer	Comment
1607	F	PHILLIPPVS; rare
1609	A	Rare
1610	F	Rare
1613	F	Rare
1614	F	PHILIPVS; rare
1615	F	PHILIPVS; rare
1618	D-F	PHILIPVS; rare

PHILIP IV, 1621–1665

Philip IV, the eldest son of Philip III and his wife, Margaret of Austria, ascended the throne in 1621. Due to reckless wars, he suffered at the hands of the French and lost valuable slices of the Spanish Empire to England and Holland. He reviled the Hapsburg decay in Spain but was indifferent to promoting commerce or education. Spain and her colonies, including New Spain, suffered from this policy. In New Spain, debt peonage benefited mainly the big *hacendados*, who, with capital at hand, were able to entice Indians to their estates by offering to pay them. In time, debt peonage and wage labor undermined the transformation of the colonial economy during the 17th century.

Several energetic rulers prevailed in New Spain during this era. Diego Carrillo de Mendoza y Pimentel, Marques de Gélves y Conde de Priego, was appointed viceroy to New Spain in 1621. He improved the safety of the roads and promoted justice. Unfortunately, in 1623 corn went up in price, and the people blamed him for the crisis. Popular displeasure due to the scarcity of corn was added to the old conflict between the viceroy and the clergy, which created more riots. By 1644 the church became an obstacle. Its numerous monasteries and convents were an expense to the economy. Religious institutions and the money lent by them on the security of real estate amounted to half the value of all property in the country. Essentially, the church was the bank of New Spain. Another problem was idle priests who had nothing to do but become nuisances to society. Church problems were ignored, and the Inquisition became a threat to education. The economy was drained by the construction of cathedrals and monasteries that were buildings of proportionate grandeur.

Silver coins were struck at the Mexico mint in denominations of 1/2, 1, 2, 4, and 8 reales. According to Dr. Alberto Francisco Pradeau's *Numismatic History of Mexico*, 1-real coins were not struck, but Frank Grove's *Coins of Mexico* and Krause's *Standard Catalog of World Coins* both show the 1-real denomination issued in 1622, 1627, 1630, 1643, 1651, 1653, and 1654. Grove lists 2 reales for 1630, 1637, 1641, 1653, 1655, and 1657, but states that he has "not seen any of the 2-reales coins." Krause shows the same dates as Grove for the 2-real denomination. New dates are still being discovered; some experts believe all denominations were made every year.

Legends on the coinage of Philip IV depict the "IV" with four I's: IIII.

1/2 Real

1/2 real, cob, 0.931 silver, 1.69 g.

Obverse: Crowned monogram of Philip IV with mintmark and assayer's initial to the left. Legend PHILIPPVS . IIII . DEI . G followed by date. *Reverse:* A ball-tipped cross with castle and lion in the quarters. Legend + HISPANIARVM . ET . INDIAR. *Mintmark:* Mº. BW-11.2, KM-22.

Date	Assayer	Comment
No date	n.v.	Date off flan
1622	D	
1642/1/0	P	
1650	P	
1653	P	
1654	P	
1656	P	
1657	P	
1658	P	
1659	P	
1661	P	
1662	P	
1667	G	

Note: n.v. = not visible.

1 Real

1 real, cob, 0.931 silver, 3.38 g.

Obverse: Crowned coat of arms of Philip IV with mintmark and assayer's initial to the left. Legend PHILIPPVS . IIII . DEI . G . followed by date. *Reverse:* A ball-tipped cross with castle and lion in the quarters. Legend + HISPANIARVM . ET . INDIARVM. *Mintmark:* Mº. BW-12.4, KM-28.

Date	Assayer	Comment
No date	n.v.	Date off flan
1622	D	
1624/3	D	
1627	D	
1630	D	
1632/2/9	D	
1633	D	
1643	P	
1651	P	
1652	P	
1653	P	
1654	P	
1657	P	
1660	P	

Note: n.v. = not visible.

Philip IV Royal 1 Real

Royal coins were struck with special dies on selected round planchets. These may not have the same legend as the regular coinage of the same date and mintmark. The choice examples were probably sent back to Spain for presentation to the king. BW-R12.4, KM-R28.

Date	*Assayer*	*Comment*
1643	*P*	

2 Reales

2 reales, cob, 0.931 silver, 6.77 g.

Obverse: Crowned coat of arms of Philip IV with mintmark and assayer's initial to the left. Legend **PHILIPPVS . IIII . DEI . G .** followed by date. *Reverse:* A ball-tipped cross with castle and lion in the quarters. Legend **+ HISPANIARVM . ET . INDIARVM.** *Mintmark:* $\overset{\circ}{\text{M}}$. BW-13.4, KM-33.

Date	Assayer	Comment
No date	n.v.	Date off flan
1641	P	
1653	P	
1654	P	
1655	P	
1657	P	
1666	G	

Note: n.v. = not visible.

4 Reales

4 reales, cob, 0.931 silver, 13.54 g.

Obverse: Crowned coat of arms of Philip IV with mintmark and assayer's initial to the left. Legend **PHILIPPVS . IIII . DEI . G .** followed by date. *Reverse:* A ball-tipped cross with castle and lion in the quarters. Legend **+HISPANIARVM. ET. INDIARVM. REX.** *Mintmark:* $\overset{\circ}{\text{M}}$. BW-14.4, KM-38.

Date	Assayer	Comment
No date	n.v.	Date off flan
1622	D	
1623/2	D	
1623	D	
1624	D	
1629	D	
1631	D	
1632	D	
1636	P	
1639	P	
1643	P	
1644	P	
1645	P	
1648	P	
1649	P	
1650	P	
1651	P	
1652	P	
1653	P	
1654	P	
1655	P	
1656	P	
1657	P	
1658	P	
1659/8	P	
1659	P	
1661	P	
1662	P	
1665	P	

Note: n.v. = not visible.

8 Reales

8 reales, cob, 0.931 silver, 27.07 g.

Obverse: Crowned coat of arms of Philip IV with mintmark and assayer's initial to the left. Legend **PHILIPVS . IIII . DEI . G .** followed by the date and a period. *Reverse:* A ball-tipped cross with castle and lion interchanged in the quarters. Legend **+HISPANIARVM . ET . INDIARVM . REX.** *Mintmark:* $\overset{\circ}{\text{M}}$. BW-15.5, KM-45.

Date	Assayer	Comment
No date	n.v.	Date off flan
1621	D	
1622/1	D	
1622	D	
1623	D	
1623/2	D	
1624/3	D	
1624	D	
1625/4	D	
1625	D	
1626	D	
1627/4	D	
1627/5	D	
1627/6	D	
1627	D	
1628/7	D	
1628	D	
1629	D	
1630	D	
1631	D	
1632	D	
1634	D	
1634	P	

Note: n.v. = not visible.

Date	Assayer	Comment
1635/4	P	
1635	P	
1636	P	
1637	P	
1639/8	P	
1639	P	
1640/39	P	
1640	P	
1641/40/39	P	
1641	P	
1642	P	
1643/2	P	
1643	P	
1644	P	
1645	P	
1646	P	
1647/6	P	
1647	P	
1648/7	P	
1648	P	
1649/8	P	
1649	P	
1650	P	
1651	P	
1652/45	P	
1652/48	P	
1652/49	P	
1652/0	P	
1652/1	P	
1652	P	
1653/2	P	
1653	P	
1654/3	P	
1654	P	
1655/4	P	
1655	P	
1656	P	
1657	P	
1658/7	P	
1658	P	
1659	P	
1660/59	P	
1660	P	
1661/0	P	
1661	P	
1662	P	
1663	P	
1664	P	
1665	P	
1666	G-P	
1666	G	
1667/6	G	
1667	G	

Philip IV Royal 8 Reales

Royal coins were struck with special dies on selected round planchets. These may not have the same legend as the regular coinage of the same date and mintmark. The choice examples were probably sent to Spain for presentation to the king. BW-R15.5, KM-R45.

Date	*Assayer*	*Comment*
1621	*D*	*PHILIPVS; rare*
1629	*D*	*Rare*
1632	*D*	*Rare*
1636	*D*	*PHILLIPVS; rare*
1639	*P*	*PHILLIPVS; rare*
1642	*P*	*PHILLIPVS; rare*
1646	*P*	*Rare*
1650	*P*	*Rare*

CHARLES II, 1665–1700

The feebleminded King Charles II, son of Philip IV, ruled for 35 years (from 1665 to 1700). His mother was Philip IV's second wife (his niece Maria, daughter of the emperor Ferdinand III). Charles was the only surviving son of his father's two marriages. He was a child of old age and genetic disease caused by the constant intermarriages of the Habsburgs. Among other defects, he had difficulty chewing, since his chin was deformed due to royal inbreeding. Charles suffered from these shortcomings; his advisers, meanwhile, became greedy and powerful and plundered Spain.

When Charles died, he was the last of the Spanish Habsburg monarchs. Spain had become an empty shell of its former glorious self. The country was wracked by foreign wars and domestic conflicts; its treasury was bare. Foreigners, mostly English merchants, profited daily from illegal trade with New Spain. Just a third of the silver taken from the New World ended up in Spanish chests. On June 8, 1692, a crowd of Indians attempted to air complaints to the viceroy or the archbishop. They were ignored, so they retaliated by burning the viceroy's palace. The fire also destroyed the municipal archives. Peace was restored by harsh, repressive measures.

Backed by an ineffective king, the crown nevertheless had several wise men who tried (with little success) to lessen the power of strong nobles and the church. Slavery was curtailed by orders and decrees. Indians were entitled to protection but had no privileges. From 1673 to 1680, Friar Payo Enriquez de Rivera Manrique was the archbishop of Mexico and viceroy of New Spain. He was a noble ruler who corrected the abuses of the officers of the treasury and curtailed piracy. Most of the revenues were spent to alleviate poverty, but the power of the church still remained an issue.

Under Charles II the authority to strike gold coins was granted on February 25, 1675. The coins were to be of 22K, or 916.666 fine.

1/2 Real

1/2 real, cob, 0.931 silver, 1.69 g.

Obverse: Crowned monogram of Charles II with mintmark to the left and assayer's initial to the right. Legend CAROLVS. II. DEI. G . followed by date. *Reverse:* A ball-tipped cross with castle and lion in the quarters. Legend +HISPANIARVM . ET . INDIAR. *Mintmark:* M°. BW-11.3, KM-23.

Date	Assayer	Comment
No date	n.v.	Date off flan
1668	G	
1669	G	
1671	G	
1673	G	
1674	G	
1677	L	
1678	L	
1681/0	L	
1681	L	
1682	L	
1683	L	
1684	L	
1685	L	
1687	L	
1689	L	
1690	L	
1691	L	
1692	L	
1694	L	
1695	L	
1697	L	

Note: n.v. = not visible.

1 Real

1 real, cob, 0.931 silver, 3.38 g.

Obverse: Crowned coat of arms of Charles II with mintmark and assayer's initial to the left. Legend CAROLVS . II . DEI . G . followed by date. *Reverse:* A ball-tipped cross with castle and lion in the quarters. Legend +HISPANIARVM . ET . INDIARVM . *Mintmark:* M°. BW-12.5, KM-29.

Date	Assayer	Comment
No date	n.v.	Date off flan
1668	G	
1670	G	
1677	G	
1688	L	
1692	L	

Note: n.v. = not visible.

Charles II Royal 1 Real

Royal coins were struck with special dies on selected round planchets.They may not have the same legend as the regular coinage of the same date and mintmark The choice examples were probably sent to Spain for presentation to the king. BW-R12.5, KM-R29.

Date	*Assayer*	*Comment*
1699	*L*	*Rare*

2 Reales

2 reales, cob, 0.931 silver, 6.77 g.

Obverse: Crowned coat of arms of Charles II with mintmark and assayer's initial to the left. Legend . CAROLVS . II . DEI . G .

followed by date. *Reverse:* A ball-tipped cross with castle and lion in the quarters. Legend +HISPANIARVM . ET . INDIARVM . REX. *Mintmark:* M̊. BW-13.5, KM-34.

Date	Assayer	Comment
No date	n.v.	Date off flan
1668	G	
1669	G	
1690	L	
1695	L	
1699	L	

Note: n.v. = not visible.

Charles II Royal 2 Reales

Royal coins were struck with special dies on selected round planchets.They may not have the same legend as the regular coinage of the same date and mintmark. The choice examples were probably sent to Spain for presentation to the king. BW-R13.5, KM-R34.

Date	*Assayer*	*Comment*
1668	*G*	*Rare*

4 Reales

4 reales, cob, 0.931 silver, 13.54 g.

Obverse: Crowned coat of arms of Charles II with mintmark and assayer's initial to the left. Legend . CAROLVS . II . DEI . G . followed by date. *Reverse:* A ball-tipped cross with castle and lion in the quarters. Legend + HISPANIARVM . ET . INDIARVM. REX. *Mintmark:* M̊. BW-14.5, KM-39.

Date	Assayer	Comment
No date	n.v.	Date off flan
1667	G	
1678	L	
1679	L	
1682	L	
1683	L	
1685	L	
1689	L	
1690	L	
1691/0	L	
1691	L	
1692	L	
1694	L	
1695	L	
1697	L	
1698	L	
1700	L	

Note: n.v. = not visible.

Charles II Royal 4 Reales

Royal coins were struck with special dies on selected round planchets. They may not have the same legend as the regular coinage of the same date and mintmark. The choice examples were probably sent to Spain for presentation to the king. BW-R14.5, KM-R39.

Date	*Assayer*	*Comment*
1678	*L*	*Rare*
1682	*L*	*Rare*
1691/0	*L*	*Rare*
1695	*L*	*Rare*

8 Reales

8 reales, cob, 0.931 silver, 27.07 g.

Obverse: Crowned coat of arms of Charles II with mintmark and assayer's initial to the left. Legend . CAROLVS . II . DEI . G . followed by the date and a period. *Reverse:* A ball-tipped cross with castle and lion interchanged in the quarters. Legend +HISPANIARVM . ET . INDIARVM . REX. *Mintmark:* M̊. BW-15.6, KM-46.

Date	Assayer	Comment
No date	n.v.	Date off flan
1667/6	G	
1667	G	
1668	G	
1669	G	
1670	G	
1671	G	
1672	G	
1673	G	
1674	G	
1675	G	
1676/5	G	Rare
1676	G	
1677	G	
1678	L	
1679	L	
1680	L	

Note: n.v. = not visible.

8 reales, BW-15.6, continued

Date	Assayer	Comment
1681/0	L	
1681	L	
1682	L	
1683	L	
1684	L	
1685	L	
1686	L	
1687	L	
1688	L	
1689	L	
1690	L	
1691	L	
1692	L	
1693	L	
1694	L	
1695	L	
1698	L	
1699	L	
1700	L	
1701	L	
No date	L	Date off flan
1690	L	
1694	L	
1695	L	
1697	L	
1698	L	
1699	L	
1700	L	
1701/0	L	

Charles II Royal 8 Reales

Royal coins were struck with special dies on selected round planchets. They may not have the same legend as the regular coinage of the same date and mintmark. The choice examples were probably sent to Spain for presentation to the king. BW-R15.6, KM-R46.

Date	*Assayer*	*Comment*
1674	*L*	*Rare*
1678	*L*	*Rare*
1681/0	*L*	*Rare*
1685	*L*	*Rare*
1689/8	*L*	*Rare*
1690	*L*	*Rare*
1691	*L*	*Rare*
1699	*L*	*Rare*
1700	*L*	*Rare*

1 Escudo

1 escudo, cob, 0.917 gold, 3.38 g.

Obverse: Crowned coat of arms of Charles II with mintmark and assayer's initial to the left. Legend . CAROLVS . II . DEI . G . followed by date. *Reverse:* A ball-tipped cross with castle and lion in the quarters. Legend + HISPANIARVM . ET . INDIARVM . REX . *Mintmark:* $\overset{\circ}{\underset{M}{x}}$. BW-16, KM-50.

2 Escudos

2 escudos, cob, 0.917 gold, 6.77 g.

Obverse: Crowned coat of arms of Charles II with mintmark and assayer's initial to the left. Legend . CAROLVS . II . DEI . G . followed by date. *Reverse:* A ball-tipped cross with castle and lion in the quarters. Legend + HISPANIARVM . ET . INDIARVM . REX . *Mintmark:* $\overset{\circ}{\underset{M}{x}}$. BW-17, KM-52.

Date	Assayer	Comment
No date	L	Date off flan
1680	L	
1681	L	
1685	L	
1690	L	
1691	L	
1693	L	
1697	L	
1695	L	
1698	L	
1700	L	
1701	L	

4 Escudos

4 escudos, cob, 0.917 gold, 13.54 g.

Obverse: Crowned coat of arms of Charles II with mintmark and assayer's initial to the left. Legend . CAROLVS . II . DEI . G . followed by date. *Reverse:* A ball-tipped cross with castle and lion in the quarters. Legend +HISPANIARVM . ET . INDIARVM . REX . *Mintmark:* $\overset{\circ}{\underset{M}{x}}$. BW-18, KM-54.

Date	Assayer	Comment
No date	L	Date off flan
1680	L	
1681	L	

Date	Assayer	Comment
1683	L	
1693	L	
1694	L	
1695	L	
1696	L	
1697	L	
1698/7	L	
1698	L	
1699/8	L	
1699	L	

8 Escudos

8 escudos, cob, 0.917 gold, 27.07 g.

Obverse: Crowned coat of arms of Charles II with mintmark and assayer's initial to the left. Legend . CAROLVS . II . DEI . GRATIA . followed by the date (note that a period follows GRATIA but not the date). *Reverse:* A ball-tipped cross with castle and lion in the quarters. Legend + HISPANIARVM . ET. INDIARVM . REX. *Mintmark:* $\overset{\circ}{\underset{M}{\times}}$. BW-19, KM-56.

Date	Assayer	Comment
No date	L	Date off flan
1691	L	
1694	L	
1695	L	
1697/6	L	
1697	L	
1698	L	
1699/8	L	
1699	L	
1700	L	
1701/0	L	

Charles II Royal 8 Escudos

Royal coins were struck with special dies on selected round planchets. They may not have the same legend as the regular coinage of the same date and mintmark. The choice examples were probably sent to Spain for presentation to the king. BW-R19, KM-R56.

Date	*Assayer*	*Comment*
1695	*L*	*Rare*
1698	*L*	*Rare*

PHILIP V, 1700–1724 (FIRST REIGN)

Charles II did not father a male heir to the throne and in his will named Philip V his successor. Philip V was the first ruler from the French Bourbon family, and was crowned during the War of Succession (1701–1713). Under the Treaty of Utrecht, he retained the Spanish throne, but Spain gave up all its possessions in Europe. He also relinquished any claim, for himself and all his descendants, on the French throne.

During the 1700s, the Bourbon rulers of Spain carried out many governmental reforms. They lowered taxes and collected them more fairly; they built roads and other public works; and the economy began to grow. As a colony, New Spain prospered during this era. The capital, Mexico City, was one of the finest metropolitan areas in the world.

Recovery of the Mexican economy was characterized by attempts to restore wealth and the public treasury, and by promotion of the cultivation of underdeveloped land. A number of laws designed to transfer farmland belonging to municipalities to poor farmers and laborers were enacted. An attempt was made to assist the peasant class, which had been sunk in ignorance and misery and had been subject to great landowners.

Also, there was a revival of traditional industries and commercial relations, and the diffusion of European culture into New Spain. To augment this, Philip V started to strengthen the treasury by putting taxes on a regular basis and by avoiding extravagance, waste, or graft in the handling of public revenues. During this era, Juan de Acuña y Bejarano, Marquis de Casa Fuerte, arrived and took the position of viceroy in 1722. He was an honest and industrious man. He established the Santo Domingo Custom House and the mint for issuing coinage. However, a major flaw prevailed. Spain had established a strict monopoly in her colonies, especially New Spain, in that they could not trade with other nations. This gave rise to smuggling and clandestine commerce. It also limited the economy of New Spain and created a danger of pirates.

Prior to 1729, the fineness of silver coinage was 0.931, but in 1729 under Philip V it was lowered to 0.916. The first reign of Philip V ended in 1724, with his abdication in favor of his 17-year-old son, Louis I. When Louis died seven months later, with no heir, Philip resumed the Spanish crown; the cob coinage of his second reign follows the coinage of Louis I in this chapter. (The milled coinage begun under Philip V is discussed in the next chapter.)

1/2 Real

1/2 real, cob, 0.931 silver, 1.69 g.

Obverse: Crowned monogram of Philip V with mintmark and assayer's initial to the left. Legend **. PHILIPPVS. V. D. G.** followed by date. *Reverse:* A ball-tipped cross with castle and lion in the quarters. Legend **. HISP. ET . INDIARVM . REX.** *Mintmark:* M̊. BW-11.4, KM-24.

Date	Assayer	Comment
No date	n.v.	Date off flan
1702	L	
1703	L	
1704	L	
1705	L	
1706	J	
1707	J	
1708	J	
1709	J	
1710	J	
1711	J	
1712	J	
1713	J	
1714	J	
1715	J	
1716	J	
1717	J	
1718/7	J	
1718	J	
1719	J	
1720	J	
1721	J	
1722	J	
1723	J	

Note: n.v. = not visible.

Philip V Royal 1/2 Real

Royal coins were struck with special dies on selected round planchets. They may not have the same legend as the regular coinage of the same date and mintmark. The choice examples were probably sent to Spain for presentation to the king. BW-R11.5, KM-R24.

Date	*Assayer*	*Comment*
1715	*J*	
1719	*J*	
1721	*J*	

1 Real

1 real, cob, 0.931 silver, 3.38 g.

Obverse: Crowned coat of arms of Philip V with mintmark and assayer's initial to the left. Legend **. PHILIPPVS . V . DEI . G .** followed by date. *Reverse:* A ball-tipped cross with castle and lion in the quarters. Legend **+ HISPANIARVM . ET. INDIARVM . REX.** *Mintmark:* M̊. BW-12.6, KM-30.

Date	Assayer	Comment
No date	n.v.	Date off flan
1702	L	
1703	L	
1704	L	
1705	L	
1706	J	
1707	J	
1708	J	
1709	J	
1710	J	
1711	J	
1712	J	
1713	J	
1714	J	
1715	J	
1716	J	
1717	J	
1718	J	
1719	J	
1720/19	J	
1720	J	
1721	J	
1722	J	
1723	J	

Note: n.v. = not visible.

Philip V Royal 1 Real

Royal coins were struck with special dies on selected round planchets. They may not have the same legend as the regular coinage of the same date and mintmark. The choice examples may have been sent to Spain for presentation to the king. BW-R12.6, KM-R30.

Date	Assayer	Comment
1715	*J*	*Rare*
1716	*J*	*Rare*
1718	*J*	*Rare*

2 Reales

2 reales, cob, 0.931 silver, 6.77 g.

Obverse: Crowned coat of arms of Philip V with mintmark and assayer's initial to the left. Legend **. PHILIPPVS V . DEI . G .** followed by date. *Reverse:* A ball-tipped cross with castle and lion in the quarters. Legend **+HISPANIARVM . ET . INDIARVM . REX.** *Mintmark:* M with small o above. BW-13.6, KM-35.

Date	Assayer	Comment
No date	L	Date off flan
1702	L	
1703	L	
1704	L	
1705	L	
1706	J	
1707	J	
1708	J	
1710	J	
1711	J	
1712	J	
1713	J	
1714	J	
1715	J	
1716	J	
1717	J	
1718	J	
1719	J	
1720	J	
1721	J	
1722	J	
1723	J	

Philip V Royal 2 Reales

Royal coins were struck with special dies on selected round planchets. They may not have the same legend as the regular coinage of the same date and mintmark. The choice examples were probably sent to Spain for presentation to the king. BW-R13.6, KM-R35.

Date	Assayer	Comment
1715	*J*	*Rare*
1716	*J*	*Rare*

4 Reales

4 reales, cob, 0.931 silver, 13.54 g.

Obverse: Crowned coat of arms of Philip V with mintmark and assayer's initial to the left. Legend *** PHILIPPVS *V* DEI * G*** followed by date. *Reverse:* A ball-tipped cross with castle and lion in the quarters. Legend **+HISPANIARVM . ET . INDIARVM . REX.** *Mintmark:* M with small o above. BW-14.6, KM-40.

Date	Assayer	Comment
No date	n.v	Date off flan
1702	L	
1703	L	
1704	L	
1705	L	
1706	L	
1707	L	
1708	J	
1709	J	
1710	J	
1711	J	
1712	J	
1713	J	
1714	J	
1715	J	
1716	J	
1717	J	
1718	J	
1719	J	
1720	J	
1721	J	
1722	J	
1723	J	

Note: n.v. = not visible.

Philip V Royal 4 Reales

Royal coins were struck with special dies on selected round planchets. They may not have the same legend as the regular coinage of the same date and mintmark. The choice examples were probably sent to Spain for presentation to the king. BW-R14.6, KM-R40.

Date	Assayer	Comment
1716	J	Rare
1719	J	Rare
1721	J	Rare
1722	J	Rare
1723	J	Rare

8 Reales

8 reales, cob, 0.931 silver, 27.07 g.

Obverse: Crowned coat of arms of Philip V with mintmark and assayer's initial to the left. Legend ∗ PHILIPPVS ∗ V ∗ DEI ∗ G ∗ followed by date. *Reverse:* A ball-tipped cross with castle and lion interchanged in the quarters. Legend +HISPANIARVM . ET . INDIARVM . REX. *Mintmark:* M̊. BW-15.7, KM-47.

Date	Assayer	Comment
No date	n.v	Date off flan
1702	L	
1703	L	
1704	L	
1705	L	
1706	J	
1708	J	
1709	J	
1710	J	
1711	J	
1712	J	
1713	J	
1714	J	
1715	J	
1716	J	
1717	J	
1718/7	J	
1719	J	
1720	J	
1721	J	
1722	J	
1723	J	

Note: n.v. = not visible.

Philip V Royal 8 Reales

Royal coins were struck with special dies on selected round planchets. They may not have the same legend as the regular coinage of the same date and mintmark. The choice examples may have been sent to Spain for presentation to the king. BW-R15.7, KM-R47.

Date	Assayer	Comment
1702	L	Rare
1703	L	Rare
1705	J	Rare
1706	J	Rare
1709	J	Rare
1711	J	Rare
1713	J	Rare
1714	J	Rare
1715	J	Rare
1716	J	Rare
1717	J	Rare
1719	J	Rare
1721	J	Rare
1722	J	Rare
1723	J	Rare

1 Escudo

1 escudo, cob, 0.917 gold, 3.38 g.

Obverse: Crowned coat of arms of Philip V with mintmark and assayer's initial to the left. Legend . PHILIPPVS . V. DEI. G . followed by date. *Reverse:* A ball-tipped cross with castle and lion in the quarters. Legend +HISPANIARVM . ET . INDIARVM . REX . *Mintmark:* M̊ (with x). BW-16.1, KM-51.

Date	Assayer	Comment
No date	n.v.	Date off flan
1702	L	
1703/2	L	
1704	L	
1707	J	
1708	J	
1709	J	
1710	J	
1711	J	
1712	J	
1713	J	

1 escudo, cob, 0.917 gold, 3.38 g.

Obverse: Crowned coat of arms of Philip V with mintmark and assayer's initial to the left. Legend .PHILIPPVS . V. D. G . followed by date. *Reverse:* A ball-tipped cross with castle and lion in the quarters. Legend +HISP . ET . INDIARVM. *Mintmark:* $\overset{\circ}{\text{M}}$. BW16.2, KM-51.2.

Date	Assayer	Comment
No date	n.v	Date off flan
1712	J	
1714	J	
1714	J	J's used for 1's in date (J7J4-J)
1715	J	

Note: n.v. = not visible.

Philip V Royal 1 Escudo

Royal coins were struck with special dies on selected round planchets. They may not have the same legend as the regular coinage of the same date and mintmark The choice examples were probably sent to Spain for presentation to the king. Mintmark: $\overset{\circ}{\text{M}}$*. BW-R16.2, KM-R51.2.*

Date	*Assayer*	*Comment*
1714	*J*	*Rare*
1715	*J*	*Rare*

2 Escudos

2 escudos, cob, 0.917 gold, 6.77 g.

Obverse: Crowned coat of arms of Philip V with mintmark and assayer's initial to the left. Legend . PHILIPPVS . V . DEI . G followed by date. *Reverse:* A ball-tipped cross with castle and lion in the quarters. Legend +HISPANIARVM . ET . INDIARVM . REX. *Mintmark:* $\overset{\circ}{\overset{\times}{\text{M}}}$. BW-17.2, KM-53.1.

Date	Assayer	Comment
No date	n.v.	Date off flan
1704	L	
1708	J	
1710	J	
1711	J	
1712	J	
1713	J	

Note: n.v. = not visible.

2 escudos, cob, 0.917 gold, 6.77 g.

Obverse: Crowned coat of arms of Philip V with mintmark and assayer's initial to the left. Legend . PHILIPPVS . V . DEI . G. followed by date. *Reverse:* A ball-tipped cross with castle and lion in the quarters. Legend +HISPANIARVM . ET . INDIARVM .REX. *Mintmark:* $\overset{\circ}{\text{M}}$. BW-17.3, KM-53.2.

Date	Assayer	Comment
No date	n.v.	Date off flan
1714	J	
1717	J	Rare
1722	J	Rare

Note: n.v. = not visible.

Philip V Royal 2 Escudos

Royal coins were struck with special dies on selected round planchets. They may not have the same legend as the regular coinage of the same date and mintmark The choice examples were probably sent to Spain for presentation to the king. BW-R17.2, KM-R53.1.

Date	*Assayer*	*Comment*
1711	*J*	*Rare*
1712	*J*	*Rare*
1722	*J*	

4 Escudos

4 escudos, cob, 0.917 gold, 13.54 g.

Obverse: Crowned coat of arms of Philip V with mintmark and assayer's initial to the left. Legend . PHILIPPVS . V . DEI. G . followed by date. *Reverse:* A ball-tipped cross with castle and lion in the quarters. Legend +HISPANIARVM . ET . INDIARVM . REX. *Mintmark:* $\overset{\circ}{\overset{\times}{\text{M}}}$. BW-18.2, KM-55.1.

Date	Assayer	Comment
No date	n.v.	Date off flan
1705	J	
1706	J	
1707	J	
1711	J	
1712	J	
1713	J	

Note: n.v. = not visible.

4 escudos, cob, 0.917 gold, 13.54 g.

Obverse: Crowned coat of arms of Philip V with mintmark and assayer's initial to the left. Legend **. PHILIPPVS . V . DEI . G .** followed by date. *Reverse:* A ball-tipped cross with castle and lion in the quarters. Legend **+HISPANIARVM . ET . INDIARVM . REX.** *Mintmark:* $\overset{\circ}{\mathrm{M}}$. BW-18.3, KM-55.2.

Date	Assayer	Comment
No date	n.v.	Date off flan
1714	J	
1715	J	
1720	J	Rare

Note: n.v. = not visible.

Philip V Royal 4 Escudos

Royal coins were struck with special dies on selected round planchets. They may not have the same legend as the regular coinage of the same date and mint mark. The choice examples were probably sent to Spain for presentation to the king.

Mintmark: $\overset{\circ}{\underset{\mathrm{M}}{\times}}$. *BW-R18.2, KM-R55.1.*

Date	*Assayer*	*Comment*
1711	*J*	*Rare*

Mintmark: $\overset{\circ}{\mathrm{M}}$. *BW-R18.3, KM-R55.2.*

Date	*Assayer*	*Comment*
1714	*J*	*Rare*

8 Escudos

8 escudos, cob, 0.917 gold, 27.07 gr.

Obverse: Crowned coat of arms of Philip V with mintmark and assayer's initial to the left. Legend **. PHILIPPVS .V . DEI . G .** followed by date. *Reverse:* A ball-tipped cross with castle and lion in the quarters. Legend **+ HISPANIARVM . ET . INDIARVM . REX.** *Mintmark:* $\overset{\circ}{\underset{\mathrm{M}}{\times}}$. BW-19.1, KM-57.1.

Date	Assayer	Comment
No date	n.v.	Date off flan
1703	L	
1706	J	
1708	J	
1709	J	
1710	J	
1711	J	
1712	J	
1713	J	

Note: n.v. = not visible.

8 escudos, cob, 0.917 gold, 27.07 g.

Obverse: Crowned coat of arms of Philip V with mintmark and assayer's initial to the left. Legend **. PHILIPVS . DEI . G .** followed by date. *Reverse:* A ball-tipped cross with castle and lion in the quarters. Legend **+ HISPANIARVM . ET . INDIARVM . REX.** *Mintmark:* $\overset{\circ}{\mathrm{M}}$. BW-19.2, KM-57.2.

Date	Assayer	Comment
No date	n.v.	Date off flan
1714	J	
1714	J	Date on reverse
1714	J	Date over GRAT on obverse
1715	J	
1717/6	J	Rare
1718	J	Rare
1720/19	J	Rare
1723	J	Rare

Note: n.v. = not visible.

Philip V Royal 8 Escudos

Royal coins were struck with special dies on selected round planchets. They may not have the same legend as the regular coinage of the same date and mintmark. The choice examples were probably sent to Spain for presentation to the king.

Mintmark: $\overset{\circ}{\underset{\mathrm{M}}{\times}}$. *BW-R19.1, KM-R57.1.*

Date	*Assayer*	*Comment*
1702	*L*	*Double-ended bar; rare*
1711	*J*	*Single-ended bar; rare*
1712	*J*	*Single-ended bar; rare*
1713	*J*	*Single-ended bar; rare*

Mintmark: $\overset{\circ}{\mathrm{M}}$. *BW-R19.3, KM-R57.3.*

Date	*Assayer*	*Comment*
1714	*J*	*Base of crown flat; rare*
1715	*J*	*Rare*
1717	*J*	*Base of crown curved; rare*
1718	*J*	*Base of crown curved; rare*
1723	*J*	*Base of crown curved; rare*

LOUIS I, 1724

The reign of Louis I was short and uneventful. The elder of two surviving sons of Philip V of Spain and María Luisa of Savoy, he ascended the throne when his father abdicated in his favor. He ruled from January 14 to August 31, 1724, when he died of smallpox. Strong ties had developed between Spain and France because the rulers of both countries were from the Bourbon family. Like Spain, New Spain was being exposed to new and different trends in European culture. As for Louis I, he was quickly forgotten, and New Spain, absorbed with mining, barely acknowledged his reign. Extensive plantations, where sugarcane and coffee became the most important crops, remained isolated and rarely received any national news.

1/2 Real

1/2 real, cob, 0.931 silver, 1.69 g.

Obverse: Crowned monogram of Louis I with mintmark and assayer's initial to the left. Legend LVDOVICVS . I . D . G . followed by date. *Reverse:* A ball-tipped cross with castle and lion in the quarters. Legend + HISPANIARVM. REX. *Mintmark:* $\overset{\circ}{\mathrm{M}}$. BW-11.7, KM-25.

Date	Assayer	Comment
1724	D	
1725	D	

Louis I Royal 1/2 Real

Royal coins were struck with special dies on selected round planchets. They may not have the same legend as the regular coinage of the same date and mintmark The choice examples were probably sent to Spain for presentation to the king. BW-R11.7, KM-R25.

Date	*Assayer*	Comment
1724	*D*	

1 Real

1 real, cob, 0.931 silver, 3.38 gr.

Obverse: Crowned coat of arms of Louis I with mintmark and assayer's initial to the left. Legend LVDOVICVS . I . DEI . G . followed by date. *Reverse:* A ball-tipped cross with castle and lion in the quarters. Legend + HISPANIARVM . ET . INDIARVM . REX. *Mintmark:* $\overset{\circ}{\mathrm{M}}$. BW-12.8, KM-A31.

Date	Assayer	Comment
1724	D	Rare
1725	D	Rare

4 Reales

4 reales, cob, 0.931 silver, 13.54 g.

Obverse: Crowned coat of arms of Louis I with mintmark and assayer's initial to the left. Legend + LVDOVICVS + I + DEI + G + followed by date. *Reverse:* A ball-tipped cross with castle and lion in the quarters. Legend +HISPANIARVM + ET + INDIARVM + REX. *Mintmark:* $\overset{\circ}{\mathrm{M}}$. BW-14.9, KM-42.

Date	Assayer	Comment
1724	D	Rare
1725	D	Rare

8 Reales

8 reales, cob, 0.931 silver, 27.07 g.

Obverse: Crowned coat of arms of Louis I with mintmark and assayer's initial to the left. Legend + LVDOVICVS + I + DEI + G + followed by date. *Reverse:* A ball-tipped cross with castle and lion interchanged in the quarters. Legend +HISPANIARVM + ET + INDIARVM + REX. *Mintmark:* $\overset{\circ}{\mathrm{M}}$. BW-15.10, KM-49.

Date	Assayer	Comment
1724	D	Rare
1725	D	Rare

2 Escudos

2 escudos, cob, 0.917 gold, 6.77 g.

Obverse: Crowned coat of arms of Louis I with mintmark and assayer's initial to the left. Legend + LVDOVICVS + I + DEI + G +. *Reverse:* A ball-tipped cross with castle and lion in the quarters. Legend + HISPAN IARVM + ET INDIARVM + REX. *Mintmark:* $\overset{\circ}{\overset{x}{\mathrm{M}}}$. BW-17.4, KM-A54.

Date	Assayer	Comment
No date	F	Rare

8 Escudos

8 escudos, cob, 0.917 gold, 27.07 g.

Obverse: Crowned coat of arms of Louis I with mintmark and assayer's initial to the left. Legend + LVDOVICVS + I + DEI + G + followed by date. *Reverse:* A ball-tipped cross with castle and lion in the quarters. Legend + HISPANIARVM + ET INDIARVM + REX. *Mintmark:* M̊. BW-19.4, KM-58.

Date	Assayer	Comment
No date	D	Rare

Louis I Royal 8 Escudos

Royal coins were struck with special dies on selected round planchets. These may not have the same legend as the regular coinage of the same date and mintmark. The choice examples were probably sent back to Spain for presentation to the king.

Mintmark: M. *BW-R19.4, KM-UL.*

Date	*Assayer*	*Comment*
1724	*D*	*Rare*
1725	*D*	*Rare*

PHILIP V, 1724–1746 (SECOND REIGN)

The first reign of Philip V (discussed earlier in this chapter) ended in 1724, when he abdicated the throne his 17-year-old son, Louis I. Louis died of smallpox seven months later, with no heir, and Philip resumed the Spanish crown. (The milled coinage begun under Philip V is discussed in the next chapter.)

1/2 Real

1/2 real, cob, 0.931 silver, 1.69 g.

Obverse: Crowned monogram of Philip V with mintmark and assayer's initial to the left. Legend . PHILIPPVS . V . D . G . followed by date. *Reverse:* a ball-tipped cross with castle and lion in the quarters. Legend . HISP . ET . INDIARVM . REX. *Mintmark:* M̊. BW-11.6, KM-25.

Date	Assayer	Comment
1724	D	
1725	D	
1726	D	
1727	D	
1728	D	
1729	R	Fineness changed to 0.916
1730	R	
1730	F	
1731	F	
1732/1	F	
1732	F	
1733/2	F	
1733	F	

Philip V Royal 1/2 Real

Royal coins were struck with special dies on selected round planchets. They may not have the same legend as the regular coinage of the same date and mintmark. The choice examples were probably sent to Spain for presentation to the king. BW-R11.5a, KM-R24a.

Date	*Assayer*	*Comment*
1726	*D*	
1727	*D*	
1730	*R*	*Normally holed*

1 Real

1 real, cob, 0.931 silver, 3.38 g.

Obverse: Crowned coat of arms of Philip V with mintmark and assayer's initial to the left. Legend . PHILIPPVS . V . DEI . G . followed by date. *Reverse:* A ball-tipped cross with castle and lion in the quarters. Legend + HISPANIARVM . ET . INDIARVM . REX. *Mintmark:* M̊. BW-12.7, KM-30a.

Date	Assayer	Comment
No date	n.v.	Date off flan
1726	J	
1727	J	
1728	J	
1729	R	Fineness changed to 0.916
1730	R	
1730	F	
1730	G	
1731	F	
1732	F	

Note: n.v. = not visible.

2 Reales

2 reales, cob, 0.931 silver, 6.77 g.

Obverse: Crowned coat of arms of Philip V with mintmark and assayer's initial to the left. Legend **. PHILIPPVS V . DEI . G.** followed by date. *Reverse:* A ball-tipped cross with castle and lion in the quarters. Legend **+HISPANIARVM . ET. INDIARVM . REX.** *Mintmark:* $\overset{o}{M}$. BW-13.7, KM-35a.

Date	Assayer	Comment
No date	n.v	Date off flan
1726	D	
1727	D	
1728	D	
1729	R	Fineness changed to 0.916
1730	R	
1730	G-R	
1730	G	
1731	F	
1731/0	F	
1732	F	
1733	F	

Note: n.v. = not visible.

Philip V Royal 2 Reales

Royal coins were struck with special dies on selected round planchets. They may not have the same legend as the regular coinage of the same date and mintmark. The choice examples were probably sent to Spain for presentation to the king. BW-R13.6a, KM-R35a.

Date	*Assayer*	*Comment*
1730	*R*	*Fineness changed to 0.916; rare*

4 Reales

4 reales, cob, 0.931 silver, 13.54 g.

Obverse: Crowned coat of arms of Philip V with mintmark and assayer's initial to the left. Legend **∗ PHILIPPVS ∗ DEI ∗ G∗** followed by date. *Reverse:* A ball-tipped cross with castle and lion in the quarters. Legend **+HISPANIARVM . ET. INDIARVM . REX.** *Mintmarks:* M, $\overset{o}{M}$. BW-14.7, KM-40a.

Date	Assayer	Comment
No date	n.v.	Date off flan
1726	D	
1727	D	
1728	D	
1729	D	Fineness changed to 0.916
1730	R	
1730	G	
1730	F-G	
1731/0	F	
1731	F	
1732/1	F	
1732	F	
1733/2	F	

Note: n.v. = not visible.

4 reales, cob, 0.931 silver, 13.54 g.

Obverse: Crowned coat of arms of Philip V with mintmark to the right and assayer's initial to the left. Legend **∗ PHILIPPVS ∗ DEI ∗ G∗** followed by date. *Reverse:* A ball-tipped cross with castle and lion in the quarters. Legend **+HISPANIARVM . ET . INDIARVM . REX.** *Mintmark:* $\overset{o}{M}$. BW-14.8, KM-40.

Date	Assayer	Comment
1728	J	
1730	J	0.916 silver

The following are Philip V clipped planchets (klippe), with a different, more ornate design. BW-14.9a, KM-41.

Date	Assayer	Comment
1733	F	
1733	M-F	
1734/3	M-F	

Philip V Royal 4 Reales

Royal coins were struck with special dies on selected round planchets. They may not have the same legend as the regular coinage of the same date and mintmark. The choice examples were probably sent to Spain for presentation to the king. BW-R14.6a, KM-UL.

Date	*Assayer*	*Comment*
1716	*J*	*Rare*
1719	*J*	*Rare*
1721	*J*	*Rare*
1722	*J*	*Rare*
1723	*J*	*Rare*
1728	*J*	
1730	*J*	*0.916 silver*

8 Reales

8 reales, cob, 0.931 silver, 27.07 g.

Obverse: Crowned coat of arms of Philip V with mintmark and assayer's initial to the left. Legend ∗ PHILIPPVS ∗ DEI ∗ G ∗ followed by date. *Reverse:* A ball-tipped cross with castle and lion interchanged in the quarters. Legend + HISPANIARVM . ET . INDIARVM . REX. *Mintmark:* $\overset{\circ}{\mathrm{M}}$. BW-15.8, KM-47a.

Date	Assayer	Comment
No date	n.v	Date off flan
1725	D	
1726	D	
1727	D	
1728	D	
1729	R	Fineness changed to 0.916
1730	R	
1730	G-R	
1730	G	
1730	F	
1731/0	F-G	
1731/29	F	
1731	F	
1732/1	F	
1732	F	
1733/2	F	
1733	F	

Note: n.v. = not visible.

Philip V Royal 8 Reales

Royal coins were struck with special dies on selected round planchets. They may not have the same legend as the regular coinage of the same date and mintmark. The choice examples may have been sent to Spain for presentation to the king. BW-R15.8, KM-R47a.

Date	*Assayer*	*Comment*
1724	*D*	*Rare*
1725	*D*	*Rare*
1726	*D*	*PHILIPPVS over LVDOVICVS; rare*
1726/5	*D*	*Rare*
1727	*D*	*Rare*
1727/3	*D*	*Rare*
1727/5	*D*	*Rare*
1729	*R*	*Rare*
1730	*R*	*Rare*
1730	*G*	*Rare*

8 reales, cob, 0.916 silver, 27.07 g.

Obverse: Crowned coat of arms of Philip V with mintmark and assayer's initial to the left. Legend ∗ PHILIPPVS ∗∗V∗∗ DEI ∗ G∗ followed by date. *Reverse:* A ball-tipped cross with castle and lion in the quarters. Legend + HISPANIARVM ∗ ET ∗ INDIARVM ∗ REX. *Mintmark:* $\overset{\circ}{\mathrm{M}}$. BW-15.9, KM-48.

Philip V clipped planchets (klippe) have a different, ornate design.

Date	Assayer	Comment
No date	n.v.	Date off flan
1733	F	
1733	M-F	
1734/3	M-F	
1734	M-F	

Note: n.v. = not visible.

1 Escudo

1 escudo, cob, 0.917 gold, 3.38 g.

Obverse: Crowned coat of arms of Philip V with mintmark and assayer's initial to the left. Legend .PHILIPPVS . V. D. G . followed by date. *Reverse:* A ball-tipped cross with castle and lion in the quarters. Legend +HISP . ET . INDIARVM. *Mintmark:* $\overset{\circ}{\mathrm{M}}$. BW16.2a, KM-51.2.

Date	Assayer	Comment
1727	J	Rare
1728	J	Rare
1730	F	
1731	F	Die-struck counterfeits exist

2 Escudos

2 escudos, cob, 0.917 gold, 6.77 g.

Obverse: Crowned coat of arms of Philip V with mintmark and assayer's initial to the left. Legend . PHILIPPVS . V . DEI . G. followed by date. *Reverse:* A ball-tipped cross with castle and lion in the quarters. Legend +HISPANIARVM . ET . INDIARVM .REX. *Mintmark:* $\overset{\circ}{\mathrm{M}}$. BW-17.3a, KM-53.2.

Date	Assayer	Comment
1729	R	Rare
1731	F	Die-struck counterfeits exist; rare

8 Escudos

8 escudos, cob, 0.917 gold, 27.07 g.

Obverse: Crowned coat of arms of Philip V with mintmark and assayer's initial to the left. Legend **. PHILIPVS . DEI . G .** followed by date. *Reverse:* A ball-tipped cross with castle and lion in the quarters. Legend + HISPANIARVM . ET . INDIARVM . REX. *Mintmark:* $\overset{\circ}{\text{M}}$. BW-19.3, KM-57.3.

Date	Assayer	Comment
1727/6	D	Rare
1728/7	D	Rare
1729	R	Rare
1730	F	Rare
1730	R	Rare
1731	F	Die strike; rare
1732	F	Die-struck counterfeits exist; rare

Selected Examples of Cob Coinage

1/2 real. 1733, F. BW-11.5, KM-24a, 16.5 mm.

1 real. 1627, D. BW-12.c, KM-28, 20 mm.

2 reales. No date, F. BW-13.2, KM-32.1, 25 mm.

4 reales. 1608/7, (F). BW-14.3, KM-37.2, 30 mm.

1 escudo. (17)14-$\overset{\circ}{\text{M}}$, J. BW-16.2, KM-51.2, 15 mm.

2 escudos. 171(4)-$\overset{\circ}{\text{M}}$, J. BW-17.3, KM-53.2, 20 mm.

4 escudos. 1713, J. BW-18.2, KM-55.1, 24 mm.

8 escudos. (1714-23). BW-19.2, KM-57.2, 37 mm.

5

Milled Coinage

In 1732, under the second reign of Philip V, New Spain ceased producing hammer-struck coinage and started issuing coins produced using a screw press. Changes at the mints took place under the leadership of the viceroy of Peru, José de Armendáriz y Perurena. New mining techniques were employed to comply with the standards established in 1728 and 1730. The new coinage of New Spain was devalued, with the 8-real coin's weight reduced to 417.6 grains at 0.9166 fineness.

The screw press required the production of milled planchets and worked by rotating a weighted lever to force upper and lower dies together with a planchet between them. Under the intense and even pressure of the press, coins were evenly and completely struck with the same thickness.

To ensure quality, two assayers supervised production. Whereas the earlier cob-series coins carried one assayer's initial, coins struck on the screw press had two assayers' initials. A collar was used to produce the edge design, which resembles a tulip, on the 8 reales. With the advent of the screw press and the use of an edge device on coins, it became very difficult for the unscrupulous to clip, file, or counterfeit the new coins.

PHILIP V, 1724–1746 (SECOND REIGN)

Philip V was the first member of France's House of Bourbon to rule Spain. (King Charles II of Spain died childless and named Philip his heir. A grandson of King Louis XIV of France, Philip had a claim to the throne via Charles II's half sister, Maria Theresa of Spain, the first wife of Louis XIV.) Philip V was crowned during the War of Succession (1701–1713). Under the Treaty of Utrecht, Philip V retained the throne and Spain lost all its possessions in Europe. Philip V would later abdicate in favor of his son, Louis I, in January 1724. Louis died of smallpox seven months later, with no heir, and Philip resumed rule in September 1724.

During the 1700s, the Bourbon rulers of Spain carried out many governmental reforms. They lowered taxes and collected them more fairly. They also built roads and instituted other public works. The economy began to grow, and as a colony, New Spain prospered. The capital, Mexico City, was one of the finest metropolitan areas in the world.

Recovery of the economy of New Spain was characterized by attempts to restore wealth and the public treasury, and by promotion of the cultivation of underdeveloped land. A number of laws were enacted that were designed to distribute farmlands belonging to municipalities among poor farmers and laborers. An attempt was made to assist the peasant class, who had been sunk in ignorance and misery thanks to powerful landowners. There was also a revival of traditional industries and commercial relations, as well as an effort to diffuse different European cultures into New Spain. To accomplish these aims, Philip V started to strengthen the treasury by collecting taxes on a regular basis and avoiding extravagance, waste, and graft in the handling of public revenues. During this era, José de Armendáriz y Perurena, the first marquis of Casa Fuerte and an honest and industrious man, arrived as viceroy in 1722. After sending the former director of the mint and assayer to jail for producing false coins, he established the Santo Domíngo Custom House, and the mint once again began to issue coinage. However, a major flaw prevailed. Spain had established a strict monopoly in her colonies, especially New Spain, so that colonies could not trade with other nations. This gave rise to smuggling and clandestine commerce. It also limited the economy of New Spain and created the danger of pirates.

Prior to 1729, the fineness of silver coinage was 0.931, but in 1729 under Philip V it was lowered to 0.916. (The cob coinage struck during the first and second reigns of Philip V is discussed in the previous chapter.)

Assayers for Philip V milled coinage were as follows:

F	Felipe Rivas de Angulo	1730–1733
F	Francisco de la Peña	1733–1784
M	Manuel de la Peña	1733–1763

1/2 Real

1/2 real, 0.9160 silver, 1.6900 g.

Obverse: Crowned coat of arms of Spain. Assayers' initials to left; no denomination shown. Legend **PHILIP .V. D . G . HISPAN . ET IND . REX.** *Reverse:* Above water and land, two crowned globes flanked by columns topped with royal crowns. Legend **VTRAQUE VNUM**, mintmark, and date. *Mintmarks:* ***M̊*** and ***M.X***. *Diameter:* 17 mm. *Edge:* Laurel leaves. BW-24.1, KM-65.

Date	Assayer	Comment
1732		No assayer or denomination; rare
1732	F	
1732	M-F	
1733	F	
1733	M-F	
1733	F	*M.X* 1733 *M.X*
1733	M-F	*M.X* 1733 *M.X*
1734/3	M-F	
1734	M-F	
1735/4	M-F	
1735	M-F	
1736	M-F	
1737	M-F	
1738	M-F	
1739	M-F	
1740/30	M-F	
1740	M-F	
1741	M-F	

1/2 real, 0.9160 silver, 1.6917 g.

Obverse: Crowned coat of arms of Spain. No denomination shown. Legend **. PHS .V .D .G . HISP. ET IND . R .** *Reverse:* Above water and land, two crowned globes flanked by columns topped with royal crowns. Legend **VTRA QUE VNUM**, date, mintmark, and assayer's initial. *Mintmark:* **.M̊.** *Diameter:* 17 mm. *Edge:* Laurel leaves. BW-24.2, KM-66.

Date	Assayer	Comment
1742	M	
1743	M	
1744/3	M	
1744	M	
1745	M	EST IND; rare
1746	M	
1747	M	

1 Real

1 real, 0.9160 silver, 3.3834 g.

Obverse: Crowned coat of arms of Spain. Assayers' initials to left of shield, denomination *I* to right. Legend * PHILIP.V. D.G. HISPAN ET IND . REX. *Reverse:* Above water and land, two crowned globes flanked by columns topped with royal crowns. Legend VTRA QUE VNUM, mintmark, and date. *Mintmarks:* *Mº* and *M.X*. *Diameter:* 20 mm. *Edge:* Laurel leaves. BW-25.1, KM-75.1.

Date	Assayer	Comment
1732		No assayer or denomination; rare
1732	F	
1733	F	*M.X*
1733	M-F	*M.X*
1733	F	Rare
1733	M-F	
1733/2	M-F	
1734/3	M-F	
1734	M-F	
1735	M-F	
1736	M-F	
1737	M-F	
1738	M-F	
1739	M-F	
1740	M-F	
1741	M-F	

1 real, 0.9160 silver, 3.3834 g.

Obverse: Crowned coat of arms of Spain. To left of shield, *R*; to right of shield, denomination *I*. Legend . PHS .V.D. G . HISP. ET IND . R . *Reverse:* Above water and land, two crowned globes flanked by columns topped with royal crowns. Legend VTRA QUE VNUM, date, mintmark, and assayer's initial. *Mintmark:* .Mº. *Diameter:* 20 mm. *Edge:* Laurel leaves. BW-25.2, KM-75.2.

Date	Assayer	Comment
1742	M	
1743	M	
1743/2	M	
1744/3	M	
1744	M	
1745	M	
1746/5	M	
1746	M	
1747	M	

2 Reales

2 reales, 0.9160 silver, 6.7668 g.

Obverse: Crowned coat of arms of Spain. Assayers' initials to left of shield; denomination *2* to right. Legend *PHILIP.V. D .G . HISPAN . ET IND . REX. *Reverse:* Above water and land, two crowned globes flanked by columns topped with royal crowns. Legend VTRA QUE VNUM, mintmark, and date. *Mintmark:* *Mº*. *Diameter:* 28 mm. *Edge:* Laurel leaves. BW-26.1, KM-84.

Date	Assayer	Comment
1732		No assayer or denomination; rare
1732	F	
1733	F	
1733	M-F	
1733	M-F	*M.X*
1733	M-F	*M.X*
1734/3	M-F	
1734	M-F	
1735/3	M-F	
1735/4	M-F	
1735	M-F	
1736/3	M-F	
1736/4	M-F	
1736/5	M-F	
1736	M-F	
1737/3	M-F	
1737	M-F	
1738/7	M-F	
1738	M-F	
1739	M-F	
1740/30	M-F	
1740	M-F	
1741	M-F	
1741/31	M-F	

2 reales, 0.9160 silver, 6.7700 g.

Obverse: Crowned coat of arms of Spain. Denomination expressed with *R* to left of shield and *2*. to right. Legend *PHS.V. D.G. HISP. ET IND . R.* *Reverse:* Above water and land, two crowned globes flanked by columns topped with royal crowns. Legend VTRA QUE VNUM, date, mintmark, and assayer's initial *M*. *Mintmark:* *Mº*. *Diameter:* 28 mm. *Edge:* Laurel leaves. BW-26.2, KM-85.

Date	Assayer	Comment
1742	M	
1743	M	
1744/3	M	
1744	M	
1745/4	M	
1745	M	HIP
1746/5	M	
1746	M	
1747	M	
1750	M	

4 Reales

4 reales, 0.9160 silver, 13.5337 g.

Obverse: Crowned coat of arms of Spain. Assayers' initials MF∗ to left of shield; to right, denomination ∗4∗. Legend ∗PHILIP. V. D.G. HISPAN. ET IND . REX. *Reverse:* Above water and land, two crowned globes flanked by columns topped with royal crowns. Legend VTRA QUE VNUM, mintmark, and date. *Mintmarks:* ∗M̊∗ and ∗M.X∗. *Diameter:* 34 mm. *Edge:* Laurel leaves. BW-27, KM-94.

Date	Assayer	Comment
1732		Specimen, no assayer or denomination; rare
1732	F	
1732	M-F	
1733/2	F	
1733	M-F	
1733	M-F	*M.X*
1733	F	*M.X* / *M.X*
1734/3	M-F	
1734	M-F	
1735/4	M-F	
1735	M-F	
1736	M-F	
1737	M-F	
1738/7	M-F	
1738	M-F	
1739	M-F	
1740/30	M-F	
1740/4	M-F	
1741	M-F	
1742	M-F	
1742/1	M-F	
1743	M-F	
1744/3	M-F	
1744	M-F	

Date	Assayer	Comment
1745	M-F	
1746	M-F	
1747	M-F	

8 Reales

8 reales, 0.9160 silver, 27.0674 g.

Obverse: Crowned coat of arms of Spain. Assayers' initials to left of shield, denomination 8 to right. Legend ∗PHILIP. V. D.G. HISPAN. ET IND. REX. *Reverse:* Above water and land, two crowned globes flanked by columns topped with royal crowns. Legend VTRA QUE VNUM, mintmark, and date. *Mintmarks:* ∗M̊∗ and ∗M.X∗. *Diameter:* 40 mm. *Edge:* Laurel leaves. BW-28.1, KM-103.

Date	Assayer	Comment
1732		No assayer or denomination
1733/2	M-F	*M.X*, large crown
1733	F	*M.X*; rare
1733	F	
1733	M-F	
1733	M-F	Large crown
1733	M-F	*M.X*, large crown; rare
1733	M-F	*M.X*, small crown
1734/3	M-F	
1734	M-F	
1735	M-F	
1736	M-F	
1737	M-F	
1738/6	M-F	
1738/7	M-F	
1738	M-F	
1739	M-F	
1740/39	M-F	
1740	M-F	
1741	M-F	
1742/32	M-F	
1742/1	M-F	
1742	M-F	
1743/2	M-F	
1743	M-F	
1744/34	M-F	
1744/3	M-F	
1744	M-F	
1745	M-F	
1746	M-F	
1747	M-F	

1 Escudo

1 escudo, gold, 3.3834 g.

Obverse: Bust of Philip V facing right. Legend **PHILIP. V. D. G . HISPAN. ET IND. REX** and date. *Reverse:* Crowned coat of arms of Philip V with denomination to the right, assayers' initials to the left. Legend **INITIUM SAPIENTIÆ TIMOR DOMINI** and mintmark *M̊*. *Diameter:* 18 mm. BW-30.1, KM-113. (Note: The gold fineness for Philip V escudos is unavailable.)

Date	Assayer	Comment
1732		No assayer or denomination
1732	F	
1733	F	
1734	M-F	
1734/3	M-F	
1735	M-F	
1736/5	M-F	
1736	M-F	
1737	M-F	
1738	M-F	
1739	M-F	
1740	M-F	
1741	M-F	
1742	M-F	
1743	M-F	
1744	M-F	
1745	M-F	
1746/5	M-F	
1747	M-F	Rare

2 Escudos

2 escudos, gold, 6.766 g.

Obverse: Armored bust of Philip V facing right. Legend **PHILIP. V. D. G. HISPAN. ET IND. REX** and date. *Reverse:* Crowned coat of arms of Philip V with denomination to the right, assayers' initials to the left. Legend **INITIUM SAPIENTIÆ TIMOR DOMINI** and mintmark *M̊*. *Diameter:* 24 mm. BW-31.1, KM-124.

Date	Assayer	Comment
1732		No assayer or denomination
1732	F	Rare
1733	F	Very scarce
1734	M-F	
1735	M-F	
1736/5	M-F	
1736	M-F	
1737	M-F	
1738	M-F	
1739	M-F	
1740/4	M-F	
1740	M-F	
1741	M-F	
1742	M-F	
1743	M-F	
1744/3	M-F	
1744	M-F	
1745	M-F	
1746	M-F	
1747	M-F	

4 Escudos

4 escudos, gold, 13.5337 g.

Obverse: Armored bust of Philip V facing right. Legend **PHILIP. V. D. G . HISPAN. ET IND. REX** and date. *Reverse:* Crowned coat of arms of Philip V with denomination to the right of shield, assayers' initials to the left. Legend **INITIUM SAPIENTIÆ TIMOR DOMINI** and mintmark *M̊*. *Diameter:* 30 mm. BW-32.1a, KM-135.

Date	Assayer	Comment
1732		No assayer or denomination; rare
1732	F	Rare
1733	F	Rare
1734/3	F-M	
1734	M-F	
1735	M-F	
1736	M-F	
1737	M-F	
1738/7	M-F	
1738	M-F	
1739	M-F	
1740	M-F	
1741	M-F	
1743	M-F	
1744	M-F	
1745	M-F	
1746	M-F	
1747	M-F	

8 Escudos

8 escudos, gold, 27.0674 g.

Obverse: Armored bust of Philip V facing right. Legend PHILIP. V. D. G . HISPAN. ET IND. REX and date. *Reverse:* Within the Order of the Golden Fleece, the crowned coat of arms of Philip V. Denomination to the right of shield, assayers' initials to the left. Legend INITIUM SAPIENTIÆ TIMOR DOMINI and mintmark *M°*. *Diameter:* 38 mm. BW-33.1, KM-148.

Date	Assayer	Comment
1732		No assayer or denomination; rare
1732	F	Rare
1733	F	Very scarce
1734	M-F	
1734/3	M-F	
1735	M-F	
1736	M-F	
1737	M-F	
1738/7	M-F	
1738	M-F	
1739	M-F	
1740	M-F	
1741	M-F	
1742	M-F	
1743	M-F	
1744	M-F	
1745	M-F	
1746	M-F	
1747	M-F	Very scarce

FERDINAND VI, 1746–1759

Ferdinand VI was born in Madrid on September 23, 1713, the younger of two surviving sons of King Philip V of Spain and Maria Luisa Gabriella of Savoy. Shortly after María Luisa's death in 1714, Philip V married Elisabeth of Parma.

As the second son of King Philip V, Ferdinand was not involved in the political intrigues of the empire. His older brother, Louis, was the heir apparent, and in fact briefly reigned as king when his father abdicated on January 14, 1724. After only seven months on the throne Louis I died of smallpox. Louis died childless, and Philip V returned to the throne because Ferdinand was not old enough to become king.

Ferdinand's stepmother, Elisabeth of Parma, wielded considerable power at court due to Philip V's ill health, and she wanted her children to inherit the throne and the fortune that went with it. Nonetheless, Ferdinand VI came to power upon the death of his father on July 9, 1746, during the War of the Austrian Succession, in which he maintained neutrality in the conflict between France and England. His first action as king was to eliminate the influence of his stepmother.

The reign of Ferdinand VI brought prestige, tranquility, and abundance to Spain. One of several reforms he instituted was the creation in 1752 of the Giro Real, a bank whose aim was to keep all foreign exchange in the hands of the royal treasury.

Ferdinand VI stimulated commerce in the Americas, attempting to end the monopoly in the Indies and the injustices of colonial trade by revamping the registering of ships. He also modernized the Spanish navy.

Assayer initials for the milled coinage of Ferdinand VI are as follows:

M	Manuel de la Peña	1733–1763
F	Francisco de la Peña	1733–1784
M	Manuel Assorin	1754–1770

1/2 Real

1/2 real, 0.9167 silver, 1.6900 g.

Obverse: Crowned coat of arms of Spain. Assayer's initial to left of shield. No denomination shown. Legend . FRD . VI . D . G . HISP . ET IND . R . *Reverse:* Above water and land, two crowned globes flanked by columns, the left topped with the imperial crown and the right with the royal crown. Legend VTRA QUE VNUM, mintmark, and date. *Mintmark:* .M°. *Diameter:* 16 mm. *Edge:* Laurel leaves. BW-24.4, KM-67.1.

Date	Assayer	Comment
1747/6	M	
1747	M	
1748/7	M	
1748	M	
1749	M	
1750	M	
1751	M	
1752	M	
1752/1	M	
1753	M	
1753/2	M	
1754	M	
1755	M	
1756/5	M	
1756	M	
1757	M	

1/2 real, 0.9167 silver, 1.6900 g.

Obverse: Crowned coat of arms of Spain. No denomination shown. Legend FRD . VI . D . G . HISP . ET IND. R . *Reverse:* Above water and land, two crowned globes flanked by columns, the left topped with the imperial crown and the right with the royal crown. Legend VTRA QUE VNUM, date, mintmark, and assayer's initial. *Mintmark:* .M°. *Diameter:* 16 mm. *Edge:* Laurel leaves. BW-24.4a, KM-67.2.

Date	Assayer	Comment
1757	M	
1758/7	M	
1758	M	
1759	M	
1760	M	

1 Real

1 real, 0.9167 silver, 3.3800 g.

Obverse: Crowned coat of arms of Spain. Denomination *1* to the right of shield, *R* to left. Legend . FRD . VI . D .G . HISP. ET IND . R . *Reverse:* Above water and land, two crowned globes flanked by columns, the left topped with the imperial crown and the right with the royal crown. Legend VTRA QUE VNUM, date, mintmark, and assayer's initial. *Mintmark:* .M°. *Diameter:* 20 mm. *Edge:* Laurel leaves. BW-25.3, KM-76.1.

Date	Assayer	Comment
1747	M	
1748/5	M	
1748/7	M	
1748	M	
1749	M	
1750/50	M	
1750	M	
1751	M	
1752	M	
1753	M	
1754	M	
1755	M	
1756	M	
1757	M	
1758/5	M	
1758	M	

1 real, 0.9167 silver, 3.3834 g.

Obverse: Crowned coat of arms of Spain. Denomination *1* to right of shield, *R* to left. Legend . FRD . VI . D . G . HISP . ET IND . R . *Reverse:* Above water and land, two crowned globes flanked by two columns, the left topped with the imperial crown and the right with the royal crown. Legend VTRA QUE VNUM, date, mintmark, and assayer's initial. *Mintmark:* .M°. *Diameter:* 20 mm. *Edge:* Laurel leaves. BW-25.3a, KM-76.2.

Date	Assayer	Comment
1757	M	
1758/7	M	
1758	M	
1759	M	
1760	M	

2 Reales

2 reales, 0.9167 silver, 6.7668 g.

Obverse: Crowned coat of arms of Spain. Denomination *2* to right of shield, *R* to left. Legend *FRD . VI . D .G . HISP . ET IND . R*. *Reverse:* Above water and land, two crowned globes flanked by columns topped with royal crowns. Legend VTRA QUE VNUM, date, mintmark, and assayer's initial. *Mintmark:* *M̊*. *Diameter:* 28 mm. *Edge:* Laurel leaves. BW-26.3a, KM-86.1.

Date	Assayer	Comment
1747	M	
1748/7	M	
1748	M	
1749	M	
1750	M	
1751/41	M	
1751	M	
1752	M	
1753/2	M	
1753	M	
1754	M	
1755/4	M	
1755	M	
1756	M	
1757/6	M	
1757	M	

2 reales, 0.9167 silver, 6.7668 g.

Obverse: Crowned coat of arms of Spain. Denomination *2* to right of shield, *R* to left. Legend *FRD . VI . D .G . HISP . ET IND . R*. *Reverse:* Above water and land, two crowned globes flanked by columns, the left topped with the imperial crown and the right with the royal crown. Legend VTRA QUE VNUM, date, mintmark, and assayer's initial. *Mintmark:* *M̊*. *Diameter:* 28 mm. *Edge:* Laurel leaves. BW-26.4, KM-86.2.

Date	Assayer	Comment
1757	M	
1758	M	
1759/8	M	
1759	M	
1760	M	

4 Reales

4 reales, 0.9167 silver, 13.5400 g.

Obverse: Crowned coat of arms of Spain. Denomination to right of shield, assayers' initials to left. Legend *FERDND . VI . D . G . HISPAN . ET IND . REX. *Reverse:* Above water and land, two crowned globes flanked by columns topped with royal crowns. Legend VTRA QUE VNUM, mintmark, and date. *Mintmark:* *M̊*. *Diameter:* 34 mm. *Edge:* Laurel leaves. BW-27.1, KM-95.

Date	Assayer	Comment
1747	M-F	
1748/7	M-F	
1748	M-F	
1749	M-F	
1750/40	M-F	
1751	M-F	
1752	M-F	
1753	M-F	
1754	M-F	
1755/4	M-F	

4 reales, 0.9167 silver, 13.540 g.

Obverse: Crowned coat of arms of Spain. Denomination to right of shield, assayers' initials to left. Legend *FERDND. VI.D.G. HISPAN . ET IND .REX. *Reverse:* Above water and land, two crowned globes flanked by columns topped with royal crowns. Legend VTRA QUE VNUM, mintmark, and date. *Mintmark:* *M̊*. *Diameter:* 34 mm. *Edge:* Laurel leaves. BW-27.2, KM-95.

Date	Assayer	Comment
1754	M-F	Left column, crown is imperial
1754	M-M	Right column, crown is royal
1755	M-M	
1756	M-M	
1757	M-M	
1758	M-M	
1759	M-M	
1760/59	M-M	
1760	M-M	

Date	Assayer	Comment
1748	M-F	
1749	M-F	
1750	F-M	
1751	F-M	

4 escudos, gold, 13.5337 g.

Obverse: Small armored bust of Ferdinand VI facing right. Legend **FERDND . VI . D . G . HISPAN . ET IND . REX** and **∗[date]∗**. *Reverse:* Crowned coat of arms of Ferdinand VI. Denomination not shown. Legend **NOMINA MAGNA SEQUOR**, assayers' initials, and mintmark **∗M̊∗**. *Diameter:* 30 mm. *Edge:* Laurel leaves. BW-32.4, KM-138.

Date	Assayer	Comment
1752	M-F	
1753	M-F	
1754	M-F	
1755	M-M	
1756	M-M	

4 escudos, gold, 13.5337 g.

Obverse: Large armored bust of Ferdinand VI facing right. Legend **FERDND . VI . D . G . HISPAN . ET IND . REX** and **∗[date]∗**. *Reverse:* Crowned coat of arms of Ferdinand VI. Denomination not shown. Legend **NOMINA MAGNA SEQUOR**, assayers' initials, and mintmark **∗M̊∗**. *Diameter:* 30 mm. *Edge:* Laurel leaves. BW-32.5, KM-139.

Date	Assayer	Comment
1757	M-M	
1758	M-M	
1759	M-M	

8 Escudos

8 escudos, gold, 27.0674 g.

Obverse: Large young armored bust of Ferdinand VI facing right. Legend **FERDND . VI . D . G . HISPAN . ET IND . REX** and **∗[date]∗**. *Reverse:* Within the collar of the Order of the Golden Fleece, the crowned coat of arms of Ferdinand VI. Denomination to the right and assayers' initials to the left. Legend **INITIUM SAPIENTIÆ TIMOR DOMINI** and mintmark **∗M̊∗**. *Diameter:* 38 mm. *Edge:* Laurel leaves. BW-33.2, KM-149.

Date	Assayer	Comment
1747	M-F	

8 escudos, gold, 27.0674 g.

Obverse: Small armored bust of Ferdinand VI facing right. Legend **FERDND . VI . D . G . HISPAN . ET IND . REX** and **∗[date]∗**. *Reverse:* Within the collar of the Order of the Golden Fleece, the crowned coat of arms of Ferdinand VI. Denomination divided by shield. Legend **NOMINA MAGNA SEQUOR**, assayers' initials, and mintmark **∗M̊∗**. *Diameter:* 38 mm. *Edge:* Laurel leaves. BW-33.3, KM-150.

Date	Assayer	Comment
1748	M-F	
1749	M-F	
1750	M-F	
1751	M-F	

8 escudos, gold, 27.0674 g.

Obverse: Small armored bust of Ferdinand VI facing right. Legend **FERDND. VI. D. G . HISPAN. ET IND. REX** and **∗[date]∗**. *Reverse:* Within the collar of the Order of the Golden Fleece, the crowned coat of arms of Ferdinand VI. Denomination not shown. Legend **NOMINA MAGNA SEQUOR**, assayers' initials, and mintmark **∗M̊∗**. *Diameter:* 38 mm. *Edge:* Laurel leaves. BW-33.4, KM-151.

Date	Assayer	Comment
1752	M-F	
1753	M-F	
1754	M-F	
1755	M-M	
1756	M-M	

8 escudos, gold, 27.0674 g.

Obverse: Medium full armored bust of Ferdinand VI facing right. Legend **FERDIND. VI. D. G . HISPAN. ET IND. REX** and **.[date].** *Reverse:* Within the collar of the Order of the Golden Fleece, the crowned coat of arms of Ferdinand VI. Denomination not shown. Legend **NOMINA MAGNA SEQUOR**, assayers' initials, and mintmark **∗M̊∗**. *Diameter:* 38 mm. *Edge:* Laurel leaves. BW-33.5, KM-152.

Date	Assayer	Comment
1757	M-M	
1758	M-M	
1759	M-M	

CHARLES III, 1759–1788

Charles III ascended the Spanish throne in 1759 upon the death of his half brother, Ferdinand VI. Charles, the first child born to King Philip V and Elisabeth of Parma, became one of Spain's most astute rulers. His reforms initiated the shift to laissez-faire economic policies, partly restoring Spain's princely grandeur. The reforms helped to improve the economy of New Spain, and the monopolistic merchants of Mexico City profited. An improving economy also helped the mining industry become more predictable.

Charles III's reign saw the creation of new centers of learning, such as the Academy of Fine Arts, the School of Mines, and the Royal Botanical Garden. The California missions were established. Expeditions were sent to Texas, and the viceroys during this period continued to improve the economy of New Spain. Juan Vicente de Güemes Padilla, Conde de Revillagigedo, who ruled as viceroy from 1788 to 1794, also took an interest in the quality of the coinage of the colony. In his capacity as viceroy, the count ordered a monumental history of the royal treasury to be written in 30 volumes. However, his successor, Miguel de la Grúa Talamanca, Marqués de Branciforte, was one of the most inept viceroys in New Spain. In the end, the tax-collecting reforms of Charles III achieved their goal but created hostility among most of the colonial population and eroded loyalty to the Spanish crown.

On September 19, 1759, a royal decree authorized changing coinage designs from the Pillar style to the Bust or Portrait style, with the bust of the king on the obverse and the royal coat of arms on the reverse, and with the Columns of Hercules added to the coat of arms. For some reason, the coins with the newly authorized designs were not struck until April 8, 1772. By secret order in March 1771 the fineness of silver coins was lowered from 0.9167 to 0.9027.

Assayer initials for the coinage of Charles III are as follows:

M	Manuel Assorin	1754–1770
F	Francisco de Rivera	1762–1770
M	Manuel de Rivera	1770–1777
F	Francisco Arance Cobos	1777–1803
M	Mariano Rodríguez	1784–1801

Pillar-Type Milled Coinage

1/2 Real

1/2 real, 0.9167 silver, 1.6900 g.

Obverse: Crowned coat of arms of Spain. Denomination not shown. Legend CAR . III . D . G . HISP . ET . IND . R. *Reverse:* Above water and land, two crowned globes flanked by columns, the left topped with the imperial crown and the right with the royal crown. Legend VTRA QUE VNUM, date, mintmark, and assayer's initial. *Mintmark:* .M°. *Diameter:* 16 mm. *Edge:* Laurel leaves. BW-24.5, KM-68.

Date	Assayer	Comment
1760	M	
1761	M	
1762	M	
1763/2	M	
1763	M	
1764	M	
1765	M	
1766	M	
1767	M	
1768/6	M	
1768	M	
1769	M	
1770	M	
1770	F	
1771	F	

1 Real

1 real, 0.9167 silver, 3.3800 g.

Obverse: Crowned coat of arms of Spain. Denomination to left and right of shield. Legend CAR . III . D .G . HISP. ET IND . R . *Reverse:* Above water and land, two crowned globes flanked by two columns, the left topped with the imperial crown and the right with the royal crown. Legend VTRA QUE VNUM, date, mintmark, and assayer's initial. *Mintmark:* .M̊. *Diameter:* 20 mm. *Edge:* Laurel leaves. BW-25.5, KM-77.

Date	Assayer	Comment
1760	M	
1761/0	M	
1762	M	
1763/2	M	
1763	M	
1764	M	
1765	M	
1766	M	
1767	M	
1768	M	
1769	M	
1770	M	
1770	F	
1771	F	

2 Reales

2 reales, 0.9167 silver, 6.7700 g.

Obverse: Crowned coat of arms of Spain. Legend +CAR. III. DD. .G . HISP. ET . IND . R +. Denomination to right. *Reverse:* Above water and land, two crowned globes flanked by two columns, the left topped with an imperial crown and the right with a royal crown. Legend VTRA QUE VNUM, date, mintmark, and assayer's initial. *Mintmark:* +M̊+. *Diameter:* 28 mm. *Edge:* Laurel leaves. BW-26.5, KM-87.

Date	Assayer	Comment
1760	M	
1761	M	
1762	M	
1763/2	M	
1763	M	
1764	M	
1765	M	
1766	M	
1767	M	
1768/6	M	
1768	M	
1769	M	
1770	M	
1770	F	Rare
1771	F	

4 Reales

4 reales, 0.9167 silver, 13.5400 g.

Obverse: Crowned coat of arms of Spain with denomination to right of shield, assayers' initials to left. Legend * CAROLVS . III . D . G . HISPAN . ET IND . REX. *Reverse:* Above water and land, two crowned globes flanked by two columns, the left topped with an imperial crown and the right with a royal crown. Legend VTRAQUE VNUM, date, and mintmark *M̊*. *Diameter:* 34 mm. *Edge:* Laurel leaves. BW-27.2, KM-96.

Date	Assayer	Comment
1760	M-M	Cross between HI and SP
1761	M-M	
1761	M-M	Cross between H and I
1762	M-M	
1762	M-F	
1763/2	M-F	
1763	M-M	
1763	M-F	
1764	M-M	
1764	M-F	
1765	M-F	
1766	M-F	
1767	M-F	
1768	M-F	
1769	M-F	
1770	M-F	
1771	M-F	
1771	F-M	

8 Reales

8 reales, 0.9027 silver, 27.0674 g.

Obverse: Crowned coat of arms of Spain. Denomination to right of shield, assayers' initials to left. Legend * CAROLVS . III . D . G . HISPAN . ET IND . REX. *Reverse:* Above water and land, two crowned globes flanked by two columns, the left topped with an imperial crown and the right with a royal crown. Legend **VTRAQUE VNUM**, mintmark, and date. *Mintmark:* M̊. *Diameter:* 38 mm. *Edge:* Laurel leaves. BW-28.4, KM-105.

Date	Assayer	Comment
1760	M-M	Tip of cross between HI and SP
1761	M-M	Tip of cross between HI and SP
1761	M-M	Tip of cross between HI and SP
1762/1	M-M	Tip of cross between H and I
1762	M-M	Tip of cross between H and I
1762	M-F	
1763/2	M-M	
1763	M-M	
1763/1	M-F	
1763/2	M-F	
1763	M-F	
1764	M-F	
1764/3	M-F	
1765	M-F	
1766	M-F	
1766/5	M-F	
1767/6	M-F	
1767	M-F	
1768/7	M-F	
1768	M-F	
1769	M-F	
1770/60	M-F	
1770	M-F	
1770	M-F	
1771	M-F	
1771	F-M	

Portrait-Type Milled Coinage

1/2 Real

1/2 real, 0.9027 silver, 1.6900 g.

Obverse: Armored, laureated bust of Charles III. Legend **CAROLUS . III . DEI . GRATIA** and **.[date].** *Reverse:* Crowned coat of arms of Spain flanked by columns wrapped in ribbon reading **PLUS VLTRA**. Legend **. HISPAN . ET IND . R.** Inverted mintmark and assayers' initials. No denomination shown. *Mintmark:* .W̊. *Diameter:* 16 mm. *Edge:* Corded. BW-24.6, KM-69.1.

Date	Assayer	Comment
1772	F-M	
1773	M-F	

1/2 real, 0.9027 silver, 1.6900 g.

Obverse: Armored, laureated bust of Charles III. Legend **CAROLUS . III . DEI . GRATIA** and **.[date].** *Reverse:* Crowned coat of arms of Spain flanked by columns wrapped in ribbon reading **PLUS VLTRA**. Legend **. HISPAN . ET IND . R .** Normal assayers' initials and mintmark. No denomination shown. *Mintmark:* M̊. *Diameter:* 16 mm. *Edge:* Corded. BW-24.7, KM-69.2.

Date	Assayer	Comment
1772	F-F	
1773	F-M	
1773	F-M	CAROLS error
1774	F-M	
1775	F-M	
1776	F-M	
1777	F-F	
1778	F-F	
1779	F-F	
1780/79	F-F	
1780	F-F	
1781	F-F	
1782/1	F-F	
1782	F-F	
1783	F-F	
1783	F-M	
1784	F-F	
1784	F-M	
1785	F-M	

1/2 real, 0.8960 silver, 1.690 g.

Obverse: Armored, laureated bust of Charles III. Legend **CAROLUS . III . DEI . GRATIA** and **.[date].** *Reverse:* Crowned coat of arms of Spain flanked by columns wrapped in ribbon reading **PLUS VLTRA**. Legend **. HISPAN . ET . IND . R .** Normal assayers' initials and mintmark. No denomination shown. *Mintmark:* M̊. *Diameter:* 16 mm. *Edge:* Corded. BW-24.8, KM-69.2a.

Date	Assayer	Comment
1786	F-M	
1787	F-M	
1788	F-M	
1789	F-M	

1 Real

1 real, 0.9027 silver, 3.3830 g.

Obverse: Armored, laureated bust of Charles III. Legend **CAROLUS . III . DEI . GRATIA** and **.[date].** *Reverse:* Crowned coat of arms of Spain flanked by columns wrapped in ribbon reading **PLUS VLTRA**. Legend **. HISPAN . ET IND . REX .** Inverted assayers' initials and mintmark, and denomination. *Mintmark:* **.W̊.** *Diameter:* 20 mm. *Edge:* Corded. BW-25.6, KM-78.1.

Date	Assayer	Comment
1772	F-M	
1773	F-M	

1 real, 0.9027 silver, 3.3830 g.

Obverse: Armored, laureated bust of Charles III. Legend **CAROLUS . III . DEI . GRATIA** and **.[date].** *Reverse:* Crowned coat of arms of Spain flanked by columns wrapped in ribbon reading **PLUS VLTRA**. Legend **. HISPAN . ET . IND . REX .** Normal assayers' initials and mintmark, and denomination. *Mintmark:* **.M̊.** *Diameter:* 20 mm. *Edge:* Corded. BW-25.7, KM-78.2.

Date	Assayer	Comment
1772	F-M	
1773	F-M	
1774	F-M	
1775	F-M	
1776	F-M	
1777	F-M	
1778	F-F	
1779	F-F	
1780	F-F	
1781	F-F	
1782	F-F	
1783	F-F	
1784	F-F	
1785	F-F	
1785	F-M	

1 real, 0.8960 silver, 3.3830 g.

Obverse: Armored, laureated bust of Charles III. Legend **CAROLUS . III . DEI . GRATIA** and **.[date].** *Reverse:* Crowned coat of arms of Spain flanked by columns wrapped in ribbon reading **PLUS VLTRA**. Legend **. HISPAN . ET IND . REX .** Normal assayers' initials and mintmark, and denomination. *Mintmark:* **.M̊.** *Diameter:* 20 mm. *Edge:* Corded. BW-25.8, KM-78.2a.

Date	Assayer	Comment
1786	F-M	
1787	F-F	
1787	F-M	
1788	F-F	
1788	F-M	
1789	F-M	

2 Reales

2 reales, 0.9027 silver, 6.7668 g.

Obverse: Armored, laureated bust of Charles III. Legend **CAROLUS . III . DEI . GRATIA** and **.[date].** *Reverse:* Crowned coat of arms of Spain flanked by columns wrapped in ribbon reading **PLUS VLTRA**. Legend **. HISPAN . ET IND . REX.** Inverted assayers' initials and mintmark, and denomination. *Mintmark:* **.W̊.** *Diameter:* 28 mm. *Edge:* Corded. BW-26.6, KM-88.1.

Date	Assayer	Comment
1772	F-M	
1773	F-M	

2 reales, 0.9027 silver, 6.7770 g.

Obverse: Armored, laureated bust of Charles III. Legend **CAROLUS . III. DEI . GRATIA** and **.[date].** *Reverse:* Crowned coat of arms of Spain flanked by columns wrapped in ribbon reading **PLUS VLTRA**. Legend **. HISPAN. ET IND . REX .** Normal assayers' initials and mintmark, and denomination. *Mintmark:* **.M̊.** *Diameter:* 28 mm. *Edge:* Corded. BW-26.8, KM-88.2.

Date	Assayer	Comment
1773	F-M	
1774	F-M	
1775	F-M	
1776	F-M	
1777	F-M	
1778	F-F	
1779	F-F	
1780	F-F	
1781	F-F	
1782	F-F	

Date	Assayer	Comment
1783	F-F	
1784	F-F	
1784	F-F	DEI GRTIA error
1784	F-M	
1785	F-M	

2 reales, 0.8960 silver, 6.7668 g.
Obverse: Armored, laureated bust of Charles III. Legend **CAROLUS . III . DEI . GRATIA** and **.[date].** *Reverse:* Crowned coat of arms of Spain flanked by columns wrapped in ribbon reading **PLUS VLTRA.** Legend **. HISPAN . ET IND . REX .** Normal assayers' initials and mintmark, and denomination. *Mintmark:* **.M̊.** *Diameter:* 28 mm. *Edge:* Corded. BW-26.8a, KM-88.2a.

Date	Assayer	Comment
1786	F-F	
1786	F-M	
1787	F-M	
1788	F-M	
1789	F-M	

4 Reales

4 reales, 0.9027 silver, 13.5337 g.
Obverse: Armored, laureated bust of Charles III. Legend **CAROLUS . III . DEI . GRATIA** and **.[date].** *Reverse:* Crowned coat of arms of Spain flanked by columns wrapped in ribbon reading **PLUS VLTRA.** Legend **. HISPAN . ET . IND . REX .** Inverted assayers' initials and mintmark, and denomination. *Mintmark:* **.W̊.** *Diameter:* 34 mm. *Edge:* Corded. BW-27.3, KM-97.1.

Date	Assayer	Comment
1772	F-M	
1773	F-M	

4 reales, 0.9027 silver, 13.5337 g.
Obverse: Armored, laureated bust of Charles III. Legend **CAROLUS . III . DEI . GRATIA** and **.[date].** *Reverse:* Crowned coat of arms of Spain flanked by columns wrapped in ribbon reading **PLUS VLTRA.** Legend **. HISPAN. ET IND REX .** Normal assayers' initials and mintmark, and denomination. *Mintmark:* **.M̊.** *Diameter:* 34 mm. *Edge:* Corded. BW 27.4, KM-97.2.

Date	Assayer	Comment
1773	F-M	
1774	F-M	
1775	F-M	
1776	F-M	
1777	F-M	
1778	F-F	
1779	F-F	
1780	F-F	
1781	F-F	
1782	F-F	
1783	F-F	
1784	F-F	
1784	F-M	
1785	F-M	

4 reales, 0.8960 silver, 13.5337 g.
Obverse: Armored, laureated bust of Charles III. Legend **CAROLUS . III . DEI . GRATIA** and **.[date].** *Reverse:* Crowned coat of arms of Spain flanked by columns wrapped in ribbon reading **PLUS VLTRA.** Legend **. HISPAN . ET . IND . REX .** Normal assayers' initials and mintmark, and denomination. *Mintmark:* **.M̊.** *Diameter:* 34 mm. *Edge:* Corded. BW-27.5, KM-97.2a.

Date	Assayer	Comment
1786	F-M	
1787	F-M	
1788	F-M	
1789	F-M	

8 Reales

8 reales, 0.9027 silver, 27.0674 g.
Obverse: Armored, laureated bust of Charles III. Legend **CAROLUS . III . DEI . GRATIA** and **.[date].** *Reverse:* Crowned coat of arms of Spain flanked by columns wrapped in ribbon reading **PLUS VLTRA.** Legend **. HISPAN . ET IND . REX .** Inverted assayers' initials and mintmark, and denomination. *Mintmark:* **.W̊.** *Diameter:* 38 mm. *Edge:* Corded. BW-28.5, KM-106.1.

Date	Assayer	Comment
1772	F-M	
1772	M-F	
1773	F-M	

8 reales, 0.9027 silver, 27.0674 g.

Obverse: Armored, laureated bust of Charles III. Legend **CAROLUS . III . DEI . GRATIA** and **.[date].** *Reverse:* Crowned coat of arms of Spain flanked by columns wrapped in ribbon reading **PLUS VLTRA**. Legend **. HISPAN . ET IND . REX .** Normal assayers' initials and mintmark, and denomination. *Mintmark:* **.M̊.** *Diameter:* 38 mm. *Edge:* Corded. BW-28.6, KM-106.2.

Date	Assayer	Comment
1773	F-M	
1774	F-M	
1775	F-M	
1776	F-M	
1777	F-M	
1777	F-F	
1778/6	F-F	
1778	F-F	
1779	F-F	
1780	F-F	
1781	F-F	
1782	F-F	
1783	F-F	
1783	F-M	
1784	F-F	
1785	F-M	

8 reales, 0.8960 silver, 27.0674 g.

Obverse: Armored, laureated bust of Charles III. Legend **CAROLUS . III . DEI . GRATIA** and **.[date].** *Reverse:* Crowned coat of arms of Spain flanked by columns wrapped in ribbon reading **PLUS VLTRA**. Legend **. HISPAN . ET IND . REX .** Normal assayers' initials and mintmark, and denomination. *Mintmark:* **.M̊.** *Diameter:* 38 mm. *Edge:* Corded. BW-28.7, KM-106.2a.

Date	Assayer	Comment
1786/5	F-M	
1786	F-M	
1787/6	F-M	
1787	F-M	
1788	F-M	
1789	F-M	

1 Escudo

1 escudo, 0.9167 gold, 3.3834 g.

Obverse: Armored bust of Charles III facing right. Legend **CAROLVS . III . D . G . HISP . ET IND . RE .** and **.[date].** *Reverse:* Crowned coat of arms of Spain. Legend **NOMINA MAGNA SEQUOR**. No denomination shown. Normal assayers' initials and mintmark **.M̊.** *Diameter:* 18 mm. *Edge:* Laurel leaves. BW-30.6, KM-116.

Date	Assayer	Comment
1760	M-M	
1761/0	M-M	
1761	M-M	

1 escudo, 0.9167 gold, 3.3834 g.

Obverse: Large armored bust of Charles III facing right. Legend **CAR . III . D . G . HISP. ET IND . R** and **.[date].** *Reverse:* Crowned coat of arms of Spain. Legend **IN . UTROG . FELIX .** No denomination shown. Normal assayers' initials and mintmark **.M̊.** *Diameter:* 18 mm. *Edge:* Laurel leaves. BW-30.7, KM-117.

Date	Assayer	Comment
1762	M-M	Rare
1762	M-F	
1763	M-M	
1763	M-F	
1764	M-F	Rare
1764	M-M	
1765	M-F	Rare
1766	M-F	Rare
1767	M-F	Rare
1768	M-F	Rare
1769	M-F	Rare
1770	M-F	Rare
1771	M-F	Rare

1 escudo, 0.9045 gold, 3.3834 g.

Obverse: Large armored bust of Charles III facing right. Legend **CAROL . III . D . G . HISP. ET IND . R .** and **.[date].** *Reverse:* Within the collar of the Order of the Golden Fleece, the crowned coat of arms of Spain, with denomination to left and right of shield. Legend **IN . UTROG . FELIX . A . D .** Inverted assayers' initials and mintmark **.W̊.** *Diameter:* 18 mm. *Edge:* Corded. BW-30.8, KM-118.1.

Date	Assayer	Comment
1772	F-M	
1773	F-M	

1 escudo, 0.9045 gold, 3.3834 g.

Obverse: Large armored bust of Charles III facing right. Legend **CAROL III. D. G . HISP. ET IND . R .** and **.[date].** *Reverse:* Within the collar of the Order of the Golden Fleece, the crowned coat of arms of Spain, with denomination to left and right of shield. Legend **IN . UTROG . FELIX . A . D .** Normal assayers' initials and mintmark **.M°.** *Diameter:* 18 mm. *Edge:* Corded. BW-30.9, KM-118.2.

Date	Assayer	Comment
1773	F-M	
1774	F-M	
1775	F-M	
1776	F-M	
1777	F-M	
1778	F-F	
1779	F-F	
1780	F-F	
1781	F-F	
1782	F-F	
1783/2	F-F	
1783	F-F	
1784	F-F	
1784	F-M	
1785	F-M	

1 escudo, 0.8750 gold, 3.3800 g.

Obverse: Large armored bust of Charles III facing right. Legend **CAROL . III . D . G . HISPAN . ET IND . R .** and date. *Reverse:* Within the collar of the Order of the Golden Fleece, the crowned coat of arms of Spain, with denomination to left and right of shield. Legend **IN . UTROG . FELIX . A . D .** Inverted assayers' initials and mintmark **.W°.** *Diameter:* 18 mm. *Edge:* Corded. BW-30.10, KM-118.2a.

Date	Assayer	Comment
1786	F-M	
1787	F-M	
1788	F-M	

2 Escudos

2 escudos, 0.9167 gold, 6.7660 g.

Obverse: Young bust of Charles III facing right. Legend **CAROLVS . III . D . G . HISPAN . ET IND . REX .** and **.[date].** *Reverse:* Crowned coat of arms of Charles III. Legend **NOMINA MAGNA SEQUOR.** No denomination shown. Normal assayers' initials and mintmark **.M°.** *Diameter:* 24 mm. *Edge:* Laurel leaves. BW-31.6, KM-128.

Date	Assayer	Comment
1760	M-M	
1761	M-M	

2 escudos, 0.9167 gold, 6.7660 g.

Obverse: Large young bust of Charles III facing right. Legend **CAROLUS . III. D. G . HISP. ET IND. REX .** and **.[date].** *Reverse:* Crowned coat of arms of Charles III. Legend **IN . UTROQ. FELIX . AUSPICE . DEO.** No denomination shown. Normal assayers' initials and mintmark **.M°.** *Diameter:* 24 mm. *Edge:* Laurel leaves. BW-31.7, KM-129.

Date	Assayer	Comment
1762	M-F	
1763	M-F	
1765	M-F	
1766	M-F	
1767	M-F	
1768	M-F	
1769	M-F	
1770	M-F	
1771	M-F	

2 escudos, 0.9167 gold, 6.7660 g.

Obverse: Armored older bust of Charles III facing right. Legend **CAROL . III . D . G . HISP. ET IND . R .** and **.[date].** *Reverse:* Within the collar of the Order of the Golden Fleece, the crowned coat of arms of Charles III, with denomination to left and right of shield. Legend **IN . UTROQ . FELIX . AUSPICE . DEO.** Inverted assayers' initials and mintmark **.W°.** *Diameter:* 24 mm. *Edge:* Corded. BW-31.11, KM-130.1.

Date	Assayer	Comment
1772	F-M	
1773	F-M	

2 escudos, 0.9167 gold, 6.7660 g.

Obverse: Large armored older bust of Charles III facing right. Legend **CAROL . III . D . G . HISPAN . ET IND . R** and **.[date].** *Reverse:* Within the collar of the Order of the Golden Fleece, the crowned coat of arms of Charles III, with denomination to left and right of shield. Legend **IN . UTROQ . FELIX . AUSPICE . DEO .** Normal assayers' initials and mintmark **.$\overset{o}{\mathrm{M}}$.** *Diameter:* 24 mm. *Edge:* Corded. BW-31.10, KM-130.2.

Date	Assayer	Comment
1773	F-M	
1774	F-M	
1775	F-M	
1776	F-M	
1777	F-M	
1778	F-F	
1779	F-F	
1780	F-F	
1781	F-F	
1782	F-F	
1783	F-F	
1784	F-F	
1784	F-M	
1785	F-M	

2 escudos, 0.8750 gold, 6.7660 g.

Obverse: Large older bust of Charles III facing right. Legend **CAROL . III . D . G . HISP . ET IND . R .** and **.[date].** *Reverse:* Within the collar of the Order of the Golden Fleece, the crowned coat of arms of Charles III, with denomination to left and right of shield. Legend **IN . UTROQ . FELIX . AUSPICE . DEO .** Inverted assayers' initials and mintmark **.$\overset{o}{\mathrm{W}}$.** *Diameter:* 24 mm. *Edge:* Corded. BW-31.10a, KM-130.2a.

Date	Assayer	Comment
1786	F-M	
1787	F-M	
1788	F-M	

2 escudos, 0.8750 gold, 6.7660 g.

Obverse: Large armored older bust of Charles III facing right. Legend **CAROL III. D. G . HISPAN. ET IND. R .** and **.[date].** *Reverse:* Within the collar of the Order of the Golden Fleece, the crowned coat of arms of Charles III, with denomination to left and right of shield. Legend **IN .UTROQ . FELIX . AUSPICE . DEO .** Normal assayers' initials and mintmark **.$\overset{o}{\mathrm{M}}$.** *Diameter:* 24 mm. *Edge:* Corded. BW-31.11a, KM-130.1a.

Date	Assayer	Comment
1788	F-M	

4 Escudos

4 escudos, 0.9167 gold, 13.5337 g.

Obverse: Young bust of Charles III facing right. Legend **. CAROLVS . III . D . G . HISPAN . ET IND . REX .** and **∗[date]∗.** *Reverse:* Crowned coat of arms of Charles III. Legend **NOMINA MAGNA SEQUORIN.** No denomination shown. Normal assayers' initials and mintmark **∗$\overset{o}{\mathrm{M}}$∗.** *Diameter:* 30 mm. *Edge:* Laurel leaves. BW-32.6, KM-140.

Date	Assayer	Comment
1760	M-M	
1761	M-M	May not exist

4 escudos, 0.9167 gold, 13.5337 g.

Obverse: Armored bust of Charles III facing right. Legend **CAROLUS . III . D . G . HISP. ET IND . REX .** and **.[date].** *Reverse:* Within the collar of the Order of the Golden Fleece, the crowned coat of arms of Charles III. Legend **IN . UTROQ . FELIX . AUSPICE . DEO .** No denomination shown. Normal assayers' initials and mintmark **.$\overset{o}{\mathrm{M}}$.** *Diameter:* 30 mm. *Edge:* Laurel leaves. BW-32.7, KM-141.

Date	Assayer	Comment
1762	M-F	Rare
1763	M-F	Rare
1764	M-F	Rare
1765	M-F	Rare
1767	M-F	Rare
1768	M-F	Rare
1769	M-F	Rare
1770	M-F	Rare
1771	M-F	Rare

4 escudos, 0.9045 gold, 13.5337 g.
Obverse: Large young laureated bust of Charles III facing right. Legend CAROL . III . D . G . HISP. ET IND . R . and .[date]. *Reverse:* Within the collar of the Order of the Golden Fleece, the crowned coat of arms of Charles III, with denomination to left and right of shield. Legend IN . UTROQ . FELIX . AUSPICE . DEO . Normal assayers' initials and mintmark .M̊. *Diameter:* 31 mm. *Edge:* Corded. BW-32.8, KM-142.1.

Date	Assayer	Comment
1772	F-M	
1773	F-M	

4 escudos, 0.9045 gold, 13.5337 g.
Obverse: Armored laureated bust of Charles III facing right. Legend CAROL . III . D . G . HISP. ET IND . R . and .[date]. *Reverse:* Within the collar of the Order of the Golden Fleece, the crowned coat of arms of Charles III, with denomination to left and right of shield. Legend IN . UTROQ . FELIX . AUSPICE . DEO . Inverted assayers' initials and mintmark .W̊. *Diameter:* 31 mm. *Edge:* Corded. BW-32.9, KM-142.2.

Date	Assayer	Comment
1773	F-M	
1774	F-M	
1775	F-M	
1776	F-M	
1777	F-M	
1778	F-F	
1779	F-F	
1780	F-F	
1781	F-F	
1782	F-F	
1783	F-F	
1784	F-F	
1784/3	F-M	
1784	F-M	
1785	F-M	

4 escudos, 0.8750 gold, 13.5337 g.
Obverse: Large armored bust of Charles III facing right. Legend CAROL . III . D . G . HISP. ET IND . R . and .[date]. *Reverse:* Within the collar of the Order of the Golden Fleece, the crowned coat of arms of Charles III, with denomination to left and right of shield. Legend IN . UTROQ . FELIX . AUSPICE . DEO . Inverted assayers' initials and mintmark .W̊. *Diameter:* 31 mm. *Edge:* Corded. BW-32.11, KM-142.2a.

Date	Assayer	Comment
1786	F-M	
1787	F-M	
1788	F-M	
1789	F-M	

4 escudos, 0.8750 gold, 13.5337 g.
Obverse: Large armored bust of Charles III facing right. Legend CAROL III. D. G . HISP. ET IND. R . and .[date]. *Reverse:* Within the collar of the Order of the Golden Fleece, the crowned coat of arms of Charles III, with denomination to left and right of shield. Legend IN . UTROQ . FELIX . AUSPICE . DEO . Normal assayers' initials and mintmark .M̊. *Diameter:* 31 mm. *Edge:* Corded. BW-32.11a, KM-142.1a.

Date	Assayer	Comment
1788	F-M	

8 Escudos

8 escudos, 0.9167 gold, 27.0674 g.
Obverse: Small young armored bust of Charles III facing right. Legend CAROLVS . III . D . G . HISPAN . ET IND . REX . and .[date]. *Reverse:* Within the collar of the Order of the Golden Fleece, the crowned coat of arms of Charles III. Legend NOMINA MAGNA SEQUOR . No denomination shown. Normal assayers' initials and mintmark *M̊*. *Diameter:* 36 mm. *Edge:* Laurel leaves. BW-33.6, KM-153.

Date	Assayer	Comment
1760	M-M	
1761	M-M	

8 escudos, 0.9167 gold, 27.0674 g.
Obverse: Young armored bust of Charles III facing right, wearing the collar of the Order of the Golden Fleece. Legend CAR OLVS . III . D . G . HISPAN . ET IND . REX . and .[date]. *Reverse:* Within the

collar of the Order of the Golden Fleece, the crowned coat of arms of Charles III. Legend NOMINA MAGNA SEQUOR. No denomination shown. Normal assayers' initials and mintmark *M̊*. *Diameter:* 36 mm. *Edge:* Laurel leaves. BW-33.7, KM-154.

Date	Assayer	Comment
1761	M-M	

8 escudos, 0.9167 gold, 27.0674 g.

Obverse: Large laureated armored bust of Charles III facing right, wearing the collar of the Order of the Golden Fleece. Legend CAROLUS . III . D . G . HISP. ET IND . REX . and .[date]. *Reverse:* Within the collar of the Order of the Golden Fleece, the crowned coat of arms of Charles III. Legend IN . UTROQ . FELIX . AUSPICE . DEO. No denomination shown. Normal assayers' initials and mintmark .M̊. *Diameter:* 36 mm. *Edge:* Laurel leaves. BW-33.8, KM-155.

Date	Assayer	Comment
1762	M-M	
1762	M-F	
1763	M-M	
1763	M-F	
1764	M-F	
1764	M-M	
1765	M-F	
1765	M-M	
1766	M-F	
1767	M-F	
1768	M-F	
1769	M-F	
1770	M-F	
1771	M-F	

8 escudos, 0.9045 gold, 27.0674 g.

Obverse: Mature laureated armored bust of Charles III facing right, wearing the collar of the Order of the Golden Fleece. Legend CAROL . III . D . G . HISP. ET. IND . R . and .[date]. *Reverse:* Within the collar of the Order of the Golden Fleece, the crowned coat of arms of Charles III, with denomination to left and right of shield. Legend IN . UTROQ . FELIX . AUSPICE . DEO. Normal assayers' initials and mintmark .M̊. *Diameter:* 36 mm. *Edge:* Corded. BW-33.13, KM-156.1.

Date	Assayer	Comment
1772	F-M	
1773	F-M	

8 escudos, 0.9167 gold, 27.0674 g.

Obverse: Mature bust of Charles III facing right, wearing the collar of the Order of the Golden Fleece. Legend CAROLUS III. D. G . HISP. ET IND. R . and .[date]. *Reverse:* Within the collar of the Order of the Golden Fleece, the crowned coat of arms of Charles III, with denomination to left and right of shield. Legend IN . UTROQ . FELIX . AUSPICE . DEO. Inverted assayers' initials and mintmark .Ŵ. *Diameter:* 36 mm. *Edge:* Laurel leaves. BW-33.10, KM-156.2.

Date	Assayer	Comment
1773	F-M	
1774	F-M	
1775	F-M	
1776	F-M	
1777	F-M	
1778	F-F	
1779	F-F	
1780	F-F	
1781	F-F	
1782	F-F	
1783	F-F	
1784	F-F	
1784	F-M	
1784	F-M	
1785	F-M	

8 escudos, 0.8750 gold, 27.0674 g.

Obverse: Large mature bust of Charles III facing right, wearing the collar of the Order of the Golden Fleece. Legend CAROL . III. D. G . HISP. ET IND. R . and date. *Reverse:* Within the collar the Order of the Golden Fleece, the crowned coat of arms of Charles III, with denomination to left and right of shield. Legend IN . UTROQ . FELIX . AUSPICE . DEO. Inverted assayers' initials and mintmark .Ŵ. *Diameter:* 36 mm. *Edge:* Laurel leaves. BW-33.11, KM-156.2a.

Date	Assayer	Comment
1786	F-M	
1787	F-M	
1788	F-M	

CHARLES IV, 1788–1808

Charles IV was born in 1748 in Portici, Italy, to Charles III of Spain and María Amalia of Saxony. He became king upon the death of his father in 1788. Initially a strong ruler, Charles IV became weak and incompetent under the control of his wife, María Luisa of Parma, and her companion, Manuel Godoy, minister of court. Godoy's and María Luisa's backing of the First Coalition against Revolutionary France triggered the French to invade and take control of Spain.

In 1808 Charles IV abdicated in favor of his son, Ferdinand VII, who had led a revolt against the French occupation. Under pressure from the French, however, Charles withdrew his own abdication and acquired Ferdinand VII's abdication in his favor. Charles IV then abdicated in favor of Napoleon, who in turn named his brother, Joseph Bonaparte, the king of Spain.

The Spanish people resisted with fierce guerilla-war tactics, the horrors of which Francisco Goya depicted in his powerful paintings. A weak Spain now had no control of New Spain or her other colonies. New Spain was asserting her independence, and the rising cost of living provided fertile soil for the seeds of revolt. The impotent Spain was a millstone around New Spain's neck.

Charles III died on December 14, 1788, but the news did not reach New Spain for several months. The mint continued to strike coins with the Charles III effigy during 1788 and 1789. A royal order of December 24, 1788, added a digit to the roman numeral III, modifying the legend to **CAROLUS IIII**, or to **CAROLUS IV**. Not until 1792 were coins issued with Charles IV's portrait.

Charles IV died in 1819. Two years later, in 1821, Mexico gained its independence from Spain.

Assayer initials for the coinage of Charles IV are as follows:

F	Francisco Arance Cobos	1777–1803
M	Mariano Rodriguez	1784–1801
T	Tomás Butrón Miranda	1801–1810
H	Henrique Buenaventura Azorín	1803–1814

1/4 Real

1/4 real, 0.8960 silver, 0.8458 g.

Obverse: Castle with mintmark to left, denomination to right, and date below. *Reverse:* Rampant lion. No legends or assayer's initial. *Mintmark:* M with small o above. *Diameter:* 11 mm. BW-23.1, KM-62.

Date	Comment
1796	
1797	
1798	
1799	
1799/8	
1800	
1801	
1802	
1803	
1804	
1805/4	
1805	
1806	
1807	
1808	

1/2 Real

1/2 real, 0.8960 silver, 1.690 g.

Obverse: Armored, laureated bust of Charles III. Legend **CAROLUS . IV. DEI . GRATIA** and **.[date].** *Reverse:* Crowned coat of arms of Spain flanked by columns wrapped in ribbons reading **PLUS VLTRA**. Legend **. HISPAN . ET IND . R .**, mintmark, and assayers' initials. No denomination shown.

Mintmark: .M°. *Diameter:* 18 mm. *Edge:* Corded. BW-24.9, KM-70.

Date	Assayer	Comment
1789	F-M	
1790	F-M	

1/2 real, 0.8960 silver, 1.690 g.

Obverse: Armored, laureated bust of Charles III. Legend **CAROLUS . IIII . DEI . GRATIA** and **.[date].** *Reverse:* Crowned coat of arms of Spain flanked by columns wrapped in ribbons reading **PLUS VLTRA**. Legend **. HISPAN . ET IND . R .**, mintmark, and assayers' initials. No denomination shown. *Mintmark:* .M°. *Diameter:* 18 mm. *Edge:* Corded. BW-24.10, KM-71.

Date	Assayer	Comment
1790	F-M	

1/2 real, 0.8960 silver, 1.690 g.

Obverse: Armored, laureated bust of Charles IV. Legend **CAROLUS . IIII . DEI . GRATIA** and **.[date].** *Reverse:* Crowned coat of arms of Spain flanked by columns wrapped in ribbons reading **PLUS VLTRA**. Legend **. HISPAN . ET IND . R .**, mintmark, and assayers' initials. No denomination shown. *Mintmark:* .M°. *Diameter:* 18 mm. *Edge:* Corded. BW-24.11, KM-72.

Date	Assayer	Comment
1792	F-M	
1793	F-M	
1794/3	F-M	
1794	F-M	
1795	F-M	
1796	F-M	
1797	F-M	
1798	F-M	
1799	F-M	
1800	F-M	
1800	F-T	
1801	F-M	
1801	F-T	
1802	F-T	
1803	F-T	
1804	F-H	
1805	T-H	
1806	T-H	
1807/6	T-H	
1807	T-H	
1808/7	T-H	
1808	T-H	

1 Real

1 real, 0.8960 silver, 3.3800 g.

Obverse: Armored, laureated bust of Charles III. Legend **CAROLUS . IV. DEI . GRATIA** and **.[date].** *Reverse:* Crowned coat of arms of Spain flanked by columns wrapped in ribbons reading **PLUS VLTRA**. Legend **. HISPAN . ET IND . REX .**, mintmark, denomination, and assayers' initials. *Mintmark:* .M°. *Diameter:* 20 mm. *Edge:* Corded. BW-25.9, KM-79.

Date	Assayer	Comment
1789	F-M	
1790	F-M	

1 real, 0.8960 silver, 3.3800 g.

Obverse: Armored, laureated bust of Charles IV. Legend **CAROLUS . IIII. DEI . GRATIA** and **.[date].** *Reverse:* Crowned coat of arms of Spain flanked by columns wrapped in ribbons reading **PLUS VLTRA**. Legend **. HISPAN . ET IND . REX .**, mintmark, denomination, and assayers' initials. *Mintmark:* .M°. *Diameter:* 20 mm. *Edge:* Corded. BW-25.10, KM-80.

Date	Assayer	Comment
1790	F-M	

1 real, 0.8960 silver, 3.3834 g.

Obverse: Armored, laureated bust of Charles IV. Legend **CAROLUS . IIII . DEI . GRATIA** and **.[date].** *Reverse:* Crowned coat of arms of Spain flanked by columns wrapped in ribbons reading **PLUS VLTRA**. Legend **. HISPAN . ET IND . REX .**, mintmark, denomination, and assayers' initials. *Mintmark:* .M°. *Diameter:* 20 mm. *Edge:* Corded. BW-25.11, KM-81.

Date	Assayer	Comment
1792	F-M	
1793	F-M	
1794	F-M	
1795	F-M	
1796	F-M	

Date	Assayer	Comment
1797/6	F-M	
1797	F-M	
1798/7	F-M	
1798	F-M	
1799	F-M	
1800	F-M	
1801	F-M	
1801	F-T	
1802	F-M	
1802	F-T	
1803	F-T	
1804	T-H	
1805	T-H	
1806	T-H	
1807/4	T-H	
1807/6	T-H	
1807	T-H	
1808/7	T-H	
1808	F-M	

2 Reales

2 reales, 0.8960 silver, 6.7700 g.

Obverse: Armored, laureated bust of Charles III. Legend **CAROLUS . IV. DEI . GRATIA** and **.[date].** *Reverse:* Crowned coat of arms of Spain flanked by columns wrapped in ribbons reading **PLUS VLTRA**. Legend **. HISPAN . ET IND . REX .**, mintmark, denomination, and assayers' initials. *Mintmark:* .$\overset{\circ}{\text{M}}$. *Diameter:* 28 mm. *Edge:* Corded. BW-26.9, KM-89.

Date	Assayer	Comment
1789	F-M	
1790	F-M	

2 reales, 0.8960 silver, 6.7700 g.

Obverse: Armored, laureated bust of Charles III. Legend **CAROLUS . IIII . DEI . GRATIA** and **.[date].** *Reverse:* Crowned coat of arms of Spain flanked by columns wrapped in ribbons reading **PLUS VLTRA**. Legend **. HISPAN . ET IND . REX .**, mintmark, denomination, and assayers' initials. *Mintmark:* .$\overset{\circ}{\text{M}}$. *Diameter:* 28 mm. *Edge:* Corded. BW-26.10, KM-90.

Date	Assayer	Comment
1790	F-M	

2 reales, 0.8960 silver, 6.7668 g.

Obverse: Large armored, laureated bust of Charles IV. Legend **CAROLUS . IIII . DEI . GRATIA** and **.[date].** *Reverse:* Crowned coat of arms of Spain flanked by columns wrapped in ribbons reading **PLUS VLTRA**. Legend **. HISPAN . ET IND . REX .**, mintmark, denomination, and assayers' initials. *Mintmark:* .$\overset{\circ}{\text{M}}$. *Diameter:* 28 mm. *Edge:* Corded. BW-26.11, KM-91.

Date	Assayer	Comment
1792	F-M	
1793	F-M	
1794	F-M	
1795	F-M	
1796	F-M	
1797	F-M	
1798	F-M	
1799/8	F-M	
1799	F-M	
1800	F-M	
1801	F-M	
1801	F-T	
1802	F-T	
1803	F-T	
1804	T-H	
1805	T-H	
1806	T-H	
1807/5	T-H	
1807	T-H	
1808/7	T-H	
1808	T-H	

4 Reales

4 reales, 0.9030 silver, 13.540 g.

Obverse: Armored, laureated bust of Charles III. Legend **CAROLUS . IV. DEI . GRATIA** and **.[date].** *Reverse:* Crowned coat of arms of Spain flanked by columns wrapped in ribbons reading **PLUS VLTRA**. Legend **. HISPAN . ET IND . REX .**, mintmark, denomination, and assayers' initials. *Mintmark:* .$\overset{\circ}{\text{M}}$. *Diameter:* 34 mm. *Edge:* Corded. BW-27.6, KM-98.

Date	Assayer	Comment
1789	F-M	
1790	F-M	

4 reales, 0.9030 silver, 13.540 g.

Obverse: Armored, laureated bust of Charles III. Legend **CAROLUS . IIII . DEI . GRATIA** and **.[date].** *Reverse:* Crowned coat of arms of Spain flanked by columns wrapped in ribbons reading **PLUS VLTRA**. Legend **. HISPAN . ET IND . REX**, mintmark, denomination, and assayers' initials. *Mintmark:* **.M°.** *Diameter:* 34 mm. *Edge:* Corded. BW-27.7, KM-99.

Date	Assayer	Comment
1790	F-M	

4 reales, 0.8960 silver, 13.540 g.

Obverse: Armored, laureated bust of Charles IV. Legend **CAROLUS . IIII . DEI . GRATIA** and **.[date].** *Reverse:* Crowned coat of arms of Spain flanked by columns wrapped in ribbons reading **PLUS VLTRA**. Legend **. HISPAN . ET IND . REX .**, mintmark, denomination, and assayers' initials. *Mintmark:* **.M°.** *Diameter:* 34 mm. *Edge:* Corded. BW-27.8, KM-100.

Date	Assayer	Comment
1792	F-M	
1793	F-M	
1794/3	F-M	
1794	F-M	
1795	F-M	
1796	F-M	
1797	F-M	
1798/7	F-M	
1798	F-M	
1799	F-M	
1800	F-M	
1801	F-M	
1801	F-T	
1802	F-T	
1803	F-T	
1803	F-M	
1804	T-H	
1805	T-H	
1806	T-H	
1807	T-H	
1808	T-H	

8 Reales

8 reales, 0.8960 silver, 27.0674 g.

Obverse: Armored, laureated bust of Charles III. Legend **CAROLUS . IV. DEI . GRATIA** and **.[date].** *Reverse:* Crowned coat of arms of Spain flanked by columns wrapped in ribbons reading **PLUS VLTRA**. Legend **. HISPAN . ET IND . REX .**, mintmark, denomination, and assayers' initials. *Mintmark:* **.M°.** *Diameter:* 40 mm. *Edge:* Corded. BW-28.8, KM-107.

Date	Assayer	Comment
1789	F-M	
1790	F-M	

8 reales, 0.8960 silver, 27.0674 g.

Obverse: Armored, laureated bust of Charles III. Legend **CAROLUS . IIII . DEI . GRATIA** and **.[date].** *Reverse:* Crowned coat of arms of Spain flanked by columns wrapped in ribbons reading **PLUS VLTRA**. Legend **. HISPAN . ET IND . REX .**, mintmark, denomination, and assayers' initials. *Mintmark:* **.M°.** *Diameter:* 40 mm. *Edge:* Corded. BW-28.9, KM-108.

Date	Assayer	Comment
1790	F-M	

8 reales, 0.8960 silver, 27.0674 g.

Obverse: Armored, laureated bust of Charles IV. Legend **CAROLUS . IIII . DEI . GRATIA** and date. *Reverse:* Crowned coat of arms of Spain flanked by columns wrapped in ribbons reading **PLUS VLTRA**. Legend **. HISPAN . ET IND . REX .**, mintmark, denomination, and assayers' initials. *Mintmark:* **.M°.** *Diameter:* 40 mm. *Edge:* Corded. BW-28.10, KM-109.

Date	Assayer	Comment
1791	F-M	
1792	F-M	
1793	F-M	
1794	F-M	
1795	F-M	
1796	F-M	
1797	F-M	
1798	F-M	
1799	F-M	
1799/7	F-M	

Date	Assayer	Comment
1800	F-M	
1801/0	F-M	
1801	F-M	
1801	F-T	
1802	F-T	
1803	F-T	
1803	T-H	
1804	T-H	CARLUS error
1805/4	T-H	
1805	T-H	Narrow date
1805	T-H	Wide date
1806	T-H	
1807/6	T-H	
1807	T-H	
1808/7	T-H	
1808	T-H	

1 Escudo

1 escudo, 0.8750 gold, 3.3834 g.

Obverse: Armored, laureated bust of Charles III facing right. Legend **CAROL . IV . D. G . HISP. ET IND . R .** and **.[date].** *Reverse:* Within the collar of the Order of the Golden Fleece, the crowned coat of arms of Spain, with denomination to left and right of shield. Legend **IN . UTROG . FELIX . A . D .**, assayers' initials, and mintmark **.M̊.** *Diameter:* 18 mm. *Edge:* Corded. BW-30.12, KM-119.

Date	Assayer	Comment
1789	F-M	
1790	F-M	

1 escudo, 0.8750 gold, 3.3834 g.

Obverse: Armored, laureated bust of Charles IV facing right. Legend **CAROL . IIII . D . G . HISP. ET IND . R .** and **.[date].** *Reverse:* Within the collar of the Order of the Golden Fleece, the crowned coat of arms of Spain, with denomination to left and right of shield. Legend **IN . UTROG . FELIX . A . D .**, assayers' initials, and mintmark **.M̊.** *Diameter:* 18 mm. *Edge:* Corded. BW-30.13, KM-120.

Date	Assayer	Comment
1792	F-M	
1793	F-M	
1794	F-M	
1795	F-M	
1796	F-M	
1797	F-M	
1798	F-M	
1799	F-M	
1800	F-M	
1801	F-M	
1801	F-T	
1802	F-T	
1803	F-T	
1804	T-H	
1805	T-H	
1806	T-H	
1807	T-H	
1808	T-H	

2 Escudos

2 escudos, 0.8750 gold, 6.7668 g.

Obverse: Armored, laureated bust of Charles III facing right. Legend **CAROL . IV. D . G . HISP. ET IND . R .** and **.[date].** *Reverse:* Within the collar of the Order of the Golden Fleece, the crowned coat of arms of Spain, with denomination to left and right of shield. Legend **IN . UTROG . FELIX . AUSPICE . DEO**, assayers' initials, and mintmark **.M̊.** *Diameter:* 23 mm. *Edge:* Corded. BW-31.12, KM-131.

Date	Assayer	Comment
1789	F-M	Very rare
1790	F-M	Very rare

2 escudos, 0.8750 gold, 6.7668 g.

Obverse: Armored, laureated bust of Charles IV facing right. Legend **CAROL . IIII . D . G . HISP. ET IND . R .** and **.[date].** *Reverse:* Within the collar of the Order of the Golden Fleece, the crowned coat of arms of Spain, with denomination to left and right of shield. Legend **IN . UTROG . FELIX . AUSPICE . DEO**, assayers' initials, and mintmark **.M̊.** *Diameter:* 23 mm. *Edge:* Corded. BW-31.12a, KM-132.

Date	Assayer	Comment
1791	F-M	.M̊. over .Ɯ̊.
1792	F-M	
1793	F-M	
1793/2	F-M	

2 escudos, BW-31.12a, continued

Date	Assayer	Comment
1794	F-M	
1795	F-M	
1796	F-M	
1797	F-M	
1798	F-M	
1799	F-M	
1800	F-M	
1801	F-T	
1802	F-T	
1803	F-T	
1804	T-H	
1805	T-H	
1806	T-H	
1807	T-H	
1808	T-H	

4 Escudos

4 escudos, 0.8750 gold, 13.5337 g.

Obverse: Armored, laureated bust of Charles III facing right. Legend CAROL . IV. D . G . HISP. ET IND . R . and .[date]. *Reverse:* Within the collar of the Order of the Golden Fleece, the crowned coat of arms of Spain, with denomination to left and right of shield. Legend IN . UTROG . FELIX . AUSPICE . DEO, assayers' initials, and mintmark .M°. *Diameter:* 30 mm. *Edge:* Corded. BW-32.13, KM-143.1.

Date	Assayer	Comment
1789	F-M	
1790	F-M	

4 escudos, 0.8750 gold, 13.5337 g.

Obverse: Armored, laureated bust of Charles III facing right. Legend CAROL . IIII . D . G . HISP. ET IND . R . and .[date]. *Reverse:* Within the collar of the Order of the Golden Fleece, the crowned coat of arms of Spain, with denomination to left and right of shield. Legend IN . UTROG . FELIX . AUSPICE . DEO, assayers' initials, and mintmark .M°. *Diameter:* 30 mm. *Edge:* Corded. BW-32.14, KM-143.2.

Date	Assayer	Comment
1790	F-M	

4 escudos, 0.8750 gold, 13.5337 g.

Obverse: Armored, laureated bust of Charles IV facing right. Legend CAROL . IIII . D . G . HISP. ET IND . R . and .[date]. *Reverse:* Within the collar of the Order of the Golden Fleece, the crowned coat of arms of Spain, with denomination to left and right of shield. Legend IN . UTROG . FELIX . AUSPICE. DEO, assayers' initials, and mintmark .M°. *Diameter:* 30 mm. *Edge:* Corded. BW-32.15, KM-144.

Date	Assayer	Comment
1791	F-M	
1792	F-M	
1793	F-M	
1794	F-M	
1795	F-M	
1796	F-M	
1797	F-M	
1798/7	F-M	
1798	F-M	
1799	F-M	
1800	F-M	
1801	F-T	
1802	F-T	
1803	F-T	
1804	T-H	
1805	T-H	
1806	T-H	
1807	T-H	
1808	T-H	

8 Escudos

8 escudos, 0.8750 gold, 27.0674 g.

Obverse: Armored, laureated bust of Charles III facing right. Legend CAROL . IV. D . G . HISP. ET IND . R . and .[date]. *Reverse:* Within the collar of the Order of the Golden Fleece, the crowned coat of arms of Spain, with denomination to left and right of shield. Legend IN . UTROG . FELIX . AUSPICE . DEO, assayers' initials, and mintmark .M°. *Diameter:* 36 mm. *Edge:* Corded. BW-33.13, KM-157.

Date	Assayer	Comment
1789	F-M	
1790	F-M	

8 escudos, 0.8750 gold, 27.0674 g. *Obverse:* Armored, laureated bust of Charles III facing right. Legend CAROL . IIII . D. G . HISP. ET IND . R . and .[date]. *Reverse:* Within the collar of the Order of the Golden Fleece, the crowned coat of arms of Spain, with denomination to left and right of shield. Legend IN . UTROG . FELIX . AUSPICE . DEO, assayers' initials, and mintmark .M°. *Diameter:* 36 mm. *Edge:* Corded. BW-33.14, KM-158.

Date	Assayer	Comment
1790	F-M	

8 escudos, 0.8750 gold, 27.0674 g. *Obverse:* Armored, laureated bust of Charles IV facing right. Legend CAROL . IIII . D . G . HISP. ET IND . R . and .[date]. *Reverse:* Within the collar of the Order of the Golden Fleece, the crowned coat of arms of Spain, with denomination to left and right of shield. Legend IN . UTROG . FELIX . AUSPICE . DEO, assayers' initials, and mintmark .M°. *Diameter:* 36 mm. *Edge:* Corded. BW-33.15, KM-159.

Date	Assayer	Comment
1791	F-M	
1792	F-M	
1793	F-M	
1794	F-M	
1795	F-M	
1796	F-M	
1797	F-M	
1798	F-M	
1799	F-M	
1800	F-M	
1801	F-M	
1801	F-T	
1802	F-T	
1803	F-T	
1804	T-H	
1805	T-H	
1806	T-H	
1807	T-H	.M°. over .N°.
1808	T-H	

FERDINAND VII, 1808–1821

Ferdinand VII was born at El Escorial, Spain, on October 14, 1784, the eldest son of Charles IV and María Luisa of Parma. He was married four times. Ferdinand VII was the last Spanish king to reign over New Spain, succeeding his father, who abdicated on March 19, 1808, in his favor. Charles IV reversed the abdication. Ferdinand VII then abdicated to his father, who in turn abdicated to Napoleon Bonaparte. Napoleon then appointed his brother, Joseph, king of Spain.

Ferdinand VII returned to Spain in 1814 and ruled until his death on September 29, 1833, in Madrid. The Inquisition grew stronger under his rule in both Spain and New Spain, and the struggle for independence began, culminating with Mexico's independence on September 16, 1821.

Assayer initials for the coinage of Ferdinand VII are as follows:

T	Tomás Butrón Miranda	1801–1810
H	Henrique Buenaventura Azorín	1803–1814
J	Joaquín Dávila Madrid	1809–1833
J	José García Ansaldo	1812–1833

1/4 Real

1/4 real, 0.8960 silver, 0.8458 g. *Obverse:* Castle with mintmark to left, denomination to right, and date below castle. *Reverse:* Rampant lion. Without assayer's initial or legends. *Mintmark:* M°. *Diameter:* 11 mm. *Edge:* Plain. BW-23.2, KM-64.

Date	Comment
1808	
1809	
1810	
1811	
1811	Copper
1812	

1/4 real, BW-23.2, continued

Date	Comment
1813	
1814	
1815	
1816	

1/2 Real

1/2 real, 0.8960 silver, 1.690 g.

Obverse: Armored laureated bust of Ferdinand VII. Legend **FERDIN .VII . DEI . GRATIA** and **.[date].** *Reverse:* Crowned coat of arms of Spain flanked by columns wrapped in ribbons reading **PLUS VLTRA**. Legend **. HISPAN . ET IND . R .**, mintmark, and assayers' initials. No denomination shown. *Mintmark:* **.$\overset{\circ}{\text{M}}$.** *Diameter:* 18 mm. *Edge:* Corded. BW-24.12, KM-73.

Date	Assayer	Comment
1808	T-H	
1809	T-H	
1810	T-H	
1810	H-J	
1811	H-J	
1811	T-H	
1812	H-J	
1812	J-J	
1813	J-J	
1813	H-J	
1814	J-J	

1/2 real, 0.8960 silver, 1.690 g.

Obverse: Draped laureated bust of Ferdinand VII. Legend **FERDIN .VII . DEI . GRATIA** and **.[date].** *Reverse:* Crowned coat of arms of Spain flanked by columns wrapped in ribbons reading **PLUS VLTRA**. Legend **. HISPAN . ET IND . R .**, mintmark, and assayers' initials. No denomination shown. *Mintmark:* **.$\overset{\circ}{\text{M}}$.** *Diameter:* 18 mm. *Edge:* Corded. BW-24.13, KM-74.

Date	Assayer	Comment
1814	J-J	
1815	J-J	
1816	J-J	
1817/6	J-J	
1817	J-J	
1818/7	J-J	
1818	J-J	
1819	J-J	
1820	J-J	
1821	J-J	

1 Real

1 real, 0.8960 silver, 3.3834 g.

Obverse: Armored laureated bust of Ferdinand VII. Legend **FERDIN . VII . DEI . GRATIA** and **.[date].** *Reverse:* Crowned coat of arms of Spain flanked by columns wrapped in ribbons reading **PLUS VLTRA**. Legend **. HISPAN . ET IND . REX .**, assayers' initials, mintmark, and denomination. *Mintmark:* **.$\overset{\circ}{\text{M}}$.** *Diameter:* 20 mm. *Edge:* Corded. BW-25.12, KM-82.

Date	Assayer	Comment
1808	T-H	
1809/8	T-H	
1809	T-H	
1810/9	T-H	
1810	T-H	
1810	H-J	
1811	T-H	
1811	H-J	
1812	H-J	
1812	J-J	
1813	H-J	
1813	J-J	
1814	H-J	
1814	J-J	

1 real, 0.8960 silver, 3.3834 g.

Obverse: Draped laureated bust of Ferdinand VII. Legend **FERDIN .VII . DEI. GRATIA** and **.[date].** *Reverse:* Crowned coat of arms of Spain flanked by columns wrapped in ribbons reading **PLUS VLTRA**. Legend **. HISPAN . ET IND . REX .**, assayers' initials, mintmark, and denomination. *Mintmark:* **.$\overset{\circ}{\text{M}}$.** *Diameter:* 20 mm. *Edge:* Corded. BW-25.13, KM-83.

Date	Assayer	Comment
1814	J-J	
1815	J-J	
1815	H-J	
1816	J-J	
1816	H-J	
1817	J-J	

Date	Assayer	Comment
1818	J-J	
1819	J-J	
1820	J-J	
1821/0	J-J	
1821	J-J	

2 Reales

2 reales, 0.8960 silver, 6.7700 g.

Obverse: Armored laureated bust of Ferdinand VII. Legend **FERDIN .VII . DEI . GRATIA** and **.[date].** *Reverse:* Crowned coat of arms of Spain flanked by columns wrapped in ribbons reading **PLUS VLTRA.** Legend **. HISPAN . ET IND . REX .**, assayers' initials, mintmark, and denomination. *Mintmark:* **.M°.** *Diameter:* 27 mm. *Edge:* Corded. BW-26.12, KM-92.

Date	Assayer	Comment
1808	T-H	
1809	T-H	
1810	T-H	
1810	H-J	
1811	T-H	
1811	H-J	
1811	H-J-T-H	

2 reales, 0.8960 silver, 6.7700 g.

Obverse: Draped laureated bust of Ferdinand VII. Legend **FERDIN . VII . DEI . GRATIA** and **.[date].** *Reverse:* Crowned coat of arms of Spain flanked by columns wrapped in ribbons reading **PLUS VLTRA.** Legend **. HISPAN . ET IND . REX .**, assayers' initials, mintmark, and denomination. *Mintmark:* **.M°.** *Diameter:* 27 mm. *Edge:* Corded. BW-26.13, KM-93.

Date	Assayer	Comment
1812	T-H	
1812	H-J	
1812	J-J	
1813	T-H	
1813	J-J	
1813	H-J	
1814	J-J	
1815	J-J	
1816	J-J	
1817	J-J	
1818	J-J	
1819	J-J	
1820	J-J	
1821/0	J-J	
1821	J-J	

4 Reales

4 reales, 0.8960 silver, 13.5400 g.

Obverse: Armored laureated bust of Ferdinand VII. Legend **FERDIN .VII . DEI . GRATIA** and **.[date].** *Reverse:* Crowned coat of arms of Spain flanked by columns wrapped in ribbons reading **PLUS VLTRA.** Legend **. HISPAN . ET IND . REX .**, assayers' initials, mintmark, and denomination. *Mintmark:* **.M°.** *Diameter:* 34 mm. *Edge:* Corded. BW-27.9, KM-101.

Date	Assayer	Comment
1809	H-J	
1810	H-J	
1811	H-J	
1812	H-J	

4 reales, 0.8960 silver, 13.5400 g.

Obverse: Draped laureated bust of Ferdinand VII. Legend **FERDIN .VII . DEI . GRATIA** and **.[date].** *Reverse:* Crowned coat of arms of Spain flanked by columns wrapped in ribbons reading **PLUS VLTRA.** Legend **. HISPAN . ET IND . REX .**, assayers' initials, mintmark, and denomination. *Mintmark:* **.M°.** *Diameter:* 34 mm. *Edge:* Corded. BW-27.10, KM-102.

Date	Assayer	Comment
1816	J-J	
1817	J-J	
1819	J-J	
1820	J-J	
1821	J-J	

8 Reales

8 reales, 0.8960 silver, 27.0674 g.

Obverse: Armored laureated bust of Ferdinand VII. Legend **FERDIN .VII . DEI . GRATIA** and **.[date].** *Reverse:* Crowned coat of arms of Spain flanked by columns wrapped in ribbons reading **PLUS VLTRA.** Legend **. HISPAN . ET IND . REX .**, assayers' initials, mintmark, and denomination.

Mintmark: .M̊. *Diameter:* 40 mm. *Edge:* Corded. BW-28.11, KM-110.

Date	Assayer	Comment
1808	T-H	
1809/8	T-H	
1809	T-H	
1809	H-J	
1810	T-H	
1810	H-J	
1810/9	H-J	
1811/0	H-J	
1811	H-J	

8 reales, 0.8960 silver, 27.0674 g.

Obverse: Draped laureated bust of Ferdinand VII. Legend **FERDIN . VII . DEI . GRATIA** and **.[date].** *Reverse:* Crowned coat of arms of Spain flanked by columns wrapped in ribbons reading **PLUS VLTRA**. Legend **. HISPAN . ET IND . REX .**, assayers' initials, mintmark, and denomination. *Mintmark:* .M̊. *Diameter:* 40 mm. *Edge:* Corded. BW-28.12, KM-111.

Date	Assayer	Comment
1811	H-J	
1812	H-J	
1812	J-J, H-J	
1812	J-J	
1813	H-J	
1813	J-J	
1814/3	H-J	
1814/3	J-J	
1814	J-J	
1815/4	J-J	
1815	J-J	
1816/5	J-J	
1816	J-J	
1817	J-J	
1818	J-J	
1819	J-J	
1820	J-J	
1821	J-J	

1/2 Escudo

1/2 escudo, 0.8750 gold, 1.6917 g.

Obverse: Undraped bust of Ferdinand VII to the right. Legend **FERD . VII . D. G . HISP. ET IND . R .** and **.[date].** *Reverse:* Within the collar of the Order of the Golden Fleece, the crowned coat of arms of Spain. Mintmark to left of collar and assayers' initials to right. Without legend or denomination. *Mintmark:* M̊. *Diameter:* 15 mm. *Edge:* Corded. BW-29.1, KM-112.

Date	Assayer	Comment
1814	J-J	
1815	J-J	
1816	J-J	
1817	J-J	
1818	J-J	
1819	J-J	
1820	J-J	

1 Escudo

1 escudo, 0.8750 gold, 3.3834 g.

Obverse: Provisional armored bust of Ferdinand VII to the right. Legend **FERDIN . VII . D. G . HISP. ET IND. R .** and **.[date].** *Reverse:* Within the collar of the Order of the Golden Fleece, the crowned coat of arms of Spain, with denomination to left and right of shield. Legend **IN . UTROQ . FELIX . A . D .**, assayers' initials, and mintmark .M̊. *Diameter:* 18 mm. *Edge:* Corded. BW-30.14, KM-121.

Date	Assayer	Comment
1809	H-J	
1810	H-J	
1811/0	H-J	
1811	H-J	
1812	H-J	

1 escudo, 0.8750 gold, 3.3834 g.

Obverse: Undraped laureated bust of Ferdinand VII to the right. Legend **FERDIN .VII . D . G . HISP. ET IND. R .** and **.[date].** *Reverse:* Within the collar of the Order of the Golden Fleece, the crowned coat of arms of Spain, with denomination to left and right of shield. Legend **IN . UTROQ . FELIX . A . D .**, assayers' initials, and mintmark .M̊. *Diameter:* 18 mm. *Edge:* Corded. BW-30.15, KM-122.

Date	Assayer	Comment
1814	H-J	
1815	H-J	
1815	J-J	
1816	J-J	

Date	Assayer	Comment
1817	J-J	
1818	J-J	
1819	J-J	
1820	J-J	

2 Escudos

2 escudos, 0.8750 gold, 6.7668 g.

Obverse: Undraped laureated bust of Ferdinand VII to the right. Legend **FERDIN . VII . D . G . HISP. ET IND . R .** and **.[date].** *Reverse:* Within the collar of the Order of the Golden Fleece, the crowned coat of arms of Spain, with denomination to left and right of shield. Legend **IN . UTROQ . FELIX . AUSPICE . DEO .**, assayers' initials, and mintmark **.M̊.** *Diameter:* 23 mm. *Edge:* Corded. BW-31.15, KM-134.

Date	Assayer	Comment
1814	H-J	
1815	J-J	
1816	J-J	
1817	J-J	
1818	J-J	
1819	J-J	
1820	J-J	
1821	J-J	

4 Escudos

4 escudos, 0.8750 gold, 13.5337 g.

Obverse: Armored laureated bust of Ferdinand VII to the right. Legend **FERDIN .VII . D . G . HISP. ET IND. R .** and **.[date].** *Reverse:* Within the collar of the Order of the Golden Fleece, the crowned coat of arms of Spain, with denomination to left and right of shield. Legend **IN . UTROQ . FELIX . AUSPICE . DEO .**, assayers' initials, and mintmark **.M̊.** *Diameter:* 30 mm. *Edge:* Corded. BW-32.15, KM-145.

Date	Assayer	Comment
1810	H-J	
1811	H-J	
1812	H-J	

4 escudos, 0.8750 gold, 13.5337 g.

Obverse: Undraped laureated bust of Ferdinand VII to the right. Legend **FERDIN . VII . D . G . HISP. ET IND . R .** and date. *Reverse:* Within the collar of the Order of the Golden Fleece, the crowned coat of arms of Spain, with denomination to left and right of shield. Legend **IN . UTROQ . FELIX . AUSPICE . DEO**, assayers' initials, and mintmark **.M̊.** *Diameter:* 30 mm. *Edge:* Corded. BW-32.16, KM-146.

Date	Assayer	Comment
1814	H-J	
1815	H-J	
1816	J-J	
1817	J-J	
1818	J-J	
1819	J-J	
1820	J-J	

8 Escudos

8 escudos, 0.8750 gold, 27.0674 g.

Obverse: Armored laureated bust of Ferdinand VII to the right. Legend **FERDIN . VII . D . G . HISP. ET IND . R .** and date. *Reverse:* Within the collar of the Order of the Golden Fleece, the crowned coat of arms of Spain, with denomination to left and right of shield. Legend **IN . UTROQ . FELIX . AUSPICE . DEO .**, assayers' initials, and mintmark **.M̊.** *Diameter:* 38 mm. *Edge:* Corded. BW-33.16, KM-160.

Date	Assayer	Comment
1808	T-H	
1809	H-J	
1810	H-J	
1811/0	H-J	
1811	H-J	
1811	J-J	
1812	J-J	

8 escudos, 0.8750 gold, 27.0674 g.

Obverse: Undraped laureated bust of Ferdinand VII to the right. Legend **FERDIN .VII . D . G . HISP. ET IND . R .** and date. *Reverse:* Within the collar of the Order of the Golden Fleece, the crowned coat of arms of Spain, with denomination to left and right of shield. Legend **IN . UTROQ . FELIX . AUSPICE . DEO .**, assayers' initials, and mintmark **.M̊.** *Diameter:* 38 mm. *Edge:* Corded. BW-33.17, KM-161.

Date	Assayer	Comment
1814	J-J	
1815	J-J	
1815	H-J	
1816	J-J	
1817	J-J	
1818	J-J	
1819	J-J	
1820	J-J	
1821	J-J	

Copper Coins of Ferdinand VII

Controversies exist regarding copper coins produced during Ferdinand VII's reign. Dr. A.F. Pradeau, in his *Numismatic History of Mexico* (1938), gives the date of the royal decree authorizing copper *vellón* coins as August 23, 1814, while Jose Manuel Sobrino, in his book *La Moneda Mexicana Su Historia* (1972), states that the decree date was March 28, 1814.

The *vellón* monetary system provided small-value copper coins, which served as money of accounts. By the second half of the 18th century, business was transacted and records were kept in *vellón* terms, as were all mint records.

Viceroy Félix María Calleja del Rey stipulated in his edict that the 2/4 *vellón* (sometimes called a *señal*) was to be equivalent to a *cuartilla*, the 1/4 to a *tlaco*, and the 1/8 to a *pilón*.

Another monetary system in use at the time was the national coinage, which fundamentally had full silver and gold value and was accepted universally. Most Mexican numismatists deal on the national standard.

An extensive study on this subject, "Understanding the Nomenclature of the Colonial Copper Coinage 1814–1821," by Ben Nibert, was published in the *Journal of Mexican Numismatics* (vol. 9, no. 4, December 2004). Nibert drew the following conclusions:

1. In discussing their denominations, the value on the coins should be used with the term *"vellon,"* indicating they represent a different accounting system—that is, 2/4 *vellon* or 2 *quartos vellon;* 1/4 *vellon* or 1 *quarto vellon* or 1 *octavo vellon*. The use of colloquial terms as values is not intended and could be confusing to the numismatist.
2. The equivalents *tlaco, pilon,* and so on are useful from a historic point of view, but 1/4, 1/8, and 1/16 are more accurate in describing actual value in relation to the existing silver coinage.

1/16 Real

1/16 real (1/8 *vellón*), copper (*pilón*).

Obverse: Mintmark and denomination with crowned monogram of Ferdinand VII. Legend FERDIN . VII . D . G . HISP . REX . and date. *Reverse:* Lion and castle within a laurel wreath. *Mintmark:* $\overset{\circ}{\text{M}}$. *Diameter:* 18 mm. *Edge:* Corded. BW-21.1, KM-59.

Date	Comment
1814	
1815/4	
1815	

1/8 Real

1/8 real (1/4 *vellón*), copper (*tlaco*).

Obverse: Mintmark and denomination with crowned monogram of Ferdinand VII. Legend FERDIN . VII . D . G . HISP . REX . and date. *Reverse:* Arms without shield within a laurel wreath. *Mintmark:* $\overset{\circ}{\text{M}}$. *Diameter:* 20 mm. *Edge:* Corded. BW-22.1, KM-63.

Date	Comment
1814	
1815	
1816	

1/4 Real

1/4 real (2/4 *vellón*), copper (*señal*).

Obverse: Mintmark and denomination with crowned monogram of Ferdinand VII. Legend FERDIN . VII . D . G . HISP . REX . and date. *Reverse:* Arms without shield within a laurel wreath. *Mintmark:* $\overset{\circ}{\text{M}}$. *Diameter:* 28 mm. *Edge:* Corded. BW-23.2a, KM-64.

Date	Comment
1814	
1815	
1816	
1818	
1821	

Pillar-Style Milled Coinage

1/4 real. 1816-$\overset{\circ}{M}$, Ferdinand VII. BW-23.2, KM-64, 12 mm.

1/2 real. 1734-$\overset{\circ}{M}$, M-F, Philip V. BW-24.1, KM-65, 17 mm.

1/2 real. 1771-$\overset{\circ}{M}$, F, Charles III. BW-24.5, KM-68, 17 mm.

1 real. 1733-MX, M-F, Philip V. BW-25.1, KM-75.1, 20 mm.

1 real. 1740-MX, M-F, Philip V. BW-25.1, KM-75.1, 20 mm.

2 reales. 1732-$\overset{\circ}{M}$, F, Philip V. BW-26.1, KM-84, 28 mm.

2 reales. 1751-$\overset{\circ}{M}$, M, Ferdinand VI. BW-26.3a, KM-86.1, 28 mm.

4 reales. 1735 $\overset{\circ}{M}$, M-F, Philip V. BW-27, KM-94, 34 mm.

Pillar-Style Milled Coinage

(continued)

4 reales. 1752-M̊, M-F, Ferdinand VI.
BW-27.1, KM-95, 34 mm.

No denomination. 1732-M̊, no assayer,
Philip V. BW-28.1, KM-103, 40 mm.

8 reales. 1733-M̊, M-F. Philip V.
BW-28.1, KM-103, 40 mm.

8 reales. 1751-M̊, M-F. Ferdinand VI.
BW-28.2, KM-104.1, 40 mm.

Bust-Style Milled Coinage

1/2 real. 1797-M̊, F-M, Charles IIII. BW-24.11, KM-72, 17 mm.

1 real. 1800-M̊, F-M, Charles IIII. BW-25.11, KM-81, 20 mm.

2 reales. 1789-M̊, F-M, Charles IV. BW-26.9, KM-89, 28 mm.

4 reales. 1799-M̊, F-M, Charles IIII. BW-27.8, KM-100, 34 mm.

8 reales. 1772-M̊, inverted M̊ and F-M, Charles III. BW-28.5, KM-106.1, 40 mm.

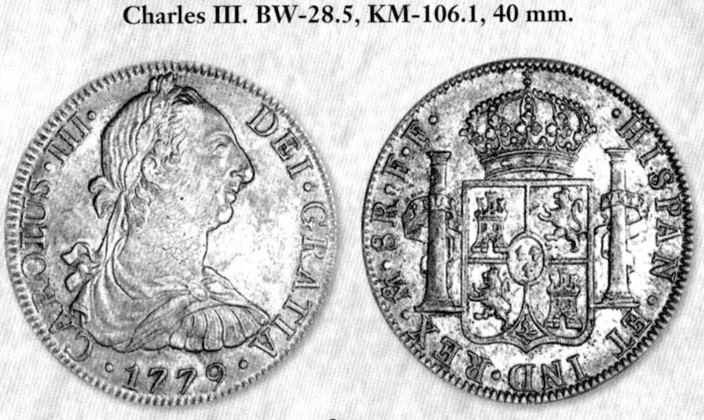

8 reales. 1779-M̊, F-F, Charles III. BW-28.6, KM-106.2, 40 mm.

Bust-Style Milled Coinage

(continued)

8 reales. 1790-$\overset{\circ}{\text{M}}$, F-M, Charles IIII. BW-28.9, KM-108, 40 mm.

1/2 escudo. 1814-$\overset{\circ}{\text{M}}$, J-J, Ferdinand VII. BW-29.1, KM-112, 15 mm.

1 escudo. 1746/5-$\overset{\circ}{\text{M}}$, M-F, Philip V. BW-30.1, KM-113, 18 mm.

1 escudo. 1747-$\overset{\circ}{\text{M}}$, M-F, Ferdinand VI. BW-30.2, KM-114, 18 mm.

1 escudo. 1776-$\overset{\circ}{\text{M}}$, F-M, Charles III. BW-30.9, KM-118.2, 18 mm.

1 escudo. 1807-$\overset{\circ}{\text{M}}$, T-H, Charles IV. BW-30.13, KM-120, 18 mm.

1 escudo. 1811-$\overset{\circ}{\text{M}}$, H-J, Ferdinand VII. BW-30.14, KM-121, 18 mm.

2 escudos. 1752-$\overset{\circ}{\text{M}}$, M-F, Ferdinand VI. BW-31.4, KM-126.2, 24 mm.

2 escudos. 1782-$\overset{\circ}{\text{M}}$, F-F, Charles III. BW-31.10, KM-130.2, 24 mm.

4 escudos. 1740/30-$\overset{o}{\text{M}}$, M-F, Philip V.
BW-32.1a, KM-135, 30 mm.

8 escudos. 1761-$\overset{o}{\text{M}}$, M-M, Charles III.
BW-33.7, KM-154, 36 mm.

8 escudos. 1806-$\overset{o}{\text{M}}$, T-H, Charles IIII.
BW-33.15, KM-159, 36 mm.

8 escudos. 1815-$\overset{o}{\text{M}}$, J-J, Ferdinand VII.
BW-33.17, KM-161, 38 mm.

6

Coinage of the War of Independence

A little background on the War of Independence is needed before we venture into the coinage of this important period of Mexico's history, which began with its birth as a republic and the advent of home rule.

New Spain was a viceroyalty of the Spanish colonial empire. Established in 1521, it primarily comprised what is known today as North America south of Canada, including all of present-day Mexico and Central America (except Panama) and most of the United States west of the Mississippi River and Florida. Mexico City served as the capital of New Spain.

New Spain was a colony of inequality, with little self-rule. The stability of the dominion of Spain was threatened by the oppressed classes, resulting in conspiracies, riots, and revolts by Creoles, Mestizos, Indians, and Africans. In time, attempts at emancipation came to a head when conspiracies and even outright plans of action proposed national unity in Mexico.

German scholar Alexander von Humboldt saw New Spain as a wealthy nation. However, beneath the glitter lay the reality of colonialism. New Spain was a dependent society wherein foreign masters wielded the baton. Inside the structure of dependency was a social pyramid determined by class and local standing. At the top of the pyramid were the elite, but they were out of step with the rest of society. For the poor and people of color, it was virtually impossible to climb the ladder.

Increasingly, however, censorship relaxed and new ideas made their way into the quiet and stagnant atmosphere of New Spain. The Jesuits in their schools taught new ideas about liberty. The expulsion of the Jesuits in 1767 weakened but did not stop the cultural movement in New Spain. During this era, the Catholic Church was still strong and its ideas were spreading.

The attitude of Spain toward the movement for Mexican rights can be summarized in a statement attributed to one of the viceroys: "For once and for all, know that you have been born to be silent and to obey, and neither to discuss nor hold opinions upon the exalted affairs of government." The Mexican population did just this for 300 years. There were protests and revolts against the Spanish, but they were neither well-organized enough nor effective enough to withstand the unmerciful retaliation of the Spanish in crushing these efforts.

The year 1801 was not a good one for the Spanish Empire to remain in either South America or New Spain. Discontent festered among rebels and Indian conspirators. The Creoles were among several factions in New Spain who had their own agendas. They wanted a government for themselves but with no structural changes, and they wanted the Mestizos (Spaniards of low socioeconomic status) to remain voiceless. A Creole social club in the town of Querétaro formed to discuss ideas for independence and brought the movement to a head. Known as the Literary Club of Querétaro, it was not opposed to the Catholic Church. Rather, its members proposed that, while still acknowledging King Ferdinand VII, they should no longer be governed by Gachupín officials, and that New Spain should enjoy equality with Spain within the Spanish Empire. Lending weight to this proposal is the fact that by this time New Spain had some independent economic muscle. In 1809 it was estimated that the colony annually exported 22 million pesos to pay for goods from Spanish merchants, who made enormous profits. New Spain also contributed royal revenues to help other colonies that were unable to meet their expenses.

The most prominent army officer in the Creole social club was Ignacio José de Allende. He reminded everyone of the chronic weakness of the viceroys and encouraged his fellow members to take matters into their own hands. At first, the struggle for independence did not exhibit well-marked or clear-cut features of social, industrial, or economic renovation. In time, however, Allende brought in parish priest Miguel Hidalgo y Costilla, from the town of Dolores. Hidalgo had read the classics and owned a respectable library that even included books on the Inquisition. This priest with piercing green eyes had sympathy for the oppressed Indians and was a man of great courage, as his actions proved. Hidalgo worked with the Indians to teach them methods of farming; the viceroy and Spanish officials disapproved, however, and cut down Hidalgo's trees and vines in retaliation.

The Querétaro conspirators planned to declare independence at the fair of San Juan de los Lagos in December 1810, but the plan was reported to Spanish officials, who issued orders on September 13 to arrest the leading conspirators. Allende was forewarned and rode to Dolores to consult with Hidalgo, and the plans for independence were changed at once. At daybreak on September 16, Hidalgo and a few supporters arrested all the Spaniards in town. Hidalgo then rang the bell of his church to summon his congregation. When they had assembled, he told them that the time to overthrow the Spaniards was at hand. The Indians, armed only with primitive weapons and led by Father Hidalgo and Allende, set off to free Mexico from the oppressive Spanish. At the next village the freedom force picked up a picture of the Virgin of Guadalupe, and it became the banner of the independence movement.

The Church later excommunicated Hidalgo. He was betrayed by a Creole officer, Francisco Ignacio Elizondo, at the wells of Baján, where he was captured on March 21, 1811. He was executed on July 30, and his head, along with the heads of other leaders of the revolt, was placed on the walls of the Alhóndiga de Granaditas in Guanajuato, where it remained until 1821. For his courageous efforts in the cause of independence, Father Hidalgo became known as the George Washington of Mexico.

Both Royalist and Insurgent coinage issues were produced during this period, with many counterstamped coins emerging from numerous states and regions. As the regions changed hands from Royalists to Insurgents, and vice versa, the available coins were counterstamped to be used under the current leader. Royalist coinage was issued from the mints of Chihuahua, Durango, Guadalajara, Guanajuato, Oaxaca, Real de Catorce, San Fernándo de Bexar, San Luis Potosí, Sombrerete, Valladolid, and Zacatecas.

The state of Oaxaca was the hotbed of the Insurgent forces in the south, and its coins were struck under adverse conditions. Several officials issued Oaxaca coins, so the varieties are endless; in addition, the conditions were ideal for them to be counterfeited, both at that time and in the years since. (During this period copper coins were supposed to be redeemable for silver coinage at a later time.) Production of Oaxaca coinage started in July 1811 and ran until October 1814. The Oaxaca copper coins can be found in all thicknesses and shapes. The authenticity of the SUD silver coinage of this period has been questioned.

In 1886, Lyman Haynes Low presented "A Sketch of the Coinage of the Mexican Revolutionary General Morelos, Based on an Important Find" to the American Numismatic and Archaeological Society. He expanded on this presentation in an 1897 book, *La Moneda del General Insurgente Don José María Morelos*, written with Nicolás León. José Luís Franco C.'s article "Variations in the Bow and Arrow of the Coins of General Morelos 1811–1814" appeared in the October–December 1971 issue of the *Sociedad Numismática de México Boletín*. Franco reported that he had examined 2,943 pieces in his study and cataloged the various aspects of the bows and arrows found on the coins. He categorized them by denomination and showed the many varieties of the various aspects of the design.

Because of the differences between minting facilities used by the various entities that issued coins, actual weights and diameters can vary from the weights and diameters given in these listings.

ROYALIST COINAGE

Chihuahua

The Chihuahua mint was established by a decree dated October 8, 1810. It issued cast 8 reales, prepared by using Mexico City coins as models and obliterating and changing the mintmark and assayers' initials. Two counterstamps are present on the obverse: on the left a T, which designates receipt by the royal treasurer; and on the right a pomegranate, placed between the crowned Pillars of Hercules. Also present is the comptroller's symbol. Standard dies were prepared for struck 8 reales in 1814 and used until 1822.

8 reales, 0.916 cast silver, 26.450 g.

Obverse: Armored, laureated bust of Ferdinand VII facing right. Legend FERDIN VII . DEI . GRATIA . [date] . *Reverse:* Crowned coat of arms of Spain flanked by columns wrapped in ribbons reading PLUS VLTRA. Legend HISPAN . ET IND . REX, mintmark CA̧, denomination, and assayers' initials. Counterstamped with T to left and a pomegranate to the right, between two columns. *Diameter:* 39 mm. BW-41.1, KM-123.

Date	Assayer	Comment
1811	R-P	
1812	R-P	
1813	R-P	

8 reales, struck silver, 27.070 g.

Obverse: Draped, laureated bust of Ferdinand VII facing right. Legend FERDIN VII . DEI . GRATIA . [date] . *Reverse:* Crowned coat of arms of Spain flanked by columns wrapped in ribbons reading PLUS VLTRA. Legend . HISPAN . ET IND . REX ., mintmark CA̧, denomination, and assayers' initials. May or may not be counterstamped with T to left and with a pomegranate to right, between two columns. All are struck on cast coins. *Diameter:* 39 mm. BW-41.2, KM-111.1.

Date	Assayer	Comment
1815	R-P	Rare
1816	R-P	
1817	R-P	
1817	M-P	
1818	R-P	
1819	R-P	
1820	R-P	
1821	R-P	
1822	R-P	

Durango

The Durango mint was established by decree of October 8, 1810, and began to issue coins in 1811. Some Durango 8 reales can be found struck on cast Chihuahua 8 reales. The pre-1816 examples are crudely struck.

1/8 real (octavo), copper.

Obverse: Crowned monogram of Ferdinand VII. *Reverse:* Legend **EN DURANGO OCTAVO DE REAL .[date].** *Diameter:* 23 mm. *Edge:* Corded. BW-42.1, KM-60.

Date	Comment
1812	
1813	
1814	Rare

1/8 real (octavo), copper.

Obverse: Crowned monogram of Ferdinand VII. *Reverse:* Above an open wreath, legend **EN DURANGO OCTAVO DE REAL .[date].** *Diameter:* 23 mm. *Edge:* Corded. BW-42.2, KM-61.

Date	Comment
1814	
1815	
1816	
1817	
1818	

1/2 real, 0.9027 silver, 1.690 g.

Obverse: Draped, laureated bust of Ferdinand VII. Legend **. FERDIN .VII . DEI . GRATIA . [date] .** *Reverse:* Crowned coat of arms of Spain flanked by columns wrapped in ribbons reading **PLUS VLTRA.** Legend **. HISPAN . ET IND . R .**, mintmark **D**, denomination, and assayers' initials. *Diameter:* 18 mm. BW-43, KM-74.1.

Date	Assayer	Comment
1813	R-M	
1814	M-Z	
1816	M-Z	

1 real, 0.9027 silver, 3.380 g.

Obverse: Draped, laureated bust of Ferdinand VII. Legend **FERDIN .VII . DEI . GRATIA . [date] .** *Reverse:* Crowned coat of arms of Spain flanked by columns wrapped in ribbons reading **PLUS VLTRA.** Legend **. HISPAN . ET . IND . REX .**, mintmark **D**, denomination, and assayers' initials. *Diameter:* 20 mm. BW-44, KM-83.1.

Date	Assayer	Comment
1813	R-M	
1814	M-Z	
1815	M-Z	
1816	R-M	

2 reales, 0.9027 silver, 6.770 g.

Obverse: Armored, laureated bust of Ferdinand VII facing right. Legend **FERD . VII . REI . DE ESP . E IND [date].** *Reverse:* Crowned coat of arms of Spain flanked by columns wrapped in ribbons reading **PLUS VLTRA.** Legend **. MON . PROV . DE DURANGO .**, denomination, and assayers' initials. *Diameter:* 27 mm. *Edge:* Corded. BW-45.1, KM-92.2.

Date	Assayer	Comment
1811	R-M	

2 reales, 0.9027 silver, 6.770 g.

Obverse: Armored, laureated bust of Ferdinand VII facing right. Legend **FERDIN .VII . DEI . GRATIA** and **. [date] .** *Reverse:* Crowned coat of arms of Spain flanked by columns wrapped in ribbons reading **PLUS VLTRA.** Legend **. HISPAN . ET IND . REX .**, mintmark **D**, denomination, and assayers' initials. *Diameter:* 28 mm. BW-45.2, KM-92.3.

Date	Assayer	Comment
1812	R-M	

2 reales, 0.9027 silver, 6.770 g.

Obverse: Draped, laureated bust of Ferdinand VII facing right. Legend **FERDIN .VII. DEI .GRATIA . [date] .** *Reverse:* Crowned coat of arms of Spain flanked by columns wrapped in ribbons reading **PLUS VLTRA.** Legend **HISPAN . ET IND . REX .**, mintmark **D**, denomination, and assayers' initials. *Diameter:* 28 mm. BW-45.3, KM-93.1.

Date	Assayer	Comment
1811	R-M	
1811	M-Z	
1812	M-Z	
1812	R-M	
1813	R-M	
1813	M-Z	
1814	M-Z	
1815	M-Z	
1815	C-G	
1816	M-Z	
1817	M-Z	
1819	C-G	

4 reales, 0.9027 silver, 13.540 g.

Obverse: Draped, laureated bust of Ferdinand VII facing right. Legend **FERDIN .VII. DEI . GRATIA. [date] .** *Reverse:* Crowned coat of arms of Spain flanked by columns wrapped in ribbons reading **PLUS VLTRA**. Legend **. HISPAN . ET IND . REX .**, mintmark **D**, denomination, and assayers' initials. *Diameter:* 34 mm. BW-46, KM-102.1.

Date	Assayer	Comment
1814	M-Z	
1816	M-Z	
1817	M-Z	

8 reales, 0.9027 silver, 27.070 g.

Obverse: Armored, laureated bust of Ferdinand VII facing right. Legend **FERDIN .VII . DEI . GRATIA . [date] .** *Reverse:* Crowned coat of arms of Spain flanked by columns wrapped in ribbons reading **PLUS VLTRA**. Legend **. HISPAN . ET IND . REX .**, mintmark **D**, denomination, and assayers' initials. *Diameter:* 40 mm. BW-47.1, KM-110.1.

Date	Assayer	Comment
1812	R-M	
1814	R-M	

8 reales, 0.9027 silver, 27.070 g.

Obverse: Draped, laureated bust of Ferdinand VII facing right. Legend **FERDIN . VII. DEI . GRATIA . [date] .** *Reverse:* Crowned coat of arms of Spain flanked by columns wrapped in ribbons reading **PLUS VLTRA**. Legend **. HISPAN . ET IND . REX .**, mintmark **D**, denomination, and assayers' initials. *Diameter:* 40 mm. BW-47.2, KM-111.2.

Date	Assayer	Comment
1811	R-M	
1812	R-M	
1812	R-M	R8
1813	R-M	
1813	R-M	.ET IN.
1813	M-Z	
1814	M-Z	
1814	R-M	
1815	M-Z	
1815	C-G	
1816	M-Z	
1817	M-Z	
1818	M-Z	
1818	R-M	
1818	C-G/R-M	
1818	C-G	
1819	C-G	
1820	C-G	
1821	C-G	
1822	C-G	

Guadalajara

The Guadalajara mint issued its first coins in 1812 and operated until April 30, 1815. The mint reopened in 1818 and remained in operation until 1822. The Guadalajara mint was the only Royalist mint to issue gold coins.

1/2 real, 0.9027 silver, 1.690 g.

Obverse: Draped, laureated bust of Ferdinand VII facing right. Legend **FERDIN .VII. DEI . GRATIA.** and **. [date] .** *Reverse:* Crowned coat of arms of Spain flanked by columns wrapped in ribbons reading **PLUS VLTRA**. Legend **. HISPAN . ET IND . R .**, mintmark **GA**, denomination, and assayers' initials. *Diameter:* 17 mm. *Edge:* Corded. BW-48, KM-74.2.

Date	Assayer	Comment
1812	M-R	Rare
1813	M-R	
1814	M-R	
1815	M-R	

1 real, 0.9027 silver, 3.380 g.

Obverse: Draped, laureated bust of Ferdinand VII facing right. Legend **FERDIN . VII . DEI . GRATIA . [date] .** *Reverse:* Crowned coat of arms of Spain flanked by columns wrapped in ribbons reading **PLUS VLTRA**. Legend **. HISPAN . ET IND . REX .**, mintmark **GA**, denomination, and assayers' initials. *Diameter:* 21 mm. *Edge:* Corded. BW-49, KM-83.2.

Date	Assayer	Comment
1813	M-R	
1814	M-R	
1815	M-R	

2 reales, 0.9027 silver, 6.770 g.

Obverse: Draped, laureated bust of Ferdinand VII facing right. Legend **FERDIN . VII . DEI . GRATIA . [date] .** *Reverse:* Crowned coat of arms of Spain flanked by columns wrapped in ribbons reading **PLUS VLTRA**. Legend **. HISPAN . ET IND . REX .**, mintmark **GA̤**, denomination, and assayers' initials. *Diameter:* 27 mm. *Edge:* Corded. BW-50, KM-93.2.

Date	Assayer	Comment
1812	M-R	
1814	M-R	
1815/4	M-R	
1815	M-R	
1821	F-S	

4 reales, 0.9027 silver, 13.540 g.

Obverse: Draped, laureated bust of Ferdinand VII facing right. Legend **FERDIN . VII . DEI . GRATIA . [date] .** *Reverse:* Crowned coat of arms of Spain flanked by columns wrapped in ribbons reading **PLUS VLTRA**. Legend **. HISPAN . ET IND . REX .**, mintmark **GA̤**, denomination, and assayers' initials. *Diameter:* 34 mm. *Edge:* Corded. BW-51.1, KM-102.2.

Date	Assayer	Comment
1814	M-R	
1815	M-R	

4 reales, 0.9027 silver, 13.540 g.

Obverse: Restyled, large draped and laureated bust of Ferdinand VII facing right. Legend **FERDIN . VII . DEI . GRATIA . [date] .** *Reverse:* Crowned coat of arms of Spain flanked by columns wrapped in ribbons reading **PLUS VLTRA**. Legend **. HISPAN . ET IND . REX .**, mintmark **GA̤**, denomination, and assayers' initials. *Diameter:* 34 mm. BW-51.2, KM-102.3.

Date	Assayer	Comment
1814	M-R	

4 reales, 0.9027 silver, 13.540 g.

Obverse: Restyled, small draped and laureated bust of Ferdinand VII facing right. Legend **FERDIN . VII . DEI . GRATIA . [date] .** *Reverse:* Crowned coat of arms of Spain flanked by columns wrapped in ribbons reading **PLUS VLTRA**. Legend **. HISPAN . ET IND . REX .**, mintmark **GA̤**, denomination, and assayers' initials. *Diameter:* 34 mm. BW-51.3, KM-102.4.

Date	Assayer	Comment
1814	M-R	

8 reales, 0.9027 silver, 27.070 g.

Obverse: Draped, laureated bust of Ferdinand VII facing right. Legend **FERDIN . VII . DEI . GRATIA . [date] .** *Reverse:* Crowned coat of arms of Spain flanked by columns wrapped in ribbons reading **PLUS VLTRA**. Legend **. HISPAN . ET IND . REX .**, mintmark **GA̤**, denomination, and assayers' initials. *Diameter:* 39 mm. *Edge:* Corded. BW-52, KM-111.3.

Date	Assayer	Comment
1812	M-R	
1812	M-R	.ET INd.
1813/2	M-R	
1813	M-R	
1814	M-R	Wide crown
1814	M-R	No . before HISPAN
1814	M-R	No . between assayers' initials
1814	M-R	Narrow crown
1815	M-R	
1818	F-S	
1821/0	F-S	
1821	F-S	
1822/1	F-S	
1822	F-S	Die varieties

4 escudos, 0.8750 gold, 13.540 g.

Obverse: Large provisional uniformed bust of Ferdinand VII facing right. Legend **FERDIN . VII . D . G . HISP. ET IND . R . [date] .** *Reverse:* Crowned coat of arms of Spain within the collar of the Order of the Golden Fleece. Denomination on both sides of shield, legend **IN . UTROQ. FELIX . . AUSPICE . DEO** around, mintmark **GA̤**, and assayers' initials. *Diameter:* 28 mm. BW-53, KM-147.

Date	Assayer	Comment
1812	M-R	Rare

8 escudos, 0.8750 gold, 27.070 g.

Obverse: Large provisional uniformed bust of Ferdinand VII facing right. Legend

FERDIN . VII . D . G . HISP. ET IND . R . [date] . *Reverse:* Crowned coat of arms of Spain within collar of the Order of the Golden Fleece. Denomination on both sides of shield, legend IN . UTROQ . FELIX . . AUSPICE . DEO around, mintmark GA, and assayers' initials. *Diameter:* 37 mm. BW-54.1, KM-162.

Date	Assayer	Comment
1812	M-R	Rare
1813	M-R	

8 escudos, 0.8750 gold, 27.070 g.

Obverse: Small provisional uniformed bust of Ferdinand VII facing right. Legend FERDIN . VII . D . G . HISP. ET IND . R . [date] . *Reverse:* Crowned coat of arms of Spain within the collar of the Order of the Golden Fleece. Denomination on both sides of shield, legend IN . UTROQ . FELIX. . AUSPICE . DEO around, mintmark GA, and assayers' initials. *Diameter:* 37 mm. BW-54.2, KM-163.

Date	Assayer	Comment
1813	M-R	

8 escudos, 0.8750 gold, 27.070 g.

Obverse: Undraped, laureated bust of Ferdinand VII facing right. Legend FERDIN . VII . D . G . HISP. ET IND . R . [date] . *Reverse:* Crowned coat of arms of Spain within the collar of the Order of the Golden Fleece. Denomination on both sides of shield, legend IN . UTROQ . FELIX .. AUSPICE . DEO around, mintmark GA, and assayers' initials. *Diameter:* 37 mm. BW-54.3, KM-161.1.

Date	Assayer	Comment
1821	F-S	

8 escudos, 0.8750 gold, 27.070 g.

Obverse: Draped, laureated bust of Ferdinand VII facing right. Legend FERDIN . VII . D . G . HISP. ET IND . R . [date] . *Reverse:* Crowned coat of arms of Spain within the collar of the Order of the Golden Fleece. Denomination on both sides of shield, legend IN . UTROQ . FELIX .. AUSPICE . DEO around, mintmark GA, and assayers' initials. *Diameter:* 37 mm. BW-54.4, KM-164.

Date	Assayer	Comment
1821	F-S	

Guanajuato

The Guanajuato mint was established December 24, 1812, and closed May 15, 1813. It was reopened by the Insurgents in April 1821.

2 reales, 0.9027 silver, 6.770 g.

Obverse: Draped, laureated bust of Ferdinand VII facing right. Legend FERDIN . VII . DEI . GRATIA and . [date] . *Reverse:* Crowned coat of arms of Spain flanked by columns wrapped in ribbons reading PLUS VLTRA. Legend . HISPAN . ET IND . REX ., mintmark G, denomination, and assayers' initials. *Diameter:* 28 mm. *Edge:* Corded. BW-55, KM-93.3.

Date	Assayer	Comment
1821	J-M	
1822	J-M	

8 reales, 0.9027 silver, 27.070 g.

Obverse: Draped, laureated bust of Ferdinand VII facing right. Legend FERDIN .VII . DEI . GRATIA . [date] . *Reverse:* Crowned coat of arms of Spain flanked by columns wrapped in ribbons reading PLUS VLTRA. Legend . HISPAN . ET IND . REX ., mintmark G, denomination, and assayers' initials. *Diameter:* 39 mm. *Edge:* Corded. BW-56, KM-111.4.

Date	Assayer	Comment
1812	J-J	
1813	J-J	
1813	J-M	
1821	J-M	
1822	J-M	
1822/0	J-M	

Nueva Vizcaya

The coins for Nueva Vizcaya were minted at the Durango mint during February and March of 1811, before the regular Durango coinage began. Nueva Vizcaya later became the state of Durango.

Unique Nueva Vizcaya edge, with cross-hatching.

8 reales, 0.9027 silver, 27.070 g.

Obverse: Crowned coat of arms of Spain flanked by columns wrapped in ribbons reading **PLUS VLTRA**. Legend **FERN . VII . REY . DE . ESP . ET IND .**, denomination, and assayers' initials. *Reverse:* Crowned coat of arms of Nueva Vizcaya. Legend **MON . PROV . DE NVEV . VIZCAYA . [date] .** *Diameter:* 41 mm. *Edge:* Unique corded. BW-57, KM-181. Rare.

Date	Assayer	Comment
1811	R-M	Varieties exist
1811	R-M	REI (not REY)
1811	R-M	NUEV. VIZCA

Oaxaca, Royalist Issues

The city of Oaxaca was experiencing a coin shortage when it became evident that the Insurgent forces were going to take over the city. The Royalist forces under Lt. General González-Saravia had a local blacksmith shop prepare 1/2-real, 1-real, and 8-reales coins, which were made briefly in 1813 before the Insurgents took control.

Oaxaca cast silver coins are suspect.

1/2 real, cast silver.

Obverse: Shield with rampant lion facing left. Legend **R. M. PROV . D . OAXACA . [date] .** *Reverse:* Cross of Jerusalem with castle in left quarter and a rampant lion facing left in the right quarter. In the lower quarters, **F♀.** and **7♀.** *Diameter:* 16 mm. BW-58, KM-166.

Date	Comment
1812	

1 real, cast silver.

Obverse: Shield with rampant lion facing left. Denomination and legend **R . M . PROV . D . OAXACA . [date] .** *Reverse:* Cross of Jerusalem with castle in left quarter and a rampant lion facing left in the right quarter. In the lower quarters, **F♀.** and **7♀.** *Diameter:* 20 mm. BW-59, KM-167.

Date	Comment
1812	

8 reales, cast silver.

Obverse: Cross of Jerusalem with castle in right quarter and a rampant lion facing right in left quarter. In the lower quarters, **F♀** and **7♀**; above and below the upright of the cross is a rosette. Legend **PROV . D .* OAXACA**, date, and denomination. *Reverse:* Shield with eight St. Andrew's crosses on the border, a rampant lion to right. Authorization mark above shield. *Diameter:* 40 mm. BW-60, KM-168.

Date	Comment
1812	A authorization mark
1812	B authorization mark
1812	C authorization mark
1812	D authorization mark
1812	K authorization mark
1812	M authorization mark
1812	Mo authorization mark, large lion
1812	N authorization mark
1812	O authorization mark
1812	R authorization mark
1812	R authorization mark, large lion
1812	V authorization mark
1812	V authorization mark, large lion
1812	Z authorization mark

Real de Catorce

Real de Catorce was a mining center in the province of San Luis Potosí. While the Royalists were in control a crude 8 reales of 1811 was issued.

8 reales, 0.9027 silver.

Obverse: Around a dotted circle, legend **EL R.D.CATORC.POR FERNA.VII. [date].** *Reverse:* Legend **+MONEDA PROVIS IONAL. VALE.** around dotted circle, and denomination. *Diameter:* 41 mm. BW-61, KM-169.

Date	Comment
1811	

San Fernándo de Bexar (San Antonio, Texas)

The 1/2-real denomination was authorized by decree of March 29, 1817, issued by Lt. Col. Manuel Prado, the military commander and governor of the province of Texas. He authorized Manuel Barrera to issue 8,000 copper coins with a value of 1/2 real. Specimens of this coin are unknown at this time.

In May 1817 the viceroy of New Spain, Juan Apodaca, appointed Antonio Martínez as the new military commander and governor of the province of Texas. On November 30, 1818, José Antonio de la Garza, the postmaster of San Fernándo de Bexar (later San Antonio, Texas), applied for a permit to coin and circulate money in the town. His permit was approved by decree dated December 6, 1818, authorizing the mintage of 500 pesos (8,000 copper *jolas*). The *jolas* were redeemed in silver over time by de la Garza, and it is believed that he threw the bagged coins into the San Antonio River to prevent them from being redeemed. Support for this theory appeared when 60 of these coins were discovered in 1959 during excavation work. This is the only coin of the Spanish colonial era to have been struck in what is now the United States.

There are two varieties of *jola:* a large-planchet variety that has a raised five-pointed star, and a small-planchet *jola* with an incuse five-pointed star. The weights and diameters are not consistent.

Small Planchet

1/2 real (*jola*), copper, small planchet, 1.4–1.5 g.

Obverse: Legend J.A.G. (for José Antonio de la Garza), denomination 1/2 lying horizontally to right on some examples and to left on others. Date 1818. *Reverse:* An incuse five-pointed star. *Diameter:* 16 mm. *Edge:* Plain. BW-62.1, KM-Tn1 (KM-170).

Date	Comment
1818	

Large Planchet

1/2 real (*jola*), copper, 1.5–1.9 g.

Obverse: Legend J.A.G. (for José Antonio de la Garza), denomination 1/2 lying horizontally to right on some and to left on others. Date 1818. *Reverse:* A raised five-pointed star. *Diameter:* 19 mm. *Edge:* Plain. BW-62.2, KM-Tn2 (KM-171).

Date	Comment
1818	

San Luis Potosí (Sierra de Pinos)

1/4 real, copper.

Obverse: Image unclear. *Reverse:* Legend STPE AVL NTANITO around, and date. Crowned horse in center. *Diameter:* 22 mm. BW-63, KM-A172.

Date	Comment
1814	

1/4 real, silver.

Obverse and reverse images unclear. BW-63.1, KM-A172a.

Date	Comment
1814	Rare

Sombrerete (Under Royalist Vargas)

The mint at Sombrerete was opened on October 8, 1810, and operated until July 16, 1811. It reopened in 1812 but closed at the end of the year. Fernándo Vargas was the mine administrator and was also in charge of the coining operation. All coins produced during his administration bear the name "Vargas."

1/2 real, 0.9027 silver.

Obverse: Two crowned globes and legend FERDIN VII SOMBRERETE. *Reverse:* Three fleurs-de-lis and legend .VARGAS ., with denomination and .[date]. below. *Diameter:* 17 mm. BW-64, KM-172.

Date	Comment
1811	
1812	

1 real, 0.9027 silver.

Obverse: Two crowned globes and legend FERDIN VII SOMBRERETE. *Reverse:* Three fleurs-de-lis and legend .VARGAS ., with denomination and .[date]. below. *Diameter:* 21 mm. BW-65, KM-173.

Date	Comment
1811	1R or R1
1812	

2 reales, 0.9027 silver.

Obverse: Crowned coat of arms of Spain within a dotted circle with the legend **R . CAXA . DE SOMBRETE** and the denomination outside the circle. *Reverse:* Legend **. VARGAS .** at top. Between small pair of columns to the left, a crowned horse's head and the letter **S**. Between small pair of columns to the right, a crowned **S** with the numeral **3** below it. Date at center between the two pairs of columns. *Diameter:* 28 mm. BW-66, KM-174.

Date	Comment
1811	

4 reales, 0.9027 silver.

Obverse: Crowned coat of arms of Spain within a dotted circle with the legend **R . CAXA . DE SOMBRETE** and the denomination outside the circle. *Reverse:* Legend **. VARGAS .** at top. Between small pair of columns to the left, a crowned horse's head and the letter **S**. Between small pair of columns to the right, a crowned **S** with the numeral **3** below it. Date at center between the two pairs of columns. *Diameter:* 33 mm. BW-67, KM-175.

Date	Comment
1812	
1812	SOMBRRETE

8 reales, 0.9027 silver.

Obverse: Crowned coat of arms of Spain within a dotted circle with the legend **R.CAXA.DE SOMBRETE** and the denomination outside the circle. *Reverse:* Legend **.VARGAS.** at top. Between small pair of columns to the left, a crowned horse's head and the letter **S**. Between small pair of columns to the right, a crowned **S** with square counterstamp **3** below it. Date at center between the two pairs of columns. *Diameter:* 39 mm. *Edge:* Corded. BW-68.2, KM-176.

Date	Comment
1810	
1811	

8 reales, 0.9027 silver.

Obverse: Crowned coat of arms of Spain within a dotted circle with the legend **R.CAXA.DE SOMBRETE** and the denomination outside the circle. *Reverse:* Legend **.VARGAS.** at top. Between small pair of columns to the left, a crowned horse's head and the letter **S**. Between small pair of columns to the right, a crowned **S** with the numeral **3** below it. Date at center between the two pairs of columns. *Diameter:* 39 mm. *Edge:* Corded. BW-68.1, KM-177.

Date	Comment
1811	
1812	

Valladolid

The province of Valladolid was established in the early colonial period and was located 25 miles east of Chichén Itzá. Small groups met there under the guise of a literary club to discuss the current Spanish rule. The club was the vanguard of the pending insurrection, which was set for December 8, 1810. However, before the action could take place the plans were exposed and members were arrested. Father Hidalgo, after being notified of the actions of the Spanish authorities, provided the spark that led to the War of Independence.

8 reales, 0.9027 silver.

Obverse: Legend *** PROVISIONAL * DE VALLADOLID.** and date. *Reverse:* Within a wreath, the crowned coat of arms of Spain. Denomination split by shield, with initials **M. O.** below the shield. *Diameter:* 39 mm. BW-69.1, KM-178.

Date	Comment
1813	Rare

8 reales, 0.9027 silver.

Obverse: Draped, laureated bust of Ferdinand VII facing right. Legend **FERDIN . VII . DEI . GRATIA** and **. [date] .** *Reverse:* Crowned coat of arms of Spain flanked by columns wrapped in ribbons reading **PLUS VLTRA.**

Legend . **HISPAN . ET IND .REX . P .D. V.** ("P.D.V." for Provisional de Valladolid). *Diameter:* 41 mm. BW-69.2, KM-179.

Date	Comment
1813	Rare

Zacatecas

The city of Zacatecas is located in a rich mining region and has been a world supplier of silver since the 1500s. On November 14, 1810, coin production started there for the Royalist movement. Some coins dated 1811 were made by the Insurgents who captured the city on April 15, 1811. The Royalists later recaptured the city on May 21, 1811. The standard Ferdinand VII Bust-type coinage was struck at the Zacatecas mint until 1822.

Moneda Provisional

1/2 real, 0.9027 silver.

Obverse: Crude crowned coat of arms of Spain flanked by columns wrapped in ribbons. Legend, around, **FERDIN VII DEI GRATIA . [date] .** *Reverse:* Hills of La Bufa and El Grillo at Zacatecas in a circle of dots. Front hill has a cross on the top and a semicircle of 7 to 15 stars ending with a ball and **L.V.O.** Around circumference, starting at nine o'clock, legend **MONEDA PROVISIONAL DE ZACATECAS.** No denomination shown. *Diameter:* 18 mm. *Edge:* Plain. BW-70.1, KM-180.

Date	Comment
1810	
1811	

1/2 real, 0.9027 silver.

Obverse: Crowned coat of arms of Spain flanked by columns wrapped in ribbons. Legend **FERDIN VII DEI GRATIA . [date] .** around. *Reverse:* Hills of La Bufa and El Grillo at Zacatecas in a circle of dots. Front hill has a cross on the top and a semicircle of 10 to 17 stars ending with a ball and **L.V.O.** Around circumference, starting at twelve o'clock, legend **MONEDA PROVISIONAL DE ZACATECAS.** Denomination not shown. *Diameter:* 18 mm. BW-70.2, KM-181.

Date	Comment
1810	
1811	

1/2 real, 0.9027 silver.

Obverse: Armored, laureated bust of Ferdinand VII facing right. Legend **FERDIN . VII . M . DEI . GRATIA . [date] .** *Reverse:* Crowned coat of arms of Spain flanked by columns wrapped in ribbons. Starting at twelve o'clock, the legend **MONEDA PROVISIONAL DE ZACATECAS.** Denomination not shown. *Diameter:* 18 mm. *Edge:* Plain. BW-70.3, KM-182.

Date	Comment
1811	
1812	

1 real, 0.9027 silver.

Obverse: Crude crowned coat of arms of Spain flanked by columns wrapped in ribbons. Legend **FERDIN . VII .DEI GRATIA .[denomination]. [date].** *Reverse:* Hills of La Bufa and El Grillo at Zacatecas in a circle of dots. Front hill has a cross on the top and a semicircle of 7 to 15 stars ending with a ball and **L.V.O.** Around circumference, starting at nine o'clock, legend **MONEDA PROVISIONAL DE ZACATECAS.** *Diameter:* 21 mm. *Edge:* Plain. BW-71.1, KM-183.

Date	Comment
1810	
1811	

1 real, 0.9027 silver.

Obverse: Crowned coat of arms of Spain flanked by columns wrapped in ribbons. Legend **FERDIN . VII . DEI . GRATIA .**, denomination, and **. [date] .** *Reverse:* Hills of La Bufa and El Grillo at Zacatecas in a circle of dots. Far hill has a cross on the top and a semicircle of 8 to 15 stars ending with a ball and **L.V.O.** Around circumference, starting at twelve o'clock, legend **MONEDA PROVISIONAL DE ZACATECAS**. *Diameter:* 21 mm. *Edge:* Plain. BW-71.2, KM-184.

Date	Comment
1810	
1811	

1 real, 0.9027 silver.

Obverse: Armored, laureated bust of Ferdinand VII facing right. Legend **FERDIN . VII . 1R . DEI . GRATIA . [date] .** *Reverse:* Crowned coat of arms of Spain flanked by columns wrapped in ribbons reading **PLUS VLTRA**. Starting at twelve o'clock, legend **MONEDA PROVISIONAL DE ZACATECAS** around circumference. *Diameter:* 21 mm. *Edge:* Plain. BW-71.3, KM-185.

Date	Comment
1811	
1812	

2 reales, 0.9027 silver.

Obverse: Crude crowned coat of arms of Spain flanked by columns wrapped in ribbons. Legend **FERDIN . VII . 2R . DEI . GRATIA . [date] .** *Reverse:* Hills of La Bufa and El Grillo at Zacatecas in a circle of dots. Far hill has a cross on the top and a semicircle of 10 to 17 stars ending with a ball and **L. V. O.** Around circumference, starting at nine o'clock, legend **MONEDA PROVISIONAL DE ZACATECAS**. *Diameter:* 28 mm. *Edge:* Plain. BW-72.1, KM-186.

Date	Comment
1810	Rare
1811	

2 reales, 0.9027 silver.

Obverse: Crowned coat of arms of Spain flanked by columns wrapped in ribbons. Legend **FERDIN . VII . 2R . DEI . GRATIA . [date] .** *Reverse:* Hills of La Bufa and El Grillo at Zacatecas in a circle of dots. Far hill has a cross and a semicircle of 15 to 17 stars ending with a ball and **L. V. O.** Around circumference, starting at twelve o'clock, legend **MONEDA PROVISIONAL DE ZACATECAS**. *Diameter:* 27 mm. *Edge:* Plain. BW-72.2, KM-187.

Date	Comment
1810	
1811	
1812	

2 reales, 0.9027 silver.

Obverse: Armored, laureated bust of Ferdinand VII facing right. Legend **FERDIN . VII . 2R . DEI . GRATIA . [date] .** *Reverse:* Crowned coat of arms of Spain flanked by columns wrapped in ribbons reading **PLUS VLTRA**. Starting at twelve o'clock, legend **MONEDA PROVISIONAL DE ZACATECAS**. *Diameter:* 26 mm. BW-72.3, KM-188.

Date	Comment
1811	
1812	

8 reales, 0.9027 silver.

Obverse: Crude crowned coat of arms of Spain flanked by columns wrapped in ribbons. Legend **FERDINANDUS . VII . DEI . GRATIA**, denomination, and **. [date] .** *Reverse:* Within a circle of dots, the hills of La Bufa and El Grillo at Zacatecas, all above a semicircle of 13 to 19 stars with a ball at each end. Above the front hill, a crucifix; below the hills, **L.V.O.** Starting at nine o'clock, legend **MONEDA . PROVISIONAL . DE . ZACATECAS .** *Diameter:* 41 mm. BW-73.1, KM-189.

Date	Comment
1810	
1811	

8 reales, 0.9027 silver.

Obverse: Crowned coat of arms of Spain flanked by columns wrapped in ribbons. Legend **FERDIN . VII . DEI . GRATIA .**, denomination, and **. [date] .** *Reverse:* Hills of La Bufa and El Grillo at Zacatecas in a circle of dots. Crown on rear mountain above a semicircle of 13 to 19 stars ending with a ball; **L.V.O.** Starting at one o'clock, legend **MONEDA PROVISIONAL DE ZACATECAS**. *Diameter:* 41 mm. BW-73.2, KM-190.

Date	Comment
1811	

8 reales, 0.9027 silver.

Obverse: Large, armored laureated bust of Ferdinand VII facing right. Legend **FERDIN . VII . 8 R. DEI GRATIA . [date] .** *Reverse:* Crowned coat of arms of Spain flanked by columns wrapped in ribbons reading **PLUS VLTRA**. Starting at one o'clock, legend **MONEDA PROVISIONAL DE ZACATECAS.** *Diameter:* 39 mm. BW-73.3, KM-191.

Date	Comment
1810	
1811	
1812	
1813	

8 reales, 0.9027 silver.

Obverse: Draped, laureated bust of Ferdinand VII facing right. Legend **FERDIN . VII . 8 R . DEI . GRATIA . [date] .** *Reverse:* Crowned coat of arms of Spain flanked by columns wrapped in ribbons reading **PLUS VLTRA**. Starting at one o'clock, legend **MONEDA PROVISIONAL DE ZACATECAS.** *Diameter:* 39 mm. BW-73.4, KM-192.

Date	Comment
1812	
1813	

Post–Moneda Provisional

1/2 real, 0.9027 silver, 1.690 g.

Obverse: Armored, laureated bust of Ferdinand VII facing right. Legend **FERDIN . VII . DEI . GRATIA . [date] .** *Reverse:* Crowned coat of arms of Spain flanked by columns wrapped in ribbons reading **PLUS VLTRA**. Legend **. HISPAN . ET IND . R . Z . M .** and assayer. Denomination not shown. *Diameter:* 18 mm. BW-70.4, KM-73.1.

Date	Assayer	Comment
1813	A-G	
1813	F-P	
1814	A-G	
1815	A-G	
1816	A-G	
1817	A-G	
1818	A-G	
1819	A-G	

1/2 real, 0.9027 silver, 1.690 g.

Obverse: Draped, laureated bust of Ferdinand VII facing right. Legend **FERDIN . VII . DEI . GRATIA . [date] .** *Reverse:* Crowned coat of arms of Spain flanked by columns wrapped in ribbons reading **PLUS VLTRA**. Legend **. HISPAN . ET IND . R . Z .** and assayer. Denomination not shown. *Diameter:* 18 mm. BW-70.5, KM-74.3.

Date	Assayer	Comment
1820	A-G	
1820	R-G	
1821	A-G	
1821	R-G	

1 real, 0.9027 silver, 3.380 g.

Obverse: Armored, laureated bust of Ferdinand VII facing right. Legend **FERDIN . VII . DEI . GRATIA . [date] .** *Reverse:* Crowned coat of arms of Spain flanked by columns wrapped in ribbons reading **PLUS VLTRA**. Legend **. HISPAN . ET IND . REX . Z . 1R .** and assayer. *Diameter:* 21 mm. BW-71.4, KM-82.1.

Date	Assayer	Comment
1813	F-P	
1813	A-G	
1814	F-P	
1814	A-G	
1815	A-G	
1816	A-G	
1817	A-G	
1818	A-G	
1819	A-G	

1 real, 0.9027 silver, 3.380 g.

Obverse: Draped, laureated bust of Ferdinand VII facing right. Legend **FERDIN . VII . DEI . GRATIA . [date].** *Reverse:* Crowned coat of arms of Spain flanked by columns wrapped in ribbons reading **PLUS VLTRA**. Legend **. HISPAN . ET IND . REX . Z . 1 R .** and assayer. *Diameter:* 21 mm. *Edge:* corded. BW-71.5, KM-83.3.

Date	Assayer	Comment
1820	A-G	
1820	R-G	
1821	A-G	
1821	A-Z	

Date	Assayer	Comment
1821	R-G	
1822	A-Z	
1822	R-G	
1822	A-G	

2 reales, 0.9027 silver, 6.770 g.

Obverse: Large armored, laureated bust of Ferdinand VII facing right. Legend **FERDIN . VII . DEI . GRATIA . [date].** *Reverse:* Crowned coat of arms of Spain flanked by columns wrapped in ribbons reading **PLUS VLTRA**. Legend **. HISPAN . ET IND . REX . Z . 2R .** and assayer. *Diameter:* 27 mm. BW-72.4, KM-UL.

Date	Assayer	Comment
1815	A-G	
1816	A-G	
1817	A-G	
1818	A-G	
1818	A-G	Small draped bust
1819	A-G	Small armored bust

2 reales, 0.9027 silver, 6.770 g.

Obverse: Large, armored, laureated bust of Ferdinand VII facing right. Legend **FERDIN . VII . DEI . GRATIA . [date].** *Reverse:* Crowned coat of arms of Spain flanked by columns wrapped in ribbons reading **PLUS VLTRA**. Legend **. HISPAN . ET IND . REX . Z . 2R .** and assayer. *Diameter:* 27 mm. BW-72.5, KM-92.1.

Date	Assayer	Comment
1813	A-G	

2 reales, 0.9027 silver, 6.770 g.

Obverse: Draped, laureated bust of Ferdinand VII facing right. Legend **FERDIN . VII . DEI . GRATIA . [date] .** *Reverse:* Crowned coat of arms of Spain flanked by columns wrapped in ribbons reading **PLUS VLTRA**. Legend **. HISPAN . ET IND . REX . Z . 2R .** and assayer. *Diameter:* 27 mm. *Edge:* Corded. BW-72.6, KM-93.4.

Date	Assayer	Comment
1819	A-G	
1819	A-G	S reversed in HISPAN
1820	A-G	
1820	R-G	
1821	A-G	
1821	A-Z/R-G	
1821	A-Z	
1821	R-G	
1822	A-Z	
1822	R-G	

2 reales, 0.9027 silver, 6.770 g.

Obverse: Small armored bust of Ferdinand VII facing right. Legend **FERDIN . VII . DEI . GRATIA . [date] .** *Reverse:* Crowned coat of arms of Spain flanked by columns wrapped in ribbons reading **PLUS VLTRA**. Legend **. HISPAN . ET IND . REX . Z . 2 R .** and assayer. *Diameter:* 27 mm. *Edge:* Corded. BW-72.7, KM-A92.

Date	Assayer	Comment
1819	A-G	

8 reales, 0.9027 silver, 27.070 g.

Obverse: Draped, laureated bust of Ferdinand VII facing right. Legend **FERDIN . VII . DEI GRATIA . [date] .** *Reverse:* Crowned coat of arms of Spain flanked by columns wrapped in ribbons reading **PLUS VLTRA**. Legend **. HISPAN . ET IND . REX . Z$**, denomination, and assayer. *Diameter:* 39 mm. *Edge:* Corded. BW-73.1, KM-111.5.

Date	Assayer	Comment
1813	F-P	
1813	A-G	
1814	A-G	
1814	A-G/F-P	
1815	A-G	
1816	A-G	
1817	A-G	
1818	A-G	
1819	A-G	
1819	A-G	GRATIA error
1820	A-G	
1820	R-G	
1821/81	R-G	
1821	R-G	
1821	A-Z/R-G	
1821	A-Z	
1822	R-G	
1822	A-Z	

8 reales, 0.9027 silver, 27.070 g.

Obverse: Draped, laureated bust of Ferdinand VII facing right. Legend **FERDIN . VII . DEI . GRATIA . [date].** *Reverse:* Crowned coat of arms of Spain flanked by columns wrapped in ribbons reading **PLUS VLTRA**. Legend **. HISPAN . ET IND . REX . Z . 8R .** Several varieties exist of the 8 reales Ferdinand VII Draped Bust–type coins. *Diameter:* 39 mm. *Edge:* Corded. BW-72.9, KM-111.6.

Date	Comment
1813	

Royalist Counterstamped Coinage

LCM: La Comandancia Militar

A rectangular counterstamp reading **LCM** was issued in various sizes from 8 mm to 21 mm. Without documentation, the meaning of LCM is unknown, but it may be "Las Cajas Militar" or "La Comandancia Militar."

2 reales, silver.

LCM counterstamp on 1809-M̊, T-H 2 reales (KM-92). BW-74.1, KM-193.1.

Date	Comment
1809	

2 reales, silver.

LCM counterstamp on 1811-M̊ 2 reales (KM-92). BW-74.1a, KM-193.2.

Date	Comment
1811	

8 reales, cast silver.

LCM counterstamp on Chihuahua 8 reales (KM-123). BW-75.1, KM-194.1.

Date	Comment
1811	Rare
1812	

8 reales, silver.

LCM counterstamp on Chihuahua 8 reales (KM-111.1), struck over KM-123. BW-75.2, KM-194.2.

Date	Comment
1815	
1817	
1820	
1821	

8 reales, silver.

LCM counterstamp on Durango 8 reales (KM-111.2). BW-75.3, KM-194.3.

Date	Comment
1812	
1821	

8 reales, silver.

LCM counterstamp on Guadalajara 8 reales (KM-111.3). BW-75.4, KM-194.4.

Date	Comment
1813	

8 reales, silver.

LCM counterstamp on Guanajuato 8 reales (KM-111.4). BW-75.5, KM-194.5.

Date	Comment
1813	

8 reales, silver.

LCM counterstamp on Nueva Vizcaya 8 reales (KM-165). BW-75.6, KM-194.6.

Date	Comment
1813	

8 reales, silver.

LCM counterstamp on Mexico 8 reales (KM-111). BW-75.7, KM-194.7.

Date	Comment
1811	
1812	
1817	
1818	
1820	

8 reales, silver.

LCM counterstamp on Sombrerete 8 reales (KM-176). BW-75.8, KM-194.8.

Date	Comment
1811	Rare
1812	

8 reales, silver.

LCM counterstamp on Zacatecas 8 reales (KM-190). BW-75.9, KM-194.9.

Date	Comment
1811	

8 reales, silver.

LCM counterstamp on Zacatecas 8 reales (KM-111.5). BW-75.10, KM-194.10.

Date	Comment
1813	
1814	
1822	

LCV: Las Cajas de Veracruz

The stamp **LCV** may indicate the royal treasury of the city of Veracruz. In 1812 the Royalist government was concerned that some of the coins it had issued were underweight. The coins found to be underweight were counterstamped with their true value (7, 7-1/4, 7-1/2, or 7-3/4 reales), with the stamp LCV alone indicating the full-weight value of 8 reales. Most of the underweight issues are believed to have been circulating counterfeits.

7 reales, silver.

LCV underweight counterstamp. BW-76, KM-195.

Date	Comment
No date	

7-1/4 reales, silver.

LCV underweight counterstamp. BW-77, KM-196.

Date	Comment
No date	Rare

7-1/2 reales, silver.

LCV underweight counterstamp. BW-78, KM-197.

Date	Comment
No date	Rare

7-3/4 reales, silver.

LCV underweight counterstamp. BW-79, KM-198.

Date	Comment
No date	Rare

8 reales, cast silver.

LCV counterstamp on 1811 Chihuahua RP 8 reales (KM-123). BW-80.1, KM-A198.

Date	Comment
1811	Rare

8 reales, silver.

LCV counterstamp on Zacatecas 8 reales (KM-191). BW-80.2, KM-199.

Date	Comment
1811	
1812	

MS (Monogram): Manuel Salcedo

General Manuel María de Salcedo was reportedly the Royalist governor of the province of Texas from 1810 to 1813. The **MS** counterstamp is said to have been placed on colonial coinage to validate its usage in Texas.

8 reales, 0.8960 silver.

MS counterstamp on Mexico 8 reales (KM-110). BW-81, KM-200.

Date	Comment
1809	
1810	
1811	

MVA: Monclova

Royalist counterstamp from Monclova, now in the state of Coahuila.

8 reales, cast silver.

MVA counterstamp on cast Mexico 8 reales (KM-110). BW-82.1, KM-202.3.

Date	Comment
1809	
1809	
1810	

8 reales, cast silver.

MVA 1812 counterstamp on Chihuahua 8 reales (KM-111.1) struck over Mexico KM-110. BW-82.2, KM-201.

Date	Comment
1809	
1816	
1821	

8 reales, silver.

MVA 1811 counterstamp on Zacatecas 8 reales (KM-189). BW-82.3, KM-202.5.

Date	Comment
1813	

8 reales, silver.

MVA 1812 counterstamp on Chihuahua 8 reales (KM-111.1) struck over cast Mexico KM-109. BW-82.4, KM-202.1.

Date	Comment
1810	

8 reales, cast silver.

MVA 1812 counterstamp on cast Mexico 8 reales (KM-109). BW-82.5, KM-202.2.

Date	Comment
1798	
1802	

INSURGENT COINAGE

Nueva Galicia

The provinces of Zacatecas and Jalisco were combined in 1531 to form the province of Nueva Galicia. The title of Nueva Galicia, which had lapsed in 1824, was revived during the War of Independence; it is now the state of Jalisco. No decrees or authorizations for this coin are currently known.

2 reales, silver.

Obverse: N.G. in center; legend + MONEDA PROVICIONAL 1813. *Reverse:* denomination in center; legend + SVPREMA . JVNTA . NACIONAL . *Diameter:* 28 mm. BW-89, KM-218.

Date	Comment
1813	Struck counterfeits exist

Oaxaca

Oaxaca was the center of the Insurgent movement under General José María Teclo Morelos y Pavón. The SUD (Spanish for "south") coinage issued from July 1811 to October 1814 was crudely prepared under adverse conditions. Most of the coins were made of copper, with the expectation that they could be redeemed in gold and silver when they became available. It is said some were issued in silver, but most silver specimens are suspect, as are the cast copper pieces. All cast copper coins with cast counterstamps are of a later period.

There are two main types and numerous varieties that have a plain field and grapevine design. The descriptive term "floriated," used in many instances, is incorrect; there are no flowers in the design, only stylized leaves and grapes.

There are several varieties of the bow-and-arrow monograms of Morelos, and we have listed a select number here.

1/2 real, struck copper.

Obverse: Bow and arrow, SUD. *Reverse:* Morelos monogram Mo, denomination, and date. Uniface issues exist. *Diameter:* 16 mm. BW-90.1, KM-219.

Date	Comment
1811	
1812	
1813	
1814	

1/2 real, struck silver.

Obverse: Bow and arrow, SUD. *Reverse:* Morelos monogram Mo, denomination, °M (for *medio*, or 1/2 real), and date. *Diameter:* 16 mm. BW-90.2, KM-220.1.

Date	Comment
1811	
1812	
1813	

1 real, struck copper.

Obverse: Bow and arrow, SUD . *Reverse:* Morelos monogram Mo, denomination . 1 R ., and date. *Diameter:* 16 mm. BW-91.1, KM-222.

Date	Comment
1811	
1812	
1813	

1 real, struck silver.

Obverse: Bow and arrow, SUD . *Reverse:* Morelos monogram Mo, denomination . 1R ., and date. *Diameter:* 20 mm. BW-91.2, KM-222a.

Date	Comment
1812	
1813	

1 real, cast silver.

Obverse: Bow and arrow, SUD . *Reverse:* Morelos monogram ℳ, denomination . 1R ., and date. Many cast silver coins may be questionable. *Diameter:* 20 mm. BW-91.3, KM-223.

Date	Comment
1812	
1813	

2 reales, struck copper.

Obverse: Bow and arrow, SUD. *Reverse:* Morelos monogram ℳ, denomination . 2 . R ., and date. *Diameter:* 26 mm. BW-92.1, KM-226.1.

Date	Comment
1811	
1811	Inverted 2
1812	
1813	
1814	

2 reales, struck silver.

Obverse: Bow and arrow, SUD. *Reverse:* Morelos monogram ℳ, denomination . 2 . R ., and date. *Diameter:* 27 mm. BW-92.2, KM-226.1a.

Date	Comment
1812	

2 reales, cast silver, ornamented fields.

Obverse: Bow and arrow, SUD. *Reverse:* Morelos monogram ℳ, denomination . 2 . R ., and date. *Diameter:* 27 mm. BW-92.3, KM-229.

Date	Comment
1812	Filled D in SUD

2 reales, struck silver, ornamented fields.

Obverse: Bow and arrow, SUD-OXA. *Reverse:* Morelos monogram ℳ, denomination . 2 . R ., and date. *Diameter:* 26 mm. BW-92.4, KM-227.

Date	Comment
1813	
1814	

2 reales, struck silver.

Obverse: Bow and arrow, SUD. OAXACA. Three large stars in field. *Reverse:* Morelos monogram ℳ, denomination . 2 . R ., and date. *Diameter:* 26 mm. BW-92.6, KM-226.2.

Date	Comment
1814	

2 reales, struck silver.

Obverse: Bow and arrow, SUD., three stars. *Reverse:* Morelos monogram ℳ, denomination . 2 . R ., and date. *Diameter:* 26 mm. BW-92.6, KM-226.2.

Date	Comment
1814	

8 reales, copper, ornamented fields.

Obverse: Bow and arrow, SUD. *Reverse:* Morelos monogram ℳ, denomination . 8 . R ., and date. *Diameter:* 38 mm. BW-93.1, KM-234.

Date	Comment
1811	
1812	
1813	
1814	

8 reales, cast silver, ornamented fields.

Obverse: Bow and arrow, SUD. *Reverse:* Morelos monogram ℳ, denomination . 8 . R ., and date. Some silver coins may be questionable. *Diameter:* 38 mm. BW-93.2, KM-235.

Date	Comment
1811	
1812	
1813	
1814	

8 reales, struck silver, ornamented fields.

Obverse: Bow and arrow, SUD. *Reverse:* Morelos monogram ℳ, denomination . 8 . R ., and date. *Diameter:* 38 mm. BW-93.3, KM-234a.

Date	Comment
1811	
1812	

8 reales, silver, plain fields.

Obverse: Bow and arrow, **. OAXACA .** above bow, eight dots under bow, **.SUD.** below bow. *Reverse:* Morelos monogram Mo, denomination **. 8 . R .**, and date. *Diameter:* 38 mm. BW-93.4, KM-233.5a.

Date	Comment
1812	

8 reales, copper.

Obverse: Bow and arrow, **.SUD.** *Reverse:* Morelos monogram Mo, denomination **. 8 . R .**, and date. *Diameter:* 38 mm. BW-93.5, KM-233.1.

Date	Comment
1812	

8 reales, copper, plain fields.

Obverse: Bow and arrow, **SUD.** *Reverse:* Morelos monogram Mo, denomination **. 8 . R .**, and date. Lines below bow slant left. *Diameter:* 38 mm. BW-93.6, KM-233.2.

Date	Comment
1812	
1813	
1814	

8 reales, struck silver, plain fields.

Obverse: Bow and arrow, **SUD.** *Reverse:* Morelos monogram Mo, denomination **. 8 . R .**, and date. *Diameter:* 37 mm. BW-93.7, KM-233.1a.

Date	Comment
1812	

8 reales, copper, plain fields.

Obverse: Bow and arrow, **SUD.** *Reverse:* Morelos monogram Mo, denomination **. 8 . R .**, and date. Lines below bow slant left. *Diameter:* 38 mm. BW-93.8, KM-233.3.

Date	Comment
1813	

8 reales, sterling silver.

Obverse: Morelos monogram Mo, denomination **. 8 . R .**, and date. *Reverse:* Lion shield with or without bow above. *Diameter:* 38 mm. BW-93.9, KM-237.

Date	Comment
1813	Rare

8 reales, copper, plain fields.

Obverse: Bow and arrow, **SUD.** *Reverse:* Morelos monogram Mo, denomination **. 8 . R .**, and date. Lines below bow slant right. *Diameter:* 38 mm. BW-93.10, KM-233.4.

Date	Comment
1813	

8 reales, cast silver.

Obverse: Bow and arrow, **SUD-OXA**. *Reverse:* Morelos monogram Mo, denomination **. 8 . R .**, and date. *Diameter:* 38 mm. BW-93.11, KM-239.

Date	Comment
1814	Rare

8 reales, copper.

Obverse: Bow and arrow, **SUD-OXA**. *Reverse:* Morelos monogram Mo, denomination **. 8 . R .**, and date. *Diameter:* 38 mm. BW-93.12, KM-240.

Date	Comment
1814	Rare

8 reales, copper.

Obverse: Bow and arrow, **SUD-OAXACA**. *Reverse:* Morelos monogram Mo, denomination **. 8 . R .**, and date. *Diameter:* 38 mm. BW-93.13, KM-241.

Date	Comment
1814	Rare

America Morelos

1/2 real, struck silver.

Obverse: Bow and arrow, legend **PROVI CIONAL DE OAXACA**. *Reverse:* On a plain field, a rampant lion to left, legend **AMER ICA MORELOS .**, and **. [date] .** *Diameter:* 16 mm. BW-90.3, KM-221.

Date	Comment
1812	
1813	

1/2 real, struck copper.

Obverse: Bow and arrow, legend **PROVI CIONAL DE OAXACA**. *Reverse:* On a plain field, a rampant lion to left, legend **AMER ICA MORELOS .**, and **. [date] .** *Diameter:* 16 mm. BW-90.4, KM-221a.

Date	Comment
1812	
1813	

1/2 real, struck copper.

Obverse: Bow and arrow, legend PROVI CIONAL DE OAXACA. *Reverse:* On a plain field, a rampant lion to left, denomination to left of lion, legend AMERICA MORELOS ., and . [date] . *Diameter:* 16 mm. BW-90.5, KM-A222.

Date	Comment
1813	

1 real, struck copper.

Obverse: Bow and arrow, SUD. *Reverse:* On a plain field, a rampant lion to left, denomination to left of lion, legend AMERICA MORELOS, and . . . [date] . . . *Diameter:* 20 mm. BW-91.5, KM-224.

Date	Comment
1813	

1 real, struck silver.

Obverse: Bow and arrow, SUD. *Reverse:* On a plain field, a rampant lion to left, denomination to left of lion, legend AMERICA MORELOS, and . . . [date] . . . *Diameter:* 20 mm. BW-91.6, KM-225.

Date	Comment
1813	Rare

2 reales, struck copper.

Obverse: Bow and arrow, T.C. SUD. *Reverse:* On a plain field, a rampant lion to left, denomination to left of lion, legend AMERICA MORELOS, and . [date] . *Diameter:* 25 mm. BW-92.7, KM-246.

Date	Comment
1814	

8 reales, struck silver.

Obverse: Morelos monogram, legend SUD. PROV. DE OAXACA, and date. *Reverse:* Lion shield with or without bow above. *Diameter:* 38 mm. BW-93.14, KM-236.

Date	Comment
1812	Rare

8 reales, cast silver.

Obverse: Shield with eight St. Andrew's crosses on its borders and a rampant lion to right; shield divides denomination. *Reverse:* On a plain field, Morelos monogram, legend PROV. DE OAXACA, and date. *Diameter:* 40 mm. BW-93.15, KM-UL.

Date	Comment
1813	Rare

Morelos T.C. (Tierra Caliente, or "Hot Country")

1/2 real, struck copper.

Obverse: Bow and arrow, .T.C.SUD. *Reverse:* Morelos monogram Mo, denomination . $\overset{\circ}{M}$. (for *medio*, or 1/2 real), and date. *Diameter:* 17 mm. BW-90.6, KM-243.

Date	Comment
1813	

1 real, struck copper.

Obverse: Bow and arrow, .T.C. SUD. *Reverse:* Morelos monogram Mo, denomination, and date. *Diameter:* 20 mm. BW-91.7, KM-244.

Date	Comment
1813	

2 reales, struck copper.

Obverse: Bow and arrow, *T* C*, and . SUD. *Reverse:* Morelos monogram Mo, denomination, and date. *Diameter:* 26 mm. BW-92.7a, KM-245.

Date	Comment
1813	

8 reales, struck copper.

Obverse: Bow and arrow, *T*C*, and *SUD*. *Reverse:* Morelos monogram Mo, denomination, and *[date]*. *Diameter:* 40 mm. BW-93.16, KM-248.

Date	Comment
1813	

8 reales, cast silver.

Obverse: Bow and arrow, * T*C*, and *SUD*. *Reverse:* Morelos monogram Mo, denomination, and *[date]*. *Diameter:* 39 mm. BW-93.17, KM-249.

Date	Comment
1813	

Morelos, Huautla

8 reales, copper.

Obverse: On a plain field, bow and arrow, SUD, and the legend MONEDA PROVI . CIONAL PS . ES . *Reverse:* On a plain field, Morelos monogram Mo, denomination, date, and legend FABRICADO EN HUAUTLA. *Diameter:* 38 mm. BW-93.18, KM-242.

Date	Comment
1812	
1813	

Zacatlán, Puebla, General Osorno

The script monogram of General José Francisco Osorno is shown on the 1813 1 real illustrated under "Insurgent Coinage" on page 115.

1/2 real, copper.

Obverse: General Osorno's monogram, Zacatlan, and date. *Reverse:* Crossed arrows within a wreath below denomination MEDIO. *Diameter:* 15 mm. BW-94.1, KM-250.

Date	Comment
1813	Rare

1 real, copper.

Obverse: General Osorno's monogram, ZACATLAN, and date. *Reverse:* Crossed arrows within wreath; denomination 1. REAL. *Diameter:* 20 mm. BW-95.1, KM-251.

Date	Comment
1813	Rare

2 reales, copper.

Obverse: General Osorno's monogram, ZACATLAN, and date. *Reverse:* Crossed arrows within a wreath; denomination 2.R. *Diameter:* 23 mm. BW-96.1, KM-252.

Date	Comment
1813	

Zongolica, Veracrúz

Two priests and a lawyer in Zongolica (located in the province of Veracrúz) wanted to join the fight for independence by raising an army. Since they were isolated from other Insurgent forces, they decided to issue their own coinage in 1/2, 1, 2, 4, and 8 reales, but only the 2- and 8-reales coins are known at this time.

2 reales, silver.

Obverse: Bow and arrow, legend VIVA FERNANDO VII Y AMERICA. *Reverse:* Crossed palm frond and sword, legend ZONGOLICA, denomination, and date. *Diameter:* 25 mm. BW-97.1, KM-253.

Date	Comment
1812	

4 reales, silver.

Obverse: Bow and arrow, legend VIVA FERNANDO VII Y AMERICA. *Reverse:* Crossed palm frond and sword, legend SONGOLICA, denomination, and date. *Diameter:* 38 mm. BW-98.1, KM-UL.

Date	Comment
1812	Unconfirmed

8 reales, silver.

Obverse: Bow and arrow, legend VIVA FERNANDO VII Y AMERICA. *Reverse:* Crossed palm frond and sword, legend SONGOLICA, denomination, and date. *Diameter:* 38 mm. BW-98.2, KM-255.

Date	Comment
(1813)	

American Congress

1 real, silver.

Obverse: Eagle with outspread wings on nopal cactus, denomination split by eagle, and legend CONGRESO AMERICANO. *Reverse:* Legend F. 7. in script on a crowned open cloak; DEPOSIT . D . L . AUCTORID . D . around circumference. *Diameter:* 20 mm. BW-83.1, KM-216.

Date	Comment
(1813)	

1 real, silver.

Obverse: Eagle with outspread wings on nopal cactus, denomination split by eagle, and legend **CONGR . AMER .** *Reverse:* Legend **F. 7 .** in script on a crowned open cloak; **DEPOS . D . L . AUT. D.** around circumference. *Diameter:* 20 mm. BW-83.2, KM-217.

Date	Comment
(1813)	

2 reales, silver.

Obverse: Eagle with outspread wings on nopal cactus, denomination split by eagle, and legend **CONGRESO AMERICANO.** *Reverse:* Legend **F. 7 .** in script on a crowned open cloak; **DEPOSIT . D . L . AUT. D .** around circumference. *Diameter:* 28 mm. BW-83.1a, KM-UL.

Date	Comment
(1813)	

National Congress

1/2 real, struck copper.

Obverse: Eagle with outspread wings on nopal cactus growing from a small, three-arch bridge. Legend **VICE . FERD . VII . DEI . GRATIA . ET . [date] .** *Reverse:* Below a hand holding a bow and arrow, a crossed halberd with a quiver and arrows; below that, a sling. Legend **S. P. CONG . NAT . IND . GUV . T . S . M .** No denomination. *Diameter:* 18 mm. BW-84.1, KM-209.

Date	Comment
1812	
1813	

1/2 real, struck, 0.9030 silver.

Obverse: Eagle with outspread wings on nopal cactus growing from a small, three-arch bridge. Legend **VICE . FERD . VII . DEI . GRATIA . ET . [date] .** *Reverse:* Below a hand holding a bow and arrow, a crossed halberd with a quiver and arrows; below that, a sling. Legend **S . P .CONG . NAT . IND . GUV . T . S . M .** No denomination. *Diameter:* 17 mm. BW-84.2, KM-210.

Date	Comment
1812	With date reading inward or outward
1813	

1 real, struck, 0.9030 silver.

Obverse: Eagle with outspread wings on nopal cactus growing from a small, three-arch bridge. Legend **VICE . FERD . VII . DEI . GRATIA . ET . [date] .** *Reverse:* Below a hand holding a bow and arrow, a crossed halberd with a quiver and arrows; below that, a sling. Legend **S. P. CONG . NAT . IND . GUV . T . 1R . S . M .** around. *Diameter:* 21 mm. BW-85.1, KM-211.

Date	Comment
1812	With date reading inward or outward
1813	

2 reales, cast copper.

Obverse: Eagle with outspread wings on nopal cactus growing from a small, three-arch bridge. Legend **VICE . FERD . VII . DEI . GRATIA . [date] .** *Reverse:* Below a hand holding a bow and arrow, a crossed halberd with a quiver and arrows; below that, a sling. Legend **+ S. P. CONG . NAT . IND . GUV . T . 2R . S . M .** around. *Diameter:* 28 mm. BW-86.1, KM-212.

Date	Comment
1812	
1813	
1814	

2 reales, struck silver.

Obverse: Eagle with outspread wings on nopal cactus growing from a small, three-arch bridge. Legend **VICE . FERD . VII . DEI . GRATIA . ET . [date] .** *Reverse:* Below a hand holding a bow and arrow, a crossed halberd with a quiver and arrows; below that, a sling. Legend **+ S. P. CONG . NAT . IND . GUV . T . 2R . S . M .** around. It is believed that these dies were intended to be used to strike a 2-escudo gold coin. *Diameter:* 28 mm. BW-86.2, KM-A213.

Date	Comment
1812	

4 reales, struck silver.

Obverse: Eagle facing front with outspread wings on nopal cactus growing from a small, three-arch bridge. Legend **VICE . FERD . VII . DEI . GRATIA . ET . [date] .** *Reverse:* Below a hand holding a bow and arrow, a crossed halberd with a quiver and arrows; below that, a sling. Legend **+ S. P. CONG . NAT . IND . GUV . T . 4R . S . M .** around. *Diameter:* 35 mm. BW-87.1, KM-214.

Date	Comment
1813	

8 reales, struck silver.

Obverse: Small eagle with outspread wings on nopal cactus growing from a small, three-arch bridge. Legend **VICE . FERD . VII . DEI . GRATIA . ET . [date] .** *Reverse:* Below a hand holding a bow and arrow, a crossed halberd with a quiver and arrows; below that, a sling. Legend **+ S. P. CONG . NAT . IND . GUV . T . 8R. S . M .** around. *Diameter:* 40 mm. BW-88.1, KM-215.1.

Date	Comment
1812	

8 reales, struck silver.

Obverse: Large eagle with outspread wings on nopal cactus growing from a small, three-arch bridge. Legend **VICE . FERD . VII . DEI . GRATIA . ET . [date] .** *Reverse:* Below a hand holding a bow and arrow, a crossed halberd with a quiver and arrows; below that, a sling. Legend **+ S. P. CONG . IND . GUV . T . 8R . S . M .** around. *Diameter:* 40 mm. BW-88.2, KM-215.2.

Date	Comment
1813	

Supreme National Congress of America (Suprema Junta de América)

On August 19, 1811, in the village of Zitácuaro in Michoacán, Ignacio López Rayón announced the formation of the first independent government of Mexico, the Supreme National Congress of America. López Rayón was president; the other two original members were José Sixto Verduzco and José María Liceaga. José Maria Morelos was named a member on June 13, 1812. This junta was supplanted by the Congress of Anáhuac in Chilpanzingo (modern spelling "Chilpancingo") on September 13, 1813.

1/2 real, struck silver.

Obverse: Eagle with outspread wings on nopal cactus growing from a small, three-arch bridge. Eagle divides denomination **M̊. R.** (*medio* real). *Reverse:* **Ame- rica** on two lines. *Diameter:* 17 mm. BW-150, KM-UL.

Date	Comment
No date	

1 real, struck silver.

Obverse: Eagle with outspread wings on nopal cactus growing from a small, three-arch bridge. Eagle divides denomination. Legend **. FERDIN . VII . DEI . GRA. . [date] .** *Reverse:* Below a hand holding a bow and arrow, a crossed halberd with a quiver and arrows; below that, a sling. Legend **+ PROV . POR LA S . JN. DE. AMERICA** around. *Diameter:* 20 mm. BW-151, KM-204.

Date	Comment
1812	

2 reales, copper.

Obverse: Eagle with outspread wings on nopal cactus growing from a small, three-arch bridge. Eagle divides denomination. Legend **FERDIN . VII . DEI . GRATIA . [date] .** *Reverse:* Below a hand holding a bow and arrow, a crossed halberd with a quiver and arrows; below that, a sling. Legend **+. PROUICIONAL . POR . LA . SUPREMA . JUNTA . D . AMERI:** around. (Note: **.D.** in legend is superimposed over capital E.) *Diameter:* 30 mm. BW-152, KM-205.

Date	Comment
1811	Copper
1812	Cast silver

8 reales, struck silver.

Obverse: Eagle with outspread wings on nopal cactus growing from a small, three-arch bridge. Eagle divides denomination. Legend FERDIN . VII . DEI . GRATIA . [date] . *Reverse:* Below a hand holding a bow and arrow, a crossed halberd with a quiver and arrows; below that, a sling. Legend +. PROUICIONAL . POR . LA . SUPREMA . JUNTA . DE . AMERICA around. *Diameter:* 35 mm. BW-153.1, KM-206.

Date	Comment
1811	
1812	

8 reales, cast silver.

Obverse: Eagle with outspread wings on nopal cactus growing from a small, three-arch bridge. Eagle divides denomination. Legend FERDIN. VII . DEI . GRATIA . [date] . *Reverse:* Below a hand holding a bow and arrow, a crossed halberd with a quiver and arrows; below that, a sling. Legend + PROUICIONAL . POR LA . SUPREMA . JUNTA . DE . AMERICA around. *Diameter:* 35 mm. BW-153.2, KM-207.

Date	Comment
1811	
1812	

8 reales, copper.

Obverse: Eagle with outspread wings on nopal cactus growing from a small three-arch bridge. Legend . FERDIN . VII . DEI . GRATIA . [date]. *Reverse:* Below a hand holding a bow and arrow, a crossed halberd with a quiver and arrows; below that, a sling. Eagle divides denomination. Legend + PROUICIONAL . POR . LA . SUPREMA . JUNTA . DE . AMERICA around. *Diameter:* 39 mm. BW-153.3, KM-208.

Date	Comment
1811	
1812	

Insurgent Counterstamped Coinage

Congress of Chilpanzingo

The Supreme National Congress of America was replaced by the Congress of Anáhuac, convened by José Maria Morelos at Chilpanzingo during the months of September, October, and November in 1813. The Congress signed a legal document formally declaring independence from Spain, while also drafting the first national constitution.

Counterstamp types for the Congress of Chilpanzingo coins are as follows:

> Type A. Hand holding a bow and arrow between a quiver with arrows, sword, and bow.
>
> Type B. Eagle on bridge.

Chilpanzingo counterstamp Type A.

Chilpanzingo counterstamp Type B.

1/2 real, silver.

Chilpanzingo counterstamp Type A, on 1812 Mexico City 1/2 real (KM-73). BW-99.1, KM-256.1.

Date	Comment
1812	

1/2 real, silver.

Chilpanzingo counterstamp Type A, on 1811 Zacatecas 1/2 real (KM-181). BW-99.1a, KM-256.2.

Date	Comment
1811	

1 real, cast silver.

Chilpanzingo counterstamp Type A, on 1803 Mexico City 1 real (KM-81). BW-99.2, KM-A257.

Date	Comment
1803	

2 reales, silver.

Chilpanzingo counterstamp Type B, on one-fourth cut of 8 reales. BW-100.1, KM-257.1.

Date	Comment
No date	Unique

2 reales, silver.

Chilpanzingo counterstamp Type B, on 1811 Zacatecas 2 reales (KM-186). BW-100.2, KM-257.2.

Date	Comment
1811	Unique

8 reales, silver.

Chilpanzingo counterstamp Type A, on 1805 TH Mexico City 8 reales (KM-109). BW-101.1, KM-258.1.

Date	Comment
1805	

8 reales, silver.

Chilpanzingo counterstamp Type A, on 1810 HJ Mexico City 8 reales (KM-110). BW-101.2, KM-258.2.

Date	Comment
1810	

8 reales, silver.

Chilpanzingo counterstamp Type A, on 1811 and 1812 HJ Mexico City 8 reales (KM-111). BW-101.3, KM-258.3.

Date	Comment
1811	
1812	

8 reales, silver.

Chilpanzingo counterstamp Type B, on 1816 RP Chihuahua 8 reales (KM-111.1). BW-101.04, KM-259.1.

Date	Comment
1816	

8 reales, silver.

Chilpanzingo counterstamp Type B, on 1811 HJ Mexico City 8 reales (KM-111). BW-101.5, KM-259.2.

Date	Comment
1811	

8 reales, silver.

Chilpanzingo counterstamp Type B, on 1813 Valladolid 8 reales (KM-178). BW-101.6, KM-259.3.

Date	Comment
1813	

8 reales, silver.

Chilpanzingo counterstamp Type B, on 1810 Zacatecas 8 reales (KM-190). BW-101.7, KM-259.4.

Date	Comment
1810	

Don José María Linares

The Insurgent counterstamp of LINA REV is thought to stand for Don José María Linares, but could possibly be Lt. Colonel Antonio Linares or San Felipe de Linares. The LINA RES counterstamp is in a 9 x 14 mm rectangle, bordered with dots.

8 reales, silver.

Counterstamp LINA RES on 1812 Mexico City JJ 8 reales (KM-110). BW-102.1, KM-263.1.

Date	Comment
1808	

8 reales, silver.

Counterstamp LINA RES on 1811 Zacatecas 8 reales (KM-190). BW-102.2, KM-263.2.

Date	Comment
1811	

8 reales, silver.

Counterstamp LINA RES on Zacatecas 8 reales (KM-191). BW-102.3, KM-263.3.

Date	Comment
1811	

General Vicente Guerrero

Insurgent hero General Vicente Guerrero was born in 1783, joined the Insurgent army in 1810 under Hermenegildo Galeana, and later was the protector of the Congress of Chilpanzingo. The counterstamp is an eagle facing left within a dotted oval.

1/2 real, silver.

Eagle counterstamped on Mexico City 1/2 real (KM-72). BW-119, KM-276.

Date	Comment
No date	

1 real, silver.

Eagle counterstamped on Mexico City 1 real (KM-78). BW-119.1, KM-277.

Date	Comment
1772	

2 reales, silver.

Eagle counterstamped on Mexico City 2 reales (KM-88). BW-120.1, KM-278.1.

Date	Comment
1784	
1798	

2 reales, silver.

Eagle counterstamped on Mexico City 2 reales (KM-91). BW-120.2, KM-278.2.

Date	Comment
1792	

8 reales, silver.

Eagle counterstamped on Zacatecas 8 reales (KM-191). BW-121.1, KM-279.

Date	Comment
1811	

ENSAIE

Coins assayed by the Insurgents' assayers were counterstamped with a 14 mm circular design of a continuous laurel wreath, with a front-facing eagle with outspread wings and head turned to the left. Below the eagle is the counterstamp ENSAIE and a sling.

8 reales, silver.

Eagle above ENSAIE counterstamped on Zacatecas 8 reales (KM-190). BW-103.1, KM-260.3.

Date	Comment
1810	
1811	

8 reales, silver.

Eagle above ENSAIE counterstamped on Zacatecas 8 reales (KM-191). BW-103.2, KM-260.4.

Date	Comment
1810	
1811	
1812	

8 reales, silver.

Eagle above ENSAIE counterstamped on Mexico City 8 reales (KM-110). BW-103.3, KM-260.1.

Date	Comment
1811	

8 reales, silver.

Eagle above ENSAIE counterstamped on Zacatecas 8 reales (KM-189). BW-103.4, KM-260.2.

Date	Comment
1811	

J.M.L. (José María Liceaga)

General José María Liceaga fortified and defended the island of Yuriria against 19 Royalist attacks between September 9 and October 31, 1812. The counterstamp is a 19 mm circle with a diagonal flagstaff and a flag with a cross. Above olive branches are the initials J.M.L. for José María Liceaga. Below for some unknown reason are the initials AP, Ds, E, PG, S, SF, SL, SM, SY, Sea, sra, V, and Ve.

1/2 real, silver.

J.M.L. counterstamped on cast Mexico City 1/2 real. Counterstamped J.M.L./S.M. on banner. BW-104, KM-A260.

Date	Comment
No date	

2 reales, silver.

J.M.L. counterstamped on Zacatecas 2 reales (KM-187). Counterstamped J.M.L./V. on banner within circle. BW-105.1, KM-261.6.

Date	Comment
1811	

2 reales, silver.

J.M.L. counterstamped on Zacatecas 2 reales (KM-187). **J.M.L./D.S.** initials on banner within circle. BW-105.2, KM-261.7.

Date	Comment
1811	

2 reales, silver.

J.M.L. counterstamped on Zacatecas 2 reales (KM-187). **J.M.L./S.M.** initials on banner within circle. BW-105.3, KM-261.8.

Date	Comment
1811	

2 reales, silver.

J.M.L. counterstamped on Zacatecas 2 reales (KM-187). Counterstamped **J.M.L./S.Y.** on banner within circle. BW-105.4, KM-261.9.

Date	Comment
1811	

2 reales, silver.

J.M.L. counterstamped on 1/4 real cut from Zacatecas 8 reales (KM-190). Counterstamped **J.M.L./Ve.** on banner within circle. BW-105.5, KM-261.1.

Date	Comment
No date	

2 reales, silver.

J.M.L. counterstamped on Zacatecas 2 reales (KM-187). Counterstamped **J.M.L./V.** on banner within circle. BW-105.6, KM-261.2.

Date	Comment
1811	

2 reales, silver.

J.M.L. counterstamped on Zacatecas 2 reales (KM-186). Counterstamped **J.M.L./DS.** on banner within circle. BW-105.7, KM-261.3.

Date	Comment
1811	

2 reales, silver.

J.M.L. counterstamped on Zacatecas 2 reales (KM-186). Counterstamped **J.M.L./S.M.** on banner within circle. BW-105.8, KM-261.4.

Date	Comment
1811	

2 reales, silver.

J.M.L. counterstamped on Zacatecas 2 reales (KM-186). Counterstamped **J.M.L./S.Y.** on banner within circle. BW-105.9, KM-261.5.

Date	Comment
1811	

8 reales, silver.

J.M.L. counterstamped on Zacatecas 8 reales (KM-190). Counterstamped **J.M.L./D.S.** on banner within circle. BW-106.1, KM-262.1.

Date	Comment
1811	

8 reales, silver.

J.M.L. counterstamped on Zacatecas 8 reales (KM-190). Counterstamped **J.M.L./S.F.** on banner within circle. BW-106.2, KM-262.4.

Date	Comment
1811	

8 reales, silver.

J.M.L. counterstamped on Zacatecas 8 reales (KM-190). Counterstamped **J.M.L./E.** on banner within circle. BW-106.3, KM-262.2.

Date	Comment
1811	

8 reales, silver.

J.M.L. counterstamped on Durango 8 reales (KM-111.2). **J.M.L./P.G.** BW-106.4, KM-262.3.

Date	Comment
1813	

8 reales, silver.

J.M.L. counterstamped on Zacatecas 8 reales (KM-190). Counterstamped **J.M.L./S.M.** within circle. BW-106.5, KM-262.5.

Date	Comment
1811	

8 reales, silver.

J.M.L. counterstamped on Zacatecas 8 reales (KM-190). **J.M.L./V. D.s., S.M., S.Y.S.L., Ve, A.P., s.r.a., Sea, P.G., S., S.M., E.** Counterstamped **J.M.L/S.M.** in circle. BW-106.6, KM-262.10.

Date	Comment
1811	

8 reales, silver.

J.M.L. counterstamped on Zacatecas 8 reales (KM-190). **J.M.L./V. D.s., S.M., S.Y.S.L., Ve, A.P., s.r.a., Sea, P.G., S., S.M., E.** Counterstamped **J.M.L/V.E.** in circle. BW-106.7, KM-262.11.

Date	Comment
1811	

8 reales, silver.

J.M.L. counterstamped on Zacatecas 8 reales (KM-190). Counterstamped **J.M.L./V.E.** within circle. BW-106.8, KM-262.6.

Date	Comment
1811	

8 reales, silver.

J.M.L. counterstamped on Guanajuato 8 reales (KM-111.4). Counterstamped **J.M.L./P.G.** within circle. BW-106.9, KM-262.12.

Date	Comment
1813	

8 reales, silver.

J.M.L. counterstamped on Zacatecas 8 reales (KM-190). **J.M.L./V., D.s., S.M., S.Y.S.L., Ve., A.P., s.r.a., Sea, P.G., S., S.M.E.** Counterstamped **J.M.L./D.S.** on banner, within circle. BW-106.10, KM-262.7.

Date	Comment
1811	

8 reales, silver.

J.M.L. counterstamped on Zacatecas 8 reales (KM-190). **J.M.L./V., D.s., S.M., S.Y.S.L., Ve., A.P., s.r.a., Sea, P.G., S., S.M., E.** Counterstamped **J.M.L./S.F.** BW-106.11, KM-262.9.

Date	Comment
1811	

8 reales, silver.

J.M.L. counterstamped on Zacatecas 8 reales (KM-190). **J.M.L./V., D.s., S.M., S.Y.S.L., Ve., A.P., s.r.a., Sea, P.G., S., S.M.E.** Counterstamped **J.M.L./V.E.** BW-106.12, KM-262.11.

Date	Comment
1811	

8 reales, silver.

J.M.L. counterstamped on Zacatecas 8 reales (KM-190). **J.M.L./V., D.s., S.M., S.Y.S.L., Ve., A.P., s.r.a., Sea, P.G., S., S.M.E.** Counterstamped **J.M.L./E.** BW-106.13, KM-262.8.

Date	Comment
1811	

L.V.S (Labor Vincit Semper)

The L.V.S. counterstamp is from an uncertain source. Some believe it stands for *Labor vincit semper* ("Work always conquers"), while others believe it to stand for "La Villa de Sombrerete." The counterstamp is a 7 x 11 mm rectangle bordered in dots, with **L.V.S.** within the rectangle.

8 reales, cast silver.

L.V.S. counterstamped on Chihuahua 8 reales (KM-123). BW-107.1, KM-264-1.

Date	Comment
1811	
1812	

8 reales, silver.

L.V.S. counterstamped on Chihuahua 8 reales (KM-111.1 overstruck on KM-123). BW-107.2, KM-264.2.

Date	Comment
1816	
1817	
1818	
1919	
182	

8 reales, silver.

L.V.S. counterstamped on Guadalajara 8 reales (KM-111.3). BW-107.3, KM-264.3.

Date	Comment
1817	

8 reales, silver.

L.V.S. counterstamped on Nueva Vizcaya 8 reales (KM-181). BW-107.4, KM-264.4.

Date	Comment
1811	

8 reales, silver.

L.V.S. counterstamped on Sombrerete 8 reales (KM-177). BW-107.5, KM-264.5.

Date	Comment
1811	
1812	

8 reales, silver.

L.V.S. counterstamped on Zacatecas 8 reales (KM-190). BW-107.6, KM-264.6.

Date	Comment
1811	

8 reales, silver.

L.V.S. counterstamped on Zacatecas 8 reales (KM-192). BW-107.7, KM-264.7.

Date	Comment
1813	

Morelos

The several styles of the Morelos counterstamp monogram are for José María Morelos y Pavón, who has been called the "Insurgent hero" and "caudillo of the Independence." His reputation as a military strategist after the famous Battle of Cuautla, along with his other military achievements, enabled the Insurgents to maintain the balance of power in their favor.

2 reales, copper.

Morelos monogram Mo, Type A, counterstamped on Oaxaca SUD (KM-226.1). BW-108, KM-A265.

Date	Comment
1812	

8 reales, silver.

Morelos monogram Mo, Type C, counterstamped on Zacatecas L.V.O. (KM-190). BW-109.1, KM-A267.

Date	Comment
1811	

8 reales, silver.

Morelos monogram Mo, Type A, counterstamped on Mexico City 8 reales (KM-109). BW-109.2, KM-265.1.

Date	Comment
1797	
1798	
1800	
1807	

8 reales, silver.

Morelos monogram Mo, Type A, counterstamped on Mexico City 8 reales (KM-110). BW-109.3, KM-265.2.

Date	Comment
1809	
1811	

8 reales, silver.

Morelos monogram Mo, Type B, counterstamped on Mexico City 8 reales (KM-111). BW-109.4, KM-265.3.

Date	Comment
1812	

8 reales, cast silver.

Morelos monogram Mo, Type A, counterstamped on Supreme National Congress 8 reales (KM-206). BW-109.5, KM-265.5.

Date	Comment
1811	

8 reales, silver.

Morelos monogram Mo, Type B, counterstamped on Guatemala 8 reales (C#67). BW-109.6, KM-266.1.

Date	Comment
1810	Rare

8 reales, silver.

Morelos monogram Mo, Type B, counterstamped on Mexico City 8 reales (KM-110). BW-109.7, KM-266.2.

Date	Comment
1809	

8 reales, silver.

Morelos monogram Mo, Type C, counterstamped on Zacatecas 8 reales (KM-189). BW-109.8, KM-267.1.

Date	Comment
1811	

8 reales, copper.

Morelos monogram Mo, Type A, counterstamped on Oaxaca SUD 8 reales (KM-233.2). BW-109.9, KM-265.4.

Date	Comment
1812	
1813	
1814	

8 reales, silver.

Morelos monogram Mo, Type A, counterstamped on Zacatecas 8 reales (KM-190). BW-109.10, KM-265.6.

Date	Comment
1811	

8 reales, silver.

Morelos monogram Mo, Type A, counterstamped on Zacatecas 8 reales (KM-191). BW-109.11, KM-265.7.

Date	Comment
1811	

8 reales, silver.

Morelos monogram Mo, Type C, counterstamped on Zacatecas 8 reales (KM-190). BW-109.12, KM-267.2.

Many available specimens with Type C Morelos monograms are considered spurious.

Date	Comment
1811	

Morelos Monograms

Type A: Stars above and below Mo monogram in circle.

Type B: Dots above and below Mo monogram.

Type C: Mo monogram in rectangle. Many specimens with Type C monograms available in the market are considered spurious.

Type D: Different style monogram, resembling the characters MLRos (somewhat overlapping).

NORTE

Ignacio López Rayón, Insurgent hero (as he was named by the Junta of Zitácuaro in 1811), was chief of the Insurgent Revolution and in charge of the Insurgent northern army after March 21, 1811.

The NORTE counterstamp issued by the Supreme National Congress and the Army of the North is 13 mm in diameter for the 1/2, 1, and 2 reales. The 8 reales is 18 mm. Within a rayed border is an eagle facing forward with outspread wings, perched on a nopal cactus; an eight-pointed star is to the left, and NORTE below.

1/2 real, silver.

NORTE counterstamped on Zacatecas 1/2 real (KM-180). BW-110, KM-268.

Date	Comment
1811	

2 reales, silver.

NORTE counterstamped on Zacatecas 2 reales (KM-187). BW-111.1, KM-269.

Date	Comment
1811	

2 reales, silver.

NORTE counterstamped on Zacatecas 2 reales (KM-188). BW-111.2, KM-A269.

Date	Comment
1812	

4 reales, silver.

NORTE counterstamped on Sombrerete 4 reales (KM-175). BW-112.1, KM-B269.

Date	Comment
1812	

8 reales, silver.

NORTE counterstamped on Zacatecas 8 reales (KM-191). BW-113.1, KM-270.4.

Date	Comment
1811	
1812	

8 reales, cast silver.

NORTE counterstamped on Chihuahua 8 reales (KM-111.1). BW-113.2, KM-270.1.

Date	Comment
1813	

8 reales, silver.

NORTE counterstamped on Guanajuato 8 reales (KM-111.4). BW-113.3, KM-270.2.

Date	Comment
1813	

8 reales, silver.

NORTE counterstamped on Zacatecas 8 reales (KM-190). BW-113.4, KM-270.3.

Date	Comment
1811	

NORTE and M. L. N.

The NORTE M. L. N. counterstamp of 15 mm is similar to the NORTE counterstamp, except for the following: it does not have a star in the field; on either side of the eagle, it has small, manlike figures; and below the eagle appear the letters M. L. N.

8 reales, silver.

NORTE M.L.N. counterstamped on Royalist 8 reales. BW-113.5, KM-UL.

Date	Comment
1811	

Osorno

The counterstamp of General José Francisco Osorno, at Zacatlán, Puebla, is a script monogram representing his last name (for an example, see the illustration of the 1813 Osorno 1 real on page 115). It measures 8 x 10 mm.

1/2 real, silver.

Osorno monogram counterstamped on Mexico City 1/2 real (KM-72). BW-114.1, KM-271.1.

Date	Comment
1798	
1802	
1806	

1/2 real, silver.

Osorno monogram counterstamped on Mexico City 1/2 real (KM-73). BW-114.2, KM-271.2.

Date	Comment
1809	

1 real, silver.

Osorno monogram counterstamped on Mexico City 1 real (KM-81). BW-115.1, KM-272.1.

Date	Comment
1803	

1 real, silver.

Osorno monogram counterstamped on Guatemala 1 real (KM-54). BW-115.2, KM-272.3.

Date	Comment
1804	

2 reales, silver.

Osorno monogram counterstamped on Mexico City 2 reales (KM-88.2a). BW-116.1a, KM-A272.1.

Date	Comment
1788	

2 reales, silver.

Osorno monogram counterstamped on Mexico City 2 reales (KM-91). BW-116.1, KM-A272.2.

Date	Comment
1808	

2 reales, silver.

Osorno monogram counterstamped on Mexico City 2 reales (KM-92). BW-116.2, KM-A272.3.

Date	Comment
1809	

2 reales, silver.

Osorno monogram counterstamped on Zacatlán 2 reales (KM-252). BW-116.3, KM-A272.4.

Date	Comment
1813	

4 reales, silver.

Osorno monogram counterstamped on Mexico City 4 reales (KM-97.2). BW-117.1, KM-273.1.

Date	Comment
1799	

4 reales, silver.

Osorno monogram counterstamped on Mexico City 4 reales (KM-100). BW-117.2, KM-273.2.

Date	Comment
1782	

8 reales, silver.

Osorno monogram counterstamped on Lima 8 reales (C#101). BW-118.1, KM-274.1.

Date	Comment
1811	

8 reales, silver.

Osorno monogram counterstamped on Mexico City 8 reales (KM-110). BW-118.2, KM-274.2.

Date	Comment
1809	
1810	
1811	

VILLA GRAN

Julián Villagrán was appointed to the rank of lieutenant general by the Supreme Government Council of America. He refused to obey the orders of the council, even going so far as to proclaim himself Julián I, emperor of Huasteca. He was captured by Royalist forces and on the orders of Viceroy Félix María Calleja del Rey was executed on June 21, 1813.

The round counterstamp is 13 mm in diameter, with VILLA GRAN (on two lines) placed within a border of dots.

2 reales, silver.

VILLA GRAN counterstamped on silver Mexico City 2 reales (KM-91). BW-125.1, KM-298.

Date	Comment
1799	
1802	

8 reales, silver.

VILLA GRAN counterstamped on silver Mexico City 8 reales (KM-109). BW-125.2, KM-275.

Date	Comment
1796	
1806	

ZMY

The origin of "ZMY" is unknown but is presumed to be Insurgent.

8 reales, silver.

ZMY counterstamped on Zacatecas 8 reales (KM-191). BW-122, KM-286.

Date	Comment
1812	

MULTIPLE COUNTERSTAMPS

Several coins bear combinations of both Insurgent and Royalist counterstamps. Most such combinations are found on cast coins from Chihuahua and Mexico City, as well as on some crude provisional issues. They were used to produce molds for casting the host coins and counterstamped by the faction that authorized them. Some were counterstamped later by other friendly forces or by opposing authorities to authorize usage in their area of operation.

S.C.M. AND C.M.S.

The initials "S.C.M." and "C.M.S." stand for "Comandancia Militar Suriana" and "Soberano Congreso Mexicano," respectively.

2 reales, silver.

Eagle with S.C.M. and C.M.S. counterstamped on Mexico City 2 reales (KM-91). BW-123, KM-289.

Date	Comment
No date	

S.C.M. AND M.d.S.

The initials "M.d.S." stand for "Militar del Sur."

2 reales, silver.

Eagle with S.C.M. and M.d.S. counterstamped on Mexico City 2 reales (KM-91). BW-124, KM-295.

Date	Comment
No date	

Osorno and VILLA GRAN

8 reales, cast silver.

Osorno monogram and VILLA GRAN counterstamped on Mexico City 2 reales (KM-110). BW-125, KM-296.

Date	Comment
1809	

8 reales, cast silver.

Osorno monogram and VILLA GRAN counterstamped on 1805 Mexico City 8 reales (KM-109). BW-125a, KM-275.

Date	Comment
1806	

J.M.L. and VTIL

2 reales, silver.

J.M.L./D.S. and VTIL counterstamped on Zacatecas 2 reales (KM-186). BW-126, KM-A286.

Date	Comment
1811	

2 reales, silver.

J.M.L./V.E. and VTIL counterstamped on Zacatecas 2 reales (KM-186). BW-127, KM-B286.

Date	Comment
1810	
1811	

Chilpanzingo and Morelos

8 reales, cast silver.

Chilpanzingo counterstamp Type A and Morelos monogram Type A on Mexico City cast 8 reales (KM-110). BW-129, KM-285.2.

Date	Comment
1810	
1811	

Chilpanzingo, L.V.S., and Morelos

8 reales, cast silver.

Chilpanzingo counterstamp Type A, L.V.S., and Morelos monogram Type A on cast Mexico City 8 reales (KM-110). BW-128, KM-C286.

Date	Comment
1809	

S.J.N.G. and VTIL

The abbreviation "S.J.N.G." stands for "Suprema Junta Nacional Gubernativa" (Supreme National Congress).

8 reales, silver.

S.J.N.G. and VTIL counterstamped on Zacatecas 8 reales (KM-190). BW-134, KM-A298.

Date	Comment
1811	

Chilpanzingo and ENSAIE

8 reales, silver.

Chilpanzingo counterstamp Type B and ENSAIE on Zacatecas 8 reales (KM-189). BW-130, KM-A297.

Date	Comment
1810	
1811	

Chilpanzingo and L.V.A.

8 reales, silver.

Chilpanzingo counterstamp Type A and L.V.A. on Mexico City 8 reales (KM-109). BW-131, KM-297.

Date	Comment
1805	

Chilpanzingo and LVS

8 reales, silver.

Chilpanzingo counterstamp Type A and LVS on Mexico City 8 reales (KM-110). BW-133, KM-281.

Date	Comment
1809	

Chilpanzingo and S.J.N.G.

8 reales, silver.

Chilpanzingo counterstamp Type B and S.J.N.G. on Zacatecas 8 reales (KM-190). BW-134.1, KM-288.2.

Date	Comment
1809	

8 reales, silver.

Chilpanzingo counterstamp Type B, **J.M.L.**, and **S.J.N.G.** on Zacatecas 8 reales (KM-191). BW-134.3, KM-UL.

Date	Comment
1811	

8 reales, silver.

Chilpanzingo counterstamp Type B and **S.J.N.G.** on Zacatecas 8 reales (KM-189). BW-134.2, KM-288.1.

Date	Comment
1811	

ENSAIE and VTIL

8 reales, silver.

ENSAIE and **VTIL** counterstamped on Zacatecas 8 reales (KM-189). BW-144, KM-290.1.

Date	Comment
1811	

8 reales, silver.

ENSAIE and **VTIL** counterstamped on Zacatecas 8 reales (KM-190). BW-135, KM-290.2.

Date	Comment
1811	

J.M.L. and VTIL

8 reales, silver.

J.M.L./D.S. and **VTIL** counterstamped on Mexico City 8 reales (KM-110). BW-136, KM-291.

Date	Comment
1810	

L.C.M. and Morelos

8 reales, cast silver.

L.C.M. and Morelos monogram Type A counterstamped on Mexico City 8 reales (KM-109). BW-137, KM-282.

Date	Comment
1792	

Morelos

8 reales, cast silver.

Morelos monogram Types A and C counterstamped on Mexico City 8 reales (KM-109). BW-138, KM-283.

Date	Comment
1805	

Morelos and Chilpanzingo

8 reales, cast silver.

Morelos monogram Type A and Chilpanzingo counterstamp Type A on Mexico City 8 reales (KM-109). BW-139, KM-284.

Date	Comment
1806	
1807	

8 reales, silver.

Morelos monogram Type A and Chilpanzingo counterstamp Type A on Mexico City 8 reales (KM-110). BW-139.1, KM-285.1.

Date	Comment
1809	

8 reales, cast silver.

Morelos monogram Type A and Chilpanzingo counterstamp Type A on Mexico City 8 reales (KM-111). BW-139.2, KM-285.3.

Date	Comment
1811	

ENSAIE and JML

8 reales, silver.

ENSAIE and **JML** counterstamped on Zacatecas **L.V.O.** 8 reales (KM-190). BW-140, KM-A290.

Date	Comment
1811	

LVS and MVA./1811.

8 reales, silver.

LVS and **MVA./1811.** counterstamped on 1817 Chihuahua 8 reales (KM-111.1). BW-140.1, KM-UL.

Date	Comment
1817	

Morelos and LVA

8 reales, cast silver.

Morelos monogram Type A and script LVA counterstamped on Mexico City 8 reales (KM-110). BW-141, KM-294.

Date	Comment
No date	

Chilpanzingo with Crown and Flag

8 reales, silver.

Chilpanzingo counterstamp Type B and circled image of crown surmounting a flag on Zacatecas 8 reales (KM-189). BW-142, KM-280.1.

Date	Comment
1811	

8 reales, silver.

Chilpanzingo counterstamp Type B and circled image of crown surmounting a flag on Zacatecas 8 reales (KM-190). BW-142.2, KM-280.2.

Date	Comment
1811	

Chilpanzingo and P.D.V.

The abbreviation "P.D.V." stands for "Provisional de Valladolid."

8 reales, silver.

Chilpanzingo counterstamp Type B and P.D.V. on Valladolid 8 reales (KM-179). BW-145, KM-287.

Date	Comment
1811	

War of Independence
ROYALIST COINAGE

Chihuahua. 8 reales, 1811. BW-41.1, KM-123, 39 mm.

Durango. 8 reales, 1820. BW-47.2, KM-111.2, 39 mm.

Guadalajara. 8 reales, 1822. BW-52, KM-111.3, 39 mm.

War of Independence—ROYALIST COINAGE
(continued)

Guanajuato.
8 reales, 1813.
BW-56,
KM-111.4,
39 mm.

Nueva
Vizcaya.
8 reales, 1811.
BW-57,
KM-181,
39 mm.

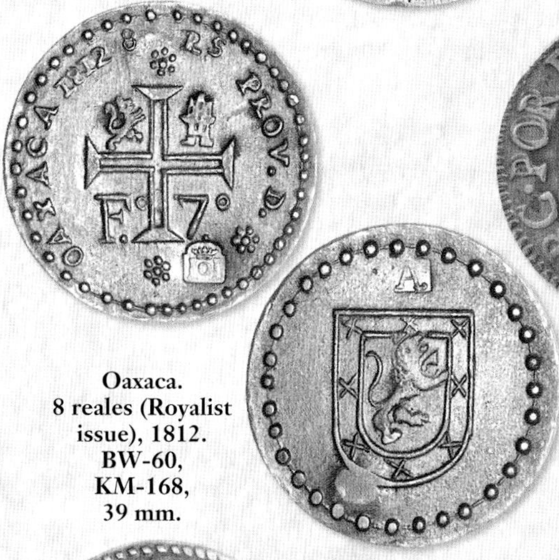

Oaxaca.
8 reales (Royalist
issue), 1812.
BW-60,
KM-168,
39 mm.

Real de
Catorce.
8 reales, 1811.
BW-61,
KM-169,
39 mm.

Sombrerete
under Royalist
VAARGAS (error).
8 reales, 1812.
BW-68,
KM-177,
39 mm.

Valladolid.
8 reales, 1813.
BW-69,
KM-178.
39 mm.

War of Independence
ROYALIST COINAGE *(continued)*

San Fernándo de Bexar (San Antonio, Texas). 1/2 real, 1818. BW-62.1, KM-Tn1 (KM-170), 16 mm.

Zacatecas Moneda Provisional. 8 reales, 1811. BW-73, KM-189, 39 mm.

Zacatecas post–Moneda Provisional. 8 reales, 1819. BW-73, KM-111.5, 39 mm.

ROYALIST COUNTERSTAMPED COINAGE

Not all counterstamped issues or varieties are listed in this volume, but verifiable issues will be listed and shown where possible in volume 3.

(No date) 8 reales, LCM counterstamp on Sombrerete 8 reales (KM-176). BW-75, KM-194.8, 39 mm.

1810 LCV and 7-3/4 reales counterstamps on $\overset{\circ}{\text{M}}$ 8 reales (KM-110). BW-79, KM-198, 39 mm.

War of Independence
INSURGENT COINAGE

Nueva Galicia. 2 reales, 1812.
BW-89, KM-218, 28 mm.

Oaxaca. 2 reales, 1814.
BW-92.6, KM-226.2, 28 mm.

Oaxaca. 8 reales (silver), 1811. BW-93, KM-235, 38 mm.

Zacatlán, Puebla. General Osorno
1 real, 1813. BW-95, KM-251, 20 mm.

American Congress. 2 reales, 1813.
BW-83, KM-UL, 28 mm.

National Congress. 2 reales (silver), 1814.
BW-86.2, KM-A213, 28 mm.

Supreme
National
Congress.
8 reales (silver),
1811. BW-153.1,
KM-206, 39 mm.

War of Independence
INSURGENT COUNTERSTAMPED COINAGE

ENSAIE on 1812 Zacatecas 8 reales, BW-103.2, KM-260.4, 39 mm.

Morelos monogram, Type A, on 1811 Zacatecas L.V.O. 8 reales, BW-109.1, KM-A267, 39 mm.

Morelos monogram, Type A, on 1811 Supreme National Congress 8 reales, BW-109.5, KM-265.5, 39 mm.

(1813) NORTE counterstamped on Zacatecas 1 real. BW-110.1, KM-82.1, 20 mm.

Chilpanzingo counterstamp, Type B, with J.M.L. and S.J.N.G. on 1811 Zacatecas 8 reales (KM-191). BW-143, KM-UL, 39 mm.

LVS and MVA./1811. counterstamped on 1817 Chihuahua 8 reales, BW-140.1, KM-UL, 40 mm.

7

Coinage of Agustín de Iturbide

Agustín de Iturbide was born September 27, 1783, in Valladolid (what is now Morelia, Michoacán). A Mexican army general and a Royalist, he nonetheless sympathized with the idea of independence. He had fought under General Torcuato Trujillo at the Battle of Monte de las Cruces and showed his leadership abilities in the war with the guerrillas in Guanajuato. In 1810 Father Miguel Hidalgo y Costilla offered Iturbide, an officer of the provisional garrison at Valladolid, a position in his army. Iturbide refused and instead joined the Royalists.

In 1820 Iturbide was sent on a military expedition in the south against General Vicente Guerrero. The clergy who had helped Iturbide obtain this command thought that after crushing the Guerrero forces, Iturbide would be made viceroy and would have a free hand. But Iturbide had his own plans—to be the liberator of Mexico. After suffering defeat by Guerrero, he decided to join the rebels after all. In February 1821, in the town of Iguala, he published a plan of independence whereby Mexico was to be an independent monarchy governed by King Ferdinand VII or some other prince. The Church was to retain its privileges, and the Criollos (Creoles) and Gachupines (native Spaniards) were henceforth to be equal. These three guarantees made up his "Plan of Iguala."

On May 19, 1822, Iturbide was proclaimed Agustín I, Constitutional Emperor of Mexico. The next year, however, was filled with political and social conflicts and infighting that weakened Iturbide's control. To give the illusion of stability, the Iturbide coinage was authorized by decree on June 11, 1822.

After less than a year of rule, Iturbide sent a message to the congress saying he had "accepted the crown only under compulsion and he now wished to abdicate." On March 19, 1823, the congress accepted his abdication and sentenced him to perpetual banishment. He spent time in Italy and England, where he wrote his memoirs.

Toward the end of 1823, Iturbide heard news of a possible invasion of Mexico by several European powers that were in support of Spain. In the spring of 1824 he informed the Mexican government that Spain was planning a reconquest and asked that he be allowed to return to Mexico to fight for independence. The government decreed that if he returned he would be executed. Iturbide was unaware of the decree and had already departed on his trip back to Mexico, with a supply of proclamations and paper money. Iturbide arrived on the coast of Tamaulipas in the summer of 1824. He proceeded peacefully to the town of Padilla, where he was arrested by one of his former lieutenants. He asked what crime he had committed to deserve this punishment, but no one would listen to him, and he was executed on July 19, 1824.

Iturbide became a hero among the Mexican reactionaries. The landowners and clergy preferred to give Iturbide, rather than Morelos and Hidalgo, the credit for winning independence. In 1838 the remains of Iturbide were moved from Padilla to their final resting place in the Cathedral of Mexico, in Mexico City.

Two measures approved between independence and the coronation of Iturbide affected the numismatics of the period. First, on November 22, 1821, the provisional government authorized the continued striking of Ferdinand VII coinage until dies for the coinage of the new government could be prepared. Second, it authorized the continued circulation of the provisional money of Zacatecas at face value. Consequently, coinage with Ferdinand VII's portrait was struck after independence.

All the coinage of Iturbide has basically the same design, but there are several varieties of eagle, legend, and placement of assayer's initials and mintmarks. There are four major Iturbide-bust types (see Obverse 1 through Obverse 4 in the list below) and two major eagle styles (small and large).

The 8 reales has five different obverses and three different reverses.

Obverse 1: Small head of a youthful-appearing Iturbide. AUGUSTIN is abbreviated to AUGUST.

Obverse 2: Large head of a mature Iturbide.

Obverse 3: Large head of Iturbide with Augustín legend spelled out as AUGUSTINUS.

Obverse 4: Medium head of Iturbide with Augustín legend spelled AUGUSTINUS.

Obverse 5: Extremely long trunk on neck; rarely encountered.

Reverse A: Small upright eagle with outspread wings, facing left. Legend MEX. I. IMPERATOR. CONSTITUT beginning at the upper right, denomination 8R, and assayer's initials J. M.

Reverse B: Large eagle (the same as on the minor coinage) with the legend the same as on Reverse A.

Reverse C: Large eagle; legend as on Reverse B, but begins at the lower left.

Varieties of the 8 reales are as follows:

Variety 1A
- Obverse 1: Small head, AUGUST.
- Reverse A: Small eagle, legend begins upper right.

Variety 1a/A
- Obverse 1a: Bust as on obverse of gold 8 escudos; otherwise as obverse 1.
- Reverse A: Small eagle, legend begins upper right.

Variety 2B
- Obverse 2: Large head, AUGUST.
- Reverse B: Large eagle, legend begins upper right.

Variety 2C
- Obverse 2: Large head, AUGUST.
- Reverse C: Large eagle, legend begins lower left.

Variety 3B
- Obverse 3: Large head, AUGUSTINUS, bust ends on a straight truncation.
- Reverse B: Large eagle, legend begins upper right.

Variety 3C
- Obverse 3: Large head, AUGUSTINUS.
- Reverse C: Large eagle, legend begins lower left.

Variety 4C
Obverse 4: Medium head, AUGUSTINUS.
Reverse C: Large eagle, legend begins lower left.

Variety 5C
Obverse 5: Extremely long trunk on neck.
Reverse C: Large eagle, legend begins lower left.

The Iturbide 8 reales was issued in 1822 in a variety of combinations of obverses and reverses. One issued has the A reverse, but the bust of the 8 escudos of 1823. The only type of 8 reales issued for 1823 was the 4C variety.

The assayer's initials that appear on all the Iturbide coinage are J.M., for Joaquin Davila Madrid. Jose Garcia Ansaldo was also an assayer, serving from 1812 to 1833, but his initials do not appear on the coinage of Iturbide.

By decree of December 20, 1822, Iturbide authorized the issuance of a million each of the 2- and 10-peso notes, and two million of the 1-peso notes. These promissory notes, redeemable in one year, were the first paper currency of Mexico. The decree specified the method of discharge of all public and governmental transactions. The basis of settlement was two-thirds coin and one-third paper currency. The public did not like using paper in place of the commonly used silver coinage, and distrust became one factor in Iturbide's collapse.

A few provisional silver coins were struck in Honduras during the reign of Iturbide. At that time, Mexico's territorial limits extended from the border of present-day Panama northward—through regions annexed on January 5, 1822, by the Capitanía General de Guatemala—and on to the northern limits of California. The only known coinage of the time is from Comayagua and Tegucigalpa, all dated 1823, found only in the 2-reales denomination. The annexation was terminated July 1, 1823, and Mexico resumed its former borders.

NUEVA VIZCAYA

1/8 real, copper, 2.5–3.5 g.

Obverse: Crowned coat of arms of Nueva Vizcaya, mintmark D, and denomination $\frac{\bullet}{8}$. *Reverse:* Legend DE LA PROVINCIA DE NUEVA VIZCAYA and 1822. *Diameter:* 17 mm. *Edge:* Plain or obliquely reeded. BW-161, KM-299.

Date	Comment
1821	
1822	
1823	

1/4 real, copper, 5.5 g.

Obverse: Crowned coat of arms of Nueva Vizcaya, mintmark D, and denomination $\frac{\bullet}{4}$. *Reverse:* Legend DE LA PROVINCIA DE NUEVA VIZCAYA and 1822. *Diameter:* 20 mm. *Edge:* Plain or obliquely reeded. BW-162, KM-300.

Date	Comment
1822	

MEXICO CITY MINT

1/2 real, 0.9027 silver, 1.692 g.

Obverse: Undraped bust of Iturbide facing right. Legend AUGUSTINUS DEI PROVI DENTIA and . M° . 1822 . *Reverse:* Imperial crowned eagle. Legend MEX . I . IMPERA TOR CONSTITUT and . J . M . Denomination not shown. *Diameter:* 16 mm. *Edge:* Corded. BW-163, KM-301.

Date	Assayer	Comment
1822	JM	
1823	JM	

1 real, 0.9027 silver, 3.384 g.

Obverse: Undraped bust of Iturbide facing right. Legend AUGUSTINUS DEI PROVI DENTIA and . M° . 1822 . *Reverse:* Imperial crowned eagle. Legend MEX . I . IMPERA TOR CONSTITUT and . 1R . J . M . *Diameter:* 20 mm. *Edge:* Corded. BW-164, KM-302.

Date	Assayer	Comment
1822	JM	

2 reales, 0.9027 silver, 6.768 g.

Obverse: Undraped bust of Iturbide facing right. Legend **AUGUSTINUS DEI PROVI DENTIA** and **. Mº . 1822 .** *Reverse:* Imperial crowned eagle. Legend **MEX . I . IMPER ATOR CONSTITUT** and **. 2R . J . M .** *Diameter:* 27 mm. *Edge:* Corded. BW-165, KM-303.

Date	Assayer	Comment
1822	JM	
1823	JM	

8 reales, 0.9027 silver, 27.073 g.

Obverse: Undraped small Iturbide bust facing right. Legend **AUGUST . . DEI . PROV** and **. Mº . 1822 .** *Reverse:* Small, upright, imperial crowned eagle. Legend **MEX . I . IMPERATOR . CONSTITUT . 8 . R . J . M .** *Diameter:* 39 mm. *Edge:* Corded. Variety 1A (Obverse 1, Reverse A). BW-166.1, KM-304.

Date	Assayer	Comment
1822	JM	
1822	JM	Proof (3 known)

8 reales, 0.9027 silver, 27.073 g.

Obverse: Undraped small Iturbide bust facing right (same bust as on the 8 escudos of 1822). Legend **AUGUST. . DEI . PROV** and **. Mº . 1822 .** *Reverse:* Small, upright, imperial crowned eagle. Legend **MEX . I . IMPERATOR . CONSTITUT . 8 . R . J . M .** *Diameter:* 39 mm. *Edge:* Corded. Variety 1a/A (Obverse 1a, Reverse A). BW-166.2, KM-305.

Date	Assayer	Comment
1822	JM	

8 reales, 0.9027 silver, 27.073 g.

Obverse: Undraped large Iturbide bust facing right. Beginning at lower left, legend **AUGUST . . DEI . PROV** and **. Mº . 1822.** *Reverse:* Large imperial crowned eagle. Legend **MEX . I . IMPERATOR . CON STITUT . 8 . R . J .M .** *Diameter:* 39 mm. *Edge:* Corded. Variety 2B (Obverse 2, Reverse B). BW-166.3, KM-306.1.

Date	Assayer	Comment
1822	JM	

8 reales, 0.9027 silver, 27.073 g.

Obverse: Undraped large Iturbide bust facing right. Beginning at lower left, legend **AUGUST . DEI . PROV** and **. Mº . 1822 .** *Reverse:* Large imperial crowned eagle with cross on crown. Legend **MEX . I . IMPERATOR . CONSTITUT . 8 . R . J .M .** *Diameter:* 39 mm. *Edge:* Corded. Variety 2B (Obverse 2, Reverse B). BW-166.4, KM-306.2.

Date	Assayer	Comment
1822	JM	

8 reales, 0.9027 silver, 27.073 g.

Obverse: Undraped large Iturbide bust facing right. Beginning at lower left, legend **AUGUSTINUS DEI PROVIDENTIA** and **. Mº . 1822 .** *Reverse:* Large imperial crowned eagle. Beginning at lower left, legend **MEX . I . IMPERATOR . CONSTITUT** and **. 8R . J . M .** *Diameter:* 39 mm. *Edge:* Corded. Variety 2C (Obverse 2, Reverse C). BW-166.5, KM-307.

Date	Assayer	Comment
1822	JM	

8 reales, 0.9027 silver, 27.073 g.

Obverse: Undraped large Iturbide bust facing right with a long, straight truncation. Beginning at lower left, legend **AUGUSTI NUS DEI PROVIDENTIA** and **. Mº . 1822 .** *Reverse:* Large imperial crowned eagle. Beginning at upper right, legend **MEX . I . IMPERATOR . CONSTITUT . 8 . R . J . M .** *Diameter:* 39 mm. *Edge:* Corded. Variety 3B (Obverse 3, Reverse B). BW-166.6, KM-308.

Date	Assayer	Comment
1822	JM	Long straight truncation
1822	JM	

8 reales, 0.9027 silver, 27.073 g.

Obverse: Undraped large Iturbide bust facing right with a long, straight truncation. Beginning at lower left, legend **AUGUSTINUS DEI PROVIDENTIA . Mº . 1822 .** *Reverse:* Large imperial crowned eagle. Beginning at lower left, legend **MEX . I . IMPERATOR . CONSTITUT** and **. 8R . J . M .** *Diameter:* 39

mm. *Edge:* Corded. Variety 3C (Obverse 3, Reverse C). BW-166.7, KM-309.

Date	Assayer	Comment
1822	JM	

8 reales, 0.9027 silver, 27.073 g.
Obverse: Undraped medium Iturbide bust facing right with irregular truncation. Beginning at lower left, legend AUGUSTI NUS DEI PROVIDENTIA and . M° . [date] . *Reverse:* Large imperial crowned eagle. Beginning at lower left, legend MEX . I . IMPERATOR . CONSTITUT and . 8R . J . M . *Diameter:* 39 mm. *Edge:* Corded. Variety 4C (Obverse 4, Reverse C). BW-166.8, KM-310.

Date	Assayer	Comment
1822	JM	
1823	JM	

8 reales, 0.9027 silver, 27.073 g.
Obverse: Medium, undraped Iturbide bust facing right with extremely long truncation. Beginning at lower left, legend AUGUSTI NUS DEI PROVIDENTIA and . M° . 1822 . *Reverse:* Large imperial crowned eagle. Beginning at lower left, legend MEX . I . IMPERATOR CONSTITUT and . 8R . J . M . *Diameter:* 39 mm. *Edge:* Corded. Variety 5C (Obverse 5, Reverse C). BW-166.9, KM-311.

Date	Assayer	Comment
1822	JM	Rare

4 escudos, 0.875 gold, 13.536 g.
Obverse: Undraped bust of Iturbide facing to the right. Legend AUGUSTINUS DEI PROVIDENTIA and . M° . 1823 . *Reverse:* Imperial crowned eagle within shield. Beginning at upper right, legend MEX . I . IMPERATOR . CONSTITUT . 4 . S . J . M . *Diameter:* 30 mm. *Edge:* Corded. BW-167, KM-312.

Date	Assayer	Comment
1823	JM	Rare

8 escudos, 0.875 gold, 27.073 g.
Obverse: Small undraped bust of Iturbide facing to the right (Type I). Legend AUGUSTI NUS DEI PROVIDENTIA and . M° . 1822 . *Reverse:* Small, upright imperial crowned eagle. Beginning at upper right, legend MEX . I . IMPERATOR . CONSTITUT . 8 . S . J . M . *Diameter:* 37 mm. *Edge:* Corded. BW-168.1, KM-313.1.

Date	Assayer	Comment
1822	JM	

8 escudos, 0.875 gold, 27.073 g.
Obverse: Small undraped bust of Iturbide facing to the right (Type I). Legend AUGSTI NUS DEI PROVIDENTIA and . M° . 1822 . *Reverse:* Small, upright imperial crowned eagle. Beginning at upper right, legend MEX . I . IMPERATOR . CONSTITUT . 8 . S . J . M . *Diameter:* 37 mm. *Edge:* Corded. BW-168.2, KM-313.2

Date	Assayer	Comment
1822	JM	AUGSTINUS error

8 escudos, 0.875 gold, 27.073 g.
Obverse: Large undraped bust of Iturbide facing to the right (Type II). Legend AUGUS TINUS DEI PROVIDENTIA and . M° . 1823 . *Reverse:* Imperial crowned eagle within shield. Legend MEX . I . IMPERATOR . CONSTITUT . 8 . S . J . M . *Diameter:* 37 mm. *Edge:* Corded. BW-168.3, KM-314.

Date	Assayer	Comment
1823	JM	

HONDURAS PROVISIONAL COINAGE

2 reales, Comayagua, silver, 5.1–5.6 g.
Obverse: Bust of Iturbide facing left. Legend ENPER[ADOR] AGUSTIN/. and . 1823 . *Reverse:* Crowned imperial eagle on nopal cactus. Legend M[ONEDA] P[ROVISIONAL] and 2R. *Diameter:* 21–22 mm. *Edge:* Plain. BW-160, KM-UL.

Date	Comment
1823	Buttrey 1*

* Buttrey numbers are from T.V. Buttrey, "Central America Under the Mexican Empire 1822–1823." *ANS Museum Notes* no. 13, 1967.

2 reales, Tegucigalpa, silver, 5.6–6.6 g.

Obverse: Early version of the Spanish coat of arms and a pointed equilateral cross. Legend TEGVSIGALPA L[IBRE] A[ÑO] and 1823. *Reverse:* Crowned imperial eagle on nopal cactus. Legend M[ONEDA] P[ROVISIONAL] and 2R. *Diameter:* 23–27 mm. *Edge:* Plain. BW-160.1, KM-UL.

Date	Comment
1823	Cross obverse, B-2; 5 known
1823	Spanish arms, B-7; 1 known

Mule of 2 reales, Tegucigalpa, silver, 5.6–6.6 g.

Obverse: Crowned imperial eagle, with the reverse of the Tegucigalpa and Comayagua coins. *Reverse:* Spanish coat of arms, crowned between the pillars of Hercules. Legend 2R M[ONEDA] TEGVSIGALPA L[IBRE] / A[ÑO] and 1823 (L and A are divided by date; A is inverted). *Diameter:* 23–27 mm. *Edge:* Plain. BW-160.2, KM-UL.

Date	Comment
1823	B-7; rare

Coinage of Agustín de Iturbide

1/8 real. 1822, NUEVA VIZCAYA. BW-160.2, KM-299, 17 mm.

1/4 real. 1822, NUEVA VIZCAYA. BW-160.3, KM-300, 20 mm.

1/2 real. 1822-M̊, JM. BW-163, KM-301, 16 mm.

1 real. 1822-M̊, JM. BW-164, KM-302, 20 mm.

2 reales. 1823-M̊, JM. BW-165, KM-303, 27 mm.

8 reales. 1822-M̊, JM. BW-166.1, KM-304, 39 mm.

8 reales. 1822-M̊, JM. BW-166.4, KM-306.2, 39 mm.

Coinage of Agustín de Iturbide

(continued)

8 reales. 1822-$\mathring{M}$, JM.
BW-166.5, KM-308, 39 mm.

8 reales. 1822-$\mathring{M}$, JM.
BW-166.7, KM-309, 39 mm.

8 reales. 1823-$\mathring{M}$, JM.
BW-166.8, KM-310, 39 mm.

4 escudos. 1823-$\mathring{M}$, JM.
BW-167, KM-312, 30 mm.

Coinage of Agustín de Iturbide
(continued)

8 escudos.
1822-$\overset{o}{M}$, JM.
BW-168.1,
KM-313.1,
Type I, 37 mm.

8 escudos.
1823-$\overset{o}{M}$, JM.
BW-168.3,
KM-314,
Type II, 37 mm.

2 reales. 182(3), COMAYAGUA.
BW-160, KM-UL, 20 mm.

2 reales. 1823, TEGVSIGALPA. KM-UL, 27 mm. *Left:* With "L. A." and cross; this is the obverse of BW-160.1. *Right:* With "L A" and Spanish coat of arms: this is the reverse of BW-160.1a. *Middle:* reverse of BW-160.1 and obverse of BW-160.1a.

8

Republic Reales Coinage

PROFILE ("HOOKNECK") EAGLE

The design for the first reales coinage of the Republic was the hookneck eagle style, also referred to as the "Profile Eagle." It was used at only three mints and for a brief period: Durango in 1824, Guanajuato in 1824 and 1825, and Mexico City in 1823 and 1824. Fineness is often expressed as 10 D$ 20 G$ (10 *dineros*, 20 *granos*, indicating a fineness of 0.90277). Several die varieties of Profile Eagle coinage exist; some are rare. An intensive study of Republic reales coinage, *Hookneck: El Aguila de Perfil*, by Clyde Hubbard and David O'Harrow, was published in 1997.

Durango

The mintmark for Profile Eagle coinage of Durango is D°. Assayer initials are as follows:

RL Unknown (1824)

1 real, 0.90277 silver, 3.380 g.

Obverse: National coat of arms. Legend . REPUBLICA . MEXICANA . *Reverse:* Radiant liberty cap, denomination, mintmark, date, assayer's initials, and 10 D$ 20 G$ (superscript "s" reversed). *Mintmark:* D°. *Diameter:* 20 mm. *Edge:* Ornamented. BW-203.3aH, KM-371.1.

Date	Assayer	Comment
1824	RL	

1 real, 0.90277 silver, 3.380 g.

Obverse: National coat of arms. Legend . REPUBLICA MEXICANA . *Reverse:* Radiant liberty cap, denomination, mintmark, date, assayer's initials, and 10 D$ 20 G$ (with normal superscript "s"). *Mintmark:* D°. *Diameter:* 20 mm. *Edge:* Ornamented. BW-203.3bH, KM-371.2.

Date	Assayer	Comment
1824	RL	Rare (3 known)

2 reales, 0.90277 silver, 6.760 g.

Obverse: National coat of arms. Legend REPUBLICA MEXICANA . *Reverse:* Radiant liberty cap, denomination, mintmark, date, assayer's initials, and 10 D$ 20 G$. *Mintmark:* D°. *Diameter:* 27 mm. *Edge:* Ornamented. BW-204.6aH, KM-373.1.

Date	Assayer	Comment
1824	RL	

2 reales, 0.90277 silver, 6.760 g.

Obverse: National coat of arms. Legend REPUBLICA MEXICANA . Thin Profile Eagle, Defiant Snake. *Reverse:* Small radiant liberty cap, denomination, mintmark, date, assayer's initials, and 10 D$ 20 G$. *Mintmark:* D. *Diameter:* 27 mm. *Edge:* Ornamented. BW-204.6bH, KM-373.2.

Date	Assayer	Comment
1824	RL	Type I (dot before 2R)

2 reales, 0.90277 silver, 6.760 g.

Obverse: National coat of arms. Legend REPUBLICA MEXICANA . Thin Profile Eagle. *Reverse:* Radiant liberty cap, denomination, mintmark, date, assayer's initials, and 10 D$ 20 G$. *Mintmark:* D. *Diameter:* 27 mm. *Edge:* Ornamented. BW-204.6cH, KM-373.3.

Date	Assayer	Comment
1824	RL	Type II (no dot before 2R)

8 reales, 0.90277 silver, 27.070 g.
Obverse: National coat of arms. Legend REPUBLICA MEXICANA . Thin Profile Eagle, Defiant Snake. *Reverse:* Medium radiant liberty cap, denomination, mintmark, date, assayer's initials, and 10 D$ 20 G$. *Mintmark:* D°. *Diameter:* 39 mm. *Edge:* Ornamented. BW-206.5H, KM-376.1.

Date	Assayer	Comment
1824	RL	

8 reales, 0.90277 silver, 27.070 g.
Obverse: National coat of arms. Legend REPUBLICA MEXICANA . Thin Profile Eagle, Defiant Snake. *Reverse:* Small radiant liberty cap, denomination, mintmark, date, assayer's initials, and 10 D$ 20 G$. *Mintmark:* D°. *Diameter:* 39 mm. *Edge:* Ornamented. BW-206.5aH, KM-376.2.

Date	Assayer	Comment
1824	RL	

8 reales, 0.90277 silver, 27.070 g.
Obverse: National coat of arms. Legend REPUBLICA MEXICANA . Thin Profile Eagle, Submissive Snake. *Reverse:* Small radiant liberty cap, denomination, mintmark, date, assayer's initials, and 10 D$ 20 G$. *Mintmark:* D°. *Diameter:* 39 mm. *Edge:* Ornamented. BW-206.5bH, KM-376.3.

Date	Assayer	Comment
1824	RL	

8 reales, 0.90277 silver, 27.070 g.
Obverse: National coat of arms. Legend REPUBLICA MEXICANA . Thin Profile Eagle, Submissive Snake. *Reverse:* Large radiant liberty cap, denomination, mintmark, date, assayer's initials, and 10 D$ 20 G$. *Mintmark:* D°. *Diameter:* 39 mm. *Edge:* Ornamented. BW-206.5cH, KM-376.4.

Date	Assayer	Comment
1824	RL	

8 reales, 0.90277 silver, 27.070 g.
Obverse: National coat of arms. Legend REPUBLICA MEXICANA . Thin Profile Eagle, Folded Snake. *Reverse:* Small radiant liberty cap, denomination, mintmark, date, assayer's initials, and 10 D$ 20 G$. *Mintmark:* D°. *Diameter:* 39 mm. *Edge:* Ornamented. BW-206.5dH, KM-376.5.

Date	Assayer	Comment
1824	RL	

8 reales, 0.90277 silver, 27.070 g.
Obverse: National coat of arms. Legend REPUBLICA MEXICANA . Thin Profile Eagle, Folded Snake. *Reverse:* Large radiant liberty cap, denomination, mintmark, date, assayer's initials, and 10 D$ 20 G$. *Mintmark:* D°. *Diameter:* 39 mm. *Edge:* Ornamented. BW-206.5eH, KM-376.6.

Date	Assayer	Comment
1824	RL	

Guanajuato

The mintmark for Profile Eagle coinage of Guanajuato is G. Assayer initials are as follows:

JJ José Mariano Jiménez (1824–1826)
JM Unknown (1824)

8 reales, 0.90277 silver, 27.070 g.
Obverse: National coat of arms. Legend REPUBLICA MEXICANA .[date]. Full-breast

The small, medium, and large Libertad cap styles, respectively, used on the reverse of Durango's 8 reales of 1824.

Profile Eagle. *Reverse:* Radiant liberty cap, ★, denomination, mintmark, assayer's initials, and **10 D$ 20 G$**. *Mintmark:* G. *Diameter:* 39 mm. *Edge:* Ornamented. BW-206.9H, KM-A376.1.

Date	Assayer	Comment
1824	JM	
1825/4	JJ	
1825	JJ	

Mexico City

The mintmark for Profile Eagle coinage of Mexico City is M°. Assayer initials are as follows:

JM José García Anzaldo (1823–1833)

? Manuel Ruiz de Tejada (?)

1/2 real, 0.90277 silver, 1.690 g.

Obverse: National coat of arms. Legend **REPUBLICA MEXICANA .** Full-breast Profile Eagle. *Reverse:* Radiant liberty cap, ★, denomination, mintmark, date, assayer's initials, and **10 D$ 20 G$**. *Mintmark:* M°. *Diameter:* 16 mm. *Edge:* Ornamented. BW-202.10H, KM-369.

Date	Assayer	Comment
1824	JM	

2 reales, 0.90277 silver, 6.760 g.

Obverse: National coat of arms. Legend **REPUBLICA MEXICANA .** Thin Profile Eagle. *Reverse:* Radiant liberty cap, denomination, mintmark, date, assayer's initials, and **10 D$ 20 G$**. *Mintmark:* M°. *Diameter:* 27 mm. *Edge:* Ornamented. BW-204.12H, KM-373.4.

Date	Assayer	Comment
1824	JM	Breast weakly struck

8 reales, 0.90277 silver, 27.070 g.

Obverse: National coat of arms. Legend **REPUBLICA MEXICANA .** Full-breast Profile Eagle. *Reverse:* Radiant liberty cap, ★, denomination, mintmark, date, assayer's initials, and **10 D$ 20 G$**. *Mintmark:* M°. *Diameter:* 39 mm. *Edge:* Colonial. BW-206.11aH, KM-A376.3.

Date	Assayer	Comment
1823	JM	Rare

8 reales, 0.90277 silver, 27.070 g.

Obverse: National coat of arms. Legend **REPUBLICA MEXICANA .** Full-breast Profile Eagle. *Reverse:* Radiant liberty cap, ★, denomination, mintmark, date, assayer's initials, and **10 D$ 20 G$**. *Mintmark:* M°. *Diameter:* 39 mm. *Edge:* Colonial. BW-206.11bH, KM-A376.4.

Date	Assayer	Comment
1823	JM	Round-top 3

8 reales, 0.90277 silver, 27.070 g.

Obverse: National coat of arms. Legend **REPULICA MEXICANA.** Full-breast Profile Eagle. *Reverse:* Radiant liberty cap, ★, denomination, mintmark, date, assayer's initials, and **10 D$ 20 G$**. *Mintmark:* M°. *Diameter:* 39 mm. *Edge:* Colonial. BW-206.11cH, KM-A376.5.

Date	Assayer	Comment
1824	JM	REPULICA error

8 escudos, 0.8750 gold, 27.070 g.

Obverse: National coat of arms in Profile Eagle. Legend **REPUBLICA MEXICANA .** Curved Tail on snake. *Reverse:* Legend **LA LIBERTAD EN LA LEY.** Above an open book, a hand holding a liberty cap on a staff; cap points to A in LIBERTAD. ★, denomination, mintmark, date, assayer's initial, and fineness **21Q$**. *Mintmark:* M°. *Diameter:* 37 mm. *Edge:* Diagonally milled. BW-212.9H, KM-382.1.

Date	Assayer	Comment
1823	JM	Type I (Curved Tail)

8 escudos, 0.8750 gold, 27.070 g.

Obverse: National coat of arms in Profile Eagle. Legend **REPUBLICA MEXICANA .** Looped Tail on snake. *Reverse:* Legend **LA LIBERTAD EN LA LEY.** Above an open book, a hand holding a staff with a liberty cap; cap points to T in LIBERTAD. ★, denomination, mintmark, date, assayer's initials, fineness **21Q$**. *Mintmark:* M°. *Diameter:* 37 mm. *Edge:* Diagonally milled. BW-212.9aH, KM-382.2.

Date	Assayer	Comment
1823	JM	Type II (Looped Tail)

Republic Profile Eagle Coinage

In the Republic Profile Eagle coinage series, there are several varieties, some major, some minor. The image gallery shows but a few of the examples that are available.

8 reales, Looped Tail (Type II) on snake. 1823-$\mathring{M}$, JM. BW-206.11H, KM-A376.2, 38 mm.

8 reales, Defiant Snake. 1824-D♀, RL. BW-206.5aH, KM-376.2, 38 mm.

8 reales, Submissive Snake. 1824-D♀, RL. BW-206.5cH, KM-376.4, 38 mm.

8 reales, Open Snake. 1824-G, JM. BW-206.9H, KM-A376.1, 38 mm.

8 reales, Folded Snake. 1824-D♀, RL. BW-206.5dH, KM-376.5, 38 mm.

8 escudos, Curved Tail (Type I) on snake. 1823-$\mathring{M}$, JM. BW-212.9H, KM-382.1, 37 mm.

UPRIGHT EAGLE

Following the abdication of Iturbide on March 20, 1823, the moderates took power and Mexico was declared an independent republic. A new congress, assembled under Miguel Ramos Arizpe, drafted a new constitution that closely followed the United States Constitution, except that Catholicism was the only religion allowed. Mexico was divided into 19 states and four territories, with each having its own governor and legislature. The new constitution also called for the president and vice president to be elected by the state legislatures. The first president, Guadalupe Victoria (born José Miguel Ramón Adaucto Fernández y Felix, he later changed his name), and his vice president, Nicolás Bravo, assumed office in the autumn of 1824.

The Republic period of Mexico's history was entwined with that of the United States on many occasions. One such occasion was the Battle of the Alamo at San Antonio, then in northern Mexico. From February 23 through March 6, 1836, some 3,000 Mexicans under General Antonio López de Santa Anna laid siege against 150 Texians (as they were then called) under Lieutenant Colonel William Barret Travis. When Travis would not surrender, the Mexican trumpets sounded the *degüello* (from the Spanish verb meaning "to slit or cut the throat," with the figurative meaning of "to show no mercy"). The Alamo was overrun, resulting in the loss of all its defenders (although some historians believe that at least two defenders survived).

Mexican and U.S. history met again during the Mexican-American War. Following the Battle of San Jacinto (April 21, 1836), Texas seceded from Mexico and declared itself the Republic of Texas. The republic was annexed by the United States in 1844 and given statehood the following year. By April 1846, Mexico and the United States were at war over possession of the disputed territory. The war ended with the February 2, 1848, ratification of the Treaty of Guadalupe Hidalgo, in which Mexico ceded Texas, California, and all the land in between to the United States for $15 million and cancellation of any unpaid claims.

During the Republic period, Mexico had several dictators and more than 70 governments. Death by natural causes was uncommon for the political leaders during this violent period, and the actions of many historical personages affected the United States and its relations with Mexico.

The real coinage of the Republic covered a period of more than 70 years, with both silver and gold coinage designs and denominations remaining basically the same. This was a fairly stable numismatic period in an unstable political era. During this period there were issues from 14 different mints with overdates, overmintmarks, and assorted other varieties.

The silver 1/4 real has a design all its own. The obverse shows the head of Liberty facing left, with the mintmark and the designer's initials. The most common initials found on the 1/4 real are LR, for Luciano Rovira of the Mexico City Mint. He created the 1/4-real dies in 1842 and was an engraver and designer. Assayer initials were RG and JG. Assayers' initials appear on all issues except for the San Luis Potosí mint. The reverse has only the 1/4 denomination and the legend REPUBLICA MEXICANA, with the date below.

The obverse design of the gold and silver coinage remained basically the same throughout the Republic period. There are many styles of national eagle from the various mints at various times. The obverse in general features the Mexican national coat of arms with REPUBLICA MEXICANA above and a wreath below. The reverse designs of the silver coinage have the liberty cap superimposed over a field of rays with the word LIBERTAD on the cap. The legend below shows the denomination, mintmark, date, assayer's initials, and 10DS 20GS (10 *dineros*, 20 *granos*, indicating a fineness of 0.90277).

The reverse design of the gold coins is different from that of the silver coinage, and is referred to collectively as the "Hand on Book" series. The motif consists of an open book of laws and a hand simultaneously pointing at the book and holding a staff with a liberty cap at its peak. The legend above is LA LIBERTAD EN LA LEY, and below it, the denomination, mintmark, date, assayer's initials, and 21Q$.

Many die-style varieties and other differences can be found on coins not listed here due to space limitations. Many years of plain-dated coins are not listed when overdates are reported.

Coinage listings are by mint, then denomination.

Alamos

The Alamos mint was located in the state of Sonora in the northwestern mining town of Alamos. Alamos was the capital city of the state of Occidente until 1830 when the state was divided into the states of Sinaloa and Sonora. The mint opened in 1864 for the issuance of federal coinage and closed in 1895.

The mintmarks for Upright Eagle coinage of Alamos are A, Å, and A$. Assayer initials are as follows:

PG	Pascual Gaxiola (1862–1868)
DL or L	Domingo Larraguibel (1866–1879)
AM	Antonio Moreno (1872–1874)
ML or L	Miguel Larraguibel (1876–1895)
ML	Manuel Larraguibel (1878–1895)
JD	Unknown (1886–?)

2 reales, 0.90277 silver, 6.760 g.

Obverse: National coat of arms. Legend REPUBLICA MEXICANA . *Reverse:* Radiant liberty cap, ★, denomination, mintmark, date, assayer's initials, and 10 D$ 20 G$. *Mintmark:* A. *Diameter:* 28 mm. *Edge:* Ornamented. BW-204.1, KM-374.

Date	Assayer	Comment
1872	AM	

8 reales, 0.90277 silver, 27.070 g.

Obverse: National coat of arms. Legend REPUBLICA MEXICANA . *Reverse:* Radiant liberty cap, ★, denomination, mintmark, date, assayer's initials, and 10 D$ 20 G$. *Mintmark:* A. *Diameter:* 39 mm. *Edge:* Ornamented. BW-206.1, KM-377.

Date	Assayer	Comment
1864	PG	
1865/4	PG	Rare
1865	PG	
1866/5	PG	Rare
1866	PG	
1866	DL	Rare
1867	DL	
1868	DL	
1869/8	DL	
1869	DL	
1870	DL	
1871	DL	
1872	AM/DL	
1872	AM	
1873	AM	
1874/3	DL	A$ mintmark
1874	DL	
1875 7/7	DL	A mintmark
1875	DL	A mintmark
1875	DL	A$ mintmark
1876	DL	
1877	DL	
1878	DL	
1879	DL	
1879	ML	
1880	ML	
1881	ML	
1882	ML	
1883	ML	
1884	ML	
1885	ML	
1886	ML	
1886/0	ML/JD	A$ - CN mintmarks
1887	ML	
1888/7	ML	
1889	ML	
1890	ML	
1891	ML	
1892/0	ML	
1892	ML	
1893	ML	
1894	ML	
1895	ML	

8 escudos, 0.8750 gold, 27.070 g.
Obverse: National coat of arms. Legend REPUBLICA MEXICANA . *Reverse:* Above an open book, a hand holding a staff with a liberty cap. Legend LA LIBERTAD EN LA LEY, ★, denomination, mintmark, date, assayer's initials, and .21 Q$. *Mintmark:* A. *Diameter:* 37 mm. *Edge:* Diagonally milled. BW-212, KM-383.

Date	Assayer	Comment
1864	PG	
1866	DL	
1868/7	DL	
1869	DL	
1870	DL	
1872	AM	Rare

Catorce

The Catorce mint, called the "Real de Catorce" during the War of Independence, was located in the state of San Luis Potosí. It was opened in 1863 by a local businessman, but since there was already another mint in the state capital of San Luis Potosí, the new mint was not well received. After some irregularities at the Catorce mint, operations ceased in 1869. Although the mint was in operation from 1863 through 1869, only the 1863 date is known.

The mintmark for Upright Eagle coinage of Catorce is CE. Assayer initials are as follows:

ML Mariano Leon (1863–?)

2 reales, 0.90277 silver, 6.760 g.
Obverse: National coat of arms. Legend REPUBLICA MEXICANA . *Reverse:* Radiant liberty cap, small ★, denomination, mintmark, date, assayer's initials, and 10 D$ 20 G$. *Mintmark:* CE. *Diameter:* 27 mm. *Edge:* Ornamented. BW-204.2, KM-374.1.

Date	Assayer	Comment
1863	ML	

4 reales, 0.90277 silver, 13.540 g.
Obverse: National coat of arms. Legend REPUBLICA MEXICANA . *Reverse:* Radiant liberty cap, small ★, denomination, mintmark, date, assayer's initials, and 10 D$ 20 G$. *Mintmark:* CE. *Diameter:* 32 mm. *Edge:* Ornamented. BW-205.1, KM-375.

Date	Assayer	Comment
1863	ML	Large C
1863	ML	Small C; rare

8 reales, 0.90277 silver, 27.070 g.
Obverse: National coat of arms. Legend REPUBLICA MEXICANA . *Reverse:* Radiant liberty cap, regular-sized ★, denomination, mintmark, date, assayer's initials, and 10 D$ 20 G$. *Mintmark:* CE. *Diameter:* 39 mm. *Edge:* Ornamented. BW-206.2, KM-377.1.

Date	Assayer	Comment
1863	ML	

Chihuahua

The Chihuahua mint was located in the capital city of the northern state of Chihuahua. The mint opened in 1831 and closed in 1895. The 4 reales was not issued from this mint.

The mintmarks for Upright Eagle coinage of Chihuahua are CA, CH, and CH^A. Assayer initials are as follows:

MR Mariano Cristobal Ramírez (1831–1834)

MJ José Mariano Jiménez (1832)

AM José Antonio Mucharraz (1833–1839)

RG Rodrigo García (1839–1856)

JC Joaquin Campa (1856–1865)

BA Bruno Arriada (1858)

FP Francisco Potts (1866)

JG José María Gómez del Campo (1866–1868)

MM Manuel Merino (1868–1895)

AV Antonio Valero (1873–1880)

EA Eduardo Avila (1877)

JM Jacobo Mucharraz (1877)

GR Guadalupe Rocha (1877)

MG Manuel Gameros (1880–1882)

PM Possibly Patrick Murphy (1880)

1/4 real, 0.90277 silver, 1.845 g.

Obverse: Bust of Liberty facing left, with mintmark to left of bust and engraver's initials to right. *Reverse:* Denomination $\frac{1}{4}$ in center of coin, legend REPUBLICA MEXICANA around, and .[date]. *Mintmark:* CẬ. *Diameter:* 12 mm. *Edge:* Plain. BW-201.1, KM-368.

Date	Assayer	Comment
1843	RG	Rare

1/2 real, 0.90277 silver, 1.690 g.

Obverse: National coat of arms surrounded by legend REPUBLICA MEXICANA. *Reverse:* Radiant liberty cap, ★, denomination, mintmark, date, assayer's initials, and 10 D$ 20 G$. *Mintmark:* CẬ. *Diameter:* 16 mm. *Edge:* Ornamented. BW-202.2, KM-370.1.

Date	Assayer	Comment
1844	RG	Rare
1845	RG	

1 real, 0.90277 silver, 3.380 g.

Obverse: National coat of arms. Legend REPUBLICA MEXICANA . *Reverse:* Radiant liberty cap, ★, denomination, mintmark, date, assayer's initials, and 10 D$ 20 G$. *Mintmark:* CẬ. *Diameter:* 20 mm. *Edge:* Ornamented. BW-203.1, KM-372.

Date	Assayer	Comment
1834	MR	Possibly unique
1834	AM	Possibly unique
1844	RG	Extremely rare
1845	RG	Extremely rare
1855	RG	Rare

2 reales, 0.90277 silver, 6.760 g.

Obverse: National coat of arms. Legend REPUBLICA MEXICANA. *Reverse:* Radiant liberty cap, ★, denomination, mintmark, date, assayer's initials, and 10 D$ 20 G$. *Mintmark:* CẬ. *Diameter:* 27 mm. *Edge:* Ornamented. BW-204.3, KM-374.2.

Date	Assayer	Comment
1832	MR	
1833	MR	
1834	MR	
1834	AM	
1835	AM	CÂ mintmark; unconfirmed
1835	AM	C mintmark error; extremely rare (3 known)
1836	AM	
1844	AM	Rare
1844	RG	3 reported
1845	RG	Rare
1855	RG	

8 reales, 0.90277 silver, 27.070 g.

Obverse: National coat of arms. Legend REPUBLICA MEXICANA . *Reverse:* Radiant liberty cap, ★, denomination, mintmark, date, assayer's initials, and 10 D$ 20 G$. *Mintmark:* CẬ. *Diameter:* 39 mm. *Edge:* Ornamented. BW-206.3, KM-377.2.

Date	Assayer	Comment
1831	MR	
1832	MR	
1833	MR	
1834	AM	
1834	MR	
1835	AM	
1836	AM	
1837	AM	
1838	AM	
1839	RG	
1840	RG	One dot after date
1840	RG	Three dots after date
1841	RG	
1842	RG	
1843	RG	
1844/1	RG	
1844	RG	
1845	RG	
1846	RG	
1847	RG	
1848	RG	
1849	RG	
1850 5/4	RG	
1850	RG	
1851	RG	
1852	RG	
1853	RG	
1854	RG	
1855/45	RG	
1855	RG	
1856	RG	
1856/5	JC	

Date	Assayer	Comment
1857	JC/RG	
1857	JC	
1858	JC	
1858	BA	
1859	JC	
1860	JC	
1861	JC	
1862	JC	
1863	JC	
1864	JC	
1865	JC	
1865	FP	
1866	JC	
1866	FP	
1867	JG	
1868	JG	
1868	MM	
1869	MM	
1870	MM	
1871/0	MM	
1871	MM	MM / inverted MM
1873	MM	
1873	MM	7 / retrograde 7
1874	MM	
1875	MM	
1876	MM	
1877	EA	
1877	GR	
1877	JM	
1877	AV	
1878	AV	
1879	AV	
1880	AV	
1880	PM	
1880	MG	Regular initials
1880	MG	Tall initials
1880	MM	
1881	MG	
1882	MG	
1882	MM	
1882	MM	Second M over sideways M
1883	MM	Sideways M
1883/2	MM	Second M over G
1883	MM	
1884/3	MM	
1884	MM	
1885/4	MM	
1885	MM	
1886	MM	
1887	MM	
1888/7	MM	
1888	MM	
1889	MM	
1890	MM	
1891/0	MM	
1891	MM	
1892	MM	
1893	MM	
1894	MM	
1895	MM	

8 escudos, 0.8750 gold, 27.070 g.

Obverse: National coat of arms. Legend REPUBLICA MEXICANA. *Reverse:* Above an open book, a hand holding a staff with a liberty cap. Legend LA LIBERTAD EN LA LEY . ★, denomination, mintmark, date, assayer's initials, and .21 QS. *Mintmark:* CA. *Diameter:* 37 mm. *Edge:* Diagonally milled. BW-212.1, KM-383.1.

Date	Assayer	Comment
1841	RG	
1842	RG	
1843	RG	
1884	RG	
1845	RG	
1846	RG	
1847	RG	
1848	RG	
1849	RG	
1850/40	RG	
1851/41	RG	
1852/42	RG	
1853/43	RG	
1854/44	RG	
1855/43	RG	
1856	RG	
1857	JC/RG	
1858	JC	
1858	BA/RG	
1859	JC/RG	
1860	JC/RG	
1861	JC	
1862	JC	
1863	JC	

8 escudos, BW-212.1, continued

Date	Assayer	Comment
1864	JC	
1865	JC	
1866	JC	
1866	FP	
1866	JG	
1867	JG	
1868	JG	Concave wings
1869	MM	Regular eagle
1870	MM	
1871/61	MM	

Culiacán

The Culiacán mint, located in the capital city of the northern state of Sinaloa, was opened in 1846 and closed in 1905, when all branch mints were closed with the coinage reform of 1905.

The mintmarks for Upright Eagle coinage of Culiacán are C, $\overset{\text{N}}{\text{C}}$, and CṆ. Assayer initials are as follows:

CE	Clemente Espinosa de los Monteros (1846–1870)
LR	Luciano Rovira* (1855)
PV	Pablo Viruega (1860–1861)
MP or P	Manuel Onofre Parodi (1873–1876)
GP	Celso Gaxiola and Manuel Onofre Parodi (1876)
JA	Unknown (1877)
CG or G	Celso Gaxiola (1876–1878)
JD or D	Juan Domínguez (1878–1882)
AM or M	Antonio Moreno (1882–1899)
F	Fernando Ferrari (1870)

* Engraver only. Luciano Rovira engraved 1/4-real coins at numerous mints for varying periods of time from 1842 through 1863. In addition, Buttrey (5th ed.), page 260, shows a pattern 1 real designed and signed by Rovira.

1/4 real, 0.90277 silver, 0.845 g.

Obverse: Bust of Liberty facing left, with mintmark to left of bust and engraver's initials to right. *Reverse:* Denomination $\frac{1}{4}$ surrounded by legend REPUBLICA MEXICANA and .[date]. *Mintmark:* C. *Diameter:* 12 mm. *Edge:* Plain. BW-201.2, KM-368.1.

Date	Engraver	Comment
1855	LR	

1/2 real, 0.90277 silver, 1.690 g.

Obverse: National coat of arms surrounded by legend REPUBLICA MEXICANA. *Reverse:* Radiant liberty cap, small ★, denomination, mintmark, date, assayer's initials, and 10 DṢ 20 GṢ. *Mintmark:* C. *Diameter:* 16 mm. *Edge:* Ornamented. BW-202.3, KM-370.2.

Date	Assayer	Comment
1846	CE	Rare
1848/7	CE	
1849/8	CE	
1849	CE	
1852	CE	
1853	CE	Unconfirmed
1853/1	CE	
1854	CE	
1856	CE	
1857/6	CE	
1857	CE	Rare
1858	CE	1R for $\frac{1}{2}$R
1860	PV	1R for $\frac{1}{2}$R; rare
1861	PV	
1863	CE	1R for $\frac{1}{2}$R; rare
1867	CE	
1869	CE	1R for $\frac{1}{2}$R

1 real, 0.90277 silver, 3.380 g.

Obverse: National coat of arms. Legend REPUBLICA MEXICANA. *Reverse:* Radiant liberty cap, small ★, denomination, mintmark, date, assayer's initials, and 10 DṢ 20 GṢ. *Mintmark:* C. *Diameter:* 20 mm. *Edge:* Ornamented. BW-203.2, KM-372.1.

Date	Assayer	Comment
1846	CE	
1848	CE	
1850	CE	
1851/0	CE	
1851	CE	Lack of overdate extremely rare (1 known)
1852/1	CE	
1853/2	CE	
1854	CE	
1856	CE	Large 6
1857/4	CE	

Date	Assayer	Comment
1857	CE	Lack of overdate extremely rare
1857/6	CE	
1858	CE	
1859	CE	
1860	PV	
1863	CE	3 known
1869	CE	

2 reales, 0.90277 silver, 6.760 g.

Obverse: National coat of arms. Legend REPUBLICA MEXICANA . *Reverse:* Radiant liberty cap, small ★, denomination, mintmark, date, assayer's initials, and 10 D$ 20 G$. *Mintmark:* C. *Diameter:* 27 mm. *Edge:* Ornamented. BW-204.5, KM-374.3.

Date	Assayer	Comment
1846	CE	
1847	CE	
1848	CE	
1850	CE	
1851/0	CE	
1852/1	CE	
1853/2	CE	
1854	CE	
1854/3	CE	
1856	CE	
1857/4	CE	
1857/6	CE	
1860	PV	
1861	PV	
1869	CE	

4 reales, 0.90277 silver, 13.540 g.

Obverse: National coat of arms. Legend REPUBLICA MEXICANA . *Reverse:* Radiant liberty cap, ★, denomination, mintmark, date, assayer's initials, and 10 D$ 20 G$. *Mintmark:* C. *Diameter:* 32 mm. *Edge:* Ornamented. BW-205.2, KM-375.1.

Date	Assayer	Comment
1846	CE	Rare
1850	CE	
1852	CE	
1857	CE	Rare; 4–6 known
1858/7	CE	Rare
1860	PV	

8 reales, 0.90277 silver, 27.070 g.

Obverse: National coat of arms. Legend REPUBLICA MEXICANA . *Reverse:* Radiant liberty cap, ★, denomination, mintmark, date, assayer's initials, and 10 D$ 20 G$. *Mintmarks:* C (1846–1874, 1882) and CN (1874–1897). *Diameter:* 39 mm. *Edge:* Ornamented. BW-206.4, KM-377.3.

Date	Assayer	Comment
1846	CE	No dot after G in 10 D$ 20 G$
1846	CE	Dot after G in 10 D$ 20 G$
1847	CE	
1848	CE	
1849	CE	G/E
1849	CE	
1850	CE	
1851	CE	
1852/1	CE	
1852	CE	
1853/0	CE	
1853	CE	Thick rays
1853	CE	MEXIGANA
1854	CE	
1854	CE	Larger eagle and liberty cap
1855/4	CE	
1855	CE	
1856	CE	
1857	CE	
1858	CE	
1859	CE	
1860/9	PV/CE	
1860	PV	
1860	CE	
1861/0	CE	
1861	PV/CE	
1861	CE	
1862	CE	
1863/2	CE	
1863	CE	
1864	CE	
1865	CE	
1866	CE	
1867	CE	
1868/7	CE	
1868	CE	
1869	CE	

8 reales, BW-206.4, continued

Date	Assayer	Comment
1870	CE	
1873	MP	
1874	MP	C mintmark
1874	MP	C^{N} mintmark
1875	MP	
1876	CG	
1876	GP	
1877	CG	
1877	CG	G^{N} mintmark error
1877	JA	
1878	CG	
1878	JD	
1878	JD	D over retrograde D
1879	JD	
1879	JD	Straight 9
1879	JD	Round 9
1880/70	JD	
1880	JD	
1881/0	JD	New die style
1881	JD	C mintmark
1881	JD	C^{N} mintmark
1882	JD	C mintmark
1882	AM	
1883	AM	
1884	AM	C^{N} mintmark
1884	AM	C mintmark
1885/6	AM	
1885	AM	C mintmark
1885	AM	C^{N} mintmark
1885	AM	G^{N} mintmark error
1886	AM	
1887	AM	
1888	AM	
1889	AM	
1890	AM	
1891	AM	
1892	AM	
1893	AM	
1894	AM	
1895	AM	
1896	AM	
1897	AM	

1/2 escudo, 0.8750 gold, 1.690 g.

Obverse: National coat of arms. Legend REPUBLICA MEXICANA. *Reverse:* Above an open book, a hand holding a staff with a liberty cap. Legend LA LIBERTAD EN LA LEY, small ★, denomination, mintmark, date, assayer's initials, and .21 QS. *Mintmark:* C. *Diameter:* 15 mm. *Edge:* Diagonally milled. BW-207, KM-378.

Date	Assayer	Comment
1848	CE	
1853	CE	
1854	CE	Restyled eagle
1856	CE	Restyled eagle
1857	CE	Restyled eagle
1859	CE	Restyled eagle
1860	CE	Restyled eagle
1862	CE	Restyled eagle
1863	CE	Restyled eagle
1866	CE	Restyled eagle
1867	CE	Restyled eagle

1 escudo, 0.8750 gold, 3.380 g.

Obverse: National coat of arms. Legend REPUBLICA MEXICANA. *Reverse:* Above an open book, a hand holding a staff with a liberty cap. Legend LA LIBERTAD EN LA LEY, small ★, denomination, mintmark, date, assayer's initials, and .21 QS. *Mintmark:* C. *Diameter:* 18 mm. *Edge:* Diagonally milled. BW-208, KM-379.

Date	Assayer	Comment
1846	CE	
1847	CE	
1848	CE	
1849/8	CE	
1850	CE	
1851	CE	
1853/1	CE	
1854	CE	
1856 5/4	CE	
1856	CE	
1857/1	CE	
1857	CE	
1861	PV	
1862	CE	
1863	CE	
1866	CE	
1870	CE	

2 escudos, 0.8750 gold, 6.770 g.

Obverse: National coat of arms. Legend REPUBLICA MEXICANA. *Reverse:* Above an open book, a hand holding a staff with a liberty cap. Legend LA LIBERTAD EN LA LEY, ★, denomination, mintmark, date, assayer's initials, and .21 Q$. *Mintmark:* C. *Diameter:* 23 mm. *Edge:* Diagonally milled. BW-209, KM-380.

Date	Assayer	Comment
1846	CE	Rare
1847	CE	Rare
1848	CE	Rare in high grade
1852	CE	Rare
1854	CE	Circulating counterfeit
1854	CE	Rare
1856/?	CE	Not 6/4, but underdate unreadable; rare
1857	CE	Rare

4 escudos, 0.8750 gold, 13.540 g.

Obverse: National coat of arms. Legend REPUBLICA MEXICANA . *Reverse:* Above an open book, a hand holding a staff with a liberty cap. Legend LA LIBERTAD EN LA LEY, ★, denomination, mintmark, date, assayer's initials, and .21 Q$. *Mintmark:* C. *Diameter:* 30 mm. *Edge:* Diagonally milled. BW-210, KM-381.

Date	Assayer	Comment
1847	CE	
1848	CE	

8 escudos, 0.8750 gold, 27.070 g.

Obverse: National coat of arms. Legend REPUBLICA MEXICANA . *Reverse:* Above an open book, a hand holding a staff with a liberty cap. Legend LA LIBERTAD EN LA LEY, ★, denomination, mintmark, date, assayer's initials, and .21 Q$. *Mintmark:* C. *Diameter:* 37 mm. *Edge:* Diagonally milled. BW-212.2, KM-383.2.

Date	Assayer	Comment
1846	CE	
1847	CE	
1848	CE	
1849	CE	
1850	CE	
1851	CE	
1852	CE	
1853/1	CE	
1853/2	CE	
1855/4	CE	
1855	CE	
1856	CE	
1857	CE	
1857	CE	No periods after C's in mintmark and assayer initials
1858	CE	
1859	CE	
1860	CE	
1860	PV	
1861	PV	
1861	CE	
1862	CE	
1863	CE	
1864	CE	
1865	CE	
1866/5	CE	
1866	CE	
1867	CE	
1868	CE	
1869	CE	
1870	CE	

Durango

In the capital of the state of Durango under colonial rule, the Durango mint opened in 1811 and remained open through 1895. Coinage began in 1824. During the 1830s and 1840s, dies prepared in France were used. They can be readily recognized because the French dies are quite different from Mexican prepared dies; among other, subtler details, the serpent's head is higher on the French dies, and the eagle's tail is shorter and square.

The mintmarks for Upright Eagle coinage of Durango are D, D̊, and D♀. During the Republic period, 14 assayers' initials were used in the Durango mint:

RL	Unknown (1825–1832)
RM	Ramón Mascarenas (1830–1848)
OMC	Octavio Martínez de Castro (1840)

LR	Luciano Rovira* (1842–1843)
CM	Clemente Morón (1848–1876)
JMR	José María Ramírez (1849–1852)
CP or P	Carlos León de la Peña (1853–1864 and 1867–1873)
LT	Unknown (1864–1865)
JMP, JP, or P	José Miguel Palma (1877)
PE or E	Pedro Espejo (1878)
TB or B	Trinidad Barrera (1878–1880)
JP	J. Miguel Palma (1880–1894)
MC or C	Manuel M. Canseco or Melchor Calderón (1882–1890)
JB	Jacobo Blanco (1885)
ND or D	Norberto Domínguez (1892–1895)
JH	Unknown (1875)

* Engraver only. Luciano Rovira engraved 1/4-real coins at numerous mints for varying periods of time from 1842 through 1863. In addition, Buttrey (5th ed.), page 260, shows a pattern 1 real designed and signed by Rovira.

1/4 real, 0.90277 silver, 0.8450 g.

Obverse: Bust of Liberty facing left, with mintmark to the left of the bust and engraver's initials to the right. *Reverse:* Denomination surrounded by legend REPUBLICA MEXICANA and .[date]. *Mintmark:* D♀. *Diameter:* 12 mm. *Edge:* Plain. BW-201.3, KM-368.2.

Date	Engraver	Comment
1842	LR	
1843	LR	

1/2 real, 0.90277 silver, 1.690 g.

Obverse: National coat of arms surrounded by legend REPUBLICA MEXICANA . *Reverse:* Radiant liberty cap, small ★, denomination, mintmark, date, assayer's initials, and 10 D$ 20 G$. *Mintmark:* D♀. *Diameter:* 16 mm. *Edge:* Ornamented. BW-202.4, KM-370.3.

Date	Assayer	Comment
1832	RM	French dies
1833/1	RM	M/L
1833	RM	
1833	RL	
1834/1	RM	
1834	RM	
1837/6/4	RM	
1837/6	RM	
1841/33	RM	
1842/32	RM	$\frac{1}{2}$ over 8R
1842/32	RM	8R instead of $\frac{1}{2}$R
1842	RM	French dies
1842	RM	Mexican dies
1843/33	RM	
1843	RM	
1845/31	RM	
1845/34	RM	
1845/35	RM	
1846	RM	
1848/5	RM	
1848/6	RM	
1849	JMR	
1850	RM	French dies; rare
1850	JMR	Rare
1851	JMR	Rare
1852/0	JMR	Rare
1852	JMR	Rare
1853	CP	Medal axis
1853	CP	Coin axis
1854	CP	
1855	CP	
1856/5	CP	
1857	CP	
1858/7	CP	
1859	CP	
1860/59	CP	
1861	CP	
1862	CP	Rare
1864	LT	
1869	CP	

1 real, 0.90277 silver, 3.380 g.

Obverse: National coat of arms. Legend REPUBLICA MEXICANA . *Reverse:* Radiant liberty cap, denomination, mintmark, date, assayer's initials, and 10 D$ 20 G$. *Mintmark:* D♀. *Diameter:* 20 mm. *Edge:* Ornamented. BW-203.3, KM-372.2.

Date	Assayer	Comment
1832/1	RM	Rare

Date	Assayer	Comment
1832	RM	M/L
1832	RM	
1834/2	RM	M/L
1834/3	RM	M/L
1834	RM	
1836/4	RM	Coin axis
1836	RM	Medal axis
1837	RM	M/L
1841	RM	M/L
1842 4/3	RM	
1843	RM	M/L
1844/34	RM	
1844	RM	Rare
1845	RM	Small date
1845	RM	Large date
1846	RM	
1847	RM	Very rare
1848/31	RM	
1848/39	RM	
1848/5	RM	
1849/8	CM	
1850	JMR	Rare
1851	JMR	
1852	JMR	Rare with 2/1/0
1853	CP	
1854/1	CP	
1854	CP	Rare
1855	CP	
1856	CP	Very rare
1857	CP	
1858	CP	
1858/7	CP	
1859	CP	
1860/59	CP	
1861	CP	
1862/1	CP	Rare
1864	LT	

2 reales, 0.90277 silver, 6.760 g.

Obverse: National coat of arms. Legend REPUBLICA MEXICANA . *Reverse:* Radiant liberty cap, denomination, mintmark, date, assayer's initials, and 10 D$ 20 G$. *Mintmark:* Dº. *Diameter:* 27 mm. *Edge:* Ornamented. BW-204.6, KM-374.4.

Date	Assayer	Comment
1826	RL	
1832	RL	Mexican dies
1832	RL	French dies
1832	RM	Post-1832 style
1834/2	RM	
1834/3	RM	
1834	RM	Very rare
1835/4	RM/RL	Rare
1841	RM	Rare
1842 4/3	RM	M/L
1842	RM	Reported, not confirmed
1843 4/3	RM	M/L
1844	RM	
1845/34	RM	M/L
1846	RM	Rare
1848/36	RM	
1848/37	RM	Reported
1849	CM	Very rare
1851	JMR/RL	
1852	JMR	
1854	CP	P/R
1855	CP	Very rare
1858	CP	
1859/8	CP	Very rare
1861	CP	Very rare

8 reales, 0.90277 silver, 27.070 g.

Obverse: National coat of arms. Legend REPUBLICA MEXICANA . *Reverse:* Radiant liberty cap, denomination, mintmark, date, assayer's initials, and 10 D$ 20 G$. *Mintmark:* Dº. *Diameter:* 39 mm. *Edge:* Ornamented. BW-206.5, KM-377.4.

Date	Assayer	Comment
1825	RL	Mexican dies
1825	RL	REPUBLICA.MEXI CANA
1826/5	RL	
1826	RL	
1827/6	RL	
1827	RL	
1828/7	RL	
1828	RL	
1829	RL	
1830	RM	B on eagle's claw
1831	RM	B on eagle's claw
1832/1	RM/RL	B on eagle's claw, Mexican dies
1832	RM/RL	REPUB MEX (spaced), French dies

8 reales, BW-206.5, continued

Date	Assayer	Comment
1833/2	RM/RL	
1833	RM	
1834/3/2	RM/RL	
1834	RM	
1835/4	RM/RL	
1835	RM	Mexican dies
1836/1	RM	
1836/4	RM	
1836	RM	M on snake
1836	RM	
1837/1	RM	
1837	RM	
1838/1	RM	
1838/7	RM	
1838	RM	
1839/1	RM	
1839/7	RM	
1839	RM	
1840/38	RM	
1840/39	RM	
1841	RM	
1841/31	RM	
1842/31	RM	B below cactus
1842/31	RM	
1842/32	RM	
1842	RM	Eagle style of 1832–1841
1842	RM	Pre-1832 eagle resumed
1842	RM	
1843/33	RM	
1843	RM	
1844	RM	
1844/34	RM	
1844/35	RM	
1845/31	RM	French dies; rare
1845/34	RM	
1845/35	RM	
1845	RM	
1846/31	RM	
1846/34	RM	
1846	RM	
1847	RM	
1848/7	RM	
1848	RM	
1849/39	CM	

Date	Assayer	Comment
1849	CM	
1849	JMR/CM	Oval 0 in fineness
1849	JMR	Oval 0 in fineness
1849	JMR	Round O in fineness
1850	JMR	
1851/0	JMR	
1851	JMR	
1852	JMR/CP	
1852	CP	
1852	JMR	
1853	JMR/CP	
1853	CP	
1854	CP	
1855	CP	
1855	CP	
1856	CP	
1857	CP	
1858	CP	
1858/7	CP	
1859	CP	
1860/59	CP	
1860	CP	
1861/0	CP	
1861	CP	
1862/1	CP	
1862	CP	
1863/1	CP	
1863/2	CP	
1863	CP	
1864	CP	
1864	LT	
1865	LT	Rare
1867	CM	
1867	CP	
1867	CP/CM	
1867	CP/LT	
1868	CP	
1869	CP	
1870/69	CP	
1870	CP	
1873	CP	
1873	CM	
1874/3	CM	
1874	CM	
1874	JH	
1875	CM	
1875	JH	

Date	Assayer	Comment
1876	CM	
1877	CM	
1877	CP	
1877	JMP	
1878	PE	
1878	TB	
1879	TB	
1880/70	TB	
1880/70	TB/JP	
1880/70	JP	
1880	TB	
1880	JP	
1881	JP	
1882	JP	
1882	MC/JP	
1882	MC	
1883/73	MC	
1883	MC	
1884/3	MC	
1884	MC	
1885	MC	
1885	JB	
1886/5	MC	
1886/3	MC	
1886	MC	
1887	MC	
1888	MC	
1889	MC	
1890	MC	
1890	JP	
1891	JP	
1892	JP	
1892	ND	
1893	ND	
1894	ND	
1895/3	ND	
1895	ND	

1/2 escudo, 0.8750 gold, 1.690 g.

Obverse: National coat of arms. Legend REPUBLICA MEXICANA. *Reverse:* Above an open book, a hand holding a staff with a liberty cap. Legend LA LIBERTAD EN LA LEY, ★, denomination, mintmark, date, assayer's initials, and .21 Q$. *Mintmark:* Dº. *Diameter:* 15 mm. *Edge:* Diagonally milled. BW-207.1, KM-378.1.

Date	Assayer	Comment
1833	RM-RL	
1834/3	RM	
1835/3	RM	
1836/4	RM	
1837	RM	
1838	RM	
1843	RM	
1844/33	RM	
1846	RM	
1848	RM	
1850/33	JMR	
1851	JMR	
1852	JMR	
1853	CP	
1854	CP	
1855	CP	
1859	CP	
1861	CP	
1864	LT	

1 escudo, 0.8750 gold, 3.380 g.

Obverse: National coat of arms. Legend REPUBLICA MEXICANA. *Reverse:* Above an open book, a hand holding a staff with a liberty cap. Legend LA LIBERTAD EN LA LEY, ★, denomination, mintmark, date, assayer's initials, and .21 Q$. *Mintmark:* Dº. *Diameter:* 18 mm. *Edge:* Diagonally milled. BW-208.1, KM-379.1.

Date	Assayer	Comment
1832	RL	
1833/2	RM/RL	
1834	RM	
1836	RM/RL	
1838	RM	
1846/38	RM	
1850	JMR	
1851/3	JMR	
1851	JMR	
1853	CP	
1854/34	CP	
1854/44	CP/RP	
1854	CP	
1855	CP	
1859	CP	
1861	CP	
1864	LT/CP	Rare

2 escudos, 0.8750 gold, 6.770 g.

Obverse: National coat of arms. Legend REPUBLICA MEXICANA. *Reverse:* Above an open book, a hand holding a staff with a liberty cap. Legend LA LIBERTAD EN LA LEY, ★, denomination, mintmark, date, assayer's initials, and .21 Q$. *Mintmark:* D♀. *Diameter:* 23 mm. *Edge:* Diagonally milled. BW-209.1, KM-380.1.

Date	Assayer	Comment
1833	RM	Rare
1837	RM	

Note: 1844 is listed by various authors but is questionable. 1832 patterns, in off metal, exist; some are gilded.

4 escudos, 0.8750 gold, 13.540 g.

Obverse: National coat of arms. Legend REPUBLICA MEXICANA . *Reverse:* Above an open book, a hand holding a staff with a liberty cap. Legend LA LIBERTAD EN LA LEY, ★, denomination, mintmark, date, assayer's initials, and .21 Q$. *Mintmark:* D♀. *Diameter:* 30 mm. *Edge:* Diagonally milled. BW-210.1, KM-381.1.

Date	Assayer	Comment
1832	RM	
1833	RM	Rare
1852	JMR	Rare

8 escudos, 0.8750 gold, 27.070 g.

Obverse: National coat of arms. Legend REPUBLICA MEXICANA . *Reverse:* Above an open book, a hand holding a staff with a liberty cap. Legend LA LIBERTAD EN LA LEY ★, additional ★, denomination, mintmark, date, assayer's initials, and .21 Q$. *Mintmark:* D♀. *Diameter:* 37 mm. *Edge:* Diagonally milled. BW-212.3, KM-383.3.

Date	Assayer	Comment
1832	RM	French dies 1832–1857
1833	RM/RL	
1834	RM	
1835/4	RM	
1836	RM/RL	
1836	RM	M on snake
1837	RM	
1838	RM	
1839	RM	
1840/30	RM/RL	
1841/30	RM	
1841/31	RM	
1841/34	RM	
1842	RM	
1842/32	RM	
1843/1	RM	
1843	RM	
1844/34	RM/RL	
1844	RM	
1845/36	RM	
1845	RM	
1846	RM	
1847	RM	
1848	CM	
1848	CM	
1849/39	CM	
1849	JMR	Rare
1850	JMR	
1851	JMR	
1852/1	JMR	
1852	CP	
1853	CP	
1854	CP	
1855/4	CP	
1856	CP	
1857	CP	French dies
1857	CP	Mexican dies 1857–1870
1858	CP	
1859	CP	
1861/0	CP	
1862	CP	
1863	CP	
1864	LT	
1866	CM	
1867	CP	
1869	CP	
1870	CP	

Estado de México

This short-lived mint, located in Tlalpan, which would soon be the capital of the state of Mexico, was open from 1828 through 1830, producing only a few coins. The mintmark for Upright Eagle coinage of Estado de México is E♀M♀. Assayer initials are as follows:

L Luis Velazquéz de la Cadena (1828–1830)

F Francisco Parodi (1828–1830)

1/2 real, 0.90277 silver, 1.690 g.

Obverse: National coat of arms. Legend REPUBLICA MEXICANA . *Reverse:* Radiant liberty cap, small ★, denomination, mintmark, date, assayer's initials, and 10 D$ 20 G$. *Mintmark:* E♀M♀. *Diameter:* 16 mm. *Edge:* Ornamented. BW-202.5, KM-370.4.

Date	Assayer	Comment
1829	L-F	

1 real, 0.90277 silver, 3.380 g.

Obverse: National coat of arms. Legend REPUBLICA MEXICANA . *Reverse:* Radiant liberty cap, small ★, denomination, mintmark, date, assayer's initials, and 10 D$ 20 G$. *Mintmark:* E♀M♀. *Diameter:* 20 mm. *Edge:* Ornamented. BW-203.4, KM-372.3.

Date	Assayer	Comment
1828	L-F	Rare

2 reales, 0.90277 silver, 6.760 g.

Obverse: National coat of arms. Legend REPUBLICA MEXICANA . *Reverse:* Radiant liberty cap, ★, denomination, mintmark, date, assayer's initials, and 10 D$ 20 G$. *Mintmark:* E♀M♀. *Diameter:* 27 mm. *Edge:* Ornamented. BW-204.7, KM-374.5.

Date	Assayer	Comment
1828	L-F	Rare

8 reales, 0.90277 silver, 27.070 g.

Obverse: National coat of arms. Legend REPUBLICA MEXICANA . *Reverse:* Radiant liberty cap, ★, denomination, mintmark, date, assayer's initials, and 10 D$ 20 G$. *Mintmark:* E♀M♀. *Diameter:* 39 mm. *Edge:* Ornamented. BW-206.6, KM-377.5.

Date	Assayer	Comment
1828	L-F	
1829	L-F	
1830/20	L-F	
1830	L-F	

2 escudos, 0.8750 gold, 6.770 g.

Obverse: National coat of arms. Legend REPUBLICA MEXICANA . *Reverse:* Above an open book, a hand holding a staff with a liberty cap. Legend LA LIBERTAD EN LA LEY, small ★, denomination, mintmark, date, assayer's initials, and .21 Q$. *Mintmark:* E♀M♀. *Diameter:* 23 mm. *Edge:* Diagonally milled. BW-209.2, KM-380.2.

This one-year type has always been valued relatively higher in the marketplace, perhaps due to the short life of the mint.

Date	Assayer	Comment
1828	L-F	

8 escudos, 0.8750 gold, 27.070 g.

Obverse: National coat of arms. Legend REPUBLICA MEXICANA . *Reverse:* Above an open book, a hand holding a staff with a liberty cap. Legend LA LIBERTAD EN LA LEY, ★, denomination, mintmark, date, assayer's initials, and .21 Q$. *Mintmark:* E♀M♀. *Diameter:* 37 mm. *Edge:* Diagonally milled. BW-212.4, KM-383.4.

Date	Assayer	Comment
1828	L-F	Rare
1829	L-F	

Guadalajara

The Guadalajara mint, located in the capital city of the state of Jalisco, began operations in 1812. Its first coinage of the Republic period was dated 1825; it continued issuing Republic-period coins until 1895.

During the reform years of the 1860s, Guadalajara was besieged by Juaristas (supporters of liberal interim president Benito Juárez) under the command of General Pedro Ogazón. The city was held by the Conservatives under the command of General Severo del Castillo. The siege lasted from September 22 to November 3, 1860. General Castillo requisitioned all of the churches' silver and ordered the director of the Guadalajara mint to coin the silver without its being assayed for fineness. The director escaped, leaving the mint's engraver, Albino del Moral, in charge. He was required to coin the silver, but he engraved a small dot next to the serpent's tail so the enforced coinage could be detected. The small dot can be found on the 1860 JG 8 reales.

After Ogazón regained Guadalajara, he ordered by decree of November 18, 1860, that all the enforced coinage be exchanged. Most of it was. The enforced coinage was 0.8190 fineness instead of 0.9027.

The mintmarks for Upright Eagle coinage of Guadalajara are G, G^{A}, Ĝ, and GA̤. Assayer initials are as follows:

FS or S	Francisco Suárez (1818–1835)
JM	Unknown (1830–1832)
JG	Juan de Dios Guzmán (1836–1839 and 1842–1867)
LP	Unknown (1831–1835)
MC	Manuel Cuevas (1839–1846)
LR	Luciano Rovira* (1844–1862)
FV	Unknown (1863)
JM	Jesus P. Manzano (1867–1869)
IC or C	Ignacio Canizo y Soto (1869–1877)
MC	Manuel Contreras (1874–1875)
JA or A	Julio Arancivia (1877–1881)
TB or B	Trinidad Barrera (1883–1884)
AH	Antonio Hernández y Prado (1884–1885)
JS or S	José S. Schiafino (1885–1895)

* Engraver only. Luciano Rovira engraved 1/4-real coins at numerous mints for varying periods of time from 1842 through 1863. In addition, Buttrey (5th ed.), page 260, shows a pattern 1 real designed and signed by Rovira.

1/4 real, silver, 0.845 g.

Obverse: Bust of Liberty facing left, with mintmark and assayer's initials. *Reverse:* Denomination surrounded by legend **REPUBLICA MEXICANA** and **.[date].** *Mintmark:* G^{A}. *Diameter:* 12 mm. *Edge:* Plain. BW-201.4, KM-368.3.

Date	Assayer	Comment
1842	JG	
1843	JG	Rare
1843	MC	
1844	MC	
1844	LR	
1845	LR	
1846	LR	
1847	LR	
1848	LR	Rare
1851	LR	
1852	LR	
1854	LR	Rare
1855	LR	Rare
1857	LR	Rare
1862	LR	Rare

1/2 real, 0.90277 silver, 1.690 g.

Obverse: National coat of arms surrounded by legend **REPUBLICA MEXICANA.** *Reverse:* Radiant liberty cap, small ★, denomination, mintmark, date, assayer's initials, and **10 D$ 20 G$.** *Mintmark:* GA̤. *Diameter:* 16 mm. *Edge:* Ornamented. BW-202.6, KM-370.5.

Date	Assayer	Comment
1825	FS	
1826	FS	
1828	FS	Reported
1828/7	FS	
1829	FS	Rare
1830/29	FS	
1831	LP	Rare
1832	FS	Medal axis
1834/3	FS	Coin axis
1835	FS/LP	5/4/3; rare
1837	JG	
1838/7	JG	
1839/7	JG/FS	9/8/7
1839	MG	Rare
1840/39	MC	
1840	MC	
1841	MC	
1841	JG	
1842	JG	Medal axis
1843/2	JG	Coin axis; rare
1843	JG	Coin axis
1843	MC/JG	
1843	MC	
1844	MC	
1845	MC	Small cap
1845	MC	Large cap

Date	Assayer	Comment
1845	JG	Small cap
1846	MC	Large cap
1846	JG	Small cap
1847	JG	
1848/7	JG	
1848	JG	
1849	JG	
1850/49	JG	
1850	JG	
1851/0	JG	
1852	JG	
1853	JG	
1854	JG	
1855/4	JG	
1855	JG	
1856	JG	
1857	JG	
1858/7	JG	
1858	JG	
1859/7	JG	
1860	JG	9/8; reported
1860/59	JG	
1861	JG	
1862/1	JG	Small A

1 real, 0.90277 silver, 3.380 g.

Obverse: National coat of arms and legend REPUBLICA MEXICANA . *Reverse:* Radiant liberty cap, ★, denomination, mintmark, date, assayer's initials, and 10 D$ 20 G$. *Mintmark:* GA. *Diameter:* 20 mm. *Edge:* Ornamented. BW-203.5, KM-372.4.

Date	Assayer	Comment
1826	FS	
1828/7	FS	
1828	FS	
1829/8/7	FS	
1829	FS	Rare
1830	FS	Rare
1831	LP	
1831	LP/FS	Rare
1832	FS	Rare
1834/3	FS	
1835	FS	Rare
1837/6	JG/FS	Rare
1837/5	FS	Rare
1838/7	JG/FS	
1839	JG	Rare
1840	MC	Rare
1840	JG	
1841	MC	Medal axis
1842/0	JG/MC	
1842	JC	Medal axis
1843	JC	Coin axis
1843	MC	Coin axis
1844	MC	
1845	JG	Rare
1846	JG	
1847/6	JG	
1847	JG	
1848	JG	Rare
1849	JG	
1850	JG	Rare
1851	JG	Very rare
1852	JG	Very rare
1853/2	JG	Rare
1854	JG	Plain date; unconfirmed
1855	JG	
1856	JG	
1857/6	JG	
1857	JG	Very rare
1858/7	JG	Rare
1859/8	JG	Rare
1859	JG	
1860/50	JG	
1861/0	JG	Rare
1861	JG	Rare
1862	JG	

2 reales, 0.90277 silver, 6.760 g.

Obverse: National coat of arms and legend REPUBLICA MEXICANA . *Reverse:* Radiant liberty cap, ★, denomination, mintmark, date, assayer's initials, and 10 D$ 20 G$. *Mintmark:* GA. *Diameter:* 27 mm. *Edge:* Ornamented. BW-204.8, KM-374.6.

Date	Assayer	Comment
1825	FS	
1826	FS	
1828/7	FS	Rare
1829	FS	Very rare
1832/0	FS/LP	
1832	FS	
1833/2	FS/LP	Rare
1834	FS	

8 reales, BW-204.8, continued

Date	Assayer	Comment
1834	FS	Rare
1835	FS	Extremely rare
1837	JG	Rare
1838	JG	Rare
1840/30	MC	
1840	MC	
1841	MC	
1842	JG	
1842/32	JG	8-pointed star
1842	JG /MC	7-pointed star
1843	JG	Plain date; unconfirmed
1843	MC/JG	
1844	MC	Rare
1845/3	MC/JG	Rare
1845/4	MC/JG	
1845	JG	
1846	JG	
1847/6	JG	
1848/7	JG	
1849	JG	
1850	JG	
1851	JG	Very rare
1852	JG	
1853/1	JG	
1854/3	JG	Very rare
1854	JG	
1855	JG	
1855/2	JG	
1856	JG	
1857	JG	Very rare
1859/8	JG	Plain date; unconfirmed
1862/1	JG	

4 reales, 0.90277 silver, 13.540 g.

Obverse: National coat of arms and legend REPUBLICA MEXICANA . *Reverse:* Radiant liberty cap, ★, denomination, mintmark, date, assayer's initials, and 10 D$ 20 G$. *Mintmark:* GA. *Diameter:* 32 mm. *Edge:* Ornamented. BW-205.3, KM-375.2.

Date	Assayer	Comment
1842/1	JG	Unconfirmed
1842	JG	Unconfirmed
1843	JG	Unconfirmed
1843	MC	
1844/3	MC	
1845	MC	
1845	JG	
1846	JG	
1847	JG	
1848	JC	Second 8 / 7
1849	JG	
1850	JG	Rare (2 known)
1852	JC	Extremely rare
1853	JG	Reported
1854	JC	Extremely rare
1854	JG	4/2 or 4/3; reported
1855	JG	Rare
1856	JG	Extremely rare
1857/6	JG	Rare
1858	JG	Very rare
1859/8	JG	Very rare
1860	JG	Extremely rare
1863/2	JG	Rare
1863	JG	

8 reales, 0.90277 silver, 27.070 g.

Obverse: National coat of arms and legend REPUBLICA MEXICANA . *Reverse:* Radiant liberty cap, ★, denomination, mintmark, date, assayer's initials, and 10 D$ 20 G$. *Mintmark:* GA. *Diameter:* 39 mm. *Edge:* Ornamented. BW-206.7, KM-377.6.

Date	Assayer	Comment
1825	FS	
1826/5	FS	
1826	FS	
1827/87	FS	
1827	FS	
1287	FS	Error
1828	FS	
1829/8	FS	
1829	FS	
1830/29	FS	
1830	FS	
1830	LP/FS	Found only with Philippine counterstamp
1831	LP	
1831	FS/LP	
1831	FS	
1832/1	FS	
1832/1	FS/LP	

Date	Assayer	Comment
1832	FS/LP	
1832	FS	
1833/2	FS/LP	
1833	FS	
1834/2	FS	
1834/3	FS	
1834	FS	
1835	FS	
1836/1	JG/FS	
1836	FS	
1836	JG/FS	
1836	JG	
1837/6	JG/FS	
1837/6	JG	
1837	JG	
1838/7	JG	
1838	JG	
1839	MC	
1839	MC/JG	
1839	JG	
1840/30	MC	
1840	MC	
1841	MC	
1842/1	JG/MC	
1842/1	JG/MC	
1842	JG	
1842	JG/MC	
1843	JG	
1843/2	MC/JG	
1843	MC	
1844	MC	
1845	MC	
1845	JG	
1846	JG	
1847	JG	
1848/7	JG	
1848	JG	
1849	JG	
1850	JG	
1851	JG	
1852	JG	
1853/2	JG	
1853	JG	Medal axis
1853	JG	Coin axis
1854/3	JG	Extremely rare
1854	JG	
1855/4	JG	
1856/4	JG	
1856	JG	
1857	JG	
1858	JG	
1859/8	JG	
1859	JG	
1860	JG	Without dot in curve of snake's tail
1860	JG	With dot in curve of snake's tail
1861	JG	Extremely rare (6 known)
1863/2	JG	
1863/4	JG	
1863	JG	
1864	JG	
1865	JG	
1867	JM	Rare
1868/7	JM	
1868	JM	
1869	JM	Rare
1869	IC	Very rare
1870/60	IC	
1870	IC	
1873	IC	
1874	IC	
1874	MC	
1875	IC	
1875	MC	
1876	IC	
1876	MC	
1877	IC	
1877	JA	
1878	JA	
1879	JA	
1880/70	FS	
1880	JA	
1880	FS	
1881	FS	
1882/1	FS	
1882	FS	
1882	TB/FS	
1882	TB	
1883	TB	
1884	TB	
1884	AH	
1885	AH	
1885	JS	
1886	JS	
1887	JS	

8 reales, BW-206.7, continued

Date	Assayer	Comment
1888	JS	
1889	JS	
1890	JS	
1891	JS	
1892/1	JS	
1892	JS	
1893	JS	
1894	JS	
1895	JS	

1/2 escudo, 0.8750 gold, 1.690 g.

Obverse: National coat of arms and legend REPUBLICA MEXICANA . *Reverse:* Above an open book, a hand holding a staff with a liberty cap. Legend LA LIBERTAD EN LA LEY, ★, denomination, mintmark GA̤, date, assayer's initials, and .21 Q$. *Diameter:* 15 mm. *Edge:* Diagonally milled. BW-207.2, KM-378.2.

Date	Assayer	Comment
1825	FS	
1829	FS	
1831	FS	
1834	FS	
1835	FS	
1837	JG	
1838	JG	
1839	JG	
1842	JG	
1847	JG	
1850	JG	
1852	JG	
1859	JG	
1861	JG	

1 escudo, 0.8750 gold, 3.380 g.

Obverse: National coat of arms and legend REPUBLICA MEXICANA . *Reverse:* Above an open book, a hand holding a staff with a liberty cap. Legend LA LIBERTAD EN LA LEY, ★, denomination, mintmark, date, assayer's initials, and .21 Q$. *Mintmark:* GA̤. *Diameter:* 18 mm. *Edge:* Diagonally milled. BW-208.2, KM-379.2.

Date	Assayer	Comment
1825	FS	
1826	FS	
1831	FS	
1834	FS	
1842	JG/MC	
1843	MC	
1847	JG	
1848/7	JG	
1849	JG	
1850	JG	
1852/1	JG	
1856	JG	
1857	JG	
1859/7	JG	
1860/59	JG	
1860	JG	

2 escudos, 0.8750 gold, 6.770 g.

Obverse: National coat of arms and legend REPUBLICA MEXICANA . *Reverse:* Above an open book, a hand holding a staff with a liberty cap. Legend LA LIBERTAD EN LA LEY, ★, denomination, mintmark, date, assayer's initials, and .21 Q$. *Mintmark:* GA̤. *Diameter:* 23 mm. *Edge:* Diagonally milled. BW-209.3, KM-380.3.

Date	Assayer	Comment
1835	FS	
1836/5	JG	
1839/5	JG	
1840	MC	Two die varieties
1841	MC	
1847/6	JG	
1848/7	JG	Rare
1850	JG	Two die varieties
1851	JG	Rare
1853	JG	Rare
1858	JG	
1859/8	JG	
1860/50	JG	
1861/59	JG	
1861/0	JG	
1863/1	JG	
1870	IC	Often seen in high grade

4 escudos, 0.8750 gold, 13.540 g.

Obverse: National coat of arms and legend REPUBLICA MEXICANA . *Reverse:* Above an open book, a hand holding a staff with a liberty cap. Legend LA LIBERTAD EN LA LEY . ★, denomination, mintmark, date, assayer's initials, and .21 Q$. *Mintmark:* GA̤.

Diameter: 30 mm. *Edge:* Diagonally milled. BW-210.2, KM-381.2.

Date	Assayer	Comment
1844	MC	
1844	JG	

8 escudos, 0.8750 gold, 27.070 g.

Obverse: National coat of arms and legend REPUBLICA MEXICANA . *Reverse:* Above an open book, a hand holding a staff with a liberty cap. Legend LA LIBERTAD EN LA LEY . ★, denomination, mintmark, date, assayer's initials, and .21 Q$. *Mintmark:* GA. *Diameter:* 27 mm. *Edge:* Diagonally milled. BW-212.5, KM-383.5.

Date	Assayer	Comment
1825	FS	
1826	FS	
1830	FS	
1836	FS	
1837	JG	
1840	MC	Rare
1843	MC	
1845	MC	Rare
1849	JG	
1850	JG	
1851	JG	
1852/1	JG	
1855	JG	
1856	JG	
1857	JG	
1861/0	JG	
1863/1	JG	
1866	JG	

Guadalupe y Calvo

Minting started in 1844 in the mining town of Guadalupe y Calvo in the state of Chihuahua. It continued until 1852, when the ore ran out and the mint closed.

The mintmark for Upright Eagle coinage of Guadalupe y Calvo is GC. Assayer initials are as follows:

MP Manuel Onofre Parodi (1844–1852)
LR Luciano Rovira* (1844)

* Engraver only. Luciano Rovira engraved 1/4-real coins at numerous mints for varying periods of time from 1842 through 1863. In addition, Buttrey (5th ed.), page 260, shows a pattern 1 real designed and signed by Rovira.

1/4 real, 0.90277 silver, 0.845 g.

Obverse: Bust of Liberty facing left, with mintmark and engraver's initials. *Reverse:* Denomination surrounded by legend REPUBLICA MEXICANA and .[date]. *Mintmark:* GC. *Diameter:* 12 mm. *Edge:* Plain. BW-201.5, KM-368.4.

Date	Engraver	Comment
1844	LR	

1/2 real, 0.90277 silver, 1.690 g.

Obverse: National coat of arms surrounded by legend REPUBLICA MEXICANA. *Reverse:* Radiant liberty cap, small ★, denomination, mintmark, date, assayer's initials, and 10 D$ 20 G$. *Mintmark:* GC. *Diameter:* 16 mm. *Edge:* Ornamented. BW-202.7, KM-370.6.

Date	Assayer	Comment
1844	MP	
1845	MP	
1846	MP	
1847	MP	
1848	MP	
1849	MP	
1850	MP	
1851	MP	

1 real, 0.90277 silver, 3.380 g.

Obverse: National coat of arms and legend REPUBLICA MEXICANA. *Reverse:* Radiant liberty cap, ★, denomination, mintmark, date, assayer's initials, and 10 D$ 20 G$. *Mintmark:* GC. *Diameter:* 20 mm. *Edge:* Ornamented. BW-203.6, KM-372.5.

Date	Assayer	Comment
1844	MP	
1845	MP	
1846	MP	
1847	MP	
1848	MP	
1849/7	MP	
1849/8	MP	
1849	MP	
1850	MP	
1851	MP	

2 reales, 0.90277 silver, 6.760 g.

Obverse: National coat of arms and legend REPUBLICA MEXICANA . *Reverse:* Radiant liberty cap, ★, denomination, mintmark, date, assayer's initials, and 10 D$ 20 G$. *Mintmark:* GC. *Diameter:* 27 mm. *Edge:* Ornamented. BW-204.9, KM-374.7.

Date	Assayer	Comment
1844	MP	
1845	MP	
1846	MP	
1847	MP	
1848	MP	
1849	MP	
1850	MP	
1851/0	MP	
1851	MP	

4 reales, 0.90277 silver, 13.540 g.

Obverse: National coat of arms and legend REPUBLICA MEXICANA . *Reverse:* Radiant liberty cap, ★, denomination, mintmark, date, assayer's initials, and 10 D$ 20 G$. *Mintmark:* GC. *Diameter:* 32 mm. *Edge:* Ornamented. BW-205.4, KM-375.3.

Date	Assayer	Comment
1844	MP	Rare
1845	MP	Rare
1846	MP	Rare
1847	MP	Rare
1849	MP	Rare
1850	MP	Rare

8 reales, 0.90277 silver, 27.070 g.

Obverse: National coat of arms and legend REPUBLICA MEXICANA . *Reverse:* Radiant liberty cap, ★, denomination, mintmark, date, assayer's initials, and 10 D$ 20 G$. *Mintmark:* GC. *Diameter:* 39 mm. *Edge:* Ornamented. BW-206.8, KM-377.7.

Date	Assayer	Comment
1844	MP	Reversed superscript s in fineness; rare
1844	MP	
1845	MP	Eagle's tail square
1845	MP	Eagle's tail round
1846	MP	Eagle's tail square
1846	MP	Eagle's tail round
1847	MP	
1848	MP	
1849	MP	
1850	MP	
1851	MP	

Date	Assayer	Comment
1852	MP	

1/2 escudo, 0.8750 gold, 1.690 g.

Obverse: National coat of arms and legend REPUBLICA MEXICANA . *Reverse:* Above an open book, a hand holding a staff with a liberty cap. Legend LA LIBERTAD EN LA LEY, small ★, denomination, mintmark, date, assayer's initials, and .21 Q$. *Mintmark:* GC. *Diameter:* 15 mm. *Edge:* Diagonally milled. BW-207.3, KM-378.3.

Date	Assayer	Comment
1846	MP	
1847	MP	
1848/7	MP	
1850	MP	
1851	MP	Revised eagle

1 escudo, 0.8750 gold, 3.380 g.

Obverse: National coat of arms and legend REPUBLICA MEXICANA . *Reverse:* Above an open book, a hand holding a staff with a liberty cap. Legend LA LIBERTAD EN LA LEY, ★, denomination, mintmark, date, assayer's initials, and .21 Q$. *Mintmark:* GC. *Diameter:* 18 mm. *Edge:* Diagonally milled. BW-208.3, KM-379.3.

Date	Assayer	Comment
1844	MP	
1845	MP	
1846	MP	
1847	MP	
1848	MP	
1849	MP	
1850	MP	
1851	MP	

2 escudos, 0.8750 gold, 6.770 g.

Obverse: National coat of arms and legend REPUBLICA MEXICANA . *Reverse:* Above an open book, a hand holding a staff with a liberty cap. Legend LA LIBERTAD EN LA LEY, ★, denomination, mintmark GC, date, assayer's initials, and .21 Q$. *Mintmark:* GC. *Diameter:* 23 mm. *Edge:* Diagonally milled. BW-209.4, KM-380.4.

Date	Assayer	Comment
1844	MP	Rare (1 known)
1847	MP	Rare
1848	MP	Rare

Date	Assayer	Comment
1849	MP	Questionable
1850	MP	

4 escudos, 0.8750 gold, 13.540 g.

Obverse: National coat of arms and legend REPUBLICA MEXICANA . *Reverse:* Above an open book, a hand holding a staff with a liberty cap. Legend LA LIBERTAD EN LA LEY, ★, denomination, mintmark, date, assayer's initials, and .21 Q$. *Mintmark:* GC. *Diameter:* 30 mm. *Edge:* Diagonally milled. BW-210.3, KM-381.3.

Date	Assayer	Comment
1844	MP	
1845	MP	
1846	MP	
1848	MP	
1850	MP	

8 escudos, 0.8750 gold, 27.070 g.

Obverse: National coat of arms and legend REPUBLICA MEXICANA . *Reverse:* Above an open book, a hand holding a staff with a liberty cap. Legend LA LIBERTAD EN LA LEY, ★, denomination, mintmark, date, assayer's initials, and .21 Q$. *Mintmark:* GC. *Diameter:* 37 mm. *Edge:* Diagonally milled. BW-212.6, KM-383.6.

Date	Assayer	Comment
1844	MP	
1845	MP	Eagle's tail square
1845	MP	Eagle's tail rounded
1846	MP	Eagle's tail squared
1846	MP	Eagle's tail rounded
1847	MP	
1848	MP	
1849	MP	
1850	MP	
1851	MP	
1852	MP	

Guanajuato

The Guanajuato mint, established in 1810 in the capital of the state of Guanajuato, was very important, as it was the Republic's most prolific producer of silver and gold coinage in all denominations.

The mintmarks for Upright Eagle coinage of Guanajuato are G, 𝔊, and G♀. Assayer initials are as follows:

JJ	José Mariano Jiménez (1825–1826)
MJ	Unknown (1826–1833)
MR	Unknown (1827–1828)
JM	Unknown (1828)
PJ	Unknown (1834–1842)
PM	Patrick Murphy (1841–1848, 1853–1861)
LR	Luciano Rovira* (1844–1862)
PF	Unknown (1848–1863)
YF	Yldefonso Flores (1862–1868)
YE	Ynocencio Espinoza (1862–1863)
FR	Faustino Ramírez (1870–1878)
SM	Unknown (1878–1879)
SB	Unknown (1880–1883)
BR	Unknown (1883–1884)
RR	Unknown (1884–1890)
RS	Rosendo Sandoval (1891–1897)

* Engraver only. Luciano Rovira engraved 1/4-real coins at numerous mints for varying periods of time from 1842 through 1863. In addition, Buttrey (5th ed.), page 260, shows a pattern 1 real designed and signed by Rovira.

1/4 real, silver, 0.845 g.

Obverse: Bust of Liberty facing left, with mintmark and engraver's initials. *Reverse:* Denomination surrounded by legend REPUBLICA MEXICANA . and .[date]. *Mintmark:* G^{O}. *Diameter:* 12 mm. *Edge:* Plain. BW-201.6, KM-368.5.

Date	Engraver	Comment
1842	PM	Assayer (not engraver); listed with engraver for this year only
1842	LR	
1843/2	LR	G^{O}/D^{O}
1843/2	LR	
1843	LR	
1844	LR	
1845	LR	
1846	LR	
1847	LR	
1848/7	LR	
1848	LR	
1849/7	LR	
1849	LR	
1850	LR	

8 reales, BW-201.6, continued

Date	Engraver	Comment
1851	LR	Retrograde R in REPUBLICA
1852	LR	
1853	LR	
1855	LR	
1856	LR	
1862	LR	
1863	LR	

1/2 real, 0.90277 silver, 1.690 g.

Obverse: National coat of arms surrounded by legend REPUBLICA MEXICANA . *Reverse:* Radiant liberty cap, ★, denomination, mintmark, date, assayer's initials, and 10 D$ 20 G$. *Mintmark:* G^{O}. *Diameter:* 16 mm. *Edge:* Ornamented. BW-202.8, KM-370.7.

Date	Assayer	Comment
1826	MJ	
1827/6	MJ	
1828	MJ	
1828/7	MR	R/J; rare
1828	MR	
1829/8	MJ	Rare
1829	MJ	
1829	MJ	N reversed in MEXICANA
1830	MJ	
1831/29	MJ	Small cap
1831	MJ	Large cap
1832	MJ	REPUBIICA error
1832/1	MJ	
1833	MJ	Round-top 3
1833	MJ	Flat-top 3
1834/3	PJ	
1834	PJ	
1835	PJ	
1836	PJ	
1837	PJ	
1838/7	PJ	
1839	PJ	Small ½
1839/8	PJ	
1839	PJ	REPUBLIGA error
1840/39	PJ	
1840	PJ	Straight J
1840	PJ	Curved J
1841/31	PJ	
1841	PJ	
1842	PJ	
1842/1	PM	
1842	PM/PJ	
1842	PM	
1843	PM	½ over 8
1843/33	PM	
1843	PM	No ★
1844/3	PM	No ★
1844	PM	No ★
1845/4	PM	No ★
1845	PM	No ★
1846/4	PM	No ★
1846/5	PM	No ★
1846	PM	No ★
1847/6	PM	No ★
1847	PM	No ★
1848	PF	No ★; rare
1848	PF/PM	No ★
1849	PF	No ★
1849	PF	No ★, MEXCANA
1850	PF	No ★
1851	PF	No ★
1852/1	PF	No ★
1852	PF	No ★
1853	PF	No ★
1854	PF	No ★
1855	PF	
1856	PF	
1856/4	PF	
1856/5	PF	
1857/6	PF	
1857	PF	Normal ★
1857	PF	Broken ★
1858/7	PF	
1858	PF	Rare
1859	PF	
1860	PF	Small ½
1860	PF	Large ½
1860/59	PF	Small ½
1860/59	PF	Large ½
1861	PF	Small ½
1861	PF	Large ½
1862/1	YE	
1862	YF	
1862/1	YE	Y/P
1862	YF	Y/P
1867	YF	
1867/57	YF/PF	

Date	Assayer	Comment
1868	YF	
1870	YF	

1 real, 0.90277 silver, 3.380 g.

Obverse: National coat of arms and legend REPUBLICA MEXICANA . *Reverse:* Radiant liberty cap, ★, denomination, mintmark, date, assayer's initials, and 10 D$ 20 G$. *Mintmark:* G. *Diameter:* 20 mm. *Edge:* Ornamented. BW-203.7, KM-372.6.

Date	Assayer	Comment
1826/5	JJ	Extremely rare (4–5 known)
1826	JJ	
1826	MJ	
1827	MJ	
1827	JM	
1828/7	MR	
1828	MR	
1828	MJ	Small 8, straight J
1828	MJ	Large 8, full J, G mintmark
1828	MR	
1829/8	MG	Small eagle
1829	MJ	Small eagle
1829	MJ	Large eagle
1830	MJ	Large letters
1830	MJ	Medium letters
1830	MJ	Small letters
1830	MJ	N in MEXICANA reversed
1831/0	MJ	N in MEXICANA reversed
1831	MJ	Large, 7-pointed ★
1831	ML	Normal, 5-pointed ★
1832/1	MJ	Large ★
1832	MJ	Normal ★
1833	MJ	Round-top 3
1833	MJ	Flat-top 3
1834	PJ	
1835	PJ	
1835	PJ	Soho Mint*
1836	PJ	
1837	PJ	
1838	PJ	Hoard date
1839	PJ	
1840/39	PJ	
1840	PJ	Soho Mint*
1841	PJ	
1842	PM	
1843	PM	Medal axis, convex wings
1843	PM	Coin axis, concave wings
1844	PM	Soho Mint*
1845/4	PM	
1845	PM	
1846	PM	
1847	PM	
1848	PF	Inverted 4; rare
1849	PF	
1850	PF	
1851	PF	
1853	PF	
1854/3	PF	Small eagle
1854	PF	Reversed 4, small eagle
1854	PF	Large eagle
1855/3	PF	
1855/4	PF	
1855	PF	
1856/5	PF	
1857/6	PF	
1857	PF	Reported
1858	PF	Rare
1860/50	PF	
1860	PF	
1861	PF	
1862	YE	
1862/1	YF	
1862	YF	
1867	YF	
1868/7	YF	G^{O} mintmark

* The Soho Mint was established in 1788 in Handsworth, West Midlands, England, by Matthew Boulton; it closed in 1850.

2 reales, 0.90277 silver, 6.760 g.

Obverse: National coat of arms and legend REPUBLICA MEXICANA . *Reverse:* Radiant liberty cap, ★, denomination, mintmark, date, assayer's initials, and 10 D$ 20 G$. *Mintmark:* G. *Diameter:* 27 mm. *Edge:* Ornamented. BW-204.10, KM-374.8.

Date	Assayer	Comment
1825	JJ	
1826	JJ	Eagle's tail square

2 reales, BW-204.10, continued

Date	Assayer	Comment
1826	JJ	Eagle's tail round
1826	MJ	
1827/6	MJ	
1827	MJ	
1828/7	MR	
1828	MJ	No ★
1828	JM	Rare
1829	MJ	
1831	MJ	
1832	MJ	
1833	MJ	
1834	PJ	
1835/4	PJ	
1835	PJ	Soho Mint
1836	PJ	
1837/6	PJ	
1837	PJ	
1838/7	PJ	Hoard date
1838	PJ	Hoard date
1839/8	PJ	
1839	PJ	
1840	PJ	
1841	PJ	
1842	PJ	Very rare
1842	PM/PJ	Reported but unconfirmed
1842	PM	Rare
1843/2	PM	Concave wings
1843	PM	Convex wings
1844	PM	
1845/4	PM	
1845	PM	
1846/5	PM	
1846	PM	
1847	PM	
1848/7	PM	
1848	PM	
1848	PF	Rare
1849/8	PF/PM	
1850/40	PF	
1850 5/4	PF	
1850	PF	
1851	PF	
1852/1	PF	
1852	PF	
1853	PF	
1854	PF	
1855	PF	★ instead of o in mintmark
1856/5	PF	
1856	PF	
1857/6	PF	
1857	PF	
1858/7	PF	
1858	PF	
1859/7	PF	
1859	PF	
1860/50	PF	
1860/59	PF	
1860	PF	
1861/57	PF	
1861/51	PF	
1861 6/5	PF	
1861	PF	
1862/1	YE	
1862	YE	
1862/57	YE	
1862	YE/PF	
1862	YF	
1863/52	YF	
1863	YF	
1867/57	YF	
1868/7	YF	

4 reales, 0.90277 silver, 13.540 g.

Obverse: National coat of arms and legend REPUBLICA MEXICANA . *Reverse:* Radiant liberty cap, ★, denomination, mintmark, date, assayer's initials, and 10 D$ 20 G$. *Mintmark:* G. *Diameter:* 32 mm. *Edge:* Ornamented. BW-205.5, KM-375.4.

Date	Assayer	Comment
1835	PJ	Soho mint
1836/5	PJ	
1836	PJ	
1837	PJ	
1838/7	PJ	
1839	PJ	
1840/30	PJ	
1840	PJ	
1841	PJ	
1841/0	PJ	Rare
1841/31	PJ	

Date	Assayer	Comment
1842	PJ	Rare
1842	PM	Rare
1843/2	PM	Eagle with convex wings, thick rays
1843	PM	Eagle with concave wings, thin rays
1844	PM	
1844/3	PM	
1845	PM	
1846/5	PM	
1847/6	PM	
1847	PM	
1848/7	PM	
1848	PM	
1849	PF	
1850	PF	
1851	PF	
1852	PF	
1853	PF	
1854	PF	Large eagle
1854	PF	Small eagle
1855 5/4	PF	
1855	PF	
1856	PF	
1857	PF	
1858	PF	
1859	PF	9 / inverted 9
1859	PF	
1860/59	PF	
1860	PF	
1861/51	PF	
1862/1	YE	
1862	YE/PF	
1862	YE	
1862/1	YF	
1862	YF	
1863/53	YF	
1863	YF/PF	
1863	YF	
1867/57	YF	
1867	YF/PF	
1867	YF	
1867 6/5	YF/PF	
1868/5	YF/PF	
1868	YF	
1868	YF/PF	
1870	FR	

8 reales, 0.90277 silver, 27.070 g.

Obverse: National coat of arms and legend REPUBLICA MEXICANA . *Reverse:* Radiant liberty cap, ★, denomination, mintmark, date, assayer's initials, and 10 D^{S} 20 G^{S}. *Mintmark:* G. *Diameter:* 39 mm. *Edge:* Ornamented. BW-206.5, KM-377.8.

Date	Assayer	Comment
1825	JJ	
1826	JJ	Straight J's
1826	JJ	Full J's
1826	MJ	
1827	MJ	
1827	MJ/JJ	
1827	MR	
1828	MJ	
1828	MR	
1829	MJ	
1830	MJ	Narrow J, oblong beading
1830	MJ	Wide J, regular beading
1831	MJ	Colon after date
1831	MJ	2 stars after date
1832	MJ	
1833	MJ	
1834	PJ	
1835	PJ	Star on cap
1835	PJ	Dot on cap
1836	PJ	
1837	PJ	
1838	PJ	
1839	PJ/JJ	
1839	PJ	
1840/30	PJ	
1840/39	RJ	
1840	PJ	
1841/31	PJ	
1841	PJ	
1842	PJ	
1842	PM/PJ	
1842	PM	
1843	PM	Dot after date
1843	PM	Triangle of dots after date
1844	PM	
1845	PM	
1846/5	PM	Eagle type of 1845

2 reales, BW-206.5, continued

Date	Assayer	Comment
1846	PM	Eagle type of 1845
1846	PM	Eagle type of 1847
1847	PM	
1848/7	PM	
1848	PM	
1848	PF	
1849	PF	
1850	PF	
1851/0	PF	
1851	PF	
1852/1	PF	
1852	PF	
1853/2	PF	
1853	PF	
1854	PF	
1855	PF	Large letters
1855	PF	Small letters
1856/5	PF	
1856	PF	
1857/6	PF	
1857	PF	
1858	PF	
1859/7	PF	
1859/8	PF	
1859	PF	
1860/50	PF	
1860/59	PF	
1860	PF	
1861/51	PF	
1861/0	PF	
1861	PF	
1862	YE/PF	
1862	YE	
1862	YF	
1862	YF/PF	
1863/53	YF	
1863	YF	
1867/57	YF	
1867	YF	
1868/58	YF	
1868	YF	
1870/60	FR	
1870	YF	
1870	FR/YF	
1870	FR	
1873	FR	G° mintmark

Date	Assayer	Comment
1874/3	FR	G° mintmark
1874	FR	G° mintmark
1875/6	FR	G° mintmark
1875	FR	G° mintmark, small circle with dot on eagle
1876/5	FR	G° mintmark
1876	FR	G° mintmark
1877	FR	
1878/7	FR	G° mintmark
1878/7	SM	S/F, G° mintmark
1878/7	SM	G° mintmark
1878	FR	G° mintmark
1878	SM	S/F, G° mintmark
1878	SM	G° mintmark
1879/8	SM	G° mintmark
1879	SM	G° mintmark
1880/70	SB	G° mintmark
1880	SB/SM	G° mintmark
1880	SB	G° mintmark
1881/0	SB	G° mintmark
1881	SB	G° mintmark
1882	SB	G° mintmark
1883	BR	G° mintmark
1883	BR/SR	G° mintmark
1883	BR/SB	G° mintmark
1884/73	BR/FR	G° mintmark
1884/3	BR	G° mintmark
1884	BR	G° mintmark
1884/74	RR/FR	G° mintmark
1885/75	RR/BR	G° mintmark
1885	RR	G° mintmark
1886/75	RR/FR	G° mintmark
1886/76	RR/FR	G° mintmark
1886/76	RR	G° mintmark
1886	RR	G° mintmark
1887	RR	G° mintmark
1888	RR	G° mintmark
1889	RR	G° mintmark
1890	RR	G° mintmark
1891	RS	S/R, circulating counterfeit, G° mintmark
1891	RS	G° mintmark
1892	RS	G° mintmark
1892	RS	G / A
1893	RS	G° mintmark

Date	Assayer	Comment
1894	RS	G^{O} mintmark
1895/1	RS	G^{O} mintmark
1895	RS	G^{O} mintmark
1896/1	RS/ML	G / A$
1896	RS	
1897	RS	G^{O} mintmark

1/2 escudo, 0.8750 gold, 1.690 g.

Obverse: National coat of arms and legend REPUBLICA MEXICANA. *Reverse:* Above an open book, a hand holding a staff with a liberty cap. Legend LA LIBERTAD EN LA LEY, denomination, mintmark, date, assayer's initials, and .21 Q$. *Mintmark:* G. *Diameter:* 15 mm. *Edge:* Diagonally milled. BW-207.4, KM-378.4.

Date	Assayer	Comment
1845	PM	
1849	PF	
1851	PF	
1852	PF	
1853	PF	
1855	PF	
1857	PF	
1858/7	PF	
1859	PF	
1860	PF	
1861	PF	
1862/1	YE	
1863	YF	

1 escudo, 0.8750 gold, 3.380 g.

Obverse: National coat of arms and legend REPUBLICA MEXICANA. *Reverse:* Above an open book, a hand holding a staff with a liberty cap. Legend LA LIBERTAD EN LA LEY, ★, denomination, mintmark, date, assayer's initials, and .21 Q$. *Mintmark:* G. *Diameter:* 18 mm. *Edge:* Diagonally milled. BW-208.4, KM-379.4.

Date	Assayer	Comment
1845	PM	
1849	PF	
1851	PF	
1853	PF	
1860	PF	
1862	YE	

2 escudos, 0.8750 gold, 6.770 g.

Obverse: National coat of arms and legend REPUBLICA MEXICANA . *Reverse:* Above an open book, a hand holding a staff with a liberty cap. Legend LA LIBERTAD EN LA LEY, ★, denomination, mintmark, date, assayer's initials, and .21 Q$. *Mintmark:* G. *Diameter:* 23 mm. *Edge:* Diagonally milled. BW-209.5, KM-380.5.

Date	Assayer	Comment
1845	PM	
1846	PM	Circulating counterfeit
1849	PF	
1853	PF	
1856	PF	Rare
1859	PF	Rare
1860	PF	
1860	PF	Circulating counterfeit, dies good, underweight
1862	YE	

4 escudos, 0.8750 gold, 13.540 g.

Obverse: National coat of arms and legend REPUBLICA MEXICANA . *Reverse:* Above an open book, a hand holding a staff with a liberty cap. Legend LA LIBERTAD EN LA LEY, ★, denomination, mintmark, date, assayer's initials, and .21 Q$. *Mintmark:* G. *Diameter:* 30 mm. *Edge:* Diagonally milled. BW-210.4, KM-381.4.

Date	Assayer	Comment
1829/8	MJ	
1829	JM	
1831	MJ	
1832	MJ	
1833	MJ	
1834	PJ	
1835	PJ	
1836	PJ	
1837	PJ	
1838	PJ	
1839	PJ	
1840	PJ	
1841	PJ	
1845	PM	
1847	PM	
1849	PF	
1851	PF	

4 escudos, BW-210.4, continued

Date	Assayer	Comment
1852	PF	
1855	PF	
1857	PF	
1858/7	PF	
1858	PF	
1859	PF	
1860	PF	
1862	YE	
1863	YF	

8 escudos, 0.8750 gold, 27.070 g.

Obverse: National coat of arms and legend REPUBLICA MEXICANA . *Reverse:* Above an open book, a hand holding a staff with a liberty cap. Legend LA LIBERTAD EN LA LEY, ★, denomination, mintmark, date, assayer's initials, and .21 Q$. *Mintmark:* G. *Diameter:* 37 mm. *Edge:* Diagonally milled. BW-212.7, KM-383.7.

Date	Assayer	Comment
1828	MJ	
1829	MJ	
1830	MJ	
1831	MJ	
1832	MJ	
1833	MJ	
1834	MJ	
1835	PJ	
1836	PJ	
1837	PJ	
1838/7	PJ	
1839/8	PJ	
1840	PJ	
1841	PJ	
1842	PJ	
1842	PM	
1844/3	PM	
1844	PM	
1845	PM	
1846	PM	
1847	PM	
1848	PM	
1848/7	PM	
1848	PF	
1849	PF	
1850	PF	
1851	PF	
1852	PF	
1853	PF	
1854	PF	
1855/4	PF	
1855	PF	
1856	PF	
1857	PF	
1858	PF	
1859	PF	
1860	PF	
1860/59	PF	
1860	PF	
1861/0	PF	
1861	PF	
1862/1	YE	
1862	YE	
1863	YF	
1863	PF	
1867	YF	
1868	YF	
1870	FR	

Hermosillo

The Hermosillo mint, located in the capital of the northern state of Sonora, opened in 1861, but 8-reales coins were struck in 1835, 1836, and 1839 with unofficial dies. The mint closed in 1895.

The mintmarks for Upright Eagle coinage of Hermosillo are H̊ and Hº. Assayer initials are as follows:

PP	Pedro Peimbert (1835–1836)
FM	Florencio Monteverde (1871–1876)
CE	Unknown (1862–?)
MP	Manuel Onofre Parodi (1866)
PR	Pablo Rubio (1866–1875)
GR	Guadalupe Rocha (1877)
AF or F	Alejandro Fourcade (1876–1877)
JA or A	Jesús Acosta (1877–1883)
FM or M	Fernando Méndez (1883–1886)
FG or G	Fausto Gaxiola (1886–1895)

1/2 real, 0.90277 silver, 1.690 g.

Obverse: National coat of arms surrounded by legend REPUBLICA MEXICANA . *Reverse:* Radiant liberty cap, (No Star), denomination, mintmark, date, assayer's initials, and 10 D$ 20 G$. *Mintmark:* H̊. *Diameter:* 16 mm. *Edge:* Ornamented. BW-202.9, KM-370.8.

Date	Assayer	Comment
1839	PP	Unique
1862	FM	Very rare
1867/1	PR/FM	6 over inverted 6
1867/2	PR	

1 real, 0.90277 silver, 3.380 g.

Obverse: National coat of arms and legend REPUBLICA MEXICANA . *Reverse:* Radiant liberty cap, ★, denomination, mintmark, date, assayer's initials, and 10 D$ 20 G$. *Mintmark:* H̊. *Diameter:* 20 mm. *Edge:* Ornamented. BW-203.8, KM-372.7.

Date	Assayer	Comment
1862	FM	Extremely rare
1867	PR	Small 7 over 1
1867	PR	Large 7 over small 7
1867	PR	No crossbar in H of mintmark
1868	PR	

2 reales, 0.90277 silver, 6.760 g.

Obverse: National coat of arms and legend REPUBLICA MEXICANA . *Reverse:* Radiant liberty cap, ★, denomination, mintmark, date, assayer's initials, and 10 D$ 20 G$. *Mintmark:* H̊. *Diameter:* 27 mm. *Edge:* Ornamented. BW-204.11, KM-374.9.

Date	Assayer	Comment
1861	FM	Very rare
1862/52	FM/CE	Hº mintmark; very rare
1867/1	PR/FM	
1867	PR	Escudo edge; rare

4 reales, 0.90277 silver, 13.540 g.

Obverse: National coat of arms and legend REPUBLICA MEXICANA . *Reverse:* Radiant liberty cap, ★, denomination, mintmark, date, assayer's initials, and 10 D$ 20 G$. *Mintmark:* H̊. *Diameter:* 32 mm. *Edge:* Ornamented. BW-205.6, KM-375.5.

Date	Assayer	Comment
1861	FM	Very rare
1862	FM	Extremely rare (2 known)
1867/1	PR/FM	Rare
1867	PR	Rare

8 reales, 0.90277 silver, 27.070 g.

Obverse: National coat of arms and legend REPUBLICA MEXICANA . *Reverse:* Radiant liberty cap, ★, denomination, mintmark, date, assayer's initials, and 10 D$ 20 G$. *Mintmark:* H̊. *Diameter:* 39 mm. *Edge:* Ornamented. BW-206.10, KM-377.9.

Date	Assayer	Comment
1835	PP	H° mintmark; rare
1836	PP	H° mintmark; rare
1839	PR	H° mintmark; unique
1861	FM	H° mintmark (narrow H), reeded edge
1861	FM	H° mintmark (wide H), reeded edge
1862	FM	H° mintmark, reeded edge, 1861–1862 die style, snake's tail right; rare
1862	FM	H° mintmark, normal edge, 1862 die style, snake's tail left; rare
1862	FM	H° mintmark, normal edge, 1862–1863 die style, snake's tail left, long ray over 8R; rare
1863	FM	H° mintmark
1864	FM	H̊ mintmark
1864	PR	
1865	FM	
1866	MP	
1866	FM	Rare
1867	PR	
1868	PR	
1869	PR	
1870	PR	
1871/0	PR	
1871	PR	
1872/1	PR	
1872	PR	
1873	PR	

8 reales, BW-206.10, continued

Date	Assayer	Comment
1874	PR	
1875	PR	
1876	AF	
1877	AF	
1877	GR	
1877	JA	
1878	JA	
1879	JA	
1880	JA	
1881	JA	
1882	JA	
1882	JA	H♀ mintmark
1883/2	JA	H^{O} mintmark
1883/2	FM/JA	H^{O} mintmark
1883	JA	H^{O} mintmark
1884/3	FM	
1884	FM	
1885	FM	
1886	FM	H^{O} mintmark
1886	FG	H^{O} mintmark
1887	FG	H^{O} mintmark
1888	FG	H^{O} mintmark
1889	FG	H^{O} mintmark
1890	FG	H^{O} mintmark
1891	FG	H^{O} mintmark
1892	FG	H^{O} mintmark
1893	FG	H^{O} mintmark
1894	FG	H^{O} mintmark
1895	FG	H^{O} mintmark

2 escudos, 0.8750 gold, 6.770 g.

Obverse: National coat of arms and legend REPUBLICA MEXICANA . *Reverse:* Above an open book, a hand holding a staff with a liberty cap. Legend LA LIBERTAD EN LA LEY, ★, denomination, mintmark, date, assayer's initials, and .21 Q§. *Mintmark:* H♀. *Diameter:* 23 mm. *Edge:* Diagonally milled. BW-209.6, KM-380.6.

Date	Assayer	Comment
1861	FM	

4 escudos, 0.8750 gold, 13.540 g.

Obverse: National coat of arms and legend REPUBLICA MEXICANA . *Reverse:* Above an open book, a hand holding a staff with a liberty cap. Legend LA LIBERTAD EN LA LEY, ★, denomination, mintmark, date, assayer's initials, and .21 Q§. *Mintmark:* H♀. *Diameter:* 30 mm *Edge:* Diagonally milled. BW-210.5, KM-381.5.

Date	Assayer	Comment
1861	FM	

8 escudos, 0.8750 gold, 27.070 g.

Obverse: National coat of arms and legend REPUBLICA MEXICANA . *Reverse:* Above an open book, a hand holding a staff with a liberty cap. Legend LA LIBERTAD EN LA LEY, ★, denomination, mintmark, date, assayer's initials, and .21 Q§. *Mintmark:* H̊. *Diameter:* 37 mm. *Edge:* Diagonally milled. BW-212.8, KM-383.8.

Date	Assayer	Comment
1863	FM	H^{O} mintmark
1864	FM	
1864	PR/FM	
1865	FM/PR	
1867	PR	
1868	PR	
1869	PR	
1870	PR	
1871	PR	
1872/1	PR	
1873	PR	

México

The Mexico mint was the first mint of the Americas, having been in operation since 1536. The Apartado mint, where this series of coins was produced, was closed for several years and now has been turned into a museum by the Casa de Moneda de México. All modern-day coinage is produced at the San Luis Potosí mint facility. The mintmark remains the traditional M̊. One would assume that the Mexico mint would have out-produced all of the branch mints, but this is not the case. A comparison of silver production in the early years shows that the Guanajuato and Zacatecas mints out-produced the Mexico mint.

The mintmarks for Upright Eagle coinage of the Mexico mint are M, M̊, and M♀. There seems to be some confusion as to matching names with assayer initials for this mint. Not all appear on the coinage, and those that do, do not appear consistently from denomination to denomination. Assayer initials for the Mexico mint are as follows:

LR (1842–1846, 1850, 1858–1863)
JM (1824–1832)
MJ (1833)
ML (1833–1836, 1837–1842)
MF (1835–1837, 1844–1847)
MM (1837–1838, 1842–1843)
RC (1847)
GC (1848–1855)
GF (1855–1857)
FH (1858–1861)
TH (1860–1861, 1863)
CH (1861–1869)
PH (1868)
MH (1873–1877)
BH (1874)

1/4 real, 0.90277 silver, 0.845 g.

Obverse: Bust of Liberty facing left, with mintmark and engraver's initials. *Reverse:* Denomination surrounded by legend, REPUBLICA MEXICANA and .[date]. *Mintmark:* Mº. *Diameter:* 12 mm. *Edge:* Plain. BW-201.7, KM-368.6.

Date	Engraver	Comment
1842	LR	
1843	LR	
1844	LR	
1845	LR	
1846	LR	
1850	LR	Rare
1858	LR	
1859	LR	
1860	LR	
1861	LR	
1862	LR	
1863	LR	

1/2 real, 0.90277 silver, 1.690 g.

Obverse: National coat of arms surrounded by legend REPUBLICA MEXICANA. *Reverse:* Radiant liberty cap, ★, denomination, mintmark, date, assayer's initials, and 10 D$ 20 G$. *Mintmark:* M̊. *Diameter:* 16 mm. *Edge:* Ornamented. BW-202.10, KM-370.9.

Date	Assayer	Comment
1824	JM	Scarce
1825	JM	
1826/5	JM	
1826	JM	Round-top 6
1826	JM	Flat-top 6
1827/6	JM	
1827	JM	Medal axis
1827	JM	Coin axis
1828/7	JM	
1828	JM	
1829/8	JM	Reported
1829	JM	
1830	JM	
1831	JM	
1832	JM	
1833	MJ	Error?
1834	ML	
1835	ML	
1836/5	ML	L/F
1836	ML	L/F
1836	ML	
1838	ML	
1839/8	ML	
1839	ML	
1840	ML	
1841	ML	
1841	ML	Two stars; extremely rare
1842	ML	
1842	MM	
1843	MM	
1844	MF	No dot after MEXICANA
1845/4	MF	
1845	MF	
1846	MF	Square wing
1846	MF	Round wing
1847	RC/RM	
1847	RC	
1848/7	GC/RC	
1849	GC	
1850/40	GC	
1850	GC	
1851	GC	
1852	GC	

1/2 real, BW-202.10, continued

Date	Assayer	Comment
1853	GC	
1854	GC	
1855	GC	
1855	GF/FC	
1856/5	GF	
1857	GF	
1858/7	FH	
1858	FH	H/C
1858	FH	
1859	FH/GF	Reported
1860	FH/GC	
1860	FH/GF	
1860	TH	
1860/59	FH	
1860	FH	
1860/59	GH	
1861	CH	
1862/51	CH/GC	Reported
1862 6/5	CH/GC	
1862	CH	H/C
1862	CH	
1863	TH	Rare
1863/55	TH/GC	
1863	CH/GC	
1863	CH	

1 real, 0.90277 silver, 3.380 g.

Obverse: National coat of arms and legend REPUBLICA MEXICANA . *Reverse:* Radiant liberty cap, ★, denomination, mintmark, date, assayer's initials, and 10 D$ 20 G$. *Mintmark:* M̊. *Diameter:* 20 mm. *Edge:* Ornamented. BW-203.9, KM-372.8.

Date	Assayer	Comment
1825	JM	
1826	JM	
1827/6	JM	
1827	JM	
1828	JM	
1830/29	JM	
1830	JM	
1831	JM	Very rare
1832	JM	
1833/2	MJ	
1850	GC	
1852	GC	Very rare
1854/2	GC	
1854	GC	
1855	GF	
1856	GF	
1857	GF	Rare
1858	FH	
1859	FH	
1861	CH	
1862	CH	
1863/2	CH	

2 reales, 0.90277 silver, 6.760 g.

Obverse: National coat of arms and legend REPUBLICA MEXICANA . *Reverse:* Radiant liberty cap, ★, denomination, mintmark, date, assayer's initials, and 10 D$ 20 G$. *Mintmark:* M̊. *Diameter:* 27 mm. *Edge:* Ornamented. BW-204.12, KM-374.10.

Date	Assayer	Comment
1824	JM	
1825	JM	
1826	JM	
1827	JM	
1828	JM	
1829/8	JM	
1829	JM	
1830	JM	
1831	JM	
1832	JM	Very rare
1833/2	MJ/JM	
1833	MJ	Very rare
1834	ML	
1836	MF	
1836	ML	
1837	ML	
1840/7	ML	
1840	ML	Very rare
1841	ML	
1842	ML	Very rare
1847	RC	Narrow legend
1847	RC	Wide legend
1848	GC	
1849	GC	
1850	GC	
1851	GC	
1852	GC	
1853	GC	

Date	Assayer	Comment
1854/44	GC	
1855	GC	
1855	GF/GC	
1855	GF	
1856/5	GF/GC	
1857	GF	
1858	FH	
1858	FH/GF	
1859	FH	
1860	FH	
1860	TH	
1861	CH	Hoard date
1861	PH	Circulating counterfeit
1862	CH	
1863	CH	
1863	TH	
1867	CH	
1868	CH	
1868	PH	

4 reales, 0.90277 silver, 13.540 g.

Obverse: National coat of arms and legend REPUBLICA MEXICANA . *Reverse:* Radiant liberty cap, ★, denomination, mintmark, date, assayer's initials, and 10 D$ 20 G$. *Mintmark:* M̊. *Diameter:* 32 mm. *Edge:* Ornamented. BW-205.7, KM-375.6.

Date	Assayer	Comment
1827/6	JM	Medal axis; rare
1827/6	JM	Coin axis; rare
1850	GC	Rare
1852	GC	Rare
1854/2	GC	Rare
1954/3	GC	Rare
1855	GF/FC	
1855	GF	
1856	GF/FC	Rare
1859	FH	
1861	CH	
1862	CH	
1863/2	CH	
1863/3	CH	
1863	CH	Rare
1867	CH	
1868	CH/PH	
1868	PH	

8 reales, 0.90277 silver, 27.070 g.

Obverse: National coat of arms and legend REPUBLICA MEXICANA . *Reverse:* Radiant liberty cap, ★, denomination, mintmark, date, assayer's initials, and 10 D$ 20 G$. *Mintmark:* M̊. *Diameter:* 39 mm. *Edge:* Ornamented. BW-206.11, KM-377.10.

Date	Assayer	Comment
1824	JM	Round tail
1824	JM	Square tail
1825	JM	
1826/5	JM	
1826	JM	10 D 20 G
1827	JM	Medal alignment
1827	JM	Coin alignment
1828	JM	
1829	JM	
1830/20	JM	
1830	JM	
1831	JM	
1832/1	JM	
1832	JM	
1833	MJ	
1833	ML	
1834/3	ML	
1834	ML	
1835	ML	Narrow date
1835	ML	Wide date
1836	ML	
1836	ML/MF	
1836	MF	
1836	MF/ML	
1837/6	ML	
1837/6	MM	
1837/6	MM/ML	
1837	ML	
1837	MM	
1838	MM	
1838	ML	
1838	ML/MM	
1839	ML	
1840	ML	
1841	ML	
1842	ML	
1842/39	MM	
1842	MM	
1843	MM	
1844	MF	

8 reales, BW-206.11, continued

Date	Assayer	Comment
1845/4	MF	
1845	MF	
1846/5	MF	
1846	MF	
1847/6	MF	
1847	RC	
1847	RC/MF	
1848	GC	
1849/8	GC	
1849	GC	
1850/40	GC	
1850	GC	
1851	GC	
1852	GC	
1853	GC	
1854	GC	
1855/4	GC	
1855	GC	
1855	GF	
1855	GF/GC	
1856/4	GF	
1856/5	GF	
1856	GF	
1857	GF	
1858	FH	
1859	FH	
1860/59	FH	
1860	FH	
1860	TH	
1861	TH	
1861	CH	
1862	CH	
1863	CH	
1863	CH/TH	
1863	TH	
1867	CH	
1868	CH	
1868	PH/CH	
1868	PH	
1869	CH	
1873	MH	
1873	MH/HH	
1874/69	MH	
1874	MH	
1874	BH/MH	
1874	BH	
1875	BH	
1876/4	BH	
1876/5	BH	
1876	BH	
1877	MH	
1877	MH/BH	
1878	MH	
1878	MH/BH	
1879/8	MH	
1879	MH	
1880/79	MH	
1880	MH	
1881/0	MH	
1881	MH	
1882/1	MH	
1882	MH	
1883/2	MH	
1883	MH	
1884/3	MH	
1884	MH	
1885	MH	
1886	MH	
1887	MH	
1888	MH	
1889	MH	
1890	AM	
1891	AM	
1892	AM	
1893	AM	
1894	AM	
1895	AM	
1895	AB	
1896	AB	
1896	AM	
1897	AM	

1/2 escudo, 0.8750 gold, 1.690 g.

Obverse: National coat of arms and legend REPUBLICA MEXICANA . *Reverse:* Above an open book, a hand holding a staff with a liberty cap. Legend LA LIBERTAD EN LA LEY, ★, denomination, mintmark, date, assayer's initials, and .21 Q S. *Mintmark:* M°. *Diameter:* 15 mm. *Edge:* Diagonally milled. BW-207.5, KM-378.5.

Date	Assayer	Comment
1825/1	JM	
1825/4	JM	
1825	JM	

Date	Assayer	Comment
1827/6	JM	
1827	JM	
1829	JM	
1831/0	JM	
1831	JM	
1832	JM	
1833	MJ	Oak and olive branches reversed
1834	ML	
1835	ML	
1838	ML	
1839	ML	
1840	ML	
1841	ML	
1842	ML	
1842	MM	
1843	MM	
1844	MF	
1845	MF	
1846/5	MF	
1846	MF	
1848	GC	
1850	GC	
1851	GC	
1852	GC	
1853	GC	
1854	GC	
1855	GF	
1856/4	GF	
1857	GF	
1858/7	FH/GF	
1858	FH	
1859	FH	
1860/59	FH	
1861	CH/FH	
1862	CH/FH	
1862	CH	
1863/57	CH/GF	
1868/58	PH	
1869/59	CH	

1 escudo, 0.8750 gold, 3.380 g.

Obverse: National coat of arms and legend REPUBLICA MEXICANA . *Reverse:* Above an open book, a hand holding a staff with a liberty cap. Legend LA LIBERTAD EN LA LEY, ★, denomination, mintmark, date, assayer's initials, and .21 Q§. *Mintmark:* Mº. *Diameter:* 18 mm. *Edge:* Diagonally milled. BW-208.5, KM-379.5.

Date	Assayer	Comment
1825	JM/FM	
1825	JM	
1827/6	JM	
1827	JM	
1830/29	JM	
1831	JM	
1832	JM	
1833	MJ	
1834	ML	
1841	ML	
1843	MM	
1845	MF	
1846/5	MF	
1848	GC	
1850	GC	
1856/4	GF	
1856/5	GF	
1856	GF	
1858	FH	
1859	FH	
1860	TH	
1861	CH	
1862	CH	
1863	TH	
1869	CH	

2 escudos, 0.8750 gold, 6.770 g.

Obverse: National coat of arms and legend REPUBLICA MEXICANA . *Reverse:* Above an open book, a hand holding a staff with a liberty cap. Legend LA LIBERTAD EN LA LEY, ★, denomination, mintmark, date, assayer's initials, and .21 Q§. *Mintmark:* Mº. *Diameter:* 23 mm. *Edge:* Diagonally milled. BW-209.7, KM-380.7.

Date	Assayer	Comment
1825	JM	Three die varieties
1827/6	JM	
1827	JM	
1830/29	JM	Rare
1833	ML	Rare
1841	ML	Rare
1844	MF	Rare
1845	MF	Rare

2 escudos, BW-209.7, continued

Date	Assayer	Comment
1846	MF	Three die varieties; rare
1848	GC	Rare
1848	GC	Circulating counterfeit
1850	GC	Rare
1856/5	GF	Rare
1858	FH	
1859	FH	Rare
1861	TH	Circulating counterfeit
1861	CH	
1862	CH	Two die varieties
1862	JM	Circulating counterfeit
1863	TH	
1868	PH	Rare
1869	CH	

4 escudos, 0.8750 gold, 13.540 g.

Obverse: National coat of arms and legend REPUBLICA MEXICANA . *Reverse:* Above an open book, a hand holding a staff with a liberty cap. Legend LA LIBERTAD EN LA LEY, ★, denomination, mintmark, date, assayer's initials, and .21 Q$. *Mintmark:* M̊. *Diameter:* 30 mm. *Edge:* Diagonally milled. BW-210.6, KM-381.6.

Date	Assayer	Comment
1825	JM	
1827	JM	
1832	JM	
1844	MF	
1850	GC	
1856	GF	
1857/6	GF	
1857	GF	
1858	FH	
1859/58	FH	
1861	CH	
1863	CH	
1868	PH	
1869	CH	

8 escudos, 0.8750 gold, 27.070 g.

Obverse: National coat of arms and legend REPUBLICA MEXICANA . *Reverse:* Above an open book, a hand holding a staff with a liberty cap. Legend LA LIBERTAD EN LA LEY, ★, denomination, mintmark, date, assayer's initials, and .21 Q$. *Mintmark:* M̊. *Diameter:* 37 mm. *Edge:* Diagonally milled. BW-212.9, KM-383.9.

Date	Assayer	Comment
1824	JM	Large-book reverse
1825	JM	Small-book reverse
1825/3	JM	
1826/5	JM	
1827	JM	
1828	JM	
1829	JM	
1830	JM	
1831	JM	
1832/1	JM	
1833	MJ	
1833	ML	
1834	ML	
1835/4	ML	
1836	ML	
1837/6	ML	
1838	ML	
1839	ML	
1840	ML	
1841	ML	
1842	ML	
1843	MM	
1844	MF	
1845	MF	
1846	MF	
1847	RC	
1848	GC	
1849	GC	
1850	GC	
1851	GC	
1852	GC	
1853	GC	
1854/44	GC	
1854/3	GC	
1855	GF	
1856/5	GF	
1856	GF	
1857	GF	
1858	FH	
1859	FH	
1860	FH	
1860	TH	
1861/51	CH	

Date	Assayer	Comment
1862	CH	
1863/53	CH	
1863/53	TH	
1867	CH	
1868	CH	
1868	PH	
1869	CH	

Oaxaca

Located in the capital of the state of Oaxaca, this mint has issued coins since the War of Independence. It was made a federal mint in 1858, but closed in 1893. During this time it issued only four denominations: silver 4 reales (1861) and 8 reales (1858–1893, excluding 1866 and 1870–1872); and 4 escudos (1861) and 8 escudos (1860–1864 and 1867–1869).

The mintmarks for Upright Eagle coinage of Oaxaca are O, Ⓐ, Ô, and OẠ. Assayer initials are as follows:

AE Agustín Endner (1859–1891)
FR Francisco de la Rosa (1861–1864)
EN Eduardo Navarro Luna (1890)

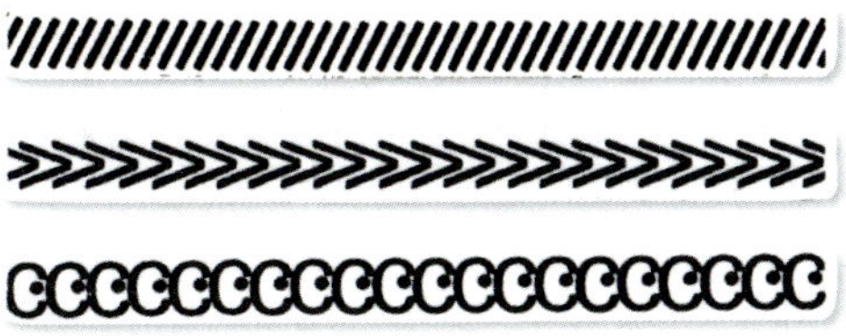

Oaxaca edge designs (top to bottom): diagonally milled, herringbone, and ornamented.

4 reales, 0.90277 silver, 13.540 g.

Obverse: National coat of arms and legend REPUBLICA MEXICANA . *Reverse:* Radiant liberty cap, ★, denomination, mintmark, date, assayer's initials, and 10 D$ 20 G$. *Mintmark:* O. *Diameter:* 32 mm. *Edge:* Diagonally milled, herringbone, or ornamented. BW-205.8, KM-375.7.

Date	Assayer	Comment
1861	FR	Diagonally milled edge; rare
1861	FR	Herringbone edge; rare
1861	FR	Ornamented edge; rare

8 reales, 0.90277 silver, 27.070 g.

Obverse: National coat of arms and legend REPUBLICA MEXICANA . *Reverse:* Radiant liberty cap, ★, denomination, mintmark, date, assayer's initials, and 10 D$ 20 G$. *Mintmark:* Ⓐ or OẠ. *Diameter:* 39 mm. *Edge:* Ornamented. BW-206.12, KM-377.11.

Date	Assayer	Comment
1858	AE	O mintmark; rare
1858	AE	Ⓐ mintmark
1859	AE	Ⓐ mintmark
1860	AE	Ⓐ mintmark
1861	FR	O mintmark
1861	FR	Ⓐ mintmark
1862	FR	O mintmark
1862	FR	Ⓐ mintmark
1863	FR	O mintmark
1863	AE	O mintmark
1863	AE	Ô mintmark
1864	FR	O mintmark
1865	AE	O mintmark
1867	AE	O mintmark
1868	AE	O mintmark
1869	AE	O mintmark
1873	AE	OẠ mintmark
1874	AE	OẠ mintmark
1875/4	AE	OẠ mintmark
1875	AE	OẠ mintmark
1876	AE	OẠ mintmark
1877	AE	OẠ mintmark
1878	AE	OẠ mintmark
1879	AE	OẠ mintmark
1880	AE	OẠ mintmark
1881	AE	OẠ mintmark
1882	AE	OẠ mintmark
1883	AE	OẠ mintmark
1884	AE	OẠ mintmark
1885	AE	OẠ mintmark
1886	AE	OẠ mintmark
1887/6	AE	OẠ mintmark
1887	AE	OẠ mintmark; rare
1888	AE	OẠ mintmark
1889	AE	OẠ mintmark
1890	AE	OẠ mintmark
1891	EN	OẠ mintmark
1892	EN	OẠ mintmark
1893	EN	OẠ mintmark

4 escudos, 0.8750 gold, 13.540 g.

Obverse: National coat of arms and legend REPUBLICA MEXICANA . *Reverse:* Above an open book, a hand holding a staff with a liberty cap. Legend LA LIBERTAD EN LA LEY, ★, denomination, mintmark, date, assayer's initials, and .21 Q$. *Mintmark:* O. *Diameter:* 30 mm. *Edge:* Diagonally milled. BW-210.7, KM-381.7.

Date	Assayer	Comment
1861	FR	

8 escudos, 0.8750 gold, 27.070 g.

Obverse: National coat of arms and legend REPUBLICA MEXICANA . *Reverse:* Above an open book, a hand holding a staff with a liberty cap. Legend LA LIBERTAD EN LA LEY, ★, denomination, mintmark, date, assayer's initials, and .21 Q$. *Mintmark:* O or Ⓞ. *Diameter:* 37 mm. *Edge:* Diagonally milled. BW-212.10, KM-383.10.

Date	Assayer	Comment
1860	AE	Ⓞ mintmark
1861	FR	O mintmark
1862	FR	O mintmark
1863	FR	O mintmark
1864	FR	O mintmark
1867	AE	O mintmark
1868	AE	O mintmark
1869	AE	O mintmark

San Luis Potosí

The San Luis Potosí mint, located in the capital city of the state of San Luis Potosí, was opened in 1827 and closed in 1893. All six real denominations were issued in silver. No gold coins were issued from this mint in this period.

The mintmarks for Upright Eagle coinage of San Luis Potosí are P, ṗ, P!, and S.L.P!. Assayer initials are as follows:

JS	Juan Sanabria (1827–1842)
AM	José Antonio Mucharraz (1838, 1843–1849)
PS	Pomposo Sanabria (1842–1843, 1848–1849, 1857–1861, 1867–1870)
SP	Possible error for PS (1849)
MC	Mariaño Catano (1849–1859)
RO	Romualdo Obregón (1859–1865)
FE	Unknown (1860)
MO	Unknown (1863)
FC	Unknown (1863)
MH	Manuel Herrera Razo (1870–1885)
CA	Carlos Aguirre Gómez (1867–1870)
BE	Blas Escontría (1879–1881)
MM	Unknown (1884)
LC	Luis Cuevas (1885–1886)
MR	Mariano Reyes (1886–1893)

1/4 real, silver, 0.8450 g.

Obverse: Bust of Liberty facing left, with mintmark. *Reverse:* Denomination surrounded by legend REPUBLICA MEXICANA and .[date]. *Mintmark:* S.L.P!. *Diameter:* 12 mm. *Edge:* Plain. BW-201.8, KM-368.7. Note: Engraver's initials were placed on the 1842 issue only.

Date	Engraver	Comment
1842	LR	
1843/2		
1843		
1844		
1845/3		
1845/4		
1845		
1847/5		
1847		
1851/47		
1851		
1854		Rare
1856		Rare
1857		Rare
1862/57		
1862		

1/2 real, 0.90277 silver, 1.690 g.

Obverse: National coat of arms surrounded by legend REPUBLICA MEXICANA . *Reverse:* Radiant liberty cap, ★, denomination, mintmark, date, assayer's initials, and 10 D$ 20G$. *Mintmark:* P!. *Diameter:* 16 mm. *Edge:* Ornamented. BW-202.11, KM-370.10.

Date	Assayer	Comment
1831	JS	
1831	JS	ṗ mintmark

Date	Assayer	Comment
1831	JS	P̍ mintmark, no ★; rare
1841/36	JS	
1841/38	JS	Reported
1842	JS	Rare
1842/1	PS/PJ	Rare
1842	PS	
1843/2	PS	
1843	PS	No ★
1843	AM	
1844	AM	
1845/4	AM	Reported
1845	AM	Very rare
1846/5	AM	
1847/6	AM	
1848	AM	
1849	MC-AM	
1849	MC	
1850/49	MC	Very rare
1850	MC	
1850	MC	P mintmark
1851	MC	
1852	MC	
1853	MC	P mintmark
1853	MC	
1854	MC	Medal axis
1854	MC	Coin axis
1855	MC	
1856	MC	
1856	MC	P mintmark
1857	MC	Rare
1857	PS	Rare
1858	MC	Rare
1858	PS	Rare
1859	MC	Very rare
1860/59	PS	
1861	RO	
1862/1	RO	
1862	RO	
1863/2	RO	

1 real, 0.90277 silver, 3.380 g.

Obverse: National coat of arms and legend REPUBLICA MEXICANA . *Reverse:* Radiant liberty cap, ★, denomination, mintmark, date, assayer's initials, and 10 D$20G$. *Mintmark:* P!. *Diameter:* 20 mm. *Edge:* Ornamented. BW-203.10, KM-372.9.

Date	Assayer	Comment
1831	JS	No ★
1831	JS	With ★
1837	JS	Reported
1837	JS	With ★; very rare
1838/7	JS	
1838	JS	Very rare
1840/39	JS	
1840	JS	
1841	JS	
1842	JS	
1842	PS	
1843	AM	
1843	PS	
1844	AM	
1845	AM	
1846/5	AM	
1847/6	AM	
1847	AM	
1848/7	AM	
1849	SP	
1849/8	SP	Rare
1849	PS	
1850	MC	
1851/0	MC	
1851	MC	
1852	MC	2/1/0
1852	MC	
1853/1	MC	
1853	MC	
1854/2	MC	Rare
1854/3	MC	
1855	MC	
1855/4	MC	
1856	MC	
1857	PS	
1857	MC	Rare
1858	MC	
1859	PS	
1860/59	PS	
1860/59	PS	S/C; rare
1861	PS	
1861	RO	
1862/1	RO	
1862	RO	

2 reales, 0.90277 silver, 6.760 g.

Obverse: National coat of arms and legend REPUBLICA MEXICANA. *Reverse:* Radiant liberty cap, ★, denomination, mintmark, date, assayer's initials, and 10 D$20G$. *Mintmark:* P!. *Diameter:* 27 mm. *Edge:* Ornamented. BW-204.13, KM-374.11.

Date	Assayer	Comment
1829	JS	P mintmark
1830/20	JS	P mintmark
1830/20	JS	P! mintmark
1837	JS	
1841	JS	
1842/1	JS	
1842	JS	
1842	PS	
1843	PS	
1843	AM	
1844	AM	
1845/4	AM	
1845	AM	Reported
1846	AM	
1849	MC	
1850	MC	
1850/49	MC	Very rare
1856	MC	
1857	MC	Very rare
1858	MC	
1859	MC	Very rare
1861	PS	
1862	RO	
1863	RO	
1863/2	RO	
1868	PS	
1869/8	PS	

4 reales, 0.90277 silver, 13.540 g.

Obverse: National coat of arms and legend REPUBLICA MEXICANA . *Reverse:* Radiant liberty cap, ★, denomination, mintmark, date, assayer's initials, and 10 D$ 20 G$. *Mintmark:* P!. *Diameter:* 32 mm. *Edge:* Ornamented. BW-205.9, KM-375.8.

Date	Assayer	Comment
1837	JS	6-pointed ★; rare
1838	JS	Rare
1842	PS	
1843/2	PS	Round-top 3
1843/2	PS	Flat-top 3
1843	PS	3 cut from 8-punch
1843	AM	
1843	PS	Normal digits and date

Date	Assayer	Comment
1844	AM	Small s
1844	AM	Large S
1845/4	AM	
1845	AM	
1846	AM	
1847	AM	
1848	AM	Extremely rare
1849	PS	Rare
1849	MC/AM	
1849	MC	
1850	MC	
1851	MC	
1852	MC	
1853	MC	
1854	MC	Rare
1855	MC	Rare
1856	MC	Rare
1857	MC	Very rare
1857	PS	Very rare
1858	MC	Extremely rare
1859	MC	Extremely rare
1860	PS	Extremely rare (1 known)
1861	PS	
1861	RO/PS	
1861/0	PS	
1862	RO	
1863	RO	
1864	RO	Extremely rare
1868	PS	
1869/8	PS	
1869	PS	

8 reales, 0.90277 silver, 27.070 g.

Obverse: National coat of arms and legend REPUBLICA MEXICANA . *Reverse:* Radiant liberty cap, ★, denomination, mintmark, date, assayer's initials, and 10 D$ 20 G$. *Mintmark:* P!. *Diameter:* 39 mm. *Edge:* Ornamented. BW-206.13, KM-377.12.

Date	Assayer	Comment
1827	JS	
1828/7	JS	
1828	JS	
1829	JS	
1830	JS	Centered-cap and low-cap varieties

Date	Assayer	Comment
1831/0	JS	
1831	JS	
1832, 3/2	JS	
1832, 8/0	JS	Very rare
1832	JS	
1833/2	JS	
1833	JS	Narrow date, planchet 37.5 mm
1833	JS	Wide date, planchet 38.5 mm
1834/3	JS	
1834	JS	Centered-cap and low-cap varieties
1835	JS	
1835	JS	8 Rs denomination
1836	JS	
1836	JS	8 Rs denomination
1837	JS	
1837	JS	8 Rs denomination
1838	JS	
1838	JS	8 Rs denomination
1839	JS	Centered-cap and low-cap varieties
1839	JS	8 Rs denomination
1840	JS	
1841	JS	
1841	JS	^{I}P mintmark error
1842/1	JS	
1842/1	JS/PS	
1842	JS	1843 eagle style
1842	PS	
1842	PS/JS	1841 eagle style
1843/2	PS	Round-top 3
1843	PS	Flat-top 3
1843	AM	Flat-top 3
1844	AM	
1845/4	AM	
1845	AM	
1846/5	AM	
1846	AM	
1847	AM	
1848	AM	
1849/8	PS/AM	
1849	PS/AM	
1849	PS	
1849	MC/PS	
1849	AM	
1849	MC	
1850	MC	
1851	MC	
1852	MC	
1853	MC	
1854	MC	
1855	MC	
1856	MC	
1857	MC	
1857	PS/MC	
1857	PS	
1858	MC/PS	
1858	PS	
1859/8	MC/PS	
1859	PS/MC	
1860	MC	
1860	RO	Rare
1860	PS	
1861	PS	
1861	RO	
1862/1	RO	
1862	RO	Round O in RO, with O/M
1862	RO	Oval 0 in R0
1862	RO	6 is an inverted 9; round O in RO
1863/2	RO	
1863/93	RO	
1863	RO	
1863	FC	
1864	RO	Rare
1867	CA	
1867	LR	
1867	PS	
1868/7	PS	
1868	PS	
1869/8	PS	
1869	PS	
1870	PS	
1873	MH	
1874/3	MH	
1874	MH	
1875	MH	
1876/5	MH	
1876	MH	
1877	MH	
1878	MH	
1879/8	MH	
1879	MH	

8 reales, BW-206.13, continued

Date	Assayer	Comment
1879	BE	
1879	MR	
1880	MR	
1880	MH	
1881	MH	
1882/1	MH	
1882	MH	
1883	MH	
1884/3	MH	
1884	MH/MM	
1884	MH	
1885/4	MH	
1885/8	MH	
1885	MH	
1885	LC	
1886	LC	
1886	MR	
1887	MR	
1888/7	MR	
1888	MR	
1889	MR	
1890	MR	
1891	MR	
1892	MR	
1893	MR	

Zacatecas

The Zacatecas mint is located in the capital city of the rich mining district in the state of Zacatecas. It was opened in October 1810 as a provisional mint during the War of Independence. The first Republic coinage was issued in 1825. The mint closed in 1905 when that year's coinage reform was instituted.

Zacatecas issued silver coinage in all denominations. The 1/4 real was issued only in 1842; the 1866 1/4-real coins bearing Zacatecas mintmarks are considered to be contemporary counterfeits. Gold coinage was produced in all denominations.

The mintmarks for Upright Eagle coinage of Zacatecas are Z, $\overset{s}{Z}$, and Z$. Assayer initials are as follows:

A	Adalco (1825–1828)
Z	Mariano Zaldívar (1825–1826)
V	José Mariano Vela (1824–1831)
O	Manuel Ochoa (1829–1867)
M	Manuel Miner (1831–1867)
LR	Luciano Rovira* (1842–?)
VL	Vicente Larrañaga (1860–1866)
JS	Possibly Jesús María Sánchez de Santa Ana (1867–1868, 1876–1886)
YH	Ygnacio Hierro (1868–1874)
JA	Juan M. Acuña (1874–1876)
FZ	Francisco de P. Zárate (1886–1897)

* Engraver only. Luciano Rovira engraved 1/4-real coins at numerous mints for varying periods of time from 1842 through 1863. In addition, Buttrey (5th ed.), page 260, shows a pattern 1 real designed and signed by Rovira.

1/4 real, silver, 0.845 g.

Obverse: Bust of Liberty facing left, with mintmark and engraver's initials. *Reverse:* Denomination surrounded by legend **REPUBLICA MEXICANA** and **.[date].** *Mintmark:* **Z**. *Diameter:* 12 mm. *Edge:* Plain. BW-201.9, KM-368.8.

Date	Engraver	Comment
1842	LR	

1/2 real, 0.90277 silver, 1.690 g.

Obverse: National coat of arms surrounded by legend **REPUBLICA MEXICANA** and the date. *Reverse:* Radiant liberty cap, ★, denomination, mintmark, date, assayer's initials, and **10 D$ 20 G$**. *Mintmark:* **Z**. *Diameter:* 16 mm. *Edge:* Ornamented. BW-202.12, KM-370.11.

Date	Assayer	Comment
1826	A-Z	
1826	A-O	
1827	A-O	
1827/7	A-O	
1828/7	A-O	
1829	A-O	
1830	O-V	
1831	O-V	
1831	O-M	
1832	O-M	
1833	O-M	Large M

Date	Assayer	Comment
1833	O-M	Normal M
1834	O-M	
1835/4	O-M	
1835	O-M	
1836	O-M	Cap of 1835
1836	O-M	Cap of 1836–1837
1837	O-M	Cap of 1835
1837	O-M	Cap of 1836–1837
1838	O-M	Medal axis
1839	O-M	
1840	O-M	Medal axis
1841	O-M	Medal axis
1841	O-M	Coin axis
1842/1	O-M	Medal axis
1842	O-M	Coin axis
1843	O-M	
1844	O-M	
1845	O-M	
1846	O-M	
1847	O-M	
1848	O-M	
1849	O-M	
1850	O-M	
1851	O-M	
1852	O-M	
1853	O-M	
1854/3	O-M	
1854	O-M	
1855/3	O-M	
1855	O-M	
1856	O-M	
1857	M-O	Z$ mintmark (1857–1869)
1858	M-O	
1859	VL	
1860	VL	
1860	M-O	
1860/50	VL	V is inverted A
1860/59	VL	V is inverted A
1861/0	VL	V is inverted A
1861	VL	V is inverted A
1862	VL	V is inverted A, no ★
1863	VL	V is inverted A
1863/1	VL	V is inverted A
1869	YH	No . after MEXICANA
1869	YH	. after MEXICANA

1 real, 0.90277 silver, 3.380 g.

Obverse: National coat of arms and legend REPUBLICA MEXICANA . *Reverse:* Radiant liberty cap, ★, denomination, mintmark, date, assayer's initials, and 10 D$ 20 G$. *Mintmark:* Z$. *Diameter:* 20 mm. *Edge:* Ornamented. BW-203.11, KM-372.10.

Date	Assayer	Comment
1826	A-Z	
1826	A-O	
1827	A-O	
1828/7	A-O	
1828	A-O	Normal A
1828	A-O	A is inverted V
1829	A-O	
1830	O-V	Small v
1830	O-V	Large V
1830	O-V	Z mintmark
1831	O-V	Rare
1831	O-M	
1832	O-M	
1833/2	O-M	
1833	O-M	
1833	O-M	REPUBLIJCA error; rare
1834/3	O-M	O/4 in assayer's mark
1834	O-M	
1835/4	O-M	Small o
1835	O-M	
1836/5	O-M	
1836	O-M	
1837	O-M	
1838	O-M	
1839	O-M	
1840	O-M	
1841	O-M	
1842/1	O-M	
1842	O-M	
1843	O-M	
1844	O-M	
1845	O-M	I/C in REPUBLICA
1846	O-M	Old-style cap and eagle
1846	O-M	New-style cap and eagle
1847	O-M	
1848	O-M	
1849	O-M	

1 real, BW-203.11, continued

Date	Assayer	Comment
1850	O-M	
1851	O-M	
1852	O-M	
1853	O-M	
1854/2	O-M	
1854	O-M	4/3/2; rare
1854/3	O-M	
1854	O-M	
1855/4	O-M	
1855	M-O	
1856	M-O	
1857	M-O	
1858	M-O	
1859	M-O	
1860	VL	V is inverted A
1861	VL	
1861	VL	V is inverted A
1862	VL	
1868	JS	Rare
1869	YH	YH/JS
1869	YH	

2 reales, 0.90277 silver, 6.760 g.

Obverse: National coat of arms and legend REPUBLICA MEXICANA. *Reverse:* Radiant liberty cap, ★, denomination, mintmark, date, assayer's initials, and 10 D$ 20 G$. *Mintmark:* Z$. *Diameter:* 27 mm. *Edge:* Ornamented. BW-204.14, KM-374.12.

Date	Assayer	Comment
1825	A-Z	
1826	A-V	A is inverted V
1826	A-Z	A is inverted V
1826	A-O	A is inverted V
1826	A-O	
1827	A-O	A is inverted V
1827	A-O	
1828/7	A-O	
1828	A-O	
1828	A-O	A is inverted V
1829	A-O	
1829	O-V	
1830	O-V	
1831	O-V	
1831	O-M	OM/OV
1831	O-M	
1832/1	O-M	
1832	O-M	
1833/27	O-M	
1833/2	O-M	
1833	O-M	
1833	O-M	3 used for S in mintmark
1834	O-M	
1835	O-M	
1836	O-M	
1837	O-M	
1837/5	O-M	3 used for S in mintmark; rare
1838	O-M	
1839	O-M	
1840	O-M	
1841/0	O-M	
1841	O-M	
1842	O-M	
1843	O-M	
1844	O-M	
1845	O-M	Small letters
1845	O-M	Large letters
1846	O-M	
1847	O-M	
1848	O-M	
1849	O-M	
1850	O-M	
1851	O-M	
1852	O-M	
1853	O-M	
1854/3	O-M	
1854	O-M	
1855/4	O-M	
1855	O-M	
1855	M-O	
1856/5	M-O	
1856	M-O	
1857	M-O	
1858	M-O	
1859	M-O	
1860/59	M-O	
1860	M-O	
1860	VL	
1861	VL	
1862	VL	
1863	M-O	
1863	VL	
1864	M-O	

Date	Assayer	Comment
1864	VL	
1865	M-O	
1867	JS	
1868	JS	
1868	YH	
1869	YH	
1870	YH	

4 reales, 0.90277 silver, 13.540 g.

Obverse: National coat of arms and legend REPUBLICA MEXICANA . *Reverse:* Radiant liberty cap, ★, denomination, mintmark, date, assayer's initials, and 10 D$ 20 G$. *Mintmark:* Z$. *Diameter:* 32 mm. *Edge:* Ornamented. BW-205.10, KM-375.9.

Date	Assayer	Comment
1830	O-M	Reported
1831	O-M	. after MEXICANA
1831	O-M	No . after MEXICANA
1832/1	O-M	
1832	O-M	
1833/2	O-M	
1833/27	O-M	
1833	O-M	
1834/3	O-M	
1834	O-M	
1835	O-M	
1836	O-M	
1837/5	O-M	
1837/6	O-M	Reported
1837	O-M	
1838/7	O-M	Rare
1839	O-M	Extremely rare
1840	O-M	Extremely rare
1841	O-M	
1842	O-M	Small letters
1842	O-M	Large letters
1843	O-M	
1844	O-M	
1845	O-M	
1846	O-M	Large OM
1846	O-M	Small OM
1847	O-M	
1848/6	O-M	
1848	O-M	
1849	O-M	
1850	O-M	
1851	O-M	
1852	O-M	
1853	O-M	
1854/3	O-M	
1854	O-M	
1855/4	O-M	
1855	O-M	Large diameter
1856	OM	Small diameter
1856	M-O	
1857/5	M-O	
1857	M-O	M/O, O/M
1857	M-O	
1858	M-O	
1859	M-O	
1860/59	M-O	
1860	M-O	
1860	VL	
1861/0	VL	
1861	VL	
1861 6/5	VL	
1862/1	VL	
1862	VL	
1863	VL	
1863	M-O	Thick O
1864	VL	
1868	JS	
1868	YH	
1869	YH	
1870	YH	

8 reales, 0.90277 silver, 27.070 g.

Obverse: National coat of arms and legend REPUBLICA MEXICANA . *Reverse:* Radiant liberty cap, ★, denomination, mintmark, date, assayer's initials, and 10 D$ 20 G$. *Mintmark:* Z$. *Diameter:* 39 mm. *Edge:* Ornamented. BW-206.14, KM-377.13.

Date	Assayer	Comment
1825	A-Z	
1826/5	A-Z	Rare
1826	A-Z	
1826	A-V	
1826/5	A-O/A-Z	
1826	A-O	
1827	A-O	
1827	A-O/A-Z	
1828	A-O	Wide date
1829	A-O	

8 reales, BW-206.14, continued

Date	Assayer	Comment
1829	O-V	
1830	O-V	
1831	O-V	
1831	O-M	
1832/1	O-M	
1832	O-M	
1833/2	O-M	
1833	O-M	
1834	O-M	Small 34 in date
1834	O-M	Medium 34 in date
1834	O-M	Large 34 in date
1835	O-M	
1836/5	O-M	
1836	O-M	
1837	O-M	
1838/7	O-M	
1838	O-M	
1839/7	O-M	
1839	O-M	
1840	O-M	
1841	O-M	
1842	O-M	Eagle style of 1841
1842	O-M	Eagle style of 1843
1843	O-M	
1843/33	O-M	
1844	O-M	
1845	O-M	
1846	O-M	
1847	O-M	
1848/7	O-M	
1848	O-M	
1849	O-M	
1850	O-M	
1851	O-M	
1852	O-M	
1853	O-M	
1854	O-M	
1855	O-M	
1855	M-O	
1856/5	M-O	
1856	M-O	
1857/5	M-O	
1857	M-O	
1858/7	M-O	
1858	M-O	
1859	M-O	

Date	Assayer	Comment
1859/8	M-O	
1859	VL/M-O	
1859	VL	
1860/50	M-O	
1860/59	M-O	
1860	M-O	
1860	VL/M-O	
1860	VL	
1861/0	VL/M-O	
1861	VL	
1861/0	VL	
1862//1	VL	
1862	VL	
1863	VL	
1863	M-O	
1864/3	VL	
1864	VL	
1864	M-O	
1865/4	M-O	
1865	M-O	
1866	VL	Circulating counterfeit
1867	JS	Rare
1868	JS	
1868	YH	
1869	YH	
1870	YH	Rare
1873	YH	
1874	YH	
1874	JA/YA	
1874	JA	
1875	JA	
1876	JA	
1876	JS	
1877	JS	
1878	JS	
1879/8	JS	
1879	JS	
1880	JS	
1881	JS	
1882/1	JS	Straight J
1882/1	JS	Full J
1882	JS	Straight J
1882	JS	Full J
1883/2	JS	
1883	JS	
1884	JS	

Date	Assayer	Comment
1885	JS	
1886/5	JS	
1886	JS	
1886	FZ	
1887	FZ	
1887	FZ	Z mintmark
1888/7	FZ	
1888	FZ	
1889	FZ	
1890	FZ	
1891	FZ	
1892/1	FZ	
1892	FZ	Narrow date
1892	FZ	Wide date
1893	FZ	
1894	FZ	
1895	FZ	
1896	FZ	
1897	FZ	

1/2 escudo, 0.8750 gold, 1.690 g.

Obverse: National coat of arms and legend REPUBLICA MEXICANA . *Reverse:* Above an open book, a hand holding a staff with a liberty cap. Legend LA LIBERTAD EN LA LEY, ★, denomination, mintmark, date, assayer's initials, and .21 Q$. *Mintmark:* Z$. *Diameter:* 15 mm. *Edge:* Diagonally milled. BW-207.6, KM-378.6.

Date	Assayer	Comment
1860	VL	
1862/1	VL	
1862	VL	

1 escudo, 0.8750 gold, 3.380 g.

Obverse: National coat of arms and legend REPUBLICA MEXICANA . *Reverse:* Above an open book, a hand holding a staff with a liberty cap. Legend LA LIBERTAD EN LA LEY, ★, denomination, mintmark, date, assayer's initials, and .21 Q$. *Mintmark:* Z$. *Diameter:* 18 mm. *Edge:* Diagonally milled. BW-208.6, KM-379.6.

Date	Assayer	Comment
1853	O-M	
1860/59	VL	V is inverted A
1860	VL	
1862	VL	

2 escudos, 0.8750 gold, 6.770 g.

Obverse: National coat of arms and legend REPUBLICA MEXICANA . *Reverse:* Above an open book, a hand holding a staff with a liberty cap. Legend LA LIBERTAD EN LA LEY, ★, denomination, mintmark, date, assayer's initials, and .21 Q$. *Mintmark:* Z$. *Diameter:* 23 mm. *Edge:* Diagonally milled. BW-209.8, KM-380.8.

Date	Assayer	Comment
1860	VL	Rare
1862	VL	
1864	M-O	Rare

4 escudos, 0.8750 gold, 13.540 g.

Obverse: National coat of arms and legend REPUBLICA MEXICANA . *Reverse:* Above an open book, a hand holding a staff with a liberty cap. Legend LA LIBERTAD EN LA LEY, ★, denomination, mintmark, date, assayer's initials, and .21 Q$. *Mintmark:* Z$. *Diameter:* 30 mm. *Edge:* Diagonally milled. BW-210.8, KM-381.8.

Date	Assayer	Comment
1860	VL	Rare
1862	VL	

8 escudos, 0.8750 gold, 27.070 g.

Obverse: National coat of arms and legend REPUBLICA MEXICANA . *Reverse:* Above an open book, a hand holding a staff with a liberty cap. Legend LA LIBERTAD EN LA LEY, ★, denomination, mintmark, date, assayer's initials, and .21 Q$. *Mintmark:* Z$. *Diameter:* 37 mm. *Edge:* Diagonally milled. BW-212.11, KM-383.11.

Date	Assayer	Comment
1858	M-O	
1859	M-O	
1860/59	VL-MO	
1860/9	M-O	
1860	M-O	
1861/0	VL	
1861	VL	
1862	VL	
1863	VL	
1863	M-O	
1864	M-O	
1865	M-O	

8 escudos, BW-212.11, continued

Date	Assayer	Comment
1868	JS	
1868	YH	
1869	YH	
1870	YH	
1871	YH	

Republic Upright Eagle Coinage

**1/4 real. 1843-MQ̣, LR.
BW-201.7,
KM-368.6, 12 mm.**

**1/2 real. 1844-P!, AM.
BW-202.11,
KM-370.1, 16 mm.**

**1 real. 1829/8/7-G, FS.
BW-203.5, KM-372.4, 20 mm.**

**2 reales. 1861-M̊, CH.
BW-204.12, KM-374.10, 27 mm.**

**4 reales. 1863-C$, ML.
BW-205.1, KM-375, 32 mm.**

**8 reales.
1878-A$, DL.
BW-206.1,
KM-377, 39 mm.**

**8 reales.
1863-C$, ML.
BW-206.2,
KM-377.1,
39 mm.**

Republic Upright Eagle Coinage

(continued)

**8 reales.
1880-CẠ, MG.
BW-206.3
KM-377.2,
39 mm.**

**8 reales.
1895-CṆ, AM.
BW-206.4,
KM-377.3,
39 mm.**

**8 reales.
1890-DỌ, MC.
BW-206.5,
KM-377.4,
39 mm.**

**8 reales.
1829-EỌMỌ,
L-F. BW-206.6,
KM-377.5,
39 mm.**

**8 reales.
1894-GẠ, JS.
BW-206.7,
KM-377.6,
39 mm.**

**8 reales.
1845-GC, MP.
BW-206.8,
KM-377.7,
39 mm.**

Republic Upright Eagle Coinage

(continued)

8 reales. 1831-G, MJ (with colon after date). BW-206.5, KM-377.8, 39 mm.

8 reales. 1894-H̊, FG. BW-206.10, KM-377.9, 39 mm.

8 reales. 1883/2-M̊, MH. BW-206.11, KM-377.10, 39 mm.

8 reales. 1874-OÅ, AE. BW-206, KM-377.11, 39 mm.

8 reales. 1885/8-P!, MH. BW-206.13, KM-377.12, 39 mm.

8 reales. 1886-Z$, JS. BW-206.14, KM-377.13, 39 mm.

Republic Upright Eagle Coinage

(continued)

1/2 escudo. 1850-D♀, JMR.
BW-207.1, KM-378.1, 15 mm.

1 escudo. 1838-D♀, RM.,
M over L. BW-208.1,
KM-379.1, 18 mm.

2 escudos. 1863-M̊, TH.
BW-209.7, KM-380.7, 23 mm.

4 escudos. 1844-GẠ, MC.
BW-210.2, KM-381.2, 30 mm.

8 escudos. 1863-C, CE.
BW-212.2, KM-383.2, 36 mm.

9

State and Federal Copper Coinage

The constitution of October 4, 1824 (establishing the Mexican republic), and related legislation recognized the states as free and sovereign in affairs within their borders. This included taxation and fiscal matters. The states were to volunteer a yearly monetary grant to the federal government for its expenses. The state legislatures elected the president, vice president, and members of the Federal Supreme Court. Thus the provinces created the nation. The next three-and-a-half decades were to be a period of conflict between those who favored a strong central government with subservient states, and those who opted for a republican system with strong and independent states.

Article 49, section IV, states that "It is the prerogative of Congress to fix and determine the weight, fineness, value, and type of monetary denomination of the country as well as of the coins issued by any of the federal states of the republic." Further legislation on November 16 gave the states the right to take charge of mints within their boundaries and the power to establish new mints if desired. However, the states were expected to conform to the law of August 1, 1823, which had established specifications for coinage. This requirement was largely ignored, with each state doing as it pleased; nevertheless, the legal mechanism of state coinage was in place.

The issuance of coinage was considered by some to be a mark of sovereignty, as coin legends such as "Estado Libre y Soberano" ("Free and Sovereign State") indicate. Ideally, by issuing copper coins the states would become financially responsible and would relieve the central government from the function of minor-coin production.

By congressional decree of March 28, 1829, the central government's first amortization (to liquidate a debt or obligation) authorized the mintage of 600,000 pesos in copper coins to redeem colonial coppers at equal exchange. The overproduction of copper coins that began in the late 1820s soon caused inflation and devaluation of the coinage, while at the same time silver became scarce in circulation.

Counterfeit copper coins flooded the market, and discounting began at 5 to 6 percent, reaching 75 percent by 1835. From July 1834 to July 1835, the face value of coppers minted increased to more than a million pesos, while the coppers in circulation reached five to six million pesos.

On October 23, 1835, the national congress passed a law revoking the rights of states to establish mints, and reducing their power to authorize them. However, the central government was not in a position to enforce this, if the states were of a mind to resist. The constitution of 1836, "Los Siete Leyes" ("The Seven Laws"), took the authority from the states and consolidated it in the central government. The states were henceforth known as *departamentos* (departments), which were controlled by Mexico City.

By decree of January 17, 1837, the government dictated that no more copper coins were to be minted in the Republic. A bank was established in 1837, to amortize circulating copper coins. This 1837 amortization brought in 43,000 pesos' worth of coins, which reportedly weighed 200 tons. Another attempt at amortization of coppers was made in 1839; it was unsuccessful due to the unstable financial situation of the country.

The situation again became critical in 1841, when from August to October, the revolution against President Anastasio Bustamante caused the collapse of law and order. There was uncontrolled devaluation, and counterfeiting was especially rampant. When Antonio López de Santa Anna returned to power he attacked the copper-money problem in several ways. Counterfeiters were court-martialed (tried in military court), and property owners caught with counterfeiting equipment were fined or jailed. A new 1/8 real was to be issued that would replace old copper coins. A plan emerged that would remove the old copper in the Department of México within 30 days of issue of the new *octavos*, and remove the old copper elsewhere in the republic within 60 days.

On December 18, 1841, the new coins began to be released. They eventually had a calming effect on the populace. Stability began to return, but the same problems would re-emerge when copper was again struck in excessive quantities. Various states attempted to solve the copper-money problem, including the state-coin-producing states of Jalisco, Zacatecas, and Guanajuato, which had their own amortizations.

On August 22, 1846, the charter of 1824 was restored. The departments were again to be known as states, with their own constitutions and elected officials. Power was decentralized, with the states resuming their importance. Nevertheless, on September 17, 1846, the national government again tried to terminate all rights that states had over mints, stating that coinage was to be its own exclusive right. Powerful states ignored the new law, and the central government lacked the muscle to enforce it.

The constitution of 1857 effectively made coinage the prerogative of the federal government. However, the troubled and chaotic times and the War of Reform (1858 to 1860) made resolute enforcement impossible. The metric coinage system was established by decree of President Benito Juárez on March 15, 1861. Coinage weights and values were specified, along with an all-new copper centavo weighing 0.32 ounce with a value of 1/100th of a peso. This would seem to have been a reaffirmation of the demise of state coinage. With the exception of the centavo in 1863, this decree was not put into effect, due to political events of the time. Finally, on November 27, 1867, after the fall of the Maximilian Empire, Juárez was able to have the 1861 law ratified and thus establish the decimal system.

Porfirio Díaz officially ended all non-federal coinage issues, including the private and municipals. A law of January 1, 1885, states that all old copper would cease to circulate. Since old specie still continued to circulate, the law was postponed on December 31, 1886. Not until January 19, 1899, did the law specifying the decimal system for the entire republic become effective.

During this period from 1824 to 1872, copper coins were issued by the following states and federal governments: Chihuahua, Durango, Guanajuato, Jalisco, Occidente, San Luis Potosí, Sinaloa, Sonora, and Zacatecas.

STATE OF CHIHUAHUA

Estado Soberano de Chihuahua

1/8 real, copper.

Obverse: Forward-facing Indian angled slightly to right, with bow, arrow, and quiver. Legend ★ ESTADO SOBERANO DE CHIHUAHUA. *Reverse:* Within a palm wreath, in two lines, the denomination $\frac{1}{8}$ and [date]. *Diameter:* 20 mm. *Edge:* Herringbone. DB-101, BW-176, KM-318.

Note: The herringbone-pattern edge used from 1833 to 1835 most often is incomplete or missing, especially on thin planchets. Stars are mostly five-pointed.

Date	Comment
1833	Fine wreath
1834	Coarse wreath
1835	Coarse wreath
1835	Fine wreath

1/4 real, copper.

Obverse: Forward-facing Indian angled slightly to right, with bow, arrow, and quiver. Legend ★ ESTADO SOBERANO DE CHIHUAHUA. *Reverse:* Within a palm wreath, in two lines, the denomination $\frac{1}{4}$ and [date]. *Diameter:* 27 mm. *Edge:* Herringbone. DB-150, BW-190, KM-340.

Date	Comment
1833	Fine wreath
1834	Coarse wreath
1835	Coarse wreath
1835/33	Fine wreath

Estado Libre de Chihuahua

1/4 real, copper.

Obverse: Forward-facing Indian angled slightly to right, with bow, arrow, and quiver. Legend ★ ESTADO LIBRE DE CHIHUAHUA. *Reverse:* Within a plain wreath, in two lines, the denomination $\frac{1}{4}$ and 1846. *Diameter:* 26 mm. *Edge:* Plain. DB-155, BW-190.1, KM-341.

Date	Comment
1846	With fractional bar
1846	Without fractional bar
1846	D over reversed D; rare

Estado de Chihuahua

1/8 real, copper.

Obverse: Forward-facing Indian angled slightly to right, with bow, arrow, and quiver. Legend ESTADO DE CHIHUAHUA ★★★★★★★★★. *Reverse:* Within a palm wreath, in two lines, the denomination $\frac{1}{8}$ and 1855. *Diameter:* 20 mm. *Edge:* Plain. DB-110, BW-176.1, KM-319.

Date	Comment
1855	

1/4 real, copper.

Obverse: Forward-facing Indian angled slightly to right, with bow, arrow, and quiver. Legend ★ ESTADO DE CHIHUAHUA ★. *Reverse:* Within a palm wreath, in two lines, the denomination $\frac{1}{4}$ and [date]. *Diameter:* 26 mm. *Edge:* Plain. DB-160, BW-190.2, KM-342.

Date	Comment
1855	
1856	

Departamento de Chihuahua

1/4 real, copper.

Obverse: Forward-facing Indian angled slightly to right, with bow, arrow, and quiver. Legend ★ DEPARTAMENTO DE. CHIHUAHUA ★. *Reverse:* Within a palm wreath, in two lines, the denomination $\frac{1}{4}$ and 1855. *Diameter:* 24 mm. *Edge:* Plain. DB-165, BW-190.3, KM-343.

Date	Comment
1855	
1855	DE over reversed DE

E. de Chihuahua

1/4 real, copper.

Obverse: Seated Liberty facing right, holding a lance. Legend E. CHIHẠ LIBERTAD. *Reverse:* Within laurel and oak wreath, in three lines, the denomination $\frac{1}{4}$ DE REAL and [date]. *Diameter:* 28 mm. *Edge:* Plain. DB-170, BW-190.4, KM-344.

Date	Comment
1860	
1861	

Date	Comment
1865	
1866	

STATE OF DURANGO

Durango

1/8 real, copper.

Obverse: Eagle with wings spread, facing right, with a serpent in its beak, perched on a small nopal cactus. Legend **1/8 D.** *Reverse:* Radiant band, incused, with date below. Legend **Libertad** in script lettering. *Diameter:* 19 mm. *Edge:* Diagonally milled. DB-201, BW-177, KM-320.

Date	Comment
1824	No overstrike
1824	Struck over Nueva Vizcaya *octavo*
1824	Struck over Nueva Vizcaya *quartilla;* rare
1828*	

* Likely a circulating counterfeit.

1/8 real, copper.

Obverse: Below a radiant liberty cap, the legend **OCTº DE R.DE Dº 1828.** *Reverse:* Forward-facing Indian angled to right, toward a flowering tree, and holding a bow, arrow, and quiver. No reverse inscription. *Diameter:* 18 mm. *Edge:* Diagonally milled. DB-210, BW-177.1, KM-321.

Date	Comment
1828	

1/4 real, copper.

Obverse: Within a half-wreath of oak and laurel, an eagle with wings outspread, facing right, with a serpent in its beak, perched on a nopal cactus. Legend **REPUBLICA MEXICANA.** *Reverse:* On a plain field, in two lines, the legend **DURANGO 1858** and $\frac{1}{4}$. *Diameter:* 27 mm. *Edge:* Arc-and-dot design, which may be indistinct or missing. DB-260, BW-191, KM-346.

Date	Comment
1858	

Estado de Durango

1/8 real, copper.

Obverse: Within a half-wreath of oak and laurel, an eagle facing right, with a serpent in its beak, perched on a nopal cactus. Legend **ESTADO DE DURANGO.** *Reverse:* Within a continuous laurel wreath and a circle, the legend **1/8 / DE REAL / 1833** in three lines. *Diameter:* 20 mm. *Edge:* Plain. DB-220, BW-177.2, KM-322.

Date	Comment
1833	

1/8 real, copper.

Obverse: Within a half-wreath of oak and laurel, an eagle with wings outspread, facing right, with a serpent in its beak, perched on a nopal cactus. Legend **REPUBLICA MEXICANA .** *Reverse:* Within a circle, the legend **8º ★ DE REAL ★**; around the circumference, **ESTADO DE DURANGO. ★ [date] ★.** *Diameter:* 19 mm. *Edge:* Herringbone. DB-250, BW-177.5, KM-325.

Date	Comment
1851	
1851*	Rounded-wing Mexican eagle, ornaments under º missing, plain edge
1852	
1852/1	
1853	Inverted 3

* Likely a circulating counterfeit.

1/4 real, copper or brass.

Obverse: Within a half-wreath of oak and laurel, an eagle with wings spread, facing right, with a serpent in its beak, perched on a nopal cactus. Legend **ESTADO DE DURANGO.** *Reverse:* Radiant liberty cap, with sprays of lilies below. Above cap, the legend **CONSTITUCION**; below cap, **1/4 . 1858.** *Diameter:* 27 mm. *Edge:* Arc-and-dot design. DB-270, BW-191.1, KM-347.

Date	Comment
1858	Copper
1858	Brass

1/4 real, copper.

Obverse: Within a half-wreath of oak and laurel, an eagle with wings spread, facing right, with a serpent in its beak, perched on a nopal cactus. Legend **ESTADO DE DURANGO.** *Reverse:* Oak and laurel sprays below. Legend **★ INDEPENDENCIA Y LIBERTAD ★** around circumference; at center, in two lines, **1/4. 1866.** *Diameter:* 27 mm. *Edge:* Arc-and-dot design. DB-285, BW-191.3, KM-349.

Date	Comment
1866	Dot after date
1866	Without dot after date

1/4 real, copper or brass.

Obverse: Within a half-wreath of oak and laurel, an eagle with wings outspread, facing right, with a serpent in its beak, perched on a nopal cactus. Legend **ESTADO DE DURANGO.** *Reverse:* In a circle within a laurel wreath, the legend **SUFRAGIO LIBRE** and **1872**; at center, **1/4.** *Diameter:* 27 mm. *Edge:* Arc-and-dot design. Coins have medal orientation. DB-290, BW-191.4, KM-350.

Date	Comment
1872	Copper
1872	Brass
1872	Copper, "R" counterstamp

Republica Mexicana (Durango)

1/8 real, copper.

Obverse: Within a half-wreath of oak and laurel, an eagle with wings spread, facing right, with a serpent in its beak, perched on nopal cactus. Legend **REPUBLICA MEXICANA.** *Reverse:* Within a continuous laurel wreath and a circle, the legend **1/8 DE REAL [date]** in three lines. *Diameter:* 19 mm. *Edge:* Plain. DB-230, BW-177.3, KM-323.

Date	Comment
1833	REPUBLIC, obverse like DB-230; rare (3 known)
1842/33	
1842	Large date
1842	Small date

Departamento de Durango

1/8 real, copper.

Obverse: Within a half-wreath of oak and laurel, an eagle with wings spread, facing right, with a serpent in its beak, perched on a nopal cactus. Legend **REPUBLICA MEXICANA.** *Reverse:* Within a circle, large **8º** with **DE REAL** in an arc below it; around the circumference, **DEPARTAMENTO DE DURANGO ★ 1845 ★.** *Diameter:* 19 mm. *Edge:* Herringbone. DB-240, BW-177.4, KM-324.

Date	Comment
1845*	
1846	Unconfirmed

* Most 1845's may be circulating counterfeits.

1/4 real, copper.

Obverse: Within a half-wreath of oak and laurel, an eagle with wings spread, facing right, with a serpent in its beak, perched on a nopal cactus. Legend **DEPARTAMENTO DE DURANGO.** *Reverse:* Around the inner circumference of a complete laurel wreath, the legend **LIBERTAD EN EL ORDEN.** At center in two lines, **1/4. / [date].** *Diameter:* 27 mm. *Edge:* Arc-and-dot design. DB-280, BW-191.2, KM-348.

Date	Comment
1860	
1866	

STATE OF GUANAJUATO

Estado Libre de Guanajuato

1/8 real, brass.

Obverse: Seated feminine figure with cornucopia in right hand and olive branch in left. Legend **ESTADO LIBRE DE GUANAJUATO** and **. UN OCTAVO .** *Reverse:* Liberty cap within radiant circle of clouds, with **. [date] .** below. *Diameter:* 20 mm. *Edge:* Incused dots. DB-301, BW-178, KM-326.

Date	Comment
1829	
1829	GRANJUATO error
1829	LIBE error
1830	
1830	GUANJUATO error
1830	Copper

1/4 real, brass.

Obverse: Seated feminine figure with cornucopia in right hand and olive branch in left. Legend **ESTADO LIBRE DE GUANAJUATO** and **. UNA CUARTILLA .** *Reverse:* Liberty cap within radiant circle of clouds, with **. [date] .** below. *Diameter:* 27 mm. *Edge:* Incused dots. DB-350, BW-192, KM-351.

Date	Comment
1828	❁ at date
1828	GUANJUATO error
1828	Dots at date
1828	UNA ❁ CUARTILLA
1829	

Estado Libre de Guanaxuato

1/8 real, copper or brass.

Obverse: Within a half-wreath of oak and laurel, an eagle with wings spread, facing right, with a serpent in its beak, perched on a nopal cactus. Legend **ESTº LIBE DE GUANAXUATO [date]** and **★ OCTAVO ★**. *Reverse:* Radiant liberty cap at top, half-wreath of laurel at bottom. At center, in a small oval, two hands holding a chisel and hammer. Around lower edge of oval, legend **OMNIA VINCIT LABOR.** *Diameter:* 25 mm. *Edge:* Plain. DB-310, BW-178.1, KM-327 and KM-328.

Date	Comment
1856	Large, copper*
1856	Small (25 mm); unconfirmed
1857	Copper
1857	Brass

* KM-327, 29 mm. All others KM-328, 25 mm.

1/4 real, copper or brass.

Obverse: Within a half-wreath of oak and laurel, an eagle with wings spread, facing right, with a serpent in its beak, perched on a nopal cactus. Legend **ESTº LIBE DE GUANAXUATO [date]** and **★ CUARTILLA ★**. *Reverse:* Radiant liberty cap at top, half-wreath of laurel at bottom. At center, in a small oval, two hands holding a chisel and hammer. Around lower edge of oval, legend **OMNIA VINCIT LABOR.** *Diameter:* 32 mm. *Edge:* Plain. DB-360, BW-192.1, KM-352.

Date	Comment
1856	Copper
1856	Copper, T in CUARTILLA not crossed
1856	Brass
1857	Copper
1857	Brass

STATE OF JALISCO, EARLY SERIES

Estado Libre de Jalisco

1/8 real, copper.

Obverse: Bow, quiver, and flag. Legend **ESTADO LIBRE DE JALISCO** and **★ 1828 ★**. *Reverse:* Seated figure of Liberty facing left and holding a liberty cap on a staff. Legend **★ UN ★ / OCTAVO**, divided by seated Liberty. *Diameter:* 21 mm. *Edge:* Diagonally milled. DB-420, BW-179, KM-329.

Date	Comment
1828	
1831	
1832/28	
1832	
1833	
1834	

1/4 real, copper.

Obverse: Bow, quiver, and flag. Legend **ESTADO LIBRE DE JALISCO** and **★ 1828 ★**. *Reverse:* Seated figure of Liberty facing left and holding a liberty cap on a staff. Legend **★ UN ★ / QUARTO ★**, divided by Liberty. *Diameter:* 28 mm. *Edge:* Diagonally milled. DB-450, BW-193, KM-353.

Date	Comment
1828	
1829/8	
1829	
1830	
1830/20	
1830/29	
1831	Rare
1832/1	Unconfirmed
1832	
1832/20	
1832/28	
1833	

1/4 real, BW-193, continued

Date	Comment
1833/2	
1834	
1835	
1835/3	
1836	Unconfirmed

Departamento de Jalisco

1/4 real, copper.

Obverse: Bow, quiver, and flag. Legend DEPARTAMENTO DE JALISCO and ★ 1836 ★. *Reverse:* Seated figure of Liberty facing left and holding a liberty cap on a staff. Legend ★ UN ★ / QUARTO ★, divided by Liberty. *Diameter:* 28 mm. *Edge:* Diagonally milled. DB-460, BW-193.1, KM-354.

Date	Comment
1836	
1836	Dept/Estado

STATE OF JALISCO, LATE SERIES

Departamento de Jalisco

1/16 real, copper.

Obverse: Bow, quiver, and flag. Legend DEPARTAMENTO DE JALISCO and ★ 1860 ★. *Reverse:* Seated figure of Liberty facing left and holding a liberty cap on a staff. Legend ★ MEDIO ★ OCTAVO ★. *Diameter:* 21 mm. *Edge:* Diagonally milled. DB-401, BW-200, KM-316.

Date	Comment
1860	

1/8 real, copper.

Obverse: Bow, quiver, and flag. Legend DEPARTAMENTO DE JALISCO and ★ [date] ★. *Reverse:* Seated figure of Liberty facing left and holding a liberty cap on a staff. Legend ★ UN ★ OCTAVO ★. *Diameter:* 28 mm. *Edge:* Diagonally milled. DB-480, BW-179.2 KM-331.

Date	Comment
1858	
1859	
1860/59	
1860	
1862	

1/4 real, copper.

Obverse: Bow, quiver, and flag. Legend DEPARTAMENTO DE JALISCO and ★ [date] ★. *Reverse:* Seated figure of Liberty facing left and holding a liberty cap on a staff. Legend ★ UNA ★ CUARTILLA ★. *Diameter:* 32 mm. *Edge:* Diagonally milled. DB-495, BW-193.3, KM-356.

Date	Comment
1858	
1859	
1859/8	Unconfirmed
1860/59	
1860	Unconfirmed

Estado Libre de Jalisco

1/16 real, copper.

Obverse: Bow, quiver, and flag. Legend ESTADO LIBRE DE JALISCO and ★ 1861 ★. *Reverse:* Seated figure of Liberty facing left and holding a liberty cap on a staff. Legend ★ MEDIO ★ OCTAVO ★. *Diameter:* 21 mm. *Edge:* Diagonally milled. DB-410, BW-200.1, KM-317.

Date	Comment
1861	

1/8 real, copper.

Obverse: Bow, quiver, and flag. Legend ESTADO LIBRE DE JALISCO and ★ [date] ★. *Reverse:* Seated figure of Liberty facing left and holding a liberty cap on a staff. Legend ★ UN ★ OCTAVO ★. *Diameter:* 28 mm. *Edge:* Diagonally milled. DB-470, BW-179.1, KM-330.

Date	Comment
1856	
1857	
1858	
1861	
1862/1	
1862	

1/4 real, copper.

Obverse: Bow, quiver, and flag. Legend ESTADO LIBRE DE JALISCO and ★ [date] ★. *Reverse:* Seated figure of Liberty facing left and holding a liberty cap on a staff. Legend ★ UNA ★ CUARTILLA. *Diameter:* 32 mm. *Edge:* Diagonally milled. DB-490, BW-193.2, KM-355.

Date	Comment
1858	
1861	
1862	

STATE OF OCCIDENTE

Estado de Occidente

1/8 real, copper.

Obverse: Eagle with wings spread, facing right, with a serpent in its beak and sprays below. Legend ESTADO DE OCCIDENTE. *Reverse:* Radiant liberty cap. Legend C [date] $\frac{1}{8}$. *Diameter:* 18 mm. *Edge:* Diagonally milled. DB-501, BW-180, KM-335.

Date	Comment
1828	Reversed S in ESTADO
1829	

Estado de Occidente / Chihuahua

1/8 real, copper.

The Occidente/Chihuahua 1/8 real *(octavo)* discovery coin was found during the 1970s at Landoras, Coahuila, Mexico, with a metal detector. It is an obvious error of unknown origin. In addition to the following specifications, the coin has a die orientation of about 95 degrees and appears to be copper. *Side 1 (Occidente):* Eagle; DB-501. *Side 2 (Chihuahua):* Indian; DB-101. *Diameter:* About 18 mm. *Weight:* 2.4 grams. *Edge:* Diagonally milled. DB-510, BW-180.1, KM-UL.

Date	Comment
No date	Unique

STATE OF SAN LUIS POTOSÍ

Estado de San Luis Potosí

1/8 real, copper.

Obverse: Seated figure of Liberty to front, holding war club in left hand and liberty cap on point of an arrow in right. Legend MEXICO LIBRE above. *Reverse:* Within wreath of laurel and oak, an open book inscribed LEY. Above book, $\frac{1}{8}$. Legend ESTADO DE SAN LUIS POTOSI . ★ and [date]. *Diameter:* 21 mm. *Edge:* Diagonally milled. DB-601, BW-181, KM-336.

Date	Comment
1829	
1830	
1831	Round-top 3
1831	Flat-top 3, normal date
1831	Large date
1859	Normal letters
1859	Small letters

Estado Libre de San Luis Potosí

1/4 real, copper.

Obverse: Seated figure of Liberty to front, holding war club in left hand and liberty cap on point of an arrow in right. Legend MEXICO LIBRE above. *Reverse:* Within wreath of laurel and oak wreath, an open book inscribed LEY. Above book, $\frac{1}{4}$. Legend ESTADO LIBRE DE SAN LUIS POTOSI . ★ and [date]. *Diameter:* 28–30 mm. *Edge:* Diagonally milled. DB-650, BW-194, KM-359.

Date	Comment
1828	
1829/28	
1829	
1830	
1832	
1832	Colonial edge
1832	Brass; rare*
1859	Large LIBRE
1859	Small LIBRE
1860/59	Unconfirmed
1860	

* Likely a circulating counterfeit.

1/4 real, copper.

Obverse: Seated figure of Liberty to front, holding war club in left hand and liberty cap on point of an arrow in right. Legend REPUBLICA MEXICANA. *Reverse:* Within an open laurel and oak wreath, an open book inscribed LIBERTAD EN LA LEY. Legend ESTADO LIBRE DE SAN LUIS POTOSI ★. and 1862. Above book, $\frac{1}{4}$. *Diameter:* 28 mm. *Edge:* Diagonally milled. DB-660, BW-194.1, KM-360.

Date	Comment
1862	
1862	LIBR error
1862	Large date

Estado Libre y Soberano de San Luis Potosí

1/4 real, copper.

Obverse: Eagle standing on cactus, facing front with wings outspread, head to right, and a serpent in its beak. Legend LIBERTAD Y REFORMA . above, sprays of oak and laurel below. *Reverse:* Within a wreath of oak and laurel, a radiant liberty cap and the value $\frac{1}{4}$. Around circumference, legend ESTADO LIBRE Y SOBERANO DE S. L. POTOSI and ★ 1867 ★. *Diameter:* 28 mm. *Edge:* Milled. DB-670, BW-194.2, KM-361.

Date	Comment
1867	
1867	AFG*
1867	Struck over 1863 one centavo
1867	Plain edge
1867	Plain edge, AFG* struck over one centavo

* For engraver Antonio Flores Grabador.

STATE OF SINALOA

Estado Libre y Soberano de Sinaloa

1/4 real, copper.

Obverse: Small Liberty head facing left within laurel wreath. Legend ESTADO LIBRE Y SOBERANO DE SINALOA ★. *Reverse:* Within an oak-and-laurel wreath, $\frac{1}{4}$ / DE REAL / [date]. *Diameter:* 27 mm. *Edge:* Milled. DB-750, BW-195, KM-363.

Date	Comment
1847	Small wreath
1847	Brass, small wreath; unconfirmed
1848	Small wreath
1848	Large date, small wreath
1859	Dot after date
1859	No dot after date
1859	Missing fractional bar
1859	No reeding; unconfirmed
1861/9	Dot at date
1861	Dot at date
1862	Dot at date
1862	BEAL error
1863	Dot at date
1864/3	Dot at date
1864	8/8, dot at date
1864/4	No dot at date
1865	Dot at date
1866/5	Dot at date
1866	Dot at date

STATE OF SONORA

Estado de Sonora, Hermosillo

1/4 real, copper.

Obverse: Between two cornucopias, an arrow with point up. Legend EST . D . SONORA . UNA . CUART ★. *Reverse:* Radiant liberty cap. Legend A DE . [date] . L . S . HERMOSILLO . *Diameter:* 21 mm. *Edge:* Diagonally milled. DB-801, BW-196, KM-364.

Date	Comment
1831	Unconfirmed
1832	
1833	
1833/2	
1834	
1835	
1835/3	
1836	
1837	Circulating counterfeit
1838	Circulating counterfeit
1840	Circulating counterfeit

Estado Libre y Soberano de Sonora

1/4 real, copper.

Obverse: Eagle standing on nopal cactus, facing front with wings outspread, head to right, and a serpent in its beak. Legend **ESTº LIBᴱ Y SOBº DE SONORA.** Oak and laurel sprays below. *Reverse:* Seated figure of Liberty facing left, holding a liberty cap on a staff. Legend **UNA CUARTILLA DE REAL . [date] .** *Diameter:* 32 mm. *Edge:* Milled. DB-850, BW-196.1, KM-365.

Date	Comment
1859*	28 mm
1859	Dots at date
1859	No dots at date
1861/59	Dot at date
1861	Dots at date
1862	Dots at date
1862/9	Repunched date
1863/2**	
1863/3**	Over inverted 3

* A 1/8 real for 1859 may exist. ** Without overdate is an altered date.

STATE OF ZACATECAS

Estado Libre Federado de Zacatecas

1/8 real, brass.

Obverse: On a monument, an open book. Legend **ESTº LIBᴱ FEDº DE ZACATECAS . [date]** and **★ OCTAVO ★**. *Reverse:* Cupid with a radiant liberty cap. Below, the hill of La Bufa with flag on top. No legend. *Diameter:* 21 mm. *Edge:* Diagonally milled. DB-901, BW-182, KM-338.

Date	Comment
1825	
1825	LEBᴱ
1827	Inverted A used for V in OCTAVO
1829	
1830	
1831	
1832	
1833	
1835	
1846	
185_	Final digit missing; rare
1850	
1851	
1852	
1858	
1859	
1862	
1863	6 in date reversed

1/4 real, brass.

Obverse: On a monument, an open book. Legend **ESTº LIBᴱ FEDº DE ZACATECAS . [date]** and **★ QUARTILLA.** *Reverse:* Cupid with a radiant liberty cap. Below, the hill of La Bufa with a flag on top. No legend. *Diameter:* 29 mm. *Edge:* Diagonally milled. DB-950, BW-197, KM-366.

Date	Comment
1824	Pattern; rare
1825	
1826	
1827	
1827/17	
1829	
1830	
1831	
1832	
1833/2	
1833	Unconfirmed
1834	
1835	
1846	
1847	
1851	Likely circulating counterfeit
185_	Digit missing; rare
1852	
1853	
1855	Rare
1858	
1859/8	
1859	
1860	
1862	
1862	Overdates unreadable
1863	

1/4 real, BW-197, continued

Date	Comment
1863/2	
1864	Likely circulating counterfeit
18_2	Digit missing; rare

Departamento de Zacatecas

1/8 real, brass.

Obverse: On a monument, an open book. Legend DEPARTAMENTO DE ZACATECAS . [date] and ★ OCTAVO ★. *Reverse:* Cupid with a radiant liberty cap. Below, the hill of La Bufa with a flag on top. No legend. *Diameter:* 21 mm. *Edge:* Diagonally milled. DB-910, BW-182.1, KM-339.

Date	Comment
1836	
1846	

1/4 real, brass.

Obverse: On a monument, an open book. Legend DEPARTAMENTO DE ZACATECAS . [date] and ★ QUARTILLA ★. *Reverse:* Cupid with a radiant liberty cap. Below, the hill of La Bufa, with a flag on top. No legend. *Diameter:* 29 mm. *Edge:* Diagonally milled. DB-960, BW-197.1, KM-367.

Date	Comment
1836	*
1845	Known only as a circulating counterfeit; rare
1846	*
1862	*

* 6 in date reversed.

REPUBLIC OF MEXICO

Republica Mexicana

1/16 real, copper or brass.

Obverse: Eagle standing on nopal cactus, facing front with wings outspread, head to right, and a serpent in its beak. Legend REPUBLICA MEXICANA. Oak and laurel sprays below. *Reverse:* Within a palm wreath, the value $\frac{1}{16}$ with M̊ . A . [date] . below. *Diameter:* 17 mm. *Edge:* Incuse rectangles. DB-1001, BW-201, KM-315.

Date	Comment
1831	
1832/1	
1832	Brass
1833/1	
1833	Brass
1835	Brass, confirmed; rare

1/8 real, copper.

Obverse: Eagle standing on nopal cactus, facing front with wings outspread, head to right, and a serpent in its beak. Legend REPUBLICA MEXICANA. Oak and laurel sprays below. *Reverse:* Within a palm wreath, the value $\frac{1}{8}$ with M̊ . A . [date] . below. *Diameter:* 21 mm. *Edge:* Incuse rectangles. DB-1010, BW-183, KM-332 and KM-333.

Date	Comment
1829	27 mm*
1829	
1830	
1831	
1832	
1833/2	
1833	
1834	
1835/4	
1835	

* KM-332; all others 21 mm, KM-333.

1/8 real, copper.

Obverse: Seated figure of Liberty facing right and holding a lance. Legend LIBERTAD. In the exergue below Liberty's seat, the engraver's mark L. ROVIRA. F. in small letters. *Reverse:* Within a wreath of laurel and oak, legend OCTAVO / DE REAL / [date]. Mintmark M̊ below wreath. *Diameter:* 30 mm. *Edge:* 1841 and 1842, lettered REPUBLICA MEXICANA; 1850 and 1861, plain. DB-1020, BW-183.1, KM-334.

Date	Comment
1841	
1842	
1850	M̊ above wreath
1861	

1/4 real, copper.

Obverse: Eagle standing on nopal cactus, facing front with wings outspread, head to right, and a serpent in its beak. Legend REPUBLICA MEXICANA. Oak and laurel sprays below. *Reverse:* Within a palm wreath, the value $\frac{1}{4}$ with $\overset{\circ}{\text{M}}$. A . [date] . below. *Diameter:* 27 mm. *Edge:* Incuse rectangles. DB-1060, BW-197.3, KM-357 and KM-358.

Date	Comment
1829	
1829	33 mm*
1830/29	
1830	
1831	
1832	
1833	
1834/3	
1834	
1835	
1836	
1837	

* DB-1050, BW-197.2, KM-357. All others 27 mm, DB-1060, BW-197.3, KM-358.

State and Federal Copper Coinage

State of Chihuahua

1/8 real.
DB-110, BW-176.1,
KM-319, 20 mm.

1/4 real.
DB-170, BW-190.4,
KM-344, 28 mm.

State of Durango

1/8 real.
DB-210, BW-177.1,
KM-321, 18 mm.

1/8 real.
DB-230, BW-177.3,
KM-323, 19 mm.

1/8 real.
DB-250, BW-177.5,
KM-325, 19 mm.

1/4 real.
DB-260, BW-191,
KM-346, 27 mm.

1/4 real.
DB-270, BW-191.1,
KM-347, 27 mm.

(State of Durango continued on next page)

State and Federal Copper Coinage

State of Durango

(continued)

1/4 real. DB-280, BW-191.2, KM-348, 27 mm.

1/4 real. DB-285, BW-191.3, KM-349, 27 mm.

1/4 real. DB-290, BW-191.4, KM-350, 27 mm.

State of Guanajuato

1/8 real. DB-301, BW-178, KM-326, 20 mm.

1/4 real. DB-350, BW-192, KM-351, 27 mm.

1/4 real. DB-360, BW-192.1, KM-352, 32 mm.

State of Jalisco (Early Series)

1/8 real. DB-420, BW-179, KM-329, 21 mm.

1/4 real. DB-450, BW-193, KM-353, 28 mm.

State and Federal Copper Coinage

State of Jalisco (Late Series)

1/16 real. DB-401, BW-200, KM-316, 21 mm.

1/8 real. DB-470, BW-179.1, KM-330, 28 mm.

1/4 real. DB-490, BW-193.2, KM-355, 32 mm.

1/4 real. DB-495, BW-193.3, KM-356, 32 mm.

State of Occidente

1/8 real. DB-501, BW-180, KM-335, 18 mm.

State of San Luis Potosí

1/8 real. DB-601, BW-181, KM-336, 21 mm.

1/4 real. DB-650, BW-194, KM-359, 28 mm.

1/4 real. DB-670, BW-670, KM-361, 28 mm.

1/4 real, over 1863 one centavo. DB-670b, BW-194.2, KM-362, 27 mm.

State and Federal Copper Coinage
(continued)

State of Sinaloa

1/4 real. DB-750, BW-195, KM-363, 27 mm.

State of Zacatecas

1/8 real. DB-901, BW-182, KM-338, 21 mm.

1/4 real. DB-950, BW-197, KM-366, 29 mm.

State of Sonora

1/4 real. DB-801, BW-196, KM-364, 21 mm.

1/4 real. DB-850, BW-196.1, KM-365, 32 mm.

Republic of Mexico

1/16 real. DB-1001, BW-201, KM-315, 17 mm.

1/8 real. DB-1010, BW-183, KM-333, 21 mm.

1/8 real. DB-1020, BW-183.1, KM-334, 30 mm.

1/4 real. DB-1050, BW-1050, KM-357, 33 mm.

10

Coinage of Emperor Maximilian

The Maximilian era of Mexico is perhaps the most romantic period of the country's colorful history, and one of the best documented. Archduke Ferdinand Maximilian of Austria was first offered the imperial crown of Mexico on October 3, 1863, but did not accept it officially until April 10, 1864, when France and Mexico signed the Miramar Treaty. The archduke was enticed to Mexico as part of an attempt to establish a French colony in the Americas, under the pretense of collecting the debt owed to France by Mexico on the so-called Jecker bonds. This scheme by Napoleon III was in defiance of the United States' Monroe Doctrine. Napoleon believed that since the United States was in the middle of a civil war, it was too preoccupied to enforce the Monroe Doctrine, and that the Confederate South, which had offered to support the French Regency government in Mexico, would win the conflict. In fact, after the American Civil War many of the Confederate troops went to Mexico to serve with Maximilian and stayed in Mexico following the fall of the empire.

In defense of Maximilian it should be brought out that he requested via letter that "The offer of the crown be from a representative majority of the Mexican people." The offer was orchestrated by General Juan N. Almonte in Mexico City. Almonte was head of the French Regency that had been established to govern Mexico until a monarch could be selected and could arrive. Almonte appealed to French general Louis Élie Frédéric Forey to comply with the Austrian archduke's request to be approved by the public before he would accept the throne. Forey convoked a supreme council, made up of 35 selected members out of the 215 who were willing to serve. On July 11, 1863, this "Junta de los Notables" approved the document that had been prepared by Forey; an additional 165 signatures were acquired before the document was presented to Maximilian on October 3, 1863.

Maximilian and his wife, Charlotte (daughter of Leopold I, King of Belgium), sailed on April 14, 1864, and arrived in Mexico on May 28. They took up residence in Chapultepec Castle and transformed it into the imperial palace. The palace today still retains some of the elegance that was established during this brief period of Mexico's history.

The political bickering among the several civil and military factions that made up the imperial government brought about the downfall of Maximilian's short reign (three years, one month, and five days). These problems, coupled with the poor judgment of his advisers, the withdrawal of Napoleon III's forces, and the mounting pressure applied by the forces of Mexico's president, Benito Juárez, resulted in the defeat of the ill-advised attempt to establish a French colony in the Americas. The U.S. government was encouraging the Juárez forces, both politically and by stacking a clandestine supply of arms and ammunition along the Texas and Arizona borders at night and leaving the surplus supplies unguarded. The next morning the supplies had disappeared and no one knew what happened.

Emperor Maximilian.

Empress Carlota.

Maximilian accepting the crown of Mexico.

In Mexico Charlotte used the Spanish translation, "Carlota," of her name. She left Mexico to plead Maximilian's cause in Europe while Maximilian stayed on and fought to save their empire. While at the Vatican to plead their case to Pope Pius IX, Empress Carlota suffered a mental collapse, and she was in mortal fear that someone was trying to kill her. Reportedly she refused to leave the Vatican at night and became the first woman to spend the night in the Vatican. Her mental problems continued and progressively became worse.

Maximilian, after a 68-day siege at the town of Querétaro, was captured through the actions of a traitor, Miguel López. He surrendered to General Mariano Escobedo on May 15, 1867, on the Hill of Bells at Querétaro. A church now stands on that spot and Mass continues to be said there for Maximilian. Along with two of his generals (Miguel Miramón and Tomás Mejía), Maximilian was brought to trial and found guilty. All three were ordered to be executed on June 16, 1867. There were efforts from all over the world on behalf of Maximilian, pleading to President Juárez to spare his life, but all the pleas were rejected. The execution took place on the morning of June 19, 1867. According to some accounts Maximilian handed out a few of the 20-peso gold coins bearing his effigy to members of the firing squad. Carlota died in Paris in 1927, never really knowing the true fate of her "Maxl" (Carlota's nickname for Maximilian) or of their dreams of an empire in Mexico. This short-lived period of Mexico's history began on April 10, 1864, with a Venetian waltz in the Miramar Palace, where Maximilian accepted the throne of Mexico; it ended June 19, 1867, on the Hill of Bells at Querétaro, Mexico, with shots from a firing squad.

The republic government had passed laws on March 15, 1857, and March 15, 1862, to establish a decimal monetary system, but by the time the French Regency was established, only the 1 centavo, 5 centavos, and 10 centavos of the republic had been struck.

The lowest denomination issued during the French intervention was the copper 1 centavo. On the obverse a Mexican crowned eagle is depicted holding a serpent in its beak and standing on a nopal ("prickly pear") cactus of 10 leaves, with two olive branches below and the legend IMPERIO MEXICANO above. The reverse has, in four lines, the denomination, date, and mintmark within an open laurel wreath. There are two varieties of the imperial crowned eagle, and both large- and small-letter varieties of the 1-centavo issue. There is no known authorization for the 1 centavo, but the date would indicate that all varieties were struck in 1864 at the mint in Mexico City. However, a complete set of dies was found at the Zacatecas mint for the 1864 M 1 centavo.

On April 8, 1864, the Regency decreed the striking of silver 5 and 10 centavos. The obverses of the coins are similar in design, except for the position of the crowned eagle. Both show the crowned eagle with a serpent in its beak standing on a nopal cactus of 10 leaves, with the legend IMPERIO MEXICANO above. The reverses of the two coins are similar, with the denomination, date, and mintmark in four lines, within a laurel wreath.

The 5 and 10 centavos do not bear the effigy of Maximilian; they depict the design as set forth in the French Regency's decree of April 8, 1864, even though most were struck after his arrival in Mexico. Both Carlota and Maximilian desired to have his effigy on the coinage of the empire, but this wish was met with opposition from within his government, mostly from José Fernando Ramírez, minister of foreign affairs and a member of the liberal wing of the government.

On April 10, 1865, Maximilian decreed that the following coins be authorized: 1/2 and 1 centavo in copper; 5, 10, 25, and 50 centavos, along with 1 peso, in silver; and 5, 10, and 20 pesos in gold. All were to have Maximilian's effigy. Out of the 10 coins authorized by the decree, only three are known to have been struck—the 50 centavos, 1 peso, and 20 pesos. All bear the dates of 1866 and 1867.

The coinage of 1865 did not have Maximilian's effigy and must have been struck under the Regency's decree rather than Maximilian's. Ramírez's resistance to using "Maxl's" effigy was overcome by Carlota, when she invited Ramírez to accompany her on a trip to the Yucatán in November of 1865. While Ramírez was away, Maximilian had the coinage struck with his effigy. Ramírez resigned his position in January 1866, with Maximilian accepting his resignation on January 29. The striking of the coins and the timing of Ramírez's resignation would suggest that he was unhappy with the manner in which Carlota had treated him.

Imperial coinage of this era does not indicate the fineness of the silver or gold, as had been the custom with the previous coinage of Mexico. The imperial coinage is also smaller in size. The 50 centavos, 1 peso, and 20 pesos are 2 millimeters smaller than their counterparts of the republic's issues. The reduction in size made the Mexican populace suspicious, and they did not want to accept the imperial coinage. The August 10, 1866, issue of the *Journal of the Empire* reported the decree that "the imperial coins are of a value equal to the republic issues, and anyone not accepting these coins would be fined."

The 50-centavo denomination was struck at the Mexico City mint only, and they all bear the date 1866. They were reportedly struck in 1867 bearing the 1866 date. The obverse bears the bust of Maximilian with the legend MAXIMILIAN EMPERADOR, and a border of small pellets. The reverse has a Mexican eagle in an imperially crowned shield with a ribbon festooned at the sides and with the legend at top. EQUIDAD EN LA JUSTICIA (Equity in Justice) appears on the shield. The legend IMPERIO MEXICANO is above, and below are the denomination, date, and mintmark.

The first 1-peso denomination of Mexico was struck under Maximilian. The obverse depicts the bust of Maximilian; on a ribbon below the effigy is the name of the designer, NAVALON, in the center; OCAMPO at the left; and SPIRITU to the right. (The letter D for designer and G for the engraver is indicated by a capital letter following the name to distinguish the role each played in creating the design.) The legend MAXIMILIANO appears to the left and EMPERADOR to the right, with a border of small pellets. The reverse contains the crowned coat of arms as designed by Luis de Salazar and approved by Maximilian on June 18, 1864. Griffins stand at each side, with crossed imperial scepter and sword in the background. The border of the shield is laureled and surrounded by the Order Chain of the Mexican Eagle. Below, on a suspended ribbon, is EQUIDAD EN LA JUSTICIA, and the legend above, IMPERIO MEXICANO, with the denomination, year, and mintmark below.

Pesos from the Potosí mint are normally crudely struck and out of shape, and in some cases exhibit poor milling. From the Potosí mint there is an interesting variety called the "Heart in Ear" variety, the result of clashed dies. The oval from the coat of arms is stamped on Maximilian's neck. The lines in the oval show strongly inside the ear, and within the lines is a heart-shaped clear spot.

There are patterns in the 50 centavos and in the peso series. The pattern 50 centavos can be distinguished not only by the strike, but by the festooned ribbons that go straight out, rather than folding back to the oval. The silver peso pattern is referred to as the "Small Letters Maximilian peso." The lettering is 2 millimeters tall; the letters of the regular issued pesos are 3 millimeters. As the patterns were struck at the Mexico City mint they are far better strikes and are normally found in Extremely Fine to Almost Uncirculated conditions.

There are copper patterns or off-metal strikes of the Small Letters peso; two of these appeared in Spink's Pablo Gerber auction in 1996. One came from the Merrill Bothamley collection and sold in the Superior auction in September 1970, lot 872. The authenticity of lot 872 was questioned at the time of the auction.

The first decimal gold coin of Mexico was the 20 pesos, also known as the "Ounce of Gold." The obverse and reverse of this coin are similar in design to those of the 1 peso, but the 20 pesos is smaller in size and has other slight differences. On the reverse there is a period between the date and the mintmark. The 20-pesos coins were first struck on August 19 and 20, 1866, and were not struck again until May 1867. All bear the 1866 date.

In 1975, the late Hal Birt Jr. of Tucson, Arizona, published an article in *La Crónica Imperial*, the official journal of the Maximilian Numismatic and Historical Society, covering the 20-peso gold coin and its known genuine varieties at that time:

> **Variety 1 (Reverse 1)**—The obverse has die scratches over MAXIMILIANO. The reverse has die cracks through IMPERIO, noticeably three from the upper half of P to E.
>
> **Variety 2 (Reverse 2)**—The obverse has a delicate die scratch nearly halfway up between E and R of EMPERADOR, with tiny raised spots over EM. The reverse has a bold raised die crack that begins at the denticle under the griffin's tail and extends five denticles toward the base of the mintmark. A wandering die crack begins at 7 o'clock, continues through the base of 20, again under the wing, over IMPE, and through MEXICA. The upper portion of 2 is flattened.
>
> **Variety 3 (Reverse 3)**—The obverse has a die scratch from the right third of the 20th bead at right of O in MAXIMILIANO to the center of the top of the head. The reverse has a bold die break under 2, about four denticles long, with what appears to be flames under the date. The second S in PESOS is barely joined at the lower curve. A Variety 3 specimen was lot 10 in the Don Bailey auction of April 27, 1975.

The empire ceased to exist on June 19, 1867, with the execution of Emperor Maximilian in the town of Querétaro. The monetary law of November 27, 1867, stated that as of September 15, 1868, the imperial coinage would cease to be legal tender. Through the requests of many state governors, this portion of the monetary law was not enforced and the imperial coinage continued to circulate in many of the states. Most of the coins disappeared from the major cities around 1870; but apparently, some of the imperial coinage circulated until 1906. The Mexican postal department issued Circular Letter 867, dated February 10, 1906, which instructed the postmasters not to accept imperial coinage in payment of postage stamps. The imperial coinage, a full decimal system based on 100 centavos to the peso (which was put into effect by an intruder into the affairs of the United States' neighbor to the south), continued in circulation into the early 21st century with only design and metal-content changes, and some changes in denomination to suit the economical situation.

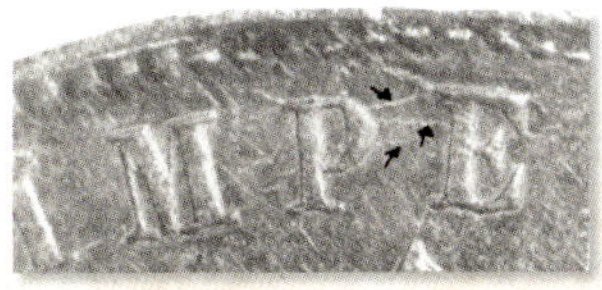

Reverse 1

Reverse 2

Reverse 3

20-peso varieties

Republic coinage continued to be struck while the French forces occupied the various states with operating mints. As this book goes to press it is unknown whether they were struck with the blessing of the imperial government or were produced after the French forces evac uated the area.

The following are the dates of French occupancy and the Republic coins released within each time span. Date ranges are from the English translation of Dr. Alberto Fracisco Pradeau's *Historia Numismatica de México* (Sociedad Numismática de México, 1970); other information from Banco de México.

Álamos (A). Occupied May 1865–August 28, 1866.
- 1865 PG 8 reales
- 1866 PG 8 reales
- 1866 DL 8 reales

Chihuahua (C^{A}, $C^{\dot{\underset{\cdot}{A}}}$). Occupied August 15, 1865–June 17, 1866.
- 1865 FP 8 reales
- 1865 JC 8 reales
- 1866 FP 8 reales
- 1866 JC 8 reales

Durango (D^{o}, $D^{\underset{\cdot}{o}}$). Occupied July 4, 1864–November 13, 1866.
- 1864 LT 1 real
- 1864 LT 8 reales
- 1864 LT 1/2 escudo
- 1864 LT 8 escudos
- 1864 CP 8 reales
- 1865 LT 8 reales
- 1866 CM 8 escudos

Guadalajara (G^{A}). Occupied January 5, 1864–December 19, 1866.
- 1864 JG 8 reales
- 1865 JG 8 reales

Guanajuato (G, $G^{\underset{\cdot}{o}}$). Occupied December 8, 1863–January 26, 1866.
- 1863 YE 1 escudo
- 1863 PF 8 escudos

Hermosillo (H^{o}, $\overset{o}{H}$). Occupied July 29, 1865–September 12, 1866.
- 1865 FM 8 escudos
- 1865 FM 8 reales

Mexico City (M^{o}, $\overset{o}{M}$). Occupied June 7, 1863–June 20, 1867.
- 1863 CH 1/2 real
- 1863 CH 1 real
- 1863 CH 2 reales
- 1863 CH 8 reales
- 1863 TH 1/2 real
- 1863 TH 1 real
- 1863 TH 8 reales

Oaxaca (O^{A}). Occupied February 8, 1865–October 31, 1866.

No issues

Real de Catorce ($C^{\underset{\cdot}{E}}$). Occupied December 25, 1863–March 1866.

No issues

San Luis Potosí ($P^{!}$, P!). Occupied December 25, 1863–December 25, 1866.
- 1863 RO 1/2 real
- 1863 RO 2 reales
- 1863 RO 4 reales
- 1863 RO 8 reales
- 1863 FC 8 reales
- 1864 RO 8 reales

Zacatecas (Z^{S}). Occupied February 6, 1864–November 29, 1866.
- 1864 VL 2 reales
- 1864 VL 4 reales
- 1864 VL 8 reales
- 1864 MO 2 reales
- 1864 MO 8 reales
- 1864 MO 8 escudos
- 1865 MO 2 reales
- 1865 MO 8 reales
- 1865 MO 8 escudos
- 1866 VL 1 real

GUANAJUATO MINT

5 centavos, 0.90277 silver, 1.3537 g.

Obverse: A crowned eagle above an oak-and-laurel wreath, holding a serpent in its beak and standing on a nopal cactus. Legend IMPERIO MEXICANO. *Reverse:* The denomination, date, and mintmark G within a laurel wreath. *Diameter:* 15 mm. *Edge:* Milled. BW-227.1, KM-385.

Date	Mintmark	Comment
1864	G	
1865	G	
1866	G	

10 centavos, 0.90277 silver, 2.7073 g.

Obverse: A crowned eagle above an oak-and-laurel wreath, holding a serpent in its beak and standing on a nopal cactus. Legend IMPERIO MEXICANO. *Reverse:* The denomination, date, and mintmark G within a laurel wreath. *Diameter:* 18 mm. *Edge:* Milled. BW-228.1, KM-386.

Date	Mintmark	Comment
1864	G	
1865	G	

1 peso, 0.90277 silver, 27.0700 g.

Obverse: Bust of Maximilian to the right with legend MAXIMILIANO EMPERADOR. *Reverse:* The imperial coat of arms, legend IMPERIO MEXICANO, denomination, date, and mintmark Gº. *Diameter:* 37 mm. *Edge:* Milled. BW-230.1, KM-388.

Date	Mintmark	Comment
1866	Gº	

MEXICO CITY MINT

1 centavo, copper.

Obverse: A crowned Mexican eagle above a half oak and laurel wreath and the legend IMPERIO MEXICANO above. *Reverse:* Within an oak-and-laurel wreath the denomination, date, and mintmark M. *Diameter:* 25 mm. *Edge:* Milled. Small Letters, BW-226, KM-384.

There are two varieties of the 1 centavo, with minor differences. The most noticeable difference is in the size of the letters (see page 205). Large Letters, BW-226.1, KM-UL.

Date	Mintmark	Comment
1864	M	Large date
1864	M	Small date

5 centavos, 0.90277 silver, 1.3537 g.

Obverse: A crowned eagle above an oak-and-laurel wreath, holding a serpent in its beak and standing on a nopal cactus. Legend IMPERIO MEXICANO. *Reverse:* The denomination, date, and mintmark M within a laurel wreath. *Diameter:* 15 mm. *Edge:* Milled. BW-227.2, KM-385.1.

Date	Mintmark	Comment
1864	M	
1866/4	M	
1866	M	

10 centavos, 0.90277 silver, 2.7073 g.

Obverse: A crowned eagle above an oak-and-laurel wreath, holding a serpent in its beak and standing on a nopal cactus. Legend IMPERIO MEXICANO. *Reverse:* The denomination, date, and mintmark M within a laurel wreath. *Diameter:* 18 mm. *Edge:* Milled. BW-228.2, KM-386.1.

Date	Mintmark	Comment
1864	M	
1866/4	M	
1866/5	M	
1866	M	

50 centavos, 0.90277 silver, 13.5365 g.

Obverse: Bust of Maximilian to the right, and the legend MAXIMILIANO EMPERADOR. *Reverse:* Abbreviated imperial coat of arms and legend IMPERIO MEXICANO, with the denomination, date, and mintmark Mº. *Diameter:* 30 mm. *Edge:* Milled. BW-229, KM-387.

Date	Mintmark	Comment
1866	Mº	

1 peso, 0.90277 silver, 27.0700 g.

Obverse: Bust of Maximilian to the right and the legend MAXIMILIANO EMPERADOR. *Reverse:* The imperial coat of arms and legend IMPERIO MEXICANO, with the denomination, date, and mintmark M̊. *Diameter:* 35 mm. *Edge:* Milled. BW-230.2, KM-388.1.

Date	Mintmark	Comment
1866	$\overset{\circ}{M}$	
1867	$\overset{\circ}{M}$	

20 pesos, 0.8750 gold, 33.840 g.

Obverse: Bust of Maximilian to the right and the legend MAXIMILIANO EMPERADOR. *Reverse:* The imperial coat of arms and legend IMPERIO MEXICANO, with the denomination, date, and mintmark $\overset{\circ}{M}$. *Diameter:* 35 mm. *Edge:* Milled. BW-231, KM-389.

Date	Mintmark	Comment
1866	$\overset{\circ}{M}$	Variety 1
1866	$\overset{\circ}{M}$	Variety 2
1866	$\overset{\circ}{M}$	Variety 3

SAN LUIS POTOSÍ

5 centavos, 0.90277 silver, 1.3537 g.

Obverse: An oak-and-laurel wreath below a crowned eagle holding a serpent in its beak and standing on a nopal cactus. Legend IMPERIO MEXICANO. *Reverse:* The denomination, date, and mintmark P, within a laurel wreath. *Diameter:* 15 mm. *Edge:* Milled. BW-227.3, KM-385.2.

Date	Mintmark	Comment
1864	P	

10 centavos, 0.90277 silver, 2.7073 g.

Obverse: An oak-and-laurel wreath below a crowned eagle holding a serpent in its beak and standing on a nopal cactus. Legend IMPERIO MEXICANO. *Reverse:* The denomination, date, and mintmark P, within a laurel wreath. *Diameter:* 18 mm. *Edge:* Milled. BW-228.3, KM-386.2.

Date	Mintmark	Comment
1864	P	

1 peso, 0.90277 silver, 27.070 g.

Obverse: Bust of Maximilian to the right and the legend MAXIMILIANO EMPERADOR. *Reverse:* The imperial coat of arms, legend IMPERIO MEXICANO, denomination, date, and mintmark P!. *Diameter:* 37 mm. *Edge:* Milled. BW-230.3, KM-388.2.

The pesos from this period are normally out of round, with doubling and other minting difficulties. A well-struck Potosí peso is scarce.

Date	Mintmark	Comment
1868	P!	

ZACATECAS

5 centavos, 0.90277 silver, 1.3537 g.

Obverse: An oak-and-laurel wreath below a crowned eagle, holding a serpent in its beak and standing on a nopal cactus. Legend IMPERIO MEXICANO. *Reverse:* The denomination, date, and mintmark Z, within a laurel wreath. *Diameter:* 15 mm. *Edge:* Milled. BW-227.4, KM-385.3.

Date	Mintmark	Comment
1865	Z	

10 centavos, 0.90277 silver, 2.7073 g.

Obverse: An oak-and-laurel wreath below a crowned eagle, holding a serpent in its beak and standing on a nopal cactus. Legend IMPERIO MEXICANO. *Reverse:* The denomination, date, and mintmark Z, within a laurel wreath. *Diameter:* 18 mm. *Edge:* Milled. BW-228.4, KM-386.3.

As a sign of repudiation of the imperial government, coins can be found with an R or some other counterstamp over the crown, or the crown in the talons of the snake.

Date	Mintmark	Comment
1865	Z	

PATTERNS

50 centavos.

A pattern 50 centavos exists. The technical information is the same on both the circulating coin and the pattern, except that the ribbon on the shield of the pattern is smaller and goes outward from the shield; on the regular issue the ribbon is draped around the shield. BW-229.1, KM-UL.

Small-letter peso.

This pattern of the Maximilian peso is the subject of a myth that the dies broke after 36 were struck, which was Maximilian's age when he was executed in 1867. BW-230.4, KM-UL.

The Coinage of Emperor Maximilian

1 centavo. 1864-M. Small Letters.
BW-226, KM-384, 25 mm.

1 centavo. 1864-M. Large Letters.
BW-226.1, KM-UL, 25 mm.

5 centavos. 1864-M. BW-227.2,
KM-385.1, 15 mm.

10 centavos. 1864-P. BW-228.3,
KM-386.2, 18 mm.

50 centavos. 1866-Mº.
BW-229, KM-387, 30 mm.

50 centavos. 1866-M̊. Pattern.
BW-229.1, KM-UL, 30 mm.

1 peso. 1866-M. BW-230.2,
KM-388.1, 37 mm.

1 peso. 1866-M̊. Small
Letters, pattern. BW-230.4,
KM-UL, 37 mm.

20 pesos. 1866-M̊. BW-231,
KM-389, 35 mm.

11

Republic Decimal Coinage

The Republic had established a decimal system of coinage by the decree of 1857, but for several years no such coinage was struck. For a young republic in a great deal of debt, bringing the many, uncoordinated sources of coinage into an all-new system was a challenge. In 1862, the Republic issued another decree calling for a decimalized currency; finally, in 1863, small quantities of 1, 5, and 10 centavos were produced at the Mexico City and San Luis Potosí mints. Not long afterward, however, the country fell under the rule of the French and Emperor Maximilian; and in April 1864 the French Regency decreed the Imperial coinage (which happened to be a decimal coinage).

After the fall of Emperor Maximilian in 1867 and the return of the Republic, the Mexican monetary system was in shambles. The branch mints were under contract to individuals, Maximilian coinage was still circulating, and up until 1873, Republic reales and escudos were still being struck at various mints (as were state and federal coppers, up until 1872). All these factors contributed to the coinage confusion.

Add to the situation the fact that, under the decimal system, 1 peso equaled 100 centavos—which made an exact exchange between the two systems difficult, especially at the lower denominations:

1/4 real = 3-1/8 centavos
1/2 real = 6-1/4 centavos
1 real = 12-1/2 centavos
2 reales = 25 centavos
4 reales = 50 centavos
8 reales = 1 peso

(There was no problem with the escudo gold, as the 1/2 escudo traded at an even 8 reales.)

With so many factors in play, persuading the Mexican public to accept a single, all-decimal coinage system would take years to accomplish.

The limited decimal coinage of the pre-Maximilian Republic had looked much like the reales coins of the same era. After the Republic was restored, the essential elements of the Imperial decimal coinage were retained. In 1869, for 25 centavos and up, the Balance Scale design was introduced on issues from Mexico City and the branch mints. The obverse design consisted of the national coat of arms (the Mexican eagle holding a snake while perched on a nopal cactus); the reverse design was the Balance Scale, and its three motifs—a sword, a two-pan scale, and a scroll with the word LEY—represented the three branches of Mexico's government (executive, judicial, and legislative, respectively). Ten different mints issued this design.

Although the public accepted the Balance Scale decimal coinage, the Balance Scale peso never took hold as a trade dollar. In 1873 the familiar and popular Liberty Cap and Rays 8 reales was restored for that purpose. It was widely used in foreign trade throughout Central America, the Near East, the Philippines, Africa, and other regions until its demise in 1897. With that one exception, Mexico's coinage from 1874 onward was a decimal currency.

In 1898 a new denomination, the Liberty Cap peso, was minted, but it was not readily accepted—the peso denomination was unfamiliar, the coin was slightly (2 mm) smaller than its predecessor, and on this small new "peso" was 902,7 (with a comma for the decimal point), indicating a silver fineness of 0.9027, rather than the familiar 10 D$ 20 G$.

As for the gold denominations, there has been much discussion as to the true rarity and values of decimal gold. Some issues have had very low mintage figures reported, yet they are not uncommon. Others with high mintage figures cannot be found. Recent research has disclosed previously uncataloged gold decimal issues, and they are reported here. Further research may disclose other previously unreported coins.

Coins are listed in this chapter alphabetically by mint, and by denomination within each mint.

When known, an assayer's full name and initials as well as years of service are listed for each mint. Although an initial for an assayer's last name usually appears on the coin, sometimes more than one assayer had the same initial for the last name. Check years of service in order to accurately identify the assayer. Occasionally two initials appear on a coin of this period. In the tables, two initals separated by a hyphen indicates two assayers identified on the coin, whereas a slash instead of a hyphen indicates an overstrike.

The fineness of decimal silver coins was minted as 902,7; for gold coins, the fineness appeared as 875.

Denominations of Republic decimal coinage are as follows:

- **1 centavo.** Three 1-centavo pattern designs were struck in 1841, 1862, and 1868. The 1841 design is similar to that of the 1863 regular coinage; the 1862 design has an eagle on the obverse and a wreath on the reverse; and the 1868 issue has the same design as on the 1869 regular coinage.

  The regular-issue 1-centavo coins were first struck in 1863 and are referred to as the Seated Liberty types. It is interesting to note that this is the only decimal issuance that does not have the word "Mexico" on the coins. The mint at Mexico City produced two styles of Seated Liberty centavo: one with a flat-top 3 and one with a round-top 3. The engraver's name, Paredes, appears on the obverse of both. The mint at San Luis Potosí produced similar centavos in 1863; these have the name of their engraver, Sanabria, on the obverse.

  When minting of the Republic decimal coinage was resumed in 1869, several mints adopted a new design—the Standing Eagle style—which they would retain through 1897.

  In 1882 the Mexican government tried to establish a new composition and design: copper-nickel coins of a much smaller size, with a bow-and-quiver motif and the denomination in roman numerals. This coinage was issued in 1, 2, and 5 centavos, and only in 1882 and 1883. Due to the distaste of the citizens, however, the design went back to the Standing Eagle style.

In 1898, the value of copper in the large Standing Eagle centavo exceeded its face value, and another new, smaller design was proposed. As soon as the design was accepted on December 21, 1899, the new 1-centavo issues were struck, but for only three days. These 1899 centavos (and their 1905 counterparts) are known to have been counterfeited.

- **2 centavos.** The copper-nickel, roman-numeral-style 2 centavos of 1882 and 1883 were issued from the Mexico City mint.
- **5 centavos.** The decimal coinage's first 5-centavo denomination was part of the limited decimal coinage struck in 1863, prior to the installation of Maximilian and the advent of the Imperial coinage. Those few 5 centavos were struck only at the San Luis Potosí mint. The obverse design resembled that of the real, with the Mexican eagle; but on the reverse, the design was changed to the date and denomination within a wreath. After the fall of Maximilian, the Mexico City mint (in 1867) and San Luis Potosí mint (in 1868) restored the full real design with Mexican eagle obverse and Liberty Cap reverse. They maintained this design until 1869, when the Republic decimal coinage—with the wreath reverse—was resumed.
- **10 centavos.** Like the 5 centavos, the 10 centavos during this period of decimal coinage were first struck in 1863 at the San Luis Potosí mint, and with the same basic designs (Mexican eagle on the obverse, date and denomination within a wreath on the reverse). And as with the 5 centavos, the reverse design reverted briefly back to the real-style Liberty Cap after the fall of Maximilian.

  In 1869 the new Standing Eagle design was adopted, with a restyled Mexican eagle on the obverse and the date and denomination within a wreath of laurel on the reverse. It was issued from 1869 through 1897 by 11 of the mints.

  In 1898 the 10-centavo obverse eagle was again restyled; the reverse stayed basically the same. The new, restyled obverse was issued from four mints up until the 1905 coinage reform.
- **20 centavos.** The 20-centavo denomination was issued in 1898 with the restyled eagle used on the 5 and 10 centavos of 1898 through 1905, and from the same mints that issued the 5 and 10 centavos. It was created to comply with an 1892 law and was intended to replace the Balance Scale 25 centavos.
- **25 centavos.** The 25-centavo denomination was first issued in 1869, in the Balance Scale design with the Mexican eagle and snake obverse. Ten different mints issued the denomination.
- **50 centavos.** The decimal 50 centavos bear the same design as the 25 centavos: the Mexican eagle on the obverse and the Balance Scale on the reverse. They were issued by nine mints.
- **1 peso (silver).** The Balance Scale peso has basically the same design as the 25- and 50-centavo coins. As discussed at the beginning of the chapter, it was intended to replace the 8 reales as a trade dollar. Designed to be two millimeters smaller than the 8 reales, the Balance Scale peso was not favorably accepted by the general public and was minted only from 1869 through 1873, by nine mints.

  The Liberty Cap style peso was another attempt to get away from the use of 8 reales in foreign trade and to remove the reales coins from the monetary system. It was struck by only four mints during its 12 years of issuance.

- **1 peso (gold).** The first mintage of the gold 1 peso was in 1870 at the Guanajuato and Mexico City mints. The design of the gold peso basically followed the designs of the 5 and 10 centavos of 1869 through 1897. It was issued up to the coinage reform of 1905, and was struck at six mints during this period.
- **2-1/2 pesos.** The 2-1/2 pesos has basically the same design as the gold 1 peso. It was issued by seven mints.
- **5 pesos.** The 5 pesos used basically the same Balance Scale design as on the 25 and 50 centavos. The Balance Scale 5 pesos were issued by eight mints.
- **10 pesos.** The 10 pesos had the same Balance Scale design that appears on the 5- and 20-peso denominations. The denomination was issued by 10 mints.
- **20 pesos.** The Balance Scale gold 20-peso coin had basically the same design as the other Balance Scale designs on denominations previously mentioned. It was issued by nine mints.

ÁLAMOS

The Álamos mint was located in the state of Sonora in the northwestern mining town of Álamos, which had been the capital city of the state of Occidente until the latter was divided into the states of Sinaloa and Sonora in 1830. The mint opened in 1864 for the issuance of federal coinage and closed in 1895.

Mintmarks for Republic decimal coinage struck at the Álamos mint are $\overset{S}{\text{A}}$ and A$^{\underline{S}}$. Assayer initials are as follows:

DL or L	Domingo Larraguibel (1874–1895)
L	Manuel Larraguibel (1878–1895)

1 centavo, copper.

Obverse: The national coat of arms, with the legend REPUBLICA MEXICANA above. *Reverse:* Within a wreath of oak and laurel, in four lines, UN / CENTAVO / [date] and mintmark $\overset{S}{\text{A}}$. *Diameter:* 25 mm. *Edge:* Plain. BW-251.3, KM-391.

Date	Comment
1875	Rare
1876	
1880	
1881	

5 centavos, 0.9027 silver, 1.353 g.

Obverse: The national coat of arms, with the legend REPUBLICA MEXICANA above and the date below. *Reverse:* At center, above a half-wreath of oak and laurel, 5 / CENTAVOS. Above the denomination, mintmark A$^{\underline{S}}$, the assayer mark (followed by a dot), and fineness 902,7. *Diameter:* 15 mm. *Edge:* Milled. BW-253.5, KM-398.

Date	Assayer	Comment
1874	DL	
1875	DL	
1876	L	
1878	L	Mule, gold peso obverse
1879	L	Mule, gold peso obverse
1880	L	Mule, gold peso obverse
1886	L	
1886	L	Mule, gold peso obverse
1887	L	
1888	L	
1889	L	
1890	L	
1891	L	
1892	L	
1893	L	
1895	L	

10 centavos, 0.9027 silver, 2.707 g.

Obverse: The national coat of arms, with the legend **REPUBLICA MEXICANA** above and the date below. *Reverse:* At center, above a half-wreath of oak and laurel, **10 / CENTAVOS.** Above the denomination, mintmark A$^{\underline{S}}$, the assayer mark (followed by a dot), and fineness **902,7**. *Diameter:* 17 mm. *Edge:* Milled. BW-254.5, KM-403.

Date	Assayer	Comment
1874	DL	
1875	L	
1876	L	
1878/5	L	
1878	L	
1879	L	
1880	L	
1882	L	
1883	L	
1884	L	
1885	L	
1886	L	
1887	L	
1888	L	
1889	L	
1890	L	
1891	L	
1891	L	Struck over 1889-H^{o}, G
1892	L	
1893	L	

25 centavos, 0.9027 silver, 6.768 g.

Obverse: The national coat of arms, with the legend **REPUBLICA MEXICANA** above and a spray of oak and laurel below; **[date]** below spray. *Reverse:* Below a small radiant liberty cap, a crossed sword and balance scale; between the pans of the scale, a scroll bearing the word **LEY**. Below the scroll, **25 CENTAVOS**, with mintmark A$^{\underline{S}}$, assayer mark **L.**, and fineness **902,7**. *Diameter:* 25 mm. *Edge:* Milled. BW-256.1, KM-406.

Date	Assayer	Comment
1874	L	
1875	L	
1876	L	
1877	L	
1878	L	
1879	L	
1880	L	
1881	L	
1882	L	
1883	L	
1884	L	
1885	L	
1886	L	
1887	L	
1888	L	
1889	L	Rare
1890	L	

50 centavos, 0.9027 silver, 13.536 g.

Obverse: The national coat of arms, with the legend **REPUBLICA MEXICANA** above and a spray of oak and laurel below; **[date]** below spray. *Reverse:* Below a small radiant liberty cap, a crossed sword and balance scale; between the pans of the scale, a scroll bearing the word **LEY**. Below the scroll, **50 CENTAVOS**, with mintmark A$^{\underline{S}}$, assayer mark **L.**, and fineness **902,7**. *Diameter:* 30 mm. *Edge:* Milled. BW-257.1, KM-407.

Date	Assayer	Comment
1875	L	
1876/5	L	
1876	L	
1877	L	
1878	L	
1879	L	
1880	L	
1881	L	
1884	L	
1885	L	A$^{\underline{S}}$ over H$^{\underline{O}}$

1 peso, 0.8750 gold, 1.692 g.

Obverse: The national coat of arms, with the legend **REPUBLICA MEXICANA** above and **1888** below. *Reverse:* At center, within an open wreath of oak and laurel, **1 / PESO.** Above the denomination, between wreath tips, assayer mark **L.**, fineness **875**, and mintmark A$^{\underline{S}}$. *Edge:* Milled. BW-258.14, KM-410.

Date	Assayer	Comment
1888	L	Struck over $\overset{o}{M}$, M; rare
1888	L	Extremely rare

2-1/2 pesos, 0.8750 gold, 4.230 g.

Obverse: The national coat of arms, with the legend **REPUBLICA MEXICANA** above and **1888** below. *Reverse:* At center, within an open wreath of oak and laurel, **2 ½ / PESOS**. Above the denomination, between wreath tips, assayer mark **L.**, fineness **875**, and mintmark **AS**. *Diameter:* 18 mm. *Edge:* Milled. BW-259.1, KM-411.

Date	Assayer	Comment
1888	L	Struck over M̊, M; rare

5 pesos, 0.8750 gold, 8.460 g.

Obverse: The national coat of arms, with the legend **REPUBLICA MEXICANA** above and a spray of oak and laurel below; **1878** below spray. *Reverse:* Below a small radiant liberty cap, a crossed sword and balance scale; between the pans of the scale, a scroll bearing the word **LEY**. Below the scroll, mintmark **AS** and assayer mark **L.**, with **CINCO PESOS** and fineness **875**. *Diameter:* 22 mm. *Edge:* Milled. BW-260.1, KM-412.

Date	Assayer	Comment
1878	L	

10 pesos, 0.8750 gold, 16.920 g.

Obverse: The national coat of arms, with the legend **REPUBLICA MEXICANA** above and a spray of oak and laurel below; **[date]** below spray. *Reverse:* Below a small radiant liberty cap, a crossed sword and balance scale; between the pans of the scale, a scroll bearing the word **LEY**. Below the scroll, mintmark **AS**, the assayer mark (followed by a dot), **DIEZ PESOS**, and fineness **875**. *Diameter:* 27 mm. *Edge:* Milled. BW-261.1, KM-413.

Date	Assayer	Comment
1874	DL	Rare
1875	DL	Rare
1875	L	Rare
1878	L	Rare
1879	L	Rare
1880	L	Rare
1881	L	Rare
1882	L	Rare
1883	L	Rare
1884	L	Rare
1885	L	Rare
1886	L	
1887	L	
1888	L	
1889	L	
1890	L	
1891	L	Rare
1893	L	
1894/3	L	
1894	L	
1895	L	Rare

20 pesos, 0.8750 gold, 33.841 g.

Obverse: The national coat of arms, with the legend **REPUBLICA MEXICANA** above and a spray of oak and laurel below; **[date]** below spray. *Reverse:* Below a small radiant liberty cap, a crossed sword and balance scale; between the pans of the scale, a scroll bearing the word **LEY**. Below the scroll, mintmark **AS** and assayer mark **L.**, with **VEINTE PESOS** and fineness **875**. *Diameter:* 34 mm. *Edge:* Milled. BW-262.1, KM-414.

Date	Assayer	Comment
1876	L	Very rare
1877	L	
1888	L	Very rare

CHIHUAHUA

Located in the capital city of the northern state of Chihuahua, this mint was opened in 1831 and closed in 1895. No 4 reales were issued from this mint.

Mintmarks for Republic decimal coinage struck at the Chihuahua mint are **CA**, **CA**, **CH**, and **CHA**. Assayer initials are as follows:

M	Manuel Merino (1868–1895)
P	Possibly Patrick Murphy (1872)
G	Manuel Gameros (1880)

5 centavos, 0.9027 silver, 1.353 g.

Obverse: The national coat of arms, with the legend REPUBLICA MEXICANA. above and a spray of oak and laurel below. *Reverse:* Within a wreath of laurel, in three lines, 5 / CENTAVOS / [date]. Below the wreath, mintmark CA. No assayer mark or fineness. *Diameter:* 15 mm. *Edge:* Diagonally milled. BW-253.1, KM-396.

Date	Comment
1868	
1869	
1870/69	
1870	

5 centavos, 0.9027 silver, 1.353 g.

Obverse: The national coat of arms, with the legend REPUBLICA MEXICANA above and the date below. *Reverse:* At center, above a half-wreath of oak and laurel, 5 / CENTAVOS. Above the denomination, between wreath tips, mintmark CA (or CH), assayer mark M., and fineness 902,7. *Diameter:* 15 mm. *Edge:* Milled. BW-253.6, KM-398.1.

Date	Assayer	Comment
1871	M	
1873	M	Crude date
1874	M	Crude date
1886	M	
1887	M	
1887	M	CA / M̊
1888	M	
1889	M	
1890	M	
1891	M	
1892	M	
1892/62	M	
1892	M	9 / inverted 9
1893	M	
1894	M	
1895	M	

10 centavos, 0.9027 silver, 2.707 g.

Obverse: The national coat of arms, with the legend REPUBLICA MEXICANA. above and a spray of oak and laurel below. *Reverse:* Within a wreath of laurel, in three lines, 10 / CENTAVOS / [date]. Below the wreath, mintmark CA. No assayer mark or fineness. *Diameter:* 18 mm. *Edge:* Diagonally milled. BW-254.2, KM-401.1.

Date	Comment
1868/7	
1868	
1869	
1870	

10 centavos, 0.9027 silver, 2.707 g.

Obverse: The national coat of arms, with the legend REPUBLICA MEXICANA above and the date below. *Reverse:* At center, above a half-wreath of oak and laurel, 10 / CENTAVOS. Above the denomination, between wreath tips, mintmark CA, the assayer mark (followed by a dot), and fineness 902,7. *Diameter:* 17 mm. *Edge:* Milled. BW-254.6, KM-403.1.

Date	Assayer	Comment
1871	M	
1873	M	Crude date
1874	M	
1880	G	G / smaller G
1881	M	Rare
1883	M	
1884	M	
1886	M	
1886/5	M	CA
1887	M	
1888	M	
1888	M	CA / M̊
1889	M	Small 89 (5-centavo typeface)
1889/8	M	
1890	M	
1890/89	M	
1891	M	
1892	M	9 / inverted 9
1892	M	
1893	M	
1894	M	
1895	M	

25 centavos, 0.9027 silver, 6.768 g.

Obverse: The national coat of arms, with the legend REPUBLICA MEXICANA above and a spray of oak and laurel below; [date] below spray. *Reverse:* Below a small radiant liberty cap, a crossed sword and balance scale; between the pans of the scale, a scroll bearing the word **LEY**. Below the scroll, **25 CENTAVOS**, with mintmark **CH** (or **CA̲**), assayer mark **M.**, and fineness **902,7**. *Diameter:* 25 mm. *Edge:* Milled. BW-256.2, KM-406.1.

Date	Assayer	Comment
1871	M	
1872	M	Very crude date
1883	M	
1885/3	M	
1885	M	
1886	M	
1887/6	M	
1887	M	
1888	M	
1889	M	

50 centavos, 0.9027 silver, 13.536 g.

Obverse: The national coat of arms, with the legend **REPUBLICA MEXICANA** above and a spray of oak and laurel below; **[date]** below spray. *Reverse:* Below a small radiant liberty cap, a crossed sword and balance scale; between the pans of the scale, a scroll bearing the word **LEY**. Below the scroll, **50 CENTAVOS**, with mintmark **CHA̲** (or **CA̲**), assayer mark **M.**, and fineness **902,7**. *Diameter:* 30 mm. *Edge:* Milled. BW-257.2, KM-407.1.

Date	Assayer	Comment
1883	M	
1884	M	
1885	M	
1886	M	
1887	M	

1 peso, 0.9027 silver, 27.073 g.

Obverse: The national coat of arms, with the legend **REPUBLICA MEXICANA** above and a spray of oak and laurel below; **[date]** below spray. *Reverse:* Below a small radiant liberty cap, a crossed sword and balance scale; between the pans of the scale, a scroll bearing the word **LEY**. Below the scroll, **UN PESO**, with mintmark **CH.**, the assayer mark (followed by a dot), and fineness **902,7**. *Diameter:* 37 mm. *Edge:* Milled. BW-258.1, KM-408.

Date	Assayer	Comment
1872	P/M	
1872	P	
1872/1	M	
1872	M	
1873	M	
1873	M/P	
1873	P	

1 peso, 0.8750 gold, 1.692 g.

Obverse: The national coat of arms, with the legend **REPUBLICA MEXICANA** above and **1888** below. *Reverse:* At center, within a wreath of oak and laurel, **1 / PESO**. Above the denomination, assayer mark **M**, fineness **875**, and mintmark **CA̲**. *Diameter:* 15 mm. *Edge:* Milled. BW-258.15, KM-410.1.

Date	Assayer	Comment
1888	M	CA̲ / M̊; rare

5 pesos, 0.8750 gold, 8.460 g.

Obverse: The national coat of arms, with the legend **REPUBLICA MEXICANA** above and a spray of oak and laurel below; **1888** below spray. *Reverse:* Below a small radiant liberty cap, a crossed sword and balance scale; between the pans of the scale, a scroll bearing the word **LEY**. Below the scroll, mintmark **CA̲** and assayer mark **M.**, with **CINCO PESOS** and fineness **875**. *Diameter:* 22 mm. *Edge:* Milled. BW-260.2, KM-412.1.

Date	Assayer	Comment
1888	M	Very rare

10 pesos, 0.8750 gold, 16.920 g.

Obverse: The national coat of arms, with the legend **REPUBLICA MEXICANA** above and a spray of oak and laurel below; **1888** below spray. *Reverse:* Below a small radiant liberty cap, a crossed sword and balance scale; between the pans of the scale, a scroll bearing the word **LEY**. Below the scroll, mintmark **CA̲** and assayer mark **M.**, with **DIEZ PESOS** and fineness **875**. *Diameter:* 27 mm. *Edge:* Milled. BW-261.2, KM-413.1.

Date	Assayer	Comment
1888	M	

20 pesos, 0.8750 gold, 33.840 g.

Obverse: The national coat of arms, with the legend **REPUBLICA MEXICANA** above and a spray of oak and laurel below; **[date]** below spray. *Reverse:* Below a small radiant liberty cap, a crossed sword and balance scale; between the pans of the scale, a scroll bearing the word **LEY**. Below the scroll, mintmark **CA̲** and assayer mark **M.**, with **VEINTE PESOS** and fineness **875**. *Diameter:* 34 mm. *Edge:* Milled. BW-262.2, KM-414.1.

Date	Assayer	Comment
1872	M	Rare
1873	M	
1874	M	
1875	M	
1876	M	
1877	M	
1882	M	
1883	M	
1884	M	
1885	M	
1887	M	
1888	M	
1889	M	
1890	M	
1891	M	
1893	M	Rare
1895	M	

CULIACÁN

The Culiacán mint, located in the capital city of the northern state of Sinaloa, opened in 1846 and closed in 1905, when all branch mints were closed with the coinage reform that year.

Mintmarks for Republic decimal coinage struck at the Culiacán mint are **C**, **CN̲**, and **$\overset{\text{N}}{\text{C}}$**. Assayer initials are as follows:

E	Clemente Espinosa de los Monteros (1846–1870)
P	Manuel Onofre Parodi (1873–1876)
G	Celso Gaxiola (1876–1878)
D	Juan Domínguez (1878–1882)
D	Unknown (1883–1884)
G	Unknown (1881–1882)
E	Unknown (1882)
AM or M	Antonio Moreno (1882–1899)
Q	Unknown (1890)
JQ or Q	Jesús S. Quiroz (1899–1903)
FV or V	Francisco Valdez (1903)
MH or H	Merced Hernández (1904)
Rp or P	Ramón Ponce de León (1904–1905)

1 centavo, copper.

Obverse: The national coat of arms, with the legend **REPUBLICA MEXICANA** above. *Reverse:* Within a wreath of oak and laurel, in four lines, **UN / CENTAVO / [date]** and mintmark **$\overset{\text{N}}{\text{C}}$**. *Diameter:* 25 mm. *Edge:* Plain. BW-251.4, KM-391.1.

Date	Comment
1874	
1875/4	
1875	
1876	
1877/6	
1877	
1880	
1881	
1897	Small N in mintmark, milled edge
1897	Large N in mintmark, milled edge

1 centavo, copper.

Obverse: The national coat of arms, with the legend **REPUBLICA MEXICANA** above and a spray of oak and laurel below. *Reverse:* At center, within a wreath of oak and laurel, the denomination ¢ (numeral 1 superimposed over a centavo symbol). Above the denomination, the date; below the wreath, mintmark **C**. *Diameter:* 20 mm. *Edge:* Plain. BW-251.12a, KM-394.

Date	Comment
1901	REPUBLICA MEXICANA (wide)
1902	REPUBLICA MEXICANA (wide)
1903	REPUBLICA MEXICANA (wide)
1903	REPUBLICAMEXICANA (close)
1904/3	REPUBLICAMEXICANA (close)
1905	REPUBLICAMEXICANA (close)

5 centavos, 0.9027 silver, 1.353 g.

Obverse: The national coat of arms, with the legend **REPUBLICA MEXICANA** above and the date below. *Reverse:* At center, above a half-wreath of oak and laurel, **5 / CENTAVOS**. Above the denomination, mintmark **CN**, the assayer mark (followed by a dot), and fineness **902,7**. *Diameter:* 15 mm. *Edge:* Milled. BW-253.7, KM-398.2.

Date	Assayer	Comment
1871	P	
1873	P	
1874	P	
1875	P	Rare
1876	P	
1886	M	
1887	M	
1888	M	
1889	M	
1890/80	M	
1890	M	
1890/9	M	
1890	D	Assayer error
1891	M	
1894	M	
1896	M	
1897	M	

5 centavos, 0.9027 silver, 1.353 g.

Obverse: The restyled national coat of arms, with the legend **REPUBLICA MEXICANA** above and the date below. *Reverse:* At center, above a half-wreath of oak and laurel, **5 / CENTAVOS**. Above the denomination, mintmark **CN**, the assayer mark (followed by a dot), and fineness **902,7**. *Diameter:* 15 mm. *Edge:* Milled. BW-253.17, KM-400.

Date	Assayer	Comment
1898	M	
1899	M	
1899	Q	
1890/800	Q	
1900	Q	Oval Q, narrow C
1900	Q	Oval Q, wide C
1900	Q	Round Q, single tail
1901	Q	
1902	Q	Heavy serifs, narrow C
1902	Q	Light serifs, wide C
1903/1	Q	
1903	Q	
1903	V	
1903/1898	V	
1904	H	
1904	H	0/9

10 centavos, 0.9027 silver, 2.707 g.

Obverse: The national coat of arms, with the legend **REPUBLICA MEXICANA** above and the date below. *Reverse:* At center, above a half-wreath of oak and laurel, **10 / CENTAVOS**. Above the denomination, mintmark **CN**, the assayer mark (followed by a dot), and fineness **902,7**. *Diameter:* 17 mm. *Edge:* Milled. BW-254.7, KM-403.2.

Date	Assayer	Comment
1871	P	Rare
1873	P	
1881	D	
1882	D	
1885	M	Mule, 2-1/2-peso obverse
1886	M	Mule, 2-1/2-peso obverse
1887	M	
1888	M	
1889	M	
1890	M	
1891	M	
1892/1	M	
1892	M	
1894	M	
1895	M	
1896	M	

10 centavos, 0.9027 silver, 2.707 g.

Obverse: The restyled national coat of arms, with the legend **REPUBLICA MEXICANA** above and the date below. *Reverse:* At center, above a half-wreath of oak and laurel, **10 / CENTAVOS**. Above the denomination, mintmark **CN̲**, the assayer mark (followed by a dot), and fineness **902,7**. *Diameter:* 17 mm. *Edge:* Milled. BW-254.16, KM-404.

Date	Assayer	Comment
1898	M	
1899	Q	Oval Q, double tail
1899	Q	Round Q, single tail
1900	Q	
1901	Q	
1902	Q	
1903	Q	
1903	V	
1904	H	

20 centavos, 0.9027 silver, 5.415 g.

Obverse: The restyled national coat of arms, with the legend **REPUBLICA MEXICANA** above and the date below. *Reverse:* At center, above a half-wreath of oak and laurel, **20 / CENTAVOS**. Above the denomination, mintmark **CN̲**, the assayer mark (followed by a dot), and fineness **902,7**. *Diameter:* 22 mm. *Edge:* Milled. BW-255.1, KM-405.

Date	Assayer	Comment
1898	M	
1899	M	
1899	Q	
1900	Q	
1901	Q	
1902/802	Q	
1902	Q	
1903	Q	
1904/3	H	
1904	H	

25 centavos, 0.9027 silver, 6.768 g.

Obverse: The national coat of arms, with the legend **REPUBLICA MEXICANA** above and a spray of oak and laurel below; **[date]** below spray. *Reverse:* Below a small radiant liberty cap, a crossed sword and balance scale; between the pans of the scale, a scroll bearing the word **LEY**. Below the scroll, **25 CENTAVOS**, with mintmark **CN̲**, the assayer mark (followed by a dot), and fineness **902,7**. *Diameter:* 25 mm. *Edge:* Milled. BW-256.3, KM-406.2.

Date	Assayer	Comment
1871	P	
1872	P	
1873	P	
1874	P	
1875	P	
1876	P	Rare
1878	D	CN̲ / G♀
1878	D	
1878	D	
1879	D	
1880	D	
1881/0	D	
1882	D	
1882	M	Rare
1883	M	
1884	M	
1885/4	M	
1886	M	
1887	M	
1888	M	
1888	M	CN̲ / M̊
1889	M	
1890	M	9/8
1890	M	
1892/0	M	
1892	M	

50 centavos, 0.9027 silver, 13.536 g.

Obverse: The national coat of arms, with the legend **REPUBLICA MEXICANA** above and a spray of oak and laurel below; **[date]** below spray. *Reverse:* Below a small radiant liberty cap, a crossed sword and balance scale; between the pans of the scale, a scroll bearing the word **LEY**. Below the scroll, **50 CENTAVOS**, with mintmark **CN̲**, the assayer mark (followed by a dot), and fineness **902,7**. *Diameter:* 30 mm. *Edge:* Milled. BW-257.3, KM-407.2.

Date	Assayer	Comment
1871	P	
1873	P	
1874	P	

Date	Assayer	Comment
1875	P	
1876	P	
1877/6	G	
1877	G	
1878	G	
1878	D	CN̲ / M̊
1878	D	
1879	D	
1879	D/G	
1880/8	D	
1880	D	
1881/0	D	
1881	D	
1881	G	
1882	D	
1882	G	
1883	D	
1885/3	M/G	
1886	M	
1886	M	
1887	M	
1888	M	
1892	M	

1 peso, 0.9027 silver, 27.073 g.

Obverse: The national coat of arms, with the legend **REPUBLICA MEXICANA** above and a spray of oak and laurel below; **[date]** below spray. *Reverse:* Below a small radiant liberty cap, a crossed sword and balance scale; between the pans of the scale, a scroll bearing the word **LEY**. Below the scroll, **UN PESO**, with mintmark **CN̲**, the assayer mark (followed by a dot), and fineness **902,7**. *Diameter:* 37 mm. *Edge:* Milled. BW-258.2, KM-408.1.

Date	Assayer	Comment
1870	E	
1871	P	
1871/11	P	
1872	P	
1873	P	Narrow date
1873	P	Wide date

1 peso, 0.9027 silver, 27.073 g.

Obverse: The national coat of arms, with the legend **REPUBLICA MEXICANA.** above and a spray of oak and laurel below. *Reverse:* At center, a large radiant liberty cap; below, ★ **UN PESO.**, with mintmark **CṆ**, the date (followed by a dot), the assayer mark (followed by a dot), and fineness **902,7**. *Diameter:* 39 mm. *Edge:* Milled. BW-258.10, KM-409.

Date	Assayer	Comment
1898	AM	
1898	AM	CṆ / M̊
1899	AM	
1899	JQ	
1900	JQ	
1901	JQ	
1902	JQ	
1903	JQ	
1903	FV	
1904	MH	
1904	RP	
1905	RP	

1 peso, 0.8750 gold, 1.692 g.

Obverse: The national coat of arms, with the legend **REPUBLICA MEXICANA** above and the date below. *Reverse:* At center, within a wreath of oak and laurel, **1 / PESO**. Above the denomination, the assayer mark (followed by a dot), fineness **875**, and mintmark **CN̲**. *Diameter:* 15 mm. *Edge:* Milled. BW-258.16, KM-410.2.

Date	Assayer	Comment
1873	P	
1875	P	Rare
1878	G	Very rare
1879	D	
1881/0	D	
1882	D	
1883	D	
1884	M	
1885	M	Extremely rare
1886/4	M	Rare
1888	M	
1889	M	Rare
1891/89	M	
1892	M	
1893	M	
1894	M	
1895	M	
1896/5	M	
1897	M	
1898	M	

1 peso, BW-258.6, continued

Date	Assayer	Comment
1898	M	C$\underline{\text{N}}$ / $\overset{\circ}{\text{M}}$
1899	Q	
1901/0	Q	
1902	Q	
1902	Q	C$\underline{\text{N}}$ / $\overset{\circ}{\text{M}}$
1904	H	
1904	H	C$\underline{\text{N}}$ / $\overset{\circ}{\text{M}}$
1905	P	

2-1/2 pesos, 0.8750 gold, 4.230 g.

Obverse: The national coat of arms, with the legend REPUBLICA MEXICANA above and 1893 below. *Reverse:* At center, within a wreath of oak and laurel, 2½ / PESOS. Above the denomination, assayer mark M., fineness 875, and mintmark C$\underline{\text{N}}$. *Diameter:* 18 mm. *Edge:* Milled. BW-259.2, KM-411.1.

Date	Assayer	Comment
1893	M	Extremely rare

5 pesos, 0.8750 gold, 8.460 g.

Obverse: The national coat of arms, with the legend REPUBLICA MEXICANA above and a spray of oak and laurel below; [date] below spray. *Reverse:* Below a small radiant liberty cap, a crossed sword and balance scale; between the pans of the scale, a scroll bearing the word LEY. Below the scroll, mintmark C$\underline{\text{N}}$ and the assayer mark (followed by a dot), with CINCO PESOS and fineness 875. *Diameter:* 22 mm. *Edge:* Milled. BW-260.3, KM-412.2.

Date	Assayer	Comment
1873	P	
1874	P	Very rare
1875	P	Rare
1876	P	Rare
1877	G	Very rare
1882	G	Reported, unconfirmed
1885	M	Rare
1888	M	
1890	M	Rare
1891	M	Very rare
1894	M	Rare
1895	M	
1900	Q	
1903	Q	

10 pesos, 0.8750 gold, 16.920 g.

Obverse: The national coat of arms, with the legend REPUBLICA MEXICANA above and a spray of oak and laurel below; [date] below spray. *Reverse:* Below a small radiant liberty cap, a crossed sword and balance scale; between the pans of the scale, a scroll bearing the word LEY. Below the scroll, mintmark C$\underline{\text{N}}$ and the assayer mark (followed by a dot), with DIEZ PESOS and fineness 875. *Diameter:* 27 mm. *Edge:* Milled. BW-261.3, KM-413.2.

Date	Assayer	Comment
1882	E	Rare
1883	M	Rare
1884	D	
1884	M	
1885	M	
1886	M	
1887	M	
1888	M	
1889	M	
1890	M	
1891	M	
1892	M	
1893	M	
1895	M	
1903	Q	

20 pesos, 0.8750 gold, 33.840 g.

Obverse: The national coat of arms, with the legend REPUBLICA MEXICANA above and a spray of oak and laurel below; [date] below spray. *Reverse:* Below a small radiant liberty cap, a crossed sword and balance scale; between the pans of the scale, a scroll bearing the word LEY. Below the scroll, mintmark C$\underline{\text{N}}$ and the assayer mark (followed by a dot), with VEINTE PESOS and fineness 875. *Diameter:* 34 mm. *Edge:* Milled. BW-262.3, KM-414.2.

Date	Assayer	Comment
1870	E	
1871	P	
1872	P	
1873	P	
1874	P	
1875	P	Very rare
1876	P	

Date	Assayer	Comment
1876	G	
1877	G	
1878	D	Rare
1881	D	
1882/1	D	
1883	M	
1884	M	
1885	M	
1886	M	
1887	M	
1888	M	
1889	M	
1890	M	
1891	M	
1892	M	
1893	M	
1894	M	
1895	M	
1896	M	
1897/6	M	
1897	M	
1898	M	
1899	M	
1899	Q	
1900	Q	
1901	Q	
1902	Q	
1903	Q	
1904	H	
1905	P	

DURANGO

In the capital of the state of Durango under colonial rule, the Durango mint opened in 1811 and remained open through 1895. Coinage began in 1824. During the 1830s and 1840s, dies prepared in France were used. They can be readily recognized because the French dies are quite different from Mexican prepared dies; among other, subtler details, the serpent's head is higher on the French dies, and the eagle's tail is shorter and square.

Mintmarks for Republic decimal coinage struck at the Durango mint are D, Dº, Dº, and D̊. Assayer initials are as follows:

M	Clemente Morón (1848–1876)
P	Carlos Miguel de la Peña (1873)
H	Unknown (1875)
P	P. José Miguel Palma (1877)
E	Pedro Espejo (1878)
B	Trinidad Barrera (1878–1880)
P	J. Miguel Palma (1880–1894)
C	Manuel M. Canseco or Melchor Calderón (1882–1890)
B	Jacobo Blanco (1885)
D	Norberto Domínguez (1892–1895)

1 centavo, copper.

Obverse: The national coat of arms, with the legend REPUBLICA MEXICANA above. *Reverse:* Within a wreath of oak and laurel, in four lines, UN / CENTAVO / [date] and mintmark D̊. *Diameter:* 25 mm. *Edge:* Milled. BW-251.5, KM-391.2.

Date	Comment
1879	
1880	
1891	
1891	D̊ / M̊

5 centavos, 0.9027 silver, 1.353 g.

Obverse: The national coat of arms, with the legend REPUBLICA MEXICANA above and the date below. *Reverse:* At center, above a half-wreath of oak and laurel, 5 / CENTAVOS. Above the denomination, mintmark Dº, the assayer mark (followed by a dot), and fineness 902,7. *Diameter:* 15 mm. *Edge:* Milled. BW-253.8, KM-398.3.

Date	Assayer	Comment
1874	M	
1877	P	

5 centavos, BW-253.8, continued

Date	Assayer	Comment
1878/7	E/P	
1879	B	
1880	B	
1881	P	
1887	C	
1888/9	C	
1888	C	
1889	C	
1890	C	
1890	P	
1891/0	P	
1891	P	
1894	D	

10 centavos, 0.9027 silver, 2.707 g.

Obverse: The national coat of arms, with the legend REPUBLICA MEXICANA above and the date below. *Reverse:* At center, above a half-wreath of oak and laurel, 10 / CENTAVOS. Above the denomination, mintmark Dº, the assayer mark (followed by a dot), and fineness 902,7. *Diameter:* 17 mm. *Edge:* Milled. BW-254.8, KM-403.3.

Date	Assayer	Comment
1878	E	
1879	B	Rare
1880/70	B	Rare
1880/79	B	Rare
1884	C	
1886	C	
1887	C	
1888	C	
1889	C	
1890	C	
1891	P	
1892	P	
1892	D	
1893	D	
1893	D/C	
1894	D	
1895	D	

25 centavos, 0.9027 silver, 6.768 g.

Obverse: The national coat of arms, with the legend REPUBLICA MEXICANA above and the date below. *Reverse:* Below a small radiant liberty cap, a crossed sword and balance scale; between the pans of the scale, a scroll bearing the word LEY. Below the scroll, 25 CENTAVOS, mintmark Dº, the assayer mark (followed by a dot), and fineness 902,7. *Diameter:* 25 mm. *Edge:* Milled. BW-256.4, KM-406.3.

Date	Assayer	Comment
1873	P	Rare
1877	P	
1878/7	E	
1878	B	Rare
1879	B	
1880	B	Rare
1882	C	
1884/2	C	
1885	C	
1886	C	
1887	C	
1888	C	
1889	C	
1890	C	

50 centavos, 0.9027 silver, 13.536 g.

Obverse: The national coat of arms, with the legend REPUBLICA MEXICANA above and the date below. *Reverse:* Below a small radiant liberty cap, a crossed sword and balance scale; between the pans of the scale, a scroll bearing the word LEY. Below the scroll, 50 CENTAVOS, mintmark Dº, the assayer mark (followed by a dot), and fineness 902,7. *Diameter:* 30 mm. *Edge:* Milled. BW-257.4, KM-407.3.

Date	Assayer	Comment
1871	P	Rare
1873	P	
1873	M/P	
1874	M	
1875	M	
1875	H	
1876/5	M	
1876	M	
1877	P	
1878	B	Rare
1879	B	Rare
1880	P	
1881	P	

Date	Assayer	Comment
1882	C	
1884/2	C	
1884	C	
1885	B	
1886	C	
1887	C	D̊/M̊
1887	C	

1 peso, 0.9027 silver, 27.073 g.

Obverse: The national coat of arms, with the legend **REPUBLICA MEXICANA** above and a spray of oak and laurel below; **[date]** below spray. *Reverse:* Below a small radiant liberty cap, a crossed sword and balance scale; between the pans of the scale, a scroll bearing the word **LEY**. Below the scroll, **UN PESO**, mintmark **Dº**, the assayer mark (followed by a dot), and fineness **902.7**. *Diameter:* 37 mm. *Edge:* Milled. BW-258.3, KM-408.2.

Date	Assayer	Comment
1870	P	
1871	P	
1872	P	
1872	PṬ	
1873	P	

2-1/2 pesos, 0.8750 gold, 4.230 g.

Obverse: The national coat of arms, with the legend **REPUBLICA MEXICANA** above and **1888** below. *Reverse:* At center, within a wreath of oak and laurel, **2½ / PESOS**. Above the denomination, assayer mark **C**, fineness **875**, and mintmark **Dº**. *Diameter:* 18 mm. *Edge:* Milled. BW-259.3, KM-411.2.

Date	Assayer	Comment
1888	C	Extremely rare

5 pesos, 0.8750 gold, 8.460 g.

Obverse: The national coat of arms, with the legend **REPUBLICA MEXICANA** above and a spray of oak and laurel below; **[date]** below spray. *Reverse:* Below a small radiant liberty cap, a crossed sword and balance scale; between the pans of the scale, a scroll bearing the word **LEY**. Below the scroll, mintmark **Dº** and the assayer mark (followed by a dot), with **CINCO PESOS** and fineness **875**. *Diameter:* 22 mm. *Edge:* Milled. BW-260.4, KM-412.3.

Date	Assayer	Comment
1873/2	P	Very rare
1877	P	Very rare
1878	E	Very rare
1878/7	B	Very rare
1879	B	Very rare
1879/7	B	Very rare

10 pesos, 0.8750 gold, 16.920 g.

Obverse: The national coat of arms, with the legend **REPUBLICA MEXICANA** above and a spray of oak and laurel below; **[date]** below spray. *Reverse:* Below a small radiant liberty cap, a crossed sword and balance scale; between the pans of the scale, a scroll bearing the word **LEY**. Below the scroll, mintmark **Dº** and the assayer mark (followed by a dot), with **DIEZ PESOS** and fineness **875**. *Diameter:* 27 mm. *Edge:* Milled. BW-261.4, KM-413.3.

Date	Assayer	Comment
1872	P	
1873/2	P	
1873/2	M/P	
1874	M	
1875	M	
1876	M	
1877	P	
1878	E	
1879	B	
1879/8	B	Very rare
1880	P	Rare
1881/79	P	
1882	P	Rare
1882	C	Very rare
1883	C	Very rare
1884	C	Very rare
1888	C	Unconfirmed

20 pesos, 0.8750 gold, 33.840 g.

Obverse: The national coat of arms, with the legend **REPUBLICA MEXICANA** above and a spray of oak and laurel below; **[date]**

below spray. *Reverse:* Below a small radiant liberty cap, a crossed sword and balance scale; between the pans of the scale, a scroll bearing the word **LEY**. Below the scroll, mintmark **Dº** and the assayer mark (followed by a dot), with **VEINTE PESOS** and fineness **875**. *Diameter:* 34 mm. *Edge:* Milled. BW-262.4, KM-414.3.

Date	Assayer	Comment
1870	P	Very rare
1871/0	P	
1871	P	
1872	PT	Very rare
1876	M	Very rare
1877	P	Very rare
1878	E	Very rare

GUADALAJARA

The Guadalajara mint was located in the capital city of the state of Jalisco. Even though it had been in operation since the colonial days, the first coinage of the Republic period was dated 1825. The mint continued issuing coins of the Republic period up to 1895.

Mintmarks for Republic decimal coinage struck at the Guadalajara mint are **GA**, **Gª**, **GẠ**, and **$\overset{A}{G}$**. Assayer initials are as follows:

C	Ignacio Cañizo y Soto (1869–1877)
A	Julio Arancivia (1877–1881)
B	Trinidad Barrera (1883–1884)
H	Antonio Hernández y Prado (1884–1885)
S	Unknown (1880–1882)
S	José S. Schiafino (1885–1895)

1 centavo, copper.

Obverse: The national coat of arms, with the legend **REPUBLICA MEXICANA** above. *Reverse:* Within a wreath of oak and laurel, in four lines, **UN / CENTAVO / [date]** and mintmark **$\overset{A}{G}$**. *Diameter:* 25 mm. *Edge:* Plain BW-251.6, KM-391.3.

Date	Comment
1872	
1873	
1874	
1875	
1876	
1877	
1878	
1881/71	
1881	
1889	$\overset{A}{G}$ / $\overset{o}{M}$
1890	

5 centavos, 0.9027 silver, 1.353 g.

Obverse: The national coat of arms, with the legend **REPUBLICA MEXICANA** above and the date below. *Reverse:* At center, above a half-wreath of oak and laurel, **5 / CENTAVOS**. Above the denomination, mintmark **Gª**, the assayer mark (followed by a dot), and fineness **902,7**. *Diameter:* 15 mm. *Edge:* Milled. BW-253.9, KM-398.4.

Date	Assayer	Comment
1877	A	
1881	S	
1886	S	
1888	S	Large Gª
1888	S	Small Gª
1889	S	
1890	S	
1891	S	
1892	S	
1893	S	

10 centavos, 0.9027 silver, 2.707 g.

Obverse: The national coat of arms, with the legend **REPUBLICA MEXICANA** above and the date below. *Reverse:* At center, above a half-wreath of oak and laurel, **10 / CENTAVOS**. Above the denomination, mintmark **Gª**, the assayer mark (followed by a dot), and fineness **902,7**. *Diameter:* 17 mm. *Edge:* Milled. BW-254.9, KM-403.4.

Date	Assayer	Comment
1871	C	
1873	C	
1874	C	

Date	Assayer	Comment
1877	A	
1881	A	
1881	S	
1883	B	
1884	H	
1884	B/S	
1884	B	
1885	H	
1886	S	
1887	S	
1888	S	
1888	S	G$^{\underline{A}}$, S over H$^{\underline{o}}$, G
1889	S	
1890	S	
1891	S	
1892	S	
1893	S	
1894	S	
1895	S	

25 centavos, 0.9027 silver, 6.768 g.

Obverse: The national coat of arms, with the legend **REPUBLICA MEXICANA** above and a spray of oak and laurel below; **[date]** below spray. *Reverse:* Below a small radiant liberty cap, a crossed sword and balance scale; between the pans of the scale, a scroll bearing the word **LEY**. Below the scroll, **25 CENTAVOS**, mintmark **G$^{\underline{A}}$**, the assayer mark (followed by a dot), and fineness **902,7**. *Diameter:* 25 mm. *Edge:* Milled. BW-256.5, KM-406.4.

Date	Assayer	Comment
1880	A	
1881/0	S	
1881	S	
1882	S	
1883/2	B/S	
1884	B	
1889	S	

1 peso, 0.9027 silver, 27.073 g.

Obverse: The national coat of arms, with the legend **REPUBLICA MEXICANA** above and a spray of oak and laurel below; **[date]** below spray. *Reverse:* Below a small radiant liberty cap, a crossed sword and balance scale; between the pans of the scale, a scroll bearing the word **LEY**. Below the scroll, **UN PESO**, mintmark **G$^{\underline{A}}$**, assayer mark **C.**, and fineness **902,7**. *Diameter:* 37 mm. *Edge:* Milled. BW-258.4, KM-408.3.

Date	Assayer	Comment
1870	C	
1871	C	
1872	C	
1873/2	C	
1873	C	

10 pesos, 0.8750 gold, 16.920 g.

Obverse: The national coat of arms, with the legend **REPUBLICA MEXICANA** above and a spray of oak and laurel below; **[date]** below spray. *Reverse:* Below a small radiant liberty cap, a crossed sword and balance scale; between the pans of the scale, a scroll bearing the word **LEY**. Below the scroll, mintmark **G$^{\underline{A}}$** and the assayer mark (followed by a dot), with **DIEZ PESOS** and fineness **875**. *Diameter:* 27 mm. *Edge:* Milled. BW-261.5, KM-413.4.

Date	Assayer	Comment
1870	C	
1871	C	
1872	C	Rare
1873	C	Very rare
1874/3	C	Very rare
1875	C	Very rare
1878	A	Very rare
1879	A	Very rare
1880	S	Very rare
1881	S	Very rare
1891	S	Very rare

GUANAJUATO

The Guanajuato mint, established in 1810 in the capital of the state of Guanajuato, was very important, as it was the Republic's most prolific producer of silver and gold coinage in all denominations.

Mintmarks for Republic decimal coinage struck at the Guanajuato mint are **G**, **G$^{\underline{o}}$**, **G^{o}**, and **𝔊**. Assayer initials are as follows:

S	Unknown (1869–1884)
M	Unknown (1876–1878)
B	Unknown (1883–1884)
R	Unknown (1877)
R	Unknown (1884–1890)
R	Unknown (1900)
RS	Unknown (1898–1900)

1 centavo, copper.

Obverse: The national coat of arms, with the legend REPUBLICA MEXICANA above. *Reverse:* Within a wreath of oak and laurel, in four lines, UN / CENTAVO / [date] and mintmark GՉ. *Diameter:* 25 mm. *Edge:* Milled. BW-251.7a, KM-391.4.

Date	Comment
1874	
1875	
1876	
1877	Rare
1878	
1880	

5 centavos, 0.9027 silver, 1.353 g.

Obverse: The national coat of arms, with the legend REPUBLICA MEXICANA above and the date below. *Reverse:* At center, above a half-wreath of oak and laurel, 5 / CENTAVOS. Above the denomination, mintmark GՉ, the assayer mark (followed by a dot), and fineness 902,7. *Diameter:* 15 mm. *Edge:* Milled. BW-253.10, KM-398.5.

Date	Assayer	Comment
1869	S	
1871	S	
1872	S	
1873	S	
1874	S	
1875	S	
1876	S	
1877	S	
1878/7	S	
1879	S	
1880	S	
1881/0	S	
1881	S	
1886	R	
1887	R	
1888	R	
1889	R	
1890	R	
1891/0	R	
1891	R	
1892	R	
1893	R	
1894	R	
1896	R	
1897	R	
1898	R	

5 centavos, 0.9027 silver, 1.353 g.

Obverse: The restyled national coat of arms, with the legend REPUBLICA MEXICANA above and the date below. *Reverse:* At center, above a half-wreath of oak and laurel, 5 / CENTAVOS. Above the denomination, mintmark GՉ, assayer mark R., and fineness 902,7. *Diameter:* 15 mm. *Edge:* Milled. BW-253.18, KM-400.1.

Date	Assayer	Comment
1898	R	Mule, gold peso obverse
1899	R	
1900	R	

10 centavos, 0.9027 silver, 2.707 g.

Obverse: The national coat of arms, with the legend REPUBLICA MEXICANA above and the date below. *Reverse:* At center, above a half-wreath of oak and laurel, 10 / CENTAVOS. Above the denomination, mintmark GՉ, the assayer mark (followed by a dot), and fineness 902,7. *Diameter:* 17 mm. *Edge:* Milled. BW-254.10, KM-403.5.

Date	Assayer	Comment
1869	S	
1871/0	S	

Date	Assayer	Comment
1872	S	
1873	S	
1874	S	
1875	S	
1876	S	
1877	S	
1878/7	S	
1878	S	
1879	S	
1880	S	
1881/71	S	
1881/0	S	
1881	S	
1882/1	S	
1883	B	
1884	B	
1884	S	
1885	R	
1886	R	
1887	R	
1888	R	
1889	R	GO / HO
1890	R	
1891	R	
1892	R	
1893/1	R	
1893	R	
1894	R	
1895	R	
1896	R	
1897	R	

10 centavos, 0.9027 silver, 2.707 g.

Obverse: The restyled national coat of arms, with the legend REPUBLICA MEXICANA above and the date below. *Reverse:* At center, above a half-wreath of oak and laurel, 10 / CENTAVOS. Above the denomination, mintmark GO, assayer mark R., and fineness 902,7. *Diameter:* 15 mm. *Edge:* Milled. BW-254.17, KM-404.1.

Date	Assayer	Comment
1898	R	
1899	R	
1900	R	

20 centavos, 0.9027 silver, 5.415 g.

Obverse: The national coat of arms, with the legend REPUBLICA MEXICANA above and the date below. *Reverse:* At center, above a half-wreath of oak and laurel, 20 / CENTAVOS. Above the denomination, mintmark GO, assayer mark R., and fineness 902,7. *Diameter:* 22 mm. *Edge:* Milled. BW-255.2, KM-405.1.

Date	Assayer	Comment
1898	R	
1899	R	
1900/800	R	

25 centavos, 0.9027 silver, 6.768 g.

Obverse: The national coat of arms, with the legend REPUBLICA MEXICANA above and a spray of oak and laurel below; [date] below spray. *Reverse:* Below a small radiant liberty cap, a crossed sword and balance scale; between the pans of the scale, a scroll bearing the word LEY. Below the scroll, 25 CENTAVOS, mintmark GO, the assayer mark (followed by a dot), and fineness 902,7. *Diameter:* 25 mm. *Edge:* Milled. BW-256.6, KM-406.5.

Date	Assayer	Comment
1870	S	
1871	S	
1872/1	S	
1872	S	
1873	S	
1874	S	
1875/4	S	
1875	S	
1876	S	
1877	S	
1878	S	
1879	S	
1880	S	
1881	S	
1882	S	
1883	B	
1884/69	B	
1884/3	B	
1884	B	
1885/65	R	
1885/69	R	
1885	R	
1886/65	R/S	GO / ZS
1886/66	R	
1886/69	R/S	

25 centavos, BW-256.6, continued

Date	Assayer	Comment
1886/5/69	R	
1886	R	
1887	R	
1888	R	
1889/8	R	
1889	R	
1889	R	GO, R / AS, L
1890	R	

50 centavos, 0.9027 silver, 13.536 g.

Obverse: The national coat of arms, with the legend **REPUBLICA MEXICANA** above and a spray of oak and laurel below; **[date]** below spray. *Reverse:* Below a small radiant liberty cap, a crossed sword and balance scale; between the pans of the scale, a scroll bearing the word **LEY**. Below the scroll, **50 CENTAVOS**, mintmark **GO**, the assayer mark (followed by a dot), and fineness **902,7**. *Diameter:* 30 mm. *Edge:* Milled. BW-257.5, KM-407.4.

Date	Assayer	Comment
1869	S	
1870	S	
1871	S	
1872/1	S	
1872	S	
1873	S	
1874	S	
1875	S	
1877	S	
1878	S	
1879	S	
1880	S	
1881/79	S	
1881	S	
1882	S	
1883/2	B/S	
1883	B	
1883	S	Rare
1884	B/S	
1885	R	
1886/5	R	
1886/5	R/B	
1886/5	R/S	
1886	R	
1887	R	

1 peso, 0.9027 silver, 27.073 g.

Obverse: The national coat of arms, with the legend **REPUBLICA MEXICANA** above and a spray of oak and laurel below; **[date]** below spray. *Reverse:* Below a small radiant liberty cap, a crossed sword and balance scale; between the pans of the scale, a scroll bearing the word **LEY**. Below the scroll, **UN PESO**, mintmark **GO**, assayer mark **S.**, and fineness **902,7**. *Diameter:* 37 mm. *Edge:* Milled. BW-258.5, KM-408.4.

Date	Assayer	Comment
1871/0	S	
1871/3	S	
1871	S	
1872	S	
1873/2	S	
1873	S	
1873	S/M	GO / MO

1 peso, 0.9027 silver, 27.073 g.

Obverse: The national coat of arms, with the legend **REPUBLICA MEXICANA.** above and a spray of oak and laurel below; **[date]** below spray. *Reverse:* At center, a large radiant liberty cap; below, **★ UN PESO.**, mintmark **GO**, the date (followed by a dot), assayer mark **R. S.**, and fineness **902,7**. *Diameter:* 39 mm. *Edge:* Milled. BW-258.11, KM-409.1.

Date	Assayer	Comment
1898	RS	
1898	RS	GO / MO
1899	RS	
1900	RS	

1 peso, 0.8750 gold, 1.692 g.

Obverse: The national coat of arms, with the legend **REPUBLICA MEXICANA** above and the date below. *Reverse:* At center, within a wreath of oak and laurel, **1 / PESO**. Above the denomination, the assayer mark, fineness **875**, and mintmark **GO**. *Diameter:* 15 mm. *Edge:* Milled. BW-258.17, KM-410.3.

Date	Assayer	Comment
1870	S	Unconfirmed
1871	S	
1888	R	
1890	R	

Date	Assayer	Comment
1892	R	
1894	R	Very rare
1895	R	
1896/5	R	
1897/6	R	
1897	R	
1898	R	Regular obverse
1898	R	Mule, 5-centavo obverse, regular reverse
1900/800	R	

2-1/2 pesos, 0.8750 gold, 4.230 g.

Obverse: The national coat of arms, with the legend REPUBLICA MEXICANA above and the date below. *Reverse:* At center, within a wreath of oak and laurel, 2½ / PESOS. Above the denomination, the assayer mark, fineness 875, and mintmark GՉ. *Diameter:* 18 mm. *Edge:* Milled. BW-259.4, KM-411.3.

Date	Assayer	Comment
1871	S	
1888	R	GՉ / MՉ

5 pesos, 0.8750 gold, 8.460 g.

Obverse: The national coat of arms, with the legend REPUBLICA MEXICANA above and a spray of oak and laurel below; [date] below spray. *Reverse:* Below a small radiant liberty cap, a crossed sword and balance scale; between the pans of the scale, a scroll bearing the word LEY. Below the scroll, mintmark GՉ and the assayer mark (followed by a dot), with CINCO PESOS and fineness 875. *Diameter:* 22 mm. *Edge:* Milled. BW-260.5, KM-412.4.

Date	Assayer	Comment
1871	S	
1887	R	Very rare
1888	R	Very rare
1893	R	Very rare

10 pesos, 0.8750 gold, 16.920 g.

Obverse: The national coat of arms, with the legend REPUBLICA MEXICANA above and a spray of oak and laurel below; [date] below spray. *Reverse:* Below a small radiant liberty cap, a crossed sword and balance scale; between the pans of the scale, a scroll bearing the word LEY. Below the scroll, mintmark GՉ and the assayer mark (followed by a dot), with DIEZ PESOS and fineness 875. *Diameter:* 27 mm. *Edge:* Milled. BW-261.6, KM-413.5.

Date	Assayer	Comment
1872	S	
1887	R	Rare
1888	R	Rare

20 pesos, 0.8750 gold, 33.840 g.

Obverse: The national coat of arms, with the legend REPUBLICA MEXICANA above and a spray of oak and laurel below; [date] below spray. *Reverse:* Below a small radiant liberty cap, a crossed sword and balance scale; between the pans of the scale, a scroll bearing the word LEY. Below the scroll, mintmark GՉ and the assayer mark (followed by a dot), with VEINTE PESOS and fineness 875. *Diameter:* 34 mm. *Edge:* Milled. BW-262.5, KM-414.4.

Date	Assayer	Comment
1870	S	
1871	S	
1872	S	
1873	S	
1874	S	
1875	S	
1876	S	
1877	M/S	Rare
1877	R	
1877	S	Rare
1877	M/S	Rare
1878	S	Rare
1879	S	Rare
1880	S	Rare
1881	S	Rare
1882	S	
1883	B	
1884	B	
1885	R	
1886	R	Very rare
1887	R	Very rare
1888	R	Very rare
1889	R	Very rare
1890	R	Very rare
1891	R	Very rare
1892	R	Very rare

20 pesos, BW-262.5, continued

Date	Assayer	Comment
1893	R	Very rare
1894	R	Very rare
1895/3	R	Very rare
1895	R	Very rare
1896	R	
1897	R	
1898	R	
1899	R	
1900	R	

HERMOSILLO

The Hermosillo mint, located in the capital of the northern state of Sonora, opened in 1861 and closed in 1895. Mintmarks for Republic decimal coinage struck at the Hermosillo mint are H̊, H♀, and Hº. Assayer initials are as follows:

R	Pablo Rubio (1866–1875)
R	Guadalupe Rocha (1877)
F	Alejandro Fourcade (1876–1877)
A	Jesús Acosta (1877–1883)
A	Unknown (1884)
M	Fernando Méndez (1883–1886)
G	Fausto Gaxiola (1886–1895)

1 centavo, copper.

Obverse: The national coat of arms, with the legend **REPUBLICA MEXICANA** above. *Reverse:* Within a wreath of oak and laurel, in four lines, **UN / CENTAVO / [date]** and mintmark H̊. *Diameter:* 25 mm. *Edge:* Plain or milled. BW-251.7, KM-391.5.

Date	Comment
1875	
1876	
1880	Short H, round O
1880	Tall H, oval 0
1881	

5 centavos, 0.9027 silver, 1.353 g.

Obverse: The national coat of arms, with the legend **REPUBLICA MEXICANA** above and the date below. *Reverse:* At center, above a half-wreath of oak and laurel, **5 / CENTAVOS**. Above the denomination, mintmark **Hº**, the assayer mark (followed by a dot), and fineness **902,7**. *Diameter:* 15 mm. *Edge:* Milled. BW-253.11, KM-398.6.

Date	Assayer	Comment
1874/69	R	
1874	R	
1878	A	
1878	A	Mule, gold peso obverse
1880	A	
1886	G	
1887	G	
1888	G	
1889	G	
1890	G	
1891	G	
1893	G	
1894	G	

10 centavos, 0.9027 silver, 2.707 g.

Obverse: The national coat of arms, with the legend **REPUBLICA MEXICANA** above and the date below. *Reverse:* At center, above a half-wreath of oak and laurel, **10 / CENTAVOS**. Above the denomination, mintmark **Hº**, the assayer mark (followed by a dot), and fineness **902,7**. *Diameter:* 17 mm. *Edge:* Milled. BW-254.11, KM-403.6.

Date	Assayer	Comment
1874	R	
1876	F	
1878	A	
1879	A	
1880	A	
1881	A	
1882/1	A	Large A in assayer initial
1882/1	A	Small A in assayer initial
1882	A	
1883	A	
1884	A	
1884	M	

Date	Assayer	Comment
1885	M	
1886	M	Rare
1886	G	
1887	G	
1888	G	
1889	G	
1890	G	
1891/80	G	
1891	G	
1892	G	
1893	G	

25 centavos, 0.9027 silver, 6.768 g.

Obverse: The national coat of arms, with the legend **REPUBLICA MEXICANA** above and a spray of oak and laurel below; **[date]** below spray. *Reverse:* Below a small radiant liberty cap, a crossed sword and balance scale; between the pans of the scale, a scroll bearing the word **LEY**. Below the scroll, **25 CENTAVOS**, mintmark **Hº**, the assayer mark (followed by a dot), and fineness **902,7**. *Diameter:* 25 mm. *Edge:* Milled. BW-256.7, KM-406.6.

Date	Assayer	Comment
1874	R	
1875	R	Rare
1876/4	F/R	
1876	F/R	
1876	F	
1877	F	
1878	A	
1879	A	
1880	A	
1881	A	
1882	A	
1883	M	
1884	M	
1885	M	
1886	G	
1887	G	
1888	G	
1889	G	
1890	G	

50 centavos, 0.9027 silver, 13.536 g.

Obverse: The national coat of arms, with the legend **REPUBLICA MEXICANA** above and a spray of oak and laurel below; **[date]** below spray. *Reverse:* Below a small radiant liberty cap, a crossed sword and balance scale; between the pans of the scale, a scroll bearing the word **LEY**. Below the scroll, **50 CENTAVOS**, mintmark **Hº**, the assayer mark (followed by a dot), and fineness **902,7**. *Diameter:* 30 mm. *Edge:* Milled. BW-257.6, KM-407.5.

Date	Assayer	Comment
1874	R	
1874/74	R	Low 7
1875/4	R	
1875	R	
1876/5	F/R	
1876	F	
1877	F	
1880/70	A	
1880	A	
1881	A	
1882	A	
1888	G	
1894	G	
1895	G	

1 peso, 0.8750 gold, 1.692 g.

Obverse: The national coat of arms, with the legend **REPUBLICA MEXICANA** above and the date below. *Reverse:* At center, within a wreath of oak and laurel, **1 / PESO**. Above the denomination, the assayer mark, fineness **875**, and mintmark **Hº**. *Diameter:* 15 mm. *Edge:* Milled. BW-258.18, KM-410.4.

Date	Assayer	Comment
1874	R	Rare
1875	R	Rare
1876	F	Rare
1888	G/M	Hº / Mº; rare

2-1/2 pesos, 0.8750 gold, 4.230 g.

Obverse: The national coat of arms, with the legend **REPUBLICA MEXICANA** above and the date below. *Reverse:* At center, within a wreath of oak and laurel, **2½ / PESOS**. Above the denomination, the assayer mark, fineness **875**, and mintmark **Hº**. *Diameter:* 18 mm. *Edge:* Milled. BW-259.5, KM-411.4.

Date	Assayer	Comment
1874	R	Extremely rare
1888	G	Extremely rare (5–6 known)

5 pesos, 0.8750 gold, 8.460 g.

Obverse: The national coat of arms, with the legend REPUBLICA MEXICANA above and a spray of oak and laurel below; [date] below spray. *Reverse:* Below a small radiant liberty cap, a crossed sword and balance scale; between the pans of the scale, a scroll bearing the word LEY. Below the scroll, mintmark Hº and the assayer mark, with CINCO PESOS and fineness 875. *Diameter:* 22 mm. *Edge:* Milled. BW-260.6, KM-412.5.

Date	Assayer	Comment
1874	R	Very rare
1877	R	Extremely rare
1877	A	Very rare
1888	G	Extremely rare

10 pesos, 0.8750 gold, 16.920 g.

Obverse: The national coat of arms, with the legend REPUBLICA MEXICANA above and a spray of oak and laurel below; [date] below spray. *Reverse:* Below a small radiant liberty cap, a crossed sword and balance scale; between the pans of the scale, a scroll bearing the word LEY. Below the scroll, mintmark Hº and the assayer mark (followed by a dot), with DIEZ PESOS and fineness 875. *Diameter:* 27 mm. *Edge:* Milled. BW-261.7, KM-413.6.

Date	Assayer	Comment
1874	R	Very rare
1876	F	Very rare
1878	A	Rare
1880	A	Very rare
1881	A	Rare

20 pesos, 0.8750 gold, 33.840 g.

Obverse: The national coat of arms, with the legend REPUBLICA MEXICANA above and a spray of oak and laurel below; [date] below spray. *Reverse:* Below a small radiant liberty cap, a crossed sword and balance scale; between the pans of the scale, a scroll bearing the word LEY. Below the scroll, mintmark Hº and the assayer mark (followed by a dot), with VEINTE PESOS and fineness 875. *Diameter:* 34 mm. *Edge:* Milled. BW-262.6, KM-414.5.

Date	Assayer	Comment
1874	R	Rare
1875	R	Rare
1876	F	Rare
1888	G	Extremely rare

MÉXICO

The Mexico mint was the first mint of the Americas, having been in operation since 1536. The Apartado mint, where this series of coins was produced, was closed in recent years and has reopened as a museum, run by the Casa de Moneda de México. All modern-day coinage is produced at the San Luis Potosí mint facility. The mintmark remains the traditional M̊. One might assume that the Mexico mint would have out-produced all of the branch mints, but this is not the case. A comparison of silver production in the early years shows that the Guanajuato and Zacatecas mints out-produced the Mexico mint.

There seems to be some confusion as to matching names with assayer initials for this mint. Not all the listed initials appear on the coinage, and those that do, do not appear consistently from denomination to denomination. Here and in chapter 8, we omit names but list the dates collectively that the initials appear on the coinage.

Mintmarks for Republic decimal coinage struck at the Mexico mint are M, Mº, and M̊. Assayer initials are as follows:

TH	(1860, 1861,1863)
CH	(1861–1869)
PH	(1868)
MH	(1873–1877)
BH	(1874)

1 centavo, copper.

Obverse: A seated figure of Liberty facing right, dividing the legend . LIBERTAD / Y REFORMA . around the edge. PAREDES on the exergue below Liberty. *Reverse:* Within a wreath of laurel, in three lines, UN / CENTAVO / 1863. Below the wreath, mintmark M̊. *Diameter:* 27 mm. *Edge:* Plain or milled. BW-251.1, KM-390.

Date	Engraver	Comment
1863	PAREDES	Flat-top 3, milled edge
1863	PAREDES	Round-top 3, milled edge
1863	PAREDES	Round-top 3, plain edge

1 centavo, copper.

Obverse: The national coat of arms, with the legend REPUBLICA MEXICANA above. *Reverse:* Within a wreath of oak and laurel, in four lines, UN / CENTAVO / [date] and mintmark M̊. *Diameter:* 25 mm. *Edge:* Milled. BW-251.8, KM-391.6.

Date	Comment
1868	Rare
1869	
1869	Plain edge
1870/69	
1870	
1871	
1872/1	
1872	
1873	
1874/3	
1874	
1874	Dot after date
1875	
1876	
1877	
1878/5	
1878/6	
1878/7	
1878	
1879/8	
1879	
1880/70	
1880	
1881	
1886	
1887	
1888/78	
1888/7	
1888	
1889	
1889/8	
1890/89	
1890/990	
1890	
1891	
1892	
1893/2	
1893	
1894/3	
1894	
1895/4	
1895	
1896	
1897	

1 centavo, copper.

Obverse: The restyled national coat of arms and the legend REPUBLICA MEXICANA. *Reverse:* Within a wreath of oak and laurel, in four lines, UN / CENTAVO / 1898 and mintmark M̊. *Diameter:* 25 mm. *Edge:* Plain. BW-251.11, KM-393.

Date	Comment
1898	

1 centavo, copper.

Obverse: The national coat of arms, with a spray of oak and laurel below and the legend REPUBLICA MEXICANA above. *Reverse:* At center, within a wreath of oak and laurel, the denomination ₵ (numeral 1 superimposed over a centavo symbol). Above the denomination, the date; below the wreath, mintmark M. *Diameter:* 20 mm. *Edge:* Plain. BW-251.15, KM-394.1.

Date	Comment
1899	
1900	Wide date
1900	Narrow date
1901	
1902/899	REPUBLICA MEXICANA (wide)
1902	REPUBLICA MEXICANA (wide)

1 centavo, BW-251.15, continued

Date	Comment
1902	REPUBLICAMEXICANA (close)
1903	REPUBLICA MEXICANA (wide)
1903	REPUBLICAMEXICANA (close)
1904/3	REPUBLICAMEXICANA (close)
1904	REPUBLICAMEXICANA (close)
1905	REPUBLICAMEXICANA (close)

1 centavo, copper-nickel.

Obverse: A crossed bow, quiver, and war-club, with the legend REPUBLICA MEXICANA above and the date below. *Reverse:* Within a wreath of oak and laurel, the denomination expressed as roman numeral I. *Diameter:* 16 mm. *Edge:* Plain. BW-251.13, KM-392.

Note: The Roman-numeral coinage of 1882 and 1883 was decreed by a congressional act of December 16, 1881, but proved to be very unpopular and was discontinued December 6, 1883.

Date	Comment
1882	
1883	

2 centavos, copper-nickel.

Obverse: A crossed bow, quiver, and war-club, with the legend REPUBLICA MEXICANA above and the date below. *Reverse:* Within a wreath of oak and laurel, the denomination expressed as roman numeral II. No mintmark or assayer initial. *Diameter:* 18 mm. *Edge:* Plain. BW-252, KM-395.

Date	Comment
1882	
1883/2	
1883	

5 centavos, copper-nickel.

Obverse: A crossed bow, quiver, and war-club, with the legend REPUBLICA MEXICANA above and the date below. *Reverse:* Within a wreath of oak and laurel, the denomination expressed as roman numeral V. No mintmark or assayer initial. *Diameter:* 20 mm. *Edge:* Plain. BW-253.16, KM-399.

Date	Comment
1882	
1883	

5 centavos, 0.9027 silver, 1.353 g.

Obverse: The national coat of arms, with the legend REPUBLICA MEXICANA above and a spray of oak and laurel below. *Reverse:* At center, a large radiant liberty cap; below, 5 CENTAVOS. [date]. and mintmark M̊. No assayer mark or fineness. *Diameter:* 15 mm. *Edge:* Ornamented. BW-253.3, KM-397.

Date	Comment
1867	
1867/3	
1868/7	
1868	

5 centavos, 0.9027 silver, 1.353 g.

Obverse: The national coat of arms, with the legend REPUBLICA MEXICANA above and the date below. *Reverse:* At center, above a half-wreath of oak and laurel, 5 / CENTAVOS. Above the denomination, mintmark Mº, the assayer mark (followed by a dot), and fineness 902,7. *Diameter:* 15 mm. *Edge:* Milled. BW-253.12, KM-398.7.

Date	Assayer	Comment
1868	C	Rare
1869	P	
1869/8	C	
1870	C	
1871	C	
1871	M	
1872	M	
1873	M	
1874/69	M	
1874	M	
1874/3	B	
1874	B	
1875	B	
1875	B/M	
1876/5	B	
1876	B	
1877/6	M	

Date	Assayer	Comment
1877	M	
1878/7	M	
1878	M	
1879/8	M	
1879	M	
1879	M	9 / inverted 9
1880/76	M/B	
1880/76	M	
1880	M	
1881/0	M	
1881	M	
1886/0	M	
1886/1	M	
1886/4	M	
1886	M	
1887	M	
1887	M	Small M
1887	M	M / large or small M
1888/7	M	
1888	M	
1889	M	
1890/89		
1890/00	M	
1890	M	
1891	M	
1892	M	
1892	M	9 / inverted 9
1893	M	
1894	M	
1895	M	
1896	B	
1897	M	

5 centavos, 0.9027 silver, 1.353 g.

Obverse: The restyled national coat of arms, with the legend REPUBLICA MEXICANA above and the date below. *Reverse:* At center, above a half-wreath of oak and laurel, 5 / CENTAVOS. Above the denomination, mintmark M̊, assayer mark M., and fineness 902,7. *Diameter:* 15 mm. *Edge:* Milled. BW-253.19, KM-400.2.

Date	Assayer	Comment
1898	M	
1899	M	
1900	M	
1901	M	
1902	M	
1902/1	M	
1903	M	
1904	M	
1904/94	M	
1905	M	

10 centavos, 0.9027 silver, 2.707 g.

Obverse: The national coat of arms, with a spray of oak and laurel below and the legend REPUBLICA MEXICANA above. *Reverse:* At center, a large radiant liberty cap; below, 10 CENTAVOS. [date]. and mintmark Mº. No assayer mark or fineness. *Diameter:* 18 mm. *Edge:* Ornamented. BW-254.3, KM-402.

Date	Comment
1867/3	
1867	
1868/7	
1868	

10 centavos, 0.9027 silver, 2.707 g.

Obverse: The national coat of arms, with the legend REPUBLICA MEXICANA above and the date below. *Reverse:* At center, above a half-wreath of oak and laurel, 10 / CENTAVOS. Above the denomination, mintmark Mº, the assayer mark (followed by a dot), and fineness 902,7. *Diameter:* 17 mm. *Edge:* Milled. BW-254.12, KM-403.7.

Date	Assayer	Comment
1869/8	C	
1869	C	
1870	C	
1871	C	
1871	M	
1872	M	
1873	M	
1874	M	
1874/64	B	
1874	B/M	
1874	B	
1875	B	
1876/5	B	
1876/5	B/M	
1876	B	
1877/6	M	
1877/6	M/B	

10 centavos, BW-254.12, continued

Date	Assayer	Comment
1877	M	
1878/7	M	
1878	M	
1879/69	M	
1879	M/C	
1879	M	
1880/79	M	
1880	M	
1881/0	M	
1881	M	
1882/1	M	
1882	M	
1883/2	M	
1884	M	
1885	M	
1886	M	
1887/6	M	
1887	M	
1888/7	M	
1888	M	Small Mº
1888	M	Large Mº
1889	M	
1890/89	M	
1890	M	
1891	M	
1892	M	
1893	M	
1893	M/C	
1894	M	
1895	M	
1896	B/C	
1896	M	
1897	M	

10 centavos, 0.9027 silver, 2.707 g.

Obverse: The restyled national coat of arms, with the legend REPUBLICA MEXICANA above and the date below. *Reverse:* At center, above a half-wreath of oak and laurel, 10 / CENTAVOS. Above the denomination, mintmark Mº, assayer mark M., and fineness 902,7. *Diameter:* 17 mm. *Edge:* Milled. BW-254.18, KM-404.2.

Date	Assayer	Comment
1898	M	
1899	M	
1900	M	
1901	M	
1902	M	
1903	M	
1904	M	
1904	M	M mintmark error
1905	M	

20 centavos, 0.9027 silver, 5.415 g.

Obverse: The national coat of arms, with the legend REPUBLICA MEXICANA above and the date below. *Reverse:* At center, above a half-wreath of oak and laurel, 20 / CENTAVOS. Above the denomination, mintmark Mº, assayer mark M., and fineness 902,7. *Diameter:* 22 mm. *Edge:* Milled. BW-255.3, KM-405.2.

Date	Assayer	Comment
1898	M	
1899	M	
1901	M	
1902	M	
1903	M	
1904	M	
1905	M	

25 centavos, 0.9027 silver, 6.768 g.

Obverse: The national coat of arms, with the legend REPUBLICA MEXICANA above and the date below. *Reverse:* Below a small radiant liberty cap, a crossed sword and balance scale; between the pans of the scale, a scroll bearing the word LEY. Below the scroll, 25 CENTAVOS, mintmark Mº, the assayer mark (followed by a dot), and fineness 902,7. *Diameter:* 25 mm. *Edge:* Milled. BW-256.8, KM-406.7.

Date	Assayer	Comment
1869	C	
1870	C	
1871	M	
1872	M	
1873/1	M	
1873	M	
1874/69	B/M	
1874/3	M	
1874	M	
1875	B	
1876/5	B	

Date	Assayer	Comment
1876	B	
1877	M	
1878/1	M	
1878/7	M	
1878	M	
1879	M	
1880	M	
1881/0	M	
1881	M	
1882	M	
1883	M	
1884	M	
1885	M	
1886/5	M	
1886	M	
1887	M	
1888	M	
1889	M	
1890	M	

50 centavos, 0.9027 silver, 13.536 g.

Obverse: The national coat of arms, with the legend **REPUBLICA MEXICANA** above and a spray of oak and laurel below; **[date]** below spray. *Reverse:* Below a small radiant liberty cap, a crossed sword and balance scale; between the pans of the scale, a scroll bearing the word **LEY**. Below the scroll, **50 CENTAVOS**, mintmark **Mº**, the assayer mark (followed by a dot), and fineness **902,7**. *Diameter:* 30 mm. *Edge:* Milled. BW-257.7, KM-407.6.

Date	Assayer	Comment
1869	C	
1870	C	
1871	C	
1871	M/C	
1872/1	M	
1872	M	
1873	M	
1874/3	M	
1874/2	B	
1874/2	B/M	
1874/3	B/M	
1874	B	
1875	B	
1876	B	
1876/5	B	

Date	Assayer	Comment
1877/2	M	
1877	M	
1878	M	
1878/7	M	
1879	M	
1880	M	
1881	M	
1882/1	M	
1883	M	
1884	M	
1885	M	
1886	M	
1886/5	M	
1887/6	M	
1887	M	
1888	M	

1 peso, 0.9027 silver, 27.073 g.

Obverse: The national coat of arms, with the legend **REPUBLICA MEXICANA** above and a spray of oak and laurel below; **[date]** below spray. *Reverse:* Below a small radiant liberty cap, a crossed sword and balance scale; between the pans of the scale, a scroll bearing the word **LEY**. Below the scroll, **UN PESO**, mintmark **Mº**, the assayer mark (followed by a dot), and fineness **902,7**. *Diameter:* 37 mm. *Edge:* Milled. BW-258.6, KM-408.5.

Date	Assayer	Comment
1869	C	
1869	C	Large LEY in scroll; pattern
1870	C	
1870	M/C	
1870/69	C	
1870	M	
1871	M	
1871/0	M	
1872/1	M	
1872	M	
1873	M	

1 peso, 0.9027 silver, 27.073 g.

Obverse: The national coat of arms, with the legend **REPUBLICA MEXICANA.** above and a spray of oak and laurel below. *Reverse:* At center, a large radiant liberty cap; below, **★ UN PESO.**, mintmark **Mº**, the date (followed by a dot), the assayer mark (followed by a dot after each initial), and fineness 902,7. *Diameter:* 39 mm. *Edge:* Milled. BW-258.12, KM-409.2.

In 1949 a reported 10,250,000 Liberty Cap pesos dated 1898 with the Mº mintmark were produced for use in the Republic of China. The Mexico mint struck 8,250,000, and the San Francisco Mint struck 2,000,000. Original strikes have 139 beads on the reverse rim, while the 1949 restrikes have 134 beads. On the originals, the 1 in the date has a straight serif and tapers to a short base; on the restrikes, the 1 has a curved serif and sits on a long thin base.

Date	Assayer	Comment
1898	AM	Original strike (139 beads)
1898	AM	1949 restrike (134 beads)
1899	AM	
1900	AM	
1901	AM	
1902/1	AM	
1902	AM	
1903	AM	
1903	MA	Error: transposed assayer initials
1904	AM	
1905	AM	
1908	AM	
1908	GV	
1909	GV	

1 peso, 0.8750 gold, 1.692 g.

Obverse: The national coat of arms, with the legend REPUBLICA MEXICANA above and the date below. *Reverse:* At center, within a wreath of oak and laurel, 1 / PESO. Above the denomination the assayer mark, fineness 875, and mintmark Mº. *Diameter:* 15 mm. *Edge:* Milled. BW-258.19, KM-410.5.

Date	Assayer	Comment
1870	C	
1871	M/C	
1872	M/C	
1872/1	M/C	
1873/1	M	
1873	M	
1874	M	
1875	B/M	
1876/5	B/M	
1877	M	
1878	M	
1879	M	
1880/70	M	
1881/71	M	
1882/72	M	
1883/72	M	
1884	M	
1885/71	M	
1885	M	
1886	M	
1887	M	
1888	M	
1889	M	
1890	M	
1891	M	
1892/0	M	
1893	M	
1894	M	
1895	M	
1895	B	
1896	B	
1896	M	
1897	M	
1898/7	M	
1899	M	
1900/800	M	
1900/890	M	
1900	M	
1901	M	
1902	M	Large date
1902	M	Small date
1903	M	
1904	M	
1905	M	

2-1/2 pesos, 0.8750 gold, 4.230 g.

Obverse: The national coat of arms, with the legend REPUBLICA MEXICANA above and the date below. *Reverse:* At center, within a wreath of oak and laurel, 2½ / PESOS. Above the denomination the assayer mark, fineness 875, and mintmark Mº. *Diameter:* 18 mm. *Edge:* Milled. BW-259.6, KM-411.5.

Date	Assayer	Comment
1870	C	Very scarce
1872	M/C	
1873/2	M	
1874	M	Rare
1874	B/M	Rare
1875	B	Rare
1876	B	Rare
1877	M	Rare
1878	M	
1879	M	
1880/79	M	
1881	M	
1882	M	
1883/73	M	
1884	M	
1885	M	
1886	M	
1887	M	
1888	M	
1889	M	
1890	M	
1891	M	
1892	M	

5 pesos, 0.8750 gold, 8.460 g.

Obverse: The national coat of arms, with the legend REPUBLICA MEXICANA above and a spray of oak and laurel below; **[date]** below spray. *Reverse:* Below a small radiant liberty cap, a crossed sword and balance scale; between the pans of the scale, a scroll bearing the word LEY. Below the scroll, mintmark Mº and the assayer mark (followed by a dot), with CINCO PESOS and fineness 875. *Diameter:* 22 mm. *Edge:* Milled. BW-260.7, KM-412.6.

Date	Assayer	Comment
1870	C	
1871/69	M	
1871/0	M	
1872	M	
1873/2	M	
1874	M	
1875	B	
1876/5	B/M	
1877	M	
1878/7	M	
1878	M	
1879/8	M	
1880	M	
1881	M	
1882	M	Rare
1883	M	Extremely rare
1884	M	
1886	M	Extremely rare
1887	M	Extremely rare
1888	M	
1889	M	
1890	M	
1891	M	
1892	M	
1893	M	
1897	M	
1898	M	
1900	M	
1901	M	
1902	M	
1903	M	
1904	M	
1905	M	

10 pesos, 0.8750 gold, 16.920 g.

Obverse: The national coat of arms, with the legend REPUBLICA MEXICANA above and a spray of oak and laurel below; **[date]** below spray. *Reverse:* Below a small radiant liberty cap, a crossed sword and balance scale; between the pans of the scale, a scroll bearing the word LEY. Below the scroll, mintmark Mº and the assayer mark (followed by a dot), with DIEZ PESOS and fineness 875. *Diameter:* 27 mm. *Edge:* Milled. BW-261.8, KM-413.7.

Date	Assayer	Comment
1870	C	
1872/1	M	
1873	M	
1874/3	M	
1875	B/M	
1878	M	
1881	M	
1882	M	
1883	M	
1884	M	
1885	M	
1886	M	

10 pesos, BW-261.8, continued

Date	Assayer	Comment
1887	M	
1888	M	
1889	M	
1890	M	
1891	M	
1892	M	Rare
1893	M	
1897	M	
1898/7	M	
1900	M	
1901	M	
1902	M	
1903	M	
1904	M	
1905	M	

20 pesos, 0.8750 gold, 33.840 g.

Obverse: The national coat of arms, with the legend **REPUBLICA MEXICANA** above and a spray of oak and laurel below; **[date]** below spray. *Reverse:* Below a small radiant liberty cap, a crossed sword and balance scale; between the pans of the scale, a scroll bearing the word **LEY**. Below the scroll, mintmark **Mº** and the assayer mark (followed by a dot), with **VEINTE PESOS** and fineness **875**. *Diameter:* 34 mm. *Edge:* Milled. BW-262.7, KM-414.6.

Date	Assayer	Comment
1870	C	
1871	M	
1872/1	M	
1872	M	
1873	M	
1874/2	M	
1874/2	B	
1875	B	
1876	B	
1877	M	
1878	M	
1879	M	
1881/0	M	
1881	M	
1882/1	M	
1882	M	
1883/1	M	
1883	M	
1884/3	M	
1884	M	
1885	M	
1886	M	
1887	M	
1888	M	
1889	M	
1890	M	
1891/0	M	
1891	M	
1892	M	
1893	M	
1894	M	
1895	M	
1896	B	
1897	M	
1898	M	
1899	M	
1900	M	
1901	M	
1902	M	
1903/2	M	
1903	M	
1904	M	
1905	M	

OAXACA

Located in the capital of the state of Oaxaca, this mint has issued coins since the War of Independence. It was made a federal mint in 1858, but closed in 1893. In the decimal series the only gold denominations struck were the 10 and 20 pesos.

Mintmarks for Republic decimal coinage struck at the Oaxaca mint are **O**, **Ⓞ**, **Ô**, and **OA̲**. There are only two assayer initial combinations for the Oaxaca issues; they are as follows:

E Agustín Endner (1859–1891)

N Eduardo Navarro Luna (1890)

1 centavo, copper.

Obverse: The national coat of arms, with the legend **REPUBLICA MEXICANA** above. *Reverse:* Within a wreath of oak and laurel, in four lines, **UN / CENTAVO / [date]** and mintmark **Ô**. *Diameter:* 25 mm. *Edge:* Milled. BW-251.9, KM-391.7.

Date	Comment
1872	
1873	
1874	
1875	

5 centavos, 0.9027 silver, 1.353 g.

Obverse: The national coat of arms, with the legend **REPUBLICA MEXICANA** above and the date below. *Reverse:* At center, above a half-wreath of oak and laurel, **5 / CENTAVOS**. Above the denomination, mintmark **OA**, the assayer mark (followed by a dot), and fineness **902,7**. *Diameter:* 15 mm. *Edge:* Milled. BW-253.13, KM-398.8.

Date	Assayer	Comment
1890	E	Rare
1890	N	

10 centavos, 0.9027 silver, 2.707 g.

Obverse: The national coat of arms, with the legend **REPUBLICA MEXICANA** above and the date below. *Reverse:* At center, above a half-wreath of oak and laurel, **10 / CENTAVOS**. Above the denomination, mintmark **OA**, the assayer mark (followed by a dot), and fineness **902,7**. *Diameter:* 17 mm. *Edge:* Milled. BW-254.13, KM-403.8.

Date	Assayer	Comment
1889	E	
1890	N	Rare
1890	E	

1 peso, 0.9027 silver, 27.073 g.

Obverse: The national coat of arms, with the legend **REPUBLICA MEXICANA** above and a spray of oak and laurel below; **[date]** below spray. *Reverse:* Below a small radiant liberty cap, a crossed sword and balance scale; between the pans of the scale, a scroll bearing the word **LEY**. Below the scroll, **UN PESO**, mintmark **OA**, assayer mark **E.**, and fineness **902,7**. *Diameter:* 37 mm. *Edge:* Milled. BW-258.7, KM-408.6.

Date	Assayer	Comment
1869	E	
1870	E	Small A in mintmark
1870	E	Large A in mintmark
1871/69	E	
1871	E	Small A in mintmark
1871	E	Large A in mintmark
1872	E	Small A in mintmark
1872	E	Large A in mintmark
1873	E	

10 pesos, 0.8750 gold, 16.920 g.

Obverse: The national coat of arms, with the legend **REPUBLICA MEXICANA** above and a spray of oak and laurel below; **[date]** below spray. *Reverse:* Below a small radiant liberty cap, a crossed sword and balance scale; between the pans of the scale, a scroll bearing the word **LEY**. Below the scroll, mintmark **OA** and assayer mark **E.**, with **DIEZ PESOS** and fineness **875**. *Diameter:* 27 mm. *Edge:* Milled. BW-261.9, KM-413.8.

Date	Assayer	Comment
1870	E	
1871	E	
1872	E	
1873	E	
1874	E	
1875	E	Rare
1876	E	Rare
1877	E	Rare
1878	E	Rare
1879	E	Rare
1880	E	Rare
1881	E	Rare
1882	E	Rare
1883	E	Rare
1884	E	Rare
1885	E	Rare
1886	E	Rare
1887	E	Rare

20 pesos, 0.8750 gold, 33.840 g.

Obverse: The national coat of arms, with the legend **REPUBLICA MEXICANA** above and a spray of oak and laurel below; **[date]** below spray. *Reverse:* Below a small radiant liberty cap, a crossed sword and balance scale; between the pans of the scale, a scroll bearing the word **LEY**. Below the scroll, mintmark **O**$\underline{\text{A}}$ and assayer mark **E.**, with **VEINTE PESOS** and fineness **875**. *Diameter:* 34 mm. *Edge:* Milled. BW-262.8, KM-414.7.

Date	Assayer	Comment
1870	E	
1871	E	
1872	E	
1888	E	Rare

SAN LUIS POTOSÍ

The San Luis Potosí mint, located in the capital city of the state of San Luis Potosí, opened in 1827 and closed in 1893. Mintmarks for Republic decimal coinage struck at the San Luis Potosí mint are **P**, **Ṗ**, **P!**, **S.L.P!**, and **S.L.P.** Assayer initials are as follows:

P or S	Pomposo Sanabria (engraver only; 1867–1870)
H	Manuel Herrera Razo (1870–1885)
G	Carlos Aguirre Gómez (1867–1870)
E	Blas Escontría (1879–1881)
C	Luis Cuevas (1885–1886)
B	Unknown (1887)
R	Mariano Reyes (1886–1893)
O	Juan R. Ochoa (1870–1873)

1 centavo, copper, 8 g.

Obverse: A seated figure of Liberty facing right, dividing the legend **. LIBERTAD / Y REFORMA .** around the edge. Engraver **SANABRIA** on the exergue below Liberty. *Reverse:* Within a wreath of laurel, in three lines, **UN / CENTAVO / 1863.** Below the wreath, mintmark **S.L.P.** *Diameter:* 26 mm. *Edge:* Milled. BW-251.2, KM-390.1.

Date	Engraver	Comment
1863	SANABRIA	

1 centavo, copper, 8 g.

Obverse: The national coat of arms, with the legend **REPUBLICA MEXICANA** above. *Reverse:* Within a wreath of oak and laurel, in four lines, **UN / CENTAVO / [date]** and mintmark **Ṗ**. *Diameter:* 25 mm. *Edge:* Milled. BW-251.10, KM-391.8.

Date	Comment
1871	Rare
1877	
1878	
1891	Ṗ / M̊
1891	

5 centavos, 0.9027 silver, 1.353 g.

Obverse: The national coat of arms, with the legend **REPUBLICA MEXICANA.** above and a spray of oak and laurel below. *Reverse:* Within a wreath of laurel, in three lines, **5 / CENTAVOS / 1863.** Below the wreath, mintmark **S.L.P.** No assayer mark or fineness. *Diameter:* 15 mm. *Edge:* Diagonally milled. BW-253.1, KM-396.1.

Date	Comment
1863	

5 centavos, 0.9027 silver, 1.353 g.

Obverse: The national coat of arms, with the legend **REPUBLICA MEXICANA.** above and a spray of oak and laurel below. *Reverse:* At center, a large radiant liberty cap; below, **5 CENTAVOS. [date].** and mintmark **P.** No assayer mark or fineness. *Diameter:* 15 mm. *Edge:* Diagonally milled. BW-253.4, KM-397.1.

Date	Comment
1868	
1869/7	
1869	

5 centavos, 0.9027 silver, 1.353 g.

Obverse: The national coat of arms, with the legend **REPUBLICA MEXICANA** above and the date below. *Reverse:* At center, above a half-wreath of oak and laurel, **5 / CENTAVOS**. Above the denomination, mintmark P!, the assayer mark (followed by a dot), and fineness 902,7. *Diameter:* 15 mm. *Edge:* Milled. BW-253.14, KM-398.9.

Date	Assayer	Comment
1869	S	
1870	G	G / $\overset{\circ}{\text{M}}$ C; rare
1870	O	
1871	O	Rare
1872	O	
1873		Rare
1874	H	
1875	H	
1876	H	
1877	H	
1878	H	
1880	H	Rare
1881	H	Rare
1886	R	
1887/0	R	
1887	R	
1888	R	
1889/7	R	
1889	R	
1890	R	
1891/89	R/B	
1891	R	
1892/89	R	
1892/0	R	
1892	R	
1893	R	

10 centavos, 0.9027 silver, 2.707 g.

Obverse: The national coat of arms, with the legend REPUBLICA MEXICANA. above and a spray of oak and laurel below. *Reverse:* Within a wreath of laurel, in three lines, 10 / CENTAVOS / 1863. Below the wreath, mintmark S.L.P. No assayer mark or fineness. *Diameter:* 18 mm. *Edge:* Diagonally milled. BW-254.2a, KM-401.2.

Date	Comment
1863	

10 centavos, 0.9027 silver, 2.707 g.

Obverse: The national coat of arms, with the legend REPUBLICA MEXICANA. above and a spray of oak and laurel below. *Reverse:* At center, a large radiant liberty cap; below, 10 CENTAVOS. [date]. and mintmark P. *Diameter:* 18 mm. *Edge:* Ornamented. BW-254.4, KM-402.1.

Date	Assayer	Comment
1868/7	P	
1868	P	
1869/7	P	

10 centavos, 0.9027 silver, 2.707 g.

Obverse: The national coat of arms, with the legend REPUBLICA MEXICANA above and the date below. *Reverse:* At center, above a half-wreath of oak and laurel, 10 / CENTAVOS. Above the denomination, mintmark P!, the assayer mark (followed by a dot), and fineness 902,7. *Diameter:* 17 mm. *Edge:* Milled. BW-254.14, KM-403.9.

Date	Assayer	Comment
1869/8	S	Rare
1870/69	O	Rare
1870	G	
1871	O	
1872	O	
1873	O	Rare
1874	H	
1875	H	
1876	H	
1877	H	
1878	H	
1879	H	
1880	H	
1881	H	
1882	H	Rare
1883	H	
1884	H	
1885	H	
1885	C	Rare
1886	C	
1886	R	
1887	R	
1888	R	
1889/7	R	
1890	R	
1891/89	R	
1891	R	
1892/0	R	
1892	R	
1893	R	

25 centavos, 0.9027 silver, 6.768 g.

Obverse: The national coat of arms, with the legend **REPUBLICA MEXICANA** above and a spray of oak and laurel below; **[date]** below spray. *Reverse:* Below a small radiant liberty cap, a crossed sword and balance scale; between the pans of the scale, a scroll bearing the word **LEY**. Below the scroll, **25 CENTAVOS**, mintmark **P!**, the assayer mark (followed by a dot), and fineness **902,7**. *Diameter:* 25 mm. *Edge:* Milled. BW-256.9, KM-406.8.

Date	Assayer	Comment
1869	S	
1870	G	
1870	O	
1871	O	
1872	O	
1873	O	
1874	H	
1875	H	
1876/5	H	
1876	H	
1877	H	
1878	H	
1879	H	
1879	E	
1880	H	
1881	H	
1881	E	Rare
1882	H	
1883	H	
1884	H	
1885	H	
1886	C	
1886	R	
1886	R	6 / inverted 6
1887	R	P! / ZS
1887	B	P! / ZS
1888	R	
1888	R	P! / ZS
1888	R/B	
1889	R	
1889	R	P! / ZS
1889	R/B	
1890	R	
1890	R/B	P! / ZS
1890	R/B	

50 centavos, 0.9027 silver, 13.536 g.

Obverse: The national coat of arms, with the legend **REPUBLICA MEXICANA** above and a spray of oak and laurel below; **[date]** below spray. *Reverse:* Below a small radiant liberty cap, a crossed sword and balance scale; between the pans of the scale, a scroll bearing the word **LEY**. Below the scroll, **50 CENTAVOS**, mintmark **P!**, the assayer mark (followed by a dot), and fineness **902,7**. *Diameter:* 30 mm. *Edge:* Milled. BW-257.8, KM-407.7.

Date	Assayer	Comment
1870	G	
1870/78	O/G	
1870	O	
1871	O/G	
1872	D/G	
1872	O	
1873	H	
1873	O	
1874	H/O	
1875	H	
1876	H	
1877	H	
1878	H	
1879/7	H	
1879	H	
1880	H	
1881	H	
1882	H	
1883	H	
1884	H	
1885/3	H	
1885/0	H	
1885/4	H	
1885	H	
1885	C	
1886/1	R	
1886	C	
1886	R	
1887	R	

1 peso, 0.9027 silver, 27.0730 g.

Obverse: The national coat of arms, with the legend **REPUBLICA MEXICANA** above and a spray of oak and laurel below; **[date]** below spray. *Reverse:* Below a small radiant liberty cap, a crossed sword and balance scale; between the pans of the scale, a scroll bearing the word **LEY**. Below the scroll, **UN PESO**, mintmark **P!**, assayer mark **S.**, and fineness **902,7**. *Diameter:* 37 mm. *Edge:* Milled. BW-258.8, KM-408.7.

Date	Assayer	Comment
1870	S	
1870	S/A	
1870	G	
1870	H	Circulating counterfeit
1870	O/G	
1870	O	
1871/69	O	
1871	O	
1871	O/G	
1872	O	
1873	O	
1873	H	

No regular-issue decimal gold coins were struck at San Luis Potosí, but there were several trial and presentation versions of gold decimal issues, as reported in *Guide Book of Mexican Coins* by T.V. Buttrey and Clyde Hubbard, 5th edition, 1989:

1888-P!, R, 1 peso, struck in silver
1888-P!, R, 2-1/2 pesos, struck in silver
1888-P!, R, 5 pesos, struck in silver
1888-P!, R, 10 pesos, struck in gold
1888-P!, R, 10 pesos, struck in silver

ZACATECAS

The Zacatecas mint is located in the capital city of the rich mining district in the state of Zacatecas. It was opened in October 1810 as a provisional mint during the War of Independence. The first Republic coinage was issued in 1825. The mint closed in 1905 when that year's coinage reform was instituted.

Mintmarks for Republic decimal coinage struck at the Zacatecas mint are **Z**, **$\overset{S}{Z}$**, and **ZS**. Assayer initials are as follows:

S	Possibly Jesús María Sánchez de Santa Ana (1876–1886)
H	Ygnacio Hierro (1868–1874)
A	Juan M. Acuña (1874–1876)
Z	Unknown (1882)
FZ or Z	Francisco de P. Zárate (1886–1897)
FM or M	Francisco Mateas (1904–1905)

1 centavo, copper.

Obverse: The national coat of arms, with the legend **REPUBLICA MEXICANA** above. *Reverse:* Within a wreath of oak and laurel, in four lines, **UN / CENTAVO / [date]** and mintmark **$\overset{S}{Z}$**. *Diameter:* 25 mm. *Edge:* Milled. BW-251.11a, KM-391.9.

Date	Comment
1872	Rare
1873	
1874/3	
1874	
1875/4	
1875	
1876	
1877	Rare
1878	
1880	
1881	

5 centavos, 0.9027 silver, 1.353 g.

Obverse: The national coat of arms, with the legend **REPUBLICA MEXICANA** above and the date below. *Reverse:* At center, above a half-wreath of oak and laurel, **5 / CENTAVOS**. Above the denomination, mintmark **ZS**, the assayer mark (followed by a dot), and fineness **902,7**. *Diameter:* 15 mm. *Edge:* Milled. BW-253.15, KM-398.10.

Date	Assayer	Comment
1870	H	
1871	H	

5 centavos, BW-253.15, continued

Date	Assayer	Comment
1871/0	H	
1872	H	
1873/2	H	
1873	H	
1874	H	
1874	A	
1875	A	
1876	A	
1876/5	S	
1876	S	
1877	S	
1878	S	
1879/8	S	
1879	S	
1880/79	S	
1880	S	
1881	S	
1886/4	S	
1886	S	
1886	Z	
1887	Z	
1888/7	Z	
1888	Z	
1889	Z	
1889	Z	9 / inverted 9
1889	Z	Struck over 1889 M$^{\underline{o}}$, M
1890	Z	
1890	Z	Struck over 1889 M$^{\underline{o}}$, M
1891	Z	
1892	Z	
1893	Z	
1894	Z	Z$^{\underline{o}}$ mintmark error
1894	Z	
1895	Z	
1896	Z	
1896	Z	6 / inverted 6
1897/6	Z	
1897	Z	
1898	Z	
1899	Z	
1900	Z	
1901	Z	
1902/1	Z	
1902	Z	
1903	Z	
1904	Z	
1904	M	
1905	M	
1905	Z	

5 centavos, 0.9027 silver, 1.353 g.

Obverse: The restyled national coat of arms, with the legend REPUBLICA MEXICANA above and the date below. *Reverse:* At center, above a half-wreath of oak and laurel, 5 / CENTAVOS. Above the denomination, mintmark Z$^{\underline{s}}$, the assayer mark (followed by a dot), and fineness 902,7. *Diameter:* 15 mm. *Edge:* Milled. BW-253.20, KM-400.3.

10 centavos, 0.9027 silver, 2.707 g.

Obverse: The national coat of arms, with the legend REPUBLICA MEXICANA above and the date below. *Reverse:* At center, above a half-wreath of oak and laurel, 10 / CENTAVOS. Above the denomination, mintmark Z$^{\underline{s}}$, the assayer mark (followed by a dot), and fineness 902,7. *Diameter:* 17 mm. *Edge:* Milled. BW-254.15, KM-403.10.

Date	Assayer	Comment
1870	H	
1871/0	H	
1871	H	
1872	H	
1873	H	
1874	A	
1874	H	
1875	A	
1876	S	
1876	A	
1877	S	Small S in mintmark
1877	S	
1878/7	S	
1878	S	
1879	S	
1880	S	
1880/79	S	
1881	S	
1881/0	S	
1882/1	S	
1882	S	
1883	S	
1883/73	S	
1884/3	S	
1884	S	
1885	S	

Date	Assayer	Comment
1885	S	Small S in mintmark
1885		No assayer mark
1886	S	
1886	Z	
1887	Z	Z mintmark
1887	Z	ZS mintmark
1888	Z	Z mintmark
1888	Z	ZS mintmark
1889/7	Z/S	
1889	Z/S	
1889	Z	
1890	Z	Z mintmark
1890	Z	ZS mintmark
1891	Z	Double S in mintmark (ZSS)
1891	Z	
1892	Z	
1893	Z	
1894	Z	
1895	Z	
1896	Z	ZS mintmark
1896	Z	Z mintmark
1897	Z	
1897/6	Z	Z mintmark
1897/6	Z	ZS mintmark

10 centavos, 0.9027 silver, 2.707 g.

Obverse: The restyled national coat of arms, with the legend **REPUBLICA MEXICANA** above and the date below. *Reverse:* At center, above a half-wreath of oak and laurel, **10 / CENTAVOS**. Above the denomination, mintmark **ZS**, the assayer mark (followed by a dot), and fineness **902,7**. *Diameter:* 17 mm. *Edge:* Milled. BW-254.19, KM-404.3.

Date	Assayer	Comment
1898	Z	
1899	Z	
1900	Z	
1901	Z	
1902	Z	
1903	Z	
1904	Z	
1904	M	
1905	M	

20 centavos, 0.9027 silver, 5.415 g.

Obverse: The national coat of arms, with the legend **REPUBLICA MEXICANA** above and the date below. *Reverse:* At center, above a half-wreath of oak and laurel, **20 / CENTAVOS**. Above the denomination, mintmark **ZS**, the assayer mark (followed by a dot), and fineness **902,7**. *Diameter:* 22 mm. *Edge:* Milled. BW-255.4, KM-405.3.

Date	Assayer	Comment
1898	Z	
1899	Z	
1900/000	Z	
1901	Z	
1902	Z	
1903	Z	
1904	Z	
1904	M	
1905	M	

25 centavos, 0.9027 silver, 6.768 g.

Obverse: The national coat of arms, with the legend **REPUBLICA MEXICANA** above and a spray of oak and laurel below; **[date]** below spray. *Reverse:* Below a small radiant liberty cap, a crossed sword and balance scale; between the pans of the scale, a scroll bearing the word **LEY**. Below the scroll, **25 CENTAVOS**, mintmark **ZS**, the assayer mark (followed by a dot), and fineness **902,7**. *Diameter:* 25 mm. *Edge:* Milled. BW-256.10, KM-406.9.

Date	Assayer	Comment
1870	H	
1871	H	
1872	H	
1873	H	
1874	A	
1874	H	
1875	A	
1876	A	
1876	S	
1877	S	
1878	S	
1879	S	
1880	S	
1881	S	
1882/1	S	
1882	S	
1883/2	S	
1883	S	
1884/3	S	

25 centavos, BW-256.10, continued

Date	Assayer	Comment
1884	S	
1885	S	
1886/5	S	
1886	S	
1886	Z	
1887	Z	
1888	Z	
1889	Z	
1890	Z	

50 centavos, 0.9027 silver, 13.536 g.

Obverse: The national coat of arms, with the legend REPUBLICA MEXICANA above and a spray of oak and laurel below; [date] below spray. *Reverse:* Below a small radiant liberty cap, a crossed sword and balance scale; between the pans of the scale, a scroll bearing the word LEY. Below the scroll, 50 CENTAVOS, mintmark ZS, the assayer mark (followed by a dot), and fineness 902,7. *Diameter:* 30 mm. *Edge:* Milled. BW-257.9, KM-407.8.

Date	Assayer	Comment
1870	H	
1871	H	
1872	H	
1873	H	
1874	A	Rare
1874	H	
1875	A	
1876	S	
1876	A	
1876/5	A	
1877	S	
1878	S	
1878/7	S	
1879	S	
1880	S	
1881	S	
1882/1	S	
1882	S	
1883	S	
1883	S	S / A in mintmark
1884/3	S	
1884	S	
1885/4	S	
1885	S	
1886	Z	
1887	Z	

1 peso, 0.9027 silver, 27.073 g.

Obverse: The national coat of arms, with the legend REPUBLICA MEXICANA above and a spray of oak and laurel below; [date] below spray. *Reverse:* Below a small radiant liberty cap, a crossed sword and balance scale; between the pans of the scale, a scroll bearing the word LEY. Below the scroll, UN PESO, mintmark ZS, assayer mark H., and fineness 902,7. *Diameter:* 37 mm. *Edge:* Milled. BW-258.9, KM-408.8.

Date	Assayer	Comment
1870	H	
1871	H	
1872	H	
1873	H	

1 peso, 0.9027 silver, 27.073 g.

Obverse: The national coat of arms, with the legend REPUBLICA MEXICANA. above and a spray of oak and laurel below. *Reverse:* At center, a large radiant liberty cap; below, ★ UN PESO., mintmark ZS, the date (followed by a dot), the assayer mark (followed by a dot after each initial), and fineness 902,7. *Diameter:* 39 mm. *Edge:* Milled. BW-258.13, KM-409.3.

Date	Assayer	Comment
1898	FZ	
1899	FZ	
1900	FZ	
1901	FZ	
1901	AZ	Rare
1902	FZ	
1903/2	FZ	
1903	FZ	
1904	FZ	
1904	FM	
1905	FM	

1 peso, 0.8750 gold, 1.692 g.

Obverse: The national coat of arms, with the legend REPUBLICA MEXICANA above and a spray of oak and laurel below. *Reverse:*

At center, within a wreath of oak and laurel, **1 / PESO**. Above the denomination, the assayer mark, fineness **875**, and mintmark **Zs**. *Diameter:* 15 mm. *Edge:* Milled. BW-258.20, KM-410.6.

Date	Assayer	Comment
1872	H	
1875/3	A	
1878	S	
1888	Z	
1889	Z	
1890	Z	

2-1/2 pesos, 0.8750 gold, 4.230 g.

Obverse: The national coat of arms, with the legend **REPUBLICA MEXICANA** above and the date below. *Reverse:* At center, within a wreath of oak and laurel, **2½ / PESOS**. Above the denomination, the assayer mark, fineness **875**, and mintmark **Zs**. *Diameter:* 18 mm. *Edge:* Milled. BW-259.7, KM-411.6.

Date	Assayer	Comment
1872	H	
1873	H	
1875/3	A	
1876/2	A	Extremely rare
1877	S	
1878	S	Rare
1880/79	S	
1888	Z	Zs / Mo; extremely rare
1889	Z	Zs / Mo
1890	Z	

5 pesos, 0.8750 gold, 8.460 g.

Obverse: The national coat of arms, with the legend **REPUBLICA MEXICANA** above and a spray of oak and laurel below; **[date]** below spray. *Reverse:* Below a radiant liberty cap, two crossed swords behind a balance scale and a scroll bearing the word **LEY**. Below the scroll, mintmark **Zs** and the assayer mark (followed by a dot), with **CINCO PESOS** and fineness **875**. *Diameter:* 22 mm. *Edge:* Milled. BW-260.8, KM-412.7.

Date	Assayer	Comment
1874	A	Rare
1875	A	Extremely rare
1877	S/A	
1878/7	S/A	
1883	S	
1888	Z	Very rare
1889	Z	
1892	Z	

10 pesos, 0.8750 gold, 16.920 g.

Obverse: The national coat of arms, with the legend **REPUBLICA MEXICANA** above and a spray of oak and laurel below; **[date]** below spray. *Reverse:* Below a radiant liberty cap, two crossed swords behind a balance scale and a scroll bearing the word **LEY**. Below the scroll, mintmark **Zs** and the assayer mark (followed by a dot), with **DIEZ PESOS** and fineness **875**. *Diameter:* 27 mm. *Edge:* Milled. BW-261.10, KM-413.9.

Date	Assayer	Comment
1871	H	
1872	H	
1873	H	
1874	H	
1875/3	A	
1876/5	S	
1877	S/H	
1878	S	
1879	S	
1880	S	
1881	S	
1882	S	
1883/2	S	
1884/3	S	
1885	S	
1886	S	
1887	Z	
1888	Z	
1889	Z	
1890	Z	
1891	Z	
1892	Z	
1893	Z	
1894	Z	
1895	Z	

20 pesos, 0.8750 gold, 33.840 g.

Obverse: The national coat of arms, with the legend **REPUBLICA MEXICANA** above and a spray of oak and laurel below; **[date]** below spray. *Reverse:* Below a radiant liberty cap, two crossed swords behind a balance scale and a scroll bearing the word LEY. Below the scroll, mintmark ZS and the assayer mark (followed by a dot), with VEINTE PESOS and fineness 875. *Diameter:* 34 mm. *Edge:* Milled. BW-262.9, KM-414.8.

Date	Assayer	Comment
1871	H	
1874	H	Rare
1875	A	Rare
1877	S	Rare
1878	S	
1888	Z	Rare
1889	Z	Extremely rare

Republic Decimal Coinage

1 centavo. 1863-M̊ (Round-Top 3). BW-251.1, KM-390, 27 mm.

1 centavo. 1863-S.L.P. BW-251.2, KM-390.1, 27 mm.

1 centavo. 1881-M̊. BW-251.8, KM-391.6, 25 mm.

1 centavo. 1883 (Mexico mint). Copper-nickel. BW-251.12, KM-392, 16 mm.

1 centavo. 1902/899-M. BW-251.13, KM-394.1, 20 mm.

2 centavos (trial strike). 1883. BW-252, KM-395, 18 mm.

5 centavos. 1867-M̊. BW-253.3, KM-397, 15 mm.

5 centavos. 1868-CA. BW-253.1, KM-396, 15 mm.

5 centavos. 1887-PI, R. BW-253.14, KM-398.9, 15 mm.

5 centavos. 1882 (Mexico mint). Copper-nickel. BW-253.16, KM-399, 20 mm.

10 centavos. 1867/3-M̊. BW-254.3, KM-402, 18 mm.

10 centavos. 1895-DO, D. BW-254.8, KM-403.3, 17 mm.

20 centavos. 1899-MO, M. BW-255.3, KM-405.2, 22 mm.

Republic Decimal Coinage
(continued)

25 centavos. 1885-MO̲, M.
BW-256.8, KM-406.7, 25 mm.

50 centavos. 1869-MO̲, C.
BW-257.7, KM-407.6, 30 mm.

1 peso.
1872-GO̲, S.
BW-258.5,
KM-408.4,
37 mm.

1 peso.
1903-CṆ, FV.
BW-258.10,
KM-409,
39 mm.

1 peso, gold.
1876/5-MO̲, B/M.
BW-259.19,
KM-410.5, 15 mm.

2-1/2 pesos. 1872-ZS̲, H.
BW-259.7, KM-411.6, 18 mm.

5 pesos. 1900-CN̲, Q.
BW-260.3, KM-412.2, 22 mm.

10 pesos. 1884-AS̲, L.
BW-261.1, KM-413, 27 mm.

20 pesos. 1898-CN̲, M.
BW-262.3, KM-414.2, 34 mm.

12

Coinage of the Revolution

There was a great deal of animosity among the potential future leaders of Mexico during the latter years of the Benito Juárez presidency. This came to a head upon the death of Juárez on July 18, 1872. Sebastián Lerdo de Tejada succeeded to the presidency and was elected to a four-year term. In 1876 he declared that he would run for reelection. Because of Lerdo de Tejada's inefficiency, Porfirio Díaz felt he could wait no longer, and in January 1876 the Porfiristas proclaimed the Plan of Tuxtepec. Their slogans were "Effective Suffrage" and "No Reelection."

After many battles between the Porfiristas and the Lerdistas, Lerdo de Tejada gave up the fight and left Mexico for the United States. On November 2, 1876, Díaz assumed the provisional presidency. From then onward (except for a four-year period from late 1880 through late 1884, when Manuel González served as president), Díaz ruled Mexico continuously, for 35 years. The Plan of Tuxtepec gave Díaz the power to rule as a dictator, and he did so. He controlled any and all aspects of Mexico, from hand-picking members of congress to eliminating potential opposition leaders (by offers of government positions or by other methods). Between 1876 and 1910, the size of the government payroll grew by 900 percent.

During the latter years of Díaz's administration there was an enormous amount of graft and corruption, and by 1910, the total United States investment in Mexico exceeded the capital owned by the Mexicans themselves.

At this point there were concerns as to who would take over as president in the event of Díaz's death. Various factions jockeyed for position, and several new political parties were formed. At the age of 80, Díaz stood for reelection and, thanks to fraudulent tactics, won another six-year term. Francisco Madero, who was from a wealthy family and who opposed Díaz's corruption, had become interested in the political scene in 1903 and by 1910 had written a book, *The Presidential Succession in 1910.* He began working against Díaz, and was jailed a month before the election. After the election Madero was released on bail and went to Texas. He published from San Antonio "The Plan of San Luis Potosí," which declared the 1910 election null and void, and he assumed the provisionary presidency and called for insurrection.

Madero's actions started various rebellions around the country and brought to light names now well-known from this period: Emiliano Zapata in Morelos; Alberto Terrazas, Abraham González, and Pascual Orozco in Chihuahua. Riding with Orozco in Chihuahua was a bandit chieftain named Francisco Pancho Villa. All of the infighting had the various factions competing against each other on all fronts, with self-proclaimed presidents coming and going, which brought in other personages such as José Victoriano Huerta Márquez, Venustiano Carranza (governor of Coahuila), Pablo González Garza, and Álvaro Obregón, to name a few.

The United States had its hand in these activities. On the basis of a report of arms headed for Veracruz, the U.S. government sent troops to that city on April 21, 1914. They seized the port to prevent the shipment of arms from getting to then-president Victoriano Huerta.

The U.S. military action, which resulted in the death of 200 Mexicans, only delayed the shipment to Huerta's troops. Huerta threatened to invade the American South, arm the African Americans, and fly the Mexican flag over the U.S. Capitol. The embargo was lifted.

While this was going on in the south of Mexico, in the north Pancho Villa and his División del Norte (Division of the North) had a steady supply of arms and munitions from the United States.

Battles between the various factions lasted for several years, with generals fighting side by side and then fighting each other. In the spring of 1916, Venustiano Carranza was the provisional president, accepted by most factions, while Zapata and Villa were still running loose. In the fall of 1916 Carranza called for a convention that resulted in the 1917 constitution. In 1920 he tried to leave Mexico, but while en route at the Indian village of Tlaxcalantongo was killed, as he slept, by Rodolfo Herrero, a local chieftain. While this was happening, the Revolutionary army entered Mexico City and declared Felipe Adolfo de la Huerta Marcor the provisional president. The Zapatistas were given the spoils of war in the lands they captured in Morelos in exchange for laying down their arms, and Zapata himself avoided capture until 1919 (when deceit prevailed where other efforts failed). Pancho Villa was given a hacienda in Chihuahua for laying down his arms, but not before he invaded Columbus, New Mexico, on March 9, 1916. Villa's actions at Columbus prompted the General Pershing Expedition of 1916, intended to capture him. However, the U.S. force was never able to do so. On July 20, 1923, at Parral, Chihuahua, Villa was ambushed by seven men and executed.

This book's listings of Revolutionary coinage, in most cases, follows the listing order in *Mexican Revolutionary Coinage, 1913–1917* (often called "the GB book") by Hugh S. Guthrie and Merrill Bothamley. Most coins have a GB reference number, but several have been recorded since the GB book was published; these are described as unlisted (UL). In the Oaxaca section, the OAX reference numbers are from *La Ventana Oaxaca: The Window to the Revolutionary Coinage of Oaxaca 1915*, by C. "Woody" Woodworth and Joe Flores. Krause-Mishler (KM) reference numbers (from the *Standard Catalogue of World Coins*) are shown where possible. Not all known Revolutionary coins are listed; groupings are jointly listed where feasible. Chihuahua coins are referenced by GB number and by VRW (Verne R. Walrafen) number (from "Chihuahua 5 and 10 Centavos," a monograph in *The Mexican Revolution Reporter*, issue 18).

The denomination and, when used, the centavo symbol may be shaded with parallel lines, which are angled in different directions depending on the variety. This shading, or "cross-hatching," will be described here simply as "shading," either horizontal, vertical, or diagonal. (Diagonal shading will be assumed to go from upper left to lower right, as "\\\\\," unless specified otherwise.)

The initials "R.M." on certain coins stand for "República Mexicana."

Because of the wide range of varieties in Mexican Revolutionary coinage, the date-by-date charts have been omitted for this introductory volume. The many varieties, along with their charts and valuations, will be explored in volume 4.

ESTADO DE AGUASCALIENTES

The state of Aguascalientes, located in the mountainous region of central Mexico, is rich in silver mines. In 1915 General Francisco Pancho Villa ordered coins to be struck for Aguascalientes. It is reported that these coins were made from a copper railroad car used to transport molasses to a local brandy factory. This would explain the occasional coin found made of brass and copper, which could have been caused by the brazing (welding with a different metal) on some sections of the tank.

1 centavo, copper, 3.21 g.

Obverse: A radiant liberty cap at center; around border, legend ESTADO DE AGUASCALIENTES / R.M. *Reverse:* Small 1915 (4 mm wide) at the top of an open wreath of laurel; at center, a diagonally shaded number 1 superimposed on an unshaded centavo symbol (¢). *Diameter:* 17.5 mm. *Edge:* Reeded. BW-276, KM-601, GB-1.

1 centavo, copper, 3.55 g.

Obverse: A radiant liberty cap at center; around border, legend ESTADO DE AGUASCALIENTES / R.M. *Reverse:* Small 1915 (4 mm wide) at the top of an open wreath of laurel; at center, a diagonally shaded number 1 superimposed on an unshaded ¢. *Diameter:* 17.5 mm. *Edge:* Plain. BW-276.1, KM-601, GB-2.

1 centavo, silver, 2.91 g.

Obverse: A radiant liberty cap at center; around border, legend ESTADO DE AGUASCALIENTES / R.M. *Reverse:* Small 1915 (4 mm wide) at the top of an open wreath of laurel; at center, a diagonally shaded number 1 superimposed on an unshaded centavo symbol (¢). Prominent die break to left of the date. *Diameter:* 17.5 mm. *Edge:* Reeded. BW-276.2, KM-UL, GB-3.

1 centavo, copper, 3.55 g.

Obverse: A radiant liberty cap at center; around border, legend ESTADO DE AGUASCALIENTES / R.M. *Reverse:* Large 1915 (5 mm wide) at the top of an open wreath of laurel; at center, a diagonally shaded number 1 superimposed on an unshaded centavo symbol (¢). *Diameter:* 17.3 mm. *Edge:* Reeded. BW-276.3, KM-601, GB-4.

1 centavo, copper, 3.55 g.

Obverse: A radiant liberty cap at center; around border, legend ESTADO DE AGUASCALIENTES / R.M. *Reverse:* Large 1915 (5 mm wide) at the top of an open wreath of laurel; at center, a diagonally shaded number 1 superimposed on an unshaded centavo symbol (¢). *Diameter:* 17.5 mm. *Edge:* Plain. BW-276.4, KM-601, GB-5.

1 centavo, silver, 2.91 g.

Obverse: A radiant liberty cap at center; around border, legend ESTADO DE AGUASCALIENTES / R.M. *Reverse:* Large 1915 (5 mm wide) at the top of an open wreath of laurel; at center, a diagonally shaded number 1 superimposed on an unshaded centavo symbol (¢). *Diameter:* 17.2 mm. *Edge:* Reeded. BW-276.5, KM-601a, GB-6.

2 centavos, copper, 4.28 g.

Obverse: A radiant liberty cap at center; around border, legend ESTADO DE AGUASCALIENTES / R.M. *Reverse:* A half-wreath of laurel at the bottom; 1915 at the top. At center, a square-front number 2 with reversed diagonal shading (direction /////), superimposed on an unshaded centavo symbol (¢). *Diameter:* 19.7 mm. *Edge:* Reeded. BW-277, KM-602.2, GB-7.

2 centavos, copper, 4.28 g.

Obverse: A radiant liberty cap at center; around border, legend ESTADO DE AGUASCALIENTES / R.M. *Reverse:* A half-wreath of laurel at the bottom; 1915 at top. At center, a square-front number 2 with reversed diagonal shading (direction /////), superimposed on an unshaded centavo symbol (¢). *Diameter:* 19.7 mm. *Edge:* Plain. BW-277.1, KM-602.2, GB-8.

2 centavos, copper, 4.28 g.

Obverse: A radiant liberty cap at center; around border, legend **ESTADO DE AGUASCALIENTES / R.M.** *Reverse:* At the top of an open wreath of laurel, a large **1915** between wreath tips. At center, a curved-front number 2 with diagonal shading, superimposed on an unshaded centavo symbol (¢). *Diameter:* 19.7 mm. *Edge:* Reeded. BW-277.2, KM-602.1, GB-9.

2 centavos, copper, 4.28 g.

Obverse: A radiant liberty cap at center; around border, legend **ESTADO DE AGUASCALIENTES / R.M.** *Reverse:* At the top of an open wreath of laurel, a large **1915** between wreath tips. At center, a curved-front number 2 with diagonal shading, superimposed on an unshaded centavo symbol (¢). *Diameter:* 19.7 mm. *Edge:* Plain. BW-277.3, KM-602.1, GB-10.

2 centavos, silver.

Obverse: A radiant liberty cap at center; around border, legend **ESTADO DE AGUASCALIENTES / R.M.** *Reverse:* At the top of an open wreath of laurel, a large **1915** between wreath tips. At center, a curved-front number 2 with diagonal shading, superimposed on an unshaded centavo symbol (¢). *Diameter:* 19.7 mm. *Edge:* Reeded. BW-277.4, KM-602.1, GB-11.

5 centavos, copper, 7.13 g.

Obverse: The national coat of arms above a spray of laurel; legend **ESTADO DE AGUASCALIENTES.** *Reverse:* **1915** at the top of an open wreath of laurel. At center, an unshaded number 5 superimposed on a horizontally shaded centavo symbol (¢) with a diagonally shaded slash. *Diameter:* 25.5 mm. *Edge:* Reeded. BW-278, KM-604.1, GB-12.

5 centavos, copper, 7.13 g.

Obverse: The national coat of arms above a spray of laurel; legend **ESTADO DE AGUASCALIENTES.** *Reverse:* **1915** at the top of an open wreath of laurel. At center, an unshaded number 5 superimposed on a horizontally shaded centavo symbol (¢) with a diagonally shaded slash. *Diameter:* 25.9 mm. *Edge:* Plain. BW-278.1, KM-604.1, GB-13.

5 centavos, copper, 7.55 g.

Obverse: The national coat of arms above a spray of laurel; legend **ESTADO DE AGUASCALIENTES.** *Reverse:* **1915** at the top of an open wreath of laurel; at center, a vertically shaded number 5 superimposed on an unshaded centavo symbol (¢). *Diameter:* 25.2 mm. *Edge:* Reeded. BW-278.2, KM-604.1, GB-14.

5 centavos, copper, 7.62 g.

Obverse: The national coat of arms above a spray of laurel; legend **ESTADO DE AGUASCALIENTES.** *Reverse:* **1915** at the top of an open wreath of laurel; at center, a vertically shaded number 5 superimposed on an unshaded centavo symbol (¢). *Diameter:* 26.1 mm. *Edge:* Plain. BW-278.3, KM-604.1, GB-15.

5 centavos, cast copper, 7.13 g.

Obverse: The national coat of arms above a spray of laurel; legend **ESTADO DE AGUASCALIENTES.** *Reverse:* **1915** at the top of an open wreath of laurel; at center, a vertically shaded number 5 superimposed on an unshaded centavo symbol (¢). *Diameter:* 26 mm. *Edge:* Reeded. BW-278.4, KM-604.1, GB-16.

5 centavos, copper, 8.35 g.

Obverse: The national coat of arms above a spray of laurel; legend **ESTADO DE AGUASCALIENTES.** *Reverse:* **1915** at the top of an open wreath of laurel; at center, a horizontally shaded number 5 superimposed on an unshaded centavo symbol (¢). *Diameter:* 25.2 mm. *Edge:* Reeded. BW-278.5, KM-604.2, GB-17.

5 centavos, copper, 6.07 g.

Obverse: The national coat of arms above a spray of laurel; legend **ESTADO DE AGUASCALIENTES.** *Reverse:* **1915** at the top of an open wreath of laurel; at center, a horizontally shaded number 5 superimposed on an unshaded centavo symbol (¢). *Diameter:* 25.6 mm. *Edge:* Plain. BW-278.6, KM-604.2, GB-18.

5 centavos, silver.

Obverse: The national coat of arms above a spray of laurel; legend ESTADO DE AGUASCALIENTES. *Reverse:* 1915 at the top of an open wreath of laurel; at center, a horizontally shaded number 5 superimposed on an unshaded centavo symbol (¢). *Diameter:* 25.5 mm. *Edge:* Reeded. BW-278.7, KM-UL, GB-19.

5 centavos, copper, 7.12 g.

Obverse: The national coat of arms above a spray of laurel; legend ESTADO DE AGUASCALIENTES. *Reverse:* Above a half-wreath of laurel, a small radiant liberty cap. On the radiance below the cap, a horizontally shaded shaded number 5; below the number, CENTAVOS / 1915. / A. *Diameter:* 25.3 mm. *Edge:* Reeded. BW-278.8, KM-603, GB-20.

5 centavos, copper, 7.13 g.

Obverse: The national coat of arms above a spray of laurel; legend ESTADO DE AGUASCALIENTES. *Reverse:* Above a half-wreath of laurel, a small radiant liberty cap. On the radiance below the cap, an unshaded number 5; below the number, CENTAVOS / 1915. / A (only a trace of the mintmark is apparent). *Diameter:* 25.3 mm. *Edge:* Plain. BW-278.9, KM-603, GB-UL.

20 centavos, copper, 10.41 g.

Obverse: Above a spray of laurel, the national coat of arms with the eagle's wings curving inward; legend ESTADO DE AGUASCALIENTES. *Reverse:* At the top, between the ends of an open wreath of laurel, a small radiant liberty cap. On the radiance below the cap, the number 20 with horizontal shading and a curved-base 2; below the number, CENTAVOS / 1915. Mintmark ₳ below the knot of the wreath's bow. *Diameter:* 29.6 mm. *Edge:* Reeded. BW-279, KM-606, GB-21.

20 centavos, cast copper, 9.53 g.

Obverse: Above a spray of laurel, the national coat of arms with the eagle's wings curving inward; legend ESTADO DE AGUASCALIENTES. *Reverse:* At the top, between the ends of an open wreath of laurel, a small radiant liberty cap. On the radiance below the cap, the number 20 with horizontal shading and a curved-base 2; below the number, CENTAVOS / 1915. Mintmark ₳ below the knot of the wreath's bow. *Diameter:* 28 mm. *Edge:* Reeded. BW-279.1, KM-606, GB-22.

20 centavos, struck copper, 9.97 g.

Obverse: Above a spray of laurel, the national coat of arms with the eagle's wings curving outward; legend ESTADO DE AGUASCALIENTES. *Reverse:* At the top, between the ends of an open wreath of laurel, a small radiant liberty cap. On the radiance below the cap, the number 20 with horizontal shading and a curved-base 2; below the number, CENTAVOS / 1915. Mintmark ₳ below the knot of the wreath's bow. *Diameter:* 29.8 mm. *Edge:* Reeded. BW-279.2, KM-606, GB-23.

20 centavos, copper, 10.64 g.

Obverse: Above a spray of laurel, the national coat of arms with the eagle's wings curving outward; legend ESTADO DE AGUASCALIENTES. *Reverse:* At the top, between the ends of an open wreath of laurel, a small radiant liberty cap. On the radiance below the cap, the number 20 with horizontal shading and a curved-base 2; below the number, CENTAVOS / 1915. Mintmark ₳ below the knot of the wreath's bow. *Diameter:* 30.3 mm. *Edge:* Plain. BW-279.3, KM-606, GB-24.

20 centavos, cast copper, 10.39 g.

Obverse: Above a spray of laurel, the national coat of arms with the eagle's wings curving outward; legend ESTADO DE AGUASCALIENTES. *Reverse:* At the top, between the ends of an open wreath of laurel, a small radiant liberty cap. On the radiance below the cap, the number 20 with horizontal shading and a curved-base 2; below the number, CENTAVOS / 1915. Mintmark ₳ below the knot of the wreath's bow. *Diameter:* 29.4 mm. *Edge:* Reeded. BW-279.4, KM-606, GB-25.

20 centavos, cast copper, 9.24 g.
Obverse: Above a spray of laurel, the national coat of arms with the eagle's wings curving outward; legend ESTADO DE AGUASCALIENTES. *Reverse:* At the top, between the ends of an open wreath of laurel, a small radiant liberty cap. On the radiance below the cap, the number **20** with horizontal shading and a curved-base 2; below the number, CENTAVOS / 1915. Mintmark A below the knot of the wreath's bow. *Diameter:* 29.4 mm. *Edge:* Plain. BW-279.5, KM-606, GB-UL.

20 centavos, copper, 13.31 g.
Obverse: Above a spray of laurel, the national coat of arms with the eagle's wings curving outward; legend ESTADO DE AGUASCALIENTES. *Reverse:* At the top, above a half-wreath of laurel, a small radiant liberty cap. On the radiance below the cap, the number **20** with horizontal shading and a flat-bottom 2; below the number, CENTAVOS / 1915. *Diameter:* 29.9 mm. *Edge:* Reeded. BW-279.6, KM-605, GB-26.

20 centavos, cast copper, 14.19 g.
Obverse: Above a spray of laurel, the national coat of arms with the eagle's wings curving outward; legend ESTADO DE AGUASCALIENTES. *Reverse:* At the top, above a half-wreath of laurel, a small radiant liberty cap. On the radiance below the cap, the number **20** with horizontal shading and a flat-bottom 2; below the number, CENTAVOS / 1915. *Diameter:* 29.1 mm. *Edge:* Reeded. BW-279.8, KM-605, GB-27.

20 centavos, cast copper, 12.00 g.
Obverse: Above a spray of laurel, the national coat of arms with the eagle's wings curving outward; legend ESTADO DE AGUASCALIENTES. *Reverse:* At the top, above a half-wreath of laurel, a small radiant liberty cap. On the radiance below the cap, the number **20** with horizontal shading and a flat-bottom 2; below the number, CENTAVOS / 1915. *Diameter:* 29.1 mm. *Edge:* Plain. BW-279.9, KM-605, GB-28.

20 centavos, silver.
Obverse: Above a spray of laurel, the national coat of arms with the eagle's wings curving outward; legend ESTADO DE AGUASCALIENTES. *Reverse:* At the top, above a half-wreath of laurel, a small radiant liberty cap. On the radiance below the cap, the number **20** with horizontal shading and a flat-bottom 2; below the number, CENTAVOS / 1915. *Diameter:* 30.8 mm. *Edge:* Plain. BW-279.7, KM-UL, GB-29.

ESTADO DE CHIHUAHUA

The state of Chihuahua is located in the arid, mountainous northern region of Mexico. It was the stronghold and base of operations for General Francisco Pancho Villa during the Revolution. In early 1914 Villa ordered the striking of millions of coins, in denominations of 5, 10, and 50 centavos, and 1 peso. A minor number of the resulting coins are dated 1915. The engravers' names can be found in small letters: SALAZAR on the obverse, and SEVILLA on the reverse. (A peso with SEVILLA on both obverse and reverse is a known counterfeit, reported to have been struck in the 1920s.)

The 5 centavos is the most common coin and accounts for all but six of the 43 known varieties of coins from Chihuahua. Copper for these coins probably came from the hacienda of Don Luis Terrazas, the governor, who was a supporter and friend of President Porfirio Díaz. The silver is said to be from bullion that was taken from the American Smelting and Refining Company's Chihuahua smelter.

Army of the North pesos were issued for Chihuahua but were struck under the supervision of General José Delgado at the Guadalajara mint.

Constitutional Army

5 centavos, brass, 6.38 g.

Obverse: A radiant liberty cap at center; legend **REPUBLICA MEXICANA / ↞E. DE CHIHA̲↠**. Engraver **SALAZAR** below the radiance. *Reverse:* An unshaded number **5** superimposed on a horizontally shaded centavo symbol (¢) with a point on the left curve; the slash on the ¢ is diagonally shaded. Legend **EJERCITO CONSTITUCIONALISTA / ↞1914↠**. *Diameter:* 25 mm. *Edge:* Plain. BW-280, KM-613a, GB-31.

5 centavos, brass, 5.89 g.

Obverse: A radiant liberty cap at center; legend **REPUBLICA MEXICANA / ↞E. DE CHIHA̲↠**. Engraver **SALAZAR** below the radiance. *Reverse:* An unshaded number **5** superimposed on a horizontally shaded centavo symbol (¢) with a pointed left curve; the slash on the ¢ is diagonally shaded. Legend **EJERCITO CONSTITUCIONALISTA / ↞.1914.↠**. The curls of the ornaments to each side of the date have dots within. *Diameter:* 25.1 mm. *Edge:* Plain. BW-280.1, KM-613a, GB-35.

5 centavos, copper, 5.90 g.

Obverse: A radiant liberty cap at center; legend **REPUBLICA MEXICANA / ↞E. DE CHIHA̲↠**. Engraver **SALAZAR** below the radiance. *Reverse:* An unshaded number **5** superimposed on a horizontally shaded centavo symbol (¢) with a rounded left curve; the slash on the ¢ is diagonally shaded. A dot is in the 5, overlapping the edge of the crossbar. Legend **EJERCITO CONSTITUCIONALISTA / ↞1914↠**. The curls of the ornaments to each side of the date have dots within. *Diameter:* 25.14 mm. *Edge:* Plain. BW-280.2, KM-613, GB-41.

5 centavos, copper, 6.40 g.

Obverse: A radiant liberty cap at center; legend **REPUBLICA MEXICANA / ↞E. DE CHIHA̲↠**. Engraver **SALAZAR** below the radiance. *Reverse:* An unshaded number **5** superimposed on a horizontally shaded centavo symbol (¢) with a rounded left curve; the slash on the ¢ is diagonally shaded. A dot is at the center of the field. Legend **EJERCITO CONSTITUCIONALISTA / ↞1915↠**. The curls of the ornaments to each side of the date have dots within. *Diameter:* 25.4 mm. *Edge:* Plain. BW-280.3, KM-613, GB-51.

5 centavos, copper, 6.3–6.9 g.

Obverse: Above a spray of oak and laurel, the national coat of arms. Legend **REPUBLICA MEXICANA**. Below the spray, engraver **M. SEVILLA**. *Reverse:* Legend **CHIHUAHUA** at top, above a half-wreath of laurel; at center, **1915 / V / CENTAVOS**. Engraver initials **M.S** above the bow on the wreath. *Diameter:* 25.5 mm. *Edge:* Plain. BW-280.4, KM-614, GB-59 and GB-60.

5 centavos, copper, 6.3–6.9 g.

Obverse: Above a spray of oak and laurel, the national coat of arms. Legend **REPUBLICA MEXICANA**. Below the spray, engraver **M. SEVILLA**. *Reverse:* An unshaded number **5** superimposed on a horizontally shaded centavo symbol (¢) with a pointed left curve; the slash on the ¢ is diagonally shaded. Legend **EJERCITO CONSTITUCIONALISTA / ↞1914↠**. *Diameter:* 25.5 mm. *Edge:* Plain. BW-280.5, KM-613b, GB-62.

5 centavos, copper, 6.3–6.9 g.

Obverse: Above a spray of oak and laurel, the national coat of arms. Legend **REPUBLICA MEXICANA**. Below the spray, engraver **M. SEVILLA**. *Reverse:* A radiant liberty cap at center; legend **REPUBLICA MEXICANA / ↞E. DE CHIHA̲↠**. Below the radiance, the name of engraver **SALAZAR**. No denomination or date. *Diameter:* 25.5 mm. *Edge:* Plain. BW-280.6, KM-UL, GB-UL.

10 centavos, copper or brass, 8.79 g.

Obverse: A radiant liberty cap at center; legend **REPUBLICA MEXICANA / ↞E. DE CHIHA̲↠**. Engraver **SALAZAR** below the radiance. *Reverse:* An unshaded number **10** superimposed on a horizontally shaded centavo symbol (¢) with rounded left curve; the slash on the ¢ is vertically shaded. Legend **EJERCITO CONSTITUCIONALISTA / ↞1915↠**. *Diameter:* 27 mm. *Edge:* Plain. BW-281, KM-615, GB-67–GB-69.

50 centavos, copper.

Obverse: A radiant liberty cap at center; legend **REPUBLICA MEXICANA / •E. DE CHIHÅ̲•**. Engraver **SALAZAR** below the radiance. *Reverse:* Legend **EJERCITO CONSTITUCIONALISTA / •1914•**. At center, an unshaded number **50** superimposed on a horizontally shaded centavo symbol (¢) with vertically shaded slash. Around the top and bottom of the denomination, the words **CINCUENTA / CENTAVOS**. *Diameter:* 30 mm. *Edge:* Reeded. BW-282p, KM-UL, GB-70.

1 peso, copper.

Obverse: A radiant liberty cap at center; legend **REPUBLICA MEXICANA / — E. DE CHIHÅ̲ —** (with the dashes representing wide, ornate flourishes on the coin). Engraver **SALAZAR** below the radiance. *Reverse:* A balance scale in front of an open book bearing the word **LEY**; below the scale and book, **→1914←**. Legend **EJERCITO CONSTITUCIONALISTA / ☼UN PESO☼**. *Diameter:* 39 mm. *Edge:* Reeded. BW-283p, KM-PN3, GB-71.

1 peso, silver.

Obverse: A radiant liberty cap at center; legend **REPUBLICA MEXICANA / — E. DE CHIHÅ̲ —** (with the dashes representing wide, ornate flourishes on the coin). Engraver **SALAZAR** below the radiance. *Reverse:* A balance scale in front of an open book bearing the word **LEY**, with **→1914←** immediately below. Legend **EJERCITO CONSTITUCIONALISTA / ☼UN PESO☼**. *Diameter:* 39 mm. *Edge:* Reeded. BW-283p.1, KM-PN4, GB-UL.

Note: Silver-clad copper issues are modern fantasies.

Hidalgo del Parral

Reports vary as to who authorized the coinage for the city of Parral. It is believed to have been General Maclovio Herrera Cano, under the authorization of Francisco Pancho Villa.

2 centavos, brass, 6.21 g.

Obverse: Two laurel branches enclosing a radiant liberty cap within a circle. At the bottom, between the ends of the branches, **1913** formed in dots. *Reverse:* At center, a circle enclosing an open wreath of laurel; between wreath tips, the number **2**, with a **C** below. (A rough backward slash across the C suggests an incorrectly rendered centavo symbol.) Outside the circle, the legend **FUERZAS CONSTITUCIONALISTAS +.** *Diameter:* 24.9 mm. *Edge:* Plain. BW-284, KM-607a, GB-74.

2 centavos, copper, 6.77 g.

Obverse: Two laurel branches enclosing a radiant liberty cap within a circle. At the bottom, between the ends of the branches, **1913** formed in dots. *Reverse:* At center, a circle enclosing an open wreath of laurel; between wreath tips, the number **2** with a **C** below. (A rough backward slash across the C suggests an incorrectly rendered centavo symbol.) Outside the circle, the legend **FUERZAS CONSTITUCIONALISTAS +.** *Diameter:* 24.9 mm. *Edge:* Plain. BW-284.1, KM-607, GB-75.

50 centavos, silver, 12.81 g.

Obverse: A crude radiant liberty cap at center. Legend **FUERZAS CONSTITUCIONA LISTAS / ☀1913☀**. *Reverse:* At center, between laurel branches, the number **50** with **CENTAVOS** below, between the ends of the branches. Above the number, a small, crude radiant sun. *Diameter:* 30 mm. *Edge:* Reeded. BW-285, KM-608, GB-76.

50 centavos, silver, 12.00 g.

Obverse: A crude radiant liberty cap at center. Legend **FUERZAS CONSTITUCIONA LISTAS / ☀1913☀**. *Reverse:* At center, between laurel branches, the number **50** with **CENTAVOS** below, between the ends of the branches. Above the number, a small, crude radiant sun. *Diameter:* 30.2 mm. *Edge:* Plain. BW-285.1, KM-609, GB-77.

1 peso, silver, 33.18 g.

Obverse: Above a half-wreath of stylized branches with berries and below an arch of small circles, the legend **H / DEL / PARRAL.** Below, in the base of the wreath, **1913.** *Reverse:* Above a half-wreath and below an arch of small dots, the number **1** dividing the word **PESO**, with both superimposed over a ball. *Diameter:* 38.6 mm. *Edge:* Plain. BW-286, KM-610, GB-78.

Note: This type is known as the "Bolita peso."

1 peso, silver, 26.09 g.

Obverse: Above a half-wreath of stylized branches with berries and below an arch of small circles, the legend **H / DEL / PARRAL.** Below, in the base of the wreath, **1913.** *Reverse:* Above a half-wreath and below an arch of small circles, a large number **1** above the word **PESO.** *Diameter:* 38.8 mm. *Edge:* Reeded. BW-286.1, KM-611, GB-79.

Note: This type is known as the "Parral peso." Well-struck counterfeits exist. On the counterfeits, the dot at the end of PESO (on the reverse) is even with the bottom of the O; on authentic coins the dot is slightly higher.

1 peso, silver, 27.3–28.85 g.

Obverse: At center, a radiant liberty cap within a double-outline circle, with **FUERZA CONSTITUCIONALISTA** surrounding. *Reverse:* Within a double-outline circle, a large number **1** superimposed on a panel bearing the word **PESO**. A trace of a wreath surrounds the double circle, with a cartouche at the top. *Diameter:* 38 mm. *Edge:* Plain. BW-286.2, KM-PN1, GB-80.

Army of the North

Next to the "Muera Huerta" peso (listed under "Cuencamé, Durango"), the most noted coin of the Mexican Revolution is the Army of the North peso, thought to have been issued from Chihuahua. Army of the North pesos, along with the 1, 2, and 5 centavos for Chihuahua, were struck at the Guadalajara mint on the orders of Pancho Villa and under the supervision of General José Delgado (who later issued a 10-centavo coin as well).

The engravers' names, Salazar and Sevilla, can be found on the Army of the North peso. Well after the Revolution ended, reproductions of the peso were struck in silver, bronze, brass, and lead, with Sevilla's name on both sides of the coin.

1 peso, silver, 29.27 g.

Obverse: Above a partial wreath of oak and laurel, the national coat of arms and legend **REPUBLICA MEXICANA.** To left of the base of the cactus, engraver **SEVILLA.** *Reverse:* A radiant liberty cap at center. Legend **EJERCITO DEL NORTE** above the cap; below, **UN PESO .**, mintmark **CH$^{\underline{A}}$**, **1915 . F. M.**, and fineness **902.7.** Below the lower rays of the liberty cap, engraver **SALAZAR.** *Diameter:* 39 mm. *Edge:* Reeded. BW-287.2, KM-619, GB-72.

Note: There is a premium value when both engravers' names are visible.

1 peso, copper.

Obverse: Above a partial wreath of oak and laurel, the national coat of arms and legend **REPUBLICA MEXICANA.** To left of the base of the cactus, engraver **SEVILLA.** *Reverse:* A radiant liberty cap at center. Legend **EJERCITO DEL NORTE** above the cap; below, **UN PESO .**, mintmark **CH$^{\underline{A}}$**, **1915 . F. M.**, and fineness **902.7.** Below the lower rays of the liberty cap, engraver **SALAZAR.** *Diameter:* 39 mm. *Edge:* Reeded. BW-287, KM-619a, GB-73.

1 peso, brass.

Obverse: Above a partial wreath of oak and laurel, the national coat of arms and legend **REPUBLICA MEXICANA.** To left of the base of the cactus, engraver **SEVILLA.** *Diameter:* 39 mm. *Edge:* Reeded. BW-287.1, KM-619b, GB-UL.

Note: This type is uniface.

ESTADO DE DURANGO

The state of Durango, located in northern Mexico, benefited from the forested Sierra Madre mountains, which fed Durango's timber industry. The agricultural community grew through the use of irrigation systems.

In addition to the coins discussed here, numerous minor varieties are to be found in the 1 and 5 centavos from Estado de Durango. They are further detailed in the Guthrie-Bothamley book, cataloged as GB-104–GB-107 (1 centavos) and GB-120–GB-134 (5 centavos).

Cuencamé, Durango

The Indian village of Cuencamé is where the famous "Muera Huerta" (Death to Huerta) coins originated, ordered by two of Pancho Villa's generals, Severino Ceniceros and Calixto Contreras. These coins showed the contempt that Pancho Villa held for President Victoriano Huerta, who had earlier ordered Villa's death by firing squad.

1 peso, copper.

Obverse: A radiant liberty cap at center. Legend ★★★ESTADOS UNIDOS MEXI CANOS★★★, with UN PESO / 1914 at bottom. *Reverse:* At the top, legend EJERCITO CONSTITUCIONALISTA. At center, above sprays of laurel, GOB. PROVISIONAL / MUERA HUERTA. *Diameter:* 39 mm. *Edge:* Crisscross pattern. BW-288, KM-UL, GB-81.

Note: This type (GB-81–GB-83) is known as the "Six Star peso."

1 peso, silver or copper.

Obverse: A radiant liberty cap at center. Legend ★★★ESTADOS UNIDOS MEXI CANOS★★★ in serif type, with UN PESO / 1914 at bottom. *Reverse:* The national coat of arms, with legend EJERCITO CONSTITU CIONALISTA • MUERA HUERTA • in sans-serif type. *Diameter:* 39 mm. *Edge:* Crisscross and partially plain. BW-288.1, KM-620, GB-82 and 83.

Note: This type (GB-81–GB-83) is known as the "Six Star peso."

1 peso, silver, 22.900 g.

Obverse: A radiant liberty cap at center. Legend ★★★ESTADOS UNIDOS MEXI CANOS★★★ in serif type, with UN PESO / 1914 at bottom. *Reverse:* The national coat of arms, with legend EJERCITO CONSTITU CIONALISTA • MUERA HUERTA • in sans-serif type. *Diameter:* 38.9 mm. *Edge:* Reeded. BW-288.2, KM-620, GB-84.

Note: The obverse and reverse have borders of dots between small triangles. Like the previous coin, this type is known as the "Six Star peso."

1 peso, silver, 23.200 g.

Obverse: A radiant liberty cap at center. Legend ESTADOS UNIDOS MEXICANOS / • 1914 • UN PESO • 1914 • in serif type. *Reverse:* The national coat of arms, with legend EJERCITO CONSTITUCIONALISTA • MUERA HUERTA • in sans-serif type. *Diameter:* 39 mm. *Edge:* Reeded. BW-288.3, KM-621, GB-85.

Note: This is a mule of the Six Star and regular Muera Huerta peso.

1 peso, silver, 23.340 g.

Obverse: A radiant liberty cap at center; legend ESTADOS UNIDOS MEXICANOS / • 1914 ● UN PESO ● 1914 •. *Reverse:* The national coat of arms with legend EJERCITO CONSTITUCIONALISTA / ● MUERA HUERTA ●. *Diameter:* 38.78 mm. *Edge:* Reeded. BW-288.4, KM-621a, GB-86.

Note: The obverse and reverse have a toothed border outside a single-outline circle. The typeface on both sides has serifs. This type is known as the "Muera Huerta peso."

1 peso, silver, 23.409 g.

Obverse: A radiant liberty cap at center; legend ESTADOS UNIDOS MEXICANOS / • 1914 • UN PESO • 1914 •. *Reverse:* The national coat of arms with legend

1 peso, silver, 23.409 g., continued
EJERCITO CONSTITUCIONALISTA / • MUERA HUERTA •. *Diameter:* 38.5 mm. *Edge:* Reeded. BW-288.5, KM-622, GB-87.

Note: The obverse has a toothed border outside a single-outline circle; the reverse has a dot-and-dash border outside a single-outline circle. The typeface on both sides has serifs.

1 peso, copper.
Obverse: A radiant liberty cap at center; legend ESTADOS UNIDOS MEXICANOS / • 1914 • UN PESO • 1914 •. *Reverse:* The national coat of arms with legend EJERCITO CONSTITUCIONALISTA / • MUERA HUERTA •. *Diameter:* 39 mm. *Edge:* Reeded. BW-288.6, KM-622, GB-89.

Note: The obverse has a toothed border outside a single-outline circle; the reverse has a dot-and-dash border outside a single-outline circle. The typeface on both sides has serifs.

20 pesos.
The 20 pesos reported in the Guthrie-Bothamley book (number 90, cast brass; number 91, gold; number 92, silver; and number 93, copper) are believed to have been struck after the Revolution period.

City of Durango

The city of Durango, founded in 1563, is the capital of the state of Durango. During the Revolution, the city was Pancho Villa's base of operations.

1 centavo, lead.
Obverse: On a plain field, the legend ƎƧTADO DE / DՈIƦ∀ИGO + (with ES and URAN in retrograde). At center, 1914. *Reverse:* Within a wreath of laurel, 1 / CEИT (with a medium-sized number 1; the 1 and N are in retrograde). *Diameter:* 20 mm. *Edge:* Plain. BW-289, KM-624, GB-94.

1 centavo, copper, 3.26 g.
Obverse: On a plain field, the legend ESTADO DE / + DURANGO +, with 1914 at center. *Reverse:* Within an open wreath of laurel, 1 / CENT (with a wide, unshaded number 1). *Diameter:* 20.3 mm. *Edge:* Plain. BW-289.1, KM-625, GB-95.

1 centavo, copper, 3.39 g.
Obverse: On a plain field, the legend ESTADO DE / + DURANGO +, with 1914 at center. *Reverse:* Within an open wreath of laurel, 1 / CENT (with an unshaded number 1). *Diameter:* 20.1 mm. *Edge:* Plain. BW-289.10, KM-625, GB-95.

1 centavo, copper, 3.12 g.
Obverse: On a plain field, the legend ESTADO DE / + DURANGO +, with 1914 at center. *Reverse:* Within an open wreath of laurel, 1 / CENT (with a wide, horizontally shaded number 1). *Diameter:* 20.1 mm. *Edge:* Plain. BW-289.2, KM-625, GB-96.

1 centavo, lead, 3.71 g.
Obverse: On a plain field, the legend ESTADO DE / + DURANGO +, with 1914 at center. *Reverse:* Within an open wreath of laurel, 1 / CENT (with a wide number 1). *Diameter:* 20 mm. *Edge:* Plain. BW-289.3, KM-625b, GB-98.

Note: The entire obverse and the reverse are incuse and in retrograde.

1 centavo, copper, 3.45 g.
Obverse: On a plain field, the legend ESTADO DE / + DURANGO +, with 1914 at center. *Reverse:* Same as the obverse: on a plain field, the legend ESTADO DE / + DURANGO +, with 1914 at center. *Diameter:* 20.27 mm. *Edge:* Plain. BW-289.4, KM-625c, GB-99.

Note: This coin is a mule of two obverses of GB-96 (BW-289.2).

1 centavo, cast lead, 3.67 g.
Obverse: On a plain field, the legend ƧTADO DE / + DURANGO + (with E of ESTADO weak or missing, and S in retrograde); at center, 1914. *Reverse:* Within a wreath of laurel, 1 / CENT (with a medium-sized numeral 1). *Diameter:* 20.5 mm. *Edge:* Plain. BW-289.5, KM-UL, GB-100.

1 centavo, copper.

Obverse: On a plain field, the legend **ESTADO DE / + DURANGO +**, with **1914** at center. *Reverse:* Within an open wreath of laurel, **I / ⊏ENT** (with a roman numeral I and a square C). *Diameter:* 20 mm. *Edge:* Plain. BW-289.6, KM-626, GB-102.

1 centavo, copper, 2.15 g.

Obverse: On a plain field, the legend **ESTADO DE / + DURANGO +**, with **1914 .** at center (dot after date is above O in DURANGO). *Reverse:* Within an open wreath of laurel, **I ⊏ENT** (with a roman numeral I and a square C). *Diameter:* 19.9 mm. *Edge:* Plain. BW-289.7, KM-626b, GB-105.

1 centavo, lead, 2.26 g.

Obverse: On a plain field, the legend **E. DE DURANGO**, with **1914** at center and ★★★ at bottom. *Reverse:* Within a dot-and-dash border, **I CEИT** (with retrograde N). *Diameter:* 20.4 mm. *Edge:* Plain. BW-289.8, KM-627a, GB-112.

1 centavo, aluminum, 1.24 g.

Obverse: At center, a small national coat of arms above a half-wreath of laurel. Legend **REPUBLICA MEXICANA** at top; **1914** at bottom. *Reverse:* On a plain field, a large number **I** with **CENTAVO.** below and the legend **ESTADO DE DURANGO.** above. *Diameter:* 20.6 mm. *Edge:* Plain. BW-289.9, KM-628, GB-113.

Note: These coins, produced for the City of Durango during the Mexican Revolution, have been misclassified since the early 1930s. All reference books have reported that they were made by the Denver Novelty Works in Denver, Colorado. Recent research by Scott Doll, however, reveals that Benziger Brothers (in Brooklyn, New York) was the producer of these coins. Only a small number of them seem to have reached the City of Durango before the end of the revolution.

5 centavos, lead.

Obverse: On a plain field, the legend **E. DE DURANGO**, with **1914** at center and ★★★ at bottom. *Reverse:* On a plain field, within a border of alternating large and small dots, **5 CVƧ** (with retrograde S). *Diameter:* 20 mm. *Edge:* Plain. BW-290, KM-633, GB-114.

5 centavos, copper, 5.94 g.

Obverse: Above a spray of laurel, the legend **ESTADO DE DURANGO**; large **1914** at center. *Reverse:* Within a circle of crosses, the denomination **5 / CENTAVOS** (with a large, thick number 5). *Diameter:* 24 mm. *Edge:* Plain. BW-290.1, KM-UL, GB-115.

5 centavos, copper, 6.20 g.

Obverse: Above a half-wreath of laurel, the legend **E. DE DURANGO** and, at center, **1914**. *Reverse:* Within a circle of crosses, the denomination **5 / CENTAVOS** (with a large, thin number 5). *Diameter:* 24 mm. *Edge:* Plain. BW-290.2, KM-630, GB-117.

5 centavos, copper, 5.40 g.

Obverse: Above a half-wreath of laurel, the legend **E. DE DURANGO** and, at center, **1914**. *Reverse:* Within a circle of crosses, the denomination **5 / ⊏ENTAVOS** (with a thick number 5 and a square C). *Diameter:* 23.7 mm. *Edge:* Plain. BW-290.3, KM-631, GB-118.

5 centavos, copper, 5.06 g.

Obverse: Above a half-wreath of laurel, the legend **E . DE DURANGO** and, at center, **1914**. *Reverse:* Within a circle of crosses, the denomination **V / CENTAVOS**. *Diameter:* 23.8 mm. *Edge:* Plain. BW-290.4, KM-632, GB-135.

5 centavos, brass, 6.84 g.

Obverse: Above a spray of laurel, the national coat of arms. Legend **REPUBLICA MEXICANA** at top, **1914** at bottom. *Reverse:* On a plain field, the denomination **5 / CENTAVOS.** (with a large, horizontally shaded number 5) and the legend **ESTADO DE DURANGO** above. *Diameter:* 25.6 mm. *Edge:* Plain. BW-290.5, KM-634, GB-139.

Note: This type was formerly misclassified as being struck at the Denver Mint; see the note to GB-113.

ESTADO DE GUERRERO

The state of Guerrero was the namesake of General Vicente Guerrero, the "Insurgent Hero" and chief of the Army of the South during the War of Independence. Located in the hills of southern Mexico, Guerrero served as the base of operations for Zapata's forces. The coinage of Guerrero, even though it bears no mintmarks or city names (except for those from Campo Morado), was struck in seven locations in temporary facilities around the state from 1914 to 1927.

Coins that can be traced to one of these seven mints are listed alphabetically, by mint. Coins that are cataloged as being from "the state of Guerrero" but are unattributable to any particular mint are listed at the end of this section.

Atlixtac, Guerrero

This temporary mint was located in a converted flour mill in the town of Atlixtac.

10 centavos, copper, 4.76–9.74 g.

Obverse: Above a half-wreath of oak and laurel, the national coat of arms and legend REPUBLICA MEXICANA. *Reverse:* At center, within an open wreath of laurel, 1915 / 10 / CENTAVOS. Above, between wreath tips, ATLIXTAC. GRO. *Diameter:* 27.5–28 mm. *Edge:* Plain. BW-313, KM-645, GB-141.

10 centavos, copper, 4.76–9.74 g.

Obverse: Above a half-wreath of oak and laurel, the national coat of arms and legend REPUBLICA MEXICANA. *Reverse:* At center, within an open wreath of laurel, 1915 / 10 / CENTAVOS (with the last two digits of the date lower than the first two). Above, between wreath tips, ATLIXTAC. GRO. *Diameter:* 27.5–28 mm. *Edge:* Plain. BW-313.1, KM-645, GB-142.

10 centavos, copper, 4.76–9.74 g.

Obverse: Above a half-wreath of oak and laurel, the national coat of arms and legend REPUBLICA MEXICANA. *Reverse:* At center, within an open wreath of laurel, 1915. / 10 / ★CENTAVOS. Above, between wreath tips, ATLIXTAC.GRO. *Diameter:* 27.5–28 mm. *Edge:* Plain. BW-313.2, KM-645, GB-143.

10 centavos, copper, 4.76–9.74 g.

Obverse: Above a half-wreath of oak and laurel, the national coat of arms and legend ★ REPUBLICA ★ MEXICANA ★. *Reverse:* At center, within an open wreath of laurel, 1915 / 10 / CENTAVOS. Above, between wreath tips, ATLIXTAC. GRO. *Diameter:* 27.5–28 mm. *Edge:* Plain. BW-313.3, KM-646, GB-144.

10 centavos, copper, 4.76–9.74 g.

Obverse: Above a half-wreath of oak and laurel, the national coat of arms and legend ★ REPUBLICA ★ MEXICANA ★. *Reverse:* At center, within an open wreath of laurel, 1915. / 10 / ★CENTAVOS. Above, between wreath tips, ATLIXTAC.GRO. *Diameter:* 27.5–28 mm. *Edge:* Plain. BW-313.4, KM-646, GB-145.

10 centavos, copper, 4.76–9.74 g.

Obverse: Above a half-wreath of oak and laurel, the national coat of arms and legend ★ REPUBLICA ★ MEXICANA ★. *Reverse:* At center, within an open wreath of laurel, 1915 / 10 / CENTAVOS (with the last two digits of the date lower than the first two). Above, between wreath tips, ATLIXTAC. GRO. *Diameter:* 27.5–28 mm. *Edge:* Plain. BW-313.5, KM-646, GB-146.

2 pesos, silver.

Obverse: At center, the national coat of arms, with sprigs of oak and laurel from the sides of the base. Legend REPUBLICA MEXICANA at top, 1914 at bottom. *Reverse:* The legend "REFORMA, LIBERTAD, JUSTICIA Y LEY" above a small radiant liberty cap. At center, ORO 0,30 / ATLIXTAC. / GRO. / • DOS PESOS . *Diameter:* 37.5 mm. *Edge:* Plain. BW-313.6, KM-UL, GB-146.5.

Cacahuatepec, Guerrero

The last-dated coins of the Revolution, from 1917, were issued from Cacahuatepec, in the state of Guerrero. The 5-, 20-, and 50-centavo coins have the legend ESTADOS UNIDOS MEXICANOS (the legend of federal coinage of the period), while the peso has REPUBLICA MEXICANOS.

5 centavos, copper, 10.16 g.

Obverse: Above a spray of oak and laurel, the national coat of arms and legend ESTADOS UNIDOS MEXICANOS. *Reverse:* Within an open wreath of laurel, an unshaded number 5 superimposed on a horizontally shaded centavo symbol (¢). At the top, 1917; G below the wreath bow. *Diameter:* 28.3 mm. *Edge:* Plain. BW-314, KM-648, GB-147.

20 centavos, silver, 3.99–6.20 g.

Obverse: Above a spray of oak and laurel, the national coat of arms and legend ESTADOS UNIDOS MEXICANOS. *Reverse:* At the top, within an open wreath of oak and laurel, a small radiant liberty cap. On the radiance below the cap, 20 / CENTAVOS / 1917, with G just below and partly between the 2 and 0 of the denomination. *Diameter:* 21.0–23.8 mm. *Edge:* Plain. BW-315, KM-649, GB-148.

50 centavos, silver, 15.46 g.

Obverse: Above a spray of oak and laurel, the national coat of arms and legend ESTADOS UNIDOS MEXICANOS. *Reverse:* At the top, within an open wreath of oak and laurel, a large radiant liberty cap. On the radiance below the cap, 50 / CENTAVOS / 1917, with GRO between 50 and CENTAVOS. *Diameter:* 30.3 mm. *Edge:* Plain. BW-316, KM-650, GB-149.

1 peso, silver, 26.81–32.05 g.

Obverse: Above a half-wreath of oak and laurel, the national coat of arms and legend REPUBLICA MEXICANA. *Reverse:* A large radiant liberty cap at center; below, legend ★UN PESO. G♀ 1917., with fineness S. 10 D$. *Diameter:* 39 mm. *Edge:* Reeded. BW-317, KM-651, GB-150.

Cacalotepec, Guerrero

20 centavos, silver, 3.89–5.73 g.

Obverse: Above a spray of oak and laurel, the national coat of arms and legend ESTADOS UNIDOS MEXICANOS. *Reverse:* At the top, within an open wreath of oak and laurel, a small radiant liberty cap. On the radiance below the cap, CACALOTEPEC / 20 / CENTAVOS / 1917, with GRO between CACALOTEPEC and 20. *Diameter:* 22.5 mm. *Edge:* Plain. BW-318, KM-652, GB-151.

Campo Morado, Guerrero

Campo Morado was a thriving mining town at the start of the Revolution, and one of Emiliano Zapata's better mints. The silver used for Campo Morado coins came from the local mines.

5 centavos, copper, 7.00 g.

Obverse: Above a spray of oak and laurel, the national coat of arms and legend ★ REPUBLICA MEXICANA. *Reverse:* At center, within an open wreath of laurel, an unshaded number 5 superimposed on an unshaded centavo symbol (¢). At the top, between wreath tips, 1915 / C.M. *Diameter:* 23.8 mm. *Edge:* Plain. BW-298, KM-653, GB-152.

10 centavos, copper or brass, 4.59 g.

Obverse: Above a half-wreath of oak and laurel, the national coat of arms and legend REPUBLICA MEXICANA. Large pads on the cactus. *Reverse:* At center, within an open wreath of laurel, 10 / CENTAVOS. At the top, between wreath tips, C.M. GRO. / 1915. *Diameter:* 25.8 mm. *Edge:* Plain. BW-299, KM-654, GB-153.

10 centavos, copper, 8.13 g.

Obverse: Above a half-wreath of oak and laurel, the national coat of arms and legend REPUBLICA MEXICANA. Small pads on the cactus. *Reverse:* At center, within an open wreath of laurel, 10 / CENTAVOS. At the top, between wreath tips, C.M. GRO. / 1915. just below. *Diameter:* 25.7 mm. *Edge:* Plain. BW-299.1, KM-654, GB-154.

20 centavos, copper, 8.52 g.
Obverse: Above a half-wreath of oak and laurel, the national coat of arms and legend REPUBLICA MEXICANA. The serpent's tail touches the cactus, while its head is close to the legend above. *Reverse:* At center, within an open wreath of laurel, ★ / 20 / CENTAVOS. At the top, between wreath tips, C.M. GRO. / 1915. *Diameter:* 27.9 mm. *Edge:* Plain. BW-300, KM-655, GB-155.

20 centavos, copper, 5.62 g.
Obverse: Above a half-wreath of oak and laurel, the national coat of arms and legend REPUBLICA MEXICANA. The serpent's tail is above the cactus; its head is farther from the legend above than on GB-155. *Reverse:* At center, within an open wreath of laurel, ★ / 20 / CENTAVOS. At the top, between wreath tips, C.M. GRO. / 1915. *Diameter:* 27.9 mm. *Edge:* Plain. BW-300.1, KM-655, GB-156.

50 centavos, copper, 10.80 g.
Obverse: At center, the national coat of arms above crossed sprays of oak and laurel. Above, legend REPUBLICA MEXICANA. Below the base, ★UN PESO (partly effaced). The snake's head ends under the left side of the C in REPUBLICA. *Reverse:* At center, within a wreath of laurel, 50 / CENTAVOS. At the top, between wreath tips, C.M. GRO. / 1915. *Diameter:* 31 mm. *Edge:* Plain. BW-301, KM-656, GB-157.

50 centavos, copper, 10.75 g.
Obverse: At center, the national coat of arms, with sprigs of oak and laurel from the sides of the base. Above, legend REPUBLICA MEXICANA. Below the base, ★UN PESO (effaced). *Reverse:* At center, within an open wreath of laurel, 50 / CENTAVOS. At the top, between wreath tips, C.M. GRO. / 1915. *Diameter:* 30.7 mm. *Edge:* Plain. BW-301.1, KM-656, GB-158.

50 centavos, copper, 10.60 g.
Obverse: At center, the national coat of arms, with sprigs of oak and laurel from the sides of the base. Above, legend ★REPUBLICA MEXICANA.★ Below the base, ★UN PESO CAMPO MO̲★ (partly effaced). *Reverse:* At center, within an open wreath of laurel, 50 / CENTAVOS. At the top, between wreath tips, C.M. GRO. / 1915. *Diameter:* 30.7 mm. *Edge:* Plain. BW-301.2, KM-656, GB-159.

50 centavos, copper, 9.67 g.
Obverse: Above a half-wreath of oak and laurel, a small national coat of arms and legend REPUBLICA MEXICANA. *Reverse:* At center, within an open wreath of laurel, 50 / CENTAVOS. At the top, between wreath tips, C.M. GRO. / 1915. Nine berries in the left branch of the wreath, eight berries in the right. *Diameter:* 30.6 mm. *Edge:* Plain. BW-301.3, KM-657, GB-160.

50 centavos, copper, 11.45 g.
Obverse: Above a half-wreath of oak and laurel, a small national coat of arms and legend REPUBLICA MEXICANA. *Reverse:* At center, within an open wreath of laurel, 50 / CENTAVOS. At the top, between wreath tips, C.M. GRO. / 1915. *Diameter:* 30.8 mm. *Edge:* Plain. BW-301.4, KM-657, GB-163.

50 centavos, copper, 11.36 g.
Obverse: Above a spray of oak and laurel, a small national coat of arms and legend ★REPUBLICA MEXICANA (with star close to the R). *Reverse:* At center, within an open wreath of laurel, 50 / CENTAVOS. At the top, between wreath tips, C.M. GRO. / 1915. Nine berries in the left branch of the wreath. *Diameter:* 30.6 mm. *Edge:* Plain. BW-301.5, KM-657, GB-165.

1 peso, silver-gold;
silver 12.420–16.050 g., gold 0.300 g.
Obverse: Above a spray of oak and laurel, the national coat of arms; within the spray, 1914. Legend ★REPUBLICA MEXICANA.★ at top; at bottom, UN PESO . CO̲ . MO̲ . GRO̲★. *Reverse:* At center, a high, small radiant liberty cap; on the radiance below the cap, fineness ORO:0,300. Legend "REFORMA, LIBERTAD, JUSTICIA Y LEY". *Diameter:* 32 mm. *Edge:* Plain. BW-302, KM-658, GB-170.

1 peso, silver-gold; silver 12.260–15.810 g., gold 0.300 g.

Obverse: At center, the national coat of arms, with sprigs of oak and laurel from the sides of the base. Legend **★REPUBLICA MEXICANA.★ / UN PESO. CAMPO Mº.** *Reverse:* At center, within a half-wreath of oak and laurel, a radiant liberty cap with **GRO.** and fineness **ORO: 0,300** above. Surrounding all, the legend **"REFORMA, LIBERTAD, JUSTICIA Y LEY" / 1914.** *Diameter:* 31 mm. *Edge:* Reeded or plain. BW-302.1, KM-659, GB-171 and GB-172.

2 pesos, silver-gold; silver 21.339 g., gold 0.595 g.

Obverse: At center, the national coat of arms, with sprigs of oak and laurel from the sides of the base. Legend **★REPUBLICA MEXICANA.★** at the top, with **DOS PESOS . G^{RO}. 1915** at the bottom. *Reverse:* At center, a sun with a face and long, single-line rays; below, a smoking volcano with a pointed top and a lower mountain at each side. In the sun's upper rays, fineness **ORO: 0,595**. Surrounding all, the legend **"REFORMA, LIBERTAD, JUSTICIA Y LEY" / Cº. Mº.** *Diameter:* 38.7 mm. *Edge:* Reeded. BW-303, KM-660, GB-174.

2 pesos, copper.

Obverse: At center, the national coat of arms, with sprigs of oak and laurel from the sides of the base. Legend **★REPUBLICA MEXICANA.★** at the top, with **DOS PESO . G^{RO}. 1915.★** at the bottom. *Reverse:* At center, a sun with a face and long, single-line rays; below, a smoking volcano with a pointed top and a lower mountain at each side. In the sun's upper rays, fineness **ORO: 0,595**. Surrounding all, the legend **"REFORMA, LIBERTAD, JUSTICIA Y LEY" / ★Cº. Mº★.** *Diameter:* 39 mm. Thick planchet. *Edge:* Plain. BW-303.1, KM-UL, GB-UL.

2 pesos, silver-gold; silver 29.440 g., gold 0.595 g.

Obverse: At center, the national coat of arms, with sprigs of oak and laurel from the sides of the base. Legend **★REPUBLICA MEXICANA·** at the top, with **★DOS PESOS· G^{RO}. 1915★** at the bottom. *Reverse:* At center, a sun with a face and long, single-line rays; below, a smoking volcano with a pointed top and a lower mountain at each side. In the sun's upper rays, fineness **ORO: 0,595**. Surrounding all, the legend **"REFORMA, LIBERTAD, JUSTICIA Y LEY" / ★C^{O}. M^{O}.★.** *Diameter:* 39 mm. *Edge:* Plain. BW-303.2, KM-661, GB-177.

2 pesos, silver, 18.27–20.08 g.

Obverse: Above a half-wreath of oak and laurel, the national coat of arms and legend **REPUBLICA MEXICANA.** *Reverse:* A large radiant liberty cap at center; below, **. DOS PESOS . C.M. GRO. 1915.** *Diameter:* 35 mm. *Edge:* Plain. BW-303.3, KM-662, GB-178.

Chilpancingo, Guerrero

Chilpancingo is the capital of the state of Guerrero and was the location of several Revolutionary battles. There are many counterfeits of the coinage of Chilpancingo.

10 centavos, cast silver, 2.52 g.

Obverse: Above a spray of oak and laurel, the national coat of arms and legend **MEZICO ESTADO G.R.O.** *Reverse:* At the top, above a half-wreath of oak and laurel, a small radiant sun with a face. At center, **10 / CENTAVOS / 1914.** *Edge:* Plain. *Diameter:* 18 mm. BW-304, KM-663, GB-180.

20 centavos, cast silver, 4.94 g.

Obverse: Above a spray of oak and laurel, the national coat of arms and legend **MEXICO ESTADO G.R.O.** *Reverse:* At the top, above a half-wreath of oak and laurel, a small radiant sun with a face. At center, **20 / CENTAVOS / 1914.** *Edge:* Plain. *Diameter:* 22 mm. BW-305, KM-664, GB-181.

Suriana, Guerrero

Suriana was a small mining camp close to Campo Morado in the state of Guerrero. Only one coin was issued from this location.

2 pesos, silver, 29.903 g.
Obverse: At center, the national coat of arms, with sprigs of oak and laurel from the sides of the base. Legend ★REPUBLICA MEXICANA.★ at the top, with DOS PESOS. G^{RO}. 1915. at the bottom. *Reverse:* At center, a sun with a face and long, single-line rays; below, a smoking volcano with a pointed top and a lower mountain at each side. In the sun's upper rays, fineness ORO: 0,595. Surrounding all, the legend "REFORMA, LIBERTAD, JUSTICIA Y LEY" / ★SURIANA. *Edge:* Reeded. *Diameter:* 39 mm. BW-312, KM-665, GB-223.

Taxco, Guerrero

The mint at Taxco, Guerrero, was the first mint used by Emiliano Zapata and the one from which he issued most of his coinage. Zapata had not only the silver resources around Taxco, but talented artisans who were able to create coinage dies, as well.

2 centavos, copper, 6.66 g.
Obverse: Above a half-wreath of oak and laurel, the national coat of arms and legend EDO. DE GRO. *Reverse:* At center, within an open wreath of laurel, an unshaded number 2 superimposed on a horizontally shaded centavo symbol (¢). At the top, between wreath tips, 1915; below bow on wreath, T̊. *Edge:* Plain. *Diameter:* 25.1 mm. BW-306, KM-667, GB-225.

5 centavos, copper, 8.56 g.
Obverse: Above a half-wreath of oak and laurel, the national coat of arms and legend ★ REPUBLICA ★ MEXICANA . ★. *Reverse:* At center, within an open wreath of laurel, an unshaded number 5 superimposed on a horizontally shaded centavo symbol (¢). At the top, ★ TAXCO. GRO . 1915. *Edge:* Plain. *Diameter:* 28 mm. BW-307, KM-668, GB-226.

10 centavos, copper, 8.26 g.
Obverse: Above a half-wreath of oak and laurel, the national coat of arms and legend ★ REPUBLICA ★ MEXICANA ·★. *Reverse:* At center, within an open wreath of laurel, 10/CENTAVOS. At the top, between wreath tips, TAXCO. GRO. 1915. *Edge:* Plain. *Diameter:* 28 mm. BW-308, KM-669, GB-227.

50 centavos, silver, 9.81 g.
Obverse: Above a half-wreath of oak and laurel, the national coat of arms and legend ★ REPUBLICA MEXICANA .★. *Reverse:* At the top, between the tips of an open wreath of laurel, a small radiant sun inscribed with 1915. At center, in three lines, _50¢ / ★ TAXCO ★ / GRO. *Edge:* Plain. *Diameter:* 27.8 mm. BW-309, KM-671, GB-228.

50 centavos, copper, 8.87 g.
Obverse: Above a half-wreath of oak and laurel, the national coat of arms and legend REPUBLICA MEXICANA. *Reverse:* At the top, between the tips of an open wreath of laurel, a small radiant sun inscribed with 1915. At center, in three lines, _50¢ / ★ TAXCO ★ / GRO. *Edge:* Plain. *Diameter:* 27.5 mm. BW-309.1, KM-UL, GB-229.

1 peso, silver-gold; silver 10.51 g., gold 0.30 g.
Obverse: The national coat of arms with sprigs of oak and laurel from the sides of the base. Legend REPUBLICA MEXICANA · / ★ UN PESO. *Reverse:* At center, within a small half-wreath of oak and laurel, a radiant liberty cap. Above the cap, in three lines, TAXCO. GRO. / ★ G. / ORO: 0.300. Surrounding all, REFORMA, LIBERTAD, JUSTICIA Y LEY . / 1915. *Edge:* Reeded. *Diameter:* 30.4 mm. BW-310, KM-672, GB-231.

1 peso, silver-gold; silver 10.51–12.79 g., gold 0.30 g.
Obverse: The national coat of arms with sprigs of oak and laurel from the sides of the base. Legend REPUBLICA MEXICANA· / ★ UN PESO. *Reverse:* At center, within a small half-wreath of oak and laurel, a radiant liberty cap; above, TAXCO.GRO. / G. / ORO: 0.300. Surrounding all, REFORMA, LIBERTAD, JUSTICIA Y LEY . / 1915. *Edge:* Reeded. *Diameter:* 30 mm. BW-310.1, KM-674, GB-236.

Estado Guerrero

The State of Guerrero, located on the southwestern coast of Mexico, was Zapata's base of operations during the Revolution. From 1914 through 1927, Zapata operated seven different mints in this state.

2 centavos, copper, 5.45 g.

Obverse: Above a spray of oak and laurel, the national coat of arms and legend REPUBLICA ★ MEXICANA. *Reverse:* At center, within an open wreath of laurel, an unshaded number 2 superimposed on a horizontally shaded centavo symbol (¢). At the top, between wreath tips, 1915. *Diameter:* 22.3 mm. *Edge:* Plain. BW-291, KM-638, GB-182.

Note: Reportedly the dies for this coin were cut by renowned engraver Meliton Gomez, who reported that in 1910 he cut the dies for several coins of the Revolution. In *Historical Notes on Coins of the Mexican Revolution 1913–1917*, J. Sanchez Garza reported that, "according to Mr. Meliton Gomez Brigadier General Jesus Salgado was the Godfather of a child baptized about mid 1915 with special coins given out to the people who attended the ceremony." (From around 1870 to around 1910 it was the custom to mint special *bolo*, or christening, pieces to give to the guests. The custom still exists, but bags of shiny new coins or packs of crisp new bank notes are given out instead.) From Garza's statement, it is assumed that the coins were struck in Taxco, although nowhere does Garza specify this.

3 centavos, copper, 4.63–6.87 g.

Obverse: Above a spray of oak and laurel, the national coat of arms and legend REPUBLICA MEXICANA. *Reverse:* At center, within an open wreath of laurel, an unshaded, flat-top 3 superimposed on an unshaded centavo symbol (¢). At the top, between wreath tips, 1915. *Diameter:* 25 mm. *Edge:* Plain. BW-291.1, KM-635, GB-183.

5 centavos, copper.

Obverse: Above a half-wreath of oak and laurel, the national coat of arms and legend REPUBLICA MEXICANA•. *Reverse:* At center, within an open wreath of laurel, an unshaded number 5 superimposed on a horizontally shaded centavo symbol (¢). At the top, between wreath tips, GRO. / 1915. *Diameter:* 26 mm. *Edge:* Plain. BW-292, KM-636, GB-184.

10 centavos, copper, 4.74 g.

Obverse: Above a half-wreath of oak and laurel, the national coat of arms and legend REPUBLICA MEXICANA•. *Reverse:* At center, within an open wreath of laurel, 10 / CENTAVOS. At the top, between wreath tips, GRO. / 1915 (with the G aligned over the 1). *Diameter:* 28 mm. *Edge:* Plain. BW-293, KM-637.2, GB-185.

10 centavos, copper, 11.37 g.

Obverse: Above a half-wreath of oak and laurel, the national coat of arms and legend REPUBLICA MEXICANA. *Reverse:* At center, within an open wreath of laurel, 10 / CENTAVOS. At the top, between wreath tips, GRO. / 1915. (with the G aligned over the 9). *Diameter:* 28.2 mm. *Edge:* Plain. BW-293.1, KM-637.2, GB-186.

10 centavos, copper.

Obverse: Above a half-wreath of oak and laurel, the national coat of arms and legend REPUBLICA MEXICANA. The letters in the legend are close together. *Reverse:* At center, within an open wreath of laurel, 10 / CENTAVOS. At the top, between wreath tips, GRO. / 1915. *Diameter:* 27 mm. *Edge:* Plain. BW-293.2, KM-637.3, GB-187.

20 centavos, copper.

Obverse: Above a half-wreath of oak and laurel, the national coat of arms and legend REPUBLICA MEXICANA. *Reverse:* At center, within an open wreath of laurel 20 / CENTAVOS. At the top, GRO / 1915. *Diameter:* 28.3 mm. *Edge:* Plain. BW-291.2, KM-UL, GB-188.

25 centavos, silver, 7.31–8.35 g.

Obverse: Within a border of dots, a crude radiant liberty cap surrounded by legend MeXIcana RePUbLICa. *Reverse:* At center, within a border of dots, the number 2•5 with **CentaVOS E.D.G. / 1915** surrounding. *Diameter:* 25 mm. *Edge:* Plain. BW-294, KM-639, GB-189.

Note: The dies for this coin were prepared by Severo Hernandez, a blacksmith whose work was unacceptable to General Jesús Salgado. Only a few coins were prepared.

50 centavos, silver, 14.5–14.8 g.

Obverse: Within a border of dots, a crude radiant liberty cap surrounded by legend **ReFORma LIbeRtad : JUStICIa / y / Ley.** *Reverse:* Within a border of dots, legend **RePUbLIca MeXICana E.**; and, within legend, **de / 50 ¢ / G. / 1915.** *Diameter:* 34 mm. *Edge:* Plain. BW-295, KM-640, GB-190.

Note: The dies for this coin were prepared by Severo Hernandez, a blacksmith whose work was unacceptable to General Jesús Salgado. Only a few coins were prepared.

1 peso, silver-gold; silver 13.030 g., gold 0.300 g.

Obverse: At center, the national coat of arms with sprigs of oak and laurel from the sides of the base. Legend **REPUBLICA MEXICANA. / ★UN PESO.** *Reverse:* Within a half-wreath of oak and laurel, a small, triangular radiant liberty cap. Above the cap's rays, **G**^RO^**·** and fineness **ORO:0,300**; surrounding all, legend **"REFORMA, LIBERTAD, JUSTICIA Y LEY" / 1914.** *Diameter:* 30.3 mm. *Edge:* Reeded. BW-296, KM-641, GB-191.

1 peso, silver-gold; silver 10.460 g., gold 0.300 g.

Obverse: At center, the national coat of arms with sprigs of oak and laurel from the sides of the base. Legend **REPUBLICA MEXICANA / ★UN PESO.** *Reverse:* Within a half-wreath of oak and laurel, a small radiant liberty cap. Above the cap's rays, **G**^RO^**·** and fineness **ORO:0,300** (with ^RO^**·** of **G**^RO^**·** set high, above the height of the **G**). Surrounding all, legend **"REFORMA, LIBERTAD, JUSTICIA Y LEY" / 1914.** *Diameter:* 29.9 mm. *Edge:* Reeded. BW-296.1, KM-642, GB-205.

2 pesos, silver-gold; silver 27.490 g., gold 0.595 g.

Obverse: At center, the national coat of arms with sprigs of oak and laurel from the sides of the base. Legend **REPUBLICA MEXICANA / ★DOS PESOS. G**^RO^**. 1914:.** *Reverse:* At center, a sun with a face and long, single-line rays; below, a smoking volcano with a rounded top and smaller mountains at each side. In the sun's upper rays, fineness **ORO: 0,595**. Surrounding all, legend **"REFORMA, LIBERTAD, JUSTICIA Y LEY".** *Diameter:* 38.8 mm. *Edge:* Reeded. BW-297, KM-643, GB-208.

2 pesos, silver-gold; silver 23.500 g., gold 0.595 g.

Obverse: At center, the national coat of arms with sprigs of oak and laurel from the sides of the base. Legend **REPUBLICA MEXICANA / ★DOS PESOS. G**^RO^**. 1914:.** *Reverse:* At center, a sun with a face and long, single-line rays; below, a smoking volcano with a high, pointed top and smaller mountains at each side. In the sun's upper rays, fineness **ORO: 0,595**. Surrounding all, legend **"REFORMA, LIBERTAD, JUSTICIA Y LEY".** *Diameter:* 38.8 mm. *Edge:* Reeded. BW-297.1, KM-644, GB-210.

Note: This coin has more rays than any other 2 pesos.

2 pesos, silver-gold; silver 28.580 g., gold 0.595 g.

Obverse: At center, the national coat of arms with sprigs of oak and laurel from the sides of the base. Legend **REPUBLICA MEXICANA / ★ DOS PESOS G**^RO^**.1914:.** *Reverse:* At center, a sun with a face and long, single-line rays; below, a smoking volcano with a rounded top and smaller mountains at each side. In the sun's upper rays, fineness **ORO: 0,595**. Surrounding all, legend **"REFORMA, LIBERTAD, JUSTICIA Y LEY".** *Diameter:* 39.2 mm. *Edge:* Reeded. BW-297.2, KM-643, GB-211.

2 pesos, silver-gold; silver 22.800 g., gold 0.595 g.

Obverse: At center, the national coat of arms with sprigs of oak and laurel from the sides of the base. Legend REPUBLICA MEXICANA / ★DOS PESOS. GRO. 1914:. *Reverse:* At center, a sun with a face and long, single-line rays; below, a smoking volcano with a high, pointed top and smaller mountains at each side. In the sun's upper rays, fineness ORO: 0,595. Surrounding all, legend "REFORMA, LIBERTAD, JUSTICIA Y LEY". *Diameter:* 39.5 mm. *Edge:* Reeded. BW-297.3, KM-644, GB-212.

2 pesos, silver-gold; silver 21.710–26.540 g., gold 0.595 g.

Obverse: At center, the national coat of arms with sprigs of oak and laurel from the sides of the base. The eagle perches on a single right-hand cactus pad. Legend REPUBLICA MEXICANA. / ★ DOS PESOOS. GRO. 1914. (with "PESOOS" error). *Reverse:* At center, a sun with a face and long, single-line rays; below, a smoking volcano with a pointed top and smaller mountains at each side. In the sun's upper rays, fineness ORO: 0,595. Surrounding all, legend "REFORMA, LIBERTAD, JUSTICIA Y LEY". *Diameter:* 39 mm. *Edge:* Reeded. BW-297.5, KM-644, GB-217.

2 pesos, silver-gold; silver 21.710–26.540 g., gold 0.595 g.

Obverse: At center, the national coat of arms with sprigs of oak and laurel from the sides of the base. The eagle perches on a right-hand cactus pad. Legend REPUBLICA MEXICANA. / ★DOS PESOS. GRO. 1914. *Reverse:* At center, a sun with a face and long, single-line rays; below, a smoking volcano with a pointed top and smaller mountains at each side. In the sun's upper rays, fineness ORO: 0,595 (one ray splits the zero). Surrounding all, legend "REFORMA, LIBERTAD, JUSTICIA Y LEY". *Diameter:* 39 mm. *Edge:* Reeded. BW-297.4, KM-644, GB-213.

2 pesos, silver-gold; silver 25.350 g., gold 0.595 g.

Obverse: At center, the national coat of arms with sprigs of oak and laurel from the sides of the base. The eagle perches on a single right-hand cactus pad, and the eagle's tail touches the laurel sprig on the right of the cactus. Legend REPUBLICA MEXICANA. / ★ DOS PESOS. GRO. 1915 ★. *Reverse:* At center, a sun with a face and long, single-line rays; below, a smoking volcano with a pointed top and smaller mountains at each side. In the sun's upper rays, fineness ORO: 0,595. Surrounding all, legend "REFORMA, LIBERTAD, JUSTICIA Y LEY". *Diameter:* 39 mm. *Edge:* Reeded. BW-297.6, KM-644, GB-220.

ESTADO DE JALISCO

The state of Jalisco is located in west-central Mexico.

Guadalajara, Jalisco

Guadalajara is the capital of the state of Jalisco. The famous Ejercito del Norte (Army of the North) pesos were struck at the Guadalajara mint rather than in Chihuahua. On January 18, 1915, Pancho Villa left Jalisco under the watch of General José Delgado, whom Villa charged with issuing 1-, 2-, and 5-centavo coins. At a later date, General Delgado had several pattern pieces of the 10 centavos and the 1 peso coined. He presented one of each to Venustiano Carranza when the latter visited Guadalajara. Delgado requested permission from Pancho Villa to coin them for regular issue, but was denied.

1 centavo, copper, 2.52 g.

Obverse: At center, a radiant liberty cap. Legend REPUBLICA MEXICANA / 1915. *Reverse:* An unshaded number 1 superimposed on the centavo symbol (¢) with radial shading (i.e., the cross-hatching lines are directed outward like the rays of a sun, from the center of the c shape). Legend EJERCITO DEL NORTE / EDO . DE JAL. *Diameter:* 19.3 mm. *Edge:* Plain. BW-319, KM-675, GB-239.

2 centavos, copper, 3.08 g.

Obverse: At center, a radiant liberty cap. Legend REPUBLICA MEXICANA / 1915. *Reverse:* An unshaded number 2 superimposed on a radially shaded centavo symbol (¢). Legend EJERCITO DEL NORTE / EDO. DE JAL. *Diameter:* 20.2 mm. *Edge:* Plain. BW-320, KM-676.1, GB-240.

5 centavos, copper, 7.18 g.

Obverse: At center, a radiant liberty cap. Legend REPUBLICA MEXICANA / 1915. *Reverse:* An unshaded number 5 superimposed on a radially shaded centavo symbol (¢). Legend EJERCITO DEL NORTE / EDO. DE JAL. *Diameter:* 24.06 mm. *Edge:* Plain. BW-321, KM-677, GB-241.

10 centavos, copper.

Obverse: At center, the coat of arms of Guadalajara, Jalisco. Legend CONSTITUCION Y REFORMAS. *Reverse:* Near the top, a small radiant liberty cap with the radiance filling the field of the coin. Below cap, on radiance, 10 / CENTAVOS / 1915, with a small G below the date. Legend GOBIERNO LIBERAL DE JALISCO . MEX. *Diameter:* 25 mm. *Edge:* Plain. BW-322, KM-678, GB-243.

1 peso, copper, pattern.

Obverse: Above a half-wreath of oak and laurel, the national coat of arms and legend REPUBLICA MEXICANA. *Reverse:* At center, a radiant liberty cap. Legend EJERCITO DEL NORTE / UN PESO. GA̭ 1915. J.D. 902.7. *Diameter:* 40 mm. *Edge:* Reeded. BW-323, KM-A678, GB-244.

Note: This coin is one of the items coined by General José Delgado for Venustiano Carranza.

ESTADO DE MÉXICO

The State of Mexico, located in the central region of Mexico, surrounds the federal district on three sides. It was known as Tenochtitlán when it was the capital of the Aztec empire.

Amecameca, Mexico

The crudest coinage of the Revolution was from Amecameca, located in the eastern region of the State of Mexico. Zapatista general Trinidad Sánchez Tenorio controlled the region and ordered the minting of 5-, 10-, 20-, 25-, and 50-centavo coins. Due to the lack of mined silver or copper to use in the minting process, metal was obtained from a railroad car that had been used to haul molasses to a local brandy factory. The coins were made by placing the planchets between two dies and striking them with a hammer, resulting in incused designs.

The abbreviation "RM" on the coins stands for "República Mexicana."

5 centavos, brass, 12.77 g.

Obverse: A crude national coat of arms with RM below, incuse in a single punch. *Reverse:* A plain field with the number 5 above the centavo symbol (¢), incuse with two punches. *Diameter:* 24.5 mm. *Edge:* Plain. BW-324, KM-680, GB-245.

5 centavos, brass, 12.55 g.

Obverse: On a plain field, legend EJERCIITO / CONVENCIONISTA. *Reverse:* A plain field with the number 5 above the centavo symbol (¢). *Diameter:* 24.5 mm. *Edge:* Plain. BW-324.1, KM-679, GB-246.

10 centavos, brass, 12.26 g.

Obverse: A crude national coat of arms with RM below, incuse in a single punch. *Reverse:* A plain field with the number 10 above the centavo symbol (¢), incuse with three punches. *Diameter:* 24.6 mm. *Edge:* Plain. BW-325, KM-681, GB-247.

20 centavos, brass, 12.78 g.

Obverse: A crude national coat of arms with RM below, incuse in a single punch. *Reverse:* A plain field with the number 20 above the centavo symbol (¢), incuse with three punches. *Diameter:* 24.7 mm. *Edge:* Plain. BW-326, KM-682, GB-248.

20 centavos, copper, 4.93 g.

Obverse: A crude national coat of arms with A.D.J. (for "Amecameca de Juárez") below. *Reverse:* A plain field with the number 20 superimposed on the centavo symbol (¢), with an underscore below. *Diameter:* 20 mm. *Edge:* Plain. BW-326.1, KM-683, GB-250.

25 centavos, brass, 12.55 g.

Obverse: On a plain field, legend EJERCITO / CONVENCIONISTA. *Reverse:* A plain field with the number 25 above the centavo symbol (¢). *Diameter:* 22 mm. *Edge:* Plain. BW-327, KM-684, GB-253.

25 centavos, copper, 6.94 g.

Obverse: Crude, incuse national coat of arms above a half-wreath of laurel and oak. *Reverse:* A plain field with the centavo symbol (¢) above the number 25. *Diameter:* 25.1 mm. *Edge:* Plain. BW-327.1, KM-685, GB-252.

40 centavos, brass.

Obverse: Crude, incuse national coat of arms above a half-wreath of laurel and oak. *Reverse:* A plain field with the number 40 and a six-sided rosette below. *Diameter:* 24 mm. *Edge:* Plain. BW-329, KM-UL, GB-UL.

50 centavos, copper, 16.38 g.

Obverse: Crude, incuse national coat of arms above a half-wreath of laurel and oak. *Reverse:* A plain field with the centavo symbol (¢) above the number number 50. *Diameter:* 28.4 mm. *Edge:* Plain. BW-328, KM-686a, GB-254.

Note: There exist hand-engraved circulating counterfeits of this type. The counterfeiter was caught and executed. Due to the crudeness of the authentic coin and its method of minting, many counterfeits circulated.

Mexico City, Mexico

Mexico City's only two coins pertaining to the Revolution were minted while the city was occupied by Zapata, who had 1 and 2 centavos struck at the Casa de Moneda de México. They are the same as the regular federal issues.

1 centavo, copper, 1.39–1.50 g.

Obverse: Above a spray of oak and laurel, the national coat of arms and legend ESTADOS UNIDOS MEXICANOS. *Reverse:* Within an open wreath of laurel, an unshaded number 1 superimposed on a horizontally shaded centavo symbol (¢). At the top, between wreath tips, 1915; below the bow on the wreath, mintmark M°. *Diameter:* 16 mm. *Edge:* Plain. BW-M328, KM-416, GB-256.

2 centavos, copper, 3.0–3.3 g.

Obverse: Above a spray of oak and laurel, the national coat of arms and legend ESTADOS UNIDOS MEXICANOS. *Reverse:* Within an open wreath of laurel, an unshaded number 2 superimposed on a horizontally shaded centavo symbol (¢). At the top, between wreath tips, 1915; below the bow on the wreath, mintmark M°. *Diameter:* 20 mm. *Edge:* Plain. BW-M329, KM-420, GB-257.

Tenancingo, Mexico

While the Zapatista forces, with limited economic resources, were in control of the city of Tenancingo, General Luciano Solís ordered the coinage of 2, 5, 10, and 20 centavos. A large water tank was the source of the copper used to make the coins. The 10 centavos dated 1916 were struck only in January, before the city fell into the hands of the Federales.

2 centavos, copper.

Obverse: Above a spray of laurel, the national coat of arms and legend ★REPUBLICA MEXICANA. *Reverse:* Within an open wreath of laurel, an unshaded number 2 superimposed on the centavo symbol (¢). At the top, between wreath tips, 1915. *Diameter:* 16 mm. *Edge:* Plain. BW-329.1, KM-688.1, GB-257.

2 centavos, copper.

Obverse: Above a spray of laurel, the national coat of arms and legend ★REPUBLICA MEXICANA. *Reverse:* Within an open wreath of laurel, an unshaded number 2 superimposed on the centavo symbol (¢). At the top, between wreath tips, 1915; below the denomination, TM (for "Teofilo Monroy," director of the mint). *Diameter:* 16 mm. *Edge:* Plain. BW-329.2, KM-688.2, GB-258.

5 centavos, copper, 2.63 g.

Obverse: Above a spray of laurel, the national coat of arms and legend REPUBLICA MEXICANA. *Reverse:* Within an open wreath of laurel, an unshaded number 5 superimposed on a horizontally shaded centavo symbol (¢). At the top, between wreath tips, 1915. *Diameter:* 19.2 mm. *Edge:* Plain. BW-330, KM-689.1, GB-259.

10 centavos, copper, 4.95 g.

Obverse: Above a spray of oak and laurel, the national coat of arms and legend REPUBLICA MEXICANA, surrounded by a denticled border. *Reverse:* Within an open wreath of laurel, an unshaded number 10 superimposed on a horizontally shaded centavo symbol (¢). At the top, between wreath tips, 1915. A denticled border surrounds all. *Diameter:* 25.3 mm. *Edge:* Plain. BW-331, KM-690.1, GB-260.

20 centavos, copper, 11.15 g.

Obverse: Above a spray of laurel, the national coat of arms and legend ★ REPUBLICA ★ MEXICANA ★. *Reverse:* At center, within a half-wreath, 20 / CENTAVOS / 1915. Above, ★ GRAL ★ L ★ SOLIS. *Diameter:* 27.9 mm. *Edge:* Plain. BW-332, KM-691, GB-261.

Texcoco, Mexico

Only a single, 1-centavo coin, made of red clay, was produced in the city of Texcoco. It is not listed in the Krause catalogs, and is only mentioned in Grove. It is shown and listed in Guthrie-Bothamley as GB-262. This is J. Sanchez Garza's plate coin (*Historical Notes on Coins of the Mexican Revolution*, 1969), which he presented to Dr. José Maria Arguelies of Mexico City. Both Neil Utberg (*Coins of Mexico, 1536–1963*, published 1963; and other titles) and Carlos Gaytán (*La Revolución Mexicana y Sus Monedas*, 1969) used Garza's photograph.

1 centavo, red clay.

Obverse: The national coat of arms above a spray of foliage. Legend ESTADOS UNIDOS MEXICANOS. *Reverse:* Within an open wreath of laurel, a double-outlined number 1 superimposed on the centavo symbol (¢), with 1915 above. *Diameter:* 22 mm. *Edge:* Plain. BW-T332, KM-UL, GB-262.

Toluca, Mexico

Next to the red clay coins of Texcoco, Toluca produced the most unusual coinage of the Revolution: the 5-centavo cardboard issue of 1915. This coin was authorized by General Gustavo Baz Prada, who was the first Revolutionary governor for the State of Mexico. Baz Prada, who was attending medical school when the Revolution broke out, joined the Huertista opposition as a sergeant and took part in several battles under orders of General Francisco V. Pacheco, one of Emiliano Zapata's main generals. Baz Prada was a general before he reached 21 years of age. His first action as a new governor was to order coins to be produced. The cardboard 5 centavos were designed and produced at the Institute of Arts (Escuela de Artes y Oficios, or EDAYO, which still exists in Toluca).

5 centavos, cardboard, 1.10 g.

Obverse: Above a half-wreath of oak and laurel, the coat of arms of Toluca. Legend ·:·ESTADO LIBRE Y SOBERANO DE MEXICO·:· / TOLUCA. *Reverse:* At center, the number 5 overlaid with a scroll inscribed CENTAVOS. Legend CIRCULARA CONFORME AL DECRETO Nº 4 DE / + III·I·915. +. *Diameter:* 28.7 mm. *Edge:* Plain. BW-333, KM-692.1, GB-263.

5 centavos, cardboard, 1.03 g.

Obverse: Above a half-wreath of oak and laurel, the coat of arms of Toluca. Legend ·:·ESTADO LIBRE Y SOBERANO DE MEXICO·:· / TOLUCA. *Reverse:* At center, the number 5 overlaid with a scroll inscribed CENTAVOS. Legend CIRCULARA CONFORME AL DECRETO Nº 4 DE / + III·I·915. +. *Diameter:* 28.5 mm. *Edge:* Plain. BW-333.1, KM-692.2, GB-263.

20 centavos, copper, 3.00 g.
Obverse: The obverse of the host coin (a 1 centavo of 1906). *Reverse:* The number **20** inside a **C**, counterstamped incused. First struck with a 20-mm flat punch, leaving a 10.5-mm incuse circle establishing the location of the value counterstamp. *Diameter:* 20.1 mm. *Edge:* Plain. BW-334, KM-693.1, GB-264.

Note: The 20- and 40-centavo coins for Toluca, counterstamped on 1- and 2-centavo coins of 1906, were said to have been used at a charity event in 1906, but they have been accepted as legitimate Revolutionary coins of the Zapatista forces.

20 centavos, copper, 2.65–2.95 g.
Obverse: The obverse of the host coin (a 1 centavo of 1906). *Reverse:* The number **20** inside a **C**, counterstamped incused. First struck with a 13.6-mm flat punch, leaving a 10.6-mm incuse circle establishing the location of the value counterstamp. *Diameter:* 20 mm. *Edge:* Plain. BW-334.1, KM-693.2, GB-265.

Note: See the note for GB-264.

20 centavos, bronze, 2.65–2.95 g.
Obverse: The obverse of the host coin (a 1 centavo of 1906). *Reverse:* The number **20** inside a **C**, counterstamped incused. First struck with a 12-mm flat punch, leaving a 10.5-mm incuse circle establishing the location of the value counterstamp. *Diameter:* 20 mm. *Edge:* Plain. BW-334.2, KM-693.2, GB-266.

Note: See the note for GB-264.

40 centavos, bronze, 5.79 g.
Obverse: The obverse of the host coin (a 2 centavos of 1906). *Reverse:* The number **40** inside a **C**, counterstamped incused. First struck with a 13.2-mm flat punch, leaving a 10.5-mm incuse circle establishing the location of the value counterstamp. There is a dot in the center of the counterstamp. *Diameter:* 25 mm. *Edge:* Plain. BW-335, KM-694, GB-267.

Note: See the note for GB-264.

40 centavos, bronze, 5.78 g.
Obverse: The obverse of the host coin (a 2 centavos of 1906). *Reverse:* The number **40** inside a **C**, counterstamped incused. First struck with a 13.2-mm flat punch, leaving a 10.5-mm incuse circle establishing the location of the value counterstamp. There is no dot in the center of the counterstamp. *Diameter:* 25 mm. *Edge:* Plain. BW-335.1, KM-694, GB-268.

Note: See the note for GB-264.

ESTADO DE MORELOS

Morelos, a state in south-central Mexico on the southern border of the Federal District, was the stronghold for Emiliano Zapata. His headquarters were located in Tlaltizapán.

Atlihuayan, Morelos

2 centavos, copper.
Obverse: Above a half-wreath of oak and laurel, the national coat of arms and legend **E. L. DE MORELOS**. *Reverse:* Within an open wreath of laurel, the number **2** superimposed on the centavo symbol (¢). At the top, between wreath tips, **1915**. *Diameter:* 23 mm. *Edge:* Plain. BW-336, KM-695, GB-269.

5 centavos, copper, 9.000 g.
Obverse: Above a half-wreath of oak and laurel, the national coat of arms and legend **REPUBLICA MEXICANA**. *Reverse:* Within a half-wreath of laurel, the number **5** superimposed on the centavo symbol (¢). At the top, **E. DE MOR. 1915**. *Diameter:* 25.9 mm. *Edge:* Plain. BW-337, KM-696, GB-270.

10 centavos, copper, 8.690 g.
Obverse: Above a half-wreath of oak and laurel, the national coat of arms and legend **REPUBLICA MEXICANA**. *Reverse:* At center, within an open wreath of laurel, the number **10** superimposed on the centavo symbol (¢). At the top, **E. DE MOR. 1915**. *Diameter:* 28 mm. *Edge:* Plain. BW-338, KM-UL, GB-271.

10 centavos, copper, 6.660 g.
Obverse: The national coat of arms. Legend REPUBLICA MEXICANA / MOR. *Reverse:* Within an open wreath of laurel, the number 10 superimposed on a wide centavo symbol (¢). Date effaced. *Diameter:* 24.4 mm. *Edge:* Reeded. BW-388.1, KM-698, GB-272.

10 centavos, copper, 5.350 g.
Obverse: The national coat of arms. Legend REPUBLICA MEXICANA / MOR. *Reverse:* Within an open wreath of laurel, the number 10 superimposed on a wide centavo symbol (¢). At the top, between wreath tips, 1915 punched into a gouged area. *Diameter:* 24.4 mm. *Edge:* Reeded. BW-338.2, KM-697, GB-273.

10 centavos, copper, 4.83–6.80 g.
Obverse: Above a spray of oak and laurel, the national coat of arms and legend REPUBLICA MEXICANA. *Reverse:* At center, within an open wreath of laurel, 10 / CENTAVOS. Above, between wreath tips, E. DE MOR. / 1915. *Diameter:* 30 mm. *Edge:* Plain. BW-338.3, KM-699, GB-275.

10 centavos, copper, 5.56–8.36 g.
Obverse: Above a half-wreath of oak and laurel, the national coat of arms and legend REPUBLICA MEXICANA. *Reverse:* At center, within an open wreath of laurel, 10 / CENTAVOS. Above, between wreath tips, MOR / 1916. *Diameter:* 28 mm. *Edge:* Plain. BW-338.4, KM-700, GB-276.

20 centavos, copper, 2.919 g.
Obverse: Above a half-wreath of oak and laurel, the national coat of arms and legend E. L. DE MORELOS. *Reverse:* At center, within an open wreath of laurel, the number 20 superimposed on the centavo symbol (¢). At the top, between wreath tips, 1915. *Diameter:* 23.6 mm. *Edge:* Plain. BW-339, KM-701, GB-277.

50 centavos, copper, 5.73–13.77 g.
Obverse: The national coat of arms. Legend REPUBLICA MEXICANA / MOR. *Reverse:* Within an open wreath of laurel, the number 50 superimposed on the centavo symbol (¢). At the top, above the wreath tips, 1915. *Diameter:* 29 mm. *Edge:* Plain. BW-340, KM-702, GB-278.

50 centavos, copper, 12.190 g.
Obverse: Above a spray of oak and laurel, the national coat of arms and legend REPUBLICA MEXICANA. *Reverse:* Within an open wreath of laurel, the number 50 superimposed on the centavo symbol (¢). At the top, above the wreath tips, 1915. *Diameter:* 28.5 mm. *Edge:* Plain. BW-340.1, KM-703, GB-279.

50 centavos, silver.
Obverse: Above a spray of oak and laurel, the national coat of arms and legend REPUBLICA MEXICANA. *Reverse:* At center, 1915 above a horizontally shaded 50; CENTAVOS at the bottom, between ends of legend .REFORMA LIBERTAD JUSTICIA Y LEY. *Diameter:* 29 mm. *Edge:* Plain. BW-340.2, KM-706, GB-280.

50 centavos, copper, 10.750 g.
Obverse: The national coat of arms, with sprigs of oak and laurel from the sides of the base. Legend REPUBLICA MEXICANA. and, below the base of the arms, MORELOS. *Reverse:* Within an open wreath of laurel, 50 / CENTAVOS. At the top, between wreath tips, 1916. *Diameter:* 30 mm. *Edge:* Plain. BW-340.3, KM-704, GB-282.

1 peso, silver.
Obverse: Above a spray of oak and laurel, the national coat of arms and legend REPUBLICA MEXICANA; below the spray, 191. Below right wing tip, engraver initials PCS. *Reverse:* Below a small radiant liberty cap, a crossed sword and balance scale; between the pans of the scale, an open book bearing the words PLAN DE AYALA 20 NOV. 1911. Surrounding all, legend REFORMA, LIBERTAD, JUSTICIA Y LEY / UN PESO. The sword handle points to the O in PESO. *Diameter:* 37 mm. *Edge:* Reeded. BW-341, KM-UL, GB-284.

1 peso, copper, 10.000 g.

Obverse: Above a spray of oak and laurel, the national coat of arms and legend **REPUBLICA MEXICANA**; below the spray, **1916**. Below right wing tip, engraver initials **PCS**. *Reverse:* Below a small radiant liberty cap, a crossed sword and balance scale; between the pans of the scale, an open book bearing the words **PLAN DE AYALA 20 NOV. 1911**. Surrounding all, legend **REFORMA, LIBERTAD, JUSTICIA Y LEY / UN PESO**. The sword handle points to the S in PESO. *Diameter:* 38 mm. *Edge:* Plain. BW-341.1, KM-UL, GB-286.

1 peso, silver.

Obverse: The national coat of arms, with sprigs of oak and laurel from the sides of the base. Legend **REPUBLICA MEXICANA. / ★ UN PESO.** *Reverse:* Within an open wreath of oak and laurel, a radiant liberty cap, with **MOR** above the cap, between wreath tips. Surrounding all, **"REFORMA, LIBERTAD, JUSTICIA Y LEY" / 1916**. *Diameter:* 31 mm. *Edge:* Plain. BW-341.2, KM-708, GB-287.

ESTADO DE OAXACA

The state of Oaxaca seceded from Mexico on June 3, 1915. The governor of the Free and Sovereign ("Libre y Soberano," or L.Y.S.) State of Oaxaca, José Inés Dávila, opened the old Oaxaca mint for coining of the new Oaxaca coins. The initials (TM) that appear on some of the Oaxaca coins are not for the engraver, but for for the director of the mint, Teofilo Monroy. The engraver was an American, living in Oaxaca, by the name of John DeCoe.

The Free and Sovereign State of Oaxaca lasted until March 6, 1916, when the forces of Venustiano Carranza entered the city of Oaxaca. Governor Dávila escaped but was later captured; he was executed on May 31, 1916.

The style of lettering on Oaxaca coinage can be found in two types:

Style 1—Thin, ragged-looking letters in the legend.

Style 2—Heavy, regular-shaped letters in the legend.

There are 10 styles for the bust of President Benito Juárez in the Oaxaca coinage:

Type 1—Bust facing forward (all others in profile)

Type 2—Bust in low relief, with long, pointed truncation

Type 3—Bust in heavy relief, with short, unfinished lapels

Type 4—Boldly outlined bust with unfinished truncation

Type 5—Bust in heavy relief, with short, unfinished lapels; centered high

Type 6—Curved bottom to bust

Type 7—Short truncation to bust, closed lapels

Type 8—Short truncation (with pronounced curve) to bust

Type 9—Medium truncation to bust, closed lapels

Type 10—Small, nude bust

The coinage of Oaxaca has a large number of varieties; due to the overview nature of this volume, only a portion of them will be listed here. A more extensive listing is presented in volume 4 of this *Whitman Encyclopedia* series.

1 centavo, copper, 1.85 g.

Obverse: Within a dotted border, legend ESTADO / L.Y.S.DE / OAXACA. *Reverse:* Within a dotted border, legend PROVISIO / NAL. UN. / CENTAVO. *Dimensions:* Rectangular, 19.7 mm x 13.4 mm. *Edge:* Plain. BW-344, KM-709, GB-289.

1 centavo, copper, 3.02 g.

Obverse: At center, a Type 1 bust of Juárez, with legend ESTADO L. Y S. DE OAXACA / ★ 1915 ★. *Reverse:* Above a spray of oak and laurel, a 9.6-mm tall number 1 superimposed on the centavo symbol (¢). At the top, MONEDA PROVISIONAL. No TM. *Diameter:* 17.9 mm. *Edge:* Corded. BW-344.1, KM-710, GB-292.

1 centavo, copper, 2.18 g.

Obverse: At center, a Type 2 bust of Juárez, with legend ESTADO L. Y S. DE OAXACA / ★ 1915 ★. *Reverse:* Above a spray of oak and laurel, an 8.8-millimeter number 1 superimposed on the centavo symbol (¢). At the top, MONEDA PROVISIONAL. No TM. *Diameter:* 18.1 mm. *Edge:* Corded. BW-344.2, KM-710, GB-293.

3 centavos, copper, 2.75 g.

Obverse: Within a single-outline border with a star inside each corner, legend ESTADO / L.Y.S. DE / OAXACA / 1915. *Reverse:* Within a single-outline border with a star inside each corner, legend PROVISIO / NAL.TRES / CENTAVOS, with the director's initials set off by ornaments at the bottom: • — TM — •. *Dimensions:* Rectangular, 24.8 mm x 16.9 mm. *Edge:* Plain. BW-345, KM-711, GB-290.

3 centavos, copper.

Obverse: Within a single-outline border with a star inside each corner, legend ESTADO / L.Y.S. DE / OAXACA / 1915. *Reverse:* Within a single-outline border with a star inside each corner, legend PROVISI / ONAL.TRES / CENTAVOS, with the director's initials set off by ornaments at the bottom: • — TM — •. *Dimensions:* Rectangular, 25 mm x 17 mm. *Edge:* Plain. BW-345.1, KM-712, GB-291.

3 centavos, copper, 2.98 g.

Obverse: At center, a Type 3 bust of Juárez, with legend ESTADO L. Y S. DE OAXACA / ★ 1915 ★. *Reverse:* Above a spray of oak and laurel, a large, flat-top number 3 with CEИTAVOS (retrograde N) below the number. At the top, MONEDA PROVISIONAL. No TM. *Diameter:* 20.2 mm. *Edge:* Corded. BW-345.2, KM-713.1, GB-296.

3 centavos, copper, 2.37 g.

Obverse: At center, a Type 3 bust of Juárez, with legend ESTADO L. Y S . DE OAXACA / ★ 1915 ★. *Reverse:* Above a spray of oak and laurel, a small, round-top number 3 with CEИTAVOS (retrograde N) below the number. At the top, MONEDA PROVISIONAL. Initials TM just above the spray, where the two halves join. *Diameter:* 20.46 mm. *Edge:* Corded. BW-345.3, KM-714, GB-299.

5 centavos, copper.

Obverse: At center, a Type 1 facing bust of Juárez, with legend ESTADO L. Y S. DE OAXACA / ★ 1915 ★. *Reverse:* Above a spray of oak and laurel, 5 / CENTAVOS. At the top, MONEDA PROVISIONAL. No TM. *Diameter:* 22 mm. *Edge:* Corded. BW-346, KM-716, GB-300.

5 centavos, brass.

Obverse: At center, ENERO, with incuse legend ESTADO DE OAXACA / 15 DE 1915 surrounding. *Reverse:* At center, the number 5, with legend REPUBLICA MEXICANA CENTAVOS surrounding. *Diameter:* 18.5 mm. *Edge:* Plain. BW-346.1, KM-715, GB-301.

Note: This unique coin was minted five months before Oaxaca seceded from the Republic and declared itself a free and sovereign state.

5 centavos, copper, 4.36 g.

Obverse: At center, a Type 5 bust of Juárez, with legend ESTADO L. Y S. DE OAXACA / ★ 1915 ★. *Reverse:* Above a spray of oak and laurel, 5 / CENTAVOS. At the top, MONEDA PROVISIONAL; below the spray, initials TM. *Diameter:* 22.1 mm. *Edge:* Corded. BW-346.2, KM-718, GB-303.

5 centavos, copper, 4.27 g.

Obverse: At center, a Type 7 bust of Juárez, with legend **ESTADO L. Y S . DE OAXACA / ★ 1915 ★**. *Reverse:* Above a spray of oak and laurel, **5 / CENTAVOS**. At the top, **MONEDA PROVISIONAL**; below the spray, initials **TM**. *Diameter:* 21.9 mm. *Edge:* Corded. BW-346.3, KM-720, GB-304.

5 centavos, copper, 4.16 g.

Obverse: At center, a Type 5 bust of Juárez, with legend **ESTADO L. Y S . DE OAXACA / ★ 1915 ★**. The word ESTADO and the date are re-engraved. *Reverse:* Above a spray of oak and laurel, **5 / CENTAVOS**. At the top, **MONEDA PROVISIONAL**; below the spray, initials **TM**. *Diameter:* 22.8 mm. *Edge:* Corded. BW-346.4, KM-UL, GB-305.

5 centavos, copper, 4.11 g.

Obverse: At center, a Type 8 bust of Juárez, with legend **ESTADO L. Y S . DE OAXACA / ★ 1915 ★**. *Reverse:* Above a spray of oak and laurel, **5 / CENTAVOS**. At the top, **MONEDA PROVISIONAL**. No **TM**. *Diameter:* 22.6 mm. *Edge:* Corded. BW-346.5, KM-721, GB-306.

5 centavos, copper, 4.13 g.

Obverse: At center, a Type 6 bust of Juárez, with legend **ESTADO L. Y S. DE OAXACA / ★ 1915 ★**. *Reverse:* Above a spray of oak and laurel, **5 / CENTAVOS**. At the top, **MONEDA PROVISIONAL**. No **TM**. *Diameter:* 22.1 mm. *Edge:* Corded. BW-346.6, KM-UL, GB-307.

5 centavos, copper.

Obverse: At center, a Type 5 bust of Juárez, with legend **ESTADO L. Y S . DE OAXACA / ★ 1915 ★**. *Reverse:* Above a spray of oak and laurel, **5 / CENTAVOS**. At the top, **MONEDA PROVISIONAL**. No **TM**. *Diameter:* 22 mm. *Edge:* Corded. BW-346.7, KM-UL, GB-UL.

10 centavos, copper, 7.96 g.

Obverse: At center, a Type 5 bust of Juárez, with legend **ESTADO L. Y S. DE OAXACA / ★ 1915 ★**. *Reverse:* Above a spray of oak and laurel, **10 / CENTAVOS**. At the top, **MONEDA PROVISIONAL**; below the spray, initials **TM**. *Diameter:* 26.1 mm. *Edge:* Corded. BW-347, KM-725, GB-312.

10 centavos, copper.

Obverse: At center, a Type 4 bust of Juárez, with legend **ESTADO L. Y S . DE OAXACA / ★ 1915 ★**. Counterstamped with 5.6-mm initials **G V** (for General García Vigil). *Reverse:* Above a spray of oak and laurel, **10 / CENTAVOS**. At the top, **MONEDA PROVISONAL**; below the spray, the initials **TM**. *Diameter:* 26.5 mm. *Edge:* Corded. BW-347.1, KM-727.3, GB-320.

10 centavos, copper.

Obverse: At center, a Type 2 bust of Juárez, with legend **ESTADO L. Y S . DE OAXACA / ★ 1915 ★**. *Reverse:* Entire reverse struck retrograde. Above a spray of oak and laurel, **10 / CENTAVOS**. At the top, **MONEDA PROVISONAL**. *Diameter:* 27.5 mm. *Edge:* Corded. BW-347.2, KM-UL, GB-323.

20 centavos, copper, 11.20 g.

Obverse: At center, a Type 5 bust of Juárez, with legend **ESTADO L. Y S . DE OAXACA / ★ 1915 ★**. *Reverse:* Above a spray of oak and laurel, **20 / CENTAVOS**. At the top, **MONEDA PROVISONAL**; below the spray, initials **TM**. *Diameter:* 27.8 mm. *Edge:* Corded. BW-348, KM-733, GB-324.

20 centavos, copper, 11.62 g.

Obverse: At center, a Type 5 bust of Juárez, with legend **ESTADO L. Y S . DE OAXACA / ★ 1915 ★**. *Reverse:* Above a spray of oak and laurel, **20 / CENTAVOS**. At the top, **MONEDA PROVISONAL**. No **TM**. *Diameter:* 29 mm. *Edge:* Corded. BW-348.1, KM-733, GB-325.

20 centavos, copper, 11.53 g.

Obverse: At center, a Type 2 bust of Juárez, with legend **ESTADO L. Y S . DE OAXACA / ★ 1915 ★**. *Reverse:* Above a spray of oak and laurel, **20 / CENTAVOS**. At the top, **MONEDA PROVISONAL**; below the spray, initials **TM**. *Diameter:* 28.6 mm. *Edge:* Corded. BW-348.2, KM-728a, GB-328.

20 centavos, copper, 11.17 g.
Obverse: At center, a Type 6 bust of Juárez, with legend ESTADO L. Y S . DE OAXACA / ★ 1915 ★. *Reverse:* Above a spray of oak and laurel, 20 / CENTAVOS. At the top, MONEDA PROVISONAL. No TM. *Diameter:* 29 mm. *Edge:* Corded. BW-348.3, KM-731.1, GB-330.

20 centavos, copper, 11.16 g.
Obverse: At center, a Type 4 bust of Juárez, with legend ESTADO L. Y S . DE OAXACA / ★ 1915 ★. *Reverse:* Above a spray of oak and laurel, 20 / CENTAVOS. At the top, MONEDA PROVISONAL. Above the denomination, a counterstamp in the form of a small, radiant liberty cap. No TM. *Diameter:* 28.3 mm. *Edge:* Corded. BW-348.4, KM-729.2, GB-331.

20 centavos, copper, 11.09 g.
Obverse: At center, a Type 4 bust of Juárez, within a border of the style of the gold 20 pesos (dots in semicircles). Legend ESTADO L. Y S . DE OAXACA. / ★ 1915 ★. *Reverse:* Above a spray of oak and laurel, 20 / CENTAVOS. At the top, MONEDA PROVISONAL. No TM. *Diameter:* 27.7 mm. *Edge:* Corded. BW-348.5, KM-729.1, GB-333.

20 centavos, copper, 11.84 g.
Obverse: At center, a Type 4 bust of Juárez, with legend ESTADO L. Y S . DE OAXACA / ★ 1915 ★. *Reverse:* Above a spray of oak and laurel, 20 / CENTAVOS. At the top, MONEDA PROVISONAL; below the spray, initials TM. *Diameter:* 31 mm. *Edge:* Corded. BW-348.6, KM-731.2, GB-334.

Note: This is the largest variety of the 20 centavos.

20 centavos, silver.
Obverse: At center, a Type 2 bust of Juárez, with legend ESTADO L. Y S . DE OAXACA / ★ 1915 ★. Incuse dots in the stars. *Reverse:* Above a spray of oak and laurel, 20 / CENTAVOS. At the top, MONEDA PROVISONAL. No TM. *Diameter:* 20 mm. *Edge:* Corded. BW-348.7, KM-728, GB-335.

50 centavos, copper.
Obverse: Within a dot-and-dash circle, a Type 9 bust of Juárez, with legend ESTADO L. Y S . DE OAXACA / ★ 1915 ★. *Reverse:* Above a spray of oak and laurel, 50 / CENTAVOS. At the top, MONEDA PROVISONAL. No TM. *Diameter:* 28.5 mm. *Edge:* Plain. BW-349, KM-739a, GB-UL.

50 centavos, silver, 4.38 g.
Obverse: At center, a Type 7 bust of Juárez, with legend ESTADO L. Y S . DE OAXACA / ★ 1915 ★. *Reverse:* Above a spray of oak and laurel, 50 / CENTAVOS. At the top, MONEDA PROVISONAL. No TM. *Diameter:* 22 mm. *Edge:* Corded. BW-349.1, KM-733, GB-336.

Note: Some later coins have the initials TM.

50 centavos, silver, 4.18 g.
Obverse: At center, a Type 7 bust of Juárez, with legend ESTADO L. Y S . DE OAXACA / ★ 1915 ★. *Reverse:* Above a spray of oak and laurel, 50 / CENTAVOS. At the top, MONEDA PROVISONAL; below the spray, initials TM. *Diameter:* 22.3 mm. *Edge:* Corded. BW-349.2, KM-736, GB-337.

50 centavos, silver, 4.55 g.
Obverse: At center, a Type 7 bust of Juárez, with legend ESTADO L. Y S . DE OAXACA / ★ 1915 ★. *Reverse:* Above a spray of oak and laurel, 50 / CENTAVOS. At the top, MONEDA PROVISONAL. No TM. *Diameter:* 22.3 mm. *Edge:* Corded. BW-349.3, KM-738, GB-338.

50 centavos, copper, 4.19 g.
Obverse: At center, a Type 8 bust of Juárez, with legend ESTADO L. Y S . DE OAXACA / ★ 1915 ★. *Reverse:* Above a spray of oak and laurel, 50 / CENTAVOS. At the top, MONEDA PROVISONAL. No TM. *Diameter:* 22.5 mm. *Edge:* Corded. BW-349.4, KM-737, GB-340.

50 centavos, copper.
Obverse: At center, a Type 8 bust of Juárez, with legend ESTADO L. Y S . DE OAXACA / ★ 1915 ★. *Reverse:* Above a spray of oak

and laurel, **50 / CENTAVOS**. At the top, **MONEDA PROVISONAL**. No **TM**. *Diameter:* 22 mm. *Edge:* Plain. BW-349.5, KM-UL, GB-341.

50 centavos, billon.

Obverse: Within a dot-and-dash circle, a Type 9 bust of Juárez, with legend **ESTADO L. Y S. DE OAXACA / ★ 1915 ★**. *Reverse:* Above a spray of oak and laurel, **50 / CENTAVOS**. At the top, **MONEDA PROVISONAL**. No **TM**. *Diameter:* 28.5 mm. *Edge:* Plain. BW-349.6, KM-739, GB-342.

50 centavos, silver, 4.21 g.

Obverse: At center, a Type 5 bust of Juárez, with legend **ESTADO L. Y S. DE OAXACA / ★ 1915 ★**. *Reverse:* Above a spray of oak and laurel, **50 / CENTAVOS**. At the top, **MONEDA PROVISONAL**. No **TM**. *Diameter:* 22.3 mm. *Edge:* Plain. BW-349.7, KM-734, GB-339.

1 peso, silver, 8.01 g.

Obverse: At center, a Type 5 bust of Juárez, with legend **ESTADO L. Y S. DE OAXACA / ★ 1915 ★**. *Reverse:* Above a spray of oak and laurel, **UN / PESO**. At the top, **MONEDA PROVISONAL**. No **TM**. *Diameter:* 26.7 mm. *Edge:* Corded. BW-350, KM-741, GB-343.

1 peso, copper.

Obverse: At center, a Type 4 bust of Juárez, with legend **ESTADO L. Y S. DE OAXACA / ★ 1915 ★**. *Reverse:* Above a spray of oak and laurel, **UN / PESO**. At the top, **MONEDA PROVISONAL**. No **TM**. *Diameter:* 22 mm. *Edge:* Plain. BW-350.1, KM-UL, GB-UL.

Note: This is a trial strike on a 5-peso planchet.

1 peso, silver, 7.86 g.

Obverse: At center, a Type 7 bust of Juárez, with legend **ESTADO L. Y S. DE OAXACA / ★ 1915 ★**. *Reverse:* Above a spray of oak and laurel, **UN / PESO**. At the top, **MONEDA PROVISONAL**; below the spray, initials **TM**. *Diameter:* 25.5 mm. *Edge:* Corded. BW-350.2, KM-743a, GB-344.

1 peso, silver, 7.49 g.

Obverse: At center, a Type 4 bust of Juárez, with legend **ESTADO L. Y S. DE OAXACA / ★ 1915 ★**. *Reverse:* Above a spray of oak and laurel, **UN / PESO**. At the top, **MONEDA PROVISONAL**. No **TM**. *Diameter:* 26.2 mm. *Edge:* Corded. BW-350.3, KM-740.1, GB-345.

1 peso, silver, 7.84 g.

Obverse: At center, a Type 4 bust of Juárez, with legend **ESTADO L. Y S. DE OAXACA / ★ 1915 ★**. *Reverse:* Above a spray of oak and laurel, **UN / PESO**. At the top, **MONEDA PROVISONAL**. No **TM**. *Diameter:* 26.3 mm. *Edge:* Corded. BW-350.4, KM-740.1, GB-346.

1 peso, silver, 7.85 g.

Obverse: At center, a Type 6 bust of Juárez, with legend **ESTADO L. Y S. DE OAXACA / ★ 1915 ★**. *Reverse:* Above a spray of oak and laurel, **UN / PESO**. At the top, **MONEDA PROVISONAL**. No **TM**. *Diameter:* 27.1 mm. *Edge:* Corded. BW-350.5, KM-742, GB-347.

1 peso, lead.

Obverse: At center, a Type 4 bust of Juárez, with legend **ESTADO L. Y S. DE OAXACA / ★ 1915 ★**. *Reverse:* Above a spray of oak and laurel, **UN / PESO**. At the top, **MONEDA PROVISONAL**. No **TM**. *Diameter:* 25.5 mm. *Edge:* Corded. BW-350.6, KM-UL, GB-349.

1 peso, copper.

Obverse: At center, a Type 6 bust of Juárez, with legend **ESTADO L. Y S. DE OAXACA / ★ 1915 ★**. *Reverse:* Above a spray of oak and laurel, **UN / PESO**. At the top, **MONEDA PROVISONAL**. No **TM**. *Diameter:* 25.5 mm. *Edge:* Plain. BW-350.7, KM-742a, GB-350.

2 pesos, silver-gold, 6.67 g.

Obverse: At center, a Type 5 bust of Juárez, with legend **ESTADO L. Y S. DE OAXACA / ★ 1915 ★**. *Reverse:* At center, above a spray of oak and laurel, a curved number **2**, encircled by finenesses **AG 0.902** and **AU 0.010** (above) and **PESOS.** (directly below). At the top, **MONEDA PROVISONAL**. Below the spray, initials **TM**. *Diameter:* 22.7 mm. *Edge:* Reeded. BW-351, KM-745, GB-351.

2 pesos, silver-gold, 6.39 g.

Obverse: At center, a Type 5 bust of Juárez, with legend **ESTADO L. Y S . DE OAXACA / ★ 1915 ★.** *Reverse:* At center, above a spray of oak and laurel, a curved number **2**, encircled by finenesses **AG 0.902** and **AU 0.010** (above) and **PESOS.** (directly below). At the top, **MONEDA PROVISONAL**. Below the spray, initials **TM**. *Diameter:* 22.4 mm. *Edge:* Reeded. BW-351.1, KM-745, GB-352.

2 pesos, copper.

Obverse: At center, a Type 10 bust of Juárez, with legend **ESTADO L. Y S . DE OAXACA / ★ 1915 ★.** *Reverse:* At center, above a spray of oak and laurel, a curved number **2**, encircled by finenesses **AG 0.902** and **AU 0.010** (above) and **PESOS.** (directly below). At the top, **MONEDA PROVISONAL**. Below the spray, initials **TM**. *Diameter:* 28.5 mm. *Edge:* Corded, with dots. BW-351.1a, KM-UL, GB-UL.

Note: Although the legend on the coin states that it is silver and gold, the composition is actually copper.

2 pesos, copper.

Obverse: At center, a Type 5 bust of Juárez, with legend **ESTADO L. Y S . DE OAXACA / ★ 1915 ★.** *Reverse:* At center, above a spray of oak and laurel, a curved number **2**, encircled by finenesses **AG 0.902** and **AU 0.010** (above) and **PESOS.** (directly below). At the top, **MONEDA PROVISONAL**. Below the spray, initials **TM**. *Diameter:* 22.5 mm. *Edge:* Plain. BW-351.2, KM-745a, GB-353.

Note: Although the legend on the coin states that it is silver and gold, the composition is actually copper.

2 pesos, silver-gold.

Obverse: At center, a Type 5 bust of Juárez, with legend **ESTADO L. Y S . DE OAXACA / ★ 1915 ★.** *Reverse:* At center, above a spray of oak and laurel, a curved number **2**, encircled by finenesses **AG 0.902** and **AU 0.010** (above) and **PESOS.** (directly below). At the top, **MONEDA PROVISONAL**. Below the spray, initials **TM**. *Diameter:* 26 mm. *Edge:* Corded. BW-351.3, KM-UL, GB-356.

2 pesos, silver, 16.39 g.

Obverse: At center, a Type 4 bust of Juárez, with legend **ESTADO L. Y S . DE OAXACA / ★ 1915 ★.** *Reverse:* Above a spray of oak and laurel, **2 / PESOS** with a shaded, curved number 2. At the top, **MONEDA PROVISONAL**; below the spray, initials **TM**. *Diameter:* 30.9 mm. *Edge:* Corded, with dots. BW-351.4, KM-744, GB-357.

2 pesos, copper.

Obverse: At center, a Type 10 bust of Juárez, with legend **ESTADO L. Y S . DE OAXACA / ★ 1915 ★.** *Reverse:* Above a spray of oak and laurel, **2 / PESOS** with an unshaded, flat number 2. At the top, **MONEDA PROVISONAL**. No **TM**. *Diameter:* 28 mm. *Edge:* Corded, with dots. BW-351.5, KM-749, GB-360.

2 pesos, silver.

Obverse: At center, a Type 7 bust of Juárez, with hand-engraved legend **ESTADO L. Y S. DE OAXACA / ★ 1915. ★.** *Reverse:* At center, below a small radiant liberty cap, a crossed sword and balance scale; between the pans of the scale, a scroll bearing the word **LEY**. Surrounding all, the hand-engraved legend **MONEDA PROVISONAL / DOS PESOS.** No **TM**. *Diameter:* 28.5 mm. *Edge:* Corded. BW-351.6, KM-UL, GB-UL.

2 pesos, silver, 13.18 g.

Obverse: At center, a Type 7 bust of Juárez, with legend **ESTADO L. Y S. DE OAXACA / ★ 1915 ★.** *Reverse:* At center, below a small radiant liberty cap, a crossed sword and balance scale; between the pans of the scale, a scroll bearing the word **LEY**. Surrounding all, the hand-engraved legend **MONEDA PROVISONAL / 2 PESOS.** No **TM**. *Diameter:* 33.6 mm. *Edge:* Corded. BW-351.7, KM-A746, GB-361.

2 pesos, silver, 14.40 g.

Obverse: At center, a Type 6 bust of Juárez, with legend ESTADO L. Y S. DE OAXACA / ★ 1915 ★. *Reverse:* At center, below a small radiant liberty cap, a crossed sword and balance scale; between the pans of the scale, a scroll bearing the word LEY. Surrounding all, the hand-engraved legend MONEDA PROVISONAL / 2 PESOS. No TM. *Diameter:* 33.7 mm. *Edge:* Corded. BW-351.8, KM-746, GB-362.

2 pesos, silver, 13.44 g.

Obverse: At center, a Type 6 bust of Juárez, with legend ESTADO L. Y S. DE OAXACA / ★ 1915 ★. *Reverse:* At center, below a small radiant liberty cap, a crossed sword and balance scale; between the pans of the scale, a scroll bearing the word LEY. Surrounding all, the hand-engraved legend MONEDA PROVISONAL. / DOS PESOS. No TM. *Diameter:* 33 mm. *Edge:* Corded. BW-351.9, KM-747.3, GB-363.

2 pesos, silver, 13.91 g.

Obverse: At center, a Type 6 bust of Juárez, with legend ESTADO L. Y S. DE OAXACA / ★ 1915. ★. *Reverse:* At center, below a small radiant liberty cap, a crossed sword and balance scale; between the pans of the scale, a scroll bearing the word LEY. Surrounding all, the hand-engraved legend MONEDA PROVISONAL / DOS PESOS. No TM. *Diameter:* 33 mm. *Edge:* Corded. BW-351.10, KM-747.1, GB-365.

2 pesos, silver, 13.44 g.

Obverse: At center, a Type 6 bust of Juárez, with legend ESTADO L. Y S. DE OAXACA / ★ 1915. ★. *Reverse:* At center, below a small radiant liberty cap, a crossed sword and balance scale; between the pans of the scale, a scroll bearing the word LEY. Surrounding all, the hand-engraved legend MONEDA PROVISONAL / DOS PESOS. No TM. *Diameter:* 33.5 mm. *Edge:* Corded. BW-351.11, KM-747.2, GB-366.

2 pesos, silver, 14.10 g.

Obverse: At center, a Type 6 bust of Juárez, with legend ESTADO L, Y S, DE OAXACA, / ★ 1915. ★. *Reverse:* At center, below a small radiant liberty cap, a crossed sword and balance scale; between the pans of the scale, a scroll bearing the word LEY. Surrounding all, the hand-engraved legend MONEDA PROVISONAL. / DOS PESOS. No TM. *Diameter:* 33.1 mm. *Edge:* Corded, with dots. BW-351.12, KM-747.3, GB-367.

5 pesos, silver-gold.

Obverse: At center, a Type 7 bust of Juárez, with legend ESTADO L. Y S. DE OAXACA / ★ 1915 ★. *Reverse:* At center, above a spray of oak and laurel, the number 5, encircled by finenesses AG 0.902 and AU 0.010 (above) and PESOS. (directly below). At the top, MONEDA PROVISONAL. Below the spray, initials TM. *Diameter:* 32 mm. *Edge:* Reeded. BW-352, KM-UL, GB-UL.

5 pesos, silver-gold, 16.97 g.

Obverse: At center, a Type 7 bust of Juárez, with legend ESTADO L. Y S. DE OAXACA / ★ 1915. ★. *Reverse:* At center, above a spray of oak and laurel, the number 5, encircled by finenesses AG 0.902 and AU 0.010 (above) and PESOS. (directly below). At the top, MONEDA PROVISONAL. Below the spray, initials TM. *Diameter:* 31.3 mm. *Edge:* Reeded. BW-352.1, KM-751, GB-368.

5 pesos, silver-gold.

Obverse: At center, a Type 7 bust of Juárez, with legend ESTADO L. Y S. DE OAXACA / ★ 1915 ★. *Reverse:* At center, above a spray of oak and laurel, the number 5, encircled by finenesses AG 0.902 and AU 0.010 (above) and PESOS. (directly below). At the top, MONEDA PROVISONAL. Below the spray, initials TM. *Diameter:* 30 mm. *Edge:* Reeded. BW-352.2, KM-UL, GB-370.

5 pesos, copper.

Obverse: At center, a Type 7 bust of Juárez, with legend ESTADO L. Y S. DE OAXACA / ★ 1915 ★. *Reverse:* At center, above a spray of oak and laurel, the number 5, encircled by finenesses AG 0.902 and AU 0.010 (above) and PESOS. (directly below). At the top, MONEDA PROVISONAL. Below the spray, initials TM. *Diameter:* 30 mm. *Edge:* Plain. BW-352.3, KM-751a, GB-371.

Note: Although the legend on the coin states that it is silver and gold, the composition is actually copper.

5 pesos, gold plated, 3.21 g.

Obverse: At center, a Type 3 bust of Juárez, with legend ESTADO L. Y S. DE OAXACA / ★ 1915 ★. *Reverse:* At center, above a spray of oak and laurel, 5 / PESOS. / 0.175 / ORO. At the top, MONEDA PROVISONAL; below the spray, initials TM. *Diameter:* 18.9 mm. *Edge:* Reeded. BW-352.4, KM-750, GB-372.

10 pesos, gold plated, 6.46 g.

Obverse: At center, a Type 5 bust of Juárez, with legend ESTADO L. Y S. DE OAXACA / ★ 1915 ★. *Reverse:* At center, above a spray of oak and laurel, 10 / PESOS / 0.175 / ORO. At the top, MONEDA PROVISONAL; below the spray, initials TM. *Diameter:* 23.4 mm. *Edge:* Reeded. BW-353, KM-UL, GB-374.

10 pesos, gold plated, 6.31 g.

Obverse: At center, a Type 5 bust of Juárez, with legend ESTADO L. Y S. DE OAXACA / ★ 1915 ★; the left star has four points. *Reverse:* At center, above a spray of oak and laurel, 10 / PESOS / 0.175 / ORO. At the top, MONEDA PROVISONAL; below the spray, initials TM. *Diameter:* 23.1 mm. *Edge:* Reeded. BW-353.1, KM-752, GB-375.

20 pesos, gold plated, 11.09 g.

Obverse: At center, a Type 5 bust of Juárez, with legend ESTADO L. Y S. DE OAXACA / ★ 1915. ★. *Reverse:* At center, above a spray of oak and laurel, 20 / PESOS / 0.175 / ORO. At the top, MONEDA PROVISONAL; below the spray, initials TM. *Diameter:* 27.5 mm. *Edge:* Reeded. BW-354, KM-753, GB-376.

20 pesos, gold plated, 11.69 g.

Obverse: At center, a Type 7 bust of Juárez, with legend ESTADO L. Y S. DE OAXACA / ★ 1915. ★. *Reverse:* At center, above a spray of oak and laurel, 20 / PESOS / 0.175 / ORO. At the top, MONEDA PROVISONAL; below the spray, initials TM. *Diameter:* 27.6 mm. *Edge:* Reeded. BW-354.1, KM-754, GB-377.

60 pesos, gold, 50.00 g.

Obverse: At center, a Type 10 bust of Juárez within an open wreath of laurel and oak. Surrounding all, legend ESTADO L. Y S. DE OAXACA / 60 PESOS ORO, within an ornate floral border. *Reverse:* At center, a radiant liberty cap over a balance scale of justice. Legend around, REPUBLICA MEXICANA 902.7 ★ T.M.★ 1916. *Diameter:* 40 mm. *Edge:* Reeded. BW-355, KM-755, GB-379.

60 pesos, silver.

Obverse: At center, a Type 10 bust of Juárez within an open wreath of laurel and oak. Surrounding all, legend ESTADO L. Y S. DE OAXACA / 60 PESOS ORO, within an ornate floral border. *Reverse:* At center, below a small radiant liberty cap, a crossed sword and balance scale; between the pans of the scale, a scroll bearing the word LEY. Legend REPUBLICA MEXICANA at top; below, fineness 902.7 with initials ★ T.M. ★ and 1916. *Diameter:* 40 mm. *Edge:* Reeded. BW-355.1, KM-755a, GB-380.

Note: Although the legend describes the coin as gold, its composition is silver.

60 pesos, copper.

Obverse: At center, a Type 10 bust of Juárez within an open wreath of laurel and oak. Surrounding all, legend ESTADO L. Y S. DE OAXACA / 60 PESOS ORO, within an ornate floral border. *Reverse:* At center, below a small radiant liberty cap, a crossed sword and balance scale; between the pans of the scale, a scroll bearing the word LEY. Legend REPUBLICA MEXICANA at top; below, fineness 902.7 with initials ★ T.M. ★ and 1916. *Diameter:* 40 mm. *Edge:* Plain. BW-355.2, KM-755b, GB-381.

Note: Although the legend describes the coin as gold, its composition is copper.

ESTADO DE PUEBLA

The state of Puebla is located southwest of Mexico City, in a region dominated by volcanoes and mountains. This is a highly industrial and educational area and is the current location of the Casa de Moneda de México.

Chiconcuautla, Puebla

The coins issued at Chiconcuautla were for the Francisco Madero Brigade, and were the only coins issued with Madero's name. The initials S.N.D.P. indicate that the coins were struck in the region of Sierra Norte de Puebla, under orders of General Esteban Márquez. The word TRANSITORIO means "transitional."

10 centavos, copper, 6.86 g.

Obverse: The national coat of arms, with 1915 below. Legend + BRIGADA FRAN CISCO I. MADERO +. *Reverse:* On a plain field, a roman numeral X superimposed on the centavo symbol (¢). Legend + TRAN SITORIO. + / S. N. DE PUEBLA. *Diameter:* 26.5 mm. *Edge:* Plain. BW-356, KM-756, GB-382.

20 centavos, copper, 8.84 g.

Obverse: The national coat of arms, with 1915 below. Legend + BRIGADA FRAN CISCO I. MADERO + / S.N.D.P. *Reverse:* At center, on a plain field, 20 / CENTAVOS. At the top, + TRANSITORIO +. *Diameter:* 29.2 mm. *Edge:* Plain. BW-357, KM-757, GB-383.

20 centavos, copper, 10.15 g.

Obverse: The national coat of arms, with 1915 below. Legend + BRIGADA FRAN CISCO I. MADERO + / S.N.D.P. *Reverse:* At center, on a plain field, 20 / CENTAVOS. At the top, TRANSITORIO. *Diameter:* 28.6 mm. *Edge:* Plain. BW-357.1, KM-758, GB-392.

Other varieties of the 20 centavos exist.

Tetela del Oro y Ocampo, Puebla

Tetela del Oro y Ocampo was a mining district located in northern Puebla. It was named in honor of Melchor Ocampo, a lawyer who served in many important positions, including as governor of Michoacán during the United States invasion in 1847. His remains are interred in the Rotonda de las Personas Ilustres in Mexico City.

2 centavos, copper, 2.34 g.

Obverse: At center, the national coat of arms, with sprigs of oak and laurel from the sides of the base. Legend REPUBLICA MEXICANA at the top, 1915 at the bottom. *Reverse:* At center, c. 2 s. ("c.s." for "centavos"). Legend TETELA DEL ORO Y OCAMPO E. PUE. *Diameter:* 17.3 mm. *Edge:* Plain. BW-358, KM-759, GB-394.

Note: Restrikes exist; they were struck with rusty dies, and the effects are obvious.

2 centavos, copper, 3.75 g.

Obverse: At center, within a circle of dots, the national coat of arms, with sprigs of oak and laurel from the sides of the base. Between the dotted circle and an outer border of dots, legend REPUBLICA MEXICANA / 1915. *Reverse:* At center, within a circle of dots, 2 / CENTAVOS. Between the dotted circle and an outer border of dots, legend TETELA DEL ORO Y OCAMPO E. DE PU. *Diameter:* 20.9 mm. *Edge:* Plain. BW-358.1, KM-760, GB-395.

5 centavos, copper, 4.41 g.

Obverse: At center, within a circle of dots, the national coat of arms, with sprigs of oak and laurel from the sides of the base. Between the dotted circle and an outer border of dots, legend REPUBLICA MEXICANA / 1915. *Reverse:* At center, within a circle of dots, 5 / CENTAVOS. Between the dotted circle and an outer border of dots, legend TETELA DEL ORO Y OCAMPO E. DE PUE. *Diameter:* 21.1 mm. *Edge:* Plain. BW-359, KM-762, GB-397.

10 centavos, copper, 2.90 g.

Obverse: At center, within a circle of dots, **10 / cs.** Between the dotted circle and an outer border of dots, legend **TETELA DEL ORO Y OCAMPO E. DE PUE.** *Reverse:* Uniface. *Diameter:* 20.1 mm. *Edge:* Plain. BW-369T, KM-763, GB-401.

20 centavos, copper, 8.13 g.

Obverse: At center, within a circle of dots, the national coat of arms, with sprigs of oak and laurel from the sides of the base. Between the dotted circle and an outer border of dots, legend **REPUBLICA MEXICANA / 1915.** *Reverse:* At center, within a circle of dots, **20 / cvs.** Between the dotted circle and an outer border of dots, legend **TETELA DEL ORO Y OCAMPO E. DE PUE.** *Diameter:* 24.1 mm. *Edge:* Plain. BW-360, KM-764, GB-402.

20 centavos, silver.

Obverse: At center, within a circle of dots, the national coat of arms, with sprigs of oak and laurel from the sides of the base. Between the dotted circle and an outer border of dots, legend **REPUBLICA MEXICANA / 1915.** *Reverse:* At center, within a circle of dots, **20 / cvs.** Between the dotted circle and an outer border of dots, legend **TETELA DEL ORO Y OCAMPO E. DE PUE.** *Diameter:* 24 mm. *Edge:* Plain. BW-360.1, KM-UL, GB-403.

ESTADO DE SINALOA

The state of Sinaloa is located on northern Mexico's western coast. Agriculture and industry make up the largest shares of the state's economy.

The first Revolutionary coins from Sinaloa were minted in June and July of 1914. The Liberty Cap pesos of 1889 to 1909 were used to sand-cast crude coins. The silver used in the castings was from El Rosario, a mine in Sinaloa, as ordered by General Rafael Buelna. The **G.C.** counterstamp stands for Gobierno Constitucionalista (Constitutional Government). Most of these coins were melted when it was discovered that the ore from which they were made contained a high content of gold.

Carlos Gaytán, in *La Revolución Mexicana y Sus Monedas* (1969), stated that in May 1965, Sir Juan de Dios Batiz had reported that all Sinaloa sand-cast pesos were made in one session in 1914—not 1913, as had previously been thought—on the orders of General Rafael Buelna (who was in Rosario, Sinaloa) and General Juan Carrasco (in the state capital, Culiacán).

20 centavos, cast silver.

The design is the same as that on the regular-issue 20 centavos of 1898–1905. *Obverse:* The national coat of arms with legend **REPUBLICA MEXICANA** above and the date below. *Reverse:* At center, above a spray of oak and laurel, **20 / CENTAVOS.** At the top, the mintmark, the assayer mark (followed by a dot), and fineness **902.7.** *Diameter:* 23 mm. *Edge:* Plain. BW-370, KM-765, GB-404.

50 centavos, cast silver, 13.18 g.

The design is the same as that on the regular-issue 50 centavos of 1905–1914. *Obverse:* Above a spray of oak and laurel, the national coat of arms, with legend **ESTADOS UNIDOS MEXICANOS.** *Reverse:* At the top, above a half-wreath of oak and laurel, a radiant liberty cap. At center, **50 / CENTAVOS,** with the date below. *Diameter:* 29.3 mm. *Edge:* Plain. BW-371, KM-766, GB-405.

50 centavos, cast silver.

The design is the same as that on the regular-issue 50 centavos of 1905–1914. *Obverse:* Above a spray of oak and laurel, the national coat of arms, with legend **ESTADOS UNIDOS MEXICANOS.** *Reverse:* At the top, above a half-wreath of oak and laurel, a radiant liberty cap. At center, **50 / CENTAVOS,** with the date below. **G.C.** counterstamp. *Diameter:* 31 mm. *Edge:* Plain. BW-371.1, KM-767, GB-407.

Note: Beware of coins with counterfeit counterstamps.

1 peso, cast silver.
The design is the same as that on the regular-issue Liberty Cap peso of 1898–1909. *Obverse:* Above a spray of oak and laurel, the national coat of arms, with legend REPUBLICA MEXICANA. *Reverse:* At center, a large radiant liberty cap, surrounded by legend with UN PESO, the mintmark, the date (followed by a dot), the assayer mark (followed by a dot), and fineness 902.7. *Diameter:* 39 mm. *Edge:* Plain. BW-372, KM-769, GB-406.

1 peso, cast silver.
The design is the same as that on the regular-issue Liberty Cap peso of 1898–1909. *Obverse:* Above a spray of oak and laurel, the national coat of arms, with legend REPUBLICA MEXICANA. *Reverse:* At center, a large radiant liberty cap, surrounded by legend with UN PESO, the mintmark, the date (followed by a dot), the assayer mark (followed by a dot), and fineness 902.7. Counterstamped G.C. *Diameter:* 39 mm. *Edge:* Plain. BW-372.1, KM-770, GB-408.

ESTADO DE ZACATECAS

The Concepción del Oro mine was located in the northeast region of the state of Zacatecas. It was the source of one of the rarest coins pertaining to the Mexican Revolution. Little is known at this time about these pieces; two varieties are known, with two known examples of each variety. The obverses of the two types are the same, while the reverses are different (Type 2 has a shorter legend, and a different cap and rays).

1 peso, silver, 22.61 g. Type 1.
Obverse: The national coat of arms, with legend REPUBLICA MEXICANA C. DEL ORO ZAC 1915. *Reverse:* At center, a radiant liberty cap. Legend LIB. IGUAL. Y JUSTICIA UN PESO. *Diameter:* 39 mm. BW-373, GB-UL, KM-UL.

1 peso, silver, 22.61 g. Type 2.
Obverse: The national coat of arms, with legend REPUBLICA MEXICANA C. DEL ORO ZAC 1915. *Reverse:* At center, a radiant liberty cap. Legend UN PESO E R (with the E and R at nine o'clock and three o'clock, respectively). *Diameter:* 39 mm. BW-374, GB-UL, KM-UL.

Coinage of the Mexican Revolution

Estado de Aguascalientes. 20 centavos. 1915. BW-279.6, KM-605, GB-26, 29.2 mm.

Estado de Chihuahua, Constitutional Army. 5 centavos. 1915. GB-55, 25 mm.

Estado de Chihuahua, Constitutional Army. 10 centavos. 1915. GB-67, 27 mm.

Estado de Chihuahua, Constitutional Army. 50 centavos. 1914. BW-282p, KM-UL, GB-70, 30 mm.

Coinage of the Mexican Revolution
(continued)

Estado de Chihuahua, Hidalgo del Parral. 2 centavos. 1914. BW-284, KM-607a, GB-74, 24.9 mm.

Estado de Chihuahua, Constitutional Army. 1 peso. 1914. BW-283p, KM-PN3, GB-71, 39 mm.

Estado de Chihuahua, Hidalgo del Parral. 50 centavos. 1913. BW-285, KM-608, GB-76, 30 mm.

Estado de Chihuahua, Hidalgo del Parral. 1 peso (the "Bolita peso"). 1913. BW-286, KM-610, GB-78, 38.6 mm.

Estado de Chihuahua, Hidalgo del Parral. 1 peso (the "Parral peso"). 1913. BW-286.1, KM-611, GB-79, 38.8 mm.

Estado de Chihuahua, Hidalgo del Parral. 1 peso. No date (1913). BW-286.2, KM-PN1, GB-80, 38 mm.

Coinage of the Mexican Revolution

(continued)

Estado de Chihuahua, Army of the North. 1 peso. 1913. BW-287.2, KM-619, GB-72, 39 mm.

Estado de Durango, Cuencamé. 1 peso (the "Six Star peso"). 1914. BW-288.1, KM-620, GB-82, 39 mm.

Estado de Durango, Cuencamé. 1 peso (a "Muera Huerta peso"). 1914. BW-288.4, KM-621a, GB-86, 38.8 mm.

Estado de Durango, City of Durango. 5 centavos. 1914. BW-290.1, KM-UL, GB-115, 24 mm.

Estado de Guerrero, Cacahuatepec. 50 centavos. 1917. BW-316, KM-650, GB-149, 30.3 mm.

Estado de Guerrero, Atlixtac. 2 pesos. 1914. BW-313.6, KM-UL, GB-146.5, 37.5 mm.

Estado de Guerrero, Cacalotepec. 20 centavos. 1917. BW-318, KM-652, GB-151, 22.5 mm.

Coinage of the Mexican Revolution

(continued)

Estado de Guerrero, Campo Morado. 50 centavos. 1915. BW-301.5, KM-657, GB-165, 30.6 mm.

Estado de Guerrero, Campo Morado. 2 pesos. 1915. BW-303, KM-660, GB-174, 38.7 mm.

Estado de Guerrero, Chilpancingo. 20 centavos. 1915. BW-305, KM-664, GB-181, 22 mm.

Estado de Guerrero, Suriana. 2 pesos. 1915. GB-224, 39 mm.

Estado de Guerrero, Taxco. 5 centavos. 1916. BW-307, KM-688, GB-226, 28 mm.

Estado de Guerrero, Taxco. 1 peso. 1915. GB-235, 30 mm.

Estado de Guerrero. 25 centavos. 1915. BW-294, KM-639, GB-189, 25 mm.

Coinage of the Mexican Revolution

(continued)

Estado de Guerrero. 2 pesos. 1914. BW-297.4, KM-644, GB-213, 38.8 mm.

Estado de Jalisco, Guadalajara. 1 centavo. 1915. BW-319, KM-675, GB-239, 19.3 mm.

Estado de Jalisco, Guadalajara. 10 centavos. 1915. BW-322, KM-678, GB-243, 25 mm.

Estado de Mexico, Amecameca. 20 centavos. No date. BW-326.1, KM-683, GB-250, 20 mm.

Estado de Mexico, Amecameca. 25 centavos. No date. BW-327.1, KM-685, GB-252, 25.1 mm.

Estado de Mexico, Mexico City. 2 centavos. 1915. BW-M329, KM-420, GB-257, 20 mm.

Estado de Mexico, Tenancingo. 5 centavos. 1915. BW-330, KM-689.1, GB-259, 19.2 mm.

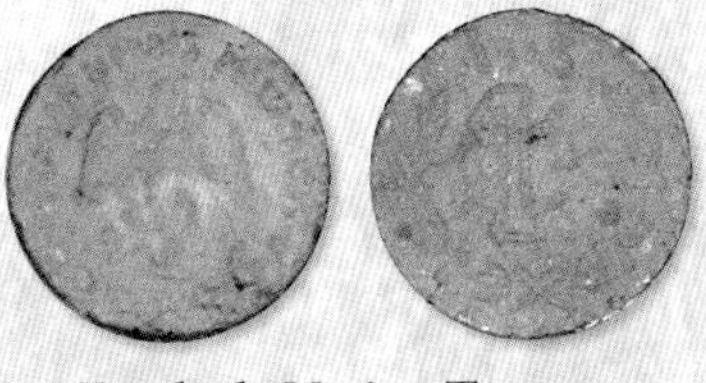

Estado de Mexico, Texcoco. 1 centavo. 1915. BW-T332, KM-UL, GB-262, 22 mm.

Estado de Mexico, Toluca. 40 centavos. 1906. BW-335.1, KM-694, GB-268, 25 mm.

Coinage of the Mexican Revolution
(continued)

Estado de Mexico, Toluca. 5 centavos. 1915.
BW-333, KM-692.1, GB-263, 28.5 mm.

Estado de Morelos, Atlihuayan. 10 centavos.
1915. BW-338.3, KM-699, GB-275, 30 mm.

Estado de Morelos, Atlihuayan. 50 centavos.
1916. BW-340.3, KM-704, GB-282, 30 mm.

Estado de Oaxaca. 3 centavos. 1915. BW-345,
KM-711, GB-290, 24.8 mm x 16.9 mm.

Estado de Oaxaca. 5 centavos. 1915.
BW-346, KM-716, GB-300, 22 mm.

Estado de Oaxaca. 10 centavos.
1915. GB-319, 27 mm.

Estado de Oaxaca. 10 centavos,
with GV counterstamp. 1915.
BW-347.1, KM-727.3, GB-320, 26.5 mm.

Estado de Oaxaca. 20 centavos. 1915. 20C,
BW-348.2, KM-728a, GB-328, 28.6 mm.

Estado de Oaxaca. 50 centavos. 1915.
BW-349.2, KM-736, GB-337, 22.3 mm.

Estado de Oaxaca. 1 peso. 1915.
BW-350.3, KM-740.1, GB-345, 26.2 mm.

Coinage of the Mexican Revolution

(continued)

Estado de Oaxaca. 2 pesos. 1915. BW-351, KM-745, GB-351, 22.7 mm.

Estado de Oaxaca. 2 pesos. 1915. BW-351.1, KM-745, GB-352, 22.4 mm.

Estado de Oaxaca. 2 pesos. 1915. BW-351.4, KM-744, GB-357, 30.9 mm.

Estado de Oaxaca. 2 pesos. 1915. BW-351.11, KM-747.2, GB-366, 33.5 mm.

Estado de Oaxaca. 5 pesos. 1915. BW-352.1, KM-751, GB-368, 31.3 mm.

Estado de Oaxaca. 10 pesos, gold plated. 1915. BW-353, KM-UL, GB-374, 23.4 mm.

Estado de Oaxaca. 20 pesos, gold plated. 1915. BW-354, KM-753, GB-376, 27.5 mm.

Estado de Oaxaca. 60 pesos. 1916. BW-355, KM-755, GB-379, 40 mm.

Coinage of the Mexican Revolution
(continued)

Estado de Puebla, Tetela del Oro y Ocampo. 5 centavos. 1915. BW-359, KM-762, GB-397, 21.1 mm.

Estado de Sinaloa. 20 centavos. No date (1915). BW-370, KM-765, GB-404, 23 mm.

Estado de Sinaloa. 1 peso. No date (1914). BW-372, KM-769, GB-406, 39 mm.

13

The Coinage Reform of 1905

At the beginning of the 20th century, the coinage of Mexico was in disarray. All the branch mints were under private contracts, the copper coins were too large and too expensive to mint for their face value, and gold and silver coins were of a fineness that was not in general use by other countries. This complicated trade: Mexican silver coinage before the reform was 0.9027 fine, whereas British sterling was 0.925 and the common fineness in the United States and most Latin American countries was 0.900. Mexican gold coins were 0.875 fine; elsewhere, they were almost universally 0.900 fine.

Leading up to the 1905 reform, the branch mints' contracts were beginning to come up for renewal—at San Luis Potosí and Oaxaca in 1893, and elsewhere in 1905. This was Mexico's opportunity to close the branch mints and move all minting operations to Mexico City, at the Apartado Mint, which had been founded by decree on May 11, 1535. The Apartado Mint had first been located at Casa de Axayácatl, the current location of the Nacional Monte de Piedad (National Pawnshop); it later moved to the location now occupied by the Palacio Nacional (National Palace). The mint was moved again in 1569 to a location on Calle de Moneda (Money Street). In March 1848 construction of the new Apartado Mint began, and the first coinage from this mint was produced on June 1, 1850.

The coinage reform of 1905 changed the status of the Apartado Mint from the Mexico City Mint to the Mexico Mint. The Legaria Mint opened in 1970, utilizing all state-of-the-art equipment to strike silver, gold, and platinum commemorative coinage as well as circulation coinage. In 1983 the San Luis Potosí Mint began supplementing the increased need for coinage minted at the Legaria facility, and continued to play a supplementary role until 1999, when minting operations were moved from Legaria to San Luis Potosí. This minting facility is the only plant that strikes coinage for Mexico displaying the famous M° mintmark.

Over the years, Mexican coinage has also been struck at various mints outside the country, including the U.S. mints in New Orleans and San Francisco and the Brooklyn, N.Y., operation of the Benziger Brothers; and the mint in Birmingham, England.

Due to the price fluctuations of precious metals, and the changing economic conditions of Mexico over the years, the size and fineness of various coins have changed from time to time to fit existing circumstances. Because of these conditions, the selections of denominations issued have also changed.

In this chapter, for each denomination we list the basic types, along with the common terms (if any) by which those types are known to collectors. We limit varieties, for the most part, to overdates, positioning of dates, and other results of the minting process; more are listed in volume 2, *Modern Coinage*, which presents the full catalog format for the 1905 coinage reform, including mintages, valuations, and additional images.

The numerous varieties in the 1905 and 1992 coinage reforms can also be found in the *Illustrated Price Guide of the Modern Mexican Coins 1905 to Date*, by Carlos Abel Amaya Guerra.

1 CENTAVO

Centavos under the Reform of 1905 fall into six basic types. The types and dates, along with the terms by which collectors commonly reference them, are as follows:

Type 1 (1905–1915)—Monogram (with the value depicted as a "monogram," in which the numeral is superimposed on a horizontally shaded centavo symbol, ¢)

Type 2 (1915)—Zapatista (like Type 1, but struck at the Mexico City Mint while it was under the control of Zapata's troops; distinguishable from Type 1 coins of 1915 by their smaller size)

Type 3 (1916–1943)—Monogram (same as Type 1, but with less tin and more zinc in the composition)

Type 4 (1944–1949)—Monogram (same as Type 3, but with even less tin and more zinc in the composition)

Type 5 (1950–1969)—Brass (with a wheat-ear design instead of a monogram on the reverse)

Type 6 (1970–1973)—Brass, Reduced (same as Type 5, but 3 mm smaller in diameter)

1 centavo, 0.950 copper, 0.040 tin, 0.010 zinc; 3 g. Type 1 (Monogram).

Obverse: The national coat of arms above a spray of oak and laurel, with legend ESTADOS UNIDOS MEXICANOS. *Reverse:* At center, within an open wreath of laurel, a large number 1 superimposed on a horizontally shaded centavo symbol (¢). At the top, between wreath tips, the date; below the wreath, mintmark M°. *Diameter:* 20 mm. *Edge:* Smooth. BW-501, KM-415.

Date	Comment
1905	
1906	Wide date
1906	Narrow date
1910	
1911	Wide date
1911	Narrow date
1912	
1913	
1914	
1915	

1 centavo, 0.950 copper, 0.025 tin, 0.025 zinc; 1.5 g. Type 2 (Zapatista).

Obverse: The national coat of arms above a spray of oak and laurel, with legend ESTADOS UNIDOS MEXICANOS. *Reverse:* At center, within an open wreath of laurel, a large number 1 superimposed on a horizontally shaded centavo symbol (¢). At the top, between wreath tips, the date; below the wreath, mintmark M°. *Diameter:* 16 mm. *Edge:* Smooth. BW-502, KM-416.

Date	Comment
1915	

1 centavo, 0.950 copper, 0.025 tin, 0.025 zinc; 3 g. Type 3 (Monogram).

Obverse: The national coat of arms above a spray of oak and laurel, with legend ESTADOS UNIDOS MEXICANOS. *Reverse:* At center, within an open wreath of laurel, a large number 1 superimposed on a horizontally shaded centavo symbol (¢). At the top, between wreath tips, the date; below the wreath, mintmark M°. *Diameter:* 20 mm. *Edge:* Smooth. BW-501.1, KM-415.

Date	Comment
1916	Narrow date
1916	Wide date
1920	
1921	
1922	
1922	Date to left

Date	Comment
1923	
1924	
1924/3	
1925	
1926	
1927	
1927/6	
1928	
1929	
1930	
1933	
1933	Low 1
1934	
1935	
1936	
1937	
1938	
1939	
1940	
1941	
1942	
1943	

1 centavo, 0.950 copper, 0.040 tin, 0.010 zinc; 3 g. Type 4 (Monogram). *Obverse:* The national coat of arms above a spray of oak and laurel, with legend ESTADOS UNIDOS MEXICANOS. *Reverse:* At center, within an open wreath of laurel, a large number 1 superimposed on a horizontally shaded centavo symbol (¢). At the top, between wreath tips, the date; below the wreath, mintmark M̊. *Diameter:* 20 mm. *Edge:* Smooth. BW-503, KM-415.

Date	Comment
1944	
1945	
1946	
1947	
1948	
1949	

1 centavo, 0.850 copper, 0.150 zinc; 2 g. Type 5 (Brass). *Obverse:* Above a spray of oak and laurel, the national coat of arms with the eagle facing left. Legend ESTADOS UNIDOS MEXICANOS. *Reverse:* A stylized sprig of wheat with three ears; the central, vertical ear divides the denomination 1 / C. At bottom left, the date; at bottom right, mintmark M̊. *Diameter:* 16 mm. *Edge:* Smooth. BW-504, KM-417.

Date	Comment
1950	
1951	
1951	Far 1
1952	
1953	
1954	
1955	
1956	
1957	
1958	
1959	
1960	
1961	
1962	
1963	
1964	
1965	
1966	
1967	
1968	
1969	

1 centavo, 0.850 copper, 0.150 zinc; 1.5 g. Type 6 (Brass, Reduced). *Obverse:* Above a spray of oak and laurel, the national coat of arms with the eagle facing left. Legend ESTADOS UNIDOS MEXICANOS. *Reverse:* A stylized sprig of wheat with three ears; the central, vertical ear divides the denomination 1 / C. At bottom left, the date; at bottom right, mintmark M̊. *Diameter:* 13 mm. *Edge:* Smooth. BW-505, KM-418.

Date	Comment
1970	
1972/0	
1972	
1973	

2 CENTAVOS

The 2 centavos under the Reform of 1905 fall into three basic types. Collectors refer to these as follows:

> Type 1 (1905 and 1906)—Bronze (with the value depicted as a monogram—in which the numeral is superimposed on a horizontally shaded centavo symbol, ¢—but described by collectors according to its metallic composition)
>
> Type 2 (1915)—Zapatista (like Type 1, but struck at the Mexico City mint while it was under the control of Zapata's troops; distinguishable from Type 1 coins of 1915 by their smaller size)
>
> Type 3 (1920–1941)—Bronze (like Type 1, but with less tin and more zinc in the composition)

2 centavos, 0.950 copper, 0.040 tin, 0.010 zinc; 6 g. Type 1 (Bronze).

Obverse: The national coat of arms above a spray of oak and laurel, with legend ESTADOS UNIDOS MEXICANOS. *Reverse:* At center, within an open wreath of laurel, a large number 2 superimposed on a horizontally shaded centavo symbol (¢). At the top, between wreath tips, the date; below the wreath, mintmark M°. *Diameter:* 25 mm. *Edge:* Smooth. BW-506, KM-419.

Date	Comment
1905	
1906	Wide date
1906	Narrow date
1906	Inverted 6

2 centavos, 0.950 copper, 0.025 tin, 0.025 zinc, 3 g. Type 2 (Zapatista).

Obverse: The national coat of arms above a spray of oak and laurel, with legend ESTADOS UNIDOS MEXICANOS. *Reverse:* At center, within an open wreath of laurel, a large number 2 superimposed on a horizontally shaded centavo symbol (¢). At the top, between wreath tips, the date; below the wreath, mintmark M°. *Diameter:* 20 mm. *Edge:* Smooth. BW-507, KM-420.

Note: These reduced-size 2-centavo coins were struck at the Mexico City mint while it was under the control of Zapata's troops, and are commonly referred to as "Zapatista" coins.

Date	Comment
1915	

2 centavos, 0.950 copper, 0.025 tin, 0.025 zinc; 6 g. Type 3 (Bronze).

Obverse: The national coat of arms above a spray of oak and laurel, with legend ESTADOS UNIDOS MEXICANOS. *Reverse:* At center, within an open wreath of laurel, a large number 2 superimposed on a horizontally shaded centavo symbol (¢). At the top, between wreath tips, the date; below the wreath, mintmark M°. *Diameter:* 25 mm. *Edge:* Smooth. BW-506.1, KM-419.

Date	Comment
1920	
1921	
1922	
1924	
1925	
1926	
1926/26	
1927	
1928	
1929	
1935	
1939	
1941	

5 CENTAVOS

The Mexican 5 centavos under the Reform of 1905 were made in seven basic types. These are commonly referenced by collectors as follows:

Type 1 (1905–1914)—Nickel (with the value depicted as 5 CENTAVOS and surrounded by a geometric border)

Type 2 (1914–1935)—Monogram (with the value depicted as a monogram, in which the numeral is superimposed on a horizontally shaded centavo symbol, ¢)

Type 3 (1936–1942)—Aztec Calendar (with the border on the reverse depicting the ancient Aztec Calendar stone)

Type 4 (1942–1955)—Josefa Grande (with a bust of Josefa Ortiz de Domínguez, insurgent supporter during the War of Independence)

Type 5 (1950)—White Josefa (with a different bust of Josefa Ortiz de Domínguez, and with more nickel in the composition, yielding a whitish appearance)

Type 6 (1954–1969)—Brass (similar to Type 5, but in brass)

Type 7 (1970–1976)—Brass, Reduced (similar to Type 6, but 2.5 mm smaller in diameter)

5 centavos, 1.00 nickel; 5 g. Type 1 (Nickel).

Obverse: The national coat of arms above a spray of oak and laurel, with legend ESTADOS UNIDOS MEXICANOS. *Reverse:* At center, a large, horizontally shaded number 5 with CENTAVOS below and the date above. Between the date and the 5, mintmark M. Surrounding all, an elaborate geometric border with an inner ring of beads. *Diameter:* 20 mm. *Edge:* Smooth. BW-508, KM-421.

Date	Comment
1905	
1906/5	
1906	
1907	
1909	
1910	
1911	Narrow date
1911	Wide date
1912	Small mintmark
1912	Large mintmark
1913	
1914	Narrow date

5 centavos, 0.950 copper, 0.025 tin, 0.025 zinc; 9 g. Type 2 (Monogram).

Obverse: The national coat of arms above a spray of oak and laurel, with legend ESTADOS UNIDOS MEXICANOS. *Reverse:* At center, within an open wreath of laurel, a large number 5 superimposed on a horizontally shaded centavo symbol (¢). At the top, between wreath tips, the date; below the wreath, mintmark M̊. *Diameter:* 28 mm. *Edge:* Smooth. BW-509, KM-422.

Date	Comment
1914	
1915	
1916	
1917	
1918	
1919	
1920	
1921	
1924	
1925	
1926	
1927	
1927	Repunched 2/2
1928	Large date
1928	Small date
1929	
1930	Large, oval 0
1930	Small, square 0
1931	
1931	Inclined 3
1933	
1934	
1935	

5 centavos, 0.800 copper, 0.200 nickel; 4 g. Type 3 (Aztec Calendar).

Obverse: Above a spray of oak and laurel, the national coat of arms with the eagle facing left. Legend **ESTADOS UNIDOS MEXICANOS**. *Reverse:* At center, a large number 5 shaded in a basket-weave pattern, with **CENTAVOS** below and the date above. Between the date and the 5, mintmark **M**. Surrounding all, a broad, elaborate border depicting the Aztec calendar. *Diameter:* 20.5 mm. *Edge:* Smooth. BW-510, KM-423.

Date	Comment
1936	
1937	
1938	
1940	
1942	

5 centavos, 0.950 copper, 0.010 tin, 0.040 zinc; 6.5 g. Type 4 (Josefa Grande).

Obverse: Above a spray of oak and laurel, the national coat of arms with the eagle facing left. Legend **ESTADOS UNIDOS MEXICANOS**. *Reverse:* A left-facing head of Josefa Ortiz de Domínguez (insurgent and supporter of the War of Independence), with **CINCO CENTAVOS / ★ [date] ★** surrounding. Mintmark M̊ in the field to the right of the head. *Diameter:* 25.5 mm. *Edge:* Smooth. BW-511, KM-424.

Date	Comment
1942	
1943	
1944	
1945	
1946	
1951	
1952	
1953	
1954	
1955	

5 centavos, 0.750 copper, 0.250 nickel; 4 g. Type 5 (White Josefa).

Obverse: Above a spray of oak and laurel, the national coat of arms with the eagle facing left. Legend **ESTADOS UNIDOS MEXICANOS**. *Reverse:* A right-facing bust of Josefa Ortiz de Domínguez (insurgent and supporter of the War of Independence). To left of the bust, **1950** and mintmark M̊. To right of the bust, the number 5 above C^{S} (centavos) with a dot below. *Diameter:* 20.5 mm. *Edge:* Smooth. BW-512, KM-425.

Date	Comment
1950	

5 centavos, 0.850 copper, 0.150 zinc; 4 g. Type 6 (Brass).

Obverse: Above a spray of oak and laurel, the national coat of arms with the eagle facing left. Legend **ESTADOS UNIDOS MEXICANOS**. *Reverse:* A right-facing bust of Josefa Ortiz de Domínguez (insurgent and supporter of the War of Independence), with **CINCO CENTAVOS** above. Mintmark M̊ and the date in the field to the right of the bust. *Diameter:* 20.5 mm. *Edge:* Smooth. BW-513, KM-426.

Date	Comment
1954	Dot back of head
1954	No dot
1955	
1956	
1957	
1958	
1959	
1960	
1960	Copper-nickel
1961	
1962	
1962	Copper-nickel
1963	
1964	
1965	
1965	Copper-nickel
1966	
1967	
1968	
1969	

5 centavos, 0.850 copper, 0.150 zinc; 2.75 g. Type 7 (Brass, Reduced).

Obverse: Above a spray of oak and laurel, the national coat of arms with the eagle facing left. Legend ESTADOS UNIDOS MEXICANOS. *Reverse:* A right-facing bust of Josefa Ortiz de Domínguez (insurgent and supporter of the War of Independence), with CINCO CENTAVOS / $\overset{o}{M}$ / [date] surrounding. *Diameter:* 18 mm. *Edge:* Smooth. BW-514, KM-427.

Date	Comment
1970	
1971	
1972	
1973	Flat-top 3
1973	Round-top 3
1974	
1975	
1976	

10 CENTAVOS

The 10 centavos under the Reform of 1905 were made in seven basic types, commonly referenced by collectors as follows:

Type 1 (1905–1914)—.800 (with small radiant liberty cap on the reverse)

Type 2 (1919)—Little .800 (like Type 1, but 3 mm smaller in diameter, and with slightly different composition)

Type 3 (1919–1921, 1935)—Large Bronze (with the value depicted as a monogram, in which the numerals are superimposed on a horizontally shaded centavo symbol, ¢)

Type 4 (1925–1935)—.720 (same as Type 2, but with reduced silver content)

Type 5 (1936–1946)—Aztec Calendar (with the border on the reverse depicting the ancient Aztec Calendar stone)

Type 6 (1955–1967)—Juárez (depicting Revolutionary president Benito Juárez)

Type 7 (1974–1980)—Ear of Corn (depicting an ear of corn or *maize*, an agricultural staple)

10 centavos, 0.800 silver, 0.200 copper; 2.5 g. Type 1 (.800).

Obverse: The national coat of arms above a spray of oak and laurel, with legend ESTADOS UNIDOS MEXICANOS. *Reverse:* At the top, above an open wreath of oak and laurel, a small radiant liberty cap. On the radiance below the cap, a horizontally shaded number 10 with CENTAVOS below; date just above the bow on the wreath. Mintmark M below and slightly between the digits of the 10. *Diameter:* 18 mm. *Edge:* Reeded. BW-515, KM-428.

Date	Comment
1905	
1906	
1907	
1907/6	
1909	
1910	
1910/00	
1911	Narrow date
1911	Wide date
1912	
1912	Low 2
1912	Narrow date
1912	Wide date
1913	
1913/2	
1914	

10 centavos, 0.800 silver, 0.200 copper; 1.8125 g. Type 2 (Little .800).

Obverse: The national coat of arms above a spray of oak and laurel, with legend ESTADOS UNIDOS MEXICANOS. *Reverse:* At the top, above an open wreath of oak and laurel, a small radiant liberty cap. On the radiance below the cap, a horizontally shaded number 10 with CENTAVOS / 1919 below. Mintmark M below and slightly between the digits of the denomination. *Diameter:* 15 mm. *Edge:* Reeded. BW-516, KM-429.

Date	Comment
1919	

10 centavos, 0.950 copper, 0.025 tin, 0.025 zinc; 12 g. Type 3 (Large Bronze).

Obverse: The national coat of arms above a spray of oak and laurel, with legend ESTADOS UNIDOS MEXICANOS. *Reverse:* At center, within an open wreath of laurel, a large number 10 superimposed on a horizontally shaded centavo symbol (¢). At the top, between wreath tips, the date; below the wreath, mintmark M̊. *Diameter:* 30.5 mm. *Edge:* Plain. BW-517, KM-430.

Date	Comment
1919	
1920	
1921	
1935	

10 centavos, 0.720 silver, 0.280 copper; 1.666 g. Type 4 (.720).

Obverse: The national coat of arms above a spray of oak and laurel, with legend ESTADOS UNIDOS MEXICANOS. *Reverse:* At the top, above an open wreath of oak and laurel, a small radiant liberty cap. On the radiance below the cap, a horizontally shaded number 10 with CENTAVOS below; date just above the bow on the wreath. Mintmark M below and slightly between the digits of the 10. *Diameter:* 15 mm. *Edge:* Reeded. BW-518, KM-431.

Date	Comment
1925	
1925/15	
1925/3	
1926	
1926/16	
1927	
1927 9/6	2/6/7
1928	
1930	
1933	
1934	
1935	

10 centavos, 0.800 copper, 0.200 nickel; 5.5 g. Type 5 (Aztec Calendar).

Obverse: Above a spray of oak and laurel, the national coat of arms with the eagle facing left. Legend ESTADOS UNIDOS MEXICANOS. *Reverse:* At center, a large number 10 shaded in a basket-weave pattern, with CENTAVOS below and the date above. Between the date and the 10, mintmark M. Surrounding all, a broad, elaborate border depicting the Aztec calendar. *Diameter:* 23.5 mm. *Edge:* Plain. BW-519, KM-432.

Date	Comment
1936	
1937	
1938	
1939	
1940	
1942	
1945	
1946	

10 centavos, 0.950 copper, 0.050 zinc; 5.5 g. Type 6 (Juárez).

Obverse: Above a spray of oak and laurel, the national coat of arms with the eagle facing left. Legend ESTADOS UNIDOS MEXICANOS. *Reverse:* A left-facing bust of Benito Juárez, with DIEZ CENTAVOS Mo [date] surrounding. *Diameter:* 23.5 mm. *Edge:* Plain. BW-520, KM-433.

Date	Comment
1955	
1956	
1957	
1959	
1966	
1967	

10 centavos, 0.750 copper, 0.250 zinc; 1.485 g. Type 7 (Ear of Corn).

Obverse: Above a spray of oak and laurel, the national coat of arms with the eagle facing left. Legend ESTADOS UNIDOS MEXICANOS. *Reverse:* At center, a partially shucked ear of corn on a plain field. In the upper part of the field, divided by the ear, 10 / Cs. In lower part, divided by the stem, the date and mintmark M̊. *Diameter:* 15 mm. *Edge:* Paired reeding. BW-521, KM-434.

Date	Comment
1974	6 rows corn, sharp stem
1975	5 rows corn, sharp stem
1976	5 rows corn, sharp stem
1977	5 rows corn, thin stem
1977	6 rows corn, blunt and thick stem
1977	6 rows corn, long and thin stem
1978	6 rows corn, blunt and thick stem
1978	5 rows corn, long and thin stem
1978	Doubled die
1979	5 rows corn, long and thin stem
1979	6 rows corn, long and thin stem
1980	6 rows corn, long and blunt stem
1980/79	Long and blunt stem

20 CENTAVOS

The 20 centavos under the Reform of 1905 were made in nine basic types. These are commonly referenced by collectors as follows:

Type 1 (1905–1914)—.800 (with small radiant liberty cap on the reverse)

Type 2 (1919)—Little .800 (like Type 1, but 3 mm smaller in diameter)

Type 3 (1920 and 1935)—Monogram (with the value depicted as a monogram, in which the numerals are superimposed on a horizontally shaded centavo symbol, ¢)

Type 4 (1920–1943)—.720 (same as Type 2, but with reduced silver content)

Type 5 (1943–1955)—Pyramid (depicting the Aztec Pyramid of the Sun at Teotihuacán)

Type 6 (1955–1971)—New Eagle (like Type 5, but with the eagle redesigned to have stylized, scale-like feathers and large feet)

Type 7 (1971–1974)—Restyled Eagle (like Type 6, but with the obverse further redesigned such that all the devices are depicted as raised outlines on a flat surface, rather than as fully contoured shapes)

Type 8 (1974–1983)—Madero (depicting Francisco Madero, first president of the Revolutionary government)

Type 9 (1983–1984)—Olmec (honoring ancient Mesoamerican culture with a depiction of an Olmec "colossal head" statue)

20 centavos, 0.800 silver, 0.200 copper; 5 g. Type 1 (.800).

Obverse: The national coat of arms above a spray of oak and laurel, with legend ESTADOS UNIDOS MEXICANOS. *Reverse:* At the top, above an open wreath of oak and laurel, a small radiant liberty cap. On the radiance below the cap, a horizontally shaded number 20 with CENTAVOS below; date just above the bow on the wreath. Mintmark M below and slightly between the digits of the 20. *Diameter:* 22 mm. *Edge:* Reeded. BW-522, KM-435.

Date	Comment
1905	
1906	
1907	Straight 7
1907	Curved 7
1908	
1910	
1911	
1912	
1913	
1914	Narrow date
1914	Wide date

20 centavos, 0.800 silver, 0.200 copper; 3.525 g. Type 2 (Little .800).

Obverse: The national coat of arms above a spray of oak and laurel, with legend ESTADOS UNIDOS MEXICANOS. *Reverse:* At the top, above an open wreath of oak and laurel, a small radiant liberty cap. On the radiance below the cap, a horizontally shaded number 20 with CENTAVOS below; 1919 just above the bow on the wreath. Mintmark M below and slightly between the digits of the 20. *Diameter:* 19 mm. *Edge:* Reeded. BW-523, KM-436.

Date	Comment
1919	

20 centavos, 0.950 copper, 0.025 tin, 0.025 zinc; 15 g. Type 3 (Monogram).

Obverse: The national coat of arms above a spray of oak and laurel, with legend ESTADOS UNIDOS MEXICANOS. *Reverse:* At center, within an open wreath of laurel, a large number 20 superimposed on a horizontally shaded centavo symbol (¢). At the top, between wreath tips, the date; below the wreath, mintmark M̊. *Diameter:* 32.5 mm. *Edge:* Plain. BW-524, KM-437.

Date	Comment
1920	
1935	

20 centavos, 0.720 silver, 0.280 copper; 3.333 g. Type 4 (.720).

Obverse: The national coat of arms above a spray of oak and laurel, with legend ESTADOS UNIDOS MEXICANOS. *Reverse:* At the top, above an open wreath of oak and laurel, a small radiant liberty cap. On the radiance below the cap, a horizontally shaded number 20 with CENTAVOS below; date just above the bow on the wreath. Mintmark M below and slightly between the digits of the 20. *Diameter:* 19 mm. *Edge:* Reeded. BW-525, KM -438.

Date	Comment
1920	
1921	
1925	
1926	
1926/5	
1927	
1928	
1930	
1933	
1934	
1935	
1937	
1939	
1940	
1941	
1942	
1943	

20 centavos, 0.950 copper, 0.040 zinc, 0.010 tin; 10 g. Type 5 (Pyramid).

Obverse: Above a spray of oak and laurel, the national coat of arms with a left-facing eagle, rendered naturalistically. Legend ESTADOS UNIDOS MEXICANOS. *Reverse:* At center, the Pyramid of the Sun, with the location TEOTIHUACAN engraved at the base and volcanoes in the background. At the top, a small radiant liberty cap; on the radiance, divided by the cap, an outlined number 20. Below the radiance, mintmark M̊. At the bottom, in two lines and flanked by two species of cactus, CENTAVOS and the date. *Diameter:* 28.5 mm. *Edge:* Plain. BW-526, KM-439.

Date	Comment
1943	
1944	
1945	
1946	
1951	0.950 copper, 0.050 zinc
1952	
1953	
1954	
1955	

20 centavos, 0.950 copper, 0.050 zinc; 10 g. Type 6 (New Eagle).

Obverse: Above a spray of oak and laurel, the national coat of arms a left-facing eagle, redesigned with stylized, scale-like feathers and large feet. Legend ESTADOS UNIDOS MEXICANOS. *Reverse:* At center, the Pyramid of the Sun, with the location TEOTIHUACAN engraved at the base and volcanoes in the background. At the top, a small radiant liberty cap; on the radiance, divided by the cap, an outlined number 20. Below the radiance, mintmark M°. At the bottom, in two lines and flanked by two species of cactus, CENTAVOS and the date. *Diameter:* 28.5 mm. *Edge:* Plain. BW-527, KM-440.

Date	Comment
1955	
1956	
1957	
1959	
1960	
1963	
1964	
1965	
1966	
1967	
1968	
1969	
1970	
1971	

20 centavos, 0.950 copper, 0.050 zinc; 9.8 g. Type 7 (Restyled Eagle).

Obverse: Above a spray of oak and laurel, the national coat of arms with a left-facing eagle, redesigned with the feathers and other elements drawn as outlines instead of in full relief. Legend ESTADOS UNIDOS MEXICANOS. *Reverse:* At center, the Pyramid of the Sun, with the location TEOTIHUACAN engraved at the base and volcanoes in the background. At the top, a small radiant liberty cap; on the radiance, divided by the cap, an outlined number 20. Below the radiance, mintmark M°. At the bottom, in two lines and flanked by two species of cactus, CENTAVOS and the date. *Diameter:* 28.5 mm. *Edge:* Plain. BW-528, KM-441.

Date	Comment
1971	
1973	
1974	

20 centavos, 0.750 copper, 0.250 nickel; 3 g. Type 8 (Madero).

Obverse: Above a spray of oak and laurel, the national coat of arms with eagle facing left, drawn in raised outlines. Legend ESTADOS UNIDOS MEXICANOS. *Reverse:* On a plain field, the head of Francisco Madero facing right, in semiprofile. To the left of the bust, mintmark M° and the date; to the right of the bust, 20c. *Diameter:* 20 mm. *Edge:* Paired reeding. BW-529, KM-442.

Date	Comment
1974	
1975	
1976	
1977	
1978	
1978	
1979	
1980	
1981	Open 8
1981	Closed 8, high date
1981	Closed 8, low date
1981/2	
1982	Long lapel
1982	Short lapel
1983	Round-top 3
1983	Flat-top 3
1983	Proof

20 centavos, 0.950 copper, 0.050 zinc; 3.04 g. Type 9 (Olmec).

Obverse: Above a spray of oak and laurel, the national coat of arms with a left-facing eagle, redesigned with feathers resembling plates of armor. Legend ESTADOS UNIDOS MEXICANOS. *Reverse:* An Olmec colossal head statue with culturo olmeco placed vertically to the left of the head, ending in a free-flowing, chainlike design that wraps fully around the head and returns to the field on the left. To the right of the head, the date superimposed over the chain; below the head, 20¢. Mintmark M° at far left. *Diameter:* 20 mm. *Edge:* Reeded. BW-530, KM-491.

Date	Comment
1983	
1983	Proof
1984	

25 CENTAVOS

The 25 centavos under the Reform of 1905 fall into two basic types. Collectors refer to these as follows:

Types 1 (1950–1953)—Scales (with the classic Balance Scale design on the reverse)

Type 2 (1964–1966)—Madero (depicting Francisco Madero, first president of the Revolutionary government)

25 centavos, 0.500 copper, 0.300 silver, 0.100 nickel, 0.100 zinc; 3.333 g. Type 1 (Scales).

Obverse: Above a spray of oak and laurel, the national coat of arms with the eagle facing left. Legend ESTADOS UNIDOS MEXICANOS. *Reverse:* Below a small radiant liberty cap, a crossed sword and balance scale; between the pans of the scale, a scroll bearing the word LEY. In the field near the top, divided by the liberty cap, 25 / Cs. At the bottom, mintmark Mo· and the date. *Diameter:* 21.5 mm. *Edge:* Reeded. BW-531, KM-443.

Date	Comment
1950	
1951	
1952	
1953	

25 centavos, 0.750 copper, 0.250 nickel; 5.5 g. Type 2 (Madero).

Obverse: Above a spray of oak and laurel, the national coat of arms with the eagle facing left. Legend ESTADOS UNIDOS MEXICANOS. *Reverse:* A bust of Francisco Madero in three-quarter profile, with VEINTICINCO CENTAVOS [date] surrounding. Mintmark M̊ to the right, near the date. *Diameter:* 23 mm. *Edge:* Reeded. BW-532, KM-444.

Date	Comment
1964	
1966	Closed beak
1966	Open beak

50 CENTAVOS

The 50 centavos under the Reform of 1905 were made in nine basic types. These are commonly referenced by collectors as follows:

Type 1 (1905–1918)—.800 (with small radiant liberty cap on the reverse)

Type 2 (1918–1919)—Reduced .800 (like Type 1, but 3 mm smaller in diameter)

Type 3 (1919–1945)—.720 (like Type 2, but with lower silver content)

Type 4 (1935)— .420 (like Type 3, but with further reduced silver content)

Type 5 (1950–1951)—Cuauhtémoc (depicting the famous Aztec leader of that name)

Type 6 (1955–1959)—Big Cuauhtémoc (with Aztec-style profile bust of the leader, and 7 mm larger in diameter than Type 5)

Type 7 (1964–1969)—Copper-nickel (like Type 6, but with a copper-nickel composition, and 8 mm smaller in diameter)

Type 8 (1970–1983)—Stylized Eagle (like Type 7, but with the obverse redesigned such that all the devices are depicted as raised outlines on a flat surface, rather than as fully contoured shapes)

Type 9 (1983)—Palenque (honoring ancient Mesoamerican culture with a depiction of the Mayan city of Palenque)

50 centavos, 0.800 silver, 0.200 copper; 12.5 g. Type 1 (.800).

Obverse: The national coat of arms above a spray of oak and laurel, with legend ESTADOS UNIDOS MEXICANOS. *Reverse:* At the top, above an open wreath of oak and laurel, a small radiant liberty cap. On the radiance below the cap, a horizontally shaded number 50 with CENTAVOS below; date just above the bow on the wreath. Mintmark M below and slightly between the digits of the 50. *Diameter:* 30 mm. *Edge:* Lettered INDEPENDENCIA Y LIBERTAD. BW-533, KM-445.

Date	Comment
1905	
1906	
1907	Curved 7
1907	Straight 7
1908	
1912	
1913	
1913/07	
1913/2	
1914	
1916	
1916	1's over inverted 1's
1917	
1918	

50 centavos, 0.800 silver, 0.200 copper; 9.06 g. Type 2 (Reduced .800).

Obverse: The national coat of arms above a spray of oak and laurel, with legend ESTADOS UNIDOS MEXICANOS. *Reverse:* At the top, above an open wreath of oak and laurel, a small radiant liberty cap. On the radiance below the cap, a horizontally shaded number 50 with CENTAVOS below; date just above the bow on the wreath. Mintmark M below and slightly between the digits of the 50. *Diameter:* 27 mm. *Edge:* Lettered INDEPENDENCIA Y LIBERTAD. BW-534, KM-446.

Date	Comment
1918	
1919	

50 centavos, 0.720 silver, 0.280 copper; 8.33 g. Type 3 (.720).

Obverse: The national coat of arms above a spray of oak and laurel, with legend ESTADOS UNIDOS MEXICANOS. *Reverse:* At the top, above an open wreath of oak and laurel, a small radiant liberty cap. On the radiance below the cap, a horizontally shaded number 50 with CENTAVOS below; date just above the bow on the wreath. Mintmark M below and slightly between the digits of the 50. *Diameter:* 27 mm. *Edge:* Lettered INDEPENDENCIA Y LIBERTAD. BW-535, KM-447.

Date	Comment
1919	
1920	
1921	
1925	
1937	
1938	
1939	
1942	
1943	
1944	
1945	

50 centavos, 0.580 copper, 0.420 silver; 7.973 g. Type 4 (.420).

Obverse: The national coat of arms above a spray of oak and laurel, with legend ESTADOS UNIDOS MEXICANOS. *Reverse:* At the top, above an open wreath of oak and laurel, a small radiant liberty cap. On the radiance below the cap, a horizontally shaded number 50 with CENTAVOS below; 1935 just above the bow on the wreath. Mintmark M below and slightly between the digits of the 50. *Diameter:* 27 mm. *Edge:* Lettered INDEPENDENCIA Y LIBERTAD BW-536, KM-448.

Date	Comment
1935	

50 centavos, 0.500 copper, 0.300 silver, 0.100 nickel, 0.100 zinc; 6.666 g. Type 5 (Cuauhtémoc).

Obverse: Above a spray of oak and laurel, the national coat of arms with the eagle facing left. Legend ESTADOS UNIDOS MEXICANOS. *Reverse:* A bust of Cuauhtémoc in three-quarter profile on a plain field, with the date to the left. Mintmark M̊ at upper right, above a small eagle diving toward the denomination, 50 / CS. *Diameter:* 26 mm. *Edge:* Reeded. BW-537, KM-449.

Date	Comment
1950	
1951	

50 centavos, 0.950 copper, 0.025 tin, 0.025 zinc; 14 g. Type 6 (Big Cuauhtémoc).

Obverse: Above a spray of oak and laurel, the national coat of arms with the eagle facing left. Legend ESTADOS UNIDOS MEXICANOS. *Reverse:* The head of Cuauhtémoc in Aztec-style headdress, with • CINCUENTA CENTAVOS • / Mo [date] surrounding. *Diameter:* 33 mm. *Edge:* Reeded. BW-538, KM-450.

Date	Comment
1955	
1956	
1957	
1959	

50 centavos, 0.750 copper, 0.250 nickel; 6.5 g. Type 7 (Copper-nickel).

Obverse: Above a spray of oak and laurel, the national coat of arms with the eagle facing left. Legend ESTADOS UNIDOS MEXICANOS. *Reverse:* The head of Cuauhtémoc in Aztec-style headdress, with • CINCUENTA CENTAVOS • / Mo [date] surrounding. *Diameter:* 25 mm. *Edge:* Reeded. BW-539, KM-451.

Date	Comment
1964	
1965	
1966	
1967	
1968	
1969	

50 centavos, 0.750 copper, 0.250 nickel; 6.5 g. Type 8 (Stylized Eagle).

Obverse: Above a spray of oak and laurel, the national coat of arms with a left-facing eagle, redesigned with the feathers and other elements drawn as outlines instead of in full relief. Legend ESTADOS UNIDOS MEXICANOS. *Reverse:* The head of Cuauhtémoc in Aztec-style headdress, with • CINCUENTA CENTAVOS • / Mo [date] surrounding. *Diameter:* 25 mm. *Edge:* Reeded. BW-540, KM-452.

Date	Comment
1970	
1971	
1972	
1975	Dots
1975	No dots
1976	Dots
1976	No dots
1977	
1978	
1979	Round 9
1979	Square 9
1980	Round 9, wide date
1980	Square 9, narrow date
1981	Rectangular 9, narrow date
1981	Round 9, wide date
1982	
1983	
1983	Proof

50 centavos, stainless steel; 4.2 g. Type 9 (Palenque).

Obverse: Above a spray of oak and laurel, the national coat of arms with a left-facing eagle, redesigned with feathers resembling plates of armor. Legend ESTADOS UNIDOS MEXICANOS. *Reverse:* The head of a Mayan of ancient Palenque; to left of the head, 50¢ PALENQUE placed vertically, with the date placed horizontally below the 5. Mintmark M̊ at far right. *Diameter:* 21.9 mm. *Edge:* Plain. BW-541, KM-492.

Date	Comment
1983	Thick snake
1983	Thin snake
1983	Proof

1 PESO

Pesos under the Reform of 1905 were made in nine basic types. These are commonly referenced by collectors as follows:

Type 1 (1910–1914)—Caballito (with an effigy of Liberty on horseback)

Type 2 (1918–1919)—.800 (with small radiant liberty cap and wreath)

Type 3 (1920–1945)—.720 (like Type 2, but with reduced silver content)

Type 4 (1947–1949)—Little Morelos (with head of War of Independence hero José María Morelos)

Type 5 (1950)—General Morelos (with bust of Morelos in three-quarter profile to left)

Type 6 (1957)—Constitution (circulating commemorative of the Constitution of 1857, with head of former president Benito Juárez facing left)

Type 7 (1957–1967)—.100 (with bust of Morelos in profile, facing right)

Type 8 (1970–1983)—Copper-nickel (with head of Morelos in profile, facing left)

Type 9 (1984–1987)—Steel (with bust of Morelos in three-quarter profile to right)

1 peso, 0.9027 silver, 0.0973 copper; 27.07 g. Type 1 (Caballito).

Obverse: The national coat of arms above a spray of oak and laurel, with legend ESTADOS UNIDOS MEXICANOS. Divided by the base of the cactus, UN / PESO. *Reverse:* Liberty in a flowing gown, riding a galloping horse while holding a torch aloft in her left hand and a branch of laurel in her right. In the background, a rising sun with long, single-line rays. At the bottom, the date with a dot to either side. *Diameter:* 39 mm. *Edge:* Lettered INDEPENDENCIA Y LIBERTAD. BW-542, KM-453.

Note: Without mintmark.

Date	Comment
1910	
1911	
1911	Short ray
1912	
1913	
1913/2	
1914	

1 peso, 0.800 silver, 0.200 copper; 18.125 g. Type 2 (.800).

Obverse: The national coat of arms above a spray of oak and laurel, with legend ESTADOS UNIDOS MEXICANOS. *Reverse:* At the top, above an open wreath of oak and laurel, a small radiant liberty cap. Below the rays, UN PESO, with mintmark M above and the date below. *Diameter:* 34 mm. *Edge:* Lettered INDEPENDENCIA Y LIBERTAD. BW-543, KM-454.

Date	Comment
1918	
1918/7	
1919	

1 peso, 0.720 silver, 0.280 copper; 16.66 g. Type 3 (.720).

Obverse: The national coat of arms above a spray of oak and laurel, with legend ESTADOS UNIDOS MEXICANOS. Near the top, divided by the eagle's head, 0.7 / 20, denoting the reduced fineness. *Reverse:* At the top, above an open wreath of oak and laurel, a small radiant liberty cap. Below the rays, UN PESO, with mintmark M above and the date below. *Diameter:* 34 mm. *Edge:* Lettered INDEPENDENCIA Y LIBERTAD. BW-544, KM-455.

Date	Comment
1920	
1920/10	
1921	
1922	
1923	
1924	
1925	
1926	
1927	

1 peso, BW-544, continued

Date	Comment
1932	Open 9
1932	Closed 9
1933	
1933/2	
1934	
1934/3	
1935	
1938	
1940	
1943	
1944	
1945	

1 peso, 0.500 silver, 0.400 copper, 0.060 nickel, 0.040 zinc; 14 g. Type 4 (Little Morelos).

Obverse: Above a spray of oak and laurel, the national coat of arms with the eagle facing left. Legend ESTADOS UNIDOS MEXICANOS. *Reverse:* The head of José Morelos facing right, with MORELOS in small letters at the base of the neck. Around the border below, •UN PESO followed by the date, mintmark Mo., weight 14 Gr., and fineness 0.500•. *Diameter:* 32 mm. *Edge:* Reeded. BW-545, KM-456.

Date	Comment
1947	
1948	
1949	
1949	Proof

1 peso, 0.500 copper, 0.300 silver, 0.100 nickel 0.100 zinc; 13.33 g. Type 5 (General Morelos).

Obverse: Above a spray of oak and laurel, the national coat of arms with a left-facing eagle. Legend ESTADOS UNIDOS MEXICANOS. *Reverse:* On a plain field, a bust of José Morelos in three-quarter profile to the left, in a general's uniform. To left of the bust, 1 / PESO / 1950 / M̊. *Diameter:* 32 mm. *Edge:* Reeded. BW-546, KM-457.

Note: Morelos's coat was unlike those of the other generals in that it had a distinctively large, high collar and no epaulets.

Date	Comment
1950	

1 peso, 0.700 copper, 0.100 silver, 0.100 nickel, 0.100 zinc; 16 g. Type 6 (Constitution).

Obverse: At center, a small national coat of arms with a left-facing eagle within an open wreath of oak and laurel. Legend • ESTADOS UNIDOS MEXICANOS • / UN PESO 1957. *Reverse:* A head of Benito Juárez facing left with legend • CENTENARIO DE LA CONSTITUCION DE MEXICO • / 1857•1957. *Diameter:* 34.5 mm. *Edge:* Lettered INDEPENDENCIA Y LIBERTAD. BW-547, KM-458.

Date	Comment
1957	

1 peso, 0.700 copper, 0.100 silver, 0.100 nickel, 0.100 zinc; 16 g. Type 7 (.100).

Obverse: At center, a small national coat of arms with a left-facing eagle within an open wreath of oak and laurel. Legend • ESTADOS UNIDOS MEXICANOS • / UN PESO [date]. *Reverse:* Within an open wreath of oak and laurel, a right-facing bust of José Morelos in a general's uniform. To left of the bust, mintmark M̊. *Diameter:* 34.5 mm. *Edge:* Lettered INDEPENDENCIA Y LIBERTAD. BW-548, KM-459.

Date	Comment
1957	
1958	
1959	
1960	
1961	
1962	
1963	
1964	
1965	
1966	
1967	

1 peso, 0.750 copper, 0.250 nickel; 9 g. Type 8 (Copper-nickel).

Obverse: Above a spray of oak and laurel, the national coat of arms with a left-facing eagle, redesigned with the feathers and other elements drawn as outlines instead of in full relief. Legend ESTADOS UNIDOS MEXICANOS. *Reverse:* On a plain field, a left-facing head of José Morelos in a general's uniform. To left of the head, UN PESO; below, the date. *Diameter:* 29 mm. *Edge:* Reeded. BW-549, KM-460.

Date	Comment
1970	Narrow date
1970	Wide date
1971	
1972	
1974	
1975	Wide date
1975	Narrow date
1976	
1977	Thick date
1977	Thin date
1978	Open 8
1978	Closed 8
1979	Thin date
1979	Thick date
1980	Closed 8, wide date
1980	Closed 8, narrow date
1980	Open 8
1981	Closed 8, narrow date
1981	Open 8, wide date
1981	Closed 8, open 9
1981	Closed 8 and 9
1982	
1983	Wide date
1983	Narrow date
1983	Open 8
1983	Proof

1 peso, stainless steel; 6.07 g. Type 9 (Steel).

Obverse: Above a spray of oak and laurel, the national coat of arms with a left-facing eagle, redesigned with feathers resembling plates of armor. Legend ESTADOS UNIDOS MEXICANOS. *Reverse:* On a plain field, a bust of José Morelos in three-quarter profile to the right, in a general's uniform. To the left of the bust, mintmark M̊; to the right, 1$ and the date. At upper right, **josé mª morelos** (in lowercase letters). *Diameter:* 24.5 mm. *Edge:* Plain. BW-550, KM-496.

Date	Comment
1984	
1985	
1986	
1987	
1987	Proof

2 PESOS

The 2 pesos under the Reform of 1905 were made both in gold and in silver:

Type 1—Victoria (depicting Mexico City's *El Ángel de la Independencia*, or the Angel of Independence, a statue based on Nike, the Greek goddess of victory)

Type 2—2 Peso Gold (with a wreath on the reverse)

2 pesos, 0.900 gold, 0.100 copper; 1.666 g. Type 2 (2 Peso Gold).

Obverse: The national coat of arms above a spray of oak and laurel, with legend ESTADOS UNIDOS MEXICANOS. *Reverse:* Within an open wreath of laurel, DOS / PESOS. At the top, between wreath tips, the date; at the bottom, below the bow on the wreath, mintmark M̊. *Diameter:* 13 mm. *Edge:* Reeded. BW-651, KM-461.

Date	Comment
1919	
1920	
1920/10	
1944	
1945	Restrike
1946	
1947	

2 pesos, 0.900 silver, 0.100 copper; 26.666 g. Type 1 (Victoria).

Obverse: Within a wreath of oak and laurel, the national coat of arms with the eagle facing left. Legend •ESTADOS•UNIDOS•MEXICANOS• / MDCCCXXI–MCMXXI (1821–1921), with the dash between the dates representing an ornament on the coin. *Reverse:* The statue known as El Ángel, with volcanoes in the background. To the left of the statue, DOS / PESOS. To the right, the coin's silver weight, **24 Gr. / PLATA / PURA**. *Diameter:* 39 mm. *Edge:* Reeded. BW-551, KM-462.

Date	Comment
1921	
1921	Feathers on knee

2-1/2 PESOS

The 2-1/2 peso gold coin under the Reform of 1905 was made in one design; collectors describe it by its denomination.

2-1/2 pesos, 0.900 gold, 0.100 copper; 2.0833 g. Type 1.

Obverse: The national coat of arms above a spray of oak and laurel, with legend **ESTADOS UNIDOS MEXICANOS**. *Reverse:* The head of Father Miguel Hidalgo y Costilla. Around the border, divided by the neck of the portrait, **DOS Y MEDIO / PESOS ★ [date]**. *Diameter:* 15.5 mm. *Edge:* Reeded. BW-652, KM-463.

Date	Comment
1918	
1919	
1920	
1920/10	
1944	
1945	Restrike
1946	
1947	
1948	

5 PESOS

The 5 pesos under the Reform of 1905 were made both in gold and in silver and, later, in base metal. The gold version, made in one design, is called "5 peso gold." The non-gold 5 pesos was produced in 10 basic types, commonly referenced by collectors as follows:

Type 1—Cuauhtémoc (depicting the famous Aztec leader of that name)

Type 2—Railroad (commemorating the opening of the Southeastern Railroad, with a depiction of a locomotive passing a plantation)

Type 3—Hidalgo (honoring the birth-bicentennial of War of Independence hero Father Miguel Hidalgo y Costilla, with his portrait in front of the church where he famously delivered the "grito de Dolores")

Type 4—Hidalgo/Wreath (depicting Father Miguel Hidalgo y Costilla within a wreath of oak and laurel)

Type 5—Hidalgo/Chico (like type 4, but with legend instead of wreath)

Type 6—Constitution (commemorating the Constitution of 1857, with a portrait of former president Benito Juárez)

Type 7—Carranza (commemorating the centennial of the birth of Revolutionary hero Venustiano Carranza)

Type 8—Guerrero (with bust of War of Independence hero General Vicente Guerrero)

Type 9—Quetzalcóatl (honoring Mesoamerican culture with depiction of the "Feathered Serpent" god Quetzalcóatl)

Type 10—Quetzalcóatl, Reduced (reduced size and new aluminum-bronze composition, with simple $5 design)

5 pesos, 0.900 gold, 0.100 copper; 4.1666 g.

Obverse: The national coat of arms above a spray of oak and laurel, with legend **ESTADOS UNIDOS MEXICANOS**. *Reverse:* The head of Miguel Hidalgo y Costilla. Around the border, divided by the neck of the portrait, **CINCO PESOS** at left, with mintmark M, a star, and the date at right. *Diameter:* 19 mm. *Edge:* lettered INDEPENDENCIA Y LIBERTAD. BW-653, KM-464.

Date	Comment
1905	
1906	
1907	
1910	
1918	
1918/7	
1919	
1920	
1955	Restrike

5 pesos, 0.900 silver, 0.100 copper; 30 g. Type 1 (Cuauhtémoc).

Obverse: The national coat of arms above a spray of oak and laurel, with legend ESTADOS UNIDOS MEXICANOS. *Reverse:* The head of Cuauhtémoc in Aztec-style headdress, facing left, with CUAUHTEMOC in small letters below the bust. Around the border, • CINCO PESOS • with weight 30 GRAMOS, fineness • LEY 0.900, mintmark • Mo, and the date. *Diameter:* 40 mm. *Edge:* Reeded. BW-552, KM-465.

Date	Comment
1947	
1948	

5 pesos, 0.900 silver, 0.100 copper; 27.777 g. Type 2 (Railroad).

Obverse: At center, a small national coat of arms above a spray of oak and laurel. Legend ESTADOS UNIDOS MEXICANOS, with CINCO PESOS below the spray. To the left of the spray, LEY above the silver weight, 0.720; to the right of the spray, PESO above the coin weight, 27 7/9 6. At the bottom, mintmark Mo and the date. *Reverse:* A complex scene with a locomotive in the foreground and a plantation with corn fields and two palm trees in the background. Behind all, a rising or setting sun inscribed 1950 and with blade-shaped rays. Surrounding all, legend INAUGURACION DEL FERROCARRIL DEL SURESTE • ("Inauguration of the Southeastern Railway"). *Diameter:* 40 mm. *Edge:* Lettered AGRICULTURA-INDUSTRIA-COMERCIO. BW-553, KM-466.

Date	Comment
1950	

5 pesos, 0.720 silver, 0.280 copper; 27.777 g. Type 3 (Hidalgo).

Obverse: At center, a small national coat of arms above a spray of oak and laurel. Legend ESTADOS UNIDOS MEXICANOS, with CINCO PESOS below the spray. To the left of the spray, PESO above the coin weight, 27 $\frac{7}{9}$ 6; to the right of the spray, LEY above the silver weight, 0.720. At the bottom, mintmark Mo and 1953. *Reverse:* Slightly to the right, a bust of Miguel Hidalgo y Costilla in three-quarter profile; to the left, the church Parroquia de Nuestra Señora de Dolores. At the top, AÑO DE HIDALGO ("Year of Hidalgo"); above the church, 1753 / 1953. *Diameter:* 40 mm. *Edge:* Lettered AGRICULTURA INDUSTRIA COMERCIO. BW-554, KM-468.

Date	Comment
1953	

5 pesos, 0.720 silver, 0.280 copper; 27.777 g. Type 4 (Hidalgo/Wreath).

Obverse: At center, a small national coat of arms above a spray of oak and laurel. Legend ESTADOS UNIDOS MEXICANOS, with CINCO PESOS below the spray. To the left of the spray, PESO above the coin weight, 27 $\frac{7}{9}$ 6; to the right of the spray, LEY above the silver weight, 0.720. At the bottom, mintmark Mo and the date. *Reverse:* Within an open wreath of laurel, the head of Miguel Hidalgo y Costilla facing left, with HIDALGO below the neck. *Diameter:* 40 mm. *Edge:* Lettered AGRICULTURA INDUSTRIA COMERCIO. BW-555, KM-467.

Date	Comment
1951	
1952	
1953	
1954	

5 pesos, 0.720 silver, 0.280 copper; 18.055 g. Type 5 (Hidalgo/Chico).

Obverse: At center, a small national coat of arms within a circle formed by a spray of oak and laurel below and the legend ESTADOS UNIDOS MEXICANOS above. Surrounding all, • CINCO PESOS • with weight 18.055 G, the date (with a dot before and after), and fineness LEY .720. *Reverse:* On a plain field, the head of Miguel Hidalgo y Costilla facing left, with legend • INDEPENDENCIA Y LIBERTAD • / HIDALGO. Mintmark M° to the right of the head. *Diameter:* 36 mm. *Edge:* Reeded. BW-556, KM-469.

Date	Comment
1955	
1956	
1957	

5 pesos, 0.720 silver, 0.280 copper; 18.05 g. Type 6 (Constitution).

Obverse: At center, a small national coat of arms within a circle formed by a spray of oak and laurel below and the legend ESTADOS UNIDOS MEXICANOS above. Surrounding all, • CINCO PESOS • with weight 18.055 G, 1957 (with a dot before and after), and fineness LEY .720. *Reverse:* The head of Benito Juárez facing left, with legend • CENTENARIO DE LA CONSTITUCION DE MEXICO • / 1857•1957. To the right of the head, mintmark M°. *Diameter:* 36 mm. *Edge:* Reeded BW-557, KM-470.

Date	Comment
1957	

5 pesos, 0.720 silver, 0.280 copper; 18.055 g. Type 7 (Carranza).

Obverse: At center, a small national coat of arms within a circle formed by a spray of oak and laurel below and the legend ESTADOS UNIDOS MEXICANOS above. Surrounding all, • CINCO PESOS • with weight 18.055 G, 1957 (with a dot before and after), and fineness LEY .720. *Reverse:* The head of Venustiano Carranza facing left, with legend • AÑO DE CARRANZA • / 1859•1959, with curling ornaments in place of the dots. To the right of the head, mintmark M°. *Diameter:* 36 mm. *Edge:* Plain. BW-558, KM-471.

Date	Comment
1959	

5 pesos, 0.750 copper, 0.250 nickel; 15 g. Type 8 (Guerrero).

Obverse: Above a spray of oak and laurel, the national coat of arms with a left-facing eagle, redesigned with the feathers and other elements drawn as outlines instead of in full relief. Legend ESTADOS UNIDOS MEXICANOS. *Reverse:* On a plain field, a bust of Vicente Guerrero facing right below legend CINCO PESOS. To the left of the bust, the date; to the right, mintmark M°. *Diameter:* 33 mm. *Edge:* Lettered INDEPENDENCIA Y LIBERTAD. BW-559, KM-472.

Date	Comment
1971	
1972	
1973	
1974	
1976	Small date
1976	Large date
1977	
1978	

5 pesos, 0.750 copper, 0.250 nickel; 10.36 g. Type 9 (Quetzalcóatl).

Obverse: Above a spray of oak and laurel, the national coat of arms with a left-facing eagle, redesigned with feathers resembling plates of armor. Legend ESTADOS UNIDOS MEXICANOS. *Reverse:* The head of the god Quetzalcóatl facing left, with mintmark M° above and QUETZALCOATL in small letters below. To the left of the head, 5 / $. At the bottom, the date. *Diameter:* 27.1 mm. *Edge:* Lettered INDEPENDENCIA Y LIBERTAD. BW-560, KM-485.

Date	Comment
1980	
1981	
1982	
1982	Proof
1983	7 known
1984	
1985	

5 pesos, 0.920 copper, 0.060 aluminum, 0.020 nickel; 3.12 g. Type 10 (Quetzalcóatl, Reduced).

Obverse: Above a spray of oak and laurel, the national coat of arms with the eagle facing left, its feathers resembling plates of armor. Legend ESTADOS UNIDOS MEXICANOS. *Reverse:* A large number 5 shaded with a screenlike pattern. To the left of the number, in three lines, the date, $, and mintmark M°. *Diameter:* 17 mm. *Edge:* Reeded. BW-561, KM-502.

Date	Comment
1985	
1987	
1988	
1988	Proof (2 known)

10 PESOS

The 10 pesos under the Reform of 1905 were made in seven basic types. The gold 10 pesos is described by its denomination. The other six types are commonly referenced by collectors as follows:

Type 1—Hidalgo Grande (large diameter, with head of Father Miguel Hidalgo y Costilla facing left)

Type 2—Constitution (commemorating the Constitution of 1857, with a portrait of former president Benito Juárez)

Type 3—Hidalgo/Madero (commemorating the 150th anniversary of independence and the 50th anniversary of the United Mexican States with a pair of portraits: Miguel Hidalgo y Costilla, hero of the War of Independence; and Francisco Madero, hero of the Revolution)

Type 4—Hidalgo, Thin (a seven-sided coin with head of Hidalgo y Costilla facing left, on a thin flan)

Type 5—Hidalgo, Thick (like Type 4, on a thicker flan)

Type 6—Hidalgo, Steel (with new metallic composition and a forward-facing head of Hidalgo y Costilla)

10 pesos, 0.900 gold, 0.100 copper; 8.333 g. Type 1a.

Obverse: The national coat of arms above a spray of oak and laurel, with legend ESTADOS UNIDOS MEXICANOS. *Reverse:* The head of Father Miguel Hidalgo y Costilla. Around the border, divided by the neck of the portrait, DIEZ PESOS to left with mintmark M to right followed by a star and the date. *Diameter:* 22.5 mm. *Edge:* Lettered. INDEPENDENCIA Y LIBERTAD. BW-654, KM-473.

Date	Comment
1905	
1906	
1907	
1908	
1910	
1916	
1917	
1919	
1920	
1959	Restrike

10 pesos, 0.900 silver, 0.100 copper; 28.888 g. Type 1 (Hidalgo Grande).

Obverse: At center, a small national coat of arms within a circle formed by a spray of oak and laurel below and the legend ESTADOS UNIDOS MEXICANOS above. Surrounding all, • DIEZ PESOS • with weight 28.888 G, the date (with a dot before and after), and fineness LEY .900. *Reverse:* On a plain field, the head of Miguel Hidalgo y Costilla facing left, with legend • INDEPENDENCIA Y LIBERTAD • / HIDALGO. Mintmark M° to the right of the head. *Diameter:* 40 mm. *Edge:* Reeded. BW-562, KM-474.

10 pesos, BW-562, continued

Date	Comment
1955	
1956	

10 pesos, 0.900 silver, 0.100 copper; 28.888 g. Type 2 (Constitution).

Obverse: At center, a small national coat of arms within a circle formed by a spray of oak and laurel below and the legend ESTADOS UNIDOS MEXICANOS above. Surrounding all, • DIEZ PESOS • with weight 28.888 G, 1957 (with a dot before and after), and fineness LEY .900. *Reverse:* The head of Benito Juárez facing left with legend • CENTENARIO DE LA CONSTITUCION DE MEXICO • / 1857•1957. Mintmark M̊ to the right of the portrait. *Diameter:* 40 mm. *Edge:* Lettered INDEPENDENCIA Y LIBERTAD. BW-563, KM-475.

Date	Comment
1957	

10 pesos, 0.900 silver, 0.100 copper; 28.888 g. Type 3 (Hidalgo/Madero).

Obverse: At center, a small national coat of arms within a circle formed by a spray of oak and laurel below and the legend ESTADOS UNIDOS MEXICANOS above. Surrounding all, • DIEZ PESOS • with weight 28.888 G, 1960 (with a dot before and after), and fineness LEY .900. Mintmark M̊ to the left of the snake in the coat of arms. *Reverse:* Busts of Miguel Hidalgo y Costilla and Francisco Madero, with HIDALGO and MADERO in small letters below. Legend • INDEPENDENCIA Y LIBERTAD • / SUFRAGIO EFECTIVO NO REELECCION. Above the portraits, the date; to the left of the portraits, 1810; to the right, 1910. *Diameter:* Seven-sided; 40 mm. *Edge:* Reeded. BW-564, KM-476.

Date	Comment
1960	

10 pesos, 0.750 copper, 0.250 nickel; 10 g. Type 4 (Hidalgo, Thin).

Obverse: Above a half-wreath of oak and laurel, the national coat of arms with a left-facing eagle, redesigned with the feathers and other elements drawn as outlines instead of in full relief. Legend ESTADOS UNIDOS MEXICANOS. *Reverse:* A left-facing head of Miguel Hidalgo y Costilla. Above, DIEZ PESOS; at lower right, the date; at lower left, mintmark M̊. *Diameter:* 30.4 mm. *Edge:* Plain. BW-565, KM-477.1.

Note: Minted on a thin flan.

Date	Comment
1974	
1974	Proof
1975	
1976	
1976	Open 6
1977	

10 pesos, 0.750 copper, 0.250 nickel; 14 g. Type 5 (Hidalgo, Thick).

Obverse: Above a half-wreath of oak and laurel, the national coat of arms with a left-facing eagle, redesigned with the feathers and other elements drawn as outlines instead of in full relief. Legend ESTADOS UNIDOS MEXICANOS. *Reverse:* A left-facing head of Miguel Hidalgo y Costilla. Above, DIEZ PESOS; at lower right, the date; at lower left, mintmark M̊. *Diameter:* Seven-sided; 30.4 mm. BW-566, KM-477.2.

Note: Minted on a thick flan.

Date	Comment
1978	
1979	
1980	
1981	
1982	
1982	Proof
1983	Proof (3 known)
1985	

10 pesos, stainless steel; 3.84 g. Type 6 (Hidalgo, Steel).

Obverse: Above a spray of oak and laurel, the national coat of arms with the eagle facing left, its feathers resembling plates of armor. Legend ESTADOS UNIDOS MEXICANOS. *Reverse:* To the right, on a plain field, a forward-facing head of Miguel Hidalgo y Costilla, with **HIDALGO** below and four dots (the number 10 in Braille) above. To the left, a large **$10** positioned vertically, with the date placed horizontally below the peso symbol. To the right, the mintmark M°. *Diameter:* 19 mm. BW-567, KM-512.

Date	Comment
1985	
1986	
1987	
1988	
1989	
1990	
1990	Proof

20 PESOS

The 20 pesos under the Reform of 1905 were made in three basic types. The gold 20 pesos is described by its denomination. The other two types are commonly referenced by collectors as follows:

Type 1—Mayan Culture type (honoring ancient Mesoamerican culture with a design from the traditional Mayan ball game)

Type 2—Victoria (with bust of former president Guadalupe Victoria)

20 pesos, 0.900 gold, 0.100 copper; 16.666 g.

Obverse: Above a spray of oak and laurel, the national coat of arms with the eagle facing left; set at an angle to right of the eagle, the date. Legend **ESTADOS UNIDOS MEXICANOS**. *Reverse:* The Aztec calendar stone, with **VEINTE PESOS** around lower edge. At the bottom, the gold weight: **★ 15 Gr. ORO PURO ★**. *Diameter:* 27.5 mm. *Edge:* Lettered **INDEPENDENCIA Y LIBERTAD**. BW-655, KM-478.

Note: Without mintmark.

Date	Comment
1917	
1918	
1919	
1920	
1920/10	
1921	
1921/11	
1959	Restrike

20 pesos, 0.750 copper, 0.250 nickel; 15.14 g. Type 1 (Mayan Culture).

Obverse: Above a spray of oak and laurel, the national coat of arms with the eagle facing left, its feathers resembling plates of armor. Legend **ESTADOS UNIDOS MEXICANOS**. *Reverse:* A simplified rendering of the round ballcourt marker from the ancient Mayan ritual ball game, with **$20** superimposed on the left side. Above the denomination, **CULTURA MAYA**; below the denomination, the date. Mintmark M° at the bottom. *Diameter:* 32 mm. *Edge:* Lettered **INDEPENDENCIA Y LIBERTAD**. BW-568, KM-486.

Date	Comment
1980	
1981	
1982	
1982	Proof
1983	Proof
1984	

20 pesos, 0.920 copper, 0.060 aluminum, 0.020 nickel; 5.86 g. Type 2 (Victoria).

Obverse: Above a spray of oak and laurel, the national coat of arms with the eagle facing left, its feathers resembling plates of armor. Legend **ESTADOS UNIDOS MEXICANOS**. *Reverse:* A bust of Guadalupe Victoria in three-quarter profile toward the left. Below the bust, in small letters, **VICTORIA**; to right of the bust, mintmark M°. Placed vertically in the field to the left of the bust, a large **$20**, with the date placed horizontally below the peso symbol ($). Near the top, five dots in the Braille configuration for "20." *Diameter:* 21 mm. *Edge:* Reeded. BW-569, KM-508.

20 pesos, BW-569, continued

Date	Comment
1985	Wide date, open 5
1985	Narrow date, open 5
1985	Wide date, closed 5
1986	
1988	
1989	
1989	Reverse doubled die
1990	
1990	Proof

25 PESOS

The 25 pesos under the Reform of 1905 were made in two basic types, commonly referenced by collectors as follows:

> Type 1—Olympics (commemorating the 1968 Summer Olympic Games in Mexico City)
>
> Type 2—Juárez (commemorating the 100th anniversary of the death of former president Benito Juárez)

See chapter 15 for non-circulating commemorative 25-peso coinage.

25 pesos, 0.720 silver, 0.280 copper; 22 g. Type 1 (Olympics).

Obverse: Above a spray of oak and laurel, the national coat of arms depicting a left-facing eagle with stylized feathers and large feet. Legend ESTADOS UNIDOS MEXICANOS. To the eagle's left, 25 / PESOS; to its right, fineness LEY / 0.720 with mintmark $\overset{\circ}{\text{M}}$ below. *Reverse:* A dancing Aztec native at center, with the five Olympic rings at the bottom. Legend JUEGOS DE LA XIX OLIMPIADA MEXICO 1968. *Diameter:* 38 mm. *Edge:* Lettered INDEPENDENCIA Y LIBERTAD. BW-570.1, 570.2, 570.3; KM-479.1, 479.2, 479.3.

Date	Comment
1968	V-1
1968	V-2
1968	V-3

25 pesos, 0.720 silver, 0.280 copper; 22 g. Type 2 (Juárez).

Obverse: Above a spray of oak and laurel, the national coat of arms with a left-facing eagle, redesigned with the feathers and other elements drawn as outlines instead of in full relief. Legend ESTADOS UNIDOS MEXICANOS. Reverse: A bust of Benito Juárez in three-quarter profile angled to the left. Legend • VEINTICINCO PESOS • with fineness LEY 0.720, mintmark M^{O}, and 1972. *Diameter:* 38 mm. *Edge:* Lettered INDEPENDENCIA Y LIBERTAD. BW-571, KM-480.

Date	Comment
1972	

50 PESOS

The 50 pesos under the Reform of 1905 were made in four basic types. Collectors refer to the gold 50 pesos as the "Centenario" (it commemorates the 100th anniversary of independence from Spain). The other three types are commonly referenced by collectors as follows:

> Type 1—Coyolxauhqui (honoring ancient Mesoamerican culture with images from the Aztec myth of Coyolxauhqui, as depicted in the Tempolo Mayor in Mexico City)
>
> Types 2—Juárez, Copper-nickel (commemorating the 100th anniversary of the death of former president Benito Juárez)
>
> Type 3—Juárez, Steel (like Type 2, but in steel composition)

See chapter 15 for non-circulating commemorative 50-peso coinage.

50 pesos, 0.900 gold, 0.100 copper; 41.6666 g. (Centenario).

Obverse: The national coat of arms above a spray of oak and laurel, with legend ESTADOS UNIDOS MEXICANOS. *Reverse:* The statue known as *El Ángel* (based on Nike, the Greek goddess of victory), with volcanoes in the background. To the left of the statue, 50 / PESOS. To the right, the coin's gold weight, 37.5 Gr. / ORO / PURO. At lower right, the date; at lower left, 1821. *Diameter:* 37 mm. *Edge:* Lettered INDEPENDENCIA Y LIBERTAD. BW-656, KM-481.

Note: Without mintmark.

Date	Comment
1921	
1922	
1923	
1924	
1925	
1926	
1927	
1928	
1929	
1930	
1931	
1943	
1944	
1945	
1946	
1947	Restrike

50 pesos, 0.750 copper, 0.250 nickel; 19.63 g. Type 1 (Coyolxauhqui).

Obverse: Above a spray of oak and laurel, the national coat of arms with the eagle facing left, its feathers resembling plates of armor. Legend ESTADOS UNIDOS MEXICANOS. *Reverse:* The mythological Coyolxauhqui; to the right, $ / 50, the date, and mintmark M°. Legend **templo mayor de méxico / • coyolxauhqui •**. *Diameter:* 36 mm. *Edge:* Reeded. BW-577, KM-490.

Date	Comment
1982	
1983	
1983	Proof
1984	
1984	Proof

50 pesos, 0.750 copper, 0.250 nickel; 8.55 g. Type 2 (Juárez, Copper-nickel).

Obverse: Above a spray of oak and laurel, the national coat of arms with the eagle facing left, its feathers resembling plates of armor. Legend ESTADOS UNIDOS MEXICANOS. *Reverse:* A bust of Benito Juárez in three-quarter profile toward the left. Below the bust, in small letters, JUAREZ; to right of the bust, mintmark M°. Placed vertically in the field to the left of the bust, a large $50, with the date placed horizontally below the peso symbol ($). Near the top, five dots in the Braille configuration for "50." *Diameter:* 23.6 mm. *Edge:* Reeded. BW-578, KM-495.

Date	Comment
1984	
1985	
1986	
1987	
1988	

50 pesos, stainless steel; 7.17 g. Type 3 (Juárez, Steel).

Obverse: Above a spray of oak and laurel, the national coat of arms with the eagle facing left, its feathers resembling plates of armor. Legend ESTADOS UNIDOS MEXICANOS. *Reverse:* A bust of Benito Juárez in three-quarter profile toward the left. Below the bust, in small letters, JUAREZ; to right of the bust, mintmark M°. Placed vertically in the field to the left of the bust, a large $50, with the date placed horizontally below the peso symbol ($). Near the top, five dots in the Braille configuration for "50." *Diameter:* 23.6 mm. *Edge:* Plain BW-579, KM-495a.

Date	Comment
1988	
1990	
1992	

100 PESOS

The 100 pesos under the Reform of 1905 were made in two basic types, commonly referenced by collectors as follows:

Type 1—Morelos (depicting War of Independence hero José María Morelos)

Type 2—Carranza (depicting Revolutionary hero Venustiano Carranza)

See chapter 15 for non-circulating commemorative 100-peso coinage.

100 pesos, 0.720 silver, 0.280 copper; 27.77 g. Type 1 (Morelos).

Obverse: Above a spray of oak and laurel, the national coat of arms with a left-facing eagle, redesigned with the feathers and other elements drawn as outlines instead of in full relief. Legend ESTADOS UNIDOS MEXICANOS. *Reverse:* A forward-facing bust of José María Morelos on a plain field. To left of the bust, CIEN / PESOS; to right, mintmark $\overset{\circ}{\text{M}}$ above the date. Below, silver weight PLATA PURA 20 G^{r}. and fineness LEY .720. *Diameter:* 39 mm. *Edge:* Reeded. BW-586, KM-483.1.

Date	Comment
1977	Low 7s
1977	High 7
1977	Level 7s
1978	
1979	
1979	Proof

100 pesos, 0.920 copper, 0.060 aluminum, 0.020 nickel; 11.97 g. Type 2 (Carranza).

Obverse: Above a spray of oak and laurel, the national coat of arms with the eagle facing left, its feathers resembling plates of armor. Legend ESTADOS UNIDOS MEXICANOS. *Reverse:* A bust of Venustiano Carranza in three-quarter profile toward the right. Below the bust, in small letters, V. CARRANZA; to left of the bust, mintmark $\overset{\circ}{\text{M}}$. Placed vertically in the field to the right of the bust, a large $100, with the date placed horizontally below the final zero. Near the top, seven dots in the Braille configuration for "100." *Diameter:* 26.5 mm. *Edge:* Paired reeding. BW-587, KM-493.

Date	Comment
1984	
1984/1984	
1985	
1986	
1987	
1987	Doubled glasses
1988	
1989	
1990	
1990	Proof
1991	
1992	

200 PESOS

The 200 pesos under the Reform of 1905 were made in three basic types, commonly referenced by collectors as follows:

Type 1—Independence (commemorating the 175th anniversary of independence from Spain)

Type 2—Revolution (commemorating the 75th anniversary of the Mexican Revolution)

Type 3—World Cup Futbol (a limited-mintage circulating coin struck in conjunction with the commemorative series discussed in the "250 Pesos" section)

See chapter 15 for non-circulating commemorative 200-peso coinage.

200 pesos, 0.750 copper, 0.250 nickel; 17.19 g. Type 1 (Independence).

Obverse: Above a spray of oak and laurel, the national coat of arms with the eagle facing left, its feathers resembling plates of armor. Legend ESTADOS UNIDOS MEXICANOS. *Reverse:* At the left, Mexico City's *Monumento de la Independencia.* To the left of the monument, 1985; to the right, four profile portraits (Ignacio Allende, Father Miguel Hidalgo y Costilla, José Morelos, and Vicente Guerrero), each with his surname beneath in small letters. Above the busts, $200; below, 175 ANIVERSARIO DE / LA INDEPENDENCIA / DE MEXICO. Mintmark M̊ at the bottom. *Diameter:* 29.6 mm. *Edge:* lettered INDEPENDENCIA Y LIBERTAD. BW-598, KM-509.

Date	Comment
1985	

200 pesos, 0.750 copper, 0.250 nickel; 17.19 g. Type 2 (Revolution).

Obverse: Above a spray of oak and laurel, the national coat of arms with the eagle facing left, its feathers resembling plates of armor. Legend ESTADOS UNIDOS MEXICANOS. *Reverse:* Four profile portraits (Emiliano Zapata, Francisco Madero, Venustiano Carranza, and Pancho Villa), each with his surname beneath in small letters. Legend 175 ANIVERSARIO DE LA REVOLUCION MEXICANA. Below the busts, $200 and 1985; at far left, mintmark M̊. *Diameter:* 29.6 mm. *Edge:* Lettered INDEPENDENCIA Y LIBERTAD. BW-599, KM-510.

Date	Comment
1985	

200 pesos, 0.750 copper, 0.250 nickel; 17.19 g. Type 3 (World Cup Futbol).

Obverse: Above a spray of oak and laurel, the national coat of arms with the eagle facing left, its feathers resembling plates of armor. Legend ESTADOS UNIDOS MEXICANOS. *Reverse:* Three football (soccer) players chasing a ball. Vertically at left, $200; at far right, mintmark M̊. Above the players, COPA MUNDIAL DE FUTBOL. At the bottom, Mexico 86 / 1986. *Diameter:* 29.5 mm. *Edge:* Reeded. BW-600, KM-525.

Date	Comment
1986	

250 PESOS

The Reform of 1905 coins of the 250-peso denomination were struck only as commemoratives in honor of the 1986 World Cup Soccer ("futbol") Games, held in Mexico City. Other denominations were struck for this commemorative series, as well; all are discussed in chapter 15, which covers non-circulating commemorative coinage of the 1905 and 1992 coinage reforms.

500 PESOS

The 500 pesos under the Reform of 1905 were made in seven basic types. Types 1 through 4 were commemoratives struck for the 1986 World Cup Soccer Games (see the previous section, "250 Pesos"). Types 5 and 7 were also commemoratives, honoring the anniversaries of the Revolution and the nationalization of the oil industry, respectively. All are discussed in chapter 15. Only Type 6, the "Madero" type, was not a commemorative, and is discussed here.

500 pesos, 0.750 copper, 0.250 nickel; 12.7 g. Type 6 (Madero).

Obverse: Above a spray of oak and laurel, the national coat of arms with the eagle facing left, its feathers resembling plates of armor. Legend ESTADOS UNIDOS MEXICANOS. *Reverse:* A bust of Francisco Madero in three-quarter profile toward the right. Below the bust, $500; to left of the bust, the date and Madero; to right of the bust, mintmark M̊. *Diameter:* 28.6 mm. *Edge:* Reeded. BW-611, KM-529.

500 pesos, BW-611, continued

Date	Comment
1986	
1987	
1988	
1988	Proof
1989	
1992	

1,000 PESOS

The 1,000 pesos under the Reform of 1905 were made in five basic types. Type 1 (World Cup Football Games), Type 2 (175th anniversary of independence), and Type 3 (50th anniversary of the nationalization of the oil industry), are commemoratives and are discussed in chapter 15. The other two types, which will be discussed here, are as follows:

Type 4—Juana (depicting 17th-century scholar, nun, and poet Juana de Asbaje)

Type 5—Atlan (depicting a representation of the legend of Aztlán, the mythological island from which the Aztecs came; "Atlan" is an incorrect spelling)

1,000 pesos, 0.920 copper, 0.060 aluminum, 0.020 nickel; 14.85 g. Type 4 (Juana).

Obverse: Above a spray of oak and laurel, the national coat of arms with the eagle facing left, its feathers resembling plates of armor. Legend ESTADOS UNIDOS MEXICANOS. *Reverse:* A bust of Juana de Asbaje in three-quarter profile toward the left, with JUANA DE ASBAJE below. Vertically at left of the bust, $1000, with the date placed horizontally below the peso symbol ($). To right of the bust, mintmark M̊. *Diameter:* 30.9 mm. *Edge:* Reeded. BW-616, KM-536.

Date	Comment
1988	
1989	
1990	
1990	Proof
1991	
1992	

1,000 pesos, 0.750 copper, 0.250 aluminum, nickel; 14.85 g. Type 5 (Atlan).

Obverse: Above a spray of oak and laurel, the national coat of arms with the eagle facing left, its feathers resembling plates of armor. Legend ESTADOS UNIDOS MEXICANOS. *Reverse:* At center, a large $1000, with mintmark M̊ below and 1988 at the bottom. At the top, the back of a boat carrying four passengers, with ATLAN directly below. *Diameter:* 22 mm. BW-617, KM-643.

Note: Although it can be found in circulation, this coin was never officially issued.

Date	Comment
1988	

2,000 PESOS

The Reform of 1905 coins of the 2,000-peso denomination were struck only as non-circulating commemoratives, in honor of the 1986 World Cup Soccer Games held in Mexico City; see chapter 15.

5,000 PESOS

The Reform of 1905 coins of the 5,000-peso denomination were struck in only one design: Type 1, Oil Industry (in honor of the 50-year anniversary of the nationalization of the oil industry).

5,000 pesos, 0.750 copper, 0.250 nickel; 17.37 g. Type 1 (Oil Industry).

Obverse: Above a spray of oak and laurel, the national coat of arms with the eagle facing left, its feathers resembling plates of armor. Legend ESTADOS UNIDOS MEXICANOS. *Reverse:* The *Fuente de Petróleos* (*Monument to the Oil Industry*, a 1952 statue in Mexico City). At the top, CINCUENTENARIO; at the bottom, EXPROPIACION PETROLERA. In the field to the left, $5000 placed vertically; to the right, 1988. Below the monument, 1938–1988 and mintmark $\overset{\text{o}}{\text{M}}$. *Diameter:* 33.4 mm. *Edge:* Reeded. BW-619, KM-531.

Date	Comment
1988	

The Coinage Reform of 1905

1 centavo. 1910 (Type 1).
BW-501, KM-415, 20 mm.

2 centavos. 1905 (Type 1).
BW-506, KM-419, 25 mm.

5 centavos. 1914 (Type 1).
BW-508, KM-421, 20 mm.

5 centavos. 1919 (Type 2).
BW-509, KM-422, 28 mm.

10 centavos. 1919 (Type 3).
BW-517, KM-430, 30.5 mm.

20 centavos. 1912 (Type 1).
BW-522, KM-435, 22 mm.

20 centavos. 1981/2 (Type 8).
BW-529, KM-442, 25 mm.

50 centavos. 1908 (Type 1).
BW-533, KM-445, 30 mm.

The Coinage Reform of 1905
(continued)

50 centavos. 1955 (Type 6). BW-538, KM-450, 33 mm.

50 centavos. 1977 (Type 8). BW-540, KM-452, 25 mm.

1 peso. 1913 (Type 1). BW-542, KM-453, 39 mm.

1 peso. 1919 (Type 2). BW-543, KM-454, 34 mm.

1 peso. 1913/2 (Type 2); detail of overdate. BW-542, KM-453.

1 peso. 1950 (Type 5). BW-546, KM-457, 32 mm.

2 pesos. 1921 (Type 1). BW-551, KM-462, 39 mm.

2 pesos. 1921 (Type 1), feathers on knee; detail. BW-551, KM-462.

The Coinage Reform of 1905
(continued)

5 pesos. 1920. BW-653, KM-464, 19 mm.

5 pesos. 1950 (Type 2). BW-553, KM-466, 40 mm.

5 pesos. 1971 (Type 8). BW-559, KM-472, 33 mm.

10 pesos. 1974 (Type 4). BW-565, KM-477.1, 30.4 mm.

20 pesos. 1919. BW-655, KM-478, 27.5 mm.

20 pesos. 1981 (Type 1). BW-568, KM-486, 32 mm.

50 pesos. 1930. BW-656, KM-481, 37 mm.

The Coinage Reform of 1905
(continued)

100 pesos. 1990 (Type 2).
BW-587, KM-493, 26.5 mm.

200 pesos. 1985 (Type 1).
BW-598, KM-509, 29.5 mm.

200 pesos. 1985 (Type 2).
BW-599, KM-510, 29.5 mm.

1,000 pesos. 1988 (Type 4).
BW-616, KM-536, 30.9 mm.

5,000 pesos. 1988 (Type 1).
BW-619, KM-531, 33.4 mm.

14

The Coinage Reform of 1992

Prior to the latter part of 1992, the inflation rate had reached new heights within Mexico. The country had issued circulating coinage in the 1,000-peso denomination, including the bronze-aluminum Juana de Asbaje (issued 1988–1992), as well as a copper-nickel 5,000 pesos issued in 1988 to commemorate the 50th anniversary of the nationalization of the oil industry. Paper money was issued in values up to 20,000 pesos to accommodate business transactions. The copper-nickel coinage began to be melted as the value of its metallic content exceeded its face value.

In early 1992, in order to stabilize the complex economy of Mexico and to better control inflation and the rate of exchange, President Carlos Salinas de Gortari requested the director general of the Casa de Moneda de México, Lic. Alfredo Lelo de Larrea y Robles, to devise a new coinage system with a newly designated monetary unit: the *nuevo peso* (new peso). In the new system the decimal was moved by three digits to eliminate the last three zeros of the current denominations (e.g., 1 new peso was the equivalent of 1,000 "old" pesos). This enabled Mexico to make use of the national currency and coinage still circulating at the time.

The commission for the new monetary system included representatives of the Casa de Moneda de México and the Banco de México, and brought together engineers, metallurgists, and artists to work on the new monetary units. Some of the items they took into consideration were portability, efficiency in the minting process, the face value as opposed to the value of the metal content (to deter hoarding), and difficulty of counterfeiting.

The decree authorizing the new monetary system was published June 22, 1992, in the *Diario Oficial de la Federación*, and became effective January 1, 1993. It covered the denominations of 5, 10, 20, and 50 centavos; and 1, 2, 5, and 10 pesos. The decree modified Article 2 and Article 5 of the monetary laws of the United States of Mexico, published in the *Diario Oficial de la Federación*, July 23, 1990.

Due to its importance to Mexican history and culture, the Aztec calendar stone (Piedra del Sol) was selected as the theme for the new coinage. The designs used for the reverses of the coins are from the various rings of the calendar stone.

On January 1, 1996, the term *nuevo* was deleted from the name of the denominations on the 1 peso and larger coins. The *nuevos pesos* continued to circulate, but the coinage struck after January 1, 1996, had only the peso symbol ($) in front of the denomination. The *nuevos pesos*, which corresponded to the monetary unit that was in effect until December 31, 1992, remained legal tender until December 31, 1995. After that date they were exchangeable at commercial banks at an equivalent of 1,000 to 1 for bank notes and coins corresponding to the new monetary unit in pesos. All the coinage of the *nuevos pesos* denomination remained the same in design, except for the dropping of the "N."

The government also made an effort to withdraw the silver-centered bimetallic coins because they were being hoarded for their silver content. There is confusion as to the final outcome of this endeavor, since some reports indicate that the government lifted the withdrawal. Circulating N$20 and N$50 coins were reported as late as 2004 in Mexico City.

In 2003, the Mexico Mint began two consecutive commemorative series in honor of the 180th anniversary of the Mexican Federation. Each series consisted of one coin for each state in the federation, with an additional coin for the Distrito Federal in the second series. In both series, the denominations were 10 pesos (silver Proofs only) and 100 pesos (bimetallic: circulating coins in silver and bronze-aluminum, and Proofs in silver and gold). The first, or "heraldic," series commenced in 2003. Each reverse featured a different state's coat of arms, and the coins were issued in descending alphabetical order, from Zacatecas through Aguascalientes.

The second, or "emblematic," series began in 2005. Each state's reverse featured images "related to architecture, art, science, fauna, flora, typical dresses or dances or geographical areas of interest peculiar to each state" (Banco de México, "The History of Coins and Banknotes in Mexico," www.banxico.org). The coins were released in normal alphabetical order, from Aguascalientes through Zacatecas. For both series in the program, the obverses bore the national coat of arms.

Numerous other circulating commemoratives were released from 2005 onward. These included the 400th anniversary of the first edition of *El Ingenioso Hidalgo Don Quijote de la Mancha*, by Miguel de Cervantes; the 470th anniversary of the Casa de Moneda de México; the 80th anniversary of the creation of the Banco de México; and the 100th anniversary of the 1905 Monetary Reform. Non-circulating commemoratives, including the Proof-only designs, are discussed in chapter 15, "Commemoratives of the Coinage Reforms of 1905 and 1992."

5 CENTAVOS

5 centavos, stainless steel, 1.58 g. Type A1.

Obverse: The national coat of arms at center, with the legend ESTADOS UNIDOS MEXICANOS above and a half-wreath of oak and laurel below. *Reverse:* On a five-sided field, at center, the denomination 5¢, the date, and the mintmark M°. To the left and below, a partial border of stylized sun-rays from the Ring of Quincunces (Anillo de los Quincunces) on the Aztec calendar stone. *Diameter:* 15.5 mm. *Edge:* Plain. BW-671, KM-546.

Date			
1992	1995	1997	2000
1993	1995, PF	1998	2001
1994	1996	1999	2002

10 CENTAVOS

10 centavos, stainless steel, 2.08 g. Type A1.

Obverse: The national coat of arms at center, with the legend ESTADOS UNIDOS MEXICANOS above and a half-wreath of oak and laurel below. *Reverse:* On a six-sided field, at center, the denomination 10¢, the date, and the mintmark M°. To the right and below, a partial border of stylized designs from the Ring of Sacrifice (Anillo del Sacrificio) on the Aztec calendar stone. *Diameter:* 17 mm. *Edge:* Plain. BW-672, KM-547.

Date			
1992	1996	2001	2006
1993	1997	2002	2007
1994	1998	2003	2008
1995	1999	2004	2009
1995, PF	2000	2005	

10 centavos, stainless steel, 2.08 g. Type A2.

Obverse: The national coat of arms at center, with the legend ESTADOS UNIDOS MEXICANOS above and a half-wreath of oak and laurel below. *Reverse:* At the center, the denomination 10¢, the date, and the mintmark M̊. To the right and below, a partial border of stylized designs from the Ring of Sacrifice (Anillo del Sacrificio) on the Aztec calendar stone. *Diameter:* 14.5 mm. *Edge:* Plain. BW-672.1, KM-934.

Date		
2009	2011	2013
2010	2012	

20 CENTAVOS

20 centavos, 0.92 copper, 0.06 aluminum, 0.02 nickel; 3.04 g. Type A1.

Obverse: The national coat of arms at center, with the legend ESTADOS UNIDOS MEXICANOS above and a half-wreath of oak and laurel below. *Reverse:* On a 12-sided field, at the center, the denomination 20¢, the date, and the mintmark M̊. From upper left to lower right, a partial border of stylized designs from Reed (Acatl), the 13th day on the Aztec calendar stone. *Diameter:* 19.5 mm, dodecagonal (12-sided). *Edge:* Plain. BW-673, KM-548.

Date			
1992	1996	2001	2006
1993	1997	2002	2007
1994	1998	2003	2008
1995	1999	2004	2009
1995, PF	2000	2005	

20 centavos, 0.92 copper, 0.06 aluminum, 0.02 nickel; 2.258 g. Type A2.

Obverse: The national coat of arms at center, with the legend ESTADOS UNIDOS MEXICANOS above and a half-wreath of oak and laurel below. *Reverse:* At the center, the denomination 20¢, the date, and the mintmark M̊. From upper left to lower right, a partial border of stylized designs from Reed (Acatl), the 13th day on the Aztec calendar stone. *Diameter:* 15.3 mm, round planchet. *Edge:* Non-continuous grooved. BW-673.1, KM-935.

Date		
2009	2011	2013
2010	2012	

50 CENTAVOS

50 centavos, 0.92 copper, 0.06 aluminum, 0.02 nickel; 4.39 g. Type A1.

Obverse: The national coat of arms at center, with the legend ESTADOS UNIDOS MEXICANOS above and a half-wreath of oak and laurel below. *Reverse:* At the center, the denomination 50¢, the date, and the mintmark M̊. From upper left, around the bottom, to upper right, a border of stylized designs from the Ring of Acceptance (Anillo de la Aceptación; a representation of the god's acceptance of sacrifice) on the Aztec calendar stone. *Diameter:* 22 mm, dodecagonal (12-sided) planchet. *Edge:* Plain. BW-674, KM-549.

Date			
1992	1996	2001	2006
1993	1997	2002	2007
1994	1998	2003	2008
1995	1999	2004	2009
1995, PF	2000	2005	

50 centavos, stainless steel, 3.103 g. Type A2.

Obverse: The national coat of arms at center, with the legend ESTADOS UNIDOS MEXICANOS above and a half-wreath of oak and laurel below. *Reverse:* At the center, the denomination 50¢, the date, and the mintmark M̊. From upper left, around the bottom, to upper right, a partial border of stylized designs from the Ring of Acceptance (Anillo de la Aceptación; a representation of the god's acceptance of sacrifice) on the Aztec calendar stone. *Diameter:* 17 mm, round planchet. *Edge:* Grooved. BW-674.1, KM-936.

Date		
2009	2011	2013
2010	2012	

1 PESO

New 1 peso, bimetallic (center, 0.92 copper, 0.06 aluminum, 0.02 nickel; outer ring, stainless steel); 3.95 g. Type A1.

Obverse: On the bronze-aluminum center, the national coat of arms; on the stainless-steel ring, the legend ESTADOS UNIDOS MEXICANOS above, with a half-wreath of oak and laurel below. *Reverse:* At the center, the denomination N$1, the date, and the mintmark M̊. On the outer ring, stylized designs from the Ring of Splendor (Anillo del Resplandor) on the Aztec calendar stone. *Diameter:* 21 mm. *Edge:* Plain. BW-675, KM-550.

Date		
1992	1994	1995, PF
1993	1995	

1 peso, bimetallic (center, 0.92 copper, 0.06 aluminum, 0.02 nickel; outer ring, stainless steel); 3.95 g. Type A2.

Obverse: On the bronze-aluminum center, the national coat of arms; on the stainless-steel ring, the legend ESTADOS UNIDOS MEXICANOS above, with a half-wreath of oak and laurel below. *Reverse:* At the center, the denomination $1, the date, and the mintmark M̊. On the outer ring, stylized designs from the Ring of Splendor (Anillo del Resplandor) on the Aztec calendar stone. *Diameter:* 21 mm. *Edge:* Plain. BW-675.1, KM-603.

Date			
1996	2001	2006	2011
1997	2002	2007	2012
1998	2003	2008	2013
1999	2004	2009	
2000	2005	2010	

2 PESOS

New 2 pesos, bimetallic (center, 0.92 copper, 0.06 aluminum, 0.02 nickel; outer ring, stainless steel); 5.19 g. Type A1.

Obverse: On the bronze-aluminum center, the national coat of arms; on the stainless-steel ring, the legend ESTADOS UNIDOS MEXICANOS above, with a half-wreath of oak and laurel below. *Reverse:* At the center, the denomination N$2, the date, and the mintmark M̊. On the outer ring, stylized designs from the Ring of Days (Anillo de los Días), the outer ring on the Aztec calendar stone. *Diameter:* 23 mm. *Edge:* Plain. BW-676, KM-551.

Date		
1992	1994	1995, PF
1993	1995	

2 pesos, bimetallic (center, 0.92 copper, 0.06 aluminum, 0.02 nickel; outer ring, stainless steel); 7.07 g. Type A2.

Obverse: On the bronze-aluminum center, the national coat of arms; on the stainless-steel ring, the legend ESTADOS UNIDOS MEXICANOS above, with a half-wreath of oak and laurel below. *Reverse:* At the center, the denomination $2, the date, and the mintmark M̊. On the outer ring, stylized designs from the Ring of Days (Anillo de los Días), the outer ring on the Aztec calendar stone. *Diameter:* 23 mm. *Edge:* Plain. BW-676.1, KM-604.

Date			
1996	2001	2006	2011
1997	2002	2007	2012
1998	2003	2008	2013
1999	2004	2009	
2000	2005	2010	

5 PESOS

New 5 pesos, bimetallic (center, 0.92 copper, 0.06 aluminum, 0.02 nickel; outer ring, stainless steel); 7.07 g. Type A1.

Obverse: On the bronze-aluminum center, the national coat of arms; on the stainless-steel ring, the legend ESTADOS UNIDOS MEXICANOS above, with a half-wreath of oak and laurel below. *Reverse:* At the center, the denomination N$5, the date, and the mintmark M̊. On the outer ring, stylized designs from the Serpent Ring (Anillo de las Serpientes) on the Aztec calendar stone. *Diameter:* 25.5 mm. *Edge:* Plain. BW-679, KM-552.

Date			
1992	1993	1994	1995, PF

5 pesos, bimetallic (center, 0.92 copper, 0.06 aluminum, 0.02 nickel; outer ring, stainless steel); 7.07 g. Type A2.

Obverse: On the bronze-aluminum center, the national coat of arms; on the stainless-steel ring, the legend ESTADOS UNIDOS MEXICANOS above, with a half-wreath of oak and laurel below. *Reverse:* At the center, the denomination $5, the date, and the mintmark M̊. On the outer ring, stylized designs from the Serpent Ring (Anillo de las Serpientes) on the Aztec calendar stone. *Diameter:* 25.5 mm. *Edge:* Plain. BW-680, KM-605.

Date			
1997	2002	2007	2012
1998	2003	2008	2013
1999	2004	2009	
2000	2005	2010	
2001	2006	2011	

The Bicentennial of Independence and the Centennial of the Revolution

Two very important series, authorized by decree on October 23, 2007, were released to commemorate the various personages in the struggle for independence and the leaders of the 1910–1920 revolution. The first issues of the two series were released in November 2008, with the remainder released through 2010. The busts of the personages are featured on the reverse.

5 pesos, bimetallic (center, 0.92 copper, 0.06 aluminum, 0.02 nickel; outer ring, stainless steel); 7.07 g. Type A24.

Obverse: On the bronze-aluminum center, the national coat of arms; on the stainless-steel outer ring, the legend ESTADOS UNIDOS MEXICANOS above, with a half-wreath of oak and laurel below. *Reverse:* At the center, a bust of one of 20 heroes of the War of Independence, with the name below and, in varying positions in the field, the date, denomination $5, and mintmark M̊. On the outer ring, BICENTENARIO DE LA INDEPENDENCIA at the top, with • MÉXICO 2010 • below. *Diameter:* 25.5 mm. *Edge:* Plain.

2008

Ignacio López Rayón, BW-680.1, KM-894

Carlos María de Bustamante, BW-680.3, KM-896

Francisco Javier Mina, BW-680.5, KM-898

Francisco Primo de Verdad y Ramos, BW-680.7, KM-900.1

Francisco Primo de Verdad y Ramos (error, without dots in legend), BW-680.7a, KM-900.2

Mariano Matamoros, BW-680.9, KM-902

Miguel Ramos Arizpe, BW-680.11, KM-904

Hermenegildo Galeana, BW-680.13, KM-906

2009

José María Cos, BW-680.15, KM-908

Pedro Moreno, BW-680.17, KM-910

Agustín de Iturbide, BW-680.19, KM-912

Nicolás Bravo, BW-680.21, KM-914

Servando Teresa de Mier, BW-680.23, KM-916

2010

Leona Vicario, BW-680.25, KM-919

Miguel Hidalgo y Costilla, BW-680.27, KM-UL

José María Morelos y Pavón, BW-680.29, KM-UL

Vicente Guerrero, BW-680.31, KM-UL

Ignacio Allende, BW-680.33, KM-UL

Guadalupe Victoria, BW-680.35, KM-UL

Josefa Ortiz de Domínguez, BW-680.37, KM-UL

5 pesos, bimetallic (center, 0.92 copper, 0.06 aluminum, 0.02 nickel; outer ring, stainless steel); 7.07 g. Type A25.

Obverse: On the bronze-aluminum center, the national coat of arms; on the stainless-steel outer ring, the legend ESTADOS UNIDOS MEXICANOS above, with a half-wreath of oak and laurel below. *Reverse:* At the center, a bust of one of 18 heroes of the Mexican Revolution, with the name below and, in varying positions in the field, the date, denomination $5, and mintmark M̊. On the outer ring, CENTENARIO DE LA REVOLUCIÓN at the top, with • MÉXICO 2010 • below. *Diameter:* 25.5 mm. *Edge:* Plain.

2008

Álvaro Obregón, BW-680.2, KM-895

José Vasconcelos, BW-680.4, KM-897

Francisco Villa, BW-680.6, KM-899

Heriberto Jara, BW-680.8, KM-901

Ricardo Flores Magón, BW-680.10, KM-903

Francisco J. Múgica, BW-680.12, KM-905

2009

Filomeno Mata, BW-680.14, KM-907

Carmen Serdán, BW-680.16, KM-909

Andrés Molina Enríquez, BW-680.18, KM-911

Luis Cabrera, BW-680.20, KM-913

Eulalio Gutiérrez, BW-680.22, KM-915

Otilio Montaño, BW-680.24, KM-917

Belisario Domínguez, BW-680.26, KM-918

2010

Francisco I. Madero, BW-680.28, KM-UL

Emiliano Zapata, BW-680.30, KM-UL

Venustiano Carranza, BW-680.32, KM-UL

La soldadera, BW-680.34, KM-UL

José María Pino Suárez, BW-680.36, KM-UL

10 PESOS

New 10 pesos, bimetallic (center, 0.925 silver, 0.075 copper; outer ring, 0.92 copper, 0.06 aluminum, 0.02 nickel); 11.138 g. Type A1.

Obverse: On the silver center, the national coat of arms; on the bronze-aluminum outer ring, the legend ESTADOS UNIDOS MEXICANOS above, with a half-wreath of oak and laurel below. *Reverse:* On the outer ring, the denomination N$10 at the top and DIEZ NUEVOS PESOS at the bottom, with the year at upper left and the mintmark M̊ at upper right. At the center, the central design on the Aztec calendar stone, which is generally believed to represent the sun god Tonatiuh. *Diameter:* 28 mm. *Edge:* Reeded. BW-681, KM-553.

Date		
1992	1994	1995, PF
1993	1995	

10 pesos, bimetallic (center, silver-plated alpaca, 0.65 copper, 0.10 nickel, 0.25 zinc; outer ring, 0.92 copper, 0.06 aluminum, 0.02 nickel); 10.329 g. Type A2.

Obverse: On the alpaca (also known as German silver) center, the national coat of arms; on the bronze-aluminum outer ring, the legend ESTADOS UNIDOS MEXICANOS above, with a half-wreath of oak and laurel below. *Reverse:* On the outer ring, the denomination $10 at the top and DIEZ PESOS at the bottom, with the year at upper left and the mintmark M̊ at upper right. At the center, the central design on the Aztec calendar stone, which is generally believed to represent the sun god Tonatiuh. *Diameter:* 28 mm. *Edge:* Reeded. BW-681.1, KM-616.

Date		
1997	1998	1999

10 pesos, bimetallic (center, silver-plated alpaca, 0.65 copper, 0.10 nickel, 0.25 zinc; outer ring, 0.92 copper, 0.06 aluminum, 0.02 nickel); 10.329 g. Type A3.

Obverse: On the alpaca (also known as German silver) center, the national coat of arms; on the bronze-aluminum outer ring, the legend ESTADOS UNIDOS MEXICANOS above, with a half-wreath of oak and laurel below. *Reverse:* On the outer ring, the denomination $10 at the top and AÑO [date] at the bottom, with the mintmark M° at far left. At the center, the central design on the Aztec calendar stone, which is generally believed to represent the sun god Tonatiuh. *Diameter:* 28 mm. *Edge:* Lettered with AÑO and the date three times. BW-681.2, KM-636.

Date	
2000	2001

10 pesos, bimetallic (center, silver-plated alpaca, 0.65 copper, 0.10 nickel, 0.25 zinc; outer ring, 0.92 copper, 0.06 aluminum, 0.02 nickel); 10.329 g. Type A4.

Obverse: On the alpaca (also known as German silver) center, the national coat of arms; on the bronze-aluminum outer ring, the legend ESTADOS UNIDOS MEXICANOS above, with a half-wreath of oak and laurel below. *Reverse:* On the outer ring, the denomination $10 at the top and DIEZ PESOS at the bottom, with the year at upper left and the mintmark M° at upper right. At the center, the central design on the Aztec calendar stone, which is generally believed to represent the sun god Tonatiuh. *Diameter:* 28 mm. *Edge:* Reeded. BW-681.3, KM-636.

Date			
2002	2006	2009	2012
2004	2007	2010	2013
2005	2008	2011	

150th Anniversary of the Battle of Puebla and the Death of General Ignacio Zaragoza

This 10-peso coin was released to commemorate the victory of 4,500 Mexican troops over a well-equipped French force of 8,000 in Puebla on May 5, 1862, at Fort Loreto and Fort Guadalupe. After losing more than 1,000 soldiers, the French withdrew to Orizaba and the coast to fight another day.

10 pesos, bimetallic (center, silver-plated alpaca, 0.65 copper, 0.10 nickel, 0.25 zinc; outer ring, 0.92 copper, 0.06 aluminum, 0.02 nickel); 10.329 g. Type 1.

Obverse: On the alpaca (also known as German silver) center, the national coat of arms; on the bronze-aluminum outer ring, the legend ESTADOS UNIDOS MEXICANOS above, with a half-wreath of oak and laurel below. *Reverse:* On the outer ring, the denomination $10 at the bottom, flanked by the dates 1862 and 2012; around the top, • 150 ANIVERSARIO DE LA BATALLA DE PUEBLA • / 5 DE MAYO. At the center, a portrait of General Ignacio Zaragoza in front of a battle scene (French invaders and Mexican troops, with the forts of Oreto and Guadalupe in the distance); mintmark M° to the right of the portrait, with GRAL. I. ZARAGOZA above. *Diameter:* 28 mm. *Edge:* Alternating plain and reeded. BW-720, KM-UL.

Date
2012

20 PESOS

New 20 pesos, bimetallic (center, 0.925 silver, 0.075 copper; outer ring, 0.92 copper, 0.06 aluminum, 0.02 nickel); 15.945 g. Type A1.

Obverse: On the silver center, the national coat of arms; on the bronze-aluminum outer ring, the legend **ESTADOS UNIDOS MEXICANOS** above, with a half-wreath of oak and laurel below. *Reverse:* On the outer ring, the denomination **N$20** at the top with a half-wreath of laurel below. At the center, a left-facing bust of Father Miguel Hidalgo y Costilla, one of the leaders of the War of Independence. To the right of the bust, the date and mintmark M°; below the neck, **HIDALGO**. *Diameter:* 32 mm. *Edge:* Reeded. BW-682, KM-561.

Date		
1993	1994	1995

20 pesos, bimetallic (center, 0.65 copper, 0.10 nickel, 0.25 zinc; outer ring, 0.92 copper, 0.06 aluminum, 0.02 nickel); 15.945 g. Type A2.

Obverse: On the alpaca (German silver) center, the national coat of arms; on the bronze-aluminum outer ring, the legend **ESTADOS UNIDOS MEXICANOS** above, with a half-wreath of oak and laurel below. *Reverse:* On the outer ring, a pattern of stylized rays and dentils from the Aztec calendar stone. At the bottom of the ring, **AÑO [date]**. At the center, the figure of Xiuhtecuhtli (the god of fire, and the owner of time). Above the figure, **FUEGO NUEVO** ("New Fire"); to the right of the figure, **$20** and the mintmark M°; below and to the right, **XIUHTECUHTLI**. *Diameter:* 32 mm. *Edge:* Alternating plain and reeded. BW-682.1, KM-637.

Date	
2000	2001

20 pesos, bimetallic (center, 0.65 copper, 0.10 nickel, 0.25 zinc; outer ring, 0.92 copper, 0.06 aluminum, 0.02 nickel); 15.996 g. Type A3.

Obverse: On the alpaca (German silver) center, the national coat of arms; on the bronze-aluminum outer ring, the legend **ESTADOS UNIDOS MEXICANOS** above, with a half-wreath of oak and laurel below. *Reverse:* To the left of center, a bust of Mexican poet and Nobel Laureate Octavio Paz in three-quarter profile facing right; in the field to the right of the bust, extending onto the outer ring, a famous verse by the poet with a reproduction of his signature below. At the top of the outer ring, **$20**, with **AÑO [date]** below and the mintmark M° at far left. *Diameter:* 32 mm. *Edge:* Alternating plain and reeded. BW-682.2, KM-638.

Date	
2000	2001

20 pesos, bimetallic (center, 0.65 copper, 0.10 nickel, 0.25 zinc; outer ring, 0.92 copper, 0.06 aluminum, 0.02 nickel); 15.996 g. Type A4.

Obverse: On the alpaca (German silver) center, the national coat of arms; on the bronze-aluminum outer ring, the legend **ESTADOS UNIDOS MEXICANOS** above, with a half-wreath of oak and laurel below. *Reverse:* To the left of center, a bust of Mexican poet and Nobel Laureate Octavio Paz in three-quarter profile with hand to chin; in the field to the right of the bust, **Premio Nobel de / Literatura / 1990**. At the top of the outer ring, **$20** with **OCTAVIO PAZ** immediately below; at the bottom, a verse by the poet and **VEINTE PESOS**. At upper left, **2010**; mintmark M° at upper right. *Diameter:* 32 mm. *Edge:* Alternating plain and reeded. BW-682.4, KM-UL.

Date
2010

100th Anniversary of the Death of Belisario Domínguez Palencia

This 20-peso coin commemorates the execution of Senator Belisario Domínguez Palencia on October 7, 1913. The distinguished senator was one of several who had spoken out against dictator Victoriano Huerta, after the latter mounted a coup against the legally elected government and murdered its president, Francisco Madero, and vice president, José María Pino Suárez.

20 pesos, bimetallic (center, silver-plated alpaca, 0.65 copper, 0.10 nickel, 0.25 zinc; outer ring, 0.92 copper, 0.06 aluminum, 0.02 nickel); 15.945 g. Type 9.

Obverse: On the alpaca (German silver) center, the national coat of arms; on the bronze-aluminum outer ring, the legend ESTADOS UNIDOS MEXICANOS above, with a half-wreath of oak and laurel below. *Reverse:* On the outer ring, the denomination $20 at the bottom; at the left, 100 ANIVERSARIO / LUCTUOSO ("100th Anniversary of His Death"); at the right, 150 ANIVERSARIO / DE SU NACIMIENTO ("150th Anniversary of His Birth"). At the center, a portrait of Senator Domínguez in three-quarter profile facing right, with the mintmark M̊ and the dates 1863–2013 to the right of the portrait. At the top of the coin, in three lines (beginning on the outer ring and continuing on the silver center), BELISARIO / DOMÍNGUEZ / ENNOBLECIÓ A LA PATRIA ("Belisario Domínguez Dignified Our Homeland"). *Diameter:* 32 mm. *Edge:* Alternating plain and reeded. BW-720.1, KM-UL.

Date
2013

100th Anniversary of Mexico's Armed Forces

20 pesos, bimetallic (center, silver-plated alpaca, 0.65 copper, 0.10 nickel, 0.25 zinc; outer ring, 0.92 copper, 0.06 aluminum, 0.02 nickel); 15.945 g. Type 1.

Obverse: On the alpaca (German silver) center, the national coat of arms; on the bronze-aluminum outer ring, the legend ESTADOS UNIDOS MEXICANOS above, with a half-wreath of oak and laurel below. *Reverse:* On the outer ring, the denomination $20 at the bottom, with VEINTE PESOS at the top; at the left, 2013; at the right, mintmark M̊. At the center, a stylized profile of a helmeted soldier flanked by the dates 1913 and 2013 and surrounded by a pattern of concentric circles. Above, the legend 100 Años del Ejército Mexicano ("100 Years of Mexico's Armed Forces"); below, 100 Años de LEALTAD ("100 Years of Loyalty"). *Diameter:* 32 mm. *Edge:* Alternating plain and reeded. BW-720.2, KM-UL.

Date
2013

50 PESOS

New 50 pesos, bimetallic (center, 0.925 silver, 0.075 copper; outer ring, 0.92 copper, 0.06 aluminum, 0.02 nickel); 33.967 g. Type A1.

Obverse: On the silver center, the national coat of arms; on the bronze-aluminum outer ring, the legend ESTADOS UNIDOS MEXICANOS above, with a half-wreath of oak and laurel below. *Reverse:* On the outer ring, the denomination N$50 at the top with a half-wreath of laurel below. At the center, in front of the Mexican flag, the busts of six young men—the "Boy Heroes," military cadets from the school in Chapultepec Castle, Mexico City, who were killed defending the castle against the Americans during the Mexican War in 1847. Below the central design, NIÑOS HÉROES; above left, the mintmark M°; above right, the date. *Diameter:* 39 mm. *Edge:* Reeded. BW-683, KM-571.

Date		
1993	1994	1995

100 PESOS

Mexican State Federation Series Number 1

100 pesos, bimetallic (center, 0.925 silver, 0.075 copper; outer ring, 0.92 copper, 0.06 aluminum, 0.02 nickel); 33.967 g. Type A1.

Obverse: On the silver center, the national coat of arms; on the bronze-aluminum outer ring, the legend ESTADOS UNIDOS MEXICANOS above, with a half-wreath of oak and laurel below. *Reverse:* At the center, a coat of arms of one of the 31 states of Mexico and the Distrito Federal, with the date above. On the outer ring, the name of the respective state at the top, with $100 at the bottom and mintmark M° at far left. *Diameter:* 39 mm. *Edge:* Alternating plain and reeded.

Note: The Proofs from this series (silver 10 pesos and bimetallic gold-and-silver 100 pesos) are cataloged in chapter 15.

Designs for series number 1 are as follows:

2003

Zacatecas, BW-684.1, KM-688
Yucatán, BW-684.2, KM-689
Veracruz, BW-684.3, KM-690
Tlaxcala, BW-684.4, KM-691

2004

Tamaulipas, BW-684.5, KM-692
Tabasco, BW-684.6, KM-693
Sonora, BW-684.7, KM-694
Sinaloa, BW-684.8, KM-695
San Luis Potosí, BW-684.9, KM-803
Querétaro, BW-684.10, KM-734
Quintana Roo, BW-684.11, KM-736
Puebla, BW-684.12, KM-738
Oaxaca, BW-684.13, KM-740
Nuevo León, BW-684.14, KM-742
Nayarit, BW-684.15, KM 744
Morelos, BW-684.16, KM-746
Michoacán, BW-684.17, KM-804
Estado de México, BW-684.18, KM-748
Jalisco, BW-684.19, KM-750

2005

Hidalgo, BW-684.20, KM-717
Guerrero, BW-684.21, KM-716
Guanajuato, BW-684.22, KM-715
Distrito Federal, BW-684.23, KM-713
Durango, BW-684.24, KM-714
Chihuahua, BW-684.25, KM-754
Chiapas, BW-684.26, KM-712
Colima, BW-684.27, KM-729
Coahuila, BW-684.28, KM-752
Campeche, BW-684.29, KM-727
Baja California Sur, BW-684.30, KM-723
Baja California, BW-684.31, KM-725
Aguascalientes, BW-684.32, KM-721

Mexican State Federation Series Number 2

100 pesos, bimetallic (center, 0.925 silver, 0.075 copper; outer ring, 0.92 copper, 0.06 aluminum, 0.02 nickel); 33.967 g. Type A3.

Obverse: On the silver center, the national coat of arms; on the bronze-aluminum outer ring, the legend ESTADOS UNIDOS MEXICANOS above, with a half-wreath of oak and laurel below. *Reverse:* At the center, a design emblematic of one of the 31 states of Mexico (plus the Distrito Federal), along with the name of the state, the date, the denomination $100, and the mintmark M°. *Diameter:* 39 mm. *Edge:* Alternating plain and reeded.

Note: The Proofs from this series (silver 10 pesos and bimetallic gold-and-silver 100 pesos) are cataloged in chapter 15.

Designs for series number 2 are as follows:

2005

Aguascalientes, BW-685.1, KM-719

Baja California, BW-685.2, KM-758

2006

Baja California Sur, BW-685.3, KM-762

Campeche, BW-685.4, KM-760

Coahuila, BW-685.5, KM-781

Colima, BW-685.6, KM-777

Chiapas, BW-685.7, KM-773

Chihuahua, BW-685.8, KM-775

Distrito Federal, BW-685.9, KM-779

Durango, BW-685.10, KM-787

Guanajuato, BW-685.11, KM-789

Guerrero, BW-685.12, KM-791

Hidalgo, BW-685.13, KM-793

Jalisco, BW-685.14, KM-795

Estado de México, BW-685.15, KM-802

Michoacán, BW-685.16, KM-785

Morelos, BW-685.17, KM-800

2007

Nayarit, BW-685.18, KM-798

Nuevo León, BW-685.19, KM-848

Oaxaca, BW-685.20, KM-849

Puebla, BW-685.21, KM-850

Querétaro, BW-685.22, KM-852

Quintana Roo, BW-685.23, KM-851

San Luis Potosí, BW-685.24, KM-853

Sinaloa, BW-685.25, KM-854

Sonora, BW-685.26, KM-855

Tabasco, BW-685.27, KM-856

Tamaulipas, BW-685.28, KM-857

Tlaxcala, BW-685.29, KM-858

Veracruz, BW-685.30, KM-859

Yucatán, BW-685.31, KM-860

Zacatecas, BW-685.32, KM-861

Other Mexican Anniversaries

The year 2005 also saw the release of circulating commemoratives in smaller series (compared to the 32 federation coins). The first of these commemorated the 400th anniversary of Miguel de Cervantes' *El Ingenioso Hidalgo Don Quijote de la Mancha* ("Don Quixote"). Three others honored events of national importance in Mexico's monetary history: the 470th anniversary of the Casa de Moneda de México; the 80th anniversary of the Banco de México; and the 100th anniversary of the 1905 Monetary Reform. (The Proof issuances of this series are listed in chapter 15.)

These coins were followed in 2006 by a 100-peso coin honoring the bicentennial of the birth of President Benito Pablo Juárez García.

400th Anniversary of "Don Quijote de la Mancha"

100 pesos, bimetallic (center, 0.925 silver, 0.075 copper; outer ring, 0.92 copper, 0.06 aluminum, 0.02 nickel); 3.967 g. Type A7.

Obverse: On the silver center, the national coat of arms; on the bronze-aluminum outer ring, the legend ESTADOS UNIDOS MEXICANOS above, with a half-wreath of oak and laurel below. *Reverse:* At the center, a reproduction of the famous engraving *Calavera Quijotesca* (a skeletal horse and rider with spear, scattering smaller skeletons in their wake), with the Mexican artist's name, J.G. POSADA, above, along with the mintmark M°. The denomination $100 is below. Around the outer ring, • DON QUIJOTE DE LA MANCHA • above, with the dates 1605–2005 (divided by 400 ANIVERSARIO) below. *Diameter:* 39 mm. *Edge:* Alternating plain and reeded. BW-690, KM-705.

100th Anniversary of the 1905 Monetary Reform

100 pesos, bimetallic (center, 0.925 silver, 0.075 copper; outer ring, 0.92 copper, 0.06 aluminum, 0.02 nickel); 3.967 g. Type A3.

Obverse: On the silver center, the national coat of arms; on the bronze-aluminum outer ring, the legend ESTADOS UNIDOS MEXICANOS above, with a half-wreath of oak and laurel below. *Reverse:* At the center, a small radiant liberty cap above the denomination $100. To the left and right, the dates 1925 and 2005, respectively, with the mintmark M̊ above right. At the top of the outer ring, REFORMA MONETARIA (Monetary Reform), above a half-wreath of oak and laurel. *Diameter:* 39 mm. *Edge:* Alternating plain and reeded. BW-686, KM-730.

470th Anniversary of the Casa de Moneda de México

100 pesos, bimetallic (center, 0.925 silver, 0.075 copper; outer ring, 0.92 copper, 0.06 aluminum, 0.02 nickel); 3.967 g. Type A4.

Obverse: On the silver center, the national coat of arms; on the bronze-aluminum outer ring, the legend ESTADOS UNIDOS MEXICANOS above, with a half-wreath of oak and laurel below. *Reverse:* Off-center to the right, a screw-style coin press, with the denomination $100 to the left. Above and below the press, the dates 1535 and 2005, respectively, with the mintmark M̊ to the right. At the top of the outer ring, CASA DE MONEDA DE MÉXICO; at the bottom, • 470 ANIVERSARIO •. *Diameter:* 39 mm. *Edge:* Alternating plain and reeded. BW-687, KM-731.

80th Anniversary of the Banco de México

100 pesos, bimetallic (center, 0.925 silver, 0.075 copper; outer ring, 0.92 copper, 0.06 aluminum, 0.02 nickel); 3.967 g. Type A5.

Obverse: On the silver center, the national coat of arms; on the bronze-aluminum outer ring, the legend ESTADOS UNIDOS MEXICANOS above, with a half-wreath of oak and laurel below. *Reverse:* At center and extending into the outer ring, the rare 1925 one-hundred-peso note of the Banco de México. Above the note, the denomination $100. At the top, the dates 1925 and 2005, separated by the logo of the Banco de México, with the mintmark M̊. At the bottom, LXXX / ANIVERSARIO (80th Anniversary). *Diameter:* 39 mm. *Edge:* Alternating plain and reeded. BW-688, KM-732.

Bicentennial of the Birth of Benito Pablo Juárez García

100 pesos, bimetallic (center, 0.925 silver, 0.075 copper; outer ring, 0.92 copper, 0.06 aluminum, 0.02 nickel); 3.967 g. Type A4.

Obverse: On the silver center, the national coat of arms; on the bronze-aluminum outer ring, the legend ESTADOS UNIDOS MEXICANOS above, with a half-wreath of oak and laurel below. *Reverse:* At center, a bust of Benito Pablo Juárez García with a facsimile of his signature below. To the left, the mintmark M̊, with 2006 to the right. Around the outer ring, BICENTENARIO DEL NATALICIO DE BENITO JUÁREZ GARCÍA / $100. *Diameter:* 39 mm. *Edge:* Alternating plain and reeded. BW-689, KM-764.

Note: Silver Proofs were not issued for this event.

The Coinage Reform of 1992

5 centavos. 1997 (Type A1).
BW-671, KM-546, 15.5 mm.

10 centavos. 1992 (Type A1).
BW-672, KM-547, 17 mm.

10 centavos. 2009 (Type A2).
BW-672, KM-UL, 14.5 mm.

20 centavos. 1995 (Type A1).
BW-673, KM-548, 19.5 mm.

20 centavos. 2005 (Type A2).
BW-673.1, KM-935, 15.3 mm.

50 centavos. 1992 (Type A1).
BW-674, KM-549, 22 mm.

50 centavos. 2010 (Type A2).
BW-674.1, KM-936, 17 mm.

New 1 peso. 1992 (Type A1).
BW-675, KM-550, 21 mm.

1 peso. 1997 (Type A2).
BW-675.1, KM-603, 21 mm.

New 2 pesos. 1992 (Type A1).
BW-676, KM-551, 23 mm.

2 pesos. 1997 (Type A2).
BW-676.1, KM-604, 23 mm.

New 5 pesos. 1992 (Type A1).
BW-679, KM 552, 25.5 mm.

5 pesos. 1997 (Type A2). BW-680,
KM-605, 25.5 mm.

The Coinage Reform of 1992
(continued)

Selections From the Independence Bicentennial $5 Series

5 pesos. Common obverse, Bicentennial of Independence series (Type A24). BW-680, 25.5 mm.

2008, Ignacio López Rayón. BW-680.1, KM-894.

2009, Agustín de Iturbide. BW-680.19, KM-912.

2010, Miguel Hidalgo y Costilla. BW-680.27, KM-UL.

2010, Ignacio Allende. BW-680.33, KM-UL.

Selections From the Revolution Centennial $5 Series

5 pesos. Common obverse, Centennial of the Revolution series (Type A25). BW-680, 25.5 mm.

2008, Francisco Villa. BW-680.6, KM-899.

2010, Venustiano Carranza. BW-680.32, KM-UL.

2010, Francisco I. Madero. BW-680.28, KM-UL.

2010, Emiliano Zapata. BW-680.30, KM-UL.

The Coinage Reform of 1992

(continued)

New 10 pesos. 1993 (Type A1).
BW-681, KM-553, 28 mm.

10 pesos. 1997 (Type A2).
BW-681.1, KM-616, 28 mm.

10 pesos. 2000 (Type A3).
BW-681.2, KM-636, 28 mm.

10 pesos. 2011 (Type A4).
BW-681.3, KM-636, 28 mm.

New 20 pesos. 1993 (Type A1).
BW-682, KM-561, 32 mm.

20 pesos. 2000 (Type A2), Xiuhtecuhtli.
BW-682.1, KM-637, 32 mm.

20 pesos. 2000 (Type A3), Octavio Paz.
BW-682.2, KM-638, 32 mm.

20 pesos. 2010 (Type A4), Octavio Paz / Premio Nobel. BW-682.4, KM-UL, 32 mm.

The Coinage Reform of 1992

(continued)

New 50 pesos. 1993 (Type A1), Niños Héroes. BW-683, KM-571, 39 mm.

Selections From Mexican State Federation $100 Series No. 1

100 pesos. Common obverse, Mexican State Federation series no. 1 (Type A1). BW-684, 39 mm.

2003, Zacatecas, BW-684.1, KM-688.

2003, Yucatán, BW-684.2, KM-689.

2003, Veracruz, BW-684.3, KM-690.

2003, Tlaxcala, BW-684.4, KM-691.

2004, Sonora, BW-684.7, KM-694.

The Coinage Reform of 1992
(continued)

Selections From Mexican State Federation $100 Series No. 2

100 pesos. Common obverse, Mexican State Federation series no. 2 (Type A3). BW-685, 39 mm.

2007, Sonora.
BW-685.26, KM-855.

2007, Tlaxcala.
BW-685.29, KM-858.

2007, Veracruz.
BW-685.30, KM-859.

2007, Yucatán.
BW-685.31, KM-860.

2007, Zacatecas.
BW-685.32, KM-861.

The Coinage Reform of 1992
(continued)

Other Mexican Circulating Commemoratives

Common obverse design; diameter varies by denomination.

10 pesos. 2012, 150th Anniversary of the Battle of Puebla and the Death of General Ignacio Zaragoza (Type 1). BW-720, KM-UL, 28 mm.

20 pesos. 2013, 100th Anniversary of the Death of Belisario Domínguez Palencia (Type 9). BW-720.1, KM-UL, 32 mm.

20 pesos. 2013, 100th Anniversary of Mexico's Armed Forces (Type 1). BW-720.2, KM-UL, 32 mm.

100 pesos. 2005, 400th Anniversary of "Don Quijote de la Mancha" (Type A7). BW-690, KM-705, 39 mm.

100 pesos. 2005, 100th Anniversary of the 1905 Monetary Reform (Type A3). BW-686, KM-730, 39 mm.

100 pesos. 2005, 470th Anniversary of the Casa de Moneda de México (Type A4). BW-687, KM-731, 39 mm.

100 pesos. 2005, 80th Anniversary of the Banco de México (Type A5). BW-688, KM-732, 39 mm.

100 pesos. 2006, Bicentennial of the Birth of Benito Pablo Juárez García (Type A6). BW-689, KM-764, 39 mm.

15

Commemoratives of the Coinage Reforms of 1905 and 1992

Mexico has issued numerous commemorative, non-circulating legal tender (NCLT) coins, both in bimetallic composition and in the precious metals silver, gold, and platinum. In most cases, both Uncirculated and Proof commemoratives are struck in precious metals, and in low mintages. Some series have circulating counterparts (listed in chapter 14), while others do not. The type numbers used by collectors and referenced herein are organized by denomination, not by series. Thus, type numbers that appear to be missing are actually listed with circulating coinage in the previous chapters, and may or may not refer to designs in the same series. (For example, in the 25-peso denomination, Type 1 is a circulating commemorative that celebrates the 1968 Summer Olympic Games in Mexico City, and Type 2 is a circulating commemorative honoring the 100th anniversary of the death of Benito Juárez. Types 3 through 7 are Proof and Brilliant Uncirculated NCLT coins commemorating the 1986 World Cup Soccer games, and are listed in the current chapter.)

The NCLT classification makes it easier to navigate import regulations through customs. Non-circulating legal tender coins are subject to customs duties, but other legal-tender coins are not. Some purists believe that NCLT coinage should not be collected or viewed as coins because they do not circulate freely. Others hold the view that since they were issued by an official decree of a legitimate government, have a valid denomination, and have legal tender status, they *are* coins and are therefore collectible.

Technical information concerning mintages and other details is covered in volume 2. The Libertad series (which does not have a denomination but does have legal tender status, by official decree) is listed in chapter 19 of the current volume.

1986 WORLD CUP FUTBOL GAMES

In 1986 Mexico was the host country for the World Cup Football (Soccer) Games, called the Copa Mundial de Futbol. The Mexico Mint commemorated this honor with both circulating and NCLT coins in 1985 and 1986.

The common obverse for this series depicts the Mexican national coat of arms with the legend ESTADOS UNIDOS MEXICANOS above and a half-wreath of oak and laurel below. The reverses feature various actions during the games, described in the following listings.

25 pesos, 1985, 0.720 silver, 7.776 g. BU, Type 3.

Diameter: 26 mm. *Edge:* Plain. *Design:* "México 86" on futbol (with fineness). BW-572, KM-497.

25 pesos, 1985, 0.925 silver, 8.406 g. PF, Types 4 and 5.

Diameter: 26 mm. *Edge:* Plain. *Designs:* Type 4, "México 86" below three ornaments (diagonally placed with futbol in front), BW-573, KM-503; Type 5, "México" below speeding futbol, BW-574, KM-514.

25 pesos, 1986, 0.925 silver, 8.406 g. PF, Types 6 and 7.

Diameter: 26 mm. *Edge:* Plain. *Designs:* Type 6, "México" on futbol (without fineness), BW-575, KM-497a; Type 7, "México" below futbol in net, BW-576, KM-519.

50 pesos, 1985, 0.720 silver, 15.552 g. BU, Type 4.

Diameter: 32 mm. *Edge:* Plain. *Design:* Player's feet chasing futbol (with fineness). BW-580, KM-498.

50 pesos, 1985, 0.925 silver, 16.831 g. PF, Types 5 and 6.

Diameter: 32 mm. *Edge:* Plain. *Designs:* Type 5, Mayan ball player with rubber ball, BW-581, KM-504; Type 6, modern player kicking futbol, BW-582, KM-515.

50 pesos, 1986, 0.925 silver, 16.831 g. PF, Types 7 and 8.

Diameter: 32 mm. *Edge:* Plain. *Designs:* Type 7, player's feet chasing futbol (without fineness), BW-583, KM-498a; Type 8, three futbols, BW-584, KM-523.

100 pesos, 1985, 0.720 silver, 31.103 g. BU, Type 3.

Diameter: 38 mm. *Edge:* Plain. *Design:* Speeding futbol with stylized ornaments (with fineness). BW-588, KM-499.

100 pesos, 1985, 0.925 silver, 32.625 g. PF, Types 4 and 5.

Diameter: 38 mm. *Edge:* Plain. *Designs:* Type 4, speeding futbol with stylized ornaments (without fineness), BW-589, KM-499a; Type 5, goalie with ball and net, BW-590, KM-505.

100 pesos, 1986, 0.925 silver, 32.625 g. PF, Types 6 and 7.

Diameter: 38 mm. *Edge:* Plain. *Designs:* Type 6, goalie holding futbol, BW-591, KM-521; Type 7, futbol and globe, BW-592, KM-524.

200 pesos, 1986, 0.999 silver, 62.206 g. BU, Type 4.

Diameter: 48 mm. *Edge:* Plain. *Design:* Futbol with two globes. BW-601, KM-526.

250 pesos, 1985, 0.900 gold, 8.640 g. BU, Types 1 and 3.

Diameter: 22 mm. *Edge:* Plain. *Designs:* Type 1, futbol with ornamented background, BW-602a, KM-500.1; Type 3, Mounted Victory with futbol in background, BW-604a, KM-506.1.

Note: Type 3 also honors **450 años de la casa de moneda** in the legend above the central device.

250 pesos, 1985, 0.900 gold, 8.640 g. PF, Type 4.

Diameter: 22 mm. *Edge:* Plain. *Design:* Mounted Victory with futbol in background. BW-605a, KM-506.2.

Note: Type 4, like Type 3, also honors **450 años de la casa de moneda** in the legend above the central device.

250 pesos, 1986, 0.900 gold, 8.640 g. BU, Type 1.

Diameter: 22 mm. *Edge:* Plain. *Design:* Futbol with ornamented background (with fineness). BW-602.1a, KM-500.1.

250 pesos, 1986, 0.900 gold, 8.640 g. PF, Type 2.

Diameter: 22 mm. *Edge:* Plain. *Design:* Futbol with ornamented background (without fineness). BW-603a, KM-500.2.

500 pesos, 1985, 0.900 gold, 17.280 g. BU, Types 1 and 3.

Diameter: 28 mm. *Edge:* Plain. *Designs:* Type 1, futbol player chasing ball in front of Aztec Calendar (with fineness), BW-606a, KM-501.1; Type 3, futbol in front of Carlos and Johanna coin (with fineness), BW-608a, KM-507.1.

500 pesos, 1985, 0.900 gold, 17.280 g. PF, Types 2 and 3.

Diameter: 28 mm. *Edge:* Plain. *Designs:* Type 2, futbol player chasing ball in front of Aztec Calendar (without fineness), BW-607.1a, KM-501.2; Type 3, futbol in front of Carlos and Johanna coin (without fineness), BW-609a, KM-507.2.

500 pesos, 1986, 0.900 gold, 17.280 g. BU, Type 1.

Diameter: 28 mm. *Edge:* Plain. *Design:* Futbol player chasing ball in front of Aztec Calendar (with fineness). BW-607a, KM-501.1.

1,000 pesos, 1986, 0.999 gold, 31.050 g. BU, Type 2.

Diameter: 30 mm. *Edge:* Plain. *Design:* Futbol with two globes. BW-614a, KM-527.

2,000 pesos, 1986, 0.999 gold, 62.200 g. BU, Type 1.

Diameter: 36 mm. *Edge:* Plain. *Design:* Futbol with two globes. BW-618a, KM-528.

175TH ANNIVERSARY OF INDEPENDENCE

In 1985 two coins were issued to commemorate the 175th anniversary of the beginning of the War of Independence: a 200-peso circulating issue in copper-nickel, and a 1,000-peso NCLT issue in 0.900 gold. The obverses depict the Mexican national coat of arms with the legend ESTADOS UNIDOS MEXICANOS above and a half-wreath of oak and laurel below. The reverses feature the conjoined busts of four heroes of the War of Independence: Ignacio Allende, Miguel Hidalgo y Costilla, José Morelos, and Vicente Guerrero, all facing left. In the background to the left is the monument *El Ángel de la Independencia (The Angel of Independence).*

1,000 pesos, 1985, 0.900 gold, 17.280 g. PF, Type 1.

Diameter: 38 mm. *Edge:* Plain. *Design:* Heroes of the War of Independence. BW-613a, KM-513.

75TH ANNIVERSARY OF THE REVOLUTION

A commemorative 200-peso copper-nickel circulating coin was issued in 1985 for the 75th anniversary of the start of the Mexican Revolution, along with a Proof 500 pesos in 0.925 silver. The obverses depict the Mexican national coat of arms with the legend ESTADOS UNIDOS MEXICANOS above and a half-wreath of oak and laurel below. The reverses feature the conjoined busts of four heroes of the Revolution: Emiliano Zapata, Francisco Madero, Venustiano Carranza, and Francisco "Pancho" Villa; in the background is the *Monumento a la Revolución (Monument of the Revolution).*

500 pesos, 1985, 0.9250 silver, 33.450 g. PF, Type 1.

Diameter: 40 mm. *Edge:* Plain. *Design:* Heroes of the Revolution. BW-610b, KM-511.

WORLD WIDE FUND FOR NATURE

In 1987, Mexico and several other countries took part in a project for the World Wide Fund for Nature (WWF; known as the World Wildlife Fund in the United States and Canada). The WWF is an organization devoted to environmental issues and to preserving endangered species. Mexico's contribution to this project was a 100-peso Proof coin in 0.720 silver. The obverse depicts the Mexican national coat of arms with the legend ESTADOS UNIDOS MEXICANOS above and a half-wreath of oak and laurel below. The reverse features the Monarch butterfly, the North American populations of which migrate thousands of miles each year between Canada and Mexico.

In 1998 Mexico participated in a joint effort to commemorate the WWF's 35th anniversary, issuing a Proof 5 pesos honoring the *lobo* (the Mexican wolf, or *Canis lupus*).

100 pesos, 1987, 0.7200 silver, 32.6250 g. PF, Type 8.
Diameter: 38 mm. *Edge:* Plain. *Design:* Monarch butterflies. BW-593.1, KM-537.

5 pesos, 1998, 0.9990 silver, 31.1035 g. PF, Type A4.
Diameter: 40 mm. *Edge:* Reeded. *Design:* *Lobo*. BW-593.2, KM-627.

50TH ANNIVERSARY OF THE NATIONALIZATION OF THE OIL INDUSTRY

In 1988 Mexico issued circulating and commemorative coins in honor of the 50th anniversary of the nationalization of the oil industry during the presidency of Lázaro Cárdenas. The Brilliant Uncirculated NCLT coins were issued in denominations of 50, 100, 500, and 1,000 pesos. The obverses depict the Mexican national coat of arms with the legend ESTADOS UNIDOS MEXICANOS above and a half-wreath of oak and laurel below. Each reverse features one of two designs: the Fuente de Petróleos (Monument to the Oil Industry, a 1952 statue in Mexico City) or a bust of Lázaro Cárdenas.

A copper-nickel circulating 5,000 pesos was also released; see chapter 13.

50 pesos, (1988), 0.999 silver, 15.550 g. BU, Type 9.
Diameter: 31 mm. *Edge:* Reeded. *Design:* Monument to the Oil Industry. BW-585, KM-532.

100 pesos, 1988, 0.999 silver, 31.103 g. BU, Type 9.
Diameter: 38 mm. *Edge:* Plain. *Design:* Lázaro Cárdenas. BW-594, KM-533.

500 pesos, 1988, 0.900 gold, 17.280 g. BU, Type 2.
Diameter: 28 mm. *Edge:* Plain. *Design:* Monument to the Oil Industry. BW-612, KM-534.

1,000 pesos, 1988, 0.900 gold, 34.559 g. BU, Type 2.
Diameter: 34.5 mm. *Edge:* Plain. *Design:* Lázaro Cárdenas. BW-615, KM-535.

SAVE THE CHILDREN FUND

Mexico, in conjunction with several other countries, issued coins to commemorate the 70th anniversary of the founding of the Save the Children Fund, with each coin featuring children in an activity characteristic of the issuing country. The obverse of Mexico's 100-peso issue bears the Mexican national coat of arms with the legend ESTADOS UNIDOS MEXICANOS above and a half-wreath of oak and laurel below. The reverse depicts three children playing piñata, a game popular with Mexican children on festive occasions.

100 pesos, 1991, 0.925 silver, 33.625 g. PF, Type 10.
Diameter: 40 mm. *Edge:* Plain. *Design:* Children playing piñata. BW-595, KM-539.

UNITED NATIONS ENVIRONMENT PROGRAMME

In 1992, to commemorate the 20th anniversary of the United Nations Environment Programme (UNEP), Mexico issued a Proof 100 pesos featuring the vaquita marina *(Phocoena sinus)*, a species of porpoise discovered in 1958 when three skulls were found on the shores of the Gulf of California. It is currently the most endangered marine mammal in the world. The obverse of the coin depicts the Mexican national coat of arms with the legend ESTADOS UNIDOS MEXICANOS above and a half-wreath of oak and laurel below.

100 pesos, 1992, 0.999 silver, 31.1035 g. PF, Type 12.
Diameter: 40 mm. *Edge:* Plain. *Design:* Vaquita marina. BW-597, KM-566.

IBEROAMERICANA SERIES

In 1991, Mexico and 13 other Latin American countries embarked on an ongoing program of coins struck for the Iberoamericana Series, which celebrates the cultures of Spain, Portugal, and the numerous countries that were at one time their colonies. Eight series have been issued in the program to date, with variations in the participating countries.

In every series, the obverse of each coin bears the coat of arms of the issuing country at center, surrounded by the coats of arms of the other countries participating in that series. The series' themes, and the designs Mexico has contributed to each series, are as follows.

Quincentennial of the Discovery of the Americas

For the first series, issued in 1991 and 1992, Mexico's contribution was the historic *Columnaria* (Pillars) design, with globes of the Eastern and Western Hemispheres between the pillars and the ships of Christopher Columbus below.

100 pesos, 1991, 0.925 silver, 27.00 g. PF, Type A2.
Diameter: 40 mm. *Edge:* Reeded. *Design:* Pillars. BW-596.1, KM-540.

100 pesos, 1992, 0.925 silver, 27.00 g. PF, Type A2.
Diameter: 40 mm. *Edge:* Reeded. *Design:* Pillars. BW-596.2, KM-540.

Endangered Native Animal Species

The second series was issued in 1994. Mexico's contribution, with the denomination N$5 to accommodate the coinage reform of 1992, depicts the Golfina turtle *(Leopidochelus Olivacea)* on the reverse.

New 5 pesos, 1994, 0.925 silver, 27.00 g. PF, Type A3.
Diameter: 40 mm. *Edge:* Reeded. *Design:* Golfina turtle. BW-596.3, KM-588.

Iberoamerican Dances and Costumes

Mexico's contribution to the third series, in 1996, depicts the Jarabe Tapatío, a traditional Mexican dance that dates from the 15th century in Spain.

5 pesos, 1997, 0.925 silver, 27.00 g. PF, Type A5.
Diameter: 40 mm. *Edge:* Reeded. *Design:* Jarabe Tapatío. BW-596.4, KM-629.

5 pesos, 1998, 0.925 silver, 27.00 g. PF, Type A5.
Diameter: 40 mm. *Edge:* Reeded. *Design:* Jarabe Tapatío. BW-596.5, KM-629.

Man and the Horse

For the fourth series, Mexico's contribution, dated 1999 but released in 2001, depicts the the Paso de la Muerte, or "Ride of Death"—a *charreada* (rodeo) event in which the *charro* (cowboy) jumps from the back of a trained horse to the bare back of an unbridled, unbroken horse while the animals are at a gallop.

5 pesos, 2000, 0.925 silver, 27.00 g. PF, Type A21.
Diameter: 40 mm. *Edge:* Reeded. *Design:* Ride of Death. BW-596.6, KM-670.

The Nautical Tradition

In the fifth series, the central figure of Mexico's coin, the *Galeón de Acapulco,* commemorates the galleons (Spanish sailing ships) that made trade possible between the Far East and Mexico during the Hernán Cortes era of the early 1500s. In front of the ship are figures that appear to be Cortes and possibily Moctezuma. In the background are the outlines of the Philippines (at left) and North America (at right), with dotted lines marking the route the galleons traveled between the Philippines and Acapulco.

5 pesos, 2003, 0.925 silver, 27.00 g. PF, Type A22.

Diameter: 40 mm. *Edge:* Reeded. *Design: Galeón de Acapulco.* BW-596.7, KM-678.

Architecture and Monuments

The reverse of Mexico's contribution to the sixth series features the Palacio de Bellas Artes (Palace of Fine Arts). The construction of this Art Nouveau–style building was begun in 1904; however, after the exterior was completed, the interior work was halted for several years, and the building was not completed until 1934.

5 pesos, 2005, 0.925 silver, 31.1035 g. PF, Type A23.

Diameter: 40 mm. *Edge:* Reeded. *Design:* Palacio de Bellas Artes. BW-596.8, KM-765.

Iberoamerican Countries in the Olympic Sports

Each country in the seventh series depicted the sports that historically have represented their Olympic spirit. Mexico's contribution celebrates Disciplinas de Oro Olimpico Mexicano (Mexican Gold-Medal Disciplines): at the left is a Mayan ball player in the game of *pelota;* on a panel at the right, symbols depict the six Olympic sports in which Mexican participants have won gold medals—boxing, diving, race-walking, swimming, equestrian events, and weight lifting

5 pesos, 2008, 0.925 silver, 31.105 g. PF, Type A24.

Diameter: 40 mm. *Edge:* Reeded. *Design:* Olympic gold-medal disciplines. BW-596.9, KM-805.

Historical Iberoamerican Coins

In the eighth series, Mexico's coin (issued in 2010 and released in 2011) carries the series name, "Monedas Historicas Iberoamericanas." In the background is a design from a historical map; superimposed over the map is Mexico's chosen historical coin, the 1 peso of 1910, known as the "Caballito"—the first peso coin issued after the Coinage Reform of 1905.

5 pesos, 2010, 0.925 silver, 27.00 g. PF, Type A25.

Diameter: 40 mm. *Edge:* Reeded. *Design:* Caballito. BW-596.10, KM-UL.

PRE-COLUMBIAN SERIES

In 1992 Mexico launched its Pre-Columbian Series: six collections commemorating six cultures of Mexico's Pre-Columbian era. There are many varieties, denominations and metal finishes in the Pre-Columbian series; these are covered in chapter 20 of this book, and in greater depth in volume 2.

In 1992 the first collection issued honored the Aztecs. Designs featured the Piedra de Tizoc (Tizoc Stone), Guerrero Águila (Eagle Warrior), Xochipilli (God of Flowers), Brasero Efigie (Brazier Effigy), Huehueteotl (God of Fire), and Jaguar / Piedra de los Soles (Jaguar / Stone of the Suns).

The Central Veracruz Collection, issued in 1993, featured the the Pirámide de el Tajín (Tajín Pyramid), Bajorrelieve de el Tajín (Bas-relief of the Tajín), Palma con Cocodrilo

(Palm With Crocodile), Anciano con Brasero (Elderly Man With Brazier), Carita Sonriente (Smiling Face), and Hacha Ceremonial (Ceremonial Hatchet).

In 1994 the Mayan Collection featured the Pirámide del Castillo (Pyramid of the Castle), Chaac-Mool (a reclining ceremonial figure), Mascarón del Dios Chaac (Mask of God Chaac), Lápida Tumba de Palenque (Gravestone of a Palenque Tomb), Dintel 26 (Lintel 26), and Personaje de Jaina (Personage of Jaina).

The next collection, issued in 1996, honored the Olmec culture, featuring the Cabeza Olmeca (Olmec Head), Señor de las Limas (Master of the Limes), Hombre Jaguar (Jaguar Man), El Luchador (The Wrestler), Hacha Ceremonial (Cermonial Ax), and Sacerdote (Priest).

The 1997 Teotihuacán Collection featured the Pirámide del Sol (Pyramid of the Sun), Disco de la Muerte (Disc of Death), Mascara (Mask), Vasija (Vessel), Jugador de Pelota (Ball Player), and Serpiente Eplumada (Feathered Serpent).

The final collection, issued in 1998, honored the Toltecs and featured the Atlantes (statues of Toltec warriors), Quetzalcóatl (Feathered Serpent), Jaguar, Sacerdote (Priest), Serpiente con Cráneo (Serpent With Skull), and Águila (Eagle).

UNICEF / FOR THE CHILDREN OF THE WORLD

Mexico in 1999 participated in a UNICEF program of the United Nations by issuing two commemorative coins, one silver, one gold. The obverses bear the Mexican national coat of arms with the legend ESTADOS UNIDOS MEXICANOS above and a half-wreath of oak and laurel below; the reverses bear the legend PARA LOS NIÑOS DEL MUNDO (For the Children of the World). The reverse of the silver 5 pesos depicts a boy and girl flying a kite; the gold 20 pesos depicts a *charrito* (little cowboy) with a lasso.

5 pesos, 1999, 0.999 silver, 31.103 g. PF, Type A6.

Diameter: 40 mm. *Edge:* Reeded. *Design:* Children flying kite. BW-601.1, KM-640.

20 pesos, 1999, 0.999 gold, 6.221 g. PF, Type A4.

Diameter: 22 mm. *Edge:* Reeded. *Design:* *Charrito* with lasso. BW-803, KM-641.

HISTORY OF NAVIGATION

In 1999 Mexico's history of navigation was commemorated on a Proof 5 pesos. The obverse has the Mexican national coat of arms with the legend ESTADOS UNIDOS MEXICANOS above and a half-wreath of oak and laurel below; the reverse depicts the sailing ship *Cuauhtémoc*, used to train cadets in the Mexican navy.

5 pesos, 1999, 0.999 silver, 19.60 g. PF, Type A16.

Diameter: 34 mm. *Edge:* Reeded. *Design:* Training ship *Cuauhtémoc.* BW-602a, KM-635.

MILLENNIUM COLLECTION

In 1999 and 2000, to commemorate the arrival of the third millennium, Mexico released its Millennium Coin Collection, consisting of three Proof 5 pesos (designed by Mexican artists in a national competition) and one Proof 10 peso (designed by the Mexico Mint). All four coins have the dual date 1999/2000, and all share a common obverse: at the center, the modern national coat of arms with the legend ESTADOS UNIDOS MEXICANOS above and a half-wreath of oak and laurel below; surrounding the central device, 10 different national coats of arms used throughout Mexico's history.

The themes for the three 5-peso coins, and the designs that won the right to represent each theme, are as follows:

Mexican History During the Second Millennium—The winning reverse design, by Olga María Vega de Ochoa, depicts a pre-Hispanic emblem from the Mixtec-Zapotec culture: the head of an eagle with three coiled serpents around it ("fisherman's jewel").

Man's Role in the Conservation of Nature in the New Millennium—Francisco Ortega Romero designed the reverse emblem: a butterfly shape formed from many different creatures, including a fish, a hummingbird, and two dolphins. Below the butterfly, two human hands spread apart, cradling the natural elements above.

World Peace in the Third Millennium—The third reverse, designed by Omar Jiménez Torres, combines the shape of a hand with the profile of a dove, carrying an olive branch in its beak.

The fourth theme in the series, "Mexico During the Second Millennium," is represented by a 10-peso coin designed by a Mexico Mint artist. It depicts three architectural masterpieces of Mexico: the library at the National University of Mexico (UNAM), the aqueduct of Querétaro, and the Mayan Observatory.

5 pesos, 1999/2000, 0.999 silver, 31.18 g. PF, Types A7–A9.

Diameter: 40 mm. *Edge:* Reeded. *Designs:* Type A7, fisherman's jewel, BW-603.1, KM-632; Type A8, butterfly, BW-603.2, KM-630; Type A9, dove, BW-603.3, KM-631.

10 pesos, 1999/2000, 0.999 silver, 62.03 g. PF, Type A3.

Diameter: 48 mm. *Edge:* Reeded. *Design:* Second millennium. BW-603.4, KM-633.

ENDANGERED SPECIES IN MEXICO COLLECTION

In 2001 the Endangered Species in Mexico (Animales en Peligro de Extinción en México) Collection was issued. The collection consists of 10 coins denominated 5 pesos in a satin finish; four are dated 2000, and the remaining six are dated 2001. The common obverse has, at the center, the modern national coat of arms with the legend ESTADOS UNIDOS MEXICANOS above and a half-wreath of oak and laurel below; surrounding the central device are 10 different national coats of arms used throughout Mexico's history. These coins were sold as a complete collection, with an informative album titled *Monedas y Especies (Coins and Species)*. A portion of the proceeds of the sale of the collection went to protecting the endangered species.

5 pesos, 2000, 0.999 silver, 31.103 g. BU, Types A11–A14.

Diameter: 40 mm. *Edge:* Reeded. *Designs:* Type A11, Royal Eagle (Águila Real), BW-604.1, KM-652; Type A12, Pronghorn (Berrendo), BW-604.2, KM-657; Type A13, River Crocodile (Cocodrilo de Río), BW-604.3, KM-655; Type A14, River Otter (Nutria de Río), BW-604.4, KM-656.

5 pesos, 2001, 0.999 silver, 31.103 g. BU, Types A15–A20.

Diameter: 40 mm. *Edge:* Reeded. *Designs:* Type A15, Black Bear (Oso Negro), BW-604.5, KM-654; Type A16, Manatee (Manatí), BW-604.6, KM-651; Type A17, Jaguar, BW-604.7, KM-658; Type A18, Harpy Eagle (Águila Arpia), BW-604.8, KM-653; Type A19, Volcano Rabbit (Zacatuche), BW-604.9, KM-660; Type A20, Prairie Dog (Perrito de las Praderas), BW-604.10, KM-659.

MEXICAN STATE FEDERATION SERIES

In 2003 Mexico joined the United States and Canada in releasing a state commemorative series. Mexico's commemoratives honored the 180th anniversary of the union of the states of the Mexican Republic into a federation. Each series consisted of one coin for each of the 31 states in the federation, with an additional coin for the Distrito Federal. The denominations were 10 pesos (silver Proofs only) and 100 pesos (bimetallic circulating coins in silver and bronze-aluminum, and bimetallic Proofs in silver and gold). For both series in the program, the obverses bore the national coat of arms with the legend ESTADOS UNIDOS MEXICANOS above and a half-wreath of oak and laurel below.

The first, or "heraldic," series commenced in 2003. Each reverse featured a different state's coat of arms, and the coins were issued in descending alphabetical order, from Zacatecas through Aguascalientes. The mintage for each circulating coin in the first series was 250,000 for each state; half of the mintage was issued within the coin's own state, and the other half around the other states of Mexico. The silver Proofs each had a mintage of 10,000 per state, with the bimetallic gold-and-silver Proofs at 1,000 per state.

The second, or "emblematic," series began in 2005. Each state's reverse featured images "related to architecture, art, science, fauna, flora, typical dresses or dances or geographical areas of interest peculiar to each state" (Banco de México, "The History of Coins and Banknotes in Mexico," www.banxico.org). The coins were released in normal alphabetical order, from Aguascalientes through Zacatecas. The mintages varied slightly, but all were approximately 150,000 per state for the Brilliant Uncirculated; 6,000 per state in Proof silver; and 600 per state in Proof bimetallic gold and silver.

The 100-peso BU issues in bimetallic silver and aluminum-bronze were struck for circulation. Although very few actually circulated, they are listed in chapter 14 with normal circulating coins, in the interest of consistency. In early 2007, when silver was US$19 to US$20 an ounce, the silver centers were popped out of a large number of the 100-peso BUs and melted, because the silver value of the center exceeded the face value of the coin.

Series Number 1

10 pesos, 0.999 silver, 31.1035 g. PF, Type A5.

Diameter: 40 mm. *Edge:* Reeded. *Designs:* As follows.

2003

Zacatecas, BW-606.1, KM-679

Yucatán, BW-606.2, KM-680

Veracruz, BW-606.3, KM-681

Tlaxcala, BW-606.4, KM-682

2004

Tamaulipas, BW-606.5, KM-683

Tabasco, BW-606.6, KM-684

Sonora, BW-606.7, KM-685

Sinaloa, BW-606.8, KM-686

San Luis Potosí, BW-606.9, KM-687

Quintana Roo, BW-606.10, KM-735

Querétaro, BW-606.11, KM-733

Puebla, BW-606.12, KM-737

Oaxaca, BW-606.13, KM-739

Nuevo León, BW-606.14, KM-741

Nayarit, BW-606.15, KM-743

Morelos, BW-606.16, KM-745

Michoacán, BW-606.17, KM-796

México (Estado de), BW-606.18, KM-747

Jalisco, BW-606.19, KM-749

2005

Hidalgo, BW-606.20, KM-711

Guerrero, BW-606.21, KM-710

Guanajuato, BW-606.22, KM-709

Durango, BW-606.23, KM-708

Distrito Federal, BW-606.24, KM-707

Colima, BW-606.25, KM-728

Coahuila, BW-606.26, KM-751

Chihuahua, BW-606.27, KM-753

Chiapas, BW-606.28, KM-706

Campeche, BW-606.29, KM-726

Baja California Sur, 606.30, KM-724

Baja California, BW-606.31, KM-722

Aguascaliente, BW-606.32, KM-720

100 pesos, bimetallic (center, 0.999 gold; outer ring, 0.999 silver), 29.169 g. Prooflike, Type A2.

Diameter: 34.5 mm. *Edge:* Paired plain and reeded. *Designs:* As follows.

2003

Zacatecas, BW-684.1, KM-696

Yucatán, BW-684.2, KM-697

Veracruz, BW-684.3, KM-698

Tlaxcala, BW-684.4, KM-699

2004

Tamaulipas, BW-684.5, KM-700

Tabasco, BW-684.6, KM-701

Sonora, BW-684.7, KM-702

Sinaloa, BW-684.8, KM-703

San Luis Potosí, BW-684.9, KM-806

Quintana Roo, BW-684.10, KM-807

Querétaro, BW-684.11, KM-808

Puebla, BW-684.12, KM-809

Oaxaca, BW-684.13, KM-810

Nuevo León, BW-684.14, KM-811

Nayarit, BW-684.15, KM-812

Morelos, BW-684.16, KM-813

Michoacán, BW-684.17, KM-814

México (Estado de), BW-684.18, KM-815

Jalisco, BW-684.19, KM-816

2005

Hidalgo, BW-684.20, KM-817

Guerrero, BW-684.21, KM-818

Guanajuato, BW-684.22, KM-819

Durango, BW-684.23, KM-820

Distrito Federal, BW-684.24, KM-821

Colima, BW-684.25, KM-824

Coahuila, BW-684.26, KM-825

Chihuahua, BW-684.27, KM-822

Chiapas, BW-684.28, KM-823

Campeche, BW-684.29, KM-826

Baja California Sur, BW-684.30, KM-827

Baja California, BW-684.31, KM-828

Aguascalientes, BW-684.32, KM-829

Series Number 2

10 pesos, 0.999 silver, 31.1035 g. PF, Type A6.

Diameter: 40 mm. *Edge:* Reeded. *Designs:* As follows.

2005

Aguascalientes, BW-609.1, KM-718

Baja California, BW-609.2, KM-757

2006

Baja California Sur, BW-609.3, KM-761

Campeche, BW-609.4, KM-759

Chiapas, BW-609.5, KM-772

Chihuahua, BW-609.6, KM-774

Coahuila, BW-609.7, KM-780

Colima, BW-609.8, KM-776

Distrito Federal, BW-609.9, KM-778

Durango, BW-609.10, KM-786

Guanajuato, BW-609.11, KM-788

Guerrero, BW-609.12, KM-790

Hidalgo, BW-609.13, KM-792

Jalisco, BW-609.14, KM-794

México (Estado de), BW-609.15, KM-830

Michoacán, BW-609.16, KM-831

Morelos, BW-609.17, KM-832

2007

Nayarit, BW-609.18, KM-833

Nuevo León, BW-609.19, KM-834

Oaxaca, BW-609.20, KM-835

Puebla, BW-609.21, KM-836

Quintana Roo, BW-609.22, KM-837

Querétaro, BW-609.23, KM-838

San Luis Potosí, BW-609.24, KM-839

Sinaloa, BW-609.25, KM-840

Sonora, BW-609.26, KM-841

Tabasco, BW-609.27, KM-842

Tamaulipas, BW-609.28, KM-843

Tlaxcala, BW-609.29, KM-844

Veracruz, BW-609.30, KM845

Yucatán, BW-609.31, KM-846

Zacatecas, BW-609.32, KM-847

100 pesos, bimetallic (center, 0.999 gold; outer ring, 0.999 silver), 29.169 g. Prooflike, Type A4.

Diameter: 34.5 mm. *Edge:* Paired plain and reeded. *Designs:* As follows.

2005

Aguascalientes, BW-685.1, KM-862

Baja California, BW-685.2, KM-863

2006

Baja California Sur, BW-685.3, KM-864

Campeche, BW-685.4, KM-865

Chiapas, BW-685.7, KM-866

Chihuahua, BW-685.8, KM-867

Coahuila, BW-685.5, KM-868

Colima, BW-685.6, KM-869

Distrito Federal, BW-685.9, KM-870

Durango, BW-685.10, KM-871

Guanajuato, BW-685.11, KM-872

Guerrero, BW-685.12, KM-873

Hidalgo, BW-685.13, KM-874

Jalisco, BW-685.14, KM-875

México (Estado de), BW-685.15, KM-876

Michoacán, BW-685.16, KM-877

Morelos, BW-685.17, KM-878

2007

Nayarit, BW-685.18, KM-879

Nuevo León, BW-685.19, KM-880

Oaxaca, BW-685.20, KM-881

Puebla, BW-685.21, KM-882

Quintana Roo, BW-685.22, KM-883

Querétaro, BW-685.23, KM-884

San Luis Potosí, BW-685.24, KM-885

Sinaloa, BW-685.25, KM-886

Sonora, BW-685.26, KM-887

Tabasco, BW-685.27, KM-888

Tamaulipas, BW-685.28, KM-889

Tlaxcala, BW-685.29, KM-890

Veracruz, BW-685.30, KM-891

Yucatán, BW-685.31, KM-892

Zacatecas, BW-685.32, KM-893

33rd International Cervantino Festival

The 33rd Festival Internacional Cervantino took place in October 2005 in Guanajuato. This multifaceted cultural festival, named in honor of Spanish writer Miguel de Cervantes Saavedra and held annually since 1972, celebrates theater, dance, music, and other art forms. A Brilliant Uncirculated 10-peso coin commemorated the 33rd renewal of the festival. All were sold exclusively at the festival, and none reached the general numismatic market. A special session was held at the festival in honor of the 400th anniversary of the publication of Cervantes' *Don Quijote de la Mancha;* commemorative coins were issued for that as well (see the next listing).

The obverse of the Cervantino Festival commemorative 10 pesos bears the national coat of arms with the legend ESTADOS UNIDOS MEXICANOS above and a half-wreath of oak and laurel below. On the reverse, Don Quixote rides his horse to the left, with the emblem of the festival below.

10 pesos, 2005, 0.999 silver, 30.500 g. BU, Type A7.

Diameter: 40 mm. *Edge:* Reeded. *Design:* 33rd Cervantino Festival. BW-757, KM-766.

400th Anniversary of *Don Quijote de la Mancha*

On June 21, 2005, Mexico issued a decree authorizing a new 20-peso coin, "El Ingenioso Hidalgo Don Quijote de la Mancha," to commemorate the 400th anniversary of publication of *Don Quijote de la Mancha*, written by Miguel de Cervantes Saavedra. (Part 1 of the book was published in 1605, the anniversary commemorated by the coin; part 2 was published in 1615.)

The obverse of the coin bears the national coat of arms with the legend ESTADOS UNIDOS MEXICANOS above and a half-wreath of oak and laurel below. The reverse design—a skeletal rider on a skeletal horse, galloping through a crowd of other skeletons and scattering the bones in their wake—is based on José Guadalupe Posada's engraving *Calavera Quijotesca*.

The Don Quixote commemorative was issued as a silver Proof 20 pesos; and as a bimetallic (silver and aluminum-bronze) 100 pesos, in three strikes: a circulating coin, a BU coin, and a Proof. There are two varieties in the 100-peso bimetallic Proof: Variety I has a thicker font, with a diamond inside the initials D, O, and Q. Variety II is the same as on the circulating issues, with a thin, stylized font on the reverse outer ring.

20 pesos, 2005, 0.999 silver, 61.30 g. PF, Type A4.

Diameter: 48 mm. *Edge:* Plain. *Design: Calavera Quijotesca.* BW-804, KM-704.

100 pesos, 2005, bimetallic (center, 0.925 silver; outer ring, aluminum-bronze), 33.30 g. BU, Type A5a.

Diameter: 39 mm. *Edge:* Paired plain and reeded. *Design: Calavera Quijotesca*, Variety I. BW-854.1, KM-705.

100 pesos, 2005, bimetallic (center, 0.925 silver; outer ring, aluminum-bronze), 33.30 g. PF, Type A5b.

Diameter: 39 mm. *Edge:* Paired plain and reeded. *Design: Calavera Quijotesca*, Variety II. BW-854.2, KM-705.

MEXICAN MONETARY ANNIVERSARIES

The year 2005 brought the anniversaries of three important events in Mexico's financial history: the 80th anniversary of the founding of the Banco de México; the 470th anniversary of the establishment of the Casa de Moneda de México; and the 100th anniversary of the Coinage Reform of 1905. These events were commemorated by a new series, the common obverse of which bears the national coat of arms with the legend ESTADOS UNIDOS MEXICANOS above and a half-wreath of oak and laurel below. All three commemoratives were produced as silver Proofs (Banco de México, 20 pesos; Casa Moneda, 10 pesos; 1905 Reform, 5 pesos) and as 100-peso circulating and Proof coins. (The circulating issues are listed in chapter 14.)

80th Anniversary of the Banco de México

The first coin in the series marked the 80th anniversary of the establishment of the Banco de México, the country's central bank and its only banknote-issuing institution. In honor of this fact, the reverse design features the Banco de México's 100-peso note of 1925 (BKM-2673). The American Bank Note Company produced this very rare note.

20 pesos, 2005, 0.999 silver, 61.500 g. PF, Type A4.

Diameter: 48 mm. *Edge:* Plain. *Design:* Banknote. BW-805, KM-767.

100 pesos, 2005, bimetallic (center, 0.925 silver; outer ring, aluminum-bronze), 33.825 g. BU, Type A6.

Diameter: 39 mm. *Edge:* Paired plain and reeded. *Design:* Banknote. BW-855, KM-732.

470th Anniversary of the Casa Moneda de México

The second issue in the series commemorates the 470th anniversary of the Casa de Moneda de México (the Mexico Mint). The oldest operating mint in the Americas, the Casa de Moneda was established by royal decree of May 11, 1535, issued by Queen Jane of Castilla. The coinage of Mexico circulated around the world and was legal tender in the United States until 1857.

The reverse design features a screw press, with the dates 1535 above and 2005 below.

10 pesos, 2005, 0.999 silver, 30.60 g. PF, Type A7.

Diameter: 40 mm. *Edge:* Plain. *Design:* Screw press. BW-856, KM-768.

100 pesos, 2005, bimetallic (center, 0.925 silver; outer ring, aluminum-bronze), 33.30 g. BU, Type A7.

Diameter: 39 mm. *Edge:* Paired plain and reeded. *Design:* Screw press. BW-858, KM-731.

100th Anniversary of the Coinage Reform of 1905

The third issue honors the 1905 reform that standardized Mexico's coinage and centralized its production. The reverse design is a small radiant liberty cap, as used on the 50 centavos and the 1 peso of the 1905 reform.

5 pesos, 2005, 0.999 silver, 15.40 g. PF, Type A2.

Diameter: 33 mm. *Edge:* Plain. *Design:* Radiant liberty cap. BW-859, KM-769.

100 pesos, 2005, bimetallic (center, 0.925 silver; outer ring, aluminum-bronze), 33.3 g. BU, Type A8.

Diameter: 39 mm. *Edge:* Paired plain and reeded. *Design:* Radiant liberty cap. BW-860, KM-730.

75TH ANNIVERSARY OF THE UNAM

This 10-peso silver Proof commemorates the 75th anniversary of the National Autonomous University (Universidad Nacional Autónoma de México, or UNAM). The obverse bears the national coat of arms with legend **ESTADOS UNIDOS MEXICANOS** above and a half-wreath of oak and laurel below. The reverse depicts several contemporary university buildings (the Rectory Tower, the main library, and the Olympic Stadium) in the background; in the foreground are stylized human figures from a work of art on the UNAM campus titled *People to University, University to People*, by David Alfaro Siqueiros. The fields of the coin are heavily frosted, with contrasting mirrored devices. This unusual coin was approved in (and is dated) 2010, but it was not released until September 29, 2011.

10 pesos, 2010, 0.999 silver, 30.7 g. Prooflike, Type 1.

Diameter: 40 mm. *Edge:* Reeded. *Design:* Campus architecture and art. BW-862, KM-UL.

BENITO JUÁREZ GARCÍA BIRTH BICENTENNIAL

In 2006 a bimetallic 100 pesos was issued to honor the birth bicentennial of Benito Juárez García, born on March 21, 1806, in San Pablo Guelatao, Oaxaca. Juárez served three terms as president from 1858 to 1872. The third term was during the empire of Maximilian, with Juárez ruling Mexico from a carriage on the move.

The obverse has the national coat of arms with the legend **ESTADOS UNIDOS MEXICANOS** above and a half-wreath of oak and laurel below; the reverse has a bust of Juárez and a facsimile of his signature. Silver Proofs were not issued for this event.

100 pesos, 2006, bimetallic (center, 0.925 silver; outer ring, aluminum-bronze), 33.967 g. BU, Type A9.

Diameter: 39 mm. *Edge:* Paired plain and reeded. *Design:* Bust of Benito Juárez. BW-860.1, KM-764.

2006 FIFA WORLD CUP, GERMANY

Two commemorative Proof coins were issued in 2006 in honor of Mexico's participation in the quadrennial International Football World Championship Tournament conducted by the Fédération Internationale de Football Association (FIFA) in Germany. Both the issues have for the obverse the national coat of arms with the legend **ESTADOS UNIDOS MEXICANOS** above and a half-wreath of oak and laurel below.

The silver 5-peso reverse features, at the left, a standing ball player *(jugador de pelota)* from the Mayan culture of Chichén Itzá, Yucatán, in ritual clothing from the classical period; the player has struck or is about to strike a rubber ball. At the right is a Mayan goal marker (a stone ring decorated with two undulating feather serpents) with a modern football (soccer ball) below it.

The gold 25-peso reverse features, at the left, a kneeling ball player in the ritual clothing of the Mayan culture of Toniná. The player faces the right of the coin, which depicts the goal marker and modern football as on the silver issue.

5 pesos, 2006, 0.999 silver, 33.30 g. PF, Type A3.

Diameter: 40 mm. *Edge:* Plain. *Design:* Mayan ball player, goal marker, and futbol. BW-861, KM-770

25 pesos, 2006, 0.999 gold, 15.55 g. PF, Type A1.

Diameter: 23 mm. *Edge:* Plain. *Design:* Kneeling Mayan ball player, goal marker, and futbol. BW-862, KM-UL.

BICENTENNIAL OF THE WAR OF INDEPENDENCE

In 2010, to commemorate the bicentennial of the War of Independence, Mexico issued two silver 20-peso Proofs, and two gold 200 pesos, one in BU and one in Proof. All three issues have for the obverse the national coat of arms with the legend ESTADOS UNIDOS MEXICANOS above and a half-wreath of oak and laurel below.

The 20-peso coins were produced with two different reverse designs. The first depicts the Parroquia de Dolores, the parish chuch where Father Miguel Hidalgo y Costilla gave the call to the populace to rise up on September 16, 1810. The second depicts the standing figures of Hidalgo y Costilla and General José María Morelos, another hero of the War of Independence.

The BU and Proof 200 pesos were produced with the same reverse design: the winged figure of Victory, from the top of the Independence Monument in Mexico City.

20 pesos, 2010, 0.999 silver, 62.0 g. PF, Type A5.

Diameter: 48 mm. *Edge:* Reeded. *Design:* Dolores Parish church. BW-805.1, KM-UL.

20 pesos, 2010, 0.999 silver, 62.0 g. PF, Type A5.

Diameter: 48 mm. *Edge:* Reeded. *Design:* Hidalgo and Morelos. BW-805.2, KM-UL.

200 pesos, 2010, 0.900 gold, 34.178 g. BU, Type A1.

Diameter: 37 mm. *Edge:* Reeded. *Design:* Independence Monument. BW-859.1, KM-UL.

200 pesos, 2010, 0.900 gold, 34.178 g. PF, Type A1.

Diameter: 37 mm. *Edge:* Reeded. *Design:* Type A1, Independence Monument. BW-859.2, KM-UL.

CENTENNIAL OF THE MEXICAN REVOLUTION

In conjunction with the Bicentennial of the War of Independence, the Centennial of the Mexican Revolution was commemorated with the issue of two Proof 10 pesos. Both issues have for the obverse the national coat of arms with the legend ESTADOS UNIDOS MEXICANOS above and a half-wreath of oak and laurel below.

Women who went with the men into combat, whether to attend to the needs of the men or to fight, were called *soldaderas*. The reverse of the first 10-peso coin depicts a *soldadera* as she stands on the steps of a railway car, looking cautiously at her surroundings.

The second reverse design consists of four Revolutionary soldiers seated in front of a locomotive.

10 pesos, 2010, 0.999 silver, 62.0 g. PF, Types A8 and A9.

Diameter: 48 mm. *Edge:* Reeded. *Designs:* Type A8, *soldadera*, BW-860.2a, KM-UL; Type A9, railroad, BW-860.3, KM-UL.

NUMISMATIC HERITAGE OF MEXICO SERIES

In 2011, the Casa de Moneda initiated a new series presenting the historical coinage of Mexico from Spanish colonial times through the modern era. The bimetallic coins were issued with a Prooflike finish; their common obverse depicts the national coat of arms on the silver center, with the legend ESTADOS UNIDOS MEXICANOS and a half-wreath of oak and laurel on the aluminum-bronze outer ring. Each reverse has a reproduction of a different historical coin, and each coin contains 1/2 ounce of sterling silver.

The designs of each series are described here using the terminology found in this book (rather than translations of the Casa de Moneda's terminology), to make it easier to find and compare the historical originals to the commemorative reproductions.

Series I

100 pesos, 2011, bimetallic (center, 0.925 sterling silver; outer ring, stainless-steel alloy), 33.967 g. Prooflike, Type A10.

Diameter: 39 mm. *Edge:* Smooth. *Designs:* As follows.

Milled Coinage, Pillars (8 reales, Philip V, 1732); BW-861.1, KM-UL

Milled Coinage, Portrait (8 reales, Charles III, 1783); BW-861.2, KM-UL

War of Independence, Insurgent Coinage, SUD (8 reales, Oaxaca); BW-861.3, KM-UL

Republic Reales Coinage, Cap and Rays (8 reales, 1824); BW-861.4, KM-UL

1905 Coinage Reform, Caballito (1 peso, 1914); BW-861.5, KM-UL

Mexican Revolution, Bolita (1 peso, Hidalgo del Parral, 1913); BW-861.6, KM-UL

Series II

100 pesos, 2012, bimetallic (center, 0.925 sterling silver; outer ring, stainless-steel alloy), 33.967 g. Prooflike, Type A11.

Diameter: 39 mm. *Edge:* Smooth. *Designs:* As follows.

Milled Coinage, Portrait, counterstamped (8 reales, Charles III, 1804); BW-862.1, KM-UL

Cob Coinage (8 reales, Philip III, 1608); BW-862.2, KM-UL

War of Independence, Royalist Moneda Provisional, L.V.O. (8 reales, Zacatecas, 1811); BW-862.3, KM-UL

Emperor Maximilian Coinage (1 peso, Mexico City, 1866); BW-862.4, KM-UL

Republic Reales Coinage, Hand on Book (8 escudos, Mexico City, 1828); BW-862.5, KM-UL

1905 Reform Coinage, Railroad (5 pesos, Mexico City, 1950); BW-862.6, KM-UL

Series III

100 pesos, 2013, bimetallic (center, 0.925 sterling silver; outer ring, stainless-steel alloy), 33.967 g. Prooflike, Type A12.

Diameter: 39 mm. *Edge:* Smooth. *Designs:* As follows.

Coinage of the Revolution, Campo Morado (2 pesos, Suriana, Guerrero, 1915); BW-863.1, KM-UL

Carlos and Johanna Coinage, Early Series (3 reales, denomination in dots, assayer R); BW-863.2, KM-UL

Republic Decimal Coinage, Balance Scale (1 peso, 1870–1873, Zacatecas); BW-863.3, KM-UL.

Republic Reales Coinage, Cap and Rays (8 reales, 1887, Cw, assayer M, chopmarked); BW-863.4, KM-UL

War of Independence, Insurgent Coinage, Supreme National Congress of America (8 reales, 1811); BW-863.5, KM-UL

Iturbide Coinage, Mexico City (8 escudos, 1822, M̊, assayer JM); BW-863.6, KM-UL.

Series IV

100 pesos, 2014, bimetallic (center, 0.925 sterling silver; outer ring, stainless-steel alloy), 33.967 g. Prooflike, Type A13.

Diameter: 39 mm. *Edge:* Smooth reeding. *Designs:* As follows.

Coinage of the Revolution, Cuencamé, Durango (Muera Huerta peso, Six Stars, 1914); BW-864.1, KM-UL

Milled Coinage, Ferdinand VI (8 escudos, 1748, M, assayer M-F); BW-864.2, KM-UL

Coinage of the Revolution, Estado de Oaxaca (gold 60 pesos, 1916); BW-864.3, KM-UL

Coinage of the War of Independence, Royalist Coinage, Oaxaca (provisional 8 reales, 1812); BW-864.4, KM-UL

Milled Coinage, Charles IV (8 reales, 1806; see volume 3 for counterstamped/punched varieties, as depicted on the commemorative); BW-864.5, KM-UL

Republic Reales Coinage, Upright Eagle, Mexico (1/4 real, 1834; see volume 3 for 1/4 real with mintmark M̊, assayer A); BW-864.6, KM-UL

CHICHÉN ITZÁ "070707" SERIES

In the fall of 2012, Banco de México released a historically important series of five coins commemorating the declaration of Chichén Itzá as a one of the "New7Wonders of the World," after a public poll conducted by the New7Wonders Foundation in Zurich, Switzerland. (The site had been declared a World Cultural Heritage Site by UNESCO in 1988.) The New7Wonders designation was issued on July 7, 2007; hence the numerals **070707**, which appear below the Casa de Moneda's mintmark on the reverse of each coin. These coins, honoring a part of Mayan cultural history, are a continuing effort on the part of the Casa de Moneda and the Banco de México to disperse Mexico's cultural history throughout the nation's coinage.

The common obverse bears, at the center, the modern national coat of arms with the legend **ESTADOS UNIDOS MEXICANOS** above and a half-wreath of oak and laurel below; surrounding the central device are 10 different national coats of arms used throughout Mexico's history.

5 pesos, 2012, 0.999 silver, 31.10 g. PF, Types A26–A28.

Diameter: 40 mm. *Edge:* Plain. *Designs:* Type A26, Casa de la Monjas (Nunnery Building), BW-870.1, KM-UL; Type A27, La Iglesia (The Church), BW-870.2, KM-UL; Type A28, Observatorio, BW-870.3, KM-UL.

10 pesos, 2012, 0.999 silver, 62.20 g. PF, Type A10.

Diameter: 48 mm. *Edge:* Plain. *Design:* Type A10, Templo de los Guerreros (Temple of Warriors). BW-870.4, KM-UL.

20 pesos, 2012, 0.999 silver, 155.51 g. PF, Type A5.

Diameter: 65 mm. *Edge:* Plain. *Design:* Type A5, Pirámide de Kukulcán (Kukulcán Pyramid, also known as "El Castillo"). BW-870.5, KM-UL.

Commemoratives of the Coinage Reforms of 1905 and 1992

The basic obverse designs for Mexican commemorative coins are shown below. (Exceptions to the basic style are noted with the reverse images, where applicable.) The extensive array of commemorative coinage is fully illustrated in volume 2.

Silver, Brilliant Uncirculated (left) and Proof (right).

Bimetallic (silver center), Brilliant Uncirculated (top) and Proof (bottom left); bimetallic (gold center), Proof (bottom right).

Gold, Brilliant Uncirculated (left) and Proof (right).

Commemoratives of the Coinage Reforms of 1905 and 1992

(continued)

Modern Mexican coat of arms center, historic Mexican coats of arms surrounding.

Mexican coat of arms center, multinational series participants' coats of arms surrounding (arms vary by countries participating).

1986 World Cup Football Games (Selected Examples)

25 pesos, PF. 1985. Type 4, BW-573, KM-503, 26 mm.

25 pesos, PF. 1985. Type 5, BW-574, KM-514, 26 mm.

50 pesos, PF. 1985. Type 5, BW-581, KM-504, 32 mm.

50 pesos, PF. 1985. Type 6, BW-582, KM-515, 32 mm.

100 pesos, PF. 1985. Type 5, BW-590, KM-505, 38 mm.

100 pesos, PF. 1986. Type 6, BW-591, KM-521, 38 mm.

250 pesos, PF. 1985. Type 4, BW-605a, KM-506.2, 22 mm.

500 pesos, PF. 1985. Type 3, BW-609a, KM 507.2, 28 mm.

2,000 pesos, BU. 1986. Type 1, BW-618a, KM-528, 36 mm.

Anniversaries of Independence and the Revolution

500 pesos, PF. 1985. Type 1, 75th Anniversary of the Mexican Revolution, BW-610b, KM-511, 40 mm.

1,000 pesos, PF. 1985. Type 1, 175th Anniversary of the War of Independence, BW-613a, KM-513, 38 mm.

200 pesos, PF. 2010. Type A1, Bicentennial of the War of Independence, BW-859, KM-UL, 37 mm.

10 pesos, PF. 2010. Type A8, Centennial of the Mexican Revolution, BW-860.2a, KM-UL, 48 mm.

10 pesos, PF. 2010. Type A9, Centennial of the Mexican Revolution, BW-860.3, KM-UL, 48 mm.

World Wide Fund for Nature

100 pesos, PF. 1987. Type 8, BW-593.1, KM-537, 38 mm.

5 pesos, PF. 1998. Type A4, BW-593.2, KM-627, 40 mm.

Nationalization of the Oil Industry (Selected Examples)

50 pesos, BU. 1988. Type 9, BW-585, KM-532, 31 mm.

1,000 pesos, BU. 1988. Type 2, BW-615, KM-535, 34.5 mm.

Save the Children Fund

100 pesos, PF. 1991. Type 10, BW-595, KM-539, 40 mm.

United Nations Environment Programme (UNEP)

100 pesos, PF. 1992. Type 12, BW-597, KM-566, 40 mm.

Iberoamericana Series (Selected Examples)

100 pesos, PF. 1992. Type A2, BW-596.2, KM-540, 40 mm.

5 pesos, PF. 2000. Type A21, BW-596.6, KM-670, 40 mm.

New 5 pesos, PF. 1994. Type A3, BW-596.3, KM-588, 40 mm.

5 pesos, PF, Type A22. 2003. "The Nautical Tradition." BW-596.7, KM-678, 40 mm.

UNICEF / For the Children of the World

5 pesos, PF, Type A6. 1999. Children flying kite, BW-601.1, KM-640, 40 mm.

20 pesos, PF, Type A4. 1999. Charrito with lasso, BW-803, KM-641, 22 mm.

History of Navigation

5 pesos, PF. 1999. Type A16, BW-602a, KM-635, 34 mm.

Millennium Collection

5 pesos, PF. 1999/2000. Type A7, BW-603.1, KM-632, 40 mm.

5 pesos, PF. 1999/2000. Type A8, BW-603.2, KM-630, 40 mm.

5 pesos, PF. 1999/2000. Type A9, BW-603.3, KM-631, 40 mm.

10 pesos, PF. 1999/2000. Type A3, BW-603.4, KM-633, 48 mm.

Endangered Species in Mexico Collection (Selected Examples)

5 pesos, BU. 2000. Type A12, BW-604.2, KM-657, 40 mm.

5 pesos, BU. 2001. Type A17, BW-604.7, KM-658, 40 mm.

5 pesos, BU. 2001. Type A18, BW-604.8, KM-653, 40 mm.

5 pesos, BU. 2001. Type A19, BW-604.9, KM-660, 40 mm.

Mexican State Confederation Series (Selected Examples)

Series 1, 10 pesos, PF. 2003. Type A5 / Zacatecas, BW-606.1, KM-679, 40 mm.

Series 1, 10 pesos, PF. 2003. Type A5 / Yucatán, BW-606.2, KM-680, 40 mm.

Series 1, 10 pesos, PF. 2003. Type A5 / Veracruz, BW-606.3, KM-681, 40 mm.

Series 1, 10 pesos, PF. 2003. Type A5 / Tamaulipas, BW-606.5, KM-683, 40 mm.

Mexican State Confederation Series (Selected Examples)

(continued)

Series 1, 100 pesos, PF. 2003. Type A2 / Tlaxcala, BW-684.4, KM-699, 34.5 mm.

Series 1, 100 pesos, PF. 2004. Type A2 / Tamaulipas, BW-684.5, KM-699, 34.5 mm.

Series 1, 100 pesos, PF. 2004. Type A2 / Tabasco, BW-684.6, KM-701, 34.5 mm.

Series 1, 100 pesos, PF. 2004. Type A2 / Sonora, BW-684.7, KM-702, 34.5 mm.

Series 2, 10 pesos, PF. 2005. Type A6 / Aguascalientes, BW-609.1, KM-718, 40 mm.

Series 2, 10 pesos, PF. 2005. Type A6 / Baja California, BW-609.2, KM-757, 40 mm.

Series 2, 10 pesos, PF. 2006. Type A6 / Baja California Sur, BW-609.3, KM-761, 40 mm.

Series 2, 10 pesos, PF. 2006. Type A6 / Campeche, BW-609.4, KM-759, 40 mm.

Mexican State Confederation Series (Selected Examples)

(continued)

Series 2, 100 pesos, PF. 2005. Type A3 / Baja California, BW-685.2, KM-863, 34.5 mm.

Series 2, 100 pesos, PF. 2006. Type A3 / Baja California Sur. BW-685.3, KM-864, 34.5 mm.

Series 2, 100 pesos, PF. 2006. Type A3 / Campeche, BW-685.4, KM-865, 34.5 mm.

Series 2, 100 pesos, PF. 2006. Type A6 / Chiapas, BW-685.7, KM-866, 34.5 mm.

Miguel de Cervantes' "Don Quixote"

10 pesos, BU. 2005. Type A7, 33rd International Cervantino Festival, BW-757, KM-766, 40 mm.

20 pesos, PF. 2005. Type A4, 400th Anniversary of *Don Quijote de la Mancha*, BW-804, KM-704, 48 mm.

100 pesos, BU. 2005. Type A5a, 400th Anniversary of *Don Quijote de la Mancha*, Variety I, BW-854.1, KM-705, 39 mm.

100 pesos, PF. 2005. Type A5b, 400th Anniversary of *Don Quijote de la Mancha*, Variety II, BW-854.2, KM-705, 39 mm.

Mexican Monetary Anniversaries

20 pesos, PF. 2005. Type A4, 80th Anniversary of the Banco de México, BW-805, KM-767, 48 mm.

100 pesos, BU. 2005. Type A6, 80th Anniversary of the Banco de México, BW-855, KM-732, 39 mm.

10 pesos, PF. 2005. Type A7, 470th Anniversary of the Casa de Moneda, BW-856, KM-768, 40 mm.

100 pesos, BU. 2005. Type A7, 470th Anniversary of the Casa de Moneda, BW-858, KM-731, 39 mm.

5 pesos, PF. 2005. Type A2, 100th Anniversary of the Coinage Reform of 1905, BW-859, KM-UL, 33 mm.

100 pesos, BU. 2005. Type A8, 100th Anniversary of the Coinage Reform of 1905, BW-860, KM-730, 39 mm.

75th Anniversary of the UNAM

10 pesos, PF. 2010. Type 1, BW-859, KM-UL, 40 mm. (Note the frosted fields and mirrored devices.)

Benito Juárez García Birth Bicentennial

100 pesos, BU. 2006.
Type A9, BW-860,
KM-764, 39 mm.

2006 FIFA World Cup, Germany

5 pesos, PF. 2006.
Type A3, BW-861,
KM-770, 40 mm.

25 pesos, PF. 2006.
Type A1, BW-862,
KM-UL, 23 mm.

Numismatic Heritage of Mexico Series (Selected Examples)

100 pesos, PF. 2011.
Type A10 / Philip V
8 reales, BW-861.1,
KM-UL, 39 mm.

100 pesos, PF. 2011.
Type A10 / War of
Independence, insurgent
SUD 8 reales, BW-861.3,
KM-UL, 39 mm.

100 pesos, PF. 2011.
Type A10 / 1905 Reform,
Caballito peso, BW-861.5,
KM-UL, 39 mm.

100 pesos, PF. 2012.
Type A11 / Philip III
cob 8 reales, BW-862.2,
KM-UL, 39 mm.

100 pesos, PF. 2012.
Type A11 / Republic
8 escudos, Hand on Book,
BW-862.5, KM-UL, 39 mm.

100 pesos, PF. 2012.
Type A11 / 1905 Coinage
Reform, 5 pesos, Railroad,
BW-862.6, KM-UL, 39 mm.

Numismatic Heritage of Mexico Series (Selected Examples)

(continued)

100 pesos, PF. 2013. Type A12 / Carlos and Johanna 3 reales, BW-863.2, KM-UL, 39 mm.

100 pesos, PF. 2013. Type A12 / Republic 8 reales, BW-863.4, KM-UL, 39 mm.

100 pesos, PF. 2013. Type A12 / War of Independence, Supreme National Congress of America, BW-863.5, KM-UL, 39 mm.

100 pesos, PF. 2014. Type A13 / Ferdinand VI 8 escudos, BW-864.2, KM-UL, 39 mm.

100 pesos, PF. 2014. Type A13 / Revolutionary 60 pesos, Oaxaca, BW-864.3, KM-UL, 39 mm.

100 pesos, PF. 2014. Type A13 / War of Independence Royalist provisional 8 reales, BW-864.4, KM-UL, 39 mm.

Chichén Itzá "070707" Series (Selected Examples)

5 pesos, PF. 2012. Type A28, BW-870.3, KM-UL, 40 mm.

10 pesos, PF. 2012. Type A10, BW-870.4, KM-UL, 48 mm.

20 pesos, PF. 2012. Type A5, BW-870.5, KM-UL, 65 mm.

16

Mint and Proof Sets

EARLY SERIES MINT SETS

The Banco de México began issuing Mint Sets in 1977 in soft plastic sheets and continued to do so until 1989. The Casa de Moneda de México strikes the coins and the Banco de México assembles the sets and distributes them. These sets technically are not Mint Sets but the bank, as well as the Mexican numismatic field in general, refers to them as Mint Sets rather than as year sets. In the early series the soft plastic pages used were not acid free and many coins from these sets have been contaminated by polyvinylchloride, commonly called PVC.

1977 Half page (9 coins). BW-MS 1, KM-BS6. BU.

1977 Full page (9 coins). BW-MS 2, KM-BS7. BU.

1978 Half page (9 coins). BW-MS 3, KM-BS8. BU.

1978 Full page (9 coins). BW-MS 4, KM-BS9. BU.

1979 Half page (8 coins). BW-MS 5, KM-BS10. BU.

1979 Full page (8 coins). BW-MS 6, KM-BS11. BU.

1980 Full page (9 coins). BW-MS 7, KM-BS12. BU.

1981 Full page (9 coins). BW-MS 8, KM-BS13. BU.

1982 Full page (7 coins). BW-MS 9, KM-BS14. BU.

1983 Full page (11 coins). BW-MS 10, KM-BS15. BU.

1983 Full page (11 coins). BW-MS 10.1, KM-BS16. BU.

1984 Full page (8 coins). BW-MS 11, KM-BS17. BU.

1985 Full page (12 coins). BW-MS 12, KM-BS18. BU.

1986 Full page (7 coins). BW-MS 13, KM-BS20. BU.

1987 Full page (9 coins). BW-MS 14, KM-BS21. BU.

1988 Full page (8 coins). BW-MS 15, KM-BS22. BU.

1989 Full page (10 coins). BW-MS 16, KM-BS23. BU.

LATE SERIES MINT SETS

Around 1992 the Banco de México began issuing Mint Sets in hard plastic cases to replace the soft plastic sheets used in the early series. The bank then re-packaged the early series (1970–1989) in the hard plastic cases and continued to use the hard cases until 2000. In some instances the sets in the hard plastic cases from 1970 to 2000 did not have examples of all coins issued in that year.

1970 (7 coins). BW-MS 17, KM-BS UL. BU.

1971 (6 coins). BW-MS 18, KM-BS UL. BU.

1972 (6 coins). BW-MS 19, KM-BS UL. BU.

1973 (5 coins). BW-MS 20, KM-BS UL. BU.

1974 (7 coins). BW-MS 21, KM-BS UL. BU.

1975 (7 coins). BW-MS 22, KM-BS UL. BU.

1976 (9 coins). BW-MS 23, KM-BS UL. BU.

1977 (9 coins). BW-MS 24, KM-BS UL. BU.

1978 (9 coins). BW-MS 25, KM-BS UL. BU.

1979 (9 coins). BW-MS 26, KM-BS UL. BU.

1980 (9 coins). BW-MS 27, KM-BS12. BU.

1981 (9 coins). BW-MS 28, KM-BS13. BU.

1982 (7 coins). BW-MS 29, KM-BS14. BU.

1983 (10 coins). BW-MS 30, KM-BS15. BU.

1983 (10 coins). BW-MS 30.1, KM-BS16. BU.

1984 (8 coins). BW-MS 31, KM-BS17. BU.

1985 (12 coins). BW-MS 32, KM-BS19. BU.

1986 (7 coins). BW-MS 33, KM-BS20. BU.

1987 (9 coins). BW-MS 34, KM-BS21. BU.

1988 (8 coins). BW-MS 35, KM-BS22. BU.

1989 (10 coins). BW-MS 36, KM-BS23. BU.

1990 (8 coins). BW-MS 37, KM-BS24. BU.

1991 (4 coins). BW-MS 38, KM-BS25. BU.

1992 (5 coins). BW-MS 39, KM-BS26. BU.

1992 (8 N$ coins). BW-MS 40, KM-BS27. BU.

1993A (7 N$ coins). BW-MS 41, KM-BS28. BU.

1993B (3 N$ coins). BW-MS 42, KM-BS29. BU.

1994A (7 N$ coins). BW-MS 43, KM-BS30. BU.

1994B (3 N$ coins). BW-MS 43.1, KM-BS31. BU.

1995 (9 N$ coins). BW-MS 44, KM-BS32. BU.

1996 (6 N$ coins). BW-MS 45, KM-BS33. BU.

1997 (8 coins). BW-MS 46, KM-BS34. BU.

1998 (8 coins). BW-MS 47, KM-BS35. BU.

1999 (8 coins). BW-MS 48, KM-BS36. BU.

CURRENT SERIES MINT SETS

In 2000 the Banco de México continued to issue annual Mint Sets, but the designs of the lightweight cardboard packaging were changed each year.

2000 (7 coins). BW-MS 49, KM-BS37. BU.

2000 (3 coins). BW-MS 50, KM-BS UL. BU.

2001 (10 coins). BW-MS 51, KM-BS38. BU.

2002 (8 coins). BW-MS 52, KM-BS39. BU.

2003 (6 coins). BW-MS 53, KM-BS40. BU.

2004 (7 coins). BW-MS 54, KM-BS UL. BU.

2005 (7 coins). BW-MS 55, KM-BS UL. BU.

2006 (7 coins). BW-MS 56, KM-BS UL. BU.

2007 (7 coins). BW-MS 57, KM-BS UL. BU.

2008 (7 coins). BW-MS 58, KM-BS UL. BU.

2009 (7 coins). BW-MS 59, KM-BS UL. BU.

2010 (7 coins). BW-MS 60, KM-BS UL. BU.

2011 (7 coins). BW-MS 61, KM-BS UL. BU.

Bicentennial of Independence and Centennial of the Revolution Mint Sets

In 2008, two 5-peso commemorative series were initiated to celebrate the Bicentennial of Independence and the Centennial of the Revolution. The lightweight cardboard packaging has designs appropriate to the area of interest. (Note: Proof Sets for the Independence and Revolution series are listed in the "Proof Sets" section.)

Bicentennial of Independence, 2008 (7 coins). BW-MS 70, KM-BS UL. BU.

Bicentennial of Independence, 2009 (6 coins). BW-MS 72, KM-BS UL. BU.

Bicentennial of Independence, 2010 (6 coins). BW-MS 74, KM-BS UL. BU.

Centennial of the Revolution, 2008 (6 coins). BW-MS 71, KM-BS UL. BU.

Centennial of the Revolution, 2009 (7 coins). BW-MS 73, KM-BS UL. BU.

Centennial of the Revolution, 2010 (5 coins). BW-MS 75, KM-BS UL. BU.

1992–1993 Presentation Mint Sets

In 1993 several Presentation Mint Sets were assembled by the Casa de Moneda de México. The nine-piece sets were presented in a wooden case with "CONO MONETARIO MEXICANO 1993" and "M̊ CASA DE MONEDA DE MÉXICO M̊" laser-engraved on the wooden case.

The Reform coinage sets contain the following coins, dated 1992 (except where noted otherwise): 5 centavos, 10 centavos (1993), 20 centavos (1993), 50 centavos, and New 1, 2, 5, 10, and 20 pesos. The number of sets assembled is unknown.

1992–1993 (9 coins). BW-PMS 1, KM-BS28. BU.

PROOF SETS

In 1983 the Casa de Moneda struck Proof Sets with 1982 and 1983 coins in the sets. The first 50 assembled sets did not contain the Proof Libertads, but did include two coins that were not used in the 998 sets with Proof Libertads: the 20 centavos of 1983 (KM-491) and the 50 centavos of 1983 (KM-492).

The seven coins contained in the Pattern Proof Sets without Libertad are as follows:

20 centavos, 1983, Type 9. BW-530, KM-491. PF.

50 centavos, 1983, Type 9. BW-541, KM-492. PF.

1 peso, 1983, Type 8. BW-549, KM-460. PF.

5 pesos, 1982, Type 9. BW-560, KM-485. PF.

10 pesos, 1982, Type 5. BW-566, KM-477.2. PF.

20 pesos, 1982, Type 1. BW-568, KM-486. PF.

50 pesos, 1983, Type 1. BW-577, KM-490. PF.

The eight coins contained in the Pattern Proof Sets with Libertad:

20 centavos, 1983, Type 8. BW-529, KM-442. PF.

50 centavos, 1983, Type 8. BW-540, KM-452. PF.

1 peso, 1983, Type 8. BW-549, KM-460. PF.

5 pesos, 1982, Type 9. BW-560, KM-485. PF.

10 pesos, 1982, Type 5. BW-566, KM-477.2. PF.

20 pesos, 1982, Type 1. BW-568, KM-486. PF.

50 pesos, 1983, Type 1. BW-577, KM-490. PF.

Libertad, 1983. BW-880, KM-494.1. PF.

Reportedly, 998 BU Libertads were withdrawn from inventory and melted to strike the Proof 1-ounce coins. The Proof Sets were packaged in facilities other than the mint, and there are some variations in the packaging.

1982–1983 "Pattern Proof Set" (8 coins). BW-PS 1, KM-PS 2. PF.

1982–1983 (7 coins, without Libertad). BW-PS 2, KM-PS 3. PF.

1982–1983 (8 coins, with Libertad). BW-PS 3, KM-PS 1. PF.

Rainbow Proof Sets

In 1989 the Casa de Moneda, under contract with a private firm, struck Proof coins in 1/4-ounce platinum, 1/2-ounce gold, and 1-ounce silver. They were packaged in nondescript, dark-blue cases outside the mint. It was reported that 3,500 Proof 1/2-ounce gold pieces were also struck, but this report appears to be erroneous, as only 738 Rainbow Proof Sets were prepared.

1989 (3 coins). BW-PS 4, KM-PS 12. PF.

1995 Proof Sets

In 1995, sets were prepared containing all circulating coinage in Proof, plus the 5 pesos, which was struck in Proof only. The sets were issued in two packaging styles but were priced the same.

1995 (8 coins). BW-PS 5, KM-UL. PF.

Bicentennial of Independence and Centennial of the Revolution Proof Sets

In 2010, Proof Sets were issued for the Bicentennial of Independence and the Centennial of the Revolution commemorative series. Each set is packaged in a velvet case (Independence, green; Revolution, red) with certificate.

Bicentennial of Independence, 2008 (7 coins). BW-PS 6, KM-UL. PF.

Bicentennial of Independence, 2009 (6 coins). BW-PS 7, KM-UL. PF.

Bicentennial of Independence, 2010 (6 coins). BW-PS 8, KM-UL. PF.

Centennial of the Revolution, 2008 (6 coins). BW-PS 9, KM-UL. PF.

Centennial of the Revolution, 2009 (7 coins). BW-PS 10, KM-UL. PF.

Centennial of the Revolution, 2010 (5 coins). BW-PS 11, KM-UL. PF.

Mint and Proof Sets

Early Series Mint Set.

Late Series Mint Set.

Current Series Mint Set.

Bicentennial of Independence Proof Set.

Centennial of the Revolution Proof Set.

1992–1993 Presentation Mint Set.

1982–1983 Proof Set With Libertad.

Rainbow Proof Set.

1995 Proof Set.

Bicentennial of Independence Proof Set.

Centennial of the Revolution Proof Set.

17

Silver Bullion Coinage

UNA ONZA

Throughout the years, Mexico has been one of the world's largest silver producers. It was always competitive in the silver trade-dollar market, with the Liberty Cap 8 reales and Liberty Cap pesos (discontinued in 1909). In an attempt to reestablish itself back in world trade-dollar activities, Mexico issued the Una Onza (One Ounce) in 1949, following up with issues in 1978 through 1980. Onzas have no legal-tender status, and are subject to customs duties and regulations. All are 40 mm in diameter, with a reeded edge; the legends are in a sans-serif typeface.

Onza, 1949. 0.925 silver, 33.625 g.

Obverse: A screw press at the center, with the legend CASA DE MONEDA DE MEXICO / 1949 surrounding. Mintmark $\overset{o}{M}$ above the press. *Reverse:* At the center, a balance scale with PESO / 33.625 / GRAMOS above the left arm and LEY / 0.925 below the pillar. The legend UNA ONZA TROY = 480 GRANOS DE PLATA PURA ★ surrounds. BW-875.1, KM-M49a.

Onza, 1978. 0.925 silver, 33.625 g. Type 1.

Obverse: A screw press at the center, with the legend CASA DE MONEDA DE MEXICO above and 1978 at lower left. Wide spacing (3 mm) between the words in DE MONEDA. *Reverse:* A balance scale at the center, surrounded by the legend UNA ONZA TROY DE PLATA PURA. Above the left arm of the scale, LEY / .925; below the pillar, PESO / 33.625 / GRAMOS. Mintmark $\overset{o}{M}$ at the bottom. BW-875.2, KM-M49b.1.

Onza, 1978. 0.925 silver, 33.625 g. Type 2.

Obverse: A screw press at the center, with the legend CASA DE MONEDA DE MEXICO above and 1978 at lower left. Close spacing (2.75 mm) between the words in DE MONEDA. *Reverse:* A balance scale at the center, surrounded by the legend UNA ONZA TROY DE PLATA PURA. Above the left arm of the scale, LEY / .925; below the pillar, PESO / 33.625 / GRAMOS. Mintmark $\overset{o}{M}$ at the bottom. BW-875.3, KM-M49b.2.

Onza, 1979. 0.925 silver, 33.625 g. Type 3.

Obverse: A screw press at the center, with the legend CASA DE MONEDA DE MEXICO above and 1979 at lower left. *Reverse:* A balance scale at the center, surrounded by the legend UNA ONZA TROY DE PLATA PURA. Left pan of scale points to U in UNA. Above the left arm of the scale, LEY / .925; below the pillar, PESO / 33.625 / GRAMOS. Mintmark $\overset{o}{M}$ at the bottom. BW-875.4, KM-M49b.3.

Onza, 1979. 0.925 silver, 33.625 g. Type 4.

Obverse: A screw press at the center, with the legend CASA DE MONEDA DE MEXICO above and 1979 at lower left. *Reverse:* A balance scale at the center, surrounded by the legend UNA ONZA TROY DE PLATA

PURA. Left pan of scale points between U and N in UNA. Above the left arm of the scale, LEY / .925; below the pillar, PESO / 33.625 / GRAMOS. Mintmark $\overset{\circ}{M}$ at the bottom. BW-875.5, KM-M49b.4.

Onza, 1980. 0.925 silver, 33.625 g. Type 5.

Obverse: A screw press at the center, with the legend CASA DE MONEDA DE MEXICO above and 1980 at lower left. *Reverse:* A balance scale at the center, surrounded by the legend UNA ONZA TROY DE PLATA PURA. Left pan of scale points to U in UNA. Above the left arm of the scale, LEY / .925; below the pillar, PESO / 33.625 / GRAMOS. Mintmark $\overset{\circ}{M}$ at the bottom. BW-875.6, KM-M49b.5.

Note: Type 5.1 has overdate 1980/2; Type 5.2 has overdate 1980/70.

Onza, 1989. 0.925 silver, 33.625 g. "El Capricho."

Obverse: A screw press at the center, with the legend CASA DE MONEDA DE MEXICO above and 1989 at lower left. *Reverse:* A balance scale at the center, surrounded by the legend UNA ONZA TROY DE PLATA PURA. Above the left arm of the scale, LEY / .925; below the pillar, PESO / 33.625 / GRAMOS. Mintmark $\overset{\circ}{M}$ at the bottom. BW-875.9, KM-UL.

Note: *Capricho* is Spanish for "caprice," and indicates that this coin is something of an anomaly. Struck on the same dies as the 1978–1980 official issues, the 1989 Proof El Capricho does not appear in the official mintage reports; the unofficial estimate is that fewer than 50 were struck.

Una Onza

1949. BW-875.1, KM-M49a, 40 mm.

1978, obverse, Type 1 (4.5 mm between words in DE MONEDA). BW-875.2, KM-M49b.1, 40 mm.

1979, reverse, Type 3 (left pan points to U in UNA). BW-875.4, KM-M49b.3, 40 mm.

1978, obverse, Type 2 (2.75 mm between words in DE MONEDA). BW-875.3, KM-M49b.2, 40 mm.

1979, reverse, Type 4 (left pan points between U and N in UNA). BW-375.5, KM-M49b.4, 40 mm.

BULLION COMMEMORATIVE SERIES

In 1987 the Casa de Moneda de México released the Bullion Commemorative Series: privately issued pieces under contract with a Texas dealer who used an obverse design slightly different than the design used on the official bullion pieces. Like the official onzas, the privately issued pieces are not legal tender and are subject to customs fees and regulations.

The obverse design for all has, as its central device, the Casa de Moneda's 16th-century coining press, as used on the official issues; the legend **CASA DE MONEDA DE MEXICO** is placed essentially as it is on the official coins. The design differs from that of the official onza in that the text is in a serif typeface; the date is directly above the press; the weight, metal, and fineness are to the left of the press; and the mintmark $\overset{\circ}{\text{M}}$ is to the right of the press. Moreover, the word **PROOF** appears in small type below the the mintmark (it does not appear on the onza).

200TH ANNIVERSARY OF THE U.S. CONSTITUTION

In 1987, one Bullion Commemorative Series featured the 200th anniversary of the U.S. Constitution; this is the series most widely found in the secondary market. The coins were struck in 0.999 silver, in weights of 1, 5, and 12 ounces; in 1/4-ounce gold; and reportedly in 12-ounce platinum (unconfirmed; the platinum issue is illustrated, but its true metallic content is unknown, and it may be silver or an off-metal pattern). The edges are reeded.

Coins in this series are as follows:

1-oz. silver. Diameter 40 mm.
BW-875.10, KM-MB37.

5-oz. silver. Diameter 65 mm.
BW-882, KM-MB38.

12-oz. silver. Diameter 80 mm.
BW-875.9.b, KM-MB39.

1/4-oz. gold. Diameter 23 mm.
BW-875.9.c, KM-UL.

Una Onza

(continued)

1980, 0/2. Type 3.1 (reverse with pan to U, obverse with 0/2 overdate). BW-875.7, KM-M49b.5.

1980 (reverse is Type 3, with pan pointing to U in UNA). BW-375.6, KM-M49b.5, 40 mm.

1980, 8/7. Type 3.2 (reverse with pan to U, obverse with 8/7 overdate). BW-875.8, KM-M49b.5.

1989. "El Capricho." BW-875.9, KM-UL, 40 mm.

Save the Giant Panda

Another issue of the 1987 Bullion Commemorative Series commemorated the fifth anniversary of the birth of "Tohui," the famous offspring of pandas Pepe and Yin Yin. At that time Tohui was the only surviving Giant Panda ever born in captivity outside the Republic of China.

The 12-ounce silver coin in the Save the Giant Panda series has a couple of additional design elements the others do not have: a serial number on the edge, and an anniversary flame on the obverse marking the fifth year since the birth of Tohui in the Chapultepec Zoo. Bronze pattern coins were made for gold 1/10-, 1/4-, 1/2-, 1-, and 5-ounce issues. A silver 5-ounce pattern was made, as well.

5-oz. silver. Diameter 65 mm. BW-896.c, KM-MB23.

12-oz. silver. Diameter 80 mm. BW-896.b, KM-MB24.

1/10-, 1/4-, 1/2-, and 1-oz. bronze. Patterns.

5-oz. silver. Pattern.

The Greatest Moments in the History of the Games

This 1988 series features 12 great events of the Olympic Summer Games through the years, and honors the athletes for their achievements. The series was issued in 2-ounce and 12-ounce 0.999 silver medallions.

2-oz. silver. Diameter 49 mm. BW-897, KM-MB51.

12-oz. silver. Diameter 80 mm. BW-897.1, KM-MB52.

Bullion Commemorative Series

200th Anniversary of the U.S. Constitution. 12-oz. silver, 1987. BW-875.9.b, KM-MB39, 80 mm. (shown reduced)

Save the Giant Panda. 12-oz. silver, 1987. BW-896.b, KM-MB24, 80 mm. (shown reduced)

The Greatest Moments in the History of the Games. 2-oz. silver, 1988. BW-897, KM-MB51, 49 mm. (shown reduced)

18

Gold Bullion Coinage

GOLD MEDALLIC COINAGE

On several occasions since the 1950s Mexico has issued gold medallic coinage, without denomination, in honor of various anniversaries or concepts. The first such coins were issued in 1953, for the 200th anniversary of the birth of Father Miguel Hidalgo y Costilla. In 1957, a similar series commemorated the centennial of the 1857 Constitution. The year 1999 saw the issuance of a coin celebrating Mexico's numismatic History of Gold, and in 2011, the Cultural Fusion Series honored Mexico's rich cultural legacy.

Miguel Hidalgo y Costilla Birth Bicentennial

On May 8, 1753, Miguel Hidalgo y Costilla was born in New Spain to a *Criollo* (Creole) family. Brought up as a Catholic, well educated, and fluent in the languages of both the ruling class and the indigenous people, he became a Jesuit priest, and at age 50 located in the parish of Dolores. He was deeply devoted to the well-being of the poor in his parish; largely indigenous, they were subjected to harsh treatment and economic restrictions by the Spanish colonial government. In 1810, Father Hidalgo y Costilla joined a plot to overthrow the government, and on September 16, he summoned his congregation and called upon them to rebel. His rousing cry of independence became known as the *grito de Dolores*, and marked the beginning of the War of Independence.

A circulating silver 5 pesos of the same design was also issued for this occasion (see chapter 13).

Hidalgo y Costilla (no denomination), 1953, 0.900 gold, 8.333 g. PF.

Obverse: The national coat of arms with the legend REPUBLICA MEXICANA above and a half-wreath of oak and laurel below. *Reverse:* A bust of Hidalgo y Costilla in three-quarter profile, with the legend AÑO DE HIDALGO above. The Dolores Church is in the background to the left, with the dates 1753 / 1953 above. *Diameter:* 22.5 mm. *Edge:* Plain. BW-654.2, KM-M91a.

Note: This coin corresponds in weight and fineness to the previously issued gold 10 pesos.

Hidalgo y Costilla (no denomination), 1953, 0.900 gold, 16.666 g. PF.

Obverse: The national coat of arms with the legend REPUBLICA MEXICANA above and a half-wreath of oak and laurel below. *Reverse:* A bust of Hidalgo y Costilla in three-quarter profile, with the legend AÑO DE HIDALGO above. The Dolores Church is in the background to the left, with the dates 1753 / 1953 above. *Diameter:* 27.5 mm. *Edge:* Plain. BW-655.3, KM-M92a.

Note: This coin corresponds in weight and fineness to the previously issued gold 20 pesos.

Centennial of the Mexican Constitution of 1857

On February 5, 1857, under the presidency of Ignacio Comonfort, the Federal Constitution of United Mexican States established the individual rights of the Mexican people and curtailed the authority of the Church. Among the constitution's 128 articles were those abolishing slavery, granting freedom of speech and other rights, and removing religious dogma from public education. Conservatives were violently opposed to these terms, and subsequent decades in Mexico would see bloody struggles between secular and religious interests.

A circulating silver 1 peso with a bust of Juárez was also issued to honor this centennial (see chapter 13).

Constitution of 1857 (no denomination), 1957, 0.900 gold, 8.333 g. PF.

Obverse: The national coat of arms with the legend REPUBLICA MEXICANA above and a half-wreath of oak and laurel below. *Reverse:* A bust of Benito Juárez in full profile; mintmark M̊ to the right of the bust, with all surrounded by the legend CENTENARIO DE LA CONSTITUCION DE MEXICO and •1857-1957•. *Diameter:* 22.5 mm. *Edge:* Plain. BW-654.3, KM-M123a.

Note: This coin corresponds in weight and fineness to the previously issued gold 10 pesos.

Constitution of 1857 (no denomination), 1957, 0.900 gold, 41.666 g. PF.

Obverse: A female figure holding a book that bears the words CONSTITUCION / 1857, superimposed over an outline of Mexico against a background of a radiant sun. The legend PRIMER / CENTENARIO / DE LA / CONSTITUCION / DE 1857 fills the upper right quarter. *Reverse:* An interior scene of Mexico's congress in session, with CON GRESO / CONSTITUYENTE above and the dates 1856–1857 in the exergue. *Diameter:* 37 mm. *Edge:* Plain. BW-656.2, KM-M122a.

Note: This coin corresponds in weight and fineness to the previously issued gold 50 pesos.

History of Gold

In 1999, a medallic coin weighing 1/20th of an ounce was issued with a design honoring Mexico's rich tradition of artistic work in gold, dating back to pre-Columbian times. The reverse of the coin depicts an Aztec man melting gold with the use of a muffle and a blow pipe; above the central figure is the word TEOCUITATL, the Nahuatl word for gold.

History of Gold (no denomination), 1999, 0.999 gold, 1.417 g. PF.

Obverse: The national coat of arms with the legend REPUBLICA MEXICANA above and a half-wreath of oak and laurel below. *Reverse:* An Aztec goldsmith, with TEOCUITLATL above, 1999 LEY 0.999 below, mintmark M̊ at left, and 1/20 / DE ONZA / ORO PURO at right. *Diameter:* 13 mm. *Edge:* Plain. BW-657, KM-UL.

Note: This coin corresponds in weight and fineness to the previously issued gold 1/20 onza.

Cultural Fusion Series

In 2011, Mexico issued the Cultural Fusion Series of 0.750 gold coins. The series sought to promote Mexico's cultural legacy, in which the indigenous and Spanish worlds were fused in a new society with its own tastes in art, architecture, transportation, food, literature, and so on.

Note: The weight and fineness of the 1/25-ounce Cultural Fusion coinage do not correspond to those of any previous issue.

Cultural Fusion (no denomination), 2011, 0.750 gold, 1.25 g. PF, Type 1.

Obverse: The national coat of arms with the legend REPUBLICA MEXICANA above and a half-wreath of oak and laurel below. *Diameter:* 13 mm. *Edge:* Plain. *Designs:* Type 1.1, Spanish and Indigenous Cultures, BW-658.1, KM-UL; Type 1.2, Architecture, BW-658.2, KM-UL; Type 1.3, Cacao, BW-658.3, KM-UL; Type 1.4, Trade, BW-658.4, KM-UL.

"GOLD COINS OF MEXICO" PROGRAM

In 1981, Mexico initiated the Gold Coins of Mexico program to compete with the Canadian 1-ounce gold Maple Leaf and the South African 1-ounce gold Krugerrand in the world market. Mexico's coins were issued in weights of 1/4, 1/2, and 1 ounce, all in 0.999 gold and bearing the same design. A small quantity of gold 1-ounce coins was issued for 1985 and 1988. The Gold Coins of Mexico program was supplanted by the Libertad program in 1991.

The common obverse design displays the national coat of arms at center, with the legend ESTADOS UNIDOS MEXICANOS above and a half-wreath of oak and laurel below. The common reverse show a full-length figure of Winged Victory with the legendary mountains Popocatépetl and Ixtaccíhuatl in the background. The fractional weight (1/4, 1/2, or 1) appears in the fineness statement to the left of the figure: [fraction] / ONZA / ORO / PURO, with

Gold Medallic Coinage

Hidalgo y Costilla, 8.333 g. 1953. BW-654.2, KM-M91a, 22.5 mm.

Hidalgo y Costilla, 16.666 g. 1953. BW-655.3, KM-M92a, 27.5 mm.

Constitution of 1857, 8.333 g. 1957. BW-654.3, KM-M123a, 22.5 mm.

History of Gold, 1.417 g. 1999. BW-657, KM-UL, 13 mm.

Constitution of 1857, 41.666 g. 1957. BW-656.2, KM-M122a, 37 mm.

Cultural Fusion Series

Common obverse.

Spanish and Indigenous Cultures, 1.25 g. 2011. BW-658.1, KM-UL, 13 mm.

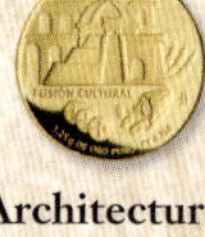
Architecture, 1.25 g. 2011. BW-658.1, KM-UL, 13 mm.

Cacao, 1.25 g. 2011. BW-658.1, KM-UL, 13 mm.

Trade, 1.25 g. 2011. BW-658.1, KM-UL, 13 mm.

[date] / Mo to the right and **MEXICO** below. The individual specifications are as follows:

1/4 oz., 1981. 8.6396 g. Diameter 22 mm. BW-G.1, KM-487.

1/2 oz., 1981. 17.2792 g. Diameter 28 mm. BW-G.2, KM-488.

1 oz., 1981. 34.5585 g. Diameter 32 mm. BW-G.3, KM-489.

1 oz., 1985. 34.5585 g. Diameter 32 mm. BW-G.3, KM-489.

1 oz., 1988. 34.5585 g. Diameter 32 mm. BW-G.3, KM-489.

Gold Coins of Mexico

1/4 oz., 1981. BW-G.1, KM-487, 22 mm.

1/2 oz., 1981. BW-G.2, KM-488, 28 mm.

1 oz., 1981. BW-G.3, KM-489, 32 mm.

19

Libertads: Silver, Gold, and Platinum

LIBERTAD SILVER

By decree of December 28, 1981, Mexico expanded on the Gold Coins of Mexico program by authorizing 1-ounce silver Libertads. These followed the same designs as the gold coins: the national coat of arms on the obverse, with Winged Victory and the legendary mountains Popocatépetl and Ixtaccíhuatl on the reverse. The edges were lettered.

In 1983 the Casa de Moneda de México issued Proof sets, each of which contained a Proof example of every circulating coin, plus the Libertad. To fill these sets, the Casa de Moneda withdrew 998 Brilliant Uncirculated Libertads from the market, melted them, and struck the planchets anew in Proof condition.

The Casa de Moneda didn't strike the 1-ounce Libertad in Proof again until 1986. In 1991, it issued fractional Libertads (1/20, 1/10, 1/4, and 1/2 ounce) in a Brilliant Uncirculated finish (sometimes referred to as a *satin finish*).

From 1993 to 1995, slight changes were made to the reverse designs. Then, in 1996, the reverse was fully redesigned: Liberty was placed upon a pediment, in three-quarter profile to the left with her arms outstretched. More of the valley of Mexico City was made visible behind her, and foliage details appeared in the foreground to either side of the pediment. The diameter was also changed, from 36 mm to 40 mm. Coins of this design are described as "New Libertads" by the mint.

In 1996, 2- and 5-ounce Brilliant Uncirculated and Proof Libertads were introduced, with the same reverse design as on the 1-ounce coin. The obverse, however, was redesigned to display Mexico's 10 different coats of arms from over the years. In 2000, the 1-ounce Libertad's obverse was change to the same design as that for the 2- and 5-ounce coins.

Although Libertads are struck with great care, varieties do exist in the series. During the years when lettered edges were used, there were occasional variations in the alignment of obverse and reverse dies during the minting process. This resulted in differing alignments between the edge lettering and the obverse and reverse designs. In addition, in the years 1982, 1983, and 1989, no decimal point was placed in the fineness.

Early Libertad Silver

1/20 oz., 1.5551 g., 0.999 silver. *Obverse:* The national coat of arms with the legend ESTADOS UNIDOS MEXICANOS above and a half-wreath of oak and laurel below. *Reverse:* Winged Victory facing forward, with the mountains Popocatépetl and Ixtaccíhuatl in the background. To Victory's left, 1/20 / ONZA; to the right, PLATA / PURA; below, [date] MEXICO LEY .999. Mintmark M° at the right, below the hand. *Diameter:* 16 mm. *Edge:* Reeded. BW-876, KM-542.

Date		
1991	1993	1994, PF
1992	1993, PF	1995
1992, PF	1994	1995, PF

1/10 oz., 3.1103 g., 0.999 silver.

Obverse: The national coat of arms with the legend ESTADOS UNIDOS MEXICANOS above and a half-wreath of oak and laurel below. *Reverse:* Winged Victory facing forward, with the mountains Popocatépetl and Ixtaccíhuatl in the background. To Victory's left, 1/10 / ONZA; to the right, PLATA / PURA; below, [date] MEXICO LEY .999. Mintmark M° at the right, below the hand. *Diameter:* 20 mm. *Edge:* Reeded. BW-877, KM-543.

Date		
1991	1993	1994, PF
1992	1993, PF	1995
1992, PF	1994	1995, PF

1/4 oz., 7.7758 g., 0.999 silver.

Obverse: The national coat of arms with the legend ESTADOS UNIDOS MEXICANOS above and a half-wreath of oak and laurel below. *Reverse:* Winged Victory facing forward, with the mountains Popocatépetl and Ixtaccíhuatl in the background. To Victory's left, 1/4 / ONZA; to the right, PLATA / PURA; below, [date] MEXICO LEY .999. Mintmark M° at the right, below the hand. *Diameter:* 25 mm. *Edge:* Reeded. BW-878, KM-544.

Date		
1991	1993	1994, PF
1992	1993, PF	1995
1992, PF	1994	1995, PF

1/2 oz., 15.5517 g., 0.999 silver.

Obverse: The national coat of arms with the legend ESTADOS UNIDOS MEXICANOS above and a half-wreath of oak and laurel below. *Reverse:* Winged Victory facing forward, with the mountains Popocatépetl and Ixtaccíhuatl in the background. To Victory's left, 1/2 / ONZA; to the right, PLATA / PURA; below, [date] MEXICO LEY .999. Mintmark M° at the right, below the hand. *Diameter:* 30 mm. *Edge:* Reeded. BW-879, KM-545.

Date		
1991	1993	1994, PF
1992	1993, PF	1995
1992, PF	1994	1995, PF

1 oz., 31.1000 g., 0.999 silver. Type 1; Lettered Edge.

Obverse: The national coat of arms with the legend ESTADOS UNIDOS MEXICANOS above and a half-wreath of oak and laurel below; eight dots on the cactus pad below the eagle's left claw. *Reverse:* Winged Victory facing forward, with the mountains Popocatépetl and Ixtaccíhuatl in the background. To Victory's left (with legends in serif type), 1 / onza; to the right, PLATA / PURA; below, [date] MEXICO Ley .999. Mintmark M° at the right, below the hand. *Diameter:* 36 mm. *Edge:* Lettered INDEPENDENCIA Y LIBERTAD. BW-880, KM-494.1.

Date	Comment
1982	No dot in fineness
1982, PF	Pattern
1983	No dot in fineness
1983, PF	
1984	
1985	
1986	
1986, PF	
1987	
1987	Doubled die
1987, PF	
1988	
1989	No dot in fineness
1989, PF	No dot in fineness

1 oz., 31.1000 g., 0.999 silver. Type 1; Reeded Edge.

Obverse: The national coat of arms with the legend ESTADOS UNIDOS MEXICANOS above and a half-wreath of oak and laurel below; eight dots on the cactus pad below the eagle's left claw. *Reverse:* Winged Victory facing forward, with the mountains Popocatépetl and Ixtaccíhuatl in the background. To Victory's left (with legends in serif type), 1 / onza; to the right, PLATA / PURA; below, [date] MEXICO Ley .999. Mintmark M° at the right, below the hand.

Diameter: 36 mm. *Edge:* Reeded. BW 880.1, KM-494.2.

Date	
1988, PF	1990, PF
1990	1991, T1

1 oz., 31.1000 g., 0.999 silver. Mule.
Obverse: The national coat of arms with the legend **ESTADOS UNIDOS MEXICANOS** above and a half-wreath of oak and laurel below; seven dots on the cactus pad below the eagle's left claw (Type 2). *Reverse:* Winged Victory facing forward, with the mountains Popocatépetl and Ixtaccíhuatl in the background. To Victory's left (Type 1, with legends in serif type), **1 / onza**; to the right, **PLATA / PURA**; below, **[date] MEXICO Ley .999**. Mintmark M̊ at the right, below the hand. *Diameter:* 36 mm. *Edge:* Reeded. BW-880.2, KM-494.5.

Date	Comment
1992	Mule (T2 obverse, T1 reverse)

1 oz., 31.1000 g., 0.999 silver.
Type 2; First Reverse Restyling.
Obverse: The national coat of arms with the legend **ESTADOS UNIDOS MEXICANOS** above and a half-wreath of oak and laurel below; seven dots on the cactus pad below the eagle's left claw. *Reverse:* Winged Victory facing forward, with the mountains Popocatépetl and Ixtaccíhuatl in the background. To Victory's left (with legends in sans-serif type), **1 / ONZA**; to the right, **PLATA / PURA**; below, **[date] MEXICO LEY .999**. Mintmark M̊ at the right, below the hand. *Diameter:* 36 mm. *Edge:* Reeded. BW-880.3, KM-494.3.

Note: "Type 2" describes changes to both the obverse and the reverse. On the obverse, there are seven dots on the cactus pad beneath the eagle's left claw (as opposed to eight on Type 1). On the reverse, the mint effected the first of two restylings, most evident in the change from serif to sans-serif typeface and an ornamental style of capitalization. The second reverse restyling, in 1996, placed Victory on a pediment, in three-quarter profile to the left, with the valley of Mexico City in the background and the mountains in the far distance. The mint calls this second design the "New Libertad"; see the next section.

Date		
1991, T2	1993	1995
1992, PF	1993, PF	1995, PF
1992	1994	
1992, PF	1994, PF	

"New Libertad" Silver

1/20 oz., 1.5551 g., 0.999 silver.
Obverse: The national coat of arms with the legend **ESTADOS UNIDOS MEXICANOS** above and a half-wreath of oak and laurel below. *Reverse:* Winged Victory on a pediment, in three-quarter profile to the left, with the valley of Mexico City in the background and, in the far distance, the mountains Popocatépetl and Ixtaccíhuatl. Legend **1/20 ONZA / PLATA PURA / [date] LEY .999** around the edge, with the phrases divided by the wings; mintmark M̊ in the field to the right. *Diameter:* 16 mm. *Edge:* Reeded. BW-876.1, KM-609.

Date			
1996	2000, PF	2005	2009, PF
1996, PF	2001	2005, PF	2010
1997	2001, PF	2006	2010, PF
1997, PF	2002	2006, PF	2011
1998	2002, PF	2007	2011, PF
1998, PF	2003	2007, PF	2013
1999	2003, PF	2008	2013, PF
1999, PF	2004	2008, PF	2014
2000	2004, PF	2009	2014, PF

1/10 oz., 3.1103 g., 0.999 silver.
Obverse: The national coat of arms with the legend **ESTADOS UNIDOS MEXICANOS** above and a half-wreath of oak and laurel below. *Reverse:* Winged Victory on a pediment, in three-quarter profile to the left, with the valley of Mexico City in the background and, in the far distance, the mountains Popocatépetl and Ixtaccíhuatl. Legend **1/10 ONZA / PLATA PURA / [date] LEY .999** around the edge, with the phrases divided by the wings; mintmark M̊ in the field to the right. *Diameter:* 20 mm. *Edge:* Reeded. BW-877.1, KM-610.

Date			
1996	2001	2006	2011
1996, PF	2001, PF	2006, PF	2011, PF
1997	2002	2007	2012
1997, PF	2002, PF	2007, PF	2013
1998	2003	2008	2013, PF
1998, PF	2003, PF	2008, PF	2014
1999	2004	2009	2014, PF
1999, PF	2004, PF	2009, PF	
2000	2005	2010	
2000, PF	2005, PF	2010, PF	

1/4 oz., 7.7758 g., 0.999 silver.

Obverse: The national coat of arms with the legend ESTADOS UNIDOS MEXICANOS above and a half-wreath of oak and laurel below. *Reverse:* Winged Victory on a pediment, in three-quarter profile to the left, with the valley of Mexico City in the background and, in the far distance, the mountains Popocatépetl and Ixtaccíhuatl. Legend 1/4 ONZA / PLATA PURA / [date] LEY .999 around the edge, with the phrases divided by wings; mintmark M̊ in the field to the right. *Diameter:* 27 mm. *Edge:* Reeded. BW-878.1, KM-611.

Date			
1996	2001	2006	2011
1996, PF	2001, PF	2006, PF	2011, PF
1997	2002	2007	2012
1997, PF	2002, PF	2007, PF	2013
1998	2003	2008	2013, PF
1998, PF	2003, PF	2008, PF	2014
1999	2004	2009	2014, PF
1999, PF	2004, PF	2009, PF	
2000	2005	2010	
2000, PF	2005, PF	2010, PF	

1/2 oz., 15.5517 g., 0.999 silver.

Obverse: The national coat of arms with the legend ESTADOS UNIDOS MEXICANOS above and a half-wreath of oak and laurel below. *Reverse:* Winged Victory on a pediment, in three-quarter profile to the left, with the valley of Mexico City in the background and, in the far distance, the mountains Popocatépetl and Ixtaccíhuatl. Legend 1/20 ONZA / PLATA PURA / [date] LEY .999 around the edge, with the phrases divided by wings; mintmark M̊ in the field to the right. *Diameter:* 33 mm. *Edge:* Reeded. BW-879.1, KM-612.

Date			
1996	2001	2006	2011
1996, PF	2001, PF	2006, PF	2011, PF
1997	2002	2007	2012
1997, PF	2002, PF	2007, PF	2013
1998	2003	2008	2013, PF
1998, PF	2003, PF	2008, PF	2014
1999	2004	2009	2014, PF
1999, PF	2004, PF	2009, PF	
2000	2005	2010	
2000, PF	2005, PF	2010, PF	

1 oz., 31.1000 g., 0.999 silver. Second Reverse Restyling.

Obverse: The national coat of arms with the legend ESTADOS UNIDOS MEXICANOS above and a half-wreath of oak and laurel below. *Reverse:* Winged Victory on a pediment, in three-quarter profile to the left, with the valley of Mexico City in the background and, in the far distance, the mountains Popocatépetl and Ixtaccíhuatl. Legend 1 ONZA / PLATA PURA / [date] LEY .999 around edge, divided by wings; mintmark M̊ in the field to the right. *Diameter:* 40 mm. *Edge:* Reeded. BW-880.5, KM-613.

Note: The "first reverse restyling" of the 1-ounce silver Libertad took place in 1991. Victory faced forward, as during previous years, but the typeface was changed from serif to sans-serif, and an ornamental style of capitalization was devised. The "second reverse restyling" was more comprehensive, and resulted in the New Libertad design.

Date			
1996	1997	1998	1999
1996, PF	1997, PF	1998, PF	1999, PF

1 oz., 31.1000 g., 0.999 silver. Obverse Restyled.

Obverse: At center, the modern national coat of arms with the legend ESTADOS UNIDOS MEXICANOS above and a half-wreath of oak and laurel below, all surrounded by a ring of Mexico's 10 historical coats of arms. *Reverse:* Winged Victory on a pediment, in three-quarter profile to the left, with the valley of Mexico City in the background and, in the far distance, the mountains Popocatépetl and Ixtaccíhuatl. Legend **1 ONZA / PLATA PURA / [date] LEY .999** around the edge, with the phrases divided by the wings; mintmark M° in the field to the right. *Diameter:* 40 mm. *Edge:* Reeded. BW-880.6, KM-639.

Date			
2000	2004	2008	2012
2000, PF	2004, PF	2008, PF	2012, PF
2001	2005	2009	2013
2001, PF	2005, PF	2009, PF	2013, PF
2002	2006	2010	2014
2002, PF	2006, PF	2010, PF	2014, PF
2003	2007	2011	
2003, PF	2007, PF	2011, PF	

2 oz., 62.2070 g., 0.999 silver.

Obverse: At center, the modern national coat of arms with the legend **ESTADOS UNIDOS MEXICANOS** above and a half-wreath of oak and laurel below, all surrounded by a ring of Mexico's 10 historical coats of arms. *Reverse:* Winged Victory on a pediment, in three-quarter profile to the left, with the valley of Mexico City in the background and, in the far distance, the mountains Popocatépetl and Ixtaccíhuatl. Legend **2 ONZAS / PLATA PURA / [date] LEY .999** around the edge, with the phrases divided by the wings; mintmark M° in the field to the right. *Diameter:* 48 mm. *Edge:* Reeded. BW-881, KM-614.

Date			
1996	2001	2006	2011
1996, PF	2001, PF	2006, PF	2011, PF
1997	2002	2007	2012
1997, PF	2002, PF	2007, PF	2013
1998	2003	2008	2013, PF
1998, PF	2003, PF	2008, PF	2014
1999	2004	2009	2014, PF
1999, PF	2004, PF	2009, PF	
2000	2005	2010	
2000, PF	2005, PF	2010, PF	

5 oz., 155.5100 g., 0.999 silver.

Obverse: At center, the modern national coat of arms with the legend **ESTADOS UNIDOS MEXICANOS** above and a half-wreath of oak and laurel below, all surrounded by a ring of Mexico's 10 historical coats of arms. *Reverse:* Winged Victory on a pediment, in three-quarter profile to the left, with the valley of Mexico City in the background and, in the far distance, the mountains Popocatépetl and Ixtaccíhuatl. Legend **5 ONZAS / PLATA PURA / [date] LEY .999** around the edge, with the phrases divided by the wings; mintmark M° in the field to the right. *Diameter:* 65 mm. *Edge:* Reeded. BW-882, KM-615.

Date			
1996	2001	2006	2011
1996, PF	2001, PF	2006, PF	2011, PF
1997	2002	2007	2012
1997, PF	2002, PF	2007, PF	2013
1998	2003	2008	2013, PF
1998, PF	2003, PF	2008, PF	2014
1999	2004	2009	2014, PF
1999, PF	2004, PF	2009, PF	
2000	2005	2010	
2000, PF	2005, PF	2010, PF	

1 Kilogram Silver

In 2002 Mexico issued a 1-kilogram Libertad coin in a Prooflike (PL) finish, with the same design as that of the 5-ounce Libertad. In 2007, a totally new kilo design was released; it featured the Aztec calendar stone on the reverse and the same coat of arms as on the 1996 5-ounce coin. Both of the kilos measure 110 mm in diameter and weigh 32.1178 ounces.

1 kg., 999.9775 g., 0.999 silver. Libertad.

Obverse: At center, the modern national coat of arms with the legend **ESTADOS UNIDOS MEXICANOS** above and a half-wreath of oak and laurel below, all surrounded by a ring of Mexico's 10 historical coats of arms. *Reverse:* Winged Victory on a pediment, in three-quarter profile to the left, with the valley of Mexico City in the background and, in the far distance, the mountains Popocatépetl and Ixtaccíhuatl. Legend **1 kg / PLATA PURA / [date] LEY .999** around the edge, with the phrases divided by the wings; mintmark M° in the field to the right.

Diameter: 110 mm. *Edge:* Reeded. BW-883, KM-677.

Note: From 2008 through 2012, kilo Libertads in Brilliant Uncirculated were issued under an exclusive agreement and sold only in Germany.

Date			
2002, PL	2007, PL	2010, PL	2013
2003, PL	2008	2011	2013, PF
2004, PL	2008, PL	2011, PL	2014
2005, PL	2009	2012	2014, PF
2006, PL	2009, PL	2012, PL	

1 kg., 999.9775 g., 0.999 silver. Aztec Calendar.

Obverse: At center, the modern national coat of arms with the legend ESTADOS UNIDOS MEXICANOS above and a half-wreath of oak and laurel below, all surrounded by a ring of Mexico's 10 historical coats of arms. *Reverse:* At center, a large reproduction of the Aztec calendar stone; above, the legend CALENDARIO AZTECA; below, $100 2011 1kg PLATA PURA LEY .999. To the right of the stone is the mintmark M°. *Diameter:* 110 mm. *Edge:* Reeded. BW-884, KM–UL.

Date			
2007, PL	2009, PL	2011, PL	2013, PL
2008, PL	2010, PL	2012, PL	

Libertad Silver

1 oz., PF, 1982. Pattern. BW-880, KM-494.1, 36 mm.

1 oz., BU, 1985. BW-880, KM-494.1, 36 mm.

1 oz., BU, 1991. Type 1. BW-880.1, KM-494.2, 36 mm (with close-up showing eight dots on the cactus pad on the reverse).

1 oz., BU, 1991. Type 2. BW-880.3, KM-494.3, 36 mm (with close-up showing seven dots on the cactus pad on the reverse).

Close-up of 1987, Doubled-Die Obverse.

"New Libertad" Silver Proofs

Common obverse design for all fractional silver Libertads, and for 1-oz. silver Libertads through 1999.

1/20 oz., PF, 2006. BW-876.1, KM-609, 16 mm.

1/10 oz., PF, 2006. BW-877.1, KM-610, 20 mm.

1/4 oz., PF, 2006. BW-878.1, KM-611, 27 mm.

1/2 oz., PF, 2006. BW-879.1, KM-612, 33 mm.

Common obverse design for 1-oz. silver Libertads after 1999, for 2- and 5-oz. Libertads, and for 1-kilo Libertads. At left, Proof; at right, Prooflike.

1 oz., PF, 2006. BW-880.6, KM-639, 40 mm.

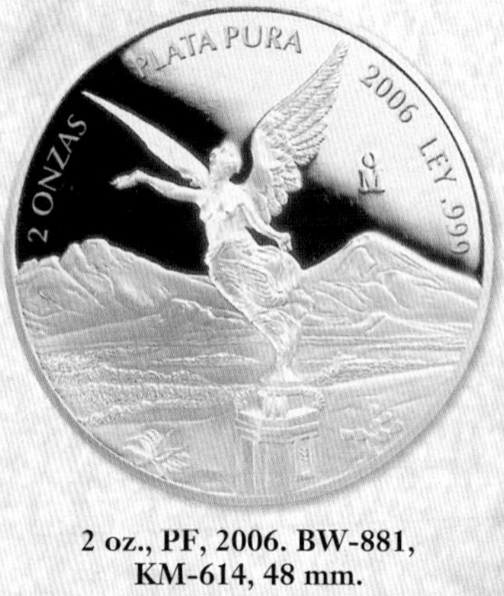

2 oz., PF, 2006. BW-881, KM-614, 48 mm.

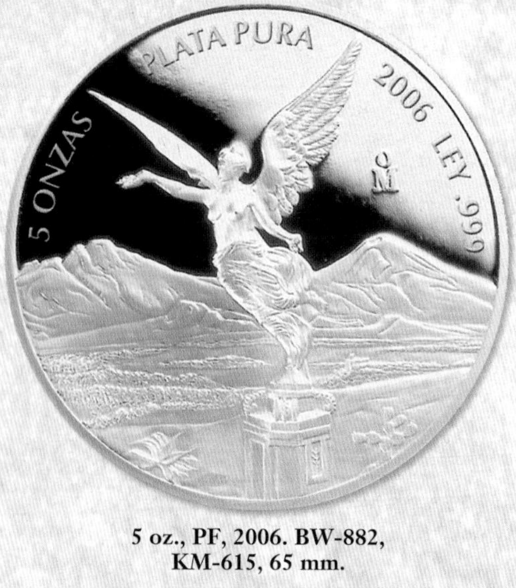

5 oz., PF, 2006. BW-882, KM-615, 65 mm.

LIBERTAD GOLD

Early Libertad Gold

Mini Libertad Gold

In 1987 and 1988, gold 1/15- and 1/20-ounce coins were issued, with an Aztec calendar on the obverse and, on the reverse, Winged Victory. Where the word "peso" appears in the legend, it refers to the weight rather than the denomination. Between the two weights and variations in the legends, seven varieties were produced.

The 1987 and 1988 fractional coins were produced under private contract between the Casa de Moneda de México and a Texas firm, and were shipped to Asia to be used in jewelry manufacturing. The mintages for the Brilliant Uncirculated and Proof versions are unknown, but are believed to be very low. Most of the unissued coins were melted in the late 1980s. Varieties 1 and 5 are rare; all others are extremely rare. These fractional gold issues can be found both cast and struck.

Fractional Libertad gold coins were not issued in the regular design (i.e., with the coat-of-arms obverse) until 1991.

Variety 1, 1/20 oz., 1.70 g., 0.900 gold.

Obverse: The Aztec calendar stone, placed just above center, with $\overset{o}{M}$ 1987 $\overset{o}{M}$ in the exergue below. *Reverse:* Winged Liberty facing forward on a plain field, surrounded by the legend CASA DE MONEDA DE MEXICO and .ORO .900 PESO 1/20 oz. *Diameter:* 13 mm. *Edge:* Reeded. BW-891, KM-530.

Date
1987

Variety 2, 1/20 oz., 1.50 g. (actual weight 1.70 g), 0.999 gold.

Obverse: The Aztec calendar stone, placed just above center, with $\overset{o}{M}$ 1987 $\overset{o}{M}$ in the exergue below. *Reverse:* Winged Liberty facing forward on a plain field, surrounded by the legend CASA DE MONEDA DE MEXICO and ORO PURO 1.500g. *Diameter:* 13 mm. *Edge:* Plain. BW-891.1, KM-UL.

Date
1987, PL

Variety 3, 1/20 oz., 1.55 g. (1.70 g. actual weight), 0.900 gold.

Obverse: The Aztec calendar stone, placed just above center, with $\overset{o}{M}$ 1987 $\overset{o}{M}$ in the exergue below. *Reverse:* Winged Liberty facing forward on a plain field, surrounded by the legend CASA DE MONEDA DE MEXICO and ORO 1.55g. *Diameter:* 13 mm. *Edge:* Plain. BW-891.2, KM-UL.

Date
1987, PF

"New Libertad" Silver Proofs
(continued)

1 kg., PL, Libertad. 2006. BW-893, KM-677, 110 mm. (shown reduced)

1 kg., PL, Aztec Calendar, 2011. BW-884, KM-UL, 110 mm. (shown reduced)

Variety 4, 1/20 oz., 1.70 g, 0.999 gold.

Obverse: The Aztec calendar stone, placed just above center, with M̊ 1988 M̊ in the exergue below. *Reverse:* Winged Liberty facing forward on a plain field, surrounded by the legend CASA DE MONEDA DE MEXICO and .ORO .999 PESO 1/20 oz. *Diameter:* 13 mm. *Edge:* Plain. BW-891.3, KM-UL.

Date
1988, PF

Variety 4, 1/20 oz., 1.70 g., 0.999 gold. Pattern.

Obverse: The Aztec calendar stone, placed just above center, with M̊ 1988 M̊ in the exergue below. *Reverse:* Winged Liberty facing forward on a plain field, surrounded by the legend CASA DE MONEDA DE MEXICO and .ORO .999 PESO 1/20 oz. A large letter P is counterstamped in the field to the left of Liberty. *Diameter:* 13 mm. *Edge:* Plain. BW-890.3, KM-UL.

Date	Comment
1988, PF	Pattern

Variety 5, 1/15 oz., 2.30 g., 0.900 gold.

Obverse: The Aztec calendar stone, placed just above center, with M̊ 1987 M̊ in the exergue below. *Reverse:* Winged Liberty facing forward on a plain field, surrounded by the legend CASA DE MONEDA DE MEXICO and .ORO .900 PESO 1/15 oz. *Diameter:* 15.6 mm. *Edge:* Plain. BW-890.1, KM-628.

Date
1987

Variety 6, 1/15 oz., 1.84 g., 0.999 gold.

Obverse: The Aztec calendar stone, placed just above center, with M̊ 1987 M̊ in the exergue below. *Reverse:* Winged Liberty facing forward on a plain field, surrounded by the legend CASA DE MONEDA DE MEXICO and ORO 1.84 g. *Diameter:* 15.6 mm. *Edge:* Plain. BW-890.2, KM-UL.

Date
1987, PF

Variety 7, 1/15 oz., 1.94 g., 0.999 gold.

Obverse: The Aztec calendar stone, placed just above center, with M̊ 1988 M̊ in the exergue below. *Reverse:* Winged Liberty facing forward on a plain field, surrounded by the legend CASA DE MONEDA DE MEXICO and ORO .999 PESO 1/15 oz. *Diameter:* 15.6 mm. *Edge:* Plain. BW-890.3, KM-UL.

Date
1988, PF

Normal Libertad Gold

Libertad 0.999 gold coins in the regular design (coat-of-arms obverse, forward-facing Winged Victory reverse) were issued in 1991, in weights of 1/20, 1/10, 1/4, 1/2, and 1 ounce. Mintage proceeded in 0.999 gold through 1993; in 1994 the fineness was changed 0.900. The gold Libertads were discontinued from 1995 through 1999. Starting in 2000, however, Brilliant Uncirculated 0.999 gold Libertads have been struck each year to date. Proof gold Libertads have been issued from 2004 to date.

1/20 oz., 1.5551 g., 0.999 gold.

Obverse: The national coat of arms with the legend ESTADOS UNIDOS MEXICANOS above and a half-wreath of oak and laurel below. *Reverse:* Winged Victory facing forward, with the mountains Popocatépetl and Ixtaccíhuatl in the background. To Victory's left, 1/20 / ONZA; to the right, ORO / PURO; below, [date] MEXICO LEY .999. Mintmark M̊ at the right, below the hand. *Diameter:* 13 mm. *Edge:* Reeded. BW-891.1a, KM-589.

Date		
1991	1992	1993

1/20 oz., 1.3990 g., 0.900 gold.

Obverse: The national coat of arms with the legend ESTADOS UNIDOS MEXICANOS above and a half-wreath of oak and laurel below. *Reverse:* Winged Victory facing forward, with the mountains Popocatépetl and Ixtaccíhuatl in the background. To Victory's left, 1/20 / ONZA; to the right, ORO / PURO; below, [date] MEXICO LEY .900. Mintmark

M̊ at the right, below the hand. *Diameter:* 13 mm. *Edge:* Reeded. BW-891.2a, KM-589.

Date
1994

1/10 oz., 3.1103 g., 0.999 gold.

Obverse: The national coat of arms with the legend ESTADOS UNIDOS MEXICANOS above and a half-wreath of oak and laurel below. *Reverse:* Winged Victory facing forward, with the mountains Popocatépetl and Ixtaccíhuatl in the background. To Victory's left, 1/10 / ONZA; to the right, ORO / PURO; below, [date] MEXICO LEY .999. Mintmark M̊ at the right, below the hand. *Diameter:* 16 mm. *Edge:* Reeded. BW-892, KM-541.

Date		
1991	1992	1993

1/10 oz., 2.7990 g., 0.900 gold.

Obverse: The national coat of arms with the legend ESTADOS UNIDOS MEXICANOS above and a half-wreath of oak and laurel below. *Reverse:* Winged Victory facing forward, with the mountains Popocatépetl and Ixtaccíhuatl in the background. To Victory's left, 1/10 / ONZA; to the right, ORO / PURO; below, [date] MEXICO LEY .900. Mintmark M̊ at the right, below the hand. *Diameter:* 16 mm. *Edge:* Reeded. BW-892.2, KM-541.

Date
1994

1/4 oz., 7.7758 g., 0.999 gold.

Obverse: The national coat of arms with the legend ESTADOS UNIDOS MEXICANOS above and a half-wreath of oak and laurel below. *Reverse:* Winged Victory facing forward, with the mountains Popocatépetl and Ixtaccíhuatl in the background. To Victory's left, 1/4 / ONZA; to the right, ORO / PURO; below, [date] MEXICO LEY .999. Mintmark M̊ at the right, below the hand. *Diameter:* 23 mm. *Edge:* Reeded. BW-893, KM-590.

Date		
1991	1992	1993

1/4 oz., 6.9980 g., 0.900 gold.

Obverse: The national coat of arms with the legend ESTADOS UNIDOS MEXICANOS above and a half-wreath of oak and laurel below. *Reverse:* Winged Victory facing forward, with the mountains Popocatépetl and Ixtaccíhuatl in the background. To Victory's left, 1/4 / ONZA; to the right, ORO / PURO; below, [date] MEXICO LEY .900 . Mintmark M̊ at the right, below the hand. *Diameter:* 23 mm. *Edge:* Reeded. BW 893.1, KM-590.

Date
1994

1/2 oz., 17.2792 g., 0.999 gold.

Obverse: The national coat of arms with the legend ESTADOS UNIDOS MEXICANOS above and a half-wreath of oak and laurel below. *Reverse:* Winged Victory facing forward, with the mountains Popocatépetl and Ixtaccíhuatl in the background. To Victory's left, 1/2 / ONZA; to the right, ORO / PURO; below, [date] MEXICO LEY .999. Mintmark M̊ at the right, below the hand. *Diameter:* 29 mm. *Edge:* Reeded. BW-894, KM-591.

Date		
1991	1992	1993

1/2 oz., 13.9960 g., 0.900 gold.

Obverse: The national coat of arms with the legend ESTADOS UNIDOS MEXICANOS above and a half-wreath of oak and laurel below. *Reverse:* Winged Victory facing forward, with the mountains Popocatépetl and Ixtaccíhuatl in the background. To Victory's left, 1/2 / ONZA; to the right, ORO / PURO; below, [date] MEXICO LEY .900. Mintmark M̊ at the right, below the hand. *Diameter:* 29 mm. *Edge:* Reeded. BW-894.1, KM-591.

Date
1994

1 oz., 31.1035 g., 0.999 gold.

Obverse: The national coat of arms with the legend ESTADOS UNIDOS MEXICANOS above and a half-wreath of oak and laurel below. *Reverse:* Winged Victory facing forward, with the mountains Popocatépetl and Ixtaccíhuatl in the background. To Victory's left, **1 / ONZA**; to the right, **ORO / PURO**; below, **[date] MEXICO LEY .999**. Mintmark M̊ at the right, below the hand. *Diameter:* 34.5 mm. *Edge:* Reeded. BW-895, KM-592.

Date		
1991	1992	1993

1 oz., 27.9900 g., 0.900 gold.

Obverse: The national coat of arms with the legend **ESTADOS UNIDOS MEXICANOS** above and a half-wreath of oak and laurel below. *Reverse:* Winged Victory facing forward, with the mountains Popocatépetl and Ixtaccíhuatl in the background. To Victory's left, **1 / ONZA**; to the right, **ORO / PURO**; below, **[date] MEXICO LEY .900**. Mintmark M̊ at the right, below the hand. *Diameter:* 34.5 mm. *Edge:* Reeded. BW-895.1, KM-592.

Date
1994

"New Libertad" Gold

1/20 oz., 1.5551 g., 0.999 gold.

Obverse: The national coat of arms with the legend **ESTADOS UNIDOS MEXICANOS** above and a half-wreath of oak and laurel below. *Reverse:* Winged Victory on a pediment, in three-quarter profile to the left, with the valley of Mexico City in the background and, in the far distance, the mountains Popocatépetl and Ixtaccíhuatl. To Victory's left, **1/20 / ONZA**; to the right, **ORO / PURO**; below, **[date] MEXICO LEY .999**. Mintmark M̊ at the right, below the hand. *Diameter:* 13 mm. BW-891.5, KM-671.

Date		
2000	2006	2009, PF
2001	2006, PF	2010
2002	2007	2010, PF
2003	2007, PF	2011
2004	2008	2011, PF
2005	2008, PF	2013
2005, PF	2009	2013, PF

1/10 oz., 3.1103 g., 0.999 gold.

Obverse: The national coat of arms with the legend **ESTADOS UNIDOS MEXICANOS** above and a half-wreath of oak and laurel below. *Reverse:* Winged Victory on a pediment, in three-quarter profile to the left, with the valley of Mexico City in the background and, in the far distance, the mountains Popocatépetl and Ixtaccíhuatl. To Victory's left, **1/10 / ONZA**; to the right, **ORO / PURO**; below, **[date] MEXICO LEY .999**. Mintmark M̊ at the right, below the hand. *Diameter:* 16 mm. *Edge:* Reeded. BW-892.5, KM-672.

Date			
2000	2005, PF	2008, PF	2011, PF
2001	2006	2009	2013
2002	2006, PF	2009, PF	2013, PF
2003	2007	2010	
2004	2007, PF	2010, PF	
2005	2008	2011	

1/4 oz., 7.7758 g., 0.999 gold.

Obverse: The national coat of arms with the legend **ESTADOS UNIDOS MEXICANOS** above and a half-wreath of oak and laurel below. *Reverse:* Winged Victory on a pediment, in three-quarter profile to the left, with the valley of Mexico City in the background and, in the far distance, the mountains Popocatépetl and Ixtaccíhuatl. To Victory's left, **1/4 / ONZA**; to the right, **ORO / PURO**; below, **[date] MEXICO LEY .999**. Mintmark M̊ at the right, below the hand. *Diameter:* 23 mm. *Edge:* Reeded. BW-893.5, KM-673.

Date			
2000	2005, PF	2008, PF	2011, PF
2001	2006	2009	2013
2002	2006, PF	2009, PF	2013, PF
2003	2007	2010	
2004	2007, PF	2010, PF	
2005	2008	2011	

1/2 oz., 15.5517 g., 0.999 gold.

Obverse: The national coat of arms with the legend **ESTADOS UNIDOS MEXICANOS** above and a half-wreath of oak and laurel below. *Reverse:* Winged Victory on a pediment, in three-quarter profile to the left, with the valley of Mexico City in the background and, in the far distance, the mountains Popocatépetl and Ixtaccíhuatl. To Victory's left, **1/2 / ONZA**; to the right, **ORO / PURO**; below, **[date] MEXICO LEY .999**. Mintmark M̊ at the right, below the hand. *Diameter:* 29 mm. *Edge:* Reeded. BW-894.5, KM-674.

Date			
2000	2005, PF	2008, PF	2011, PF
2001	2006	2009	2013
2002	2006, PF	2009, PF	2013, PF
2003	2007	2010	
2004	2007, PF	2010, PF	
2005	2008	2011	

1 oz., 31.1035 g., 0.999 gold.

Obverse: The national coat of arms with the legend **ESTADOS UNIDOS MEXICANOS** above and a half-wreath of oak and laurel below, all surrounded by a ring of Mexico's 10 historical coats of arms. *Reverse:* Winged Victory on a pediment, in three-quarter profile to the left, with the valley of Mexico City in the background and, in the far distance, the mountains Popocatépetl and Ixtaccíhuatl. To Victory's left, **1 / ONZA**; to the right, **ORO / PURO**; below, **[date] MEXICO LEY .999**. Mintmark M̊ at the right, below the hand. *Diameter:* 34.5 mm. *Edge:* Reeded. BW-895.5, KM-675.

Date			
2000	2005, PF	2008, PF	2011, PF
2001	2006	2009	2013
2002	2006, PF	2009, PF	2013, PF
2003	2007	2010	
2004	2007, PF	2010, PF	
2005	2008	2011	

1 Kilogram Gold

In 2012, the Banco de México released a 200-peso Proof 0.999 gold coin, the largest gold coin ever released by Mexico. It was part of a multi-coin program (including silver commemorative 20 pesos and gold commemorative 200 pesos) issued in honor of the 200th anniversary of the beginning of the War of Independence. A limited mintage of 200 of the 1-kilo coins was authorized.

200 pesos, 1 kg., 0.999 gold. Bicentenario.

Obverse: At center, the modern national coat of arms with the legend **ESTADOS UNIDOS MEXICANOS** above and a half-wreath of oak and laurel below, all surrounded by a ring of Mexico's 10 historical coats of arms. *Reverse:* At center, the Winged Victory figure from the Columna de la Independencia (Column of the Independence). The legends **BICENTENARIO** appear at the top and **1kg ORO PURO** at the left. To the right of Victory's shoulder, **1810 / – / 2010**; below that, **200 / PESOS**. Mintmark M̊ at bottom right. *Diameter:* 90 mm. *Edge:* Lettered **INDEPENDENCIA Y LIBERTAD**. BW-898, KM-UL.

Date
2012, PF

PLATINUM COINAGE

Libertad Platinum

In 1987, the Casa de Moneda struck 1/4-ounce platinum coins under private contract. They were to be a part of the three-piece "Rainbow Proof Set" (see chapter 16).

1/4 oz., Libertad, 7.7775 g., 0.999 platinum.

Obverse: The national coat of arms with the legend **ESTADOS UNIDOS MEXICANOS** above and a half-wreath of oak and laurel

Libertad Gold

Mini Libertad Gold

Variety 1, 1/20 oz. 1987.
BW-891, KM-530, 13 mm.

Variety 2, 1/20 oz. 1987.
BW-891.1, KM-UL, 13 mm.

Variety 3, 1/20 oz. 1987.
BW-891.2, KM-UL, 13 mm.

Variety 4, 1/20 oz. Pattern. 1987.
BW-890.3, KM-UL, 13 mm.

Variety 5, 1/15 oz. 1987.
BW-890.1, KM-628, 15.6 mm.

Variety 6, 1/15 oz. 1987.
BW-890.2, KM-UL, 15.6 mm.

Variety 7, 1/15 oz. 1988.
BW-890.3, KM-UL, 15.6 mm.

"New Libertad" Gold Proofs

Common obverse design for all gold New Libertads.

1/20 oz., 2006.
BW-891.5,
KM-671,
13 mm.

1/10 oz., 2006.
BW-892.5,
KM-672,
16 mm.

1/4 oz., 2006. BW-893.5,
KM-673, 23 mm.

1/2 oz., 2006. BW-894.5,
KM-674, 29 mm.

1 oz., 2006. BW-895.5,
KM-675, 34.5 mm.

200 pesos, 1 kg., 2010. BW-898,
KM-UL, 90 mm. (shown reduced)

below. *Reverse:* Winged Victory facing forward, with the mountains Popocatépetl and Ixtaccíhuatl in the background. To Victory's left, **1/4 / onza**; to the right, **PLATINO / PURO**; below, **1989 MEXICO LEY .999**. Mintmark M̊ at the right, below the hand. *Diameter:* 27 mm. BW-898.1, KM-538.

Date
1989, PF

Non-Libertad Platinum

One-ounce platinum Proofs were struck in 1987; a very limited number of platinum specimens (five reported) were struck with 50-peso Centenario dies. No records that have been found to date explain these pieces.

1 oz., 31.103 g. 0.999 platinum. Screw Press.

Obverse: A historical national coat of arms with the legend **REPUBLICA MEXICANA** above and a spray of oak and laurel below. *Reverse:* At the center, a coinage screw press, with **ONE OUNCE / PLATINUM / 999.5** under the left arm of the press and **UNA ONZA / PLATINO / 999.5** under the right, all surrounded by the legend **CASA DE MONEDA DE MEXICO** and **1987**. Mintmark M̊ above the press, the letter **P** below. *Diameter:* 38 mm. BW-898.5, KM-UL.

Date
1987, PF

50 pesos, 41.300 g., 0.999 platinum. Centenario.

Obverse: A historical national coat of arms with the legend **REPUBLICA MEXICANA** above and a spray of oak and laurel below. *Reverse:* Winged Victory facing forward, with the legendary mountains of Popocatépetl and Ixlaccíhuatl in the background. At Victory's left, **50 / PESOS**; at her right, **37.5Gr / ORO / PURO**; at the bottom, the dates **1821** and **1947** at either side of her feet. *Diameter:* 38 mm. BW-897, KM-UL.

Date
1987

Platinum Coinage

Libertad Platinum

1/4 oz., 1989. BW-895, KM-539, 27 mm.

Non-Libertad Platinum

1 oz., 1987. BW-897, KM-UL, 38 mm.

50 pesos, 41.3 g., 1947. BW-897, KM-UL, 38 mm.

20

Pre-Columbian Collections

At the American Numismatic Association's convention in Baltimore, on July 28, 1993, the Banco de México held a press conference to announce the beginning of the Pre-Columbian Coin Program. The series was timed to coincide with the 500th anniversary of Christopher Columbus's arrival in the Americas in 1492. This series of commemorative coins honored six pre-Columbian civilizations: the Aztec, Central Veracrúz, Maya, Olmec, Teotihuacán, and Toltec cultures. Each collection comprises the following:

- three silver coins of a single design, in weights of 1/4, 1/2, and 1 ounce (sold individually and in sets);
- three additional silver 1-ounce designs;
- one silver 5-ounce design; and
- three gold coins of a single design, in weights of 1/4, 1/2, and 1 ounce (sold individually and in sets).

Note that coins of the same weight and metal may have different denominations across the collections (and even within collections, due to the Coinage Reform of 1992). The program spanned the years 1992 through 1998; the only year during this time when none of the collections were issued was 1995.

In 1994, design changes were authorized on the Brilliant Uncirculated and Proof versions of three of the coins: the Brasero Efigie in the Aztec Collection, the Anciano con Brasero in the Central Veracrúz Collection, and the Hombre Jaguar in the Olmec Collection. Previously, the date and mintmark had been at the left and right of the main image (Type I); after the design change, both the date and the mintmark are side by side to the left of the main image (Type II).

The uniform specifications of this large and popular series make it easy to summarize the details as follows:

Ounces	Denominations	Weight	Diameter
Silver (0.999 fine)			
1/4 oz.	N$1, $1, $25	7.7700 g.	27 mm
1/2 oz.	N$2, $2, $50	15.5517 g.	33 mm
1 oz.	N$5, $5, $100	31.1030 g.	40 mm
5 oz.	N$10, $10, $10,000	155.3100 g.	65 mm
Gold (0.999 fine)			
1/4 oz.	N$25, $25, $250	7.7758 g.	23 mm
1/2 oz.	N$50, $50, $500	15.5517 g.	29 mm
1 oz.	N$100, $100, $1,000	31.1035 g.	35 mm

AZTEC COLLECTION

The first series, released in 1992, honored the Aztecs, who ruled a mighty empire in Mexico during the 1400s and early 1500s. The Aztecs developed cities as large as any in Europe at that time; Tenochtitlán, the ruling city (and the largest), occupied an island in Lake Texcoco. Canals crisscrossed the city, and roads linked it to the mainland. Little remains of the former lake, and present-day Mexico City occupies the basin.

Tenochtitlán was a center for commerce, from which merchants trekked to the lowlands to trade manufactured products for agricultural goods. The Aztecs and other cultures in the region used cacao beans and additional widely accepted items for money. To worship their hundreds of divinities, they built towering temples, created huge sculptures, and held ceremonies featuring bloody human sacrifices. The Aztec culture observed a 260-day religious calendar and a 365-day solar calendar, which consisted of 18 months of 20 days each (plus five extra days).

In 1519 the Spanish explorer Hernán Cortés landed on the east coast of Mexico and marched inland to the Aztec capital. His forces were joined by numerous Indians who had been conquered by the Aztecs and forced to pay them heavy tributes. (Among these new allies were the Totonacs, discussed in the Central Veracrúz section). The Aztecs fought back and in 1520 drove the Spaniards from Tenochtitlán; but Cortés ultimately prevailed, and the Aztec empire ceased to exist in 1521.

The common obverse design for the Aztec Collection consists of the national coat of arms with ESTADOS UNIDOS MEXICANOS above and a half-wreath of oak and laurel below, set on a semicircular field with a flat lower edge. (The reverse field is the same shape.) Surrounding the field is a stylized ornamental border; at the bottom appear the weight (in *onzas*); the metal (*plata* or *oro*); and the fineness, LEY 0.999. The edges are reeded.

Silver Issues

Eagle Warrior (1/4, 1/2, and 1 oz.)

The silver Guerrero Águila (Eagle Warrior) design, in three weights, was first issued in 1992. The eagle-warrior held an elite position in the Aztec army. The eagle helmet depicted on the coin was part of the uniform, and indicated the warriors' devotion to Huitzilopochtli—the god of war and of the sun, the hero-warrior, and the special guardian of Tenochtitlán. Originally issued in Proof only in 1992, the Eagle Warrior designs were issued later in the year in Brilliant Uncirculated.

The original 25-, 50-, and 100-peso denominations of the coins were made illegal by the Coinage Reform of 1992. In 1993 the mint issued modified coins in denominations of N$1, N$2, and N$5, in both Brilliant Uncirculated and Proof.

1/4 oz., 25 pesos, 0.999 silver, 7.7758 g.

Reverse: At the center of the field, an eagle-warrior in three-quarter profile to the right, with mintmark M̊ at left, 1992 at right, and legend GUERRERO AGUILA below. Surrounding the field, a stylized ornamental border with $25 below. *Diameter:* 27 mm. BW-900, KM-554.

Date	Comment
1992	
1992, PF	

1/2 oz., 50 pesos, 0.999 silver, 15.5517 g.

Reverse: At the center of the field, an eagle-warrior in three-quarter profile to the right, with mintmark M̊ at left, 1992 at right, and legend GUERRERO AGUILA below. Surrounding the field, a stylized ornamental border with $50 below. *Diameter:* 33 mm. BW-901, KM-555.

Date	Comment
1992	
1992, PF	

1 oz., 100 pesos, 0.999 silver, 31.1030 g.

Reverse: At the center of the field, an eagle-warrior in three-quarter profile to the right, with mintmark M̊ at left, **1992** at right, and legend **GUERRERO AGUILA** below. Surrounding the field, a stylized ornamental border with **$100** below. *Diameter:* 40 mm. BW-902, KM-556.

Date	Comment
1992	
1992, PF	

1/4 oz., New 1 peso, 0.999 silver, 7.7700 g.

Reverse: At the center of the field, an eagle-warrior in three-quarter profile to the right, with mintmark M̊ at left, **1993** at right, and legend **GUERRERO AGUILA** below. Surrounding the field, a stylized ornamental border with **N$1** below. *Diameter:* 27 mm. BW-907, KM-644.

Date	Comment
1993	
1993, PF	

1/2 oz., New 2 pesos, 0.999 silver, 15.5517 g.

Reverse: At the center of the field, an eagle-warrior in three-quarter profile to the right, with mintmark M̊ at left, **1993** at right, and legend **GUERRERO AGUILA** below. Surrounding the field, a stylized ornamental border with **N$2** below. *Diameter:* 33 mm. BW-908, KM-645.

Date	Comment
1993	
1993, PF	

Brazier Effigy (1 oz.)

Effigy braziers depicted various gods and were used for incense and other fire-related rituals. The Brasero Efigie (Brazier Effigy) design depicts such a vessel honoring Tlaloc, the god of rain and creation and one of the most important Aztec deities. The Aztecs believed that Tlaloc's tears flowed down his cheeks and regenerated the crops and fields.

1 oz., 100 pesos, 0.999 silver, 31.1030 g.

Reverse: At the center of the field, a brazier effigy of the god Tlaloc, with **1992** at left, mintmark M̊ at right, and **BRASERO EFIGIE** below. Surrounding the field, a stylized ornamental border with **$100** below. *Diameter:* 40 mm. BW-902.1, KM-563.

Date	Comment
1992	
1992, PF	

1 oz., New 5 pesos, 0.999 silver, 31.1030 g.

Reverse: At the center of the field, a brazier effigy of the god Tlaloc, with **1993** at left and mintmark M̊ at right, and **BRASERO EFIGIE** below. Surrounding the field, a stylized ornamental border with **N$5** below. *Diameter:* 40 mm. BW-909.2, KM-648.

Note: Type I is described above. On Type II coins, the mintmark and date are both at the left.

Date	Comment
1993	Type I
1993	Type II
1993, PF	Type I
1993, PF	Type II

God of Fire (1 oz.)

The Cult of Fire was among the oldest in Mesoamerica. Its god, Huehuetéotl, was also known as the protector of the earth, the old deity, and the old god of fire. The Huehuetéotl sculpture depicted on the coins represents the association between the gods of fire and the gods of water, who together governed the center of the universe and maintained the balance of the cosmos.

1 oz., 100 pesos, 0.999 silver, 31.1030 g.

Reverse: At the center of the field, a sculpture of Huehuetéotl, with **1992** at left, mintmark M̊ at right, and **HUEHUETEOTL** below. Surrounding the field, a stylized ornamental border with **$100** below. *Diameter:* 40 mm. BW-909.2a, KM-564.

Date	Comment
1992	
1992, PF	

1 oz., New 5 pesos, 0.999 silver, 31.1030 g.

Reverse: At the center of the field, a sculpture of Huehuetéotl, with **1993** at left, mintmark M° at right, and **HUEHUETEOTL** below. Surrounding the field, a stylized ornamental border with **N$5** below. *Diameter:* 40 mm. BW-909.3, KM-649.

Date	Comment
1993	
1993, PF	

God of Flowers (1 oz.)

Xochipilli, the god of flowers, symbolized the renovation of society and nature, and his body was tattooed all over with floral designs. The Aztecs performed intricate rites to dedicate their gardens to him. They even fought *guerras floridas* (flower wars)—covenants between neighboring rival communities that helped them obtain victims to sacrifice to Xochipilli.

The coins were originally issued dated 1992, in Proof only. As with the Guerrero Águila coins, the original denomination (in this case, 100 pesos only) was made illegal by the Coinage Reform of 1992. In 1993 the mint issued modified coins in the new-5-peso denomination, in both Brilliant Uncirculated and Proof.

1 oz., 100 pesos, 0.999 silver, 31.1030 g.

Reverse: At the center of the field, a sculpture of Xochipilli, with **1992** at left, mintmark M° at right, and **XOCHIPILLI** below. Surrounding the field, a stylized ornamental border with **$100** below. *Diameter:* 40 mm. BW-909.3, KM-562.

Date	Comment
1992, PF	

1 oz., New 5 pesos, 0.999 silver, 31.1030 g.

Reverse: At the center of the field, a sculpture of Xochipilli, with **1992** at left, mintmark M° at right, and **XOCHIPILLI** below. Surrounding the field, a stylized ornamental border with **N$5** below. *Diameter:* 40 mm. BW-909.4, KM-647.

Date	Comment
1993	
1993, PF	

Tizoc Stone (5 oz.)

The Piedra de Tizoc, or Tizoc stone, is a large monolith that was discovered in the Templo Mayor. Its designs celebrated the victories of Tizoc, who was the Aztec emperor from 1481 to 1486. It may also symbolize the ritual passing of the throne from Tizoc to his brother Ahuitzotl after Tizoc's untimely death. The Piedra de Tizoc design uses a motif that is repeated 14 times around the edge of the original stone: two male warrior figures, the one on the left (possibly Tizoc) garbed as an Aztec god, holding the one on the right—a defeated, non-Aztec god—by the hair.

5 oz., 10,000 pesos, 0.999 silver, 155.3100 g.

Reverse: At the center of the field, a relief design of two male warrior figures with the date at left, mintmark M° at right, and **PIEDRA DE TIZOC** below. Surrounding the field, a stylized ornamental border with **$10000** below. *Diameter:* 65 mm. BW-906, KM-557.

Date	Comment
1992	
1993, PF	

5 oz., New 10 pesos, 1993, 0.999 silver, 155.3100 g.

Reverse: At the center of the field, a relief design of two male warrior figures with the date at left, mintmark M° at right, and **PIEDRA DE TIZOC** below. Surrounding the field, a stylized ornamental border with **N$10** below. *Diameter:* 65 mm. BW-910, KM-650.

Date	Comment
1992, PF	Error; issued 1993, dated 1992
1993	
1993, PF	

Gold Issues

Jaguar / Stone of the Suns (1/4, 1/2, and 1 oz.)

The Piedra de los Soles (Stone of the Suns) depicts the Aztec creation myth, which held that prior to the current epoch the earth had four others, with a new incarnation of the sun god for each epoch. The first of these four prior ages is symbolized on the stone by a jaguar and the number 4 (rendered as four large dots). On the coin, as on the stone, only three of the numerals are visible, as one of the corners of the sculpture is damaged.

1/4 oz., 250 pesos, 0.999 gold, 7.7758 g.

Reverse: At the center of the field, a relief design with the head of a jaguar in profile to the left and three dots surrounding. Mintmark M̊ at the left of the head, 1992 at the right, and JAGUAR / PIEDRA DE LOS SOLES below. Surrounding the field, a stylized ornamental border with $250 below. *Diameter:* 23 mm. BW903, KM-558.

Date	Comment
1992	
1992, PF	

1/2 oz., 500 pesos, 0.999 gold, 15.5517 g.

Reverse: At the center of the field, a relief design with the head of a jaguar in profile to the left and three dots surrounding. Mintmark M̊ at the left of the head, 1992 at the right, and JAGUAR / PIEDRA DE LOS SOLES below. Surrounding the field, a stylized ornamental border with $500 below. *Diameter:* 29 mm. BW-904, KM-559.

Date	Comment
1992	
1992, PF	

1 oz., 1,000 pesos, 0.999 gold, 31.1035 g.

Reverse: At the center of the field, a relief design with the head of a jaguar in profile to the left and three dots surrounding. Mintmark M̊ at the left of the head, 1992 at the right, and JAGUAR / PIEDRA DE LOS SOLES below. Surrounding the field, a stylized ornamental border with $1000 below. *Diameter:* 35 mm. BW-905, KM-560.

Date	Comment
1992	
1992, PF	

CENTRAL VERACRÚZ COLLECTION

The Totonac people built a complex civilization in the region of what is now the State of Veracrúz. During the 15th century they were forcibly absorbed into the Aztec empire and required to pay tribute, in the form of both goods and humans (for slaves or sacrifice), to the Aztec capital, Tenochtitlán. The Totonacs were among those who joined the forces of Hernán Cortés in defeating the Aztecs (see the section on the Aztec Collection).

The Totonacs' largest city, El Tajín, covered at least 2,600 acres. Its massive, pyramidal stone temples and palaces ranged around the open plazas of a mighty political center. As in other Mesoamerican cultures, Totonac priests maintained a complex religion in which numerous capricious gods, both good and evil, inhabited the sky, earth, and underworld. The economy of Central Veracrúz was agricultural, and the Totonacs' exports included feathers, pelts, and honey. Cacao beans were used for monetary exchange.

The first Central Veracrúz issues appeared later in 1992 than the Aztec issues, and they were denominated in new pesos from the outset; there was no need to reissue them to conform with the Coinage Reform of 1992.

The common obverse design for the Central Veracrúz Collection consists of the national coat of arms with ESTADOS UNIDOS MEXICANOS above and a half-wreath of oak and laurel below, set on a rectangular field with rounded ends. (The reverse field is the same shape.) Surrounding the field is a stylized ornamental border; at the bottom appear the weight (in *onzas*); the metal (*plata* or *oro*); and the fineness, LEY 0.999. The edges are reeded.

Silver Issues

Bas-Relief of El Tajín (1/4, 1/2, and 1 oz.)

In the central section of El Tajín are the remains of 13 courts for the ritual ballgame, indicating the game's importance to the Totonacs. On the vertical walls of the south ball court is a bas-relief (the Bajorrelieve de El Tajín) in the double-outline linear style, with scenes of the ceremonial game interwoven with scrolls and bands. A section from this bas-relief is depicted on the matching group of silver coins of the Central Veracrúz Collection.

1/4 oz., New 1 peso, 0.999 silver, 7.7700 g.

Reverse: At the center of the field, a section of decorative bas-relief; incorporated into the relief, at upper left and right (respectively), 1993 and mintmark M̊. In the field below the relief, BAJORRELIEVE DE EL TAJIN. Surrounding the field, an ornamental border with N$1 below. *Diameter:* 27 mm. BW-911, KM-567.

Date	Comment
1993	
1993, PF	

1/2 oz., New 2 pesos, 0.999 silver, 15.5517 g.

Reverse: At the center of the field, a section of decorative bas-relief; incorporated into the relief, at upper left and right (respectively), 1993 and mintmark M̊. In the field below the relief, BAJORRELIEVE DE EL TAJIN. Surrounding the field, an ornamental border with N$2 below. *Diameter:* 33 mm. BW-912, KM-568.

Date	Comment
1993	
1993, PF	

1 oz., New 5 pesos, 0.999 silver, 31.1030 g.

Reverse: At the center of the field, a section of decorative bas-relief; incorporated into the relief, at upper left and right (respectively), 1993 and mintmark M̊. In the field below the relief, BAJORRELIEVE DE EL TAJIN. Surrounding the field, an ornamental border with N$5 below. *Diameter:* 40 mm. BW-913, KM-569.

Date	Comment
1993	
1993, PF	

Palm With Crocodile (1 oz.)

The Palma con Cocodrilo (Palm With Crocodile) design reflects both the Gulf Coast landscape, where the Totonac civilization developed, and the Totonacs' fascination with the crocodile. The creature is viewed from above; its tail curls back around in imitation of a palm frond.

1 oz., New 5 pesos, 0.999 silver, 31.1030 g.

Reverse: At the center of the field, the figure of a crocodile with curled tale. In the field at upper left, 1993; mintmark M̊ at upper right; and PALMA CON COCODRILO at the bottom. Surrounding the field, an ornamental border with N$5 below. *Diameter:* Diameter 40 mm. BW-913.1, KM-582.

Date	Comment
1993	
1993, PF	

Smiling Face (1 oz.)

The Carita Sonriente (Smiling Face) is one of the most widely found art products of the Central Veracrúz pre-Hispanic culture. These small, terra-cotta figurines, with their distinctive triangular heads and puffy, smiling faces, are often found in tombs. Explanations for their purpose vary: one is that they were thought to have magical powers that would aid the dead in the afterlife. Another suggests they represent drugged individuals (hence the puffy features) being prepared for sacrifice.

1 oz., New 5 pesos, 0.999 silver, 31.1030 g.

Reverse: At the center of the field, the head of a Smiling Face figurine. In the field to the left, 1993; mintmark M̊ to the right; and CARITA SONRIENTE at the bottom.

Surrounding the field, an ornamental border with **N$5** below. *Diameter:* 40 mm. BW-913.2, KM-584.

Date	Comment
1993	
1993, PF	

Old Man With Brazier (1 oz.)

The Anciano con Brasero (Old Man With Brazier)—a seated elderly man with a brazier atop his head—represented the god of fire. These sculptures, found in the Centro de las Mesas in the state of Veracrúz, are made of terra-cotta, sometimes at life size. They have strong elements of both Totonac and Teotihuacán styles, indicating the strong relationship between the two cultures.

1 oz., New 5 pesos, 0.999 silver, 31.1030 g.

Reverse: At the center of the field, an old man sitting cross-legged and balancing a large brazier on his head. In the field to the left, **1993**; mintmark M̊ to the right; and **ANCIANO CON BRASERO** at the bottom. Surrounding the field, an ornamental border with **N$5** below. *Diameter:* 40 mm. BW-913.3, KM-583.

Note: Type I is described above. On Type II coins, the mintmark and date are both at the left.

Date	Comment
1993	Type I
1993	Type II
1993, PF	Type I
1993, PF	Type II

Pyramid of the Niches (5 oz.)

The design on the 5-ounce coin, called the Pirámide de El Tajín (Tajín Pyramid), depicts the Pyramid of the Niches located in the Totonac city. The stepped pyramids of El Tajín are visually dramatic, a quality enhanced by the niches and jutting cornices on the tiers. The Pyramid of the Niches has a total of 365 such niches, suggesting its use for calendar and ritual purposes.

5 oz., New 10 pesos, 0.999 silver, 155.515 g.

Reverse: At the center of the field, the Pyramid of the Niches. In the field to the left, **1993**; mintmark M̊ to the right; and **PIRAMIDE DE EL TAJIN** at the bottom. Surrounding the field, an ornamental border with **N$10** below. *Diameter:* 65 mm. BW-914, KM-570.

Date	Comment
1993	
1993, PF	

Gold Issues

Ceremonial Hatchet (1/4, 1/2, and 1 oz.)

The three gold pieces depict the Hacha Ceremonial (Ceremonial Hatchet): an axhead in the form of a man's head, flattened in profile and wearing a helmet that is probably associated with the *juego de pelota* (the Mesoamerican ball game). The fish shape of the helmet signifies the importance of the ocean in the Central Veracrúz culture.

1/4 oz., New 25 pesos, 1993, 0.999 gold, 7.7758 g.

Reverse: At the center of the field, a profile of a man wearing a fish helmet. In the field to the left, **1993**; mintmark M̊ to the right; and **HACHA CEREMONIAL** at the bottom. Surrounding the field, an ornamental border with **N$25** below. *Diameter:* 23 mm. BW-915, KM-585.

Date	Comment
1993	
1993, PF	

1/2 oz., New 50 pesos, 0.999 gold, 15.5517 g.

Reverse: At the center of the field, a profile of a man wearing a fish helmet. In the field to the left, **1993**; mintmark M̊ to the right; and **HACHA CEREMONIAL** at the bottom. Surrounding the field, an ornamental border with **N$50** below. *Diameter:* 29 mm. BW-916, KM-586.

Date	Comment
1993	
1993, PF	

1 oz., New 100 pesos, 0.999 gold, 31.1030 g.

Reverse: At the center of the field, a profile of a man wearing a fish helmet. In the field to the left, 1993; mintmark M̊ to the right; and HACHA CEREMONIAL at the bottom. Surrounding the field, an ornamental border with N$100 below. *Diameter:* 35 mm. BW-917, KM-587.

Date	Comment
1993	
1993, PF	

MAYAN COLLECTION

The third collection in the series honors the Mayan culture, which dates from 320 A.D. and occupied areas in what are now Yucatán, Guatemala, and southeast Mexico. Their economy was largely agricultural, with the population centered around multiple city-states like Tikal, Chichén Itzá, and Palenque.

The Mayans built huge pyramids with stepped sides that led to the ornate stone temples located at the top. The interiors were decorated with intricate murals and hieroglyphics, and in fact the Mayans are noted for having the only fully developed written language known in the pre-Columbian Americas. During the 11th and 12th centuries the Mayans were subdued by the Toltecs, which resulted in the Maya-Tolteca civilization.

The common obverse design for the Mayan Collection consists of the national coat of arms with ESTADOS UNIDOS MEXICANOS above and a half-wreath of oak and laurel below, set on a hexagonal (six-sided) field. (The reverse field is the same shape.) Surrounding the field is a stylized ornamental border; at the bottom appear the weight (in *onzas*); the metal (*plata* or *oro*); and the fineness, LEY 0.999. The edges are reeded.

Silver Issues

Chaac-Mool (1/4, 1/2, and 1 oz.)

The three-piece silver group depicts a characteristic sculpture of Chichén Itzá: the Chaac-Mool. The figure is a man half-sitting, half-lying on his back. His elbows are on the ground, and his hands hold a tray or plate on his abdomen. His face is turned sharply to look over one shoulder (in the case of the coin design, toward the viewer). The Chaac-Mool may have been associated with Mayan sacrificial rituals.

1/4 oz., New 1 peso, 0.999 silver, 7.7700 g.

Reverse: At the center of the field, a Chaac-Mool figure, with 1994 to the left, mintmark M̊ to the right, and CHAAC-MOOL below. A stylized ornamental border surrounds the field on five sides, crossing into the field on the uppermost, sixth side; at the bottom, N$1. *Diameter:* 27 mm. BW-918, KM-572.

Date	Comment
1994	
1994, PF	

1/2 oz., New 2 pesos, 0.999 silver, 15.5517 g.

Reverse: At the center of the field, a Chaac-Mool figure, with 1994 to the left, mintmark M̊ to the right, and CHAAC-MOOL below. A stylized ornamental border surrounds the field on five sides, crossing into the field on the uppermost, sixth side; at the bottom, N$2. *Diameter:* 33 mm. BW-919, KM-573.

Date	Comment
1994	
1994, PF	

1 oz., New 5 pesos, 0.999 silver, 31.1030 g.

Reverse: At the center of the field, a Chaac-Mool figure, with 1994 to the left, mintmark M̊ to the right, and CHAAC-MOOL below. A stylized ornamental border surrounds the field on five sides, crossing into the field on the uppermost, sixth side; at the botto m, N$5. *Diameter:* 40 mm. BW-920, KM-574.

Date	Comment
1994	
1994, PF	

Lintel 26 (1 oz.)

The ruins of the ancient Mayan city Yaxchilán, in what is now the state of Chiapas, are famous for the sculpted lintels above the doorways. Archaeologists describe these important sculptures by number; the mint chose Dintel (Lintel) 26 as the subject of this 1-ounce coin. The sculpture, which dates to about 726 A.D., depicts a ritual scene in which a woman gives the head (or a mask) of a jaguar to a dignitary or high priest.

1 oz., New 5 pesos, 0.999 silver, 31.1030 g.

Reverse: At the center of the field, an ornamental segment of Lintel 26, with 1994 to the left, mintmark M̊ to the right, and DINTEL 26 below. A stylized ornamental border surrounds the field on five sides, crossing into the field on the uppermost, sixth side; at the bottom, N$5. *Diameter:* 40 mm. BW-920.1, KM-578.

Date	Comment
1994	
1994, PF	

Gravestone of a Palenque Tomb (1 oz.)

This 1-ounce coin's design, Lápida Tumba de Palenque (Gravestone of a Palenque Tomb), is taken from the bas-relief slab covering the sarcophagus of the Mayan ruler Pakal. The central figure of the design is the body of Pakal, who lies atop the monster of the sun at the base of the Tree of the World, as he prepares to journey to the afterlife.

1 oz., New 5 pesos, 0.999 silver, 31.1030 g.

Reverse: At the center of the field, an ornamental segment of Pakal's tomb, with 1994 to the left, mintmark M̊ to the right, and LAPIDA TUMBA / DE PALENQUE below. A stylized ornamental border surrounds the field on five sides, crossing into the field on the uppermost, sixth side; at the bottom, N$5. *Diameter:* 40 mm. BW-920.2, KM-575.

Date	Comment
1994	
1994, PF	

Mask of the God Chaac (1 oz.)

This design depicts the Mascarón del Dios Chaac (Mask of the God Chaac, the Mayan rain god), found on the façade of the Temple of Kabah in the Yucatán peninsula. The Mayan people made this their most persistent decorative element; indeed, it is repeated by the hundreds on the walls of the temple, which is also known as the Temple of the Masks.

1 oz., New 5 pesos, 0.999 silver, 31.1030 g.

Reverse: At the center of the field, the mask of Chaac, with 1994 to the left, mintmark M̊ to the right, and MASCARON / DEL DIOS CHAAC below. A stylized ornamental border surrounds the field on five sides, crossing into the field on the uppermost, sixth side; at the bottom, N$5. *Diameter:* 40 mm. BW-920.3, KM-577.

Date	Comment
1994	
1994, PF	

Pyramid of the Castle (5 oz.)

The 5-ounce silver Mayan Collection coin depicts the stepped Pirámide del Castillo (Pyramid of the Castle), dedicated to the Mayan god Kukulcán. As the Mayan version of Quetzalcoatl, Kukulcán was the creator of the universe and was related to the four seasons. The name is also associated with the deified personality of a mythical king who restored the city of Chichén Itzá.

There are two varieties of this coin. The common variety is dated 1994, with the legend PIRAMIDE / DEL / CASTILLO. The 1993 variety has the legend PIRAMIDE / DEL CASTILLO / CHICHEN-ITZA. When originally released in 1993 it was cataloged as "extended legend," but it was soon found to be an error. All unsold specimens were melted; it is estimated that approximately 25 to 30 were not survived.

5 oz., New 10 pesos, 0.999 silver, 155.3100 g.

Reverse: At the center of the field, the Pyramid of the Castle, with **1994** to the left, mintmark M̊ to the right, and **PIRAMIDE / DEL / CASTILLO** below. A stylized ornamental border surrounds the field on five sides, crossing into the field on the uppermost, sixth side; at the bottom, **N$10**. *Diameter:* 65 mm. BW-921, KM-576.

Date	Comment
1993, PF	Error
1994	
1994, PF	

Gold Issues

Personage of Jaina (1/4, 1/2, and 1 oz.)

The design on the three gold coins, called Personaje de Jaina, is based on the small, naturalistic, terra-cotta figurines sculpted by the Mayans. Thousands have been found on the small island of Jaina, which was used by the Mayans of Yucatán as a burial ground during the third and fourth centuries. Although many more have been found elsewhere, they are commonly known as Jaina figurines. The one reproduced on the coin depicts a civil dignitary sitting on a throne.

1/4 oz., New 25 pesos, 0.999 gold, 7.7758 g.

Reverse: At the center of the field, a Jaina figurine, with **1994** to the left, mintmark M̊ to the right, and **PERSONAJE / DE JAINA** below. A stylized ornamental border surrounds the field on five sides, crossing into the field on the uppermost, sixth side; at the bottom, **N$25**. *Diameter:* 23 mm. BW-922, KM-579.

Date	Comment
1994	
1994, PF	

1/2 oz., New 50 pesos, 0.999 gold, 15.5517 g.

Reverse: At the center of the field, a Jaina figurine, with **1994** to the left, mintmark M̊ to the right, and **PERSONAJE / DE JAINA** below. A stylized ornamental border surrounds the field on five sides, crossing into the field on the uppermost, sixth side; at the bottom, **N$50**. *Diameter:* 29 mm. BW-923, KM-580.

Date	Comment
1994	
1994, PF	

1 oz., New 100 pesos, 0.999 gold, 31.1035 g.

Reverse: At the center of the field, a Jaina figurine, with **1994** to the left, mintmark M̊ to the right, and **PERSONAJE / DE JAINA** below. A stylized ornamental border surrounds the field on five sides, crossing into the field on the uppermost, sixth side; at the bottom, **N$100**. *Diameter:* 35 mm. BW-924, KM-581.

Date	Comment
1994	
1994, PF	

OLMEC COLLECTION

The fourth collection in the program honored the Olmec culture, which flourished in central Mexico and parts of Guatemala, Honduras, and Costa Rica around 1200 to 300 B.C. The Olmec archaeological sites are located in the tropical lowlands close to the Gulf of Mexico.

Olmec society was hierarchical, with wealth and status determining social class. The higher social class of rulers, priests, and skilled artisans lived in the larger towns; the farmers in the surrounding rural areas provided the food for the higher classes in the cities.

The best-known Olmec artworks are the monumental basalt sculptures of heads, human figures, thrones, and supernatural creatures. Amazingly, the sculptures are carved from stones that are not from the lowlands region, but were moved from the mountains some 60 miles distant.

The colossal heads found at San Lorenzo are the oldest known representations of Olmec rulers. These massive stones asserted the ruler's superhuman powers, and their expressive faces may have been realistic portraits of specific personages.

The common obverse design for the Olmec Collection consists of the national coat of arms with ESTADOS UNIDOS MEXICANOS above and a half-wreath of oak and laurel below, set on a square field with slightly convex sides. (The reverse field is the same shape.) Surrounding the field is a stylized ornamental border; at the bottom appear the weight (in *onzas*); the metal (*plata* or *oro*); and the fineness, LEY 0.999. The edges are reeded.

Silver Issues

Master of the Limes (1/4, 1/2, and 1 oz.)

Señor de las Limas (Master of the Limes) is the central motif on the three-piece silver group of coins in this collection. It is modeled after the original Señor de las Limas, a greenstone sculpture of a seated priest with a baby jaguar-human in his arms. It was found in the Valley of the Limes in the region of Veracrúz. According to archaeologists, the sculpture is related to fertility and maternity rituals.

1/4 oz., 1 peso, 0.999 silver, 7.7700 g.

Reverse: At the center of the field, the Master of the Limes figure. To the left, 1996; to the right, mintmark M̊; below, SEÑOR DE LAS LIMAS. Surrounding the field, an ornamental border with $1 below. *Diameter:* 27 mm. BW-925, KM-593.

Date	Comment
1996	
1996, PF	
1998	

1/2 oz., 2 pesos, 0.999 silver, 15.5517 g.

Reverse: At the center of the field, the Master of the Limes figure. To the left, 1996; to the right, mintmark M̊; below, SEÑOR DE LAS LIMAS. Surrounding the field, an ornamental border with $2 below. *Diameter:* 33 mm. BW-926, M-594.

Date	Comment
1996	
1996, PF	
1998	

1 oz., 5 pesos, 0.999 silver, 31.1030 g.

Reverse: At the center of the field, the Master of the Limes figure. To the left, 1996; to the right, mintmark M̊; below, SEÑOR DE LAS LIMAS. Surrounding the field, an ornamental border with $5 below. *Diameter:* 40 mm. BW-927, KM-595.

Date	Comment
1996	
1996, PF	
1998	

Jaguar-Man (1 oz.)

These figures are some of the finest examples of Olmec sculpture and can be found in a number of poses. The most common, and the one used on the Hombre Jaguar (Jaguar-Man) coin, is the seated personage wearing a helmet. The facial features resemble those of a jaguar, which was the center of most Olmec rituals.

1 oz., 5 pesos, 0.999 silver, 31.1030 g.

Reverse: At the center of the field, the Jaguar-Man figure. To the left, 1996; to the right, mintmark M̊; below, HOMBRE JAGUAR. Surrounding the field, an ornamental border with $5 below. *Diameter:* 40 mm. BW-927.3, KM-596.

Date	Comment
1996	Type I
1996	Type II (KM-UL)
1996, PF	Type I
1996, PF	Type II (KM-UL)
1998	

The Wrestler (1 oz.)

The stone sculpture known as El Luchador (The Wrestler) was found in the state of Veracrúz near the Rio Uxpanapa. The sculpture is 66 cm high and represents a seated man with his arms at shoulder height, elbows bent, hands in fists—a dynamic attitude, as if he is playing some sort of sport or fighting.

1 oz., 5 pesos, 0.999 silver, 31.1030 g.

Reverse: At the center of the field, the seated figure of the Wrestler. To the left, 1996; to the right, mintmark M°; below, EL LUCHADOR. Surrounding the field, an ornamental border with $5 below. *Diameter:* 40 mm. BW-927.1, KM-597.

Date	Comment
1996	
1996, PF	
1998	

Ceremonial Ax (1 oz.)

The Olmec Hacha Ceremonial (Ceremonial Ax) shown on the coin is a humanlike figure, often made of greenstone. The facial features are like those of the Jaguar-Man; when the figure is viewed in profile, the body tapers at the bottom to a wedge. A cleft is often carved into the back and top of the head. Ceremonial axes may have been used for rituals pertaining to agriculture.

1 oz., 5 pesos, 0.999 silver, 31.1030 g.

Reverse: At the center of the field, the Ceremonial Ax figure. To the left, 1996; to the right, mintmark M°; below, HACHA CEREMONIAL. Surrounding the field, an ornamental border with $5 below. *Diameter:* 40 mm. BW-927.2, KM-598.

Date	Comment
1996	
1996, PF	
1998	

Olmec Head (5 oz.)

The design on the 5-ounce coin depicts one of the most iconic sculptures of the Olmec culture: the Cabeza Olmeca, or Olmec Head. To date only 16 of these colossal heads have been found. Their weight ranges from 9 to 11 metric tons, and their height is from 1.6 m to 3 m. Archaeologists are uncertain whether these heads represent gods, priest, or rulers.

5 oz., 10 pesos, 0.999 silver, 155.3100 g.

Reverse: At the center of the field, an Olmec Head. To the left, 1996; to the right, mintmark M°; below, CABEZA OLMECA. Surrounding the field, an ornamental border with $10 below. *Diameter:* 65 mm. BW-928, KM-599.

Date	Comment
1996	
1996, PF	
1998	

Gold Issues

Priest (1/4, 1/2, and 1 oz.)

The central motif on the gold coins in the Olmec Collection is the Sacerdote (Priest), a bas-relief figure found at the ancient ruins of La Venta. In the sculpture, a priest or high dignitary is seated in profile, and is surrounded by a massive, undulating feathered serpent.

1/4 oz., 25 pesos, 0.999 gold, 7.7758 g.

Reverse: At the center of the field, the seated Priest surrounded by a feathered serpent. To the left, 1996; to the right, mintmark M°; below, SACERDOTE. Surrounding the field, an ornamental border with $25 below. *Diameter:* 23 mm. BW-929, KM-600.

Date	Comment
1996	
1996, PF	

**1/2 oz., 50 pesos,
0.999 gold, 15.5517 g.**

Reverse: At the center of the field, the seated Priest surrounded by a feathered serpent. To the left, **1996**; to the right, mintmark M̊; below, SACERDOTE. Surrounding the field, an ornamental border with **$50** below. *Diameter:* 29 mm. BW-930, KM-601.

Date	Comment
1996	
1996, PF	

**1 oz., 100 pesos,
0.999 gold, 31.1035 g.**

Reverse: At the center of the field, the seated Priest surrounded by a feathered serpent. To the left, **1996**; to the right, mintmark M̊; below, SACERDOTE. Surrounding the field, an ornamental border with **$100** below. *Diameter:* 35 mm. BW-931, KM-602.

Date	Comment
1996	
1996, PF	

TEOTIHUACÁN COLLECTION

Around the second century B.C., in the valley of Mexico, several settlements joined to form the first urban center: Teotihuacán. Teotihuacán had at its peak had more than 2,000 structures and a population of more than 100,000. Extending from modern-day Sinaloa in western Mexico to Guatemala in the southeast, it was the largest city in the world prior to the 1400s. It was also the religious center of Mesoamerica.

Teotihuacán was a planned city, laid out on a complex grid. Multi-family homes were common. The primary street through the city was the Avenue of the Dead, with the Pyramid of the Moon at one end; the Pyramid of the Sun farther down the avenue; and the Ciudadela (a sunken, enclosed compound that may have been a marketplace), with the Temple of Quetzalcóatl, still farther along.

The city reached its greatest splendor from 350 A.D. to 650 A.D., then suddenly declined. The final dissolution occurred about 700 A.D. Some archaeologists believe a great fire decimated almost every structure in the city.

The common obverse design for the Teotihuacán Collection consists of the national coat of arms with ESTADOS UNIDOS MEXICANOS above and a half-wreath of oak and laurel below, set in a horizontal oval field. (The reverse field is the same shape.) Surrounding the field is a stylized ornamental border; at the bottom appear the weight (in *onzas*); the metal (*plata* or *oro*); and the fineness, LEY 0.999.

Silver Issues

Disc of Death (1/4, 1/2, and 1 oz.)

The three-piece silver set in this collection features the Disco de la Muerte (Disc of Death): an extraordinary stone sculpture depicting a human skull at the center with rays radiating outward. The disc was damaged at some point, broken around the edges, perhaps during a raid during the decline of the city.

**1/4 oz., 1 peso,
0.999 silver, 7.7700 g.**

Reverse: At the center of the field, the broken Disc of Death. To the left, the date; to the right, mintmark M̊; below, DISCO DE LA MUERTE. Surrounding the field, an ornamental border with **$1** below. *Diameter:* 27 mm. BW-932, KM-617.

Date	Comment
1997	
1997, PF	
1998	
1998, PF	

**1/2 oz., 2 pesos,
0.999 silver, 15.5517 g.**

Reverse: At the center of the field, the broken Disc of Death. To the left, the date; to the right, mintmark M̊; below, DISCO DE LA MUERTE. Surrounding the field, an ornamental border with $2 below. *Diameter:* 33 mm. BW-933, KM-618.

Date	Comment
1997	
1997, PF	
1998	
1998, PF	

1 oz., 5 pesos, 0.999 silver, 31.1035 g.

Reverse: At the center of the field, the broken Disc of Death. To the left, the date; to the right, mintmark M̊; below, DISCO DE LA MUERTE. Surrounding the field, an ornamental border with $5 below. *Diameter:* 40 mm. BW-934, KM-619.

Date	Comment
1997	
1997, PF	
1998	
1998, PF	

Mask (1 oz.)

A magnificent stone Mascara (Mask) like the one depicted on the coin was part of the funerary dress for the high-ranking people of the Teotihuacán culture.

1 oz., 5 pesos, 0.999 silver, 31.1030 g.

Reverse: At the center of the field, a funeral mask. To the left, the date; to the right, mintmark M̊; below, MASCARA. Surrounding the field, an ornamental border with $5 below. *Diameter:* 40 mm. BW-934.1, KM-620.

Date	Comment
1997	
1997, PF	
1998	
1998, PF	

Vessel (1 oz.)

The design of this coin, called Vasija (Vessel), is based on a Teotihuacáno vase or container shaped as a seated human figure. The vessel illustrates one of many types of human-shaped figurines. Their significance is unknown, although it is believed they were gods or high-ranking individuals.

1 oz., 5 pesos, 0.999 silver, 31.1030 g.

Reverse: At the center of the field, a human-shaped vessel. To the left, the date; to the right, mintmark M̊; below, VASIJA. Surrounding the field, an ornamental border with $5 below. *Diameter:* 40 mm. BW-934.2, KM-621.

Date	Comment
1997	
1997, PF	
1998	
1998, PF	

Ball Player (1 oz.)

The reclining Jugador de Pelota (Ball Player) figure on this coin is based on a figurine molded in the orange ceramic clay that was common at a certain stage of the Teotihuacán culture. The figurines were important to the Teotihuacán commercial system, which extended to almost all of the Mesoamerican regions.

1 oz., 5 pesos, 0.999 silver, 31.1030 g.

Reverse: At the center of the field, the figure of a reclining ball player. To the left, the date; to the right, mintmark M̊; below, JUGADOR DE PELOTA. Surrounding the field, an ornamental border with $5 below. *Diameter:* 40 mm. BW-934.3, KM-622.

Date	Comment
1997	
1997, PF	
1998	
1998, PF	

Pyramid of the Sun (5 oz.)

The 5-ounce coin for this collection features the Pirámide del Sol (Pyramid of the Sun), an ambitious monument dedicated to the sun and important to the Teotihuacános. Its orientation is based on astronomical considerations, and deviates slightly on the north side.

5 oz., 10 pesos, 0.999 silver, 155.3100 g.

Reverse: At the center of the field, the Pyramid of the Sun. At upper left, the date; at upper right, mintmark M̊; below, PIRAMIDE DEL SOL. Surrounding the field, an ornamental border with $5 below. *Diameter:* 65 mm. BW-935, KM-623.

Date	Comment
1997	
1997, PF	
1998	

Gold Issues

Feathered Serpent (1/4, 1/2, and 1 oz.)

The design depicted on the three gold coins is a detail from the Temple of Quetzalcóatl. The Serpiente Emplumada (Feathered Serpent) was one of the most powerful gods of the Teotihuacán culture, and the subject of special rituals.

1/4 oz., 25 pesos, 0.999 gold, 7.7758 g.

Reverse: At the center of the field, the feathered serpent-god Quetzalcóatl. To the left, the date; to the right, mintmark M̊; below, SERPIENTE EMPLUMADA. Surrounding the field, an ornamental border with $25 below. *Diameter:* 23 mm. BW-936, KM-624.

Date	Comment
1997, PF	
1998	

1/2 oz., 50 pesos, 0.999 gold, 15.5517 g.

Reverse: At the center of the field, the feathered serpent-god Quetzalcóatl. To the left, the date; to the right, mintmark M̊; below, SERPIENTE EMPLUMADA. Surrounding the field, an ornamental border with $50 below. *Diameter:* 29 mm. BW-937, KM-625.

Date	Comment
1997, PF	
1998	

1 oz., 100 pesos, 0.999 gold, 31.1035 g.

Reverse: At the center of the field, the feathered serpent-god Quetzalcóatl. To the left, the date; to the right, mintmark M̊; below, SERPIENTE EMPLUMADA. Surrounding the field, an ornamental border with $100 below. *Diameter:* 34.5 mm. BW-938, KM-626.

Date	Comment
1997, PF	
1998	

TOLTEC COLLECTION

The complex Toltec civilization occupied the region of Tula in 713 A.D. The Toltecs left a legacy of a vast wealth and beauty in a majestic archaeological zone. Some of the advances they made in the arts are still conserved in the walls of the buildings.

The Toltecs established an advanced educational system that attracted students from as far away as what is now Central America. The Toltecs worshipped the feathered serpent-god Quetzalcóatl, along with Tezcatlipoca, god of the night and darkness; Tlaloc, god of the rain and vegetation; Centeotl, god of corn; Itzpapalotl ("Obsidian Butterfly"), a fearsome warrior goddess; and Tonatiuh, or the sun god. Invading Chichimec tribes destroyed the Toltec Empire in 1200 A.D.

The common obverse design for the Toltec Collection consists of the national coat of arms with ESTADOS UNIDOS MEXICANOS above and a half-wreath of oak and laurel below, set on an irregular five-sided field with slightly convex sides. (The reverse field is the same shape.) Surrounding the field is a stylized ornamental border; at the bottom appear the weight (in *onzas*); the metal (*plata* or *oro*); and the fineness, LEY 0.999.

Silver Issues

Jaguar (1/4, 1/2, and 1 oz.)

The three silver coins depict a bas-relief sculpture of a jaguar, an animal revered by the Toltecs.

1/4 oz., 1 peso, 0.999 silver, 7.7700 g.

Reverse: At the center of the field, a sculpture of a jaguar. To the left, 1998; to the right, mintmark M°; below, JAGUAR. Surrounding the field, an ornamental border with $1 below. *Diameter:* 27 mm. BW-939, KM-661.

Date	Comment
1998	
1998, PF	

1/2 oz., 2 pesos, 0.999 silver, 15.5517 g.

Reverse: At the center of the field, a sculpture of a jaguar. To the left, 1998; to the right, mintmark M°; below, JAGUAR. Surrounding the field, an ornamental border with $2 below. *Diameter:* 33 mm. BW-940, KM-662.

Date	Comment
1998	
1998, PF	

1 oz., 5 pesos, 0.999 silver, 31.1030 g.

Reverse: At the center of the field, a sculpture of a jaguar. To the left, 1998; to the right, mintmark M°; below, JAGUAR. Surrounding the field, an ornamental border with $5 below. *Diameter:* 40 mm. BW-941, KM-663.

Date	Comment
1998	
1998, PF	

Quetzalcóatl (1 oz.)

The first silver 1-ounce coin in the Toltec Collection depicts the birth of Ce Acatl Topiltzin Quetzalcóatl. Tradition relates that he was a leader of the Toltecs and led them to build a great city, dominating several territories with power and wealth once they were established. He established the cult of the serpent and discontinued human sacrifices during his reign.

1 oz., 5 pesos, 0.999 silver, 31.1030 g.

Reverse: At the center of the field, a sculpture of the birth of Quetzalcóatl. To the left, 1998; to the right, mintmark M°; below, QUETZALCOATL. Surrounding the field, an ornamental border with $5 below. *Diameter:* 40 mm. BW-941.1, KM-665.

Date	Comment
1998	
1998, PF	

Priest (1 oz.)

This coin design, Sacerdote (Priest), depicts one of the great Toltec Atlantean figures (carved stone columns in the shapes of warriors), this one in the form of a priest. Priests within the Toltec culture had a very important social status. They had a direct relation with the gods they venerated and adopted the names and virtues of the gods they represented.

1 oz., 5 pesos, 0.999 silver, 31.1030 g.

Reverse: At the center of the field, an Atlantean priest figure. To the left, 1998; to the right, mintmark M°; below, SACERDOTE. Surrounding the field, an ornamental border with $5 below. *Diameter:* 40 mm. BW-941.2, KM-664.

Date	Comment
1998	
1998, PF	

Serpent With Skull (1 oz.)

The Serpiente con Cráneo (Serpent With Skull) motif shows a detail of the Coatepantli, or "Serpent Wall," found at the Tula site in Hidalgo. The sculpture is a bas-relief of a serpent devouring a human skull. (On the wall, the relief alternates with images of eagles eating bloody hearts.)

1 oz., 5 pesos, 0.999 silver, 31.1030 g.

Reverse: At the center of the field, a serpent devouring a human skull. To the left, **1998**; to the right, mintmark M̊; below, **SERPIENTE CON CRANEO**. Surrounding the field, an ornamental border with **$5** below. *Diameter:* 40 mm. BW-941.3, KM-666.

Date	Comment
1998	
1998, PF	

Atlantean Figures (5 oz.)

The silver 5-ounce Toltec coin has a representation of the Atlantes statues, found in the temple of Quetzalcóatl in the archaeological zone of Tula in central Mexico. The statues, which overlook an ancient city dating back to 713 B.C., are Toltec warriors; they hold in their right hands weapons that fire darts, and in their left hands, several arrows. Each warrior wears a chest shield in the shape of a butterfly, a skirt tied in front with a wide belt, and a circular back shield representing the sun.

5 oz., 10 pesos, 0.999 silver, 155.7300 g.

Reverse: At the center of the field, two Atlantean warrior figures with pillar. To the left, **1998**; to the right, mintmark M̊; below, **ATLANTES**. Surrounding the field, an ornamental border with **$10** below. *Diameter:* 65 mm. BW-942, KM-634.

Date	Comment
1998	

Gold Issues

Eagle (1/4, 1/2, and 1 oz.)

The central device on the three gold coins of the Toltec Collection is a fragment of sculpture depicting the Águila (Eagle) eating a heart. The eagle was one of the Toltecs' most revered creatures.

1/4 oz., 25 pesos, 0.999 gold, 7.7758 g.

Reverse: At the center of the field, an eagle devouring a heart. To the left, **1998**; to the right, mintmark M̊; below, **AGUILA**. Surrounding the field, an ornamental border with **$25** below. *Diameter:* 23 mm. BW-943, KM-667.

Date	Comment
1998	
1998, PF	

1/2 oz., 50 pesos, 0.999 gold, 15.5517 g.

Reverse: At the center of the field, an eagle devouring a heart. To the left, **1998**; to the right, mintmark M̊; below, **AGUILA**. Surrounding the field, an ornamental border with **$50** below. *Diameter:* 29 mm. BW-944, KM-668.

Date	Comment
1998	
1998, PF	

1 oz., 100 pesos, 0.999 gold, 31.1035 g.

Reverse: At the center of the field, an eagle devouring a heart. To the left, **1998**; to the right, mintmark M̊; below, **AGUILA**. Surrounding the field, an ornamental border with **$100** below. *Diameter:* 34.5 mm. BW-945, KM-669.

Date	Comment
1998	
1998, PF	

Aztec Collection

Common obverse (silver); weight varies.

Eagle Warrior (Guerrero Águila). 1 oz., $100, PF. 1992. BW-902, KM-556, 40 mm.

Brazier Effigy (Brasero Efigie). 1 oz., $100, PF. 1992. BW-902.1, KM-563, 40 mm.

God of Fire (Huehuetéotl). 1 oz., $100, PF. 1992. BW-909.2, KM-564, 40 mm.

God of Flowers (Xochipilli). 1 oz., $100, PF. 1992. BW-909.3, KM-562, 40 mm.

Tizoc Stone (Piedra de Tizoc). 5 oz., $10,000, PF. BW-906, KM-557, 65 mm. (shown reduced)

Common obverse (gold); weight varies.

Jaguar / Stone of the Suns (Jaguar / Piedra de los Soles). 1 oz., $1,000, PF. 1992. BW-905, KM-560, 35 mm.

Central Veracrúz Collection

Common obverse (silver); weight varies.

Bas-Relief of El Tajín (Bajorrelieve de El Tajín). 1 oz., N$5, PF. BW-913, KM-569, 40 mm.

Palm With Crocodile (Palma con Cocodrilo). 1 oz., N$5, PF. 1993. BW-913.1, KM-582, 40 mm.

Smiling Face (Carita Sonriente). 1 oz., N$5, PF. 1993. BW-913.2, KM-584, 40 mm.

Old Man With Brazier (Anciano con Brasero, Type I). 1 oz., N$5, PF. 1993. BW-913.3, KM-583, 40 mm.

Pyramid of the Niches (Piramide de El Tajín). 5 oz., N$10, PF. 1993. BW-914, KM-570, 65 mm. (shown reduced)

Common obverse (gold); weight varies.

Ceremonial Hatchet (Hacha Ceremonial). 1 oz., N$100, PF. BW-917, KM-587, 35 mm.

Mayan Collection

Common obverse (silver); weight varies.

Chaac-Mool. 1 oz., N$5, PF. 1994. BW-920, KM-574, 40 mm.

Lintel 26 (Dintel 26). 1 oz., N$5, PF. 1994. BW-920.1, KM-578, 40 mm.

Gravestone of a Palenque Tomb (Lapida Tumba de Palenque). 1 oz., N$5, PF. 1994. BW-920.2, KM-575, 40 mm.

Mask of the God Chaac (Mascarón del Dios Chaac). 1 oz., N$5, PF. 1994. BW-920.3, KM-577, 40 mm.

Pyramid of the Castle (Pirámide del Castillo). 5 oz., N$10, PF. 1994. BW-921, KM-576, 65 mm. (shown reduced)

Pyramid of the Castle (Pirámide del Castillo), error. 5 oz., N$10, PF. 1993. BW-921.1, KM-UL, 65 mm. (shown reduced)

Common obverse (gold); weight varies.

Personage of Jaina (Personaje de Jaina). 1 oz., N$100, PF. BW-924, KM-581, 35 mm.

Olmec Collection

Common obverse (silver); weight varies.

Master of the Limes (Señor de las Limas). 1 oz., $5, PF. 1996. BW-927, KM-595, 40 mm.

Jaguar-Man (Hombre Jaguar), Type I. 1 oz., $5, PF. 1996. BW-927.3, KM-596, 40 mm.

Jaguar-Man (Hombre Jaguar), Type II. 1 oz., $5, PF. 1996. BW-927.3, KM-596, 40 mm.

The Wrestler (El Luchador). 1 oz., $5, PF. 1996. BW-927.1, KM-597, 40 mm.

Ceremonial Ax (Hacha Ceremonial). 1 oz., $5, PF. 1996. BW-927.1, KM-598, 40 mm.

Olmec Head (Cabeza Olmeca). $10, 5 oz., PF. 1996. BW-928, KM-599, 65 mm. (shown reduced)

Common obverse (gold); weight varies.

Priest (Sacerdote). $100, 1 oz., PF. 1996. BW-931, KM-602, 35 mm.

Teotihuacán Collection

Common obverse (silver); weight varies.

Disc of Death (Disco de la Muerte). 1 oz., $5, PF. 1997. BW-934, KM-619, 40 mm.

Mask (Mascara). 1 oz., $5, PF. 1997. BW-934.1, KM-620, 40 mm.

Vessel (Vasija). 1 oz., $5, PF. 1997. BW-934.2, KM-621, 40 mm.

Ball Player (Jugador de Pelota). 1 oz., $5, PF. 1997. BW-934.3, KM-622, 40 mm.

Pyramid of the Sun (Pirámide del Sol). 5 oz., $10, PF. 1997. BW-935, KM-623, 65 mm. (shown reduced)

Common obverse (gold); weight varies.

Feathered Serpent (Serpiente Emplumada). 1 oz., $100, PF. 1997. BW-938, KM-626, 35 mm.

Toltec Collection

Common obverse (silver); weight varies.

Jaguar. 1 oz., $5, PF. 1998. BW-941, KM-663, 40 mm.

Quetzalóatl. 1 oz., $5, PF. 1998. BW-941.1, KM-665, 40 mm.

Priest (Sacerdote). 1 oz., $5, PF. 1998. BW-941.2, KM-664, 40 mm.

Serpent With Skull (Serpiente con Cráneo). 1 oz., $5, PF. 1998. BW-941.3, KM-666, 40 mm.

Atlantean Figures (Atlantes). 5 oz., $10, PF. 1998. BW-942, KM-634, 65 mm. (shown reduced)

Common obverse (gold); weight varies.

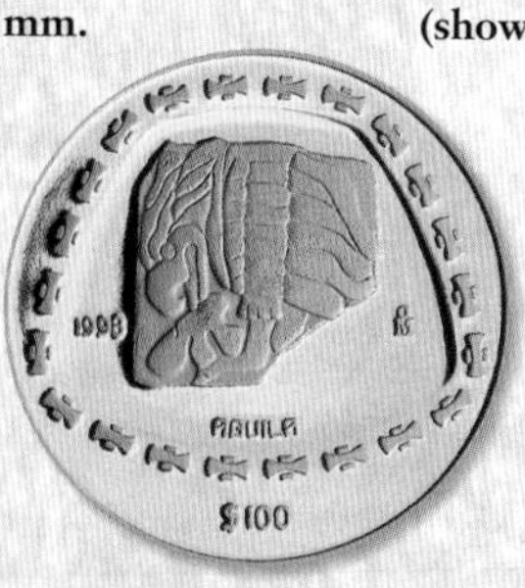

Eagle (Águila). 1 oz., $100, 1998. BW-945, KM-669, 35 mm.

21

Tokens of Mexico

The existence of tokens in Mexico dates back before 1821, as described in the earliest publication on the subject by a Mexican numismatic researcher: *Los Tlacos Coloniales* (Manuel Romero de Terreros, 1935). Prior to that publication, the Fonrobert Collection, containing hacienda tokens and auctioned in Berlin in 1878, served as the main source of information on the subject.

The use of tokens arose in the time of the hacienda system, an economic arrangement that resembled European feudalism. When Spain began to colonize the New World, the Crown favored certain individuals with large land grants. The new owner would forcibly remove the native people from his land, then hire them to work for him in a condition akin to serfdom—or often, slavery. The increasing power of the landowners, or *hacendados*, and their treatment of the peasants who labored under them, set the stage for the Mexican Revolution.

The *hacendado* often paid the workers in tokens that were good only at the hacienda's company store. Moreover, outside the haciendas there was a general shortage of smaller-denomination coins (below the value of 1/4 real) in circulation. Municipal governments and town merchants addressed this problem by issuing tokens of their own—easy enough to do, since all that was needed to produce them was copper, a means to melt it, and molds in which to pour it. The many issues of these various producers have led to the specialty of token collecting within Mexican numismatics.

During the years there have been various publications of token articles, most of them focused on particular regions. Examples are as follows:

Birt, Hal, Jr. *Tokens and Medals of Sonora, Mexico.* 1990.

Brunk, Gregory G. "Some Apparently Unlisted Mexican Hacienda Tokens." *Token and Medal Society Journal*, vol. 18, no. 4, 1978.

Castanada, José. "Baja California Tokens." *Plus Ultra*, 1978.

Eklund, O.P., and Sidney P. Noe. *Hacienda Tokens of Mexico.* 1949.

Grove, Frank W. *Tokens of Mexico.* 1989.

Leslie, Elwin C. "The Municipal Coins of Colima." *U.S. Mexican Numismatic Association Journal*, vol. 12, no. 1, March 2007. Reprint.

Leslie, Elwin C., and Alberto Francisco Pradeau. *Henequen Plantation Tokens of the Yucatán Peninsula.* 1972.

Leslie, Elwin C., and Erma Stevens. *Privately Issued Storecards and Tokens, State of Sonora, Mexico.* 1970.

Pradeau, Alberto Francisco. *Los Tlacos y Pilones Mexicanos.* 1963.

Romero de Terreros, Manuel. *Las Monedas de Necesidad del Estado de Michoacán.* 1955.

Romero de Terreros, Manuel. *Los Tlacos Coloniales: Ensayo Numismático.* 1935.

Rulau, Russell. *Latin American Tokens* (2nd ed.). 2000.

Salmerón, Antonio Deana. "Las Contraseñas del Cafetal Guatimoc." *Monedas,* no. 33, 1967.

Sobrino, José Manuel. *La Moneda Mexicana: Su Historia.* 1972

Verrey, Claudio C. *Fichas de las Fincas Cafetaleras de Chiapas.* 1988.

Verrey, Claudio C. *Fichas de Sonora.* (No date).

Verrey, Claudio C. *Monedas Municipales y Particulares de San Luis Potosí.* 1988.

Worthington, Richard D. *Catalogue of the Trade Tokens of Chihuahua, Mexico.* 1990.

The tokens in the following listings are selections from Frank W. Grove's *Tokens of Mexico,* published in 1989. Attribution numbers beginning with "G-" are from Grove; "MRdt," from Manuel Romero de Terreros; "N-," Sidney P. Noe.

Albares. Cast bronze.

Obverse: In crude lettering within a border of large dots, ALBA / RES. Uniface. *Diameter:* 23 mm. G-27.

A Morfin, State of Michoacán. Bronze.

Obverse: At center, a bow and two crossed arrows, surrounded by the legend A MORFIN / 1854. *Reverse:* Within a wreath, the value $\frac{1}{8}$ and the legend CHILCHOTA. *Diameter:* 21 mm. G-62.

Ario, State of Michoacán. Bronze.

Obverse: At center, a bust facing right, surrounded by the legend MUNICIPALIDAD DE ARIO / 1838. *Reverse:* At center, within a laurel wreath, the value $\frac{1}{8}$. *Diameter:* 24 mm. G-91.

Ario, State of Michoacán. Bronze.

Obverse: At center, a radiant liberty cap, surrounded by the legend MUNICIPALIDAD DE ARIO / 1857. *Reverse:* At center, within a wreath, the value $\frac{1}{8}$. *Diameter:* 23 mm. G-92.

Ario, State of Michoacán. Bronze.

Obverse: At center, a monument, surrounded by the legend MUNICIPALIDAD DE ARIO / 1866. *Reverse:* At center, within a wreath of oak and laurel, the value $\frac{1}{8}$. *Diameter:* 23 mm. G-95.

Ca. M. de la Velardena. Nickel.

Obverse: On an octagonal planchet, the legend CA. M. DE LA / * / VELARDENA -.- with MADE BY HEIDEMANN MFG. CO. S.A. TEX. in small type below. *Reverse:* At center, the value 25¢, surrounded by the legend BUENO POR / EN MERCANCIAS. *Diameter:* 25 mm. G-2000.

Cocupao (now Quiroga), State of Michoacán. Bronze.

Obverse: At center, El Tziate, a wooded mountain in Michoacán, with the legend MUNICIPAL DE COCUPAO above and AÑO DE 1851 below the mountain *Reverse:* At center, the value $\frac{1}{8}$ with a half wreath of laurel and olive below and a pair of clasped hands above. *Diameter:* 23 mm. G-221.

Hacienda de Buenavista, State of Michoacán. Bronze.

Obverse: At center, the monogram J F V (Jose Francisco Velarde) in elaborate script, surrounded by the legend HACIENDA DE / BUENAVISTA. *Reverse:* At center, within a horizontal oval, 1848. *Diameter:* 24 mm. G-431.

Hacienda San Rafael, State of Michoacán. Bronze.

Obverse: At center, the monogram Y C in script type, surrounded by the legend HACIENDA DE SAN RAFAEL ★. *Reverse:* At center, within a wreath of laurel and oak, the value $\frac{1}{4}$, with 1847 between the wreath tips above. *Diameter:* 24 mm. G-435.

Hacienda Tipitaro, State of Michoacán. Bronze.

Obverse: At center, a sharp peak, flanked by trees, rising from water; two flying birds above the left tree. The legend HACIENDA DE TIPITARO surrounds. *Reverse:* At center, a pedestal with a basket of flowers on top, surrounded by the legend MEDIO REAL AÑO DE 1846. *Diameter:* 24 mm. MRdt 100, G-443.

Hacienda Tomendán, State of Michoacán. Bronze.

Obverse: At center, above a spray of foliage, a hill with a cross on top, surrounded by a wreath and the legend HACIENDA DE TOMENDAN. (The letter H is partly obscured in the tip of the spray.) *Reverse:* Filling the top and center of the field, a hand holding a balance scale, with the value $\frac{1}{2}$ at the bottom. *Diameter:* 20 mm. MRdt 103, G-445.

Licores S.A., State of Baja California. Bronze.

Obverse: At center, an incused 5, surrounded by the legend LICORES S.A. / TIJUANA B. C. *Reverse:* At center, an incused 5, surrounded by the legend SUCURSALES / ENSENADA MEXICALI B.C. *Diameter:* 24 mm. G-1701.

Mendoza. Bronze.

Obverse: At center, MEN / DOZA / 1801, with indistinct ornaments above. Uniface. *Diameter:* 27 mm. N-257, G-567.

Mesquite. Brass.

Obverse: At center, within a milled border, MES- / QVITE, with indistinct ornaments below. Uniface. *Diameter:* 19 mm. G-574.

Pátzcuaro, State of Michoacán. Brass.

Obverse: At center, within an ornate border, Janitzio Island (in Lake Pátzcuaro) forms the background, with the value $\frac{1}{8}$ above; in the foreground, a fisherman in a boat between two ducks. The legend MUNICIPO DE PAZTCUARO surrounds. *Reverse:* At center, a woman facing right and holding a string of fish. *Diameter:* 23 mm. MRdt 43, G-683.

Penychet. Cast bronze.

Obverse: At center, in crude letters, PENY / CHET. *Reverse:* At center, in crude letters, legend AÑO. / DE / 1808. *Diameter:* 29 mm. N-317, G-694.

El Pilón, State of Michoacán. Bronze.

Obverse: At center, within a laurel wreath, the sun setting behind a mountain (El Pilón); all surrounded by the legend TANTEO DEL PILON / ★UN OCTAVO★. *Reverse:* Within a laurel wreath, the script initials AA, with surrounding legend CONSTANCIA AL TRABAJO / ★1861★. *Diameter:* 20 mm. MRdt 50, G-713.

Ponce, Luís. Bronze.

Obverse: At center, a six-armed cross surrounded by the legend LUIS POИCE / -XXX- (with inverted N). *Reverse:* Above a central ornament of four ovals, the legend \MEXICO/ at the top (with the slash or bar characters very long, extending from the legend to the center ornament), and O ZXXX O below. *Diameter:* 22 mm. G-728.

Pueblo de los Dolores. Bronze.

Obverse: On an irregular planchet, within an ornate border and below starlike ornaments, the legend PVEBL / DE.LOS / DOLO / RES. Uniface. *Diameter:* 28 mm x 30 mm. G-744.

Santa Clara, State of Michoacán. Bronze.

Obverse: At center, above a spray of foliage, a radiant liberty cap with the legend Santa Clara above and 1856 below. *Reverse:* At center, above a spray of foliage, $\frac{1}{8}$ with the legend FONDO MUNICIPAL surrounding. *Diameter:* 22 mm. G-884.

Tacámbaro, State of Michoacán. Bronze.

Obverse: At center, above a spray of palm, $\frac{1}{8}$ with the legend TACAMBARO above. *Reverse:* An irregular, doughnut-like shape described by Grove as "a rock in a lake." *Diameter:* 21 mm. MRdt 66, G-937.

Tanhuato, State of Michoacán. Bronze.

Obverse: The Mexican eagle above a half wreath of oak and laurel, with the legend MUNICIPIO DE TANHUATO. above. *Reverse:* At center, within a wreath of laurel, the value $\frac{1}{8}$ with ★1871★ below. Between the wreath tips, a small radiant liberty cap. *Diameter:* 24 mm. MRdt 74, G-942.

Taretan, State of Michoacán. Bronze.

Obverse: At center, above a half wreath of palm and oak, 1831 and the value $\frac{1}{8}$, with TARETAN above. Uniface. *Diameter:* 22 mm. G-948.

Yaxcopoil, State of Yucatán. Brass.

Obverse: At center, in incused letters, YAXCOPOIL / XII. *Reverse:* Monogram FC (Fernando Cervera). *Diameter:* 22 mm. G-2012.

Tokens of Mexico

Because many of the tokens available in the marketplace today lack details, making identification difficult, line drawings are shown along with photos of the tokens.

Albares. Uniface. G-27, 23 mm.

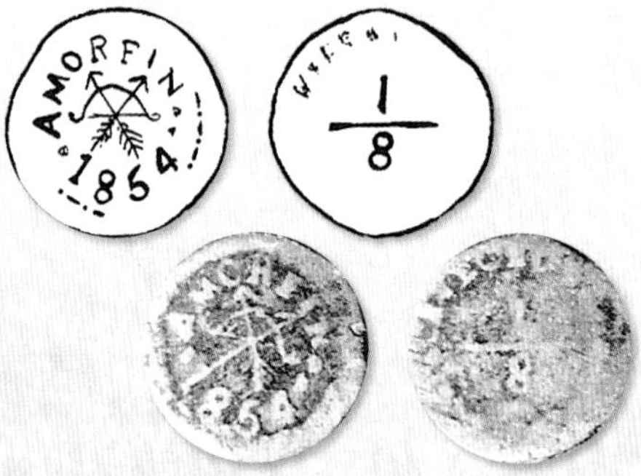

A Morfin, State of Michoacán. G-62, 21 mm.

Ario, State of Michoacán. G-91, 24 mm.

Ario, State of Michoacán. G-92, 23 mm.

Ario, State of Michoacán. G-95, 23 mm.

Tokens of Mexico
(continued)

Ca. M. de la Velardena. G-2000, 25 mm.

Cocupao (now Quiroga), State of Michoacán. G-221, 23 mm.

Hacienda de Buenavista, State of Michoacán. G-431, 24 mm.

Hacienda San Rafael, State of Michoacán. G-435, 24 mm.

Hacienda Tipitaro, State of Michoacán. MRdt 100, G-443, 24 mm.

Hacienda Tomendán, State of Michoacán. MRdt 103, G-445, 20 mm.

Tokens of Mexico
(continued)

Licores S.A., State of Baja California. G-1701, 24 mm.

Mendoza. Uniface. N-257, G-567, 27 mm.

Mesquite. Uniface. G-574, 19 mm.

Pátzcuaro, State of Michoacán. MRdt 43, G-683, 23 mm.

Penychet. N-317, G-694, 29 mm.

El Pilón, State of Michoacán. MRdt 50, G-713, 20 mm.

Luís Ponce. G-728, 22 mm.

Tokens of Mexico
(continued)

Pueblo de los Dolores. Uniface.
G-744, 28 mm x 30 mm.

Santa Clara, State of Michoacán. G-884, 22 mm.

Tacámbaro, State of Michoacán. MRdt 66, G-937, 21 mm.

Tanhuato, State of Michoacán. MRdt 74, G-942, 24 mm.

Taretan, State of Michoacán. Uniface. G-948, 22 mm.

Yaxcopoil, State of Yucatán. G-2012, 22 mm.

22

VARIETY AND ERROR COINS

The collector specialty of mint errors and varieties has been a fast-growing one, helped along in recent years by the 2008 release of *The Illustrated Price Guide of the Modern Mexican Coins, 1905 to Date, Including Errors and Varieties*, by Carlos Abel Amaya Guerra. Error and variety coins—some showing minor deviations from the norm, some showing major ones—exist for every era of Mexican numismatics, particularly the 20th century. Although early-20th-century error coins of Mexico are scarce and seldom turn up in the marketplace, large quantities start turning up from around the mid-1970s.

The difference between die varieties and mint errors, as described by numismatic author Bill O'Rourke, is as follows (slightly edited for consistency with usage in this volume):

> A *die variety* is usually a variation in a coin's design from what was originally intended. Die varieties can be traced back to specific dies or hubs. Thus, coins that are commonly called doubled dies; overmintmarks and/or assayer's initials; and repunched mintmarks, dates, and/or assayer's initials all fall into the die-variety classification.
>
> An *error* is a direct result of the mechanical minting process itself. Off-center strikes and coins struck on incomplete or wrong planchets are considered errors.

Most of the descriptions of error coins are self-explanatory—for example, "multiple strike," "off center," and "wrong planchet." A few may need explanation, however:

> *brockage*—A mirror image of the design from one face of the coin impressed into its opposite face. This is caused when a coin is struck but does not eject from the die; when a fresh planchet is moved into place, the original coin is between the planchet and the die, and the image from the struck coin is pressed into the new planchet.
>
> *lamination*—A spot where the metal has separated partly or fully from the coin's surface. This is caused when grease or debris is present in the strip of metal as it is rolled out to make the planchets, and the metal at the surface cannot adhere properly to the material below. (Compare to a *cud*, described next.)
>
> *cud*—A lump on the coin's surface caused by the breaking away of part of the original die, such that the metal is not impressed at that location.
>
> *broadstrike*—A coin that was struck outside the retaining collar, such that it spreads to larger-than normal size.

clipped planchet—A coin that is missing a divot of metal, giving it something of a "bitten cookie" appearance, in which the edge of the missing piece may be smooth or ragged. This is caused before the striking stage, when the planchet is incorrectly punched out of the strip of metal.

The major die varieties for each coin type are listed elsewhere in this book, so the present chapter will not go into great detail on the subject (although the image gallery does depict an example of a variety versus a mint error, and gives a basic sampling of the different types of errors). Volume 2 presents a larger selection of modern errors and varieties.

Variety and Error Coins

Double-struck State of Sonora copper 1/4 real, 1832. (Note the difference between this, an error during the minting process, and a variety created by a different die, shown at right.)

Doubled-die obverse, 1-ounce Libertad, 1987 (close-up).

1 peso, 1975, struck on 50-cent planchet.

Triple-struck State of Chihuahua 1/4 real, 1835.

Triple-struck 1 peso, 1981.

Brockage on reverse of an off center 20 pesos, 1981.

Off-center 20 pesos, 1981.

Clipped planchet, 1 peso, 1981.

23

Patterns, Trial Strikes, and Experimental Pieces

To discuss these special noncirculating issues, it's necessary to understand a few bits of minting terminology. The following definitions are based on those in J. Hewitt Judd's *United States Pattern, Experimental and Trial Pieces* (various editions). Dr. Judd's terminology is widely accepted in American numismatics, and because they describe more-or-less universal minting methods, they're appropriate for use with Mexican coinage, as well.

The broadest term to describe these coins is *essay* (or *essai*, in its original, French spelling), which refers to any coin that is struck with official mint dies but is not a regular issue. Essays can be roughly grouped into three categories: patterns, experimental srikes, and *pieces de caprice*.

In simplest terms, a *pattern* is an official design proof, intended for consideration for a new denomination or a new or revised design for an existing coin. Patterns are scrutinized by decision-makers both within and outside the mint. An *experimental strike* is also official, but made for the mint personnel's use in evaluating a possible change in planchet diameter, format, shape, thickness, etc. A *piece de caprice* (often called a *fantasy coin*) is a coin struck with official mint equipment and facilities, but without the mint's authorization, for the purpose of a financial or other reward.

The term *trial strike* can describe either a pattern coin or an experimental one. A trial strike is a test of an official die but in an "off" metal—that is, a metal other than the one intended for circulation. Thus, a trial is often called an *off-metal strike*, which should not be confused with the type of mint error of the same name. (An error is a coin struck in the wrong metal by mistake and subsequently issued; whereas an off-metal pattern or experimental strike is intentional.)

Most of the patterns, trial strikes, and experimental issues from the Republic reales and decimal series, along with their gold counterparts, have been well documented in T.V. Buttrey and Clyde Hubbard's *Guide Book of Mexican Coins 1822 to Date* (6th ed.). A representative selection of these earlier issues is listed here, in date order, along with some that are more current. ("Gerber numbers" in the following list reference the catalog numbers in the Pablo Gerber, Sr., auction of June 1996.)

1769-M̊, 1/2 grano. Copper, pattern. *Obverse:* At center, the crowned coat of arms of Spain. To the left of the shield, G̊ ("grano"); to the right, the denomination $\frac{1}{2}$. Legend CAROLVS•III•INDIAR•REX•. *Reverse:* An eagle above three globes, with surrounding legend •SINE ME REGNA FATISC• ("Without Me Kingdoms Totter") and M̊•1769•M̊. *Edge:* Plain. *Diameter:* 21.5 mm. BW-960 P, KM-PnC1.

1769-M°, 1 grano. Copper, pattern.

Obverse: At center, the crowned coat of arms of Spain. To the left of the shield, G° ("grano"); to the right, the denomination I. Legend CAROLVS·III·INDIAR·REX·. *Reverse:* An eagle above three globes, with surrounding legend ·SINE ME REGNA FATISCUNT· ("Without Me Kingdoms Totter") and M°·1769·M°. *Edge:* Plain. *Diameter:* 27.25 mm. BW-961 P, Gerber-405, KM-PnD1.

1827-G°, WW, 8 reales. Silver, Proof pattern.

Obverse: The national coat of arms with upright eagle above a half wreath of oak and laurel, and the legend REPUBLICA MEXICANA around the top. *Reverse:* At center, a small radiant liberty cap with the legend 8 R: G°: 1827 :W:W: 10 D$ 20 G$ below. *Edge:* Plain. *Diameter:* 40 mm. BW-962 P, Gerber-413, KM-Pn12.

Note: "WW" in the reverse legend is engraver William Wyon (Royal Mint, London).

1829-P^{I}, JS, 8 reales. Silver, Proof pattern.

Obverse: The national coat of arms with upright eagle above a half wreath of oak and laurel, and the legend REPUBLICA MEXICANA around the top. *Reverse:* At center, a small radiant liberty cap with the legend ★8 R·P! 1829 · J· S· 10 D$20 G$ below. *Edge:* Plain. *Diameter:* 37 mm. BW-963 P, Gerber-416, KM-Pn20.

Note: "JS" in the reverse legend is assayer Juan N. Sanabria (believed to be at the Royal Mint, London).

183_-G, 8 reales. Copper, Proof pattern trial strike.

Obverse: The national coat of arms with upright eagle above a half wreath of oak and laurel, and the legend REPUBLICA MEXICANA around the top. *Reverse:* At center, a small radiant liberty cap with the incomplete legend ★8 R·G·183 [empty space] ·10 D$ 20 G$. *Edge:* Plain. *Diameter:* 39 mm. BW-964 P, KM-Pn24.

1831-G, MJ, 8 escudos. Copper, Proof pattern.

Obverse: The national coat of arms with upright eagle above a half wreath of oak and laurel, and the legend REPUBLICA MEXICANA around the top. *Reverse:* Above an open book that bears the word LEY, a hand holding a staff with a liberty cap. Surrounding legend LA LIBERTAD EN LA LEY and ★8E G. 1831.M.J.21Q$. *Edge:* Plain. *Diameter:* 38 mm. GBW-965.P, Gerber-421, KM-Pn28.

Note: The identity of "MJ" in the legend is unknown; the pattern was created at Soho Mint, Birmingham, England.

1832-D°, LR, 4 escudos. Brass, pattern.

Obverse: The national coat of arms with upright eagle above a half wreath of oak and laurel, and the legend REPUBLICA MEXICANA around the top. *Reverse:* Above an open book that bears the word LEY, a hand holding a staff with a liberty cap. Legend LA LIBERTAD EN LA LEY and ★4E· D°· 1832·L·R·21Q$. *Edge:* Plain. *Diameter:* 30 mm. BW-966.P, Gerber-424, KM-Pn34.

Note: The identity of "LR" in the reverse legend is unknown.

1836, 1/4 real. Copper, Proof pattern.

Obverse: The national coat of arms with upright eagle above a half wreath of oak and laurel, and the legend REPUBLICA MEXICANA around the top. *Reverse:* A large radiant liberty cap with the radiance emanating from a ring of clouds. Above, the denomination UNA ★ CUARTILLA; below, 1836. *Edge:* Plain. *Diameter:* 27.5 mm. BW-967.P, KM-Pn53.

1841-M°, 1 centavo. Copper, pattern.

Obverse: A seated figure of Liberty facing right, with a spear in her left hand and an ax and fasces propped behind the seat. In the exerge below, L. ROVIRA F. (with the *F* standing for *Fecit*, or "made it"). *Reverse:* At center, within a wreath of oak and laurel, 1 / CENTAVO / 1841 / M°. *Edge:* Plain. *Diameter:* 30 mm. BW-968.P, Gerber-432, KM-Pn60.

Note: "L. Rovira" on the obverse is engraver Luciano Rovera; "F." stands for the Latin *Fecit*, meaning "made it."

(1850). Copper, pattern "salesman's sample."

Obverse: The national coat of arms with upright eagle above a half wreath of oak and laurel, and the legend MONNAIE MEXICAINE (Mexican Currency) around the top. *Reverse:* At center, within a wreath of oak and laurel, EUĢ KURTZ / MECANICIEN. / A PARIS. (Eugene Kurtz Machine Company in Paris). *Edge:* Plain. *Diameter:* 38 mm. BW-969.P, KM-PnUL.

1851-C, CE, 8 reales. Copper, pattern.

Obverse: The national coat of arms with upright eagle above a half wreath of oak and laurel, and the legend REPUBLICA MEXICANA around the top. *Reverse:* At center, a large radiant liberty cap, with the legend ★8R . C . 1851 . C . E . 10 D^S·20 G^S· below. *Edge:* Plain. *Diameter:* 40 mm. BW-970.P, Gerber-438, KM-PnA.74.

Note: "CE" in the reverse legend is assayer Clemente Espinosa.

1866-(M̊), 1 peso. Silver, pattern (Small Letters). Uniface.

Reverse: Profile portrait of Emperor Maximilian, with the legend MAXIMILIANO EMPERADOR surrounding and, below the portrait, a small ribbon. *Edge:* Reeded. *Diameter:* 37 mm. BW-971.P, Gerber-451, KM-Pn100.

1869-Mº, C, 1 peso. Copper, off-metal strike.

Obverse: The national coat of arms with upright eagle above a half wreath of oak and laurel, along with the legend REPUBLICA MEXICANA around the top and 1869 below. *Reverse:* Below a small radiant liberty cap, a crossed sword and balance scale; between the pans of the scale, a scroll bearing the word LEY. Below the scroll, UN PESO Mº C. 902.7. *Edge:* Plain. *Diameter:* 37 mm. BW-972.P, Gerber-460, KM-Pn118.

Note: The identity of assayer "C" in the reverse legend is unknown.

1870-Mº, B, 20 pesos. Copper, pattern.

Obverse: The national coat of arms with upright eagle above a half wreath of oak and laurel, along with the legend REPUBLICA MEXICANA around the top and 1870 below. *Reverse:* Below a small radiant liberty cap, a crossed sword and balance scale; between the pans of the scale, a scroll bearing the word LEY. Below the scroll, Mº C. VEINTE PESOS 875. *Edge:* Plain. *Diameter:* 34.5 mm. BW-973.P, KM-Pn123.

Note: The identity of assayer "C" in the reverse legend is unknown.

1875-Mº, B, 20 pesos. Copper, off-metal strike.

Obverse: The national coat of arms with upright eagle above a half wreath of oak and laurel, along with the legend REPUBLICA MEXICANA around the top and 1875 below. *Reverse:* Below a small radiant liberty cap, a crossed sword and balance scale; between the pans of the scale, a scroll bearing the word LEY. Below the scroll, Mº B. VEINTE PESOS 875. *Edge:* Plain. *Diameter:* 36 mm. BW-974.P, Gerber-467, KM-Pn132.

Note: The identity of assayer "B" in the reverse legend is unknown.

1889-Mº, AM, 1 peso. White metal, pattern.

Obverse: The national coat of arms with upright eagle above a half wreath of oak and laurel, and the legend REPUBLICA MEXICANA around the top. *Reverse:* At center, a large radiant liberty cap, with the legend ★UN PESO·Mº1889·A·M·902,7. *Edge:* Plain. *Diameter:* 37 mm. BW-975.P, Gerber-477, KM-Pn152.

Note: This coin is part of an 1889 set of white-metal decimal patterns by AM (identity unknown). Other denominations in the set were 1, 20, and 50 centavos; and 2-1/2, 10, and 20 pesos.

1907, 50 centavos. Silver, pattern.

Obverse: The national coat of arms with upright eagle above a spray of oak and laurel, and the legend ESTADOS UNIDOS MEXICANOS around the top. Divided by the base of the cactus, 50 / ¢; to the right of the centavo symbol, in small letters, ESSAI. *Reverse:* Liberty in a flowing gown, riding a galloping horse to the left while holding a torch aloft in her left hand and a branch of laurel in her right. In the background, a rising sun with long, single-line rays. In the exergue, CH PillEt (engraver Charles Pillet) to the left, and ESSAI in small letters to the right. At the bottom, •1907•. *Edge:* Plain or lettered. *Diameter:* 30 mm. BW-976.P, KM-Pn173.

Note: Engraved in Paris.

1909, 1 peso. Silver, pattern.

Obverse: The national coat of arms with upright eagle above a spray of oak and laurel, and the legend ESTADOS UNIDOS MEXICANOS around the top. Divided by the base of the cactus, UN / PESO; in the exergue to the right, in small letters, ESSAI. *Reverse:* Liberty in a flowing gown, riding a galloping horse to the left while holding a torch aloft in her left hand and a branch of laurel in her right. In the background, a rising sun with long, single-line rays. In the exergue, CH PillEt (engraver Charles Pillet) to the left, and ESSAI in small leters to the right. At the bottom, •1909•. *Edge:* Lettered-incused, INDEPENDENCIA Y LIBERTAD. *Diameter:* 39 mm. BW-977.P, KM-Pn179.

Note: Like the preceding pattern, engraved in Paris. Very rare.

1916, 20 pesos. Copper, pattern.

Obverse: The national coat of arms with upright eagle above a half wreath of oak and laurel, and the legend REPUBLICA MEXICANA around the top. *Reverse:* At center, the Aztec Calendar Stone, surrounded by the legend 20 PESOS 16.7185 X 0.9 = 15.047 Au. / ★1916★. *Edge:* Plain. *Diameter:* 28 mm. BW-978.P, Gerber-488, KM-Pn189.

1936-Mº, 1 peso. Silver, Proof pattern.

Obverse: The national coat of arms with a left-facing eagle above a spray of oak and laurel, and the legend ESTADOS UNIDOS MEXICANOS around the top. *Reverse:* Filling the center and right of the field, a profile portrait of José María Morelos facing right, with mintmark Mº below the neck. Filling the left part of the field, the vertical legend 0.720★UN PESO★1936. *Edge:* Plain. *Diameter:* 22 mm. BW-979.P, KM-Pn191.

Note: Extremely rare.

1945-Mº, 50 centavos. Nickel, Proof pattern.

Obverse: The national coat of arms with a left-facing eagle above a spray of oak and laurel, and the legend ESTADOS UNIDOS MEXICANOS around the top and mintmark Mº above the eagle's head. *Reverse:* Large profile portrait of Benito Juárez facing left, with the legend CINCUENTA CENTAVOS . 1945 surrounding. *Edge:* Plain. *Diameter:* 28 mm. BW-980.P, Gerber-490, KM-Pn192.

1947-Mo, 5 pesos. Silver, Proof pattern.

Obverse: The national coat of arms with a left-facing eagle above a spray of oak and laurel, and the legend ESTADOS UNIDOS MEXICANOS around the top. *Reverse:* Below a small radiant liberty cap, a crossed sword and balance scale; between the pans of the scale, a scroll bearing the word LEY. The legend 30 GRAMOS LEY 0.900 Mo / • CINCO PESOS • 1947 surrounds. *Edge:* Plain. *Diameter:* 40 mm. BW-981.P, Gerber-491, KM-Pn195.

1947, Una Onza. Silver, Proof pattern.

Obverse: At the center, a balance scale with PESO / 33.625 / GRAMOS in small letters above the left arm and LEY / 0.925 below the pillar. The legend ★ UNA ONZA TROY = 480 GRANOS DE PLATA PURA surrounds. *Reverse:* A screw press at the center, with the legend CASA DE MONEDA DE MEXICO / 1947 surrounding. Mintmark Mº above the press. *Edge:* Plain. *Diameter:* 40 mm. BW-982.P, Gerber-492, KM-Pn196.

Note: Very rare.

1950-Mo, 5 pesos. Silver, pattern (Closed Wreath).

Obverse: At center, a small national coat of arms with left-facing eagle above a spray of oak and laurel. Above, the legend ESTADOS UNIDOS MEXICANOS; below, CINCO PESOS / Mo 1950. In small letters to the left of the spray, LEY / 0.620; in small letters to the right of the spray, PESO / 27 7/9 G. *Reverse:* A left-facing profile portrait of Miguel Hidalgo y Costilla, within a closed wreath of laurel. *Edge:* Lettered (COMERCIO AGRICULTURA INDUSTRIA). *Diameter:* 40 mm. BW-983.P, Gerber-494, KM-PnUL.

1950-Mo, 5 pesos. Silver, pattern (Open Wreath).

Obverse: At center, a small national coat of arms with left-facing eagle above a spray of oak and laurel. Above, the legend ESTADOS UNIDOS MEXICANOS; below, CINCO PESOS / Mo 1950. In small letters to the left of the spray, LEY / 0.620; in small letters to the right of the spray, PESO / 27 7/9 G. *Reverse:* A left-facing profile portrait of Miguel Hidalgo y Costilla with HIDALGO in small letters beneath the neck and mintmark M° to the right, all within an open wreath of laurel. *Edge:* Lettered (COMERCIO AGRICULTURA INDUSTRIA). *Diameter:* 40 mm. BW-984.P, Gerber-495, KM-Pn197.

1978-M°, 20 pesos. Copper, Proof pattern.

Obverse: Above a half wreath of oak and laurel, the national coat of arms with a left-facing eagle whose feathers and other elements are drawn as outlines instead of in full relief. Above, the legend ESTADOS UNIDOS MEXICANOS. *Reverse:* Slightly above center, a stylized Aztec depiction of Coyolxauhqui, with mintmark M° to the right and VEINTE PESOS / 1978 below. *Edge:* Plain. *Diameter:* 36 mm. BW-985.P, KM-PnUL.

Note: Very rare.

1980-M°, 10 pesos. Silver, Proof pattern.

Obverse: Above a half wreath of oak and laurel, the national coat of arms with a left-facing eagle whose feathers and other elements are drawn as outlines instead of in full relief. Above, the legend ESTADOS UNIDOS MEXICANOS. *Reverse:* Slightly above center, a stylized Aztec depiction of Coyolxauhqui, with mintmark M° to the right and DIEZ PESOS / 1980 below. *Edge:* Plain. *Diameter:* 30 mm. BW-986.P, KM-Pn220.

Note: Very rare.

1980-M°, 10 pesos. Brass, Proof pattern.

Obverse: Above a half wreath of oak and laurel, the national coat of arms with a left-facing eagle whose feathers and other elements are drawn as outlines instead of in full relief. Above, the legend ESTADOS UNIDOS MEXICANOS. *Reverse:* A stylized Mesoamerican head, with DIEZ PESOS below and 1980 above. Mintmark M° immediately below the head. *Edge:* Plain. *Diameter:* 30 mm. BW-987.P, KM-Pn221.

Note: Very rare.

1980-M°, 20 pesos. Silver, pattern trial strike. Uniface (reverse).

Reverse: A simplified rendering of the round ballcourt marker from the ancient Mayan ritual ball game, with $20 superimposed on the left side. Above the denomination, CULTURA MAYA; below the denomination, the date. Mintmark M° at the bottom. *Edge:* Plain. *Diameter:* 30 mm. BW-988.P, KM-Pn222.

Note: This pattern can also be found in copper and brass.

1985-M°, 1 peso. Silver, pattern.

Obverse: The national coat of arms with a left-facing eagle above a half wreath of oak and laurel, and the legend ESTADOS UNIDOS MEXICANOS around the top. *Reverse:* In a field divided by a vertical line, the left two-thirds holds a stylized rendering of the main emblems of the SUD coinage from the War of Independence; the right third holds the mintmark M̊, **1985**, and the denomination **$1**. *Edge:* Plain. *Diameter:* 15 mm. BW-989.P, KM-Pn234.

1985-M̊, 500 pesos. Copper, Proof pattern.

Obverse: The national coat of arms with a left-facing eagle above a half wreath of oak and laurel, and the legend **ESTADOS UNIDOS MEXICANOS** around the top. *Reverse:* Facing left, the conjoined busts of four heroes of the Revolution: Emiliano Zapata, Francisco Madero, Venustiano Carranza, and Francisco "Pancho" Villa, each with his surname beneath in small letters; in the background, the top of the *Monumento a la Revolución (Monument of the Revolution).* The legend **75 ANIVERSARIO DE LA REVOLUCION MEXICANA** surrounds, with mintmark M̊ at far left and **$500 / 1985** at the bottom. *Edge:* Plain. *Diameter:* 38 mm. BW-990.P, KM-PnUL.

Note: Very rare.

1987-M̊, 100 pesos. Copper, Proof pattern.

Obverse: The national coat of arms with a left-facing eagle above a half wreath of oak and laurel, and the legend **ESTADOS UNIDOS MEXICANOS** around the top. *Reverse:* At center, the words **mariposa monarcha** (Monarch butterfly), surrounded by 10 butterflies of successively increasing size. At top right, **1987 / $100 /** M̊. *Edge:* Plain. *Diameter:* 38 mm. BW-991.P, KM-Pn238.

1990-M̊, 50,000 pesos. Silver, Proof pattern.

Obverse: The national coat of arms with a left-facing eagle above a half wreath of oak and laurel, and the legend **ESTADOS UNIDOS MEXICANOS** around the top. *Reverse:* A portrait of Emiliano Zapata in three-quarter profile, with **$50,000** above, M̊ **/ EMILIANO / ZAPATA** at left, and **1990** at right. *Edge:* Plain. *Diameter:* 38 mm. BW-992.P, KM-Pn244.

Note: Very rare.

1990-M̊, 50,000 pesos. Brass, pattern.

Obverse: The national coat of arms with a left-facing eagle above a half wreath of oak and laurel, and the legend **ESTADOS UNIDOS MEXICANOS** around the top. *Reverse:* A portrait of Emiliano Zapata in three-quarter profile, with **$50,000** above, M̊ **/ EMILIANO / ZAPATA** at left, and **1990** at right. *Edge:* Plain. *Diameter:* 38 mm. BW-993.P, KM-Pn242a.

Note: Rare.

1990-M̊, 50,000 pesos. Copper-nickel, Proof pattern.

Obverse: The national coat of arms with a left-facing eagle above a half wreath of oak and laurel, and the legend **ESTADOS UNIDOS MEXICANOS** around the top. *Reverse:* A portrait of Emiliano Zapata in three-quarter profile, with **$50,000** above, M̊ **/ EMILIANO / ZAPATA** at left, and **1990** at right. *Edge:* Plain. *Diameter:* 38 mm. BW-994.P, KM-Pn242b.

1990-M̊, 100,000 pesos. Silver, Proof pattern.

Obverse: Above a half wreath of oak and laurel, the national coat of arms with a left-facing eagle whose feathers and other elements are drawn as outlines instead of in full relief. Above, the legend **ESTADOS UNIDOS MEXICANOS.** *Reverse:* At center, a bust of Plutarco Calles in three-quarter profile to the right, with **PLUTARCO E. CALLES** below. **$100000** placed vertically in the field to the left, with **1990** immediately below the peso symbol; in the field to the right, M̊ **/ Ley 0.900**. *Edge:* Plain. *Diameter:* 39 mm. BW-995.P, KM-Pn245.

Note: Very rare.

1991-M̊, 2,000 pesos. Bimetallic, pattern.

Obverse: At center, the national coat of arms with a left-facing eagle. Surrounding the eagle, struck on a path that overlaps both metals, the legend **ESTADOS UNIDOS MEXICANOS** above and a half wreath of oak and laurel below. *Reverse:* At center,

Mexico City's *Monumento a la Revolucion*, with 1991 below and mintmark M̊ to the right. On the surrounding ring, the legend MONUMENTO A LA REVOLUCION, with $2,000 at the bottom. *Edge:* Plain. *Diameter:* 21 mm. BW-996.P, KM-Pn252.

Patterns, Trial Strikes, and Experimental Pieces

1/2 grano. 1769-M̊. Copper. BW-960 P, KM-PnC1, 21.5 mm.

1 grano. 1769-M̊. Copper. BW-961 P, Gerber-405, KM-PnD1, 27.25 mm. (The example pictured has been holed.)

8 reales. 1827-G̊, WW. Silver. BW-962 P, Gerber-413, KM-Pn12, 40 mm.

8 reales. 1829-P^{I}, JS. Silver. BW-963 P, Gerber-416, KM-Pn20, 37 mm.

8 reales. 183_-G. Copper. BW-964 P, KM-Pn24, 39 mm.

8 escudos. 1831-G, MJ. Copper. BW-965 P, Gerber-421, KM-Pn28, 38 mm.

Patterns, Trial Strikes, and Experimental Pieces

(continued)

4 escudos. 1832-D♀, LR. Brass. BW-966 P, Gerber-424, KM-Pn34, 30 mm.

1/4 real. 1836. Copper. BW-967 P, KM-Pn53, 27.5 mm

1 centavo. 1841-M♀. Copper. BW-968 P, Gerber-432, KM-Pn60, 30 mm.

"Salesman's sample." (1850). Copper. BW-969 P, KM-PnUL, 38 mm.

8 reales. 1851-C, CE. Copper. BW-970 P, Gerber-438, KM-PnA.74, 40 mm.

1 peso. (1866). Silver (uniface). BW-971 P, Gerber-451, KM-Pn100, 37 mm.

Patterns, Trial Strikes, and Experimental Pieces

(continued)

1 peso. 1869-M♀, C. Copper. BW-972 P, Gerber-460, KM-Pn118, 37 mm.

20 pesos. 1870-M♀, B. Copper. BW-973 P, KM-Pn123, 34.5 mm.

20 pesos. 1875-M♀, B. Copper. BW-974 P, Gerber-467, KM-Pn132, 36 mm.

1 peso. 1889-M♀, AM. White metal. BW-975 P, Gerber-477, KM-Pn152, 37 mm.

50 centavos. 1907. Silver. BW-976 P, KM-Pn173, 30 mm.

Patterns, Trial Strikes, and Experimental Pieces

(continued)

1 peso. 1909. Silver. BW-977 P, KM-Pn179, 39 mm.

20 pesos. 1916-($\mathring{M}$). Copper. BW-978 P, Gerber-488, KM-Pn189, 28 mm.

1 peso. 1936-$\mathring{M}$. Silver. BW-979 P, KM-Pn191, 22 mm.

50 centavos. 1945. Nickel. BW-980 P, Gerber-490, KM-Pn192, 28 mm.

5 pesos. 1947-Mo. Silver. BW-981 P, Gerber-491, KM-Pn196, 40 mm.

Una Onza. 1947. Silver. BW-982 P, Gerber-492, KM-Pn196, 40 mm.

Patterns, Trial Strikes, and Experimental Pieces

(continued)

5 pesos. 1950-Mo. Silver, Closed Wreath. BW-983 P, Gerber-494, KM-PnUL, 40 mm.

5 pesos. 1950-Mo. Silver, Open Wreath. BW-984 P, Gerber-495, KM-Pn197, 40 mm.

20 pesos. 1978-M̊. Copper. BW-985 P, KM-PnUL, 36 mm.

10 pesos. 1980-M̊. Silver. BW-986 P, KM-Pn220, 30 mm.

10 pesos. 1980-M̊. Brass. BW-987 P, KM-Pn221, 30 mm.

1980, $20, M̊. Silver (uniface). BW-988 P, KM-Pn222, 30 mm.

1 peso. 1985-M̊. Silver. BW-989 P, KM-Pn234, 15 mm.

Patterns, Trial Strikes, and Experimental Pieces
(continued)

500 pesos. 1985-Mo. Copper. BW-990 P, KM-PnUL, 38 mm.

100 pesos. 1987-Mo. Copper. BW-991 P, KM-Pn238, 38 mm.

50,000 pesos. 1990-Mo. Silver. BW-992 P, KM-Pn244, 38 mm.

50,000 pesos. 1990-Mo. Brass. BW-993 P, KM-Pn242a, 38 mm.

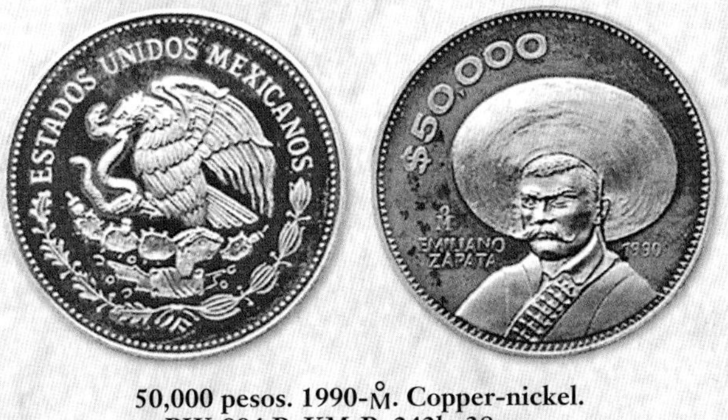

50,000 pesos. 1990-Mo. Copper-nickel. BW-994 P, KM-Pn242b, 38 mm.

Patterns, Trial Strikes, and Experimental Pieces

(continued)

100,000 pesos. 1990-Mº. Silver. BW-995 P, KM-Pn245, 39 mm.

**2,000 pesos. 1991-Mº. Bimetallic.
BW-996 P, KM-Pn252, 21 mm.**

24

Medals of Mexico

Medallic art is often connected with numismatics, even though medals are purely commemorative or honorific and, unlike tokens, are not used as currency. Even so, the two collecting fields often overlap—there is a natural association between their physical formats, and medals are often issued by the very bodies (state, regional, and local governments; merchants; etc.) that issue coins and tokens. In addition, the motivation behind the designs is often strongly related. The art on both coins and medals can reinforce the authority of a governing body and remind the population of its character (or to use a purely modern term, its "branding"). Prior to the era of electricity and swift travel, coins and medals also played a role in spreading the news: who the current ruler is, where the seat of power is located, and so on. Finally, the people and facilities who produce coins are often the ones employed to create medals. French engraver Charles Pillet, for example, engraved several of the medals described in this chapter as well as the Mexican peso of 1910 to 1921; and both private and government mints strike medals.

This chapter presents a small but representative sample of the medals that have been produced in and for Mexico from the colonial era to the present.

PROCLAMATION MEDALS

Proclamation medals were issued in New Spain throughout the Spanish colonial period, usually to celebrate the coronation of a new king, but sometimes to mark other events during his reign. Some were issued by private individuals; others were issued by professional, trade, religious, municipal, or other groups. The medals demonstrated the issuers' loyalty to the king, and spread the news of the coronation or other event to the populace. This section covers proclamation medals issued from the reign of Philip V (proclaimed king of Spain in November 1700) through that of Ferdinand VII (which, within Mexico, ended with the declaration of the nation's independence on September 16, 1821).

Proclamation medals can be found in many sizes and metals, including gold, silver, bronze, and their alloys. Some of the bronze and silver medals are gold plated. Only a few selected examples are shown in this volume; for an in-depth study, Frank W. Grove's *Medals of Mexico, Volume 1: Medals of the Spanish Kings* (1976) is a good source. G-numbers within this chapter are from the aforementioned work.

King Philip V (1700–1724; 1724–1746)

1701, Mexico City, cast silver. *Obverse:* Armored bust of Philip V to the right, wearing a wig and robe of state. The legend PHILIP:V:DG:HISPANIARVM: REX:AN:1701 surrounds. *Reverse:* The coat of arms of Mexico City (capital of New Spain) beneath an eagle facing right, with the legend IMPERATOR · + INDIARVM ·

surrounding and MEX / ICO at the center, divided by the castle. *Diameter:* 30 mm. *Other formats:* Solid gold; gold plated. G-PV-1.

King Louis I (1724)

1724, Mexico City, gold-plated cast silver.

Obverse: Within a circle, a half-length figure of Louis I in three-quarter profile to the left, with hat and wig, and wearing the collar of the Order of the Golden Fleece. The legend LVDOVICUS*I*D. G. HISPANIARVM REX + surrounds. *Reverse:* Within a circle, the coat of arms of Mexico City beneath an eagle facing right, all surrounded by the legend IMPERATOR * INDIARVM:MEXICI: 1724 +. *Diameter:* 61 mm. G-LI-4.

King Ferdinand VI (1746–1759)

1747, Córdoba, cast silver.

Obverse: Armored bust of Ferdinand VI in profile to the right, wearing a wig and the Order of the Golden Fleece. The legend FERDINAND VI.DG.HISPA. ET.INDIAR. REX: surrounds. *Reverse:* The coat of arms of Spain, surrounded by the legend IMPERATOR IN DIARUM.ꝞDCORDOUA. 1747. (Emperor of the Indies, Villa de Córdoba, 1747). *Diameter:* 32 mm. G-F6-14.

1747, Guadalajara, el Colegio Hispano, cast silver.

Obverse: Bust of Ferdinand VI to the front, wearing a wig; the legend FERDIN. VI•D• G•HISP•ETIND•REX• surrounds. *Reverse:* To the left, a portion of the coat of arms of Guadalajara; to the right, the three bars from the coat of arms of Bishop Juan Gómez de Parada. The legend CIVI• GVADALAX•COL•HISP•1747 surrounds. *Diameter:* 37 mm. G-F6-17.

1747, Puebla, cast silver.

Obverse: Within a circle, a bust of Ferdinand VI in profile to the left, wearing a hat and wig. The legend FERDINADVS VI DG.ISPANIAN̥ REX. *Reverse:* Within a circle, a bust of Queen Barbara to the front, surrounded by the legend PROCLAMTIO. 1747.NGELOPOLIS (with a composite AN character for the first two letters in ANGELOPOLIS—i.e., Puebla). *Diameter:* 29 mm. G-F6-30.

King Charles III (1759–1788)

1760, Mexico City, silver.

Obverse: Armored bust of Charles III in profile to the right, wearing a wig. The legend CAROL.III .D.G . HISPAN . REX MEXIC . PROCL 1760 surrounds. *Reverse:* An ornamental coat of arms of Mexico City with the legend INSIGN FIDELIT ET PVBL LÆTI. In the exergue below the coat of arms, engraver A.B. Madero / F. *Diameter:* 43.5 mm. *Other formats:* Bronze (44 mm); gold-plated bronze (43 mm). G-K-1.

(No date), al Mérito, gold.

Obverse: Laureate bust of Charles III in profile to the right, wearing the collar of the Order of the Golden Fleece. The legend CARLOS III • REY DE ESP • EMP • DE LAS INDIAS • surrounds. Below the bust, engraver A . GILL . MEDINA . *Reverse:* At center, within a wreath of laurel, AL / MERITO. *Diameter:* 58 mm. *Other formats:* Silver; bronze. G-K-92.

King Charles IV (1788–1808)

1789, Mexico City, el Arzobispo (inverted date), gold.

Obverse: An undraped, laureate bust of Charles IV in profile to the right, surrounded by the legend * CAROLO * IV * HISP * ET * IND * REG * MEX * PROCL * AN * 1789*. In the exergue below the bust, engraver GIL. *Reverse:* A laureate bust of Queen María Louisa in profile to the left, surrounded by the legend * LVDOV * REG * AVSPICE * and * ALF * ARCH * MEX*. *Diameter:* 41 mm. *Other formats:* Silver; bronze. G-C-20.

Note: When the legend circles the field and ends with part of the information at the bottom, at about the 6 o'clock position, that part of the legend is often turned right-side up so it can be read without the coin's having to be turned. Here, the date falls in the 6 o'clock position but continues in the path of the legend, so that it appears upside-down (inverted).

1790, Guanajuato, silver.

Obverse: Bust of Charles IV in profile to the right, wearing the collar of the Order of the Golden Fleece. The legend ∗A∗ CARLOS∗IV∗REY∗CATOLICO∗ surrounds. Below the bust, engraver G. A. GIL. *Reverse:* The coat of arms of Guanajuato, surrounded by the legend FUE·PROCLAMADO·POR·LA·NOBLE·CIUDAD·Đ·GUANAXUATO·EN 25·DE·DIZIEMBRE·DE·1790. *Diameter:* 47 mm. *Other formats:* Bronze. G-C-72.

King Ferdinand VII (1808, 1813–1833)

1808, Mexico City, gold.

Obverse: Bust of Ferdinand VII in profile to the right, wearing the collar of the Order of the Golden Fleece. The legend A·FERNANDO·VII·REY DE ESPAÑA Y DE INDIAS· surrounds. Below the bust, in script, engraver F. GORDILLO F. Mº. *Reverse:* The coat of arms of Mexico City, with a feminine Indian figure to the left and an eagle holding a snake in its beak to the right. The legend EN SU EXALTACION AL TRONO LA CIUDAD DE MEXICO. surrounds. In the exergue below, EN 13 DE AGOSTO / DE 1808. *Diameter:* 43 mm. *Other formats:* Silver; bronze. G-F-1.

1809, Mexico City, la Universidad, silver.

Obverse: Bust of Fernando VII in profile to the left, wearing an ornate coat and the Order of the Golden Fleece. Legend ∗FERDINANDVS VII BORBONIVS REX CATHOLICVS∗. Below the edge of the shoulder, in script, engraver J. GUERRERO. *Reverse:* Seated figure of Minerva in three-quarter profile to the left, with a shield at her left side and a lance in her right hand; in the background, books, a globe, and an owl. The legend POES · ET · ELOQVENT · CERT · CONST · MEX · ACAD · surrounds. In the exergue below, J.M. GUERRERO INVENTO Y / G. EN M̊. A. DE 1809. *Diameter:* 50 mm. *Other formats:* Bronze. G-F-38.

Note: This medal was struck as an award for participants in a literary contest organized by the university.

Proclamation Medals

Philip V, 1701, Mexico City. G-PV-1, 30 mm.

Louis I, 1724, Mexico City. G-LI-4, 61 mm. (shown reduced)

Proclamation Medals
(continued)

Charles III, 1760, Mexico City. G-K-1, 43.5 mm.

Charles III, no date, al Mérito. G-K-92, 58 mm. (shown reduced)

Charles IV, 1789, Mexico City, el Arzobispo. G-C-20, 41 mm.

Charles IV, 1790, Guanajuato. G-C-72, 47 mm.

POST-COLONIAL MEDALS

In 1821, to mark the occasion of the end of Spanish rule, the Republic of Mexico struck its first medal, now referenced by its legend, "Proclamación de la Indepedencia," in Mexico City. Since that time, both the Casa de Moneda and private mints have struck a large number of medals honoring events and personages of Mexico. (The Casa de Moneda did not place mintmarks on medals before 1946; as a result, its pre-1946 medals are indistinguishable from private issues.)

Numerous articles have been written on this subject, but few books. Carlos Perez-Maldonado's *Medallas de México* (1945) was one of these, but it is now unavailable. In 1972 Frank W. Grove published *Medals of Mexico, Volume 2: 1821–1971*, and it became a standard in the field. Copies can still be found, but medals of the past four decades are obviously not included.

This chapter presents a selection from the wide array of post-colonial medals, to provide insight into the diversity of the subject matter and the artistic endeavors of the designers in the field. In *Medals of Mexico*, the entries are grouped into seven types, based on their subject matter: events; business or commercial; expositions or fairs; Masonic lodges; personages; *bolos* (christening pieces); and scholastic awards. Because this chapter presents a much smaller selection, and for consistency with the rest of this volume, the listings after each general discussion are in date order. G-numbers are from Grove.

Proclamation Medals

(continued)

Ferdinand VII, 1808, Mexico City. G-F-1, 43 mm.

Ferdinand VII, 1809, Mexico City, la Universidad. G-F-38, 50 mm. (shown reduced)

19th Century

Agustín de Iturbide led the Army of Three Guarantees into Mexico City on September 27, 1821. With independence now an accomplished fact, Iturbide persuaded enough members of the congress to award him the Imperial Crown of Mexico, and he was made emperor on July 21, 1822. One of Mexico's earliest medals, dated 1821, was struck in honor of the first year of his reign.

As one would imagine, the great figures of Mexico's first Republic were (and still are) popular medallic subjects. Guadalupe Victoria, as the first president of Mexico, appeared on the first of many such medals: the 1824 "Águila de Perfil" medal, with two reverse designs—the Profile ("Hookneck") Eagle and the Upright Eagle. In due time, Vicente Guerrero, Santa Anna, and others were captured in medallic art.

During the French intervention of 1863 through 1867, a great many medals were issued to honor Emperor Maximilian and Empress Carlota. These included commemorations of events initiated by the emperor, awards given in his name, and posthumous events in his honor. One elaborate medal, struck in 1875, celebrates the unveiling of a statue of Maximilian at the Miramare Castle in Trieste, Italy.

From the 19th century to the present, scores of *fantasy medals* have been struck with Maximilian's image. Minted in varying degrees of fineness in gold or silver, they appear in Internet auctions on a regular basis. Especially common are 10-mm fantasies with no denomination, often described as "1865, gold one peso of Maximilian"—completely inaccurate, as the gold 1 peso was never decreed during the Maximilian era. They are sometimes listed, more accurately, as "fantasy pesos." Another Maximilian fantasy that shows up in online auctions is a silver medal depicting the busts of Maximilian and Carlota within a circle of symbols on the obverse, and with an Aztec calendar on the reverse.

The republic was restored in 1867. Benito Juárez arrived in San Luis Potosí on February 21, as the French troops were withdrawing. On July 1, after the fall and execution of Maximilian, Juárez moved his government to Mexico City. The medal "Juárez en su Vuelta a San Luis Potosí" commemorated the occasion.

Events and achievements of a nonpolitical nature were also honored with medallic art. One example is the July 1855 commencement of construction on the first railroad from Mexico City to the Gulf of Mexico. The event was marked with the "Ferrocarril Hacia el Golfo" medal. The numerous expositions and fairs that have taken place in Mexico, or with the works and culture of Mexico as a subject, were popular subjects. Prior to 1900, most such medals depicted a maiden on the obverse and a legend describing the event on the reverse, as with the 1899 Coyoacán "Exposición General de Agricultura" medal. The design trend changed soon thereafter, and scenes depicting the event's focus, such as animals, farming, or art, became popular on exposition medals in the 20th century.

From the 1870s until the early 1900s, it was customary to have a *bolo* medal made to honor the christening of a child. These normally have the date of birth or christening and the name of the child, as well the names of the parents and godparents. One *bolo*, dated 1882 and made for Geronimo Treviño, has U.S. connections. Geronimo's mother, Roberta Augusta Ord, was the daughter of U.S. Major General Edward O.C. Ord, a Civil War commander who also fought in the Indian wars. (Fort Ord, California, was named after him.) Roberta married Mexican General Geronimo Treviño on July 20, 1880. The two generals had originally become acquainted in their efforts to foster mutual understanding and peaceful relations among the people in the Mexican-American border area.

Scholastic awards were important within Mexico and date back to 1854. The medals were struck in gold, silver, and bronze in various sizes. One popular design was "El Gobierno de la Union," issued in silver in numerous varieties from the late 1860s to the early 1910s.

Mexico has probably produced more religious medals than all the other types combined. A typical subject is the Virgin of Guadalupe, patroness of Mexico. She is depicted as she appeared on a peasant's cloak in 1531, which lies preserved under bulletproof glass in the Basílica de Nuestra Señora de Guadalupe in Mexico City: as a full-length figure, hands clasped, standing in a crescent moon that is borne up by an angel. The radiance around her typically keeps to a narrow margin, and is wreathed in an oval of clouds, as on the cloak.

1821, Mexico City, Proclamación de la Independencia, silver.

Obverse: The legend **MEJICO / EN LA SOLEMNE / PROCLAMACION / DE LA INDEPENDEN- / CIA DEL IMPERIO / A 27 DE OCTUBRE / DE 1821.** *Reverse:* Crowned imperial eagle turned partway to the left, with wings spread, perched on a nopal cactus. On a rock below the cactus, engraver **J. GUERRERO**. *Diameter:* 34 mm. *Other formats:* Bronze. G-5.

1821, Mexico City, Augustín, Emperador de México, silver.

Obverse: An uncrowned eagle turned partway to the left, with wings spread, perched on a fringed banner reading **AGVSTINO • DE • ITURBIDE / LIBERTATIS • PATRIAE / VINDICI • STRENVO / MEXICAN • IMPER • AN • I •**. Below the fringe, **Dedicada por el Mismo Artifice**. *Reverse:* The figure of an Indian princess, representing Mexico, presenting a sword, sash, and laurel wreath to Iturbide. Above the figures, a radiant cloud with religious symbols at its center. The legend **PRO RELIGIONE / ET PATRIA ∗**, divided by the cloud, surrounds. In the exergue below, engraver **José Guerrero** and **N! de M̊ • / A • de 1821 •**. *Diameter:* 57 mm. *Other formats:* Bronze; lead (uniface reverse trial strike, 58 mm). G-7.

1824, Guadalupe Victoria, Águila de Perfil, gold.

Obverse: Bust of Guadalupe Victoria in profile to the right, wearing a military dress coat, surrounded by the legend **EL EXMO.S.D.GUADALUPE VICTORIA PRESIDEIOÐLA-** (the inscription is continued on the reverse). *Reverse:* At center, the national coat of arms with eagle in profile to the left; above, the continuation of the obverse inscription, **REPUBLICA MEXICANA.** Surrounding all, in small letters, **J. GUERRERO DIBUJO Y GRABO EN MEXICO A. DE 1824 Y LA DEDICA AL MERITO Y PATRIOTISMO DEL MISMO SR.** *Diameter:* 40 mm. *Other formats:* Silver (41 mm); bronze (41 mm). G-70.

Note: This medal with the same obverse but an Upright Eagle on the reverse is G-71 (40 mm, struck in silver and in bronze).

1855, Ferrocarril Hacia el Golfo, gold-plated bronze.

Obverse: At center, a locomotive traveling to the right, with the legend **PRIVILIGIO DE LOS SRES • MOSSO HERMANOS Y CA** above. Below the tracks, in the exergue, **MEXICO / 1855.** *Reverse:* A lengthy statement, in 12 lines, that begins with **PRIMER CAMINO DE FIERRO DE LA CAPITAL DE LA REPUB**CA **HACIA EL GOLFO DE MEXICO.** *Diameter:* 46 mm. *Other formats:* Bronze, without gold plating. G-97.

(No date), Maximiliano y Carlota (fantasy), silver.

Obverse: Jugate busts of Maximilian and Carlota in profile to the left within a circle of decorative symbols, with the legend **MAXIMILIANO + Y + CARLOTA** around the top. *Reverse:* The Aztec Calendar Stone, with no inscription. *Diameter:* 37 mm. G-170.

Note: Any medal of Maximilian and Carlota that has the Calendar Stone on the reverse should be viewed with suspicion, as it is almost certainly a fantasy.

1867, Juárez en su Vuelta a San Luis Potosí, silver.

Obverse: The legend AL / C° PRESIDENTE / BENITO JUAREZ / EN SU VUELTA / A SN LUIS POTOSI / FEBRERO DE. / 1867. Below the date, A. FLORET G. *Reverse:* The Mexican eagle in profile to the right, wings spread, with a small radiant liberty cap above and military armaments below. *Diameter:* 47 mm. *Other formats:* Bronze (48 mm); silver or bronze, without engraver (47 mm). G-180.

1870, El Gobierno de la Union, silver.

Obverse: At center, an arrangement of symbols representing the Arts and Sciences: a book, laid flat, with a globe, a partial architectural column, and a lyre laid on top; on a scroll draped over the column, the word PREMIO. Above, the legend EL GOBIERNO DE LA UNION; below, MEXICO 1870. Beneath the spine of the book, engraver NAVALON. *Reverse:* Within a wreath of laurel, the legend AL / TALENTO Y LA / APLICACION. *Diameter:* 45 mm. G-S-70.

Note: This basic design is found in several varieties, all in silver, at diameters of 45.5–46 mm (G-S-68 through G-S-111).

1875, Statue to Maximilian, gold.

Obverse: At center, a small bust of Maximilian in profile to the left, set within an elaborate medallion. Four large angels divide the medallion into equal sections; in each section, a host of smaller angels, with an inscription in Italian below them in the medallion's border. The inscription positioned below the bust reads A MASSIMILIANO D'AUSTRIA / IMPERATORE DEL MESSICO / MDCCCLXXV. *Reverse:* The statue to Maximilian in Trieste, surrounded by the legend ERECTO IN TRIESTE PER LIBERALITA D'AMMIRATORI NAZIONALI E STRANIERI. At lower right, engraver J. TAUTENHAYN. *Diameter:* 71 mm. *Other formats:* Silver; bronze. G-149.

Note: On the obverse, an inscription in small letters surrounds the bust and presents the date of death as June 16, 1867—the date Maximilian was originally due to be executed. The actual date of execution was June 19, 1867.

1882, Geronimo Treviño, silver.

Obverse: In the lower half of a circle, the sea; on its horizon, a radiant star at center and five mountain peaks to the right. Above, within the circle, the legend GERONIMO / TREVINO embracing a script monogram of the initials GT. Outside the circle, surrounding all, ★NACIO EL 3 DE SETIEMBRE DE 1882. *Reverse:* On a plain field, the legends SUS PADRES, / GERONIMO TREVINO / Y BERTHA A. ORD. and Se Bautizó en Monterey. / Padrinos, / Porfirio Diaz / y Carmen Romero / Rubio / DE DIAZ. *Diameter:* 26.5 mm. G-Pb-86.

1895, Guadalupe, Coronata, bronze.

Obverse: The Virgin of Guadalupe being crowned by angels, all surrounded by the legend B. V. GUADALUPENSIS QUALIS APPARUIT AN. 1531. *Reverse:* Interior of the Basilica de Guadalupe, surrounded by the legend + TEMPLUM GUADALUPENSE NUPER INSTARATUM CUM B. M.V. SOLEMNI RITU CORONATA EST AN. 1895. In the exergue, engraver JOHNSON. *Diameter:* 46 mm. G-P-193.

1899, Coyoacán, Exposición General de Agricultura, bronze.

Obverse: Within a floral wreath, the legend EXPOSICION GENERAL / DE / AGRICULTURA / EN COYOACAN / 1899. *Reverse:* In the foreground, a seated feminine figure in profile to the left, holding a wreath in her extended right hand. In the near background, flowers, a shock of wheat, and a plow; in the background, the Exposition Building. At lower left, below the figure's foot, engraver E. MORAL. *Diameter:* 49 mm. G-E-120.

20th Century

In the early 1900s, a feeling of unrest was building among the Mexican people. The dictatorship of Porfirio Díaz , beginning in

1876, had been a time of relative stability and progress, but the expansion of industry and infrastructure had come at the expense of the working class. Although the cities were growing, in the countryside the wealth was increasingly concentrated in the hands of a few *hacendados*, leaving small farmers and landless peasants impoverished and powerless. During his lengthy and stable (if repressive) rule, Díaz was featured on no fewer than 27 medals, including many of those celebrating the Centennial of Independence of Mexico.

The 1910 centennial generated numerous commemorative medals, 26 of which are listed in the Grove work. The medals for this historic occasion were often large or ambitious in design. The densely engraved "Centenario de la Independencia, Centurion," has complex, three-dimensional scenes on both sides; the medal known as "Independencia, Díaz y Hidalgo, grande," at 80 mm, is likewise striking, if more conventional in design.

During the 1920s, medallic art began to have a distinctly 20th-century feel. In 1925, a medal struck by the Casa de Moneda honors the "VI Centenario de la Fundación de la Ciudad de México"—the 600th anniversary of Mexico City's founding—by combining traditional native designs with informal typography. Earlier medals used simple, dignified typefaces, either serif or sans-serif, with occasional script flourishes. Part of the obverse legend on the "VI Centenario" medal appears as if it were taken from a native carving; the reverse legend is in the Art Nouveau style of the day.

Eight years later, the design of the 1933 "Vuelo de Barberan y Collar" medal represented another leap forward in design style; the legend on the obverse and the globe on the reverse look very much like something from a contemporary news reel. Issued by the Casa de Moneda, the medal honors two Mexican pilots who, earlier that year, flew from Spain to Cuba in a single-engine plane. Ten days later, they flew out of Havana for Mexico City, but they never arrived at their destination, and no trace of the plane was ever found.

Medallic production continue steadily for decades, commemorating heroes of the War of Independence and the Revolution, new Olympic games, anniversaries of states and battles, major agricultural expositions, and so on. Then, in the 1960s, demand for this form of honorific art shot upward. The Mexico Mint and private mints in Mexico (like the Casa de Baron) and the United States issued medals for almost any event, real or imaginary; conventions held by clubs and travel agents' organizations, youth sporting events, and so on joined historical subjects on medals.

After the 1960s, medal issues decreased, although medals continued to be struck by both the Casa de Moneda and various private mints. As soccer is the national sport, a number of medals were struck to remember the 1970 World Cup, which was held in Mexico but won by Brazil. The Brazilian company Medallas Yáñez issued "Fut-bol, Copa Jules Rimet, Brazil," with the obverse depicting both the Jules Rimet Cup in gold and the crossed flags of Brazil and Mexico.

The roster of beautiful and collectible medals of Mexico could fill several volumes. Perhaps the most fitting to close the chapter in the book on numismatics is one struck with a coin on it. Several medals with coins in the design have been struck for numismatic organizations in Mexico, both by the Casa de Moneda and by private mints. The Sociedad Numismatica de México initiated a Coins on Medals series in 1971, with the obverse and reverse of each medal depicting the obverse and reverse of a historic Mexican coin—a concept similar to that of the Numismatic Heritage of Mexico Series of commemorative coins (see chapter 15). The medals were issued intermittently up to the late 1990s, ending with a total of 20 medals, a handful of which are quite rare. The 1973 issue listed here depicts an 8 reales of Charles III. In 1999 the Sociedad Numismatica began a new series of Coins on Medals.

1910, Centenario de la Independencia, Centurion, gold.

Obverse: Beneath a tree, an angel crowning a bust of Father Hidalgo held aloft by two figures (representing Law and Peace). In the background at left, the Cathedral in Mexico City; at right, the peak of Popocatépetl. Above the scene, the legend CENTENARIO DE LA INDEPENDENCIA MEXICANA; below, 1910. Beneath the mountain peak, modeler M. CENTURION. *Reverse:* Father Hidalgo leading several followers, who carry torches, drums, and staffs, to the left. In the background to the right, the Church of Dolores. Above, the legend 16 DE SEPTIEMBRE DE 1810. *Diameter:* 50 mm. *Other formats:* Silver; bronze. G-380.

1910, Independencia, Díaz y Hidalgo (grande), gold-plated bronze.

Obverse: A standing feminine figure holding a wreath above the legend at right: EN CONMEMORACION DEL / CENTENARIO DE LA / INDEPENDENCIA NACIONAL / SIENDO PRESIDENTE / DE LA REPUBLICA EL C. GRAL / DON PoRFIRIO DIAZ. *Reverse:* A standing figure of Hidalgo facing forward in front of a desk, his left hand on a chair back, his right gesturing to books on the desk. In the background above the desk, a framed picture of the Virgin of Guadalupe. The legend PADRE TE LLAMA EL PUEBLO MEXICANO : TU LE DISTE LA VIDA,NOBLE ANCIANO! Below, an oval bearing the national eagle and wreathed in laurel, with 1810 and 1910 to the left and right, respectively. *Diameter:* 80 mm. G-391.

1925, VI Centenario de la Fundación de la Ciudad de Mexico, gold.

Obverse: The Mexico City coat of arms granted by Carlos V in 1553, surrounded by a stylized border of Mesoamerican emblems. The legend SEXTO CENTENARIO / DE LA FUNDACION DE LA CIUDAD DE MEXICO is above; the first two words are shaped as if carved among the emblems. *Reverse:* Within a stylized border of Mesoamerican emblems, the Mexican eagle in profile to the right, wings raised, a snake in its beak, perching on a nopal cactus amid water and reeds. A small, catlike animal crouches below the cactus to the right. In the border above, H. AYUNTAMIENTO CONSTITUCIONAL DE MEXICO; below, 1325*1925. *Diameter:* 50 mm. *Other formats:* Bronze; silver. G-450.

1933, Vuelo de Barberán y Collar, silver.

Obverse: At center, the legend ESPAÑA / BARBERAN-COLLAR / MEXICO / 1933; around the circumference, VENCIO IN LA TIERRA•VENCIO EN EL MAR•VENCE EN EL AIRE. At the bottom, a spray of laurel. *Reverse:* A globe with the continents outlined, a small biplane, and an arc representing the route from Spain to Mexico. *Diameter:* 37 mm. G-479.

1970, Fut-bol, Copa Jules Rimet, Brazil, silver.

Obverse: At center, a gilded image of the Jules Rimet Cup with a small futbol to the right and the enameled flags of Mexico and Brazil below. The legend IX CAMPEONATO MUNDIAL DE FUT-BOL and ' COPA JULES RIMET ' surrounds. At the lower left corner of the Mexican flag, designer initials REV. *Reverse:* At center, the enameled flag of Brazil within a stylized wreath of laurel; between the wreath tips, 1958•1962•1970. Around the perimeter, the enameled flags of the 15 other participating nations, with the word CAMPEON above the wreath. *Diameter:* 62 mm. *Other formats:* Enameled silver (MEXICO 0.925 incused in edge). G-1075.

1973, Conmemorativa de la Moneda Mexicana, Busto de 8 Reales, gold.

Obverse: At center, the obverse of a 1772 Charles III 8 reales with bust of the king in profile, in a frosted finish. Around the perimeter, on a mirrored field, ♦ CONMEMORATIVA DE LA MONEDA MEXICANA ♦ and 1772 1821 / BUSTO DE 8 REALES. *Reverse:* At center, the reverse of the 8 reales with crowned coat of arms of Spain between pillars, in a frosted finish. Around the perimeter, on a mirrored field, PRIMUM NUMISMA AMERICÆ and SOCIEDAD NUMISMATICA DE MEXICO. At far left, 1973; at far right, M̊. *Diameter:* 38.5 mm. *Other formats:* Silver. G-UL.

Post-Colonial Medals

Mexico City, Proclamación de la Independencia, 1821. G-5, 34 mm.

Mexico City, Augustín, Emperador de México, 1821. G-7, 57 mm. (shown reduced)

Guadalupe Victoria, Águila de Perfil, 1824. G-70, 40 mm.

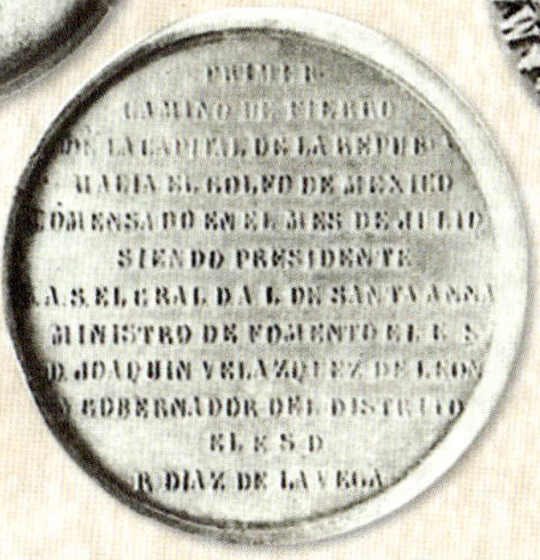

Ferrocarril Hacia el Golfo, 1855. G-97, 46 mm. (shown reduced)

Maximiliano y Carlota (fantasy), no date. G-170, 37 mm.

Post-Colonial Medals

(continued)

Juárez en su Vuelta a San Luis Potosí, 1867. G-180, 47 mm. (shown reduced)

El Gobierno de la Union, 1870. G-S-70, 45 mm.

Statue to Maximilian, 1875. G-149, 71 mm. (shown reduced)

Geronimo Treviño, 1882. G-Pb-86, 26.5 mm.

Guadalupe, Coronata, 1895. G-P-193, 46 mm. (shown reduced)

Coyoacán, Exposición General de Agricultura, 1899. G-E-120, 49 mm. (shown reduced)

Post-Colonial Medals
(continued)

Centenario de la Independencia, Centurion, 1910. G-380, 50 mm. (shown reduced)

Independencia, Díaz y Hidalgo (grande), 1910. G-391, 80 mm. (shown reduced)

VI Centenario de la Fundación de la Ciudad de Mexico, 1925. G-450, 50 mm. (shown reduced)

Vuelo de Barberán y Collar, 1933. G-479, 37 mm.

Fut-bol, Copa Jules Rimet, Brazil, 1970. G-1075, 62 mm. (shown reduced)

Conmemorativa de la Moneda Mexicana, Busto de 8 Reales, 1973. G-UL, 38.5 mm.

25

Orders and Decorations of Mexico

The orders, decorations, and awards of Mexico are included in this book to show the broad scope of Mexican numismatics. Ignacio López Rayón (1773–1832), chief of the Insurgent Revolution (so named by the Junta de Zitácuaro), established the Order of Hidalgo and the Order of Allende, the first military orders of Mexico. The Imperial Order of Guadalupe was established February 20, 1822, by Emperor Agustín de Iturbide. It was restored by Santa Anna on November 11, 1854, and Emperor Maximilian on September 29, 1863. However, it was discontinued after the fall of each ruler. Other well-known orders are the Imperial Order of San Carlos, established by Emperor Maximilian, April 10, 1865; the Imperial Order of the Mexican Eagle, established January 1, 1865, also by Emperor Maximilian; and the Mexican Order of the Aztec Eagle, established December 29, 1933, by the Mexican government.

During the Spanish colonial period many colleges and institutions issued medals and/or cloth "escudos," or "shields" (the cloth escudo was sewn on the left sleeve of the military jacket) for various events. During the War of Independence several decorations, medals, and cloth escudos were issued for engagements at various cities and locations. All are very scarce.

After the War of Independence there were several conflicts, local disputes, Indian uprisings, and other events for which decorations or medals were awarded. During the Mexican War (La Invasion Norteamerica), several decorations and a few cloth escudos were issued. Like the Spanish colonial issues, they are scarce and difficult to find. In 1848 the United States Mint issued medals to commemorate Generals Zachary Taylor and Winfield Scott. The National Association of Veterans of the Mexican War (NAVMW) issued shields and table medals to their members at conventions. The U.S. federal government never awarded medals to any Mexican War veterans except to Generals Scott and Taylor. New York and South Carolina awarded medals to the Mexican War veterans who served from those states. The last meeting of the NAVMW was held in 1910 in Indianapolis.

The French intervention of 1862–1867 produced several orders and decorations issued by both the Republic and the Imperial sides in the conflict. Few medals or decorations were issued during the Mexican Revolution of 1910–1920, although several decorations were issued for members of the Veteranos de la Revolución. The 1914 Veracrúz, Segunda Invasión Norteamericana created a few more decorations and table medals from both the Mexican and the U.S. sides.

Note: Table medals are not worn, but displayed.

Orders and Decorations of Mexico

Imperial Order of the Mexican Eagle, Commander Neck Badge, Grove-O-32 46 x 40 mm (shown reduced).

Imperial Order of the Mexican Eagle, Breast Star, G-O-31, 95 mm (shown reduced).

Imperial Order of Guadalupe, Commander Neck Badge, G-O-25, 38 x 70 mm (shown reduced).

Imperial Order of Guadalupe, Breast Star, G-O-18, 82 mm (shown reduced).

Imperial Order of Guadalupe, gold Officer's Badge, G-O-26, 40 x 37 mm (shown reduced).

Imperial Order of Guadalupe, Grand Cross Sash with badge, G-O-19. Badge 38 x 70 mm (shown reduced).

Orders and Decorations of Mexico

(continued)

Maximilian Silver Civil Merit Medal, G-D-252a, 33 mm (shown reduced).

Imperial Order of San Carlos. Established by decree of April 10, 1865, as an award for ladies' charitable acts or merit. First Class. G-O-36, 66 x 50 mm (shown reduced).

Mexican Order of the Aztec Eagle. Established in 1933 as an award to distinguished foreigners. Grand Cross set. G-O-41 and 42, sash badge 63 mm, breast star 63 mm (shown reduced).

The goal of the 1916 Pershing Expedition into Mexico was to capture Pancho Villa, who invaded the United States with a raid on Columbus, N.M. National Guard troops from many states and cities across the the United States participated in the expedition. Most of these entities issued medals.

French Medal for Mexico. Awarded to the French Forces who fought with Maximilian. G-D-290a and G-D-290a (miniature), 31 mm and 11 mm, respectively (shown reduced).

Cross of Loyalty Carranza, awarded to troops that accompanied Carranza when he fled Mexico City in May 1920. G-D-430, 46 x 43 mm (shown reduced).

Veteran of the Revolution Badge, 1910–1914. G-D-361, 68 mm (shown reduced).

Orders and Decorations of Mexico

(continued)

Revolutionary Cross of Merit, 1st Period, awarded to those who fought against the Diaz government, November 19, 1910–May 15, 1911. G-D-356, badge 50 mm (shown reduced).

Revolutionary Cross of Merit, 2nd Period, awarded to those who fought against the Huerta government, February 20, 1913–August 15, 1914. G-D-357, 50 mm (shown reduced).

Veterano De La Revolution (Cross for the Veterans of the Revolution), 1910–1914. G-D-361, 41 mm (shown reduced).

26

Bullion Values of Gold and Silver Coins

The following charts show the value of silver and gold Mexican coins, based purely on their precious-metal content; their values as collectibles are *not* included in the figures here. Although the charts capture significant changes in coin specifications, they do not account for slight variations in the fineness and weight of coins in the colonial era.

SILVER COINS

	Fineness	Oz. Silver	Current Bullion Value						
			$17	$18	$19	$20	$21	$22	$23
Milled Coinage, Pillar Style									
1/2 R	0.917	0.0498	$0.85	$0.90	$0.95	$1.00	$1.05	$1.10	$1.15
1 R	0.917	0.9960	16.93	17.93	18.92	19.92	20.92	21.91	22.91
2 R	0.917	0.1995	3.39	3.59	3.79	3.99	4.19	4.39	4.59
4 R	0.917	0.3992	6.79	7.19	7.58	7.98	8.38	8.78	9.18
8 R	0.917	0.7980	13.57	14.36	15.16	15.96	16.76	17.56	18.35
Milled Coinage, Portrait Style									
1/4 R	0.896	0.0244	0.41	0.44	0.46	0.49	0.51	0.54	0.56
1/2 R	0.903	0.0491	0.83	0.88	0.93	0.98	1.03	1.08	1.13
1 R	0.903	0.0982	1.67	1.77	1.87	1.96	2.06	2.16	2.26
2 R	0.903	0.1965	3.34	3.54	3.73	3.93	4.13	4.32	4.52
4 R	0.903	0.3931	6.68	7.08	7.47	7.86	8.26	8.65	9.04
8 R	0.903	0.7858	13.36	14.14	14.93	15.72	16.50	17.29	18.07
Iturbide Coinage									
1/2 R	0.903	0.0490	0.83	0.88	0.93	0.98	1.03	1.08	1.13
1 R	0.903	0.0981	1.67	1.77	1.86	1.96	2.06	2.16	2.26
2 R	0.903	0.1964	3.34	3.54	3.73	3.93	4.12	4.32	4.52
8 R	0.903	0.7858	13.36	14.14	14.93	15.72	16.50	17.29	18.07

	Fineness	Oz. Silver	Current Bullion Value						
			$17	$18	$19	$20	$21	$22	$23
Republic Reales Coinage									
1/4 R	0.903	0.0245	$0.42	$0.44	$0.47	$0.49	$0.51	$0.54	$0.56
1/2 R	0.903	0.0491	0.83	0.88	0.93	0.98	1.03	1.08	1.13
1 R	0.903	0.0981	1.67	1.77	1.86	1.96	2.06	2.16	2.26
2 R	0.903	0.1962	3.34	3.53	3.73	3.92	4.12	4.32	4.51
4 R	0.903	0.3925	6.67	7.07	7.46	7.85	8.24	8.64	9.03
8 R	0.903	0.7859	13.36	14.15	14.93	15.72	16.50	17.29	18.08
Maximillian Coinage									
5¢	0.903	0.0393	0.67	0.71	0.75	0.79	0.83	0.86	0.90
10¢	0.903	0.0786	1.34	1.41	1.49	1.57	1.65	1.73	1.81
50¢	0.903	0.3930	6.68	7.07	7.47	7.86	8.25	8.65	9.04
$1	0.903	0.7859	13.36	14.15	14.93	15.72	16.50	17.29	18.08
Republic Decimal Coinage									
5¢	0.903	0.0392	0.67	0.71	0.74	0.78	0.82	0.86	0.90
5¢, restyled	0.903	0.0392	0.67	0.71	0.74	0.78	0.82	0.86	0.90
10¢	0.903	0.0785	1.33	1.41	1.49	1.57	1.65	1.73	1.81
10¢, restyled	0.903	0.0785	1.33	1.41	1.49	1.57	1.65	1.73	1.81
20¢	0.903	0.1572	2.67	2.83	2.99	3.14	3.30	3.46	3.62
25¢	0.903	0.1965	3.34	3.54	3.73	3.93	4.13	4.32	4.52
50¢	0.903	0.3930	6.68	7.07	7.47	7.86	8.25	8.65	9.04
$1, Balance Scale	0.903	0.7860	13.36	14.15	14.93	15.72	16.51	17.29	18.08
$1, Liberty Cap	0.903	0.7860	13.36	14.15	14.93	15.72	16.51	17.29	18.08
1905 Coinage Reform									
10¢, .800 (T1)	0.800	0.0643	1.09	1.16	1.22	1.29	1.35	1.41	1.48
10¢, Little .800 (T2)	0.800	0.0466	0.79	0.84	0.89	0.93	0.98	1.03	1.07
10¢, .720 (T4)	0.720	0.0386	0.66	0.69	0.73	0.77	0.81	0.85	0.89
20¢, .800 (T1)	0.800	0.1286	2.19	2.31	2.44	2.57	2.70	2.83	2.96
20¢, Little .800 (T2)	0.800	0.0907	1.54	1.63	1.72	1.81	1.90	2.00	2.09
20¢, .720 (T4)	0.720	0.0772	1.31	1.39	1.47	1.54	1.62	1.70	1.78
25¢, Scales (T1)	0.300	0.0321	0.55	0.58	0.61	0.64	0.67	0.71	0.74

	Fineness	Oz. Silver	Current Bullion Value						
			$17	$18	$19	$20	$21	$22	$23
1905 Coinage Reform ***(continued)***									
50¢, .800 (T1)	0.800	0.3215	$5.47	$5.79	$6.11	$6.43	$6.75	$7.07	$7.39
50¢, Reduced .800 (T2)	0.800	0.2330	3.96	4.19	4.43	4.66	4.89	5.13	5.36
50¢, .720 (T3)	0.720	0.1928	3.28	3.47	3.66	3.86	4.05	4.24	4.43
50¢, .420 (T4)	0.420	0.1077	1.83	1.94	2.05	2.15	2.26	2.37	2.48
50¢, Cuauhtémoc (T5)	0.300	0.0643	1.09	1.16	1.22	1.29	1.35	1.41	1.48
$1, Caballito (T1)	0.903	0.7859	13.36	14.15	14.93	15.72	16.50	17.29	18.08
$1, .800 (T2)	0.800	0.4662	7.93	8.39	8.86	9.32	9.79	10.26	10.72
$1, .720 (T3)	0.720	0.3857	6.56	6.94	7.33	7.71	8.10	8.49	8.87
$1, Little Morelos (T4)	0.500	0.2251	3.83	4.05	4.28	4.50	4.73	4.95	5.18
$1, General Morelos (T5)	0.300	0.1286	2.19	2.31	2.44	2.57	2.70	2.83	2.96
$1, Constitution (T6)	0.100	0.0514	0.87	0.93	0.98	1.03	1.08	1.13	1.18
$1, .100 (T7)	0.100	0.0514	0.87	0.93	0.98	1.03	1.08	1.13	1.18
$2, Victoria (T1)	0.900	0.7716	13.12	13.89	14.66	15.43	16.20	16.98	17.75
$5, Cuauhtémoc (T1)	0.900	0.8681	14.76	15.63	16.49	17.36	18.23	19.10	19.97
$5, Railroad (T2)	0.720	0.6430	10.93	11.57	12.22	12.86	13.50	14.15	14.79
$5, Hidalgo (T3)	0.720	0.6430	10.93	11.57	12.22	12.86	13.50	14.15	14.79
$5, Hidalgo/ Wreath (T4)	0.720	0.6430	10.93	11.57	12.22	12.86	13.50	14.15	14.79
$5, Hidalgo/ Chico (T5)	0.720	0.4179	7.10	7.52	7.94	8.36	8.78	9.19	9.61
$5, Constitution (T6)	0.720	0.4178	7.10	7.52	7.94	8.36	8.77	9.19	9.61
$5, Carranza (T7)	0.720	0.4179	7.10	7.52	7.94	8.36	8.78	9.19	9.61
$10, Hidalgo Grande (T1)	0.900	0.8359	14.21	15.05	15.88	16.72	17.55	18.39	19.23
$10, Constitution (T2)	0.900	0.8359	14.21	15.05	15.88	16.72	17.55	18.39	19.23

	Fineness	Oz. Silver	Current Bullion Value						
			$17	$18	$19	$20	$21	$22	$23
1905 Coinage Reform *(continued)*									
$10, Hidalgo/ Madero (T3)	0.900	0.8359	14.21	15.05	15.88	16.72	17.55	18.39	19.23
$25, Olympics (T1)	0.720	0.5093	8.66	9.17	9.68	10.19	10.70	11.20	11.71
$25, Juårez (T2)	0.720	0.5093	8.66	9.17	9.68	10.19	10.70	11.20	11.71
$100, Morelos	0.720	0.6428	10.93	11.57	12.21	12.86	13.50	14.14	14.78
Una Onza	0.925	1.0000	17.00	18.00	19.00	20.00	21.00	22.00	23.00
1992 Coinage Reform									
N$10, silver center (T-A1)	0.925	0.1667	2.83	3.00	3.17	3.33	3.50	3.67	3.83
N$20, silver center (T-A1)	0.925	0.2500	4.25	4.50	4.75	5.00	5.25	5.50	5.75
N$50, silver center (T-A1)	0.925	0.5000	8.50	9.00	9.50	10.00	10.50	11.00	11.50

GOLD COINS

	Fineness	Oz. Gold	Current Bullion Value						
			$1,100	$1,200	$1,300	$1,400	$1,500	$1,600	$1,700
Milled Coinage, Portrait Style									
1/2 E	0.875	0.0476	$52.36	$57.12	$61.88	$66.64	$71.40	$76.16	$80.92
1 E	0.875	0.0951	104.61	114.12	123.63	133.14	142.65	152.16	161.67
1 E	0.905	0.0984	108.24	118.08	127.92	137.76	147.60	157.44	167.28
1 E	0.917	0.0998	109.78	119.76	129.74	139.72	149.70	159.68	169.66
2 E	0.875	0.1903	209.33	228.36	247.39	266.42	285.45	304.48	323.51
2 E	0.917	0.1995	219.45	239.40	259.35	279.30	299.25	319.20	339.15
4 E	0.875	0.3807	418.77	456.84	494.91	532.98	571.05	609.12	647.19
4 E	0.905	0.3938	433.18	472.56	511.94	551.32	590.70	630.08	669.46
4 E	0.917	0.3990	438.90	478.80	518.70	558.60	598.50	638.40	678.30
8 E	0.875	0.7615	837.65	913.80	989.95	1,066.10	1,142.25	1,218.40	1,294.55
8 E	0.905	0.7876	866.36	945.12	1,023.88	1,102.64	1,181.40	1,260.16	1,338.92
8 E	0.917	0.7980	877.80	957.60	1,037.40	1,117.20	1,197.00	1,276.80	1,356.60

	Fineness	Oz. Gold	Current Bullion Value						
			$1,100	**$1,200**	**$1,300**	**$1,400**	**$1,500**	**$1,600**	**$1,700**
Iturbide Coinage									
4 E	0.875	0.3808	$418.88	$456.96	$495.04	$533.12	$571.20	$609.28	$647.36
8 E	0.875	0.7616	837.76	913.92	990.08	1,066.24	1,142.40	1,218.56	1,294.72
Republic Escudos Coinage									
1/2 E	0.875	0.0475	52.25	57.00	61.75	66.50	71.25	76.00	80.75
1 E	0.875	0.0951	104.61	114.12	123.63	133.14	142.65	152.16	161.67
2 E	0.875	0.1905	209.55	228.60	247.65	266.70	285.75	304.80	323.85
4 E	0.875	0.3809	418.99	457.08	495.17	533.26	571.35	609.44	647.53
8 E	0.875	0.7615	837.65	913.80	989.95	1,066.10	1,142.25	1,218.40	1,294.55
Maximillian Coinage									
$20	0.875	0.9520	1,047.20	1,142.40	1,237.60	1,332.80	1,428.00	1,523.20	1,618.40
Republic Decimal Coinage									
$1	0.875	0.0476	52.36	57.12	61.88	66.64	71.40	76.16	80.92
$2.50	0.875	0.1190	130.90	142.80	154.70	166.60	178.50	190.40	202.30
$5	0.875	0.2380	261.80	285.60	309.40	333.20	357.00	380.80	404.60
$10	0.875	0.4760	523.60	571.20	618.80	666.40	714.00	761.60	809.20
$20	0.875	0.9520	1,047.20	1,142.40	1,237.60	1,332.80	1,428.00	1,523.20	1,618.40
1905 Coinage Reform									
$2	0.900	0.0482	53.02	57.84	62.66	67.48	72.30	77.12	81.94
$2.50	0.900	0.0603	66.33	72.36	78.39	84.42	90.45	96.48	102.51
$5	0.900	0.1206	132.66	144.72	156.78	168.84	180.90	192.96	205.02
$10	0.900	0.2411	265.21	289.32	313.43	337.54	361.65	385.76	409.87
$20	0.900	0.4822	530.42	578.64	626.86	675.08	723.30	771.52	819.74
$50	0.900	1.2057	1,326.27	1,446.84	1,567.41	1,687.98	1,808.55	1,929.12	2,049.69

27

Paper Money of Mexico

Space does not allow us extensive coverage of the complex history of paper money in Mexico. Instead, this chapter will sketch a brief history of the four periods in which it is grouped by collectors—pre-Revolutionary, Revolutionary, post-Revolutionary, and Banco de México—and provide illustrations that suggest the broad range designs. To explore the subject in detail, the reader is referred to the major works in the field, as follows.

Many of the publications that study early Mexican paper money are out of print and can be difficult to find. Carlos Gaytan's 1965 *Billetes de Mexico* served as a foundation for most of these, including multiple works by Gaytan; *The Standard Catalog of Mexican Coins, Paper Money, and Medals*, by George W. Vogt (1978); and *Historia del Papel Moneda en México*, by José Antonio Batiz Vazquez (1984).

One very important resource for more than 25 years was *The Complete Encyclopedia of Mexican Paper Money*, by Duane Douglas, Claudio Verrery, and Alberto Hidalgo (1982). When published, this was the most comprehensive reference available, covering the complete history of paper money. It was replaced by *Mexican Paper Money 2010*—a thorough revision of the *Complete Encyclopedia*, by Cory Frampton, Duane Douglas, Alberto Hidalgo, and Elmer Powell. The "M" numbers for notes illustrated in this chapter are from the system in these two works.

For more on the paper money issued by the Banco de México since its founding in 1925, including series, sub-series, proofs, and specimens, see Duane Douglas's *Paper Money of Mexico* (3rd ed., 2002); and *The Mexican Bank Note* (1999), published by the Banco de México.

Banking in Mexico was first established during the Spanish colonial period with the Banco de Avio de Minas and, later, the Banco de Avio, but neither bank issued paper money. During the War of Independence, those who did not flee New Spain with their fortunes chose to hide their gold and silver for safekeeping. Warfare and looting disrupted production at the mines, and precious-metal coinage became increasingly hard to come by. As discussed in chapter 6, both the Royalists and the Insurgents decided to produce their own coinage. It was during this time that three different styles of a *medio* (half-real) note, printed in black on cardboard, emerged in San Miguel el Grande, Guanajuato. Only one of each style is known to exist; each is dated July or August 1813, and each is hand-signed. It is unknown whether the signatures belonged to military officers, merchants, or officials—what is known is that these three small notes are the earliest available examples of paper money in Mexico.

The first *official* issuance of paper money in Mexico took place during the reign of Agustín de Iturbide, who headed country that was in grave economic trouble. Having failed at turning the economy around by other means, Iturbide resorted to issuing paper currency. His decree of December 20, 1822, authorized 1-, 2-, and 10-peso notes, acceptance of which was required by law. The public disliked the idea of paper money, which had no intrinsic value, especially when it was being forced upon them, and the notes were demonetized immediately after Iturbide stepped down.

The ongoing financial hardships of the new Federal Republic required officials to give paper money another try. The new notes were printed on the backs of canceled Papal bulls of indulgence, in the hope that this would give the notes legitimacy by association (and that it would deter counterfeiting). Even that was not enough to gain the public's faith, and the notes soon had to be withdrawn.

Decades passed before paper money was attempted again, this time 1864, during the French Intervention. The first issuer was the Banco de Londres y América del Sur (Bank of London and South America). The fact that a tangible, profitable institution was accountable for the value of the paper, and that acceptance of the notes was purely voluntary, made the new currency much more acceptable to the public. Following the example of the Banco de Londres, other banking facilities began to appear within Mexico, and other kinds of financial instruments, like public bonds certificates of deposit, began to emerge. Soon, notes were being issued not only by banks but by municipalities, merchants, and others. In addition to denominations in centavos, pesos, and in some places reales, notes were issued in novel values like 1 real *de carne* (in meat); 4 reales *de mercancias* (in merchandise); 1,000 grams of gold; and dual denominations, like 12-1/2 centavos and 1 real; 25 centavos and 2 reales; and 50 centavos and 4 reales.

During the rule of Porfirio Díaz, the banking system became stronger and more organized, and in 1897 the Law of Credit Institutions required each state to have at least one private bank that issued notes (in addition to the Banco Nacional de México). Backed by the value of precious metal, the notes were issued in denominations from 1 to 1,000 pesos.

The political, economic, and military upheavals of the Mexican Revolution, which began on November 20, 1910, led once again to the hoarding of coins; and as the banking system fell apart, the value of banknotes disintegrated.

The first paper money of the Revolution was issued on April 26, 1913, in Piedras Negras, Coahuila, but confusion and distrust were the result. Although the banks agreed at first to issue currency to wage the war, once the Revolutionary forces occupied their regions, they closed their branches and refused to honor the notes. Venustiano Carranza issued several decrees stating that banks in the areas under his control were required to remain open. When the banks refused, Carranza ordered that they be taken over. Problems continued until the September 24, 1913, banking reform, when President Carranza decreed that the exclusive right to issue currency rested solely with the Constitutional Government, and that, when the Revolution was over, a single state bank of issue would be established. Any bank or issuer of currency not controlled by the government would be terminated.

On February 5, 1917, the Constitutional Congress ratified a new constitution in Querétaro. Article 28 of the constitution dictated that, as soon as the required metallic reserve was met, the Banco de México would be authorized as the only paper-money-issuing bank in the country. Economic and political conditions within Mexico were such that the requirements were not met until August 28, 1925, when the bank was finally established with one billion pesos and backed by a like amount in gold. President Plutarco Elías Calles authorized official operations on September 1, 1925, and the notes issued that day were printed by the American Bank Note Company.

The Banco de México notes replaced all other state and local issues; and since 1925, it has been the central bank and the only bank of issue. Its purposes are to issue currency, regulate monetary circulation within Mexico, to establish interest rates, and to regulate foreign exchange. To date, it has had seven issues of currency. In 2001 the bank issued its first polymer (plastic) note, in the 20 pesos denomination.

Paper Money of Mexico
Pre-Revolutionary

Chihuahua, El Banco Minero, 20 pesos, 1914. BW-1-CHI-20 P, BK-CHI-100, M-135c. 184 x 82 mm. (shown reduced)

Chiapas, Banco de Chiapas, 20 pesos, Specimen. BW-1-CHP-20 Ps, BK-CHIP-5, M-67s. 184 x 82 mm. (shown reduced)

Paper Money of Mexico

Pre-Revolutionary

(continued)

Distrito Federal, El Banco de Londres y México, 1,000 pesos. BW-1-DF-1000 P, BK-DF-122, M-277a. 184 x 82mm. (shown reduced)

Revolutionary

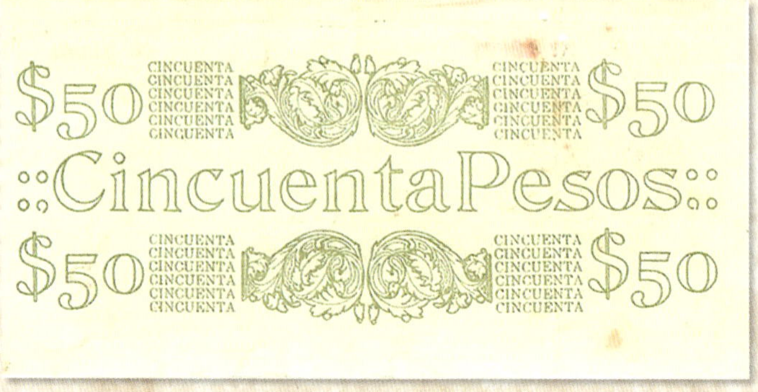

Chihuahua, Tesorería General del Estado, 50 pesos, 1913. BW-2-CHI-50 P, MI-CHI-29, M-909a. 123 x 61 mm.

Paper Money of Mexico
Revolutionary
(continued)

Distrito Federal, Gobierno Constitcionalista, 100 pesos, 1915, Specimen. BW-2-DF-100 Ps, SI-DF9.3, M-1260s. 178 x 86 mm. (shown reduced)

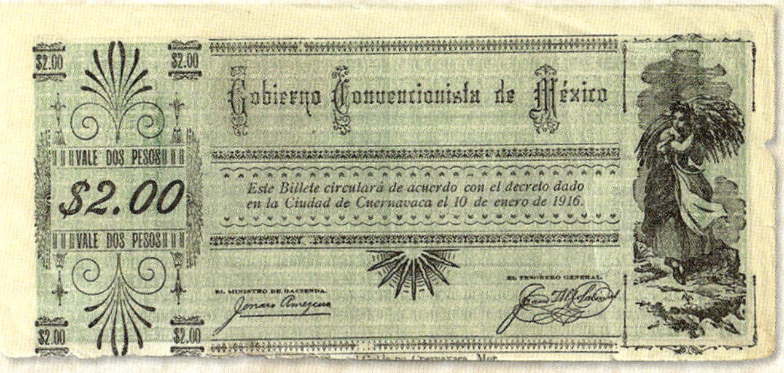

Morelos, Gobierno Convencionista de México, 2 pesos, 1916. BW-2-MOR-2 P, SI-MOR-15, M-3201. 193 x 87 mm. (shown reduced)

Paper Money of Mexico

Post-Revolutionary

Distrito Federal, 1 peso, 1920. BW-3-DF-1 P, PT-DF-2, M-4285. 133 x 62 mm. (shown reduced)

Jalisco, 10 pesos, no date [1926 and 1927]. BW-3-JAL-10 P, PT-JAL-29, M-4354. 156 x 70 mm. (shown reduced)

Paper Money of Mexico
Post-Revolutionary
(continued)

Jalisco, 50 pesos, 1927. BW-3-JAL-50 P, PT-JAL-38, M-4365. 150 x 88 mm. (shown reduced)

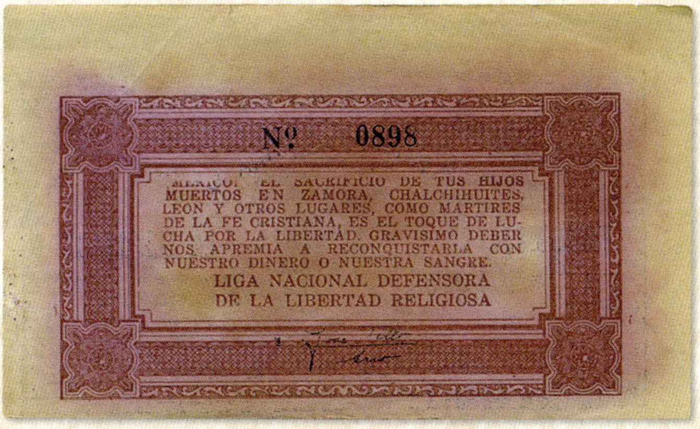

Paper Money of Mexico

Banco de México

20 nuevo pesos, 1992. BW-4-MEX-20 P, BKM-1992. 129 x 66 mm. (shown reduced)

20 pesos, 2001. Polymer composition. BW-4-MEX-20 P, BKM-2001. 129 x 66 mm. (shown reduced)

Paper Money of Mexico

Banco de México

(continued)

**50,000 pesos, 1990.
BW-4-MEX-50000 P,
BKM-UL. 156 x 68 mm.
(shown reduced)**

**200 pesos, 2010.
BW-4-MEX-200 P, BKM-2010.
70.5 x 141 mm. (shown reduced)**

GLOSSARY

alloy—A combination of two or more metals.

annulet—Literally, "little circle"; a decoration that resembles a small ring. On colonial coinage, a small ring with a dot in the center.

armored—Describes a portrait in which the subject wears armor, to indicate military strength.

assayer—One who analyzes and certifies metallic composition.

assayer mark—The initials or other mark of an assayer, placed on a coin to guarantee its metallic composition.

Balance Scale design—A coinage motif consisting of a small radiant liberty cap above a crossed sword and balance scale; between the pans of the scale is a scroll bearing the word LEY (law). Commonly used on Republic decimal coinage.

bas relief—A type of sculpture in which the design is raised above, but still attached to, the field behind it. Commonly found on architecture and sometimes seen on medallic art.

blank—A disc of metal before it is impressed with the design of a coin or medal.

bolo (Spanish)—A christening medal; common during the 19th and early 20th centuries in Mexico.

bullion—Pure, unalloyed metal in bulk form (bars, ingots, etc.).

bullion coinage—Coins struck from pure or nearly pure metal, for sale to collectors and investors at a premium above their metal value.

bust—A term that loosely describes a portrait that is smaller than half-length (i.e., from the chest up). Generally assumes that at least part of one shoulder is included, but some numismatists apply the term to portraits that end at the neck.

Bust coinage—See "Portrait coinage."

BW-number—Bailey-Whitman number (from the *Whitman Encyclopedia of Mexican Money*, by D. and L. Bailey).

cabo de barra (Spanish)—literally, "the end of the bar." In the cob-coinage era, planchets were clipped from the end of a bar of refined gold or silver, then weighed and, if necessary, filed or clipped to bring them to the proper weight before striking.

cacahoat (Nahuatl)—Cacao beans, a medium of exchange in the Anáhuac era.

cacahuapinol (Nahuatl)—Flour made of corn and cacao used as a medium of exchange in the Anáhuac era.

canutillos (Spanish)—The hollow quills of large feathers, filled with gold dust and sealed at each end; used as a medium of exchange in the Anáhuac era.

Casa Moneda de México—The official mint of Mexico.

cast coinage—Coins made by the pouring of liquid metal into a mold made from an original coin; usually cruder in appearance than struck coinage.

centavo—The smallest fraction of a peso; 1 peso equals 100 centavos.

chiampinoli—A kind of plant meal used as a medium of exchange in the Anáhuac era.

cob—An early type of coin, struck with a hammer; in Mexico, cobs were issued from about 1580 to 1732. As no restraining collar was used, the planchets spread into irregular shapes when struck.

collar—An outer ring that confines a blank or planchet, such that it does not spread as it is struck by the coin press. The collar can have a design or lettering that is impressed into the edge of the coin.

commemorative coin—A legal-tender coin struck to honor or celebrate an event, a person, or an idea. A commemorative coin can be circulating or non-circulating legal tender; the latter are sold at a premium above their face value.

coppers—Early copper coins of low face value.

counterstamp—A mark struck onto the obverse or reverse of an existing coin to "claim" it for use by a different government, or to change its value.

cud—A raised portion of metal at the edge of a coin where the edge of its die was broken; when the coin was struck, the metal flowed into the broken area.

cuartilla (Spanish)—Silver quarter-real.

cuentas (Spanish)—Jade beads used as a medium of exchange in the Anáhuac era.

currency—The system of money in general use in a given country. In numismatics, *currency* often refers to paper money.

decimal coinage—A coinage system whose base unit is divided into sub-units of 10, 100, or 1,000.

die—The piece of metal that imparts the design to the planchet when it is struck. Both the design and the relief are reversed, because they will be transferred in mirror image to the coin.

diesinker—One who engraves coinage dies.

die variety—A minor alteration of a coin's basic design.

dineros—A medieval measurement of fineness, in which pure silver was designated 12 *dineros*. One dinero equals 24 *granos*.

dot—A coin ornament consisting of a small, filled circle. It may be used as punctuation or simply as a word or line divider.

doubled die—A coinage die that has received two misaligned impressions, which are passed on to the coins struck from that die. Also refers to the resulting coins.

draped—Describes a portrait in which the subject is draped in a loose, flowing garment, reminiscent of ancient gods or rulers.

edge—The "third side" of the coin, often impressed with lettering or ornaments.

effigy—In numismatics, a depiction of a specific person on a coin.

error—A malformed or other incorrectly made coin caused by a mistake during the cutting or striking of the blank.

escudo—The base unit of Mexican pre-decimal gold coinage; 1 gold escudo equaled 16 silver reales.

essay (French *essai*)—Any coin that is struck with official mint dies but is not a regular issue.

exergue—The portion of a coin beneath the main design, often separated from the design by a line. Often used for the date or the engraver's name.

experimental strike—A sample strike performed by the mint to test a possible change in planchet diameter, format, shape, thickness, etc.

fantasy coin—A coin struck with official mint equipment and facilities, but without the mint's authorization, for the purpose of financial or other reward.

field—The plain background against which a coin's design is visible.

fineness—The purity of the precious metal in a coin. Expressed in thousandths: e.g., 99% or .990.

flan—A blank or planchet.

GB-number—Guthrie-Bothamley number (from *Mexican Revolutionary Coinage, 1913–1917*, by H. Guthrie and M. Bothamley).

G-number—Grove number (from the numerous titles by F.W. Grove).

gramos (Spanish)—Grams.

granos (Spanish)—Grains. In the medieval system of describing fineness, 24 *granos* equaled 1 *dinero;* pure silver was graded 12 *dineros.*

hammered coinage—Coins made by striking the planchet between the two dies with a large hammer.

Hand on Book design—Suspended over an open book, a hand holding a staff with a liberty cap on the point; the book is usually inscribed LA LIBERTAD EN LA LEY. The design was prominently used on gold escudos of the Republic.

hoe money—A flat, one-piece metal blade used as a medium of exchange in the Anáhuac era. Also called "Aztec hoe money," "ax money," or *tajaderas* (Spanish for "chopping knives").

Hookneck Eagle design—See Profile Eagle design.

incuse—Describes a design that is pressed into the surface of the coin, as opposed to raised above it (i.e., in relief).

jolas—Half-real coins issued under Spanish rule in San Fernando de Bexar (now San Antonio, Texas) in 1818.

jugate (Latin)—Paired; in numismatics, two portraits paired on one side of a coin, often in profile with one partially superimposed over the other.

KM-number—Krause-Mishler number (from the *Standard Catalogue of World Coins*, by C. Krause and C. Mishler).

laureate (Latin)—Laureled; a portrait in which the head wears a laurel wreath, indicating the subject is victorious.

legal tender—The official money of a government or authorizing body.

legend—An inscription on a coin.

lettered edge—An edge design in words, rather than the usual reeding or other ornament.

Libertad—The name given to the standard Mexican bullion series authorized in the late 20th century; also, any coin of that series.

liberty cap—In ancient Rome, the brimless cap, or *pileus*, worn by emancipated slaves. Widely adopted as a symbol of freedom; often inscribed with the word "Liberty" (in Spanish, "Libertad").

Liberty Cap design—A coin design consisting solely of a liberty cap, usually surrounded by radiance. Does not apply to designs that incorporate a liberty cap is into a complex motif (e.g., the Hand on Book design). Used prominently on silver reales coinage of the Republic.

lozenge—A coinage ornament resembling a diamond shape.

mailed—Describes a portrait in which the subject wears mail (chain armor) to indicate military strength.

maravedi—A small denomination during the era of Carlos and Johanna; coins were struck in 2 and 4 maravedies.

mascle—A coinage ornament consisting of a lozenge with a smaller diamond shape in the center.

medio (Spanish)—Half; a half-real coin.

milled coinage—In general, any coinage that is struck by machine instead of by hand; in particular, the screw-press coinage issued from 1732 through 1821, supplanting cob (stamped) coinage.

mintmark—A symbol on a coin indicating the mint at which it was struck.

mule—A coin struck from two dies that were not originally meant to be paired.

non-circulating legal tender (NCLT)—A coin that is legally valid for commercial use but is not intended for that purpose and is never or almost never seen in circulation. Proof and commemorative coins, for example, are NCLT coinage; they are struck with extra care and are sold to the public at a premium above their face value.

norte (Spanish)—North.

nuevo peso—New peso, a transitional denomination devised in 1992; the decimal point in the value was moved three places to the left of its former location, and the new denomination was indicated with an N before the peso symbol (e.g., N$5).

OAX-number—Reference number from *La Venta Oaxaca*, by C. Woodworth.

obverse—The front, or "heads," side of the coin. In Mexican numismatics, the obverse typically (but not always) is the side bearing the coat of arms.

octavo—A 1/8-real coin.

off metal—A strike on a metal other than the one intended for circulation.

onza (Spanish)—Ounce. See also the Mexican bullion coin called "Una Onza."

oro (Spanish)—Gold.

overdate—A die on which some or all of the numerals in the date are superimposed over older ones. Also, a coin struck from such a die.

overstrike—An impression struck on an already-struck coin, but with a different die.

patolquechtli—Pieces of cotton fabric used as a medium of exchange in the Anáhuac era.

pattern—A coinage sample, officially sanctioned but not for circulation, created to test a new or revised design, denomination, or metal.

peso—The base unit of Mexican decimal coinage.

piece of eight—A Spanish milled 8-real coin.

Pillar coinage—Spanish-colonial coins issued in Mexico from 1732 through 1771, bearing on their obverse the Spanish coat of arms flanked by two columns or pillars.

pilón—A small copper coin of Ferdinand VII, with the value of 1/16 real.

planchet—A disc of metal intended to be struck with a coin design.

plata (Spanish)—Silver.

platino (Spanish)—Platinum.

Plus Ultra (Latin)—A popular colonial-era coin inscription meaning "farther beyond," or, more loosely, "there are lands farther beyond these." Often depicted as "PLVS VLTRA," as in Latin inscriptions.

pomegranate—An ornament commonly found on Spanish-colonial coins. In Christian symbolism, the fruit represents many things, including fertility, the suffering and resurrection of Jesus, and the bringing together of many individuals in one church.

Portrait coinage—Spanish-colonial coins issued in Mexico from 1772 through 1821, bearing on their obverse a portrait of the issuing king. Also called "Bust coinage."

Profile Eagle design—The design of the first reales coinage of the Republic, issued from 1823 to 1825. In the national coat of arms on the obverse, the eagle faces to the left, in profile, with its neck bent forward and its wings raised above its back; often called the "Hookneck Eagle" due to the pronounced curve of the eagle's neck.

Proof—Coins struck with special care for sale to collectors at a premium above their face value.

pura (Spanish)—Pure.

quatrefoil—A coinage ornament resembling a four-petaled flower.

real—The base unit of Mexican pre-decimal silver coinage.

relief—The portion of a coin's design that is raised above the surface.

reverse—The back, or "tails," side of a coin. In Mexican numismatics, the reverse typically (but not always) holds the date, mintmark, and value.

rim—The raised portion around the perimeter of a coin's obverse or reverse, which protects the design from wear.

rondule—A coin ornament that resembles a small ring with an empty center.

royal strikes—Perfectly round cob coins with unusually sharp strikes. They may have been intended as proof of workmanship for the king.

screw press—An early pressing machine of simple design, in which the upper plate is driven toward the lower plate by means of a large, perpendicular screw.

seigniorage—The difference between a coin's production cost and its face value.

señal—A small copper coin of Ferdinand VII, with the value of 1/4 real.

tajadera—See "hoe money."

Texas *jolas*—Half-real coins issued under Spanish rule in San Fernando de Bexar (now San Antonio, Texas) in 1818.

tlaco—A small copper coin of Ferdinand VII, with the value of 1/8 real.

token—A privately issued coin-like object used in trade; not an official government issue.

truncation—The sharply cut-off edge at the bottom of a bust or portrait.

sud (Spanish)—South.

Una Onza—The Mexican silver one-ounce bullion series issued in 1949, 1978–1980, and 1989.

Upright Eagle design—The style of the national coat of arms on most of the Republic real and escudo coinage, save for a brief time during which the Profile Eagle was used. The Upright Eagle stands with head up and turned to the right, its breast facing forward and its wings spread open to the sides.

vellón (Spanish)—A system of small-value coins created to facilitate business transactions and record-keeping.

VRW-number—Verne R. Walrafen number (from "Chihuahua 5 and 10 Centavos," by V.R. Walrafen).

Bibliography

Amaya Guerra, Carlos Abel. *Illustrated Price Guide of the Modern Mexican Coins, 1905 to Date, Including Errors and Varieties.* Mexico City: Author, 2008.

Bailey, Don. "The Numismatics of Spanish Colonial Mexico." *Coin World*, November 1987.

Bailey, Don. *State and Federal Copper and Brass Coinage of Mexico, 1824–1872.* Hemet, Calif.: Don Bailey Institute for Mexican Numismatic and Historical Research, 2008.

Beals, Gary. *Numismatic Terms of Spain and Spanish America.* Author, 1966.

Buttrey, T.V. "Central America Under the Mexican Empire, 1822–1823." *American Numismatic Association Museum Notes*, vol. 13, pp. 231–250, 1967.

Buttrey, T.V., and Clyde Hubbard. *A Guide Book of Mexican Coins 1822 to Date* (6th ed.). Iola, Wisc.: Krause, 1992.

Diccionario Porrúa de Historia, Biografía, y Geografía de México (6th ed.). Four volumes. Mexico City: Editorial Porrúa,1986.

Fernández Garza, Mauricio. *Las Monedas Municipales y Su Contexto Histórico.* Monterrey, México: Sociedad Numismática de Monterrey, 1979.

Frampton, Cory, Duane Douglas, Alberto Hidalgo & Elmer Powell. *Mexican Paper Money.* Carefree, Ariz.: Mexican Coin Company, 2010.

Gaytán, Carlos. *La Revolución Mexicana y Sus Monedas.* Mexico: Editorial Diana, 1969.

Grove, Frank W. *Coins of Mexico.* Lawrence, Mass.: Quarterman, 1981.

Grove, Frank W. *Medals of Mexico*, vols.1–3. Ontario, Calif.: Author, 1973–1976.

Guthrie, Hugh S., and Merrill Bothamley. *Mexican Revolutionary Coinage, 1913–1917.* Beverly Hills, Calif.: Superior Stamp & Coin Company, 1976.

Krause, Chester L., and Clifford Mishler. *Standard Catalog of World Coins: Spain, Portugal, and the New World.* Iola, Wis.: Krause Publications, 2002.

Woodworth, C. Woody, and Joe Flores. *La Ventana Oaxaca: The Window to the Revolutionary Coinage of Oaxaca 1915.* Authors, 1988.

McNickle, A.J.S. 1962. *Spanish Colonial Coins of North America Mexico Mint.* Mexico City: Sociedad Numismática de México, 1962.

Ortíz, Manuel Angel. *Fundamentals of Mexican Numismatics.* Sociedad Numismática de México.

Pradeau, Alberto Francisco. *Historia Numismática de México de 1823 a 1950.* Vols. 1–4. Sociedad Numismática de México, 1970.

Romero de Terreros y Vinet, Manuel. *Las Artes Industriales en la Nueva España* (rev. ed.). Mexico City: Banco Nacional de México, 1982.

Sánchez Garza, J. *Historical Notes on Coins of the Mexican Revolution 1913*–1917. Imprenta Formal, 1932.

Utberg, Neil. *Coins of Mexico, 1536–1963.* Author, 1963.

Vázquez-Gómez, Juana. 1997. *Dictionary of Mexican Rulers, 1325–1997.* Westport, Conn.: Greenwood, 1997.

Walrafen, Verne R. "Chihuahua 5 and 10 Centavos." *The Mexican Revolution Reporter*, issue 18, August 1980.

Wise, L.F., and E.W. Egan. *Kings, Rulers, and Statesmen.* New York: Sterling, 1967.

ACKNOWLEDGEMENTS

The authors would like to thank the following individuals and organizations for their invaluable help in bringing this book together:

Diane Alatorre
Carlos Abel Amaya Guerra
American Numismatic Association's Edward C. Rochette Money Museum
Banco de México
Robert Briggs
Dave Busse
Casa de Moneda de México
Roger Charteris Reyes
Juan Cristóbal Díaz Negrete
Scott Doll
Duane Douglas
Cory Frampton
Fundación Carlos Slim
Manuel Galán Medina
Ira Goldberg
Larry Goldberg
Luis M. Gómez-Wulschner
Russel H. Goodyear
Heritage Auctions
Ann Hernandez
Alberto Hidalgo
Max Keech
Jeff Lewis
Richard A. Long
Greg B. Meyer
Alfonso Miranda
Museo Soumaya
Ignacio Pineda
Kent Ponterio
Richard Ponterio
Ponterio & Associates
Elmer Powell
J.R. Rollo
Cori Sedwick Downing
Daniel Frank Sedwick
Alex Siegel
Spink America
Stack's Bowers Galleries
Cathy Stovall
Mike Stovall
Pat Stovall

We would also like to give special thanks to Scott Long for being there when we needed him. Our sincerest apologies if, by some oversight, we've failed to acknowledge any of the contributors to this book.

Whitman Publishing would like to thank Ricardo Camara Sanchez, Miguel Colón Ortiz, Beth Deisher, Myrna Garcia-Clemmons, Patricia Hoyos, Larry Lee, Robert Lemke, Tom Mulvaney, Martha Perusek, Diana Plattner, José Luis Ramirez-Damian, and Maria de los Remedios Gómez Arnau, for their contributions to this project.

ABOUT THE AUTHORS

Born and reared in south-central Michigan, Don Bailey joined the Marine Corps during the Korean War. When he retired from the Marines, he lived in Yuma, Arizona, where he was introduced to the vastly interesting history of Mexico. He started collecting U.S. coins in the early 1960s, but soon turned exclusively to Mexican numismatics, concentrating at first on the coinage of Maximilian and the French Intervention. Since 1979 he has been very active in the Mexican numismatic field as a full-time dealer, attending most of the major coin shows in the United States and Mexico. His wife, Lois, has been his full-time business and research partner.

In 1967, Don started the Maximilian Numismatic and Historical Society, which prospered for several years until burnout and a waning of collector interest in specialty organizations took their toll. He published his first article, on the subject of Mexican numismatics, that same year. Since then he has written on other subjects (including the story of the 1980s forger and murderer Mark Hoffman), but Mexican history and numismatics have always been his focus. He has written articles and columns for *World Coin News*, *Coin World*, and other publications, and served as *Coin World*'s "Mexican Trends" analyst. He has also been a contributor to major references on Mexican numismatics, including the *Standard Catalog of Mexican Coins*, *Standard Catalog of World Coins*, and *Tokens of Latin America;* Frank W. Grove's numerous volumes on medals, decorations, and tokens of Mexico; and the *Guide Book of Mexican Coins*, by T.V. Buttrey and Clyde Hubbard, to name a few.

Don has been a member of, and an officer in, many numismatic organizations. He is a life member of the American Numismatic Association and has been a member of the Sociedad Numismatica de México for more than 40 years, serving for a number of those years as the society's official representative in the United States. He has worked with the Banco de México and the Casa de Moneda de México to promote their products and numismatic materials, and in 1974 he was appointed to the U.S. Assay Commission.

Don has been the recipient of the ANA's Presidential Award, the Sociedad Numismatica's José Tamborrel Jr. Award (twice), and the Sociedad's Alberto Francisco Pradeau Award. *Numismatic News* named him a Numismatic Ambassador in 1980. On September 27, 2001, Don received the Orden Mexicana del Águila Azteca (Mexican Order of the Aztec Eagle), the highest honor bestowed on a foreigner by the government of Mexico.

In June of 1997, Don, Joe Flores, and Sal Falcone organized the United States Mexican Numismatic Association, and Don served for many years as its executive director and the editor of its quarterly publication, the *Mexican Numismatic Journal.* The Sociedad Numismatica honored the association with the Dr. Alberto Francisco Pradeau award for promoting Mexican numismatics.

According to Don, "These fifty years have been a ball. Fifty years of working, if one can use that term, in a field that you really enjoy is all that one can ask. My wife, Lois, is a vital part of the operation. Without her assistance and encouragement the goals we have achieved would have been impossible to reach."

INDEX